# Social Stratification
# and Inequality

*Eighth Edition*

# Social Stratification and Inequality

## Class Conflict in Historical, Comparative, and Global Perspective

**Harold R. Kerbo**

*California Polytechnic State University*

*San Luis Obispo*

The McGraw-Hill Companies

Connect
Learn
Succeed™

SOCIAL STRATIFICATION AND INEQUALITY: CLASS CONFLICT IN HISTORICAL,
COMPARATIVE, AND GLOBAL PERSPECTIVE, EIGHTH EDITION

2 3 4 5 6 7 8 9 0 DOC/DOC 1 0 9 8 7 6 5 4 3 2 1

ISBN 978-0-07-811165-5
MHID 0-07-811165-X

Vice President & Editor-in-Chief: *Michael Ryan*
Vice President EDP/Central Publishing Services: *Kimberly Meriwether David*
Editorial Director: *William Glass*
Sponsoring Editor: *Gina Boedeker*
Executive Marketing Manager: *Pamela S. Cooper*
Editorial Coordinator: *Nikki Weissman*
Senior Project Manager: *Lisa A. Bruflodt*
Design Coordinator: *Brenda A. Rolwes*
Cover Designer: *Studio Montage, St. Louis, Missouri*
Buyer: *Susan K. Culbertson*
Media Project Manager: *Sridevi Palani*
Compositor: *Glyph International*
Typeface: *10/12 Times*
Printer: *R. R. Donnelley*

**Library of Congress Cataloging-in-Publication Data**

Kerbo, Harold R.
  Social stratification and inequality: class conflict in historical,
comparative, and global perspective / Harold R. Kerbo.—8th ed.
    p. cm.
  ISBN 978-0-07-811165-5 (alk. paper)
  1. Social classes—United States.   2. Social conflict—United States.
  3. Equality—United States.   4. Social mobility—United States.   I. Title.
  HN90.S6K47 2011
  305.50973—dc22                                                          2010049100

www.mhhe.com

*For Kathy, Nicole, and Emily*

# Preface

I have been accustomed to beginning this preface by noting that since the first edition of this book in the early 1980s inequality has grown every year. Before the 1980s, income inequality and other indicators of standards of living in the United States were in line with other industrial nations of the world. Since 1980, the United States has become the most unequal advanced nation in the world, with levels of inequality more in line with those of poor countries around the world.

While this is still the case in 2010, events from 2008 suggest the United States may be at one of those turning points experienced in the past 100 years. The high inequality of the 1920s (about equal to the inequality today) was followed by the Great Depression and then the New Deal reforms, which reduced income inequality and increased the influence of working people from the 1930s through the 1960s. The relative decline of the United States in the world from the 1970s stimulated the Reagan "revolution" from 1980, increasing inequality and worsening conditions for the bottom 50 percent of Americans for almost the next 30 years. Then in 2008 the financial crisis and "Great Recession" brought anger toward the corporate elite and government intervention to restrict the corporate elite, somewhat reminiscent of the New Deal reforms of the 1930s. And 2008 brought a very different president, Barack Obama, and a very different faction of the political elite into power. In contrast to more than 100 years of political administrations in the United States, few people with corporate elite backgrounds have been appointed to high government positions (such as the president's cabinet) by President Obama.

By 2010, however, one might say "the more things change, the more they remain the same." But it is far too early for such a statement. Most forms of inequality in the stratification system have yet to be much affected. There are still too many conflicting forces at work in the United States. Some new policies have the potential for reducing class inequalities in future years, but economic conditions are yet to settle into a pattern. Quick government action to bail out large financial institutions whose behavior caused the financial crisis of 2008 led to a resumption of huge financial corporate profits by 2009. But the 10 percent unemployment for middle and working class Americans created by the financial crisis was almost unchanged by the end of 2010. Like recessions of recent decades, it has taken longer and longer for unemployment to go back down. Thus income inequality figures remain little changed so far.

Is the American stratification system in transition again? Or will the class inequalities of power in recent decades be able to thwart such a transition? The United States is in "interesting times." And perhaps in no better times for trying to understand the

American stratification system and the forces for change or resistant to change. These are no less "interesting times" to attempt a better understanding of the global economy and the place of the United States within it. Throughout the book we will consider what has changed in the American stratification system and the potential for reversing these changes of increasing class inequalities year after year for more than 30 years.

This eighth edition of *Social Stratification and Inequality* has been updated throughout. Outdated material, such as the extensive coverage of the old status attainment and social mobility models, has been replaced with income and wealth mobility research. A significant reduction has been made in the chapters on social stratification in Japan and Germany with the merging of former Chapters 15 and 16. In several places new material has been added, for example on global inequalities and potential changes with the new Obama administration, and new research has been added in almost every chapter since the seventh edition of this book.

Like the first edition, the basic orientation of this book continues to follow a general conflict perspective. This is not to say that other perspectives have been neglected, but I continue to believe that a conflict perspective of some variety is most useful in understanding the subject matter of social stratification. A central, often violent, question about social stratification continues to be how valued goods and services are to be distributed in a society and in the world. This underlying conflict is sometimes hidden, sometimes tamed, but nevertheless behind all systems of social stratification. When overt conflict over the distribution of valued goods and services is relatively low, it only means that the system of stratification has been somewhat successful in managing such conflict (at least for a time). As I completed work on this edition, I had just returned from doing research on poverty in Southeast Asia. I had seen firsthand in Thailand how political violence can escalate between the rich and poor, not when the poor are getting poorer but when the gap between the rich and poor is seen as less legitimate and is no longer tolerated. This is in contrast to much higher poverty in neighboring Cambodia, where no such rebellion is likely any time soon because ruling elites are more able to violently repress and silence the poor.

Seeing third world poverty up close, meeting people in small villages and huge urban slums, I have come to realize that the antiglobalization protesters and some parts of the modern world system theory have it only partially correct. It is clear that extreme poverty in many countries contributes to inequality and poverty here in the United States. Corporations can move their operations away from U.S. locations to countries where the average wage is $1 a day or less. Some of these corporations now produce their products in "sweatshops" accurately described by global protesters. However, we must understand that the extreme poverty of more than a billion people is so extensive that they are fighting to get jobs in those sweatshops; landing a job in such places is a clear step up in their lives. Parents in rich countries such as the United States may hope their sons and daughters grow up with a good college education and become doctors, lawyers, and such. Millions of parents in third world countries hope their sons and daughters simply live through childhood, and can then better their lives with a job in one of those sweatshops. World opinion and global protesters also are only partially correct in charging that the policies of rich nations and their multinational corporations are contributors to global inequality and poverty. This is often, but not always, the case.

Why do we find some poorer countries with extensive multinational corporate investment from rich countries, such as Thailand and Vietnam, with huge decreases in poverty over the years, while other nations in the same region (such as Laos, Myanmar, and Cambodia) continue to have the worst levels of poverty and hopelessness in the world? With global inequality and poverty growing rapidly in many regions, conflict theories accurately predict that there is a danger it will explode into more and more political violence and terrorism. Now more than ever, we need to better understand why some countries are able to bring their people out of poverty, while the people of many more countries remain ensnared in poverty and a cycle of misery that threatens to kill many millions of people and throw the world into wars potentially more deadly than those of the 20th century. These are lofty questions, perhaps, but they are among those we must attempt to answer.

## ✴ Acknowledgments

Let me again acknowledge my debt to the many social scientists whose works are discussed and cited in the pages of this book. Without their knowledge and hard work, a book such as this would be impossible. I would also like to thank Erik Olin Wright and David Grusky, who made their way through the Center for the Study of Social Stratification at Tohoku University while I was there. Both have given their permission for me to use some of their recent and as yet unpublished research on the shrinking middle class in the United States (see Chapter 8). As usual, my old friend G. William Domhoff has given me many good ideas on the subject of social stratification over the years, as well as in recent months while I was working on this book's revision. I also want to acknowledge the help provided by an Abe Research Fellowship funded over a 2-year period through the Japan Foundation in Tokyo and the Social Science Research Council in New York. The Abe Fellowship enabled me to spend several months, mostly in poor villages, in Thailand, Vietnam, Laos, and Cambodia, to gather information about poverty and what is being done to reduce it in Thailand, Laos, and Vietnam, as well as understand why there is almost no poverty reduction in the countryside in Cambodia. For his advice and support with my research in Thailand, I would like to thank my old friend Uthai Dulyakasem, president of Silpakorn University. In Cambodia an old friend, Professor Bunnak at the Royal University of Phnom Penh, made my research possible and provided me with a very good translator and research assistant, Mr. Channarith (Rith). In Vietnam, I would like to thank President Bui Van Ga at Da Nang University and two very good research assistants, Thao Nguyen and Le Van Chon. Again, I want to thank my old friend Patrick Ziltener from the University of Zurich (and now also at the Economics Ministry of Switzerland) for many comments and information that went into the revision of this book. A new friend, Professor Oleg Oguben from Moscow State University, gave me valuable information and comments while I was on a lecture tour in Moscow and while he was a visiting professor at my university. Finally, I would like to thank my McGraw-Hill editor, Gina Boedeker, and developmental editor, Jolynn Kilburg, who helped make work on this eighth edition much easier and more pleasant.

Last, but certainly not least, McGraw-Hill and I would like to extend our thanks to the reviewers of the eighth edition for their insightful and helpful comments:

Matthew Aronson, Colorado State University
Nicole Braun, Grand Valley State University
Cliff Brown, University of New Hampshire
Penelope Canan, University of Central Florida
James Crone, Hanover College
Nicholas Dempsey, Eckerd College
Chad Gesser, Owensboro Community and Technical College
Gerry Grzyb, University of Wisconsin–Oshkosh
Floyd Hammack, New York University
Pamela Kaye, Principia College
B. Mitchell Peck, University of Oklahoma–Norman
Barbara Wells, Maryville College
William Weston, Centre College

*Harold R. Kerbo*

# Contents

# Introduction

# Perspectives and Concepts in the Study of Social Stratification

In recent decades more Americans have moved into the upper middle class, living in homes like the one shown in the top photo. But at the same time, many more Americans have been falling into lower-class positions and living in homes more like those in the bottom photo, if they are not homeless. The United States now has the highest rate of inequality among all advanced industrial societies in the world, and it continues to grow.

*SOURCES:* Top: © Photodisc/PunchStock, bottom: © Harold Kerbo

## Chapter Outline

❖ Michael

❖ David

❖ Definitions and Concepts

❖ Social Stratification in the Modern World System

❖ The Organization of Chapters

❖ Summary

In understanding human beings and human societies, no subject is more important than social stratification. A system of social stratification and occupational ranking helps shape how people live, their opportunities for a better life, their mental health and life expectancy, and much more (Weeden and Grusky 2005). On a more general level, a system of social stratification has an important influence on events such as war and peace, economic expansion or stagnation, unemployment and inflation, and government policies of many kinds.

Most people, of course, are aware of the fact that some people are rich while others are poor. But people in general are usually less aware of the rather systematic social forces that structure such outcomes. They prefer to think that people themselves are responsible for their lot in life. This type of belief is especially strong among the nonpoor and whites in the United States, with its values of freedom and individualism. Most people, too, are aware of the fact that some individuals have more influence than others, with the power to shape national issues of war and peace, economic well-being, and general social welfare. But, again, people are usually much less aware of how a system of stratification forms the basis for such influence. They prefer to think that great men and women determine historical events; the possibility that great men and women are themselves a product of a system of social stratification is less obvious to most people. And finally, most people are aware of racial, ethnic, and gender inequalities. Especially because of America's racial and ethnic diversity, there is no doubt greater awareness of this inequality here than in most places in the world. However, it is also because of the reality of these inequalities and their significance in American society that there are so many ideologies and misconceptions about these inequalities. Most people do not fully understand the structural nature of these inequalities and often misjudge the level of inequality based on occupation, race, ethnicity, and gender (Osberg and Smeeding 2006).

We can begin our study of social stratification on the level of individual life histories. Individual life histories alone, of course, can tell us very little about an overall *system* of social stratification. It should also be recognized that the subject of sociology, and thus social stratification, is concerned with group properties, social structures, and social forces. In other words, sociology is concerned primarily with groups or aggregates of people, not individual biographies. For example, if sociologists want to understand crime or mental illness, they are interested in the social forces that help produce such phenomena. On an individual level, many *unique* influences may be shaping human behavior. Thus, to increase the power of our explanations or sociological theories, we concern ourselves with more general social forces that affect many people in a nation and globally. As in any science, our intent is to get the most general explanations or understanding out of the smallest number of variables in our theories.

With this in mind, however, we can examine individual biographies as examples, and for the questions they raise. For maximum effect, let us consider a life history on each extreme of the stratification system in the United States. The contexts of these life histories and their details may seem a bit dated now, but as we will see, they highlight principles of social stratification that are even more important in the United States today.

# ⚔ Michael

Michael was born in August 1965, in the low-income, predominantly black area of Los Angeles called Watts. There is some distinction in the place and timing of Michael's birth not only because he was born 6 months after his mother began a jail term but also because his birth occurred a few days after one of the worst race riots in U.S. history—a race riot that was only one of the first of over 300 that sprang up, one after another, through out 1968 (Salert and Sprague 1980). Given these circumstances, we have a rather detailed description of Michael's early life provided by Richard Meyers of the *Los Angeles Times;* it is a life history that parallels the troubled history of the low-income urban area of Los Angeles since Michael was born (see the *Los Angeles Times,* August 10, 1980).

Michael's mother was involved in a daily struggle to find money for food and shelter for herself and a 1-year-old child with a disability when a knife fight led to her arrest and jail term. Despite considerable pressure to the contrary, Michael's mother, Judy, did not give up her baby born while in prison. Michael and his brother were placed in separate foster homes until Judy could care for her children adequately. During his 3 years in the foster home, Michael was healthy and developed with the likes and dislikes of any young child—he "hated green peas and haircuts"; he loved his toys, dog, and ice cream; and he enjoyed playing with his foster father's tools.

Judy was out of prison after 3 years, but she was also out of work and had no place to live. For the next 17 months she lived in 10 different locations—including her mother's apartment, two foster homes, her stepfather's back porch, and a truck. With an unemployment rate of 20 percent in the area at the time, jobs were extremely scarce. She reports working for a time with a temporary government work project, and for a time as an aide in a parole office. She also tried her hand at being a pimp for gay men, which brought her considerably more money but also a life she rejected in order to provide a home for her children. Pregnant again at age 18, she gave up hustling for welfare and her children.

Judy was happy when Michael was returned to her, although she wept for many days when Michael cried for his foster parents. She began receiving a welfare check, like 265,221 other people in the area. But the amount received, despite California's more "generous" assistance level, was inadequate for her needs and the needs of three children. (At the time in California, a mother with three children could receive less than $400 per month with a basic welfare grant under Aid to Families with Dependent Children and including food stamps.) Judy and her three children were forced to live with relatives in a three-bedroom apartment that was home for 13 people.

To some extent, Judy and Michael's prospects improved when Judy married a man who was employed as a janitor. They moved to a rented apartment of their own in a low-income housing project. Like most mothers, Judy loved her children and did her best to provide for them. Michael remembers she always wrote "I love you" on his lunch sack when he began school. She saved to buy Christmas presents for the kids and did volunteer work at Michael's preschool.

With marriage Judy had her fourth child. But as is too often the case for many poor children, the relatively good times did not last. Judy's marriage began breaking up and she turned to drugs. The children were chased by rats in the apartment, rats that sometimes woke them up at night, and Michael was bitten by a tarantula. Again they moved, and again Judy was alone with her children.

Their new apartment was not much better, but the rats were less of a problem. Judy was back on the welfare rolls, and the area they lived in was one of the most crime-prone and violent. Judy first placed Michael in a Catholic school to keep him away from the crime and gangs in the public school, but it did not last. Both Judy and Michael describe being embarrassed when comparing themselves with the parents and children in this new school, with the embarrassment reaching a peak when Judy could not afford 11 cents for the required pencil and eraser at the school. Michael was placed in the public school.

When he was 7 years old, Michael saw a man killed for the first time. The man was driving an ice cream truck in front of Michael's apartment when several young boys stopped the truck, beat the man, and took $12. Other residents in the area took all the ice cream out of the truck. This was only the first of many people Michael saw killed before he was 15.

Michael's 16-month-old sister died when she fell down their apartment stairs. Judy dealt with the death with much grief and alcohol. Shortly afterward, when Michael was in the third grade, he was again placed in a foster home. This time it was because of a child abuse charge against Judy. Michael had broken his arm but was unable to convince anyone that it had happened in a fall away from home. Again Judy found it difficult to live with her life. Michael remembers crying night after night for his mother. The alleged child abuse, however, did appear unfounded, and Michael was returned to Judy after a judge became convinced of her innocence.

At about this time Michael also found the influence of street gangs difficult to resist. He was arrested for shoplifting when he was in third grade. By the time he was 10 there were other arrests and gang fights for Michael. By age 15 he had experienced anger over his mother's beating and gang rape by young boys, he had seen more men killed, and he had to bear the fact that his and his mother's possessions were stolen time and time again. He had seen his mother sick because of hunger, and he had stolen food. Michael still lived in the area of the 1965 Watts riot, which in the 1990s had an even higher rate of crime. Also, by the age of 15, Michael was in jail; 9 months after the story on Michael appeared in the *Los Angeles Times* his mother was found shot to death.

The future for Michael, along with that of millions of children in similar circumstances in this country, does not look good. Judging from the experience of most middle-aged men in the area of Watts, we might expect Michael to be in and out of the unemployment lines throughout his life; when work is found it will be low-paid and low-skilled. Given changes in the U.S. economy, as Michael was coming of age, the pay for low-skilled workers will become even lower in coming years, if such work can be found at all. Of course, there is a strong possibility that he will be in and out of prison as well, if not killed, like many young people in places such as Watts, where the leading cause of death for men is gunshot.

We can feel sorry and angry for, and about, Judy and Michael; but sorrow and anger are not the intent of the preceding description. It is meant to illustrate not just the misfortunes of one family but the experience of many families who are poor (of no matter what race) in the United States. Such experiences are no doubt varied, for, contrary to popular belief, the poor represent a diverse segment of our population. But the poor do have many common problems that are presented by their common position at the bottom of the stratification system in an affluent society. We will consider the questions this case presents for the study of social stratification after we examine the case of David.

---

# ✄ David

David was born at the other end of the stratification system in this country—at the top. His parents were not only rich, but they were among the superrich and powerful. David was born in 1915, the youngest of six children. His father had assets of at least $0.5 billion, which he had inherited from his father (Collier and Horowitz 1976:133). David, like Michael, grew up in a number of dwellings, though, as might be expected, there were many differences. For one, the several dwellings that David grew up in were all owned by his family—at the same time. The homes were substantially less crowded than Michael's first home (three bedrooms for 13 people), and it is rather doubtful that they had rats, spiders, and cockroaches.

First, there was the family's New York City townhouse on Fifth Avenue. Then, for the weekends, there was the Pocantico Hills estate in New York. The 3,500-acre Pocantico estate is five times the size of Central Park in New York City, with a 250-acre park of its own. At Pocantico, David and his brothers and sister could "go to the stone stables and have the riding master take them out on the trails; they could check out one of the fleet of electric cars that sailed silently around the grounds" (Collier and Horowitz 1976:182). It took $50,000 a year to maintain the "Big House" on this estate, and a total of $500,000 per year to maintain the whole estate.

During the summers David's family spent most of their time at their estate in Seal Harbor, Maine. Here the children could go sailing in the family's many boats or go on long walks to the "cabin" deep in the woods on the estate (Collier and Horowitz 1976:181–182). Finally, if they really wanted to get away, there was a home in the Virgin Islands, a Venezuelan ranch, and a ranch in the Grand Teton Mountains (Dye 1979:158).

We would expect that David was much like Michael as a 2-year-old child. He was curious about his environment, he loved to play with his toys, and, though never mentioned in biographies, we might expect that he liked ice cream. But David had a much wider and safer environment to explore, and his toys were more numerous and expensive. After this young age, the differences grew much wider. David did not grow up with street crime and violence, it is doubtful he ever saw a man killed, and his schools were much different. He went to the elite Lincoln School near the Pocantico Hills estate, then attended Harvard and the London School of Economics, and earned a PhD in economics at the University of Chicago (Kutz 1974:71).

As a young child, David appeared serious and "responsible," and he was informally selected from among his brothers to carry on the family business interests (Collier and Horowitz 1976:220; Dye 1979:158). After World War II David began work at his uncle's bank as an assistant manager of the foreign department. He spent 3 years at that job, and in 1950 he was promoted to vice president. By 1952 he was senior vice president; in 1962, president; and in 1969, chair of the board and chief executive officer (Kutz 1974:73–99). He retired from these positions in 1981.

Before retirement, David Rockefeller was described as the most powerful private citizen in the United States—"the only man who would have to step down to become President of the United States" (Collier and Horowitz 1976:431; Dye 1979:157–158). As one corporate executive put it to the *Wall Street Journal* (April 3, 1981), Mr. Rockefeller "is the equivalent of a head of state. He is the chairman of the board of the Eastern establishment." All this is an exaggeration—at least to some degree. At Chase Manhattan Bank David Rockefeller chaired a board of directors that included men from top positions at American Express Company, Chrysler, Continental Corporation, Equitable Life Assurance, Exxon, General Electric, General Motors, IBM, Sears Roebuck, Standard Oil of Indiana, Union Carbide, and United States Steel (U.S. Senate Committee on Governmental Affairs 1978b:898). In addition, the bank's trust department controlled significant stock in such companies as Exxon, IT&T, Morgan Bank, Standard Oil of California, Mobil, and Aetna Life and Casualty (U.S. Senate Committee on Governmental Affairs 1978a).

David Rockefeller has also served as chair of the Museum of Modern Art, on the board of Harvard University, as a trustee of the Carnegie Foundation, a trustee of the University of Chicago and the John F. Kennedy Library, and as director of the Council on Foreign Relations (Dye 1979:159). He repeatedly turned down cabinet posts offered by Presidents Kennedy, Johnson, and Nixon (Collier and Horowitz 1976:403).

David Rockefeller is noted for his hard work, but he does have the time and means to play. He is part owner of a French vineyard; in his Pocantico home, he has "a renowned temperature-controlled [wine] cellar sealed with a bank-vault door." He owns three 40-foot boats at his Seal Harbor estate in Maine, and he has one of the best collections of impressionist and postimpressionist paintings (Collier and Horowitz 1976:321). One must not forget his beetle collection (bugs, not Beatle records); dating back to his childhood days, his collection is reported to be one of the best in the world, with two species named after him (Collier and Horowitz 1976:221).

Added to all this, David's personal real estate holdings included residences in Manhattan and Pocantico, the vacation homes at Seal Harbor and in the Caribbean, a sheep ranch in Australia, and several thousand acres in the Virgin Islands and the Brazilian interior (Collier and Horowitz 1976:423). It is difficult to obtain precise figures on the total wealth of people like David Rockefeller, but one "conservative" estimate of the present Rockefeller family wealth (excluding family holdings in real estate and financial institutions) was $4 billion (Kutz 1974:71).

The two life histories just described illustrated examples of a very rich and a very poor family. And it might be well to note that we can find many more people in Michael's position than we can in David Rockefeller's position. But these two life histories have been presented for a more important reason; they suggest several questions that must be considered in any study of social stratification.

**1.** Most basic, of course, is the question, *Why* is Michael so poor while David Rockefeller is so rich? A popular explanation (especially in the United States) for wealth and poverty is directed toward individual qualities. The rich, it is often believed, are rich because of their superior talents and motivation. The poor, in turn, are believed to be poor because of their lack of talent and motivation and their low moral qualities. It is doubtful that anyone would question the exceptional talent of David Rockefeller. But the key question is how this talent developed or where it came from. Also, we must ask how many among the poor have exceptional talent, or even average talent, that is never given a chance to develop. If a poor child were adopted at birth by a family like the Rockefellers, how would this child turn out? Will the poor children adopted by actress Angelina Jolie from Vietnam, Africa, and Cambodia have more opportunities in life than they otherwise would have? Similarly, what if David Rockefeller had been adopted by a poor family? Unless we are willing to say that most rich people are usually biologically superior in some way (which is absurd), we must look further. In the two cases just described, social background differences are obvious. But this presents further questions.

**2.** How does class background influence how people turn out or where they end up in the class system? Does class background primarily influence opportunities for more and better education, job opportunities, and opportunities for more income; does it also shape personal characteristics like intelligence, aspirations, and self-evaluations? Family class background is often used as an explanation for social conditions like poverty and crime, as well as for why some people end up affluent and in respected positions in the society. But this is only a partial explanation. With this explanation we may blame Michael's mother for the way Michael ended up: Despite her love for Michael, why was she in jail when Michael was born? Why did she have children she could not support? Why did she allow Michael to get involved with gangs? By themselves, however, such questions provide little help in a *general* understanding of inequality and social stratification. On one hand, if we blame Judy for Michael's outcome, we may have to blame Judy's parents, and their parents, until we go back to the early slaves. (Do we blame them for being captured and sold as slaves?) On the other hand, we must not forget what Judy had to face in raising Michael. These questions lead us to other questions.

**3.** Why do social backgrounds differ? In essence, we have returned to our first question without making much progress. At this point we must ask questions about the nature of society rather than of individuals. What are the political, economic, and social forces that help produce inequality and social stratification? In related questions we must ask if inequality is somehow necessary and beneficial for overall society. Or is inequality best understood as a conflict relation, with the greater power of the more affluent producing their greater share of valued goods and services? Even if we find inequality to be beneficial in some way, we must also ask if the *degree* of inequality we find in the United States (the highest in the industrialized world) is beneficial for overall society. Or does the degree of inequality in this country primarily benefit the more affluent, resulting in the exploitation of others?

**4.** With our example of David and Michael, especially in the United States, we have to ask, How much does race matter? What if David Rockefeller had come from a black family? Would he have been able to attain the high position and power he had before retiring? And are things different in the United States since the 1950s when David Rockefeller started his rapid move up the corporate ladder? Could one of the top banks in the United States be headed by a black person today? And what about Michael's poverty? Was he kept poor primarily because he is black? Would a white boy born poor have a better chance to move out of poverty than Michael had? All of these questions ask, Does race matter? Certainly the answers must be yes. But how much, and is it changing? These are the more difficult questions that students of social stratification must ask.

**5.** In a related vein, what if it had been Mary Rockefeller instead of David? Even if born in such a wealthy and powerful upper-class family, would a woman be able to attain the power David Rockefeller attained? Again, is this situation changing in the American society since David Rockefeller was a young man and on his way to the top of the corporate world? And what if Michael had been a Mary, and still poor and black? How could life have been different? Would there have been different chances to get a job, obtain welfare, escape crime? Again these are difficult questions, but all very important ones in the study of social stratification in the United States, as well as in any other country in the world.

**6.** Putting aside questions concerning the causes of inequality, we have others pertaining to the maintenance of inequality. For example, why is it that many of the poor either accept or tolerate their low position? A question often posed is, Why do people on the bottom rebel? Perhaps a more important question (given over 35 million poor in this country) is, Why do the poor so seldom rebel? Blacks and other minorities did rebel in the 1960s, and from time to time have done so again, as in South Central Los Angeles in 1992. But most of the poor in this country are white, and the black rebellion has subsided (to some degree for now) without (as we will see later) significant improvement for most blacks.

**7.** With respect to the brief biographies of Michael and of David Rockefeller, could we find similar biographies in other countries today? In other words, how similar or different are the level of inequality and the system of social stratification in this country compared with others, past and present?

**8.** With the increasing global economy we must ask about the effects of the global stratification system on the life chances of individuals. Does it matter that David Rockefeller was a banker in a rich country rather than in a Latin American or Asian nation? Do the immense global inequalities result in higher profits for corporate executives and wealthy stockholders in rich nations like the United States? How about people like Michael? Are the incomes and job prospects of less affluent Americans affected by the existence of so many poor people in the world?

**9.** Finally, with respect to David Rockefeller's former power in this society (and the world), what was the basis of his power, and that of others like him? Was this power more an outcome of his family wealth, or of his institutional position with Chase Manhattan Bank (the second-largest bank in the United States before he retired)?

As we will see in coming chapters, questions such as these have no simple answers. But these questions are among the most important that a serious examination of social stratification must attempt to answer. There is an even more general question, however, from which the others follow. As Lenski (1966) put it, the study of social stratification is an attempt to answer the questions of *who gets what, and why.* We want to know why some (like the Rockefellers) get a much greater share of these resources. Is it a matter of hard work? When we ask such a question, it becomes necessary to link personal misfortune (such as Michael's) and fortune (such as David Rockefeller's) with more general social arrangements or social structure. It is this task that will guide what follows.

# ⚔ Definitions and Concepts

Before proceeding, there is the usual matter of basic definitions and concepts. Because a few words or concepts may be used differently by social scientists than by others in the society, or even by other social scientists, we must be precise. At the same time, we have to avoid overdoing the definitions and concepts now or we will only compound the confusion. For this reason our discussion at this point is as brief as possible. We define only the most important terms and concepts, leaving others for discussion as appropriate. Further, we define the terms and concepts that follow as simply as possible. Complexity and additional specification may be added in later chapters when such specification becomes necessary and useful.

## Social Stratification and Inequality

We must begin with a most basic concept that describes a necessary precondition for social stratification but that must not be confused with social stratification. This condition is **social differentiation,** which occurs, quite simply, when we find people with distinct individual qualities and social roles. People are differentiated in terms of biological characteristics such as sex, size, strength, and agility; and in every society they are differentiated (at least to some degree) by social roles, work tasks, or occupations. Some people do the hunting, others chop wood, and still others care for children or gather plants in the forest. As societies become technologically more complex, the division of labor increases—the number of tasks, occupations, and roles also grows. In short, an increased division of labor means more differentiation.

It is important to recognize that social differentiation does not necessarily suggest that differences in personal qualities or work roles are ranked on a hierarchy, or are evaluated differently. As Heller (1969:3) noted, "Positions may be differentiated from one another and yet not *ranked* relative to each other. For example, in our society the position of the adolescent is generally not considered superior to that of infant, merely different." Social differentiation, however, sets the stage for inequality and social stratification.

**Social inequality** is the condition whereby people have unequal access to valued resources, services, and positions in the society. Such inequality can emerge in terms of how individuals and groups are themselves ranked and evaluated by others, but, most important, social inequality is related to differing positions in a social structure. Social inequality often emerges from social differentiation for two basic reasons. On one hand, because of the human capacity to apply meaning to events and things, to develop judgments of what is "good," "bad," or preferable, social evaluation is often applied to differences. Thus, individual characteristics and different positions or roles may be valued unequally or ranked from superior to inferior. In this sense we refer to social inequality in terms of prestige or honor. As we will see in subsequent chapters, it is only in this limited respect that we can say social inequality has been present in all human societies.

On the other hand, and more important, inequality may emerge from social differentiation because some roles or social positions place some people in a position to acquire a greater share of valued goods and services. In this case we refer to inequality in terms of the access to favored positions in the society, although social evaluation or prestige will usually follow as a secondary matter because people who have positions that are favored in the society will be evaluated highly.

For example, in societies where physical strength is important in providing the necessities of life, the strong may be able successfully to demand greater rewards and, consequently, greater respect. In more complex societies with an expanded division of labor, those in the position of coordinating and organizing the work of others obtain more authority. Such authority will be used to acquire greater rewards. Also, acquiring a surplus of goods and services in and of itself usually leads to even more rewards. This is because an unequal exchange may develop. When some people control what others want and need, they are able to demand additional goods and services in return for distributing these necessities.

We come finally to the most important concept for our purpose—social stratification. As the root term suggests, this concept implies *strata.* By adding the term *social* we are saying that human beings in social positions are stratified from high to low as strata of rock are layered one upon another. But at this point social stratification is not clearly distinguished from social inequality, so we must mean something more if separate terms are used. **Social stratification** means that inequality has been hardened or *institutionalized,* and there is a *system of social relationships* that determines who gets what, and why. When we say *institutionalized,* we mean that a system of layered hierarchy has been established. People have come to expect that individuals and groups with certain positions will be able to demand more influence and respect and accumulate a greater share of goods and services. Such inequality may or may not be accepted equally by a majority in the society, but it is recognized as the way things are.

By a system of social stratification we also mean that something like rules have been developed that "explain" how rewards are distributed and why they are distributed in such a way. For example, the rules may explain that some individuals receive greater rewards because they are the human representatives of some god or because they are believed to contribute more to the well-being of the total society.

When class or strata placement is primarily hereditary, we refer to such placement as **ascription.** That is, people are placed in positions in a stratification system because of qualities beyond their control (for example, because of race, gender, or class at birth). When class or strata placement is due primarily to qualities that can be controlled by individuals, we refer to such placement as **achievement.** That is, people obtain their place in the stratification system because they have merit, because they live up to certain ideals, or because they follow certain achievement rules. However, as we will see, in most societies strata placement is based on a varying mixture of ascription and achievement.

And in the United States in particular we will see that the ascriptive factors of race, gender, and ethnicity have certainly not gone away and must be examined to understand social stratification and inequality today.

## Class Divisions and Social Mobility

Because much of our concern in coming chapters is the stratification systems of industrial societies, a brief introductory comment is necessary with respect to class divisions and social mobility. (Again, more detail is added when needed.) The concept of class, as we will see, has provoked much controversy among sociologists. Generally, we can define **class** as a grouping of individuals with similar positions and similar political and economic interests within the stratification system. The controversy over class involves such factors as (1) the most important criteria in distinguishing classes, (2) the number of class divisions that exist, (3) the extent to which individuals (themselves) must recognize these divisions if they are to be meaningful, and (4) whether or not class divisions (as defined here) even exist in the United States and other industrial societies (Weeden and Grusky 2005).

In coming chapters we present evidence supporting the dominant view that class is a meaningful and very important concept in the context of the United States, and that class divisions are based on three main criteria: a person's position in the **occupational structure,** a person's position in **authority structures** (how many people a person must take orders from versus how many people a person can give orders to), and a person's ownership of property (or, more specifically, the ownership of property that produces profit, such as stock ownership), which we can call the **property structure.** These three criteria tend to intersect, producing more or less distinct class divisions.

A typical listing of class divisions in the United States is made primarily in terms of occupational and economic divisions. Given that the United States is an industrial capitalist nation, such divisions are of prime importance in the stratification system. These class divisions are often labeled upper class, upper middle class, lower middle class, working class, and lower class. Similar labels, specifying occupation more distinctly, are capitalist class (upper class), higher nonmanual (higher white collar), lower nonmanual (lower white collar), skilled manual (skilled blue collar), and unskilled manual (unskilled blue collar).

Because of our stress on the three intersecting criteria for class location (occupation, authority, property), a slightly altered class breakdown is employed. This class breakdown provides more recognition of the fact that the United States is a bureaucratized industrial society as well as a capitalistic industrial society. That is, people are ranked by authority as well as by occupational and economic standing.

The **upper class** is used to signify those families high in property ownership, with high authority flowing from such ownership. These are the old established families with significant ownership of major corporations, such as the Rockefellers, the Du Ponts, the Mellons, and the Fords.

The **corporate class** is used to signify people with high authority and power in major corporations (and often government), usually without extensive ownership in these corporations. These people include top corporate executives (presidents, vice presidents, and so on) and corporate board members. There is some evidence that the upper class is shrinking in importance while this corporate class is growing in importance.

The **middle class** is used to signify those with relatively little property, but high to middle positions in occupation (nonmanual labor) and authority. Further distinction is made with respect to the upper middle class (lesser corporate managers, doctors, lawyers, and so forth) and lower middle class (office workers, clerks, salespeople).

The **working class** is used to signify people with little or no property, middle to low positions in occupation (manual labor), and little or no authority. A further distinction is made with respect to skilled and unskilled manual workers. At times the term **lower class** is used to signify those individuals with no property, who are often unemployed and have no authority (that is, the poor).

The rather ambiguous term **status** should be discussed in conjunction with class. This term is ambiguous because sociologists often use it to mean different things. On one hand, status is often used to indicate positions in a social structure—for example, student, teacher, father, child—with certain rights and duties attached to such positions. On the other hand, status is often used to indicate something like class position within a hierarchy. In this usage, however, the criterion of status consists of occupational prestige, or the popularly ranked esteem and respect associated with high to low occupational attainment. In subsequent chapters we use the term status in this second sense.

Any analysis of a class system is incomplete without due consideration of social mobility. As we will see, a class system may in part be distinguished from other types of stratification systems because of the greater possibility of achievement or changes in class placement. In reality, of course, ascription is never eliminated, and what exists is a varied mixture of achievement and ascription. **Social mobility** may be defined as individual or group movement within the class system. We can speak of both vertical and horizontal mobility, or the movement of individuals up and down the class system compared with their movement across positions of roughly equal rank.

Given that class systems are based (at least to some degree) on achievement, we would expect them to display extensive patterns of vertical social mobility. Combining this expectation with the American stress on equality of opportunity, we can understand why the study of social mobility has become almost an obsession among American sociologists. We have numerous studies designed to measure the extent of vertical mobility in the United States, as well as many studies attempting to measure the exact mixture of achievement versus ascriptive factors that determine where people end up in the class system.

We may note at this point that research indicates social mobility has been extensive in the United States, although most of it is short-range. Now, however, there is clear evidence that social mobility in the United States began to slow considerably beginning in the 1980s. But the extent of mobility continues to vary, depending on where we look in the class system (top, middle, or bottom) and by race. However, the research also indicates that both ascriptive factors (such as race and family class background) and achievement factors (such as educational attainment) play a part in class placement in the United States, with ascriptive factors playing a larger part than our values proclaim.

# ✸ Social Stratification in the Modern World System

Now that we have defined some of the basic terms related to our subject matter, we have a final subject that in one way or another runs throughout the coming chapters on various aspects of social stratification. We can introduce this subject by noting the current historic shift in progress in the United States—a shift directly related to social stratification and inequality. The economic shift is related to the relative economic decline of the United States beginning in the 1970s in what is called the **modern world system** or global economy. This relative decline of the United States in the world economy stimulated support for what was known as *Reaganomics* in the 1980s. As we will see in more detail, while average Americans became more and more afraid for their security and the future well-being of their children, the corporate class also became more involved in politics in an attempt to reverse the decline in U.S. profits and markets around the world (Micklethwait and Wooldridge 2004; Blyth 2002; Useem 1984). Reaganomics in part contributed to the increase in income and wealth inequality that had already begun in the United States because of changes in the world economy.

From the beginning of the 1980s, the United States already had the highest level of income inequality among industrial nations. As we will see in the next chapter, by 2009 this inequality was substantially higher and still growing in the first years of the 21st century. A major cause of this inequality has been a big loss of jobs to Americans—jobs that paid an average income. But added to this job loss was job growth at both the higher and lower ends of the income scale, from the 1980s and through the 2000s, primarily at the lower end. One's math skills need not be very advanced to figure out that these changes will result in greater inequality.

As the United States came out of the long recession by the early 1990s, there were other changes pushing the inequality figures higher still. At first, with economic recovery in 1993 and early 1994 there was economic growth (as measured in gross national product, or GNP), as there must be when coming out of any recession. But there was a new twist: Few jobs were accompanying the economic growth. When some new jobs finally appeared in the second half of 1994, however, there were more differences. For example, about half of the new jobs were "soft jobs"—jobs that were temporary, part-time, with low wages, and usually with few if any benefits such as medical insurance.

Also strange when considering this recession had ended in the early 1990s was and increase in American poverty for a few more years. The poverty rate, which had been 12.8 percent of the American population before the recession began in 1989, moved to 14.2 percent by 1991, 14.8 percent in 1992, and then to 15.1 percent *when the recession was declared over.* Along with the increasing rate of poverty was a continued decline in average family income through 1996, which was down 7 percent between 1989 and 1994. Job losses for Americans in the middle-income scale continued through the early and mid-1990s, but there was again something different: While jobs at the lower-income levels continued to increase, jobs at the upper-income levels—primarily technical, professional, and managerial jobs—also began increasing even more in contrast to the 1980s. For the Americans able to take such jobs this was great news. But our math skills again do not have to be very advanced to recognize the trend in even greater income and wealth inequality in the United States. And perhaps most important of all, these changes since the 1970s are almost certainly not temporary, but reflect a major shift in the nature of social stratification in the United States.

During the second half of the 1990s the United States reversed its relative economic decline compared to Europe and Japan, ravaged with economic stagnation. The U.S. economy was booming, with unemployment dipping into the 4 percent range—a rate unheard of for many decades. But the news was not all so good. The incomes of people on the bottom in the United States continued to stagnate, while the incomes of those in the upper range continued to grow rapidly, making for ever-growing income inequality throughout the late 1990s. Not until the last 2 years of the longest economic boom in American history did people in the lowest economic positions finally make some slight gains in income and poverty reduction. This was not supposed to happen in an economic boom with such low unemployment.

By the end of 2001, however, the U.S. economy quickly stopped its downturn and slowly began to grow again. However, another curious thing happened: The U.S. economy was into 2 years of slow economic recovery by the fall of 2003 as unemployment and poverty continued to increase. By the end of 2006 only modest job gains had occurred. It was the longest period of economic recovery in American history without a drop in unemployment (*Wall Street Journal,* August 13, 2003; *New York Times,* July 21 and September 4, 2003, January 6 and January 10, 2004). There was a loss of over 3 million American jobs while corporate profits surged, and an additional one and a half million Americans fell into poverty. This situation was simply a continuation of trends that sped up during the long economic boom of the 1990s. In previous economic recessions corporations cut back production, laid off workers, and cut inventory to save profits as they rode out the recession. When a recession was over corporations would start rehiring workers to increase production to take advantage of the new demand for goods. This time was different. With more freedom to move around the world, more U.S. industrial corporations figured they could beat the recession by cutting costs with low-wage third world labor. The recession, in other words, further drove U.S. corporations to close operations in America and move overseas. With a strong economy through 2006, U.S. corporations are not hiring as many American workers as before but are increasing capacity in relocated factories by hiring more workers in places like China. Chinese workers, in other words, are benefiting from the U.S. economic recovery while American workers remain unemployed as U.S. corporate profits surge.

Toward the end of 2008 the United States was faced with its worst economic crisis since the Great Depression of the 1930s. Several large financial firms had to be bailed out with "TARP" money from the federal government, many receiving as much as $45 billion. General Motors also had to be bailed out and went into Chapter 11 bankruptcy. The stock market lost one-third of its value in just a few months. Millions of Americans lost their homes. The unemployment rate shot up to over 10 percent compared to the 5 percent or so for more than a decade. By 2010 the economy was slowly improving, and it is clear that without quick action by Congress and the federal government the United States would have led the world into another big depression. In the first months of 2010, however, the unemployment rate stayed close to 10 percent. It is difficult to predict what the future will bring, but it is likely the return of lost jobs will be as slow as during the last two recessions. And as with the previous two recessions, it is very likely that many of those lost jobs will never return. China, for example, contin-ues its rapid economic growth, now making more and more of the goods that used to be produced in the United States.

It is possible, of course, that the severity of the U.S. economic crisis that began in 2008 will move the country in a different direction as happened during, and because of, the Great Depression of the 1930s. The Obama administration has been trying to push in this new direction with laws to regulate the behavior of big corporations that stimu-lated the economic crisis and to limit the huge CEO salaries that are far ahead of those in Europe and Japan (as we see in detail in the next chapter). Other laws and raising the minimum wage *could* allow for a reduction of income inequality in the United States, which has increased every year since 1980. But it is too early to know how much, if any, of this will happen, as Republicans in Congress are united against almost all legis-lation proposed by the Obama administration. In addition, the lessons of how the U.S. economy became competitive with Europe and Japan during the 1980s are still strong in the minds of the corporate elite and conservative politicians.

As we will see, there is abundant evidence that the U.S. economy had been doing well compared to Japan and Europe since the 1980s *because* the wages, benefits, and job security of American workers were *so low* compared to those of workers in these other countries. In other words, large increases in inequalities in the United States helped revive the U.S. economy in the 1990s. The lesson *may* be that in the future capitalist economies will have to compete with each other in the modern world system by making workers' wages and benefits lower and keeping them low—a possible lesson that wor-ries European workers, as I found during interviews with German trade union leaders. All over Europe, in fact, the first years of the 21st century have brought massive strikes to prevent European corporations and governments from following the American lead in cutting wages and benefits. In May of 2003, for example, a nationwide strike in Austria shut down all major services. These Austrian employees were voicing their disapproval of attempts by their government to cut pensions to help reduce corporate taxes. My classes were cancelled at the University of Vienna because of the strike, so we moved to the streets to watch the thousands of Austrians marching in protest. Many signs as well as media interviews made it clear these Austrian workers, like those in France, Germany, Italy, and other major European countries, will work hard to stop their governments from allowing the trend toward lower wages and benefits seen in the United States.

A major question for social stratification systems through the 21st century is also related to increasing global competition in the modern world system. Will the Europeans be able to remain competitive with much higher wages and benefits, or will they be forced to make their people poorer, as American workers have become?

With the cold war over and the Berlin Wall down, the "them versus us" mental-ity directed toward the old Soviet Union is gone. It has been replaced, however, with a greater recognition of large differences among capitalist nations. In other words, it is no longer simply capitalism versus communism, but competition among differing forms of organizations in the capitalist world economy. These differences among capitalist nations, as we will see, also involve differences in their systems of social stratification. Thus, we can also say that there has been a historic shift in the American stratification system and the place of the United States in the modern world system. To understand the current system of social stratification in this country as well as the future of this system, we *must* pay close attention to differences among nations and to trends in globalization, or in our terms, in the modern world system. We do so throughout coming chapters, but especially in chapters on the modern world system and comparative social stratification involving Japan, Germany, China, and poor countries of this world.

It is becoming more and more difficult for the affluent to ignore the huge level of world inequality. While that long economic boom was going on in the United States at the end of the 20th century, and while Americans at the bottom levels of the stratification system were not seeing many improvements in their lives, a very large segment of the world's population was becoming much poorer. As we will see, the new **Purchasing Power Parity (PPP)** index allows us to get a much more realistic picture of differing standards of living and rates of poverty around the world. Using this estimate, international agencies now calculate that there are *more than 1 billion people in the world living on less than what $1 a day would buy in the United States!* This number has been going up rapidly in the world for more than a century, and continues to increase in many world regions as we move through the first years of the 21st century (World Bank 2006a). While this high level of poverty and income inequality has dropped slightly in recent years, the change is almost completely due to economic development with poverty reduction in the two countries with the world's largest populations, China and India (Firebaugh and Goesling 2004; World Bank 2006b, 2007). In other world regions, especially in sub-Saharan Africa, poverty rates are getting higher. We also see there are data clearly showing a relationship between world poverty and such things as war and terrorism. International opinion polls find that most people in the world believe that the United States is to some degree responsible for this increasing world poverty (*New York Times,* June 3, 2003; December 5, 2002). New research covered in Chapters 14 and 16 indicates that there is some truth in these beliefs. But the situation, as usual, is more complex; some less-developed countries in the world are able to participate in the global economy, accept hundreds of multinational corporations in their borders, and drastically reduce the poverty of their people. For many other less-developed countries, however, opening to the global economy and the stratification of nations behind it leaves them worse off in the long run—their national assets are stripped away and their people become poorer. Understanding the differences between these less-developed countries (such as Thailand, Vietnam, China, and Taiwan, compared to Burma, Haiti, and the Congo) can be among the most important contributions of sociology to the world (Kerbo 2005, 2006).

## ⚹ The Organization of Chapters

With some of the major issues in the study of social stratification having been outlined and basic terms having been defined, it is useful to give an idea of the order in which major issues are approached. In Part One of this book, after the present introductory chapter, we consider the extent of inequality in the United States. Our concern in Chapter 2 is the degree to which valued goods and services, health, political influence, and other important aspects of life are unequally distributed. In Chapter 3 the focus is on the history of inequality in human societies. We examine how inequality and systems of social stratification evolved from the earliest societies thousands of years ago up to the present.

The chapters in Part Two present various theories of social stratification and theoretical controversies. Chapter 4 examines the classical theories of Marx and Weber, and Chapter 5 examines current functional and conflict theories.

Part Three is concerned primarily with structures of social stratification in modern industrial societies, especially the United States. By structures we mean the various class positions and the logic of how power and wealth hang together in modern societies. Chapters 6 through 11 are devoted to major classes in the United States—the upper class, corporate class, middle and working classes, as well as the poor, and the effects of gender, race, and ethnic status on social stratification in Chapters 10 and 11.

Part Four on the processes of social stratification follows. Chapters 12 and 13 concern the subjects of social mobility and the legitimation of inequality, or how inequality is made acceptable or tolerable, especially for those toward the bottom of the stratification system.

Part Five compares systems of social stratification in other nations, as well as focusing on the relation between social stratification and the modern world system. We begin with Chapter 14 on the modern world system, competition by the dominant core nations through recent history, and such questions as the existence of a global corporate class or upper class today. Chapter 15 pertains to social stratification in Japan and Germany. Particularly because Japan is the first industrial society without a Western cultural tradition, an examination of its class system provides an interesting test of our ideas about social stratification developed in Western societies. While there are some important differences, in this case the many similarities in Western and Japanese social stratification are very interesting. With respect to Germany, there are again basic similarities to social stratification systems found throughout the industrialized world. But there also are some significant differences, especially with respect to overall inequality and the power of the working class. In both countries, therefore, many stereotypes about inequality and social stratification obtained with a focus on only one nation are exposed, helping us gain a better understanding of our subject of social stratification.

Finally, with global inequalities and poverty increasing in many parts of the world, we must understand how a modern world system, or global stratification system, shapes the lives of people in poorer countries. We need to know why misery and poverty are going up in some countries while others have made dramatic gains in poverty reduction. In summary, in recent decades most African countries have been getting much poorer, most Latin American countries have had economic development that benefits only the more affluent, while many nations in East and Southeast Asia have had dramatic gains in *both* poverty reduction and economic development benefiting the more affluent. Thailand, China, and Vietnam have been specifically praised by agencies like the World Bank and United Nations for their economic development and impressive poverty reduction in recent decades. But the old "Asian economic miracle" story focused on Asian cultural characteristics is far too simple, especially when we find neighboring countries today with identical cultural heritages with vastly different economic prospects and levels of poverty. In Chapter 16 we explore how the less-developed nations brought into the global economy can be exploited by the rich of this world. And we see how some nations have thrown off the negative effects of the colonial exploitation of previous centuries to enter the modern world system from a position of more strength to protect their interests and those of their people.

## Summary

The beginning contrast between Michael and David Rockefeller raised a number of questions about the nature of social stratification. These questions especially indicate that the nature of the society and social structure must be the focal points for understanding social stratification, or "who gets what, and why." A number of basic definitions were then given, especially definitions of social differentiation, social inequality, and social stratification. The major class divisions in modern industrial societies—the upper class, corporate class, middle class, working class, and the lower class or the poor—were described, along with the dynamics of social mobility. The chapter concluded with a description of the modern world system, or what can be called world stratification. The nature of a particular country's system of social stratification can no longer be fully understood without reference to that country's position in the modern world system. The relative decline of the United States in the modern world system in past decades was a major cause of growing inequality, especially the shrinking middle-class or middle-income positions in this country. Now we see that the relative economic decline of the United States in the modern world economy was suspended in the later years of the 1990s compared to Europe and Japan because of continuing increases in inequality in the United States, with wages, benefits, and job security all declining for workers in the lower half of the stratification system. Finally with growing global inequality, we must understand the effects of globalization and the modern world system.

# Dimensions of Inequality in the United States

In this chapter we see more details about the growing inequality in the United States compared to other postindustrial nations. In none of these other nations do we see such contrasts of high standards of living and homelessness at the same time.

*SOURCES:* Left: © McGraw-Hill Companies, Inc./Gary He, photographer; right: Royalty-Free/CORBIS

## Chapter Outline

❖ **Income and Wealth Inequality**

❖ **Inequality in Basic Necessities**

❖ **Health Inequalities**

❖ **Unequal Political Outputs**

❖ **Dimensions of Inequality: A Conclusion**

❖ **Summary**

A few years ago I met an American friend of mine at a train station in California. He had been living in Japan for 10 years, and except for a couple of short visits to Hawaii, had not been in the United States during those 10 years. He arrived in San Francisco, spent a few days across the bay in Oakland, and traveled by train to Los Angeles and then all the way across the country to spend a few weeks gathering information in Washington, D.C. Upon arriving in California, and then more so as he traveled across the United States, he was shocked at the poverty and signs of inequality he saw everywhere. "This is not the country I remember," he told me. "It almost seems like a third world country today." A couple of years later, while I was living in Germany, American relatives who came for a visit asked, "So where do the poor people live?" They were unaware that, such as there are, I had already shown them.

These are not uncommon reactions. Indeed, in the United States we find a mix of third world and first world characteristics more than in other industrial nations. Traveling around this country, you find the third world and first world in separate regions, with people of first world America trying to isolate themselves from what they find in the other. The third world regions, it must be stressed, are not mostly due to recent immigration: The vast majority of poor people in the United States were born of parents whose ancestors had been Americans for many generations.

As noted briefly in the previous chapter, the United States may be beginning another shift that will have a profound impact on the nature of social stratification in this country. During the 1920s the level of inequality in the United States was at a high point, similar to the levels of inequality existing in this country today. The Great Depression of the 1930s and then World War II led to major political and economic changes that brought inequality down to the average among the industrial nations of the world by the 1950s and 1960s. From the beginning of the 1980s, however, political and economic changes have been pushing the United States toward more inequality and less equality of opportunity every year. There are many indications that these trends could shift yet again. The election of Barack Obama as President of the United States in 2008 and the worst economic crisis since the Great Depression of the 1930s have come together in a "perfect storm." The growing inequalities of wealth, income, and opportunity in the United States may soon be reversed through new political and economic policies. The possible changes in the American system of social stratification remain difficult to judge using new Census Bureau income inequality data for 2009. But in this chapter and others to follow, we identify the possible signs that could in time produce these changes and consider them in detail.

It is time to turn to some details of the inequality in the United States compared with earlier history and compared with other countries. But it must be stressed that our intent in this chapter is primarily *descriptive;* in later chapters we offer explanations for why U.S. inequality is so high and rising. We begin by describing the distribution of income and wealth, then proceed to standards of living and health. In the final section we describe inequalities in government services and the tax policies that lead to inequalities in who pays for these services. These types of inequalities are among the most important, although by no means the only ones of importance. There are, for example, other non-material inequalities, even important inequalities in self-respect and happiness, related to the stratification system. These factors are examined in other chapters. And, of course, for American society, there are very important inequalities of all types based on gender, race, and ethnic status. A few of these are considered in this chapter. Because of the importance of these subjects, though, much more detail about gender, race, and ethnic inequalities and their causes is presented in Chapters 10 and 11. The patterns of inequality examined here provide a base image of inequality in a Western industrial society, which will make further study of social stratification more meaningful.

# ❊ Income and Wealth Inequality

Two of the most important types of inequality are inequalities of income and wealth. These are of major importance because it is income and wealth that bring other valued goods and services, not to mention the basic necessities of life. The relationship between income and necessities like food, shelter, and health care is described after our discussion of income and wealth. Income and wealth, however, are also generalized commodities that, depending on the quantity and how they are used, bring power and influence. The relationship income and wealth have to power and influence is the subject of later chapters.

By *income* we mean money, wages, and payments that periodically are received as returns from an occupation or investments. Income is the means by which most Americans and other people obtain the necessities and simple luxuries of life; a wage or salary (rather than investments) sustains the vast majority of people in the world. *Wealth* is accumulated assets in the form of various types of valued goods, such as real estate, stocks, bonds, or money held in reserve. Wealth is anything of economic value that is bought, sold, stocked for future disposition, or invested to bring an economic return. As might be expected, most people have little or no wealth; whatever they have attained in the form of wages and salaries cannot be accumulated because it must be used for immediate necessities. Income is certainly distributed in an unequal manner in the United States, but wealth is distributed even more unequally. It is useful to note that, of course, wealth can be turned into income when people have a lot of it, as is the case with people who have over $1 million incomes per year, who on average obtain only 33 percent of that income through employment (Hacker 1997:84).

## Income Inequality

A simple method of considering income inequality is by looking at a population distribution within specified income categories. Table 2-1 presents such a distribution for all

## TABLE 2-1

### Percentage Annual Income Distribution of Households by Race and Ethnic Status, 2009

| | Percent | | | | |
|---|---|---|---|---|---|
| | **All families** | **White families** | **Black families** | **Hispanic origin** | **Asian** |
| Under $15,000 | 13.0 | 11.4 | 23.4 | 16.5 | 11.7 |
| $15,000–$24,999 | 11.9 | 11.6 | 15.4 | 15.2 | 7.9 |
| $25,000–$34,999 | 11.1 | 10.8 | 13.4 | 14.3 | 8.2 |
| $35,000–$49,999 | 14.1 | 14.2 | 14.5 | 15.4 | 11.1 |
| $50,000–$74,999 | 18.1 | 18.7 | 15.2 | 17.6 | 16.9 |
| $75,000–$99,999 | 11.5 | 12.0 | 8.7 | 9.1 | 11.1 |
| $100,000–$149,999 | 11.9 | 12.6 | 6.3 | 7.8 | 16.9 |
| $150,000–$199,999 | 4.4 | 4.7 | 1.8 | 2.2 | 7.8 |
| $200,000 & over | 3.8 | 4.1 | 1.2 | 1.7 | 7.7 |

SOURCE: U.S. Bureau of the Census. *Income, Poverty, and Health Insurance Coverage in the United States, 2009.* (2010: Table A-1).

families (as well as for whites, blacks, and Hispanics) in the United States as of 2009. Of the millions of households, for example, 13.0 percent had annual incomes of less than $15,000; 11.9 percent had incomes between $15,000 and $29,999; and, at the other end of the spectrum, 3.8 percent had incomes of $200,000 or more. And it is worth noting that while the percentage of Americans in the low-income categories have changed very little, the category of $100,000 and over has increased much more than any other category in the past several years.

As we will see in later chapters, an important issue in the study of social stratification and inequality, especially in the United States, is inequality by race and ethnic origin. Race, ethnicity, and class are related to each other in complex ways, with racial divisions often having, to some degree, class divisions at their base. But for now we first need to consider the level of income inequality by race and Hispanic origin. In Table 2-1 we find that both blacks and Hispanics had a higher percentage of people with incomes of $15,000 or less in 2009, and a much lower percentage with incomes of $100,000 or more compared with whites. The biggest contrast in Table 2-1, however, is the much higher percentage of Asian American households with incomes of $100,000 or more in 2009. We also consider some reasons for this in Chapter 11 on race and ethnic inequalities.

In contrast to considering the distribution of people or families within income categories (as in Table 2-1), we can consider the distribution of total income among select population categories. A standard method of doing so is to divide the population into income fifths (20 percent population segments) and compare population shares with income shares. Table 2-2 presents this information for 2009. In this year the lowest fifth of households in the United States received 3.4 percent of the income, the next-lowest

**TABLE 2-2**

## Percentage of Aggregate Household Income Received by Each Fifth, 2009

| All households | Percentage of aggregate income |
|---|---|
| Lowest fifth | 3.4% |
| Second fifth | 8.6 |
| Middle fifth | 14.6 |
| Fourth fifth | 23.2 |
| Highest fifth | 50.3 |

SOURCE: U.S. Bureau of the Census, *Income, Poverty, and Health Insurance Coverage in the United States: 2009* (2010: Table 1-3).

fifth received 8.6 percent, and the highest fifth received 50.3 percent of all income. In other words, the lowest 20 percent of households received only 3.4 percent of the total income, while the highest 20 percent of households received 50.3 percent of the total.

The vast majority of people in this country must depend on some type of employment (as opposed to wealth) for their income, and the occupational structure is of primary importance in creating an unequal distribution of income. Table 2-3 presents the median incomes within general occupational categories for 2009. For males, the highest occupational category (executive, administrative, and managerial occupations) shows an average annual income of $70,183 while the lowest, production workers, shows an average wage of $36,772. It is also important to note that for females the highest figure is substantially lower than that for men, $51,014. Roughly the same income discrepancy is found between males and females with respect to education level in Table 2-3. As we will see in later chapters, part of the male–female inequality is due to sex discrimination, but this discrimination operates also within the occupational structure in a number of important ways.

The extent of income inequality by occupation is severely underestimated in Table 2-3 because we are considering only very general occupational categories. Within each occupational category many people are making much less and others much more than is indicated by the median. This underestimation is especially evident at the top, where many managers of major corporations have exceptionally high salaries. As we will see later, top managers of large American corporations have annual incomes far exceeding incomes of the top managers of all other industrial nations, something few Americans realize (Osberg and Smeeding 2006). The average total income of the CEOs of 200 of America's largest corporations in 2005 averaged over $11 million (Pearl, Meyer and Partners 2006:6; also see Mishel, Bernstein, and Allegretto 2007: Table 3-46). Just between 1998 and 2005 this top CEO salary increased 169 percent (Mishel, Bernstein, and Shierholz 2009: Table 3-42). Almost half of this total compensation is in the form of stock options, which are tax deductible for the corporation, and are highly restricted or prohibited in other industrial nations. Among the 100 highest-paid corporate executives

## TABLE 2-3

### Median Annual Income by Occupational Category and Education, Male and Female, 2009

| | Annual wages | |
|---|---|---|
| Occupation | Male | Female |
| Executive, administrative, and managerial | $70,183 | $51,014 |
| Professional | 66,369 | 48,856 |
| Service occupations | 30,953 | 23,302 |
| Sales and office occupations | 47,312 | 29,823 |
| Natural resource production | 26,589 | 21,134 |
| Production | 36,772 | 25,244 |

| | Median annual income | |
|---|---|---|
| Educational level | | |
| Less than high school | $29,023 | $21,226 |
| High school graduate | 39,478 | 29,150 |
| Some college | 47,097 | 34,087 |
| Bachelor's degree | 71,466 | 51,878 |

SOURCE: U.S. Bureau of the Census, *Income, Poverty, and Health Insurance Coverage in the United States, 2009* (2010: Table A-5).

in the United States during 2009, however, you did not have to include stock options to keep them all in the multimillion-dollar annual pay category. The highest paid CEO in 2009 was Lawrence Ellison of Oracle Corporation with over $550 million for the year (www.forbes.com/lists/). The second highest paid was Ray Irani of Occidental Petroleum with over $220 million. At number ten was Robert Lane at Deere and Company at over $61 million. The longest economic boom in American history, from the early 1990s to 2001, was very kind to American CEOs: The gap between the average worker's pay and that of top corporate executives has shown a staggering increase from 40 to 1 in 1990 to 419 to 1 in 1998. After a slight drop in the first years of the 21st century, this increase in top manager compensation resumed its upward pace, rising again by 10 percent for 2005, during a time when the average income of the average American remained almost flat (Pearl, Meyer, and Partners 2006:1). If the same wage increase that top executives received for the 1990s had been given to average workers, their pay would have gone from an average of $29,000 in 1990 to $110,000 in 1998. Instead, however, average worker pay increased only slightly in the decades of the 1990s. And as we will see in more detail later, the poorest Americans saw only very small gains in their standard of living finally during the last 2 years of this long economic boom, with their minuscule gains quickly eroded by an economic downturn in 2001 in the face of massive reductions in the welfare system put in place during 1996. With the slow recovery from 2001 until 2007, these gains were not maintained. In fact, although corporate profits were going up steadily between 2001 and 2008, the real average income of Americans changed very little.

Until the big American financial institutions set off the U.S. and global economic crisis of 2008–2009 with their unsound banking policies, few Americans knew much about top corporate salaries (Osberg and Smeeding 2006). That situation changed dramatically once these big financial institutions began failing and required huge bailouts by the federal government. The news media began asking questions about the very high CEO salaries and bonuses, especially in a time when these CEOs were performing very badly, and so did top government officials. Investigations showed that even as these financial institutions were losing billions of dollars and receiving billions of dollars in taxpayers' money in bailouts (TARP funds), the big salaries and bonuses continued. For example, while Bank of America received $45 billion in government bailout money in 2008, the company gave $1 million or more each to 172 top managers, and $64 million in bonuses to its top four managers (State Attorney General of New York 2009). And it must be remembered that this is bonus money on top of their regular salaries, which are usually in the hundreds of thousands of dollars. Bank of America was far from alone. Citigroup lost over $27 billion in 2008 and received $45 billion in government bailout money while giving 738 managers at least $1 million each in bonuses. The top four executives at Citigroup received a combined total of $43 million in bonuses. Goldman Sachs received $10 billion in government bailout money while giving a total of more than $45 million in bonuses to its top four executives. J. P. Morgan Chase received $25 billion in bailout money while giving a total of more than $74 million to its top four executives. Merrill Lynch suffered losses of more than $27 billion in 2008 and had to be taken over by Bank of America to survive. While this was happening, Merrill Lynch's top four executives received a total of more than $120 million in bonuses. At Morgan Stanley it was $10 billion in bailout money while its top four executives received a total of $73 million in bonuses. This behavior by the executives of big U.S. financial institutions set off public and government calls to increase regulation on these banks not seen since the Great Depression of the 1930s in this country. These corporate executive salaries and bonuses are by far the highest in the world in the last few decades.

Having considered some aspects of current income inequality, we now go on to three further questions: (1) What was the previous pattern of income inequality in the United States? (2) How does the United States compare with other industrialized nations in this respect? (3) Has the distribution of income in this country become more or less unequal, or has it remained the same over the years? This last question has become one of the most important in recent decades and pertains to a troubling trend in the nature of inequality in the United States.

## Trends in U.S. Income Inequality

Income inequality was reduced somewhat during the 1930s and early 1940s due to depression reforms and full employment during World War II. The most significant change occurred within the top 20 percent and the top 5 percent of families, who had their share of income reduced from 54.4 percent and 30 percent, respectively, in 1929 to 44 percent and 17.2 percent by 1945 (Turner and Starnes 1976:51). There was a slight decrease in

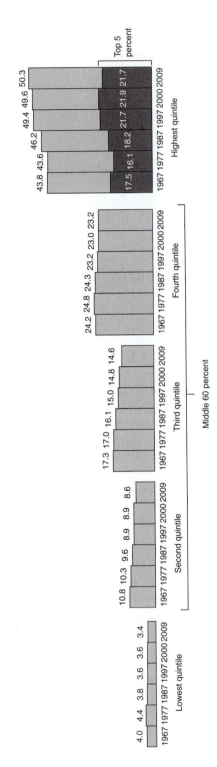

**FIGURE 2-1** *Percentage of Aggregate Household Income by Income Fifths and Top 5 Percent, 1967–2009*

*SOURCE:* U.S. Bureau of the Census, *Money Income in the United States: 2000* (2001: Table A-2); *Income, Poverty, and Health Insurance Coverage, 2009* (2010: Table 3).

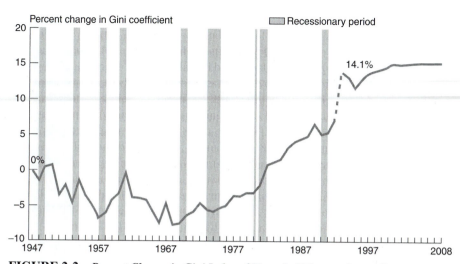

**FIGURE 2-2**   *Percent Change in Gini Index of Household Income Inequality, 1967–2008*

*SOURCE:* U.S. Bureau of the Census, *Measuring 50 Years of Economic Change* (1998:30): U.S. Bureau of the Census, *Income, Poverty, and Health Care Coverage in the U.S. 2008* (2009:38).

income inequality between 1947 and 1975. The percentage of income going to the bottom 20 percent of the people increased somewhat, and the percentage of income going to the top 20 percent and top 5 percent of the people decreased. *However,* as noted in the beginning of this chapter, there has been significant change since 1980. A significant increase has occurred in income inequality between 1980 and 2009 because, as they say, the income rich have been getting richer while the income poor have been getting poorer. As we see in Figure 2-1, by 2008 the bottom income group now has only 3.4 percent of the income, compared with 4.4 percent in 1977, and the top 20 percent income group now has 50.3 percent of all income, compared with only 43.6 percent in 1977.

Figure 2-2 indicates this growing inequality by using data from what is known as a **Gini index** to measure income inequality. With Figure 2-2 we can see that income inequality in the United States was lower between 1967 and through the 1970s, but then rose dramatically in the 1980s and 1990s. A Gini index score of 0.0 indicates complete equality in a society, while a Gini index score of 1.0 would indicate one person or family has all the income. In 1980 this Gini index for the United States stood at 0.331 and had increased to 0.469 by 2005 (U.S. Bureau of the Census 2006b:40).

Another way to consider this growing income inequality is by looking at changes in income for 20 percent (fifths) income segments over time. Figure 2-3 shows what was happening during the 1980s, the years when economic changes and Reaganomics tax and welfare policy changes were creating the most dramatic transformation in income inequality in the United States. As can be seen, the lower-income groups were losing income while the top groups were making significant gains. In fact, while the bottom 60 percent of Americans were losing income in the 1980s, the top 5 percent gained over 15 percent in income and the top 1 percent of people made gains of about 63 percent of their income.

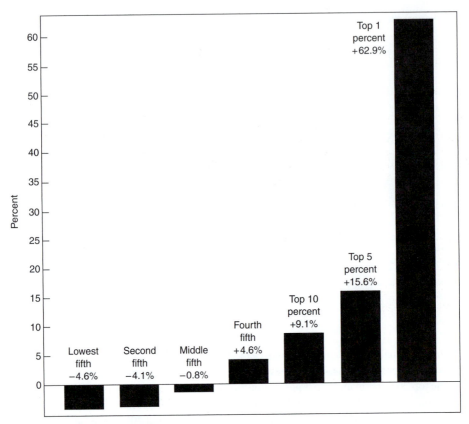

**FIGURE 2-3**   *Income Gains and Losses, 1980–1989*

*SOURCE:* Mishel and Bernstein (1993:48).

The changes for a longer time period are shown in Figure 2-4. We see that from 1967 to 2000 all income segments lost shares of income except the top 20 percent of people, who gained over 13 percent in this 33-year period. What is most interesting about Figure 2-4 is that the highest shrinking of income shares is found among the middle-income groups, with the second fifth losing most at more than 17 percent. This is a clear indication of what is often called the shrinking middle class in American society.

This is not the place to get into a full explanation of why income inequality has grown significantly since 1980, but we can briefly cover some of the most important reasons. These reasons fall into two main categories: (1) political policies since the late 1970s and (2) changes in the U.S. economy. Among the political policies that increased income inequality were changes in tax policies (reducing taxes for the wealthy, while taxes for lower-income groups increased) and cuts in transfer payments such as the means-tested welfare programs for the poor (Mishel and Bernstein 1993; Moller et al. 2003; Alderson and Nielsen 2002; Goesling 2001; Harrison and Bluestone 1988). As Figure 2-5 indicates,

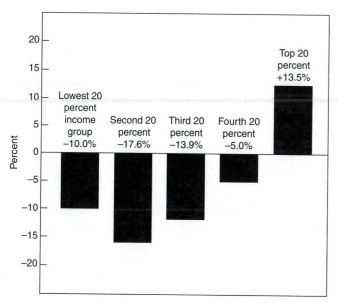

**FIGURE 2-4**    *Income Gains and Losses, 1967–2000*

*SOURCE:* U.S. Bureau of the Census, *Money Income in the U.S., 2000* (2001:11).

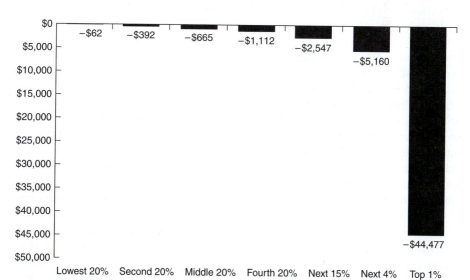

**FIGURE 2-5**    *Tax Savings by Income Groups from Bush Income Tax Cuts to 2006*

*SOURCE:* Mishel, Bernstein, and Allegretto (2007) http://www.stateofworkingamerica.org (April 2007).

these tax cuts continued during the George W. Bush administration, an administration that will probably go down in history as making more tax cuts than any previous president. The impact on income inequality is clear from just one example of the 2003 tax cuts. A major political impact on increasing inequality can be seen in the shrinking U.S. minimum wage. Whereas the minimum wage was just under $8 in 1968 (using 2000 dollar equivalents to correct for inflation), it was only $5.15 by 2000 (U.S. Department of Commerce 2004:225). In fact, this federal minimum wage had fallen to $4.65 at the end of the Reagan years in 1989, to be raised only slightly during the Clinton presidency. The U.S. Congress has deliberately avoided allowing the minimum wage to keep pace with the cost of living, thus keeping wages of the poorest American workers lower. However, we come to another of those indicators of future change in the American stratification system with the Obama presidency. The minimum wage was given is biggest boost in decades, moving from $5.15 an hour to $7.25 an hour in 2009. In real 2009 dollars, this raised the minimum wage to where it was at the beginning of the Reagan administration in 1981 (Mishel, Bernstein, and Shierholz 2009:209).

Among the most important changes in the economy, as noted earlier, has been the reduction in middle-paying jobs in the 1980s and 1990s, while jobs in both the highest-paid and lowest-paid areas of the economy increased (Mishel, Bernstein, and Schmitt 1999, 2001; Mishel, Bernstein, and Boushey 2003; Thurow 1987). Further, of all the new jobs created in the economy from 1979 to 1986, over 55 percent had wages at the poverty level or below (Bluestone 1988). Finally, ranking jobs into those with highest to lowest average pay, Wright and Dwyer (2003) found large differences of the net number of jobs from the 1960s to early 2000s. During the 1960s, those jobs in the top 20 percent in terms of pay increased most, with additional large increases in jobs in the next two 20 percent groups in terms of pay. By the 1990s and early 2000s, however, the net number of jobs with the lowest pay and the highest pay were increasing most, with middle-paying jobs substantially lower.

## *Comparative Income Inequality*

Our next question pertains to what the U.S. income inequality looks like compared with that of other industrial nations. In the beginning, it is useful to point out that during the 1960s the United States was generally ranked about midway in terms of income inequality when compared with other industrial nations (Jain 1975). France had the highest amount of income inequality at the time, with West Germany, England, and Australia showing the lowest levels in the 1960s.

By the 1970s the United States had taken a slight lead to have the highest income inequality among all industrial nations, and has held the lead ever since, moving further away from most other nations. For example, while the bottom 10 percent of people held 1.8 percent of income and the top 10 percent of people held over 30 percent, the figures for Sweden were 3.7 and 20 percent in the late 1990s (World Bank 2000: Table 5). In Japan it was 4.8 and 21.7, while it was 3.3 and 23.7 in Germany. As usual, among the major industrial nations, Great Britain was closest to the United States, but with 2.6 percent of the income going to the bottom 10 percent of people and 27.3 going to the top 10 percent of people.

Tables 2-4 and 2-5 show us more clearly what has been happening in recent decades. Table 2-4 shows that the United States was already the most unequal country

## TABLE 2-4

### Comparative Income Inequality, Top to Bottom 20 Percent Income Groups, Early 1980s

| Country | Percentage of national income held by: | |
| --- | --- | --- |
| | **Bottom 20 percent** | **Top 20 percent** |
| Denmark | 5.4% | 38.6% |
| Belgium | 7.9 | 36.0 |
| Sweden | 8.0 | 36.9 |
| Italy | 6.8 | 41.0 |
| Germany | 6.8 | 38.7 |
| Spain | 6.9 | 40.0 |
| The Netherlands | 6.9 | 38.3 |
| France | 6.3 | 40.8 |
| United Kingdom | 5.8 | 39.5 |
| United States | 4.7 | 40.9 |

*SOURCE:* Data are for years in the late 1970s to early 1980s and come from the World Bank, *World Development Report 1990* (1990:236).

## TABLE 2-5

### Comparative Income Inequality, Top to Bottom 10 Percent Income Groups, and Gini Index 2007

| Country | Percent of national income held by: | | Gini Index |
| --- | --- | --- | --- |
| | **Bottom 10 percent** | **Top 10 percent** | |
| Austria | 3.3% | 23.0% | .29 |
| Denmark | 2.6 | 21.3 | .24 |
| Belgium | 3.4 | 28.1 | .33 |
| Sweden | 3.6 | 22.0 | .25 |
| Italy | 2.3 | 26.8 | .36 |
| Germany | 3.2 | 22.1 | .28 |
| Spain | 2.6 | 26.6 | .34 |
| The Netherlands | 2.5 | 22.9 | .31 |
| France | 2.8 | 25.1 | .32 |
| United Kingdom | 2.1 | 28.5 | .36 |
| United States | 1.9 | 29.9 | .41 |

*SOURCE:* United Nations, *Human Development Report, 2009* (2009: Table M).

during the early 1980s, but not by so much. In fact, while the bottom 20 percent of people in Italy received more of the income than the bottom 20 percent of Americans, the top 20 percent of people in Italy received slightly more of the national income than the American top 20 percent. A Table 2.5 shows, the United States had moved way ahead of these other nations in 2007. In fact, we find that many of the countries in Europe have become more equal.

Even more striking is how the bottom 10 percent of Americans rank with the rest of the world. Using 2002 World Bank data, the Web service NationMaster compiled tables showing the percent of national income going to the bottom 10 percent of people in 100 countries around the world (http://www.nationmaster.com/graph-T/eco_inc_dis_poo_10). Of the rich nations, Japan had the highest percent of its income going to the bottom 10 percent of its people. The United States is the only rich nation far down the list, 85th out of 100 nations. Admittedly, the 1.8 percent of national income going to the bottom 10 percent of Americans is more real income (in buying power) than the 1.8 percent of national income going to the bottom 10 percent in poor African nations like Burundi and Mali. Still, it is the gap between the rich and the poor that is most striking in the United States when compared even to poor countries in this world.

Another standard way of comparing income and wages across nations is to consider wages (including the value of benefits such as health care coverage) of manufacturing employees. When we do so for 2007, the most recent data, all of the manufacturing employees in the major nations of Europe, plus Canada and Australia, had higher wages than American workers (U.S. Bureau of the Census, 2010b: Table 1318). German workers, for example, had wages that were 166 percent of those of American workers, with wages in Norway 180 percent of those in the United States. For Europe as a whole, manufacturing wages were 133 percent of those in the United States. But there is an increasing problem even with this method of comparing wages because the percentage of middle-paying manufacturing workers in the United States is shrinking compared to Europe, where these middle-paying jobs are shrinking less if at all. In contrast, the United States is adding a much greater percentage of lower-paying jobs compared to European countries (Wright and Dwyer 2003). It is this shrinking of U.S. middle-paying jobs, as we see in more detail in Chapter 8, that is increasing much of the inequality in this country.

The biggest contrast for the United States, though, is shown in Table 2-6. American top executives are way above all other top executives in the world. As we see in more detail in coming chapters, this increasing inequality in the United States compared to other industrial nations is partly due to a complex mix of U.S. government cuts in social programs, reduced taxes on the rich, and changes in the global economy (Moran 2006; Lobao and Hooks 2003; Beckfield 2006; Brady and Denniston 2006; Brady, Beckfield, and Seeleib-Kaiser 2005; Brady 2006, 2005, 2003a; Kerbo 2006: Chapter 3).

The late 1990s and 2000s were times of controversial CEO pay increases in Europe, primarily in response to the much higher compensation for CEOs of U.S. corporations (Cheffins 2003). But Table 2-6 shows European executives have a long way to go to catch their American counterparts. The top half of Table 2-6 compares the basic salaries of CEOs in the 300 largest corporations across the advanced industrial nations. The bottom half of Table 2-6 includes a smaller group of advanced industrial nations

## TABLE 2-6

### Comparative CEO Basic Salary and Total Compensation, 1988–2005

| Country | Basic CEO salary, 1988–2005 | | |
|---|---|---|---|
| | **1988** | **2003** | **2005** |
| Australia | $180,760 | $737,162 | $707,747 |
| Belgium | 383,718 | 739,700 | 987,387 |
| Canada | 423,358 | 944,375 | 1,068,964 |
| France | 404,331 | 780,380 | 1,202,145 |
| Germany | 412,259 | 1,013,171 | 1,181,292 |
| Italy | 342,492 | 893,035 | 1,137,326 |
| Japan | 502,639 | 484,909 | 543,564 |
| The Netherlands | 396,403 | 716,387 | 862,711 |
| New Zealand | | 476,926 | 396,456 |
| Spain | 352,006 | 658,039 | 697,691 |
| Sweden | 234,670 | 743,160 | 948,990 |
| Switzerland | 510,567 | 1,263,450 | 1,390,899 |
| United Kingdom | 453,485 | 881,047 | 1,184,936 |
| **United States** | **805,490** | **2,386,762** | **2,164,952** |
| Non-U.S. average | 383,057 | 794,749 | 946,931 |

*SOURCE*: Table constructed from Towers Perrin data in Mishel, Bernstein, and Allegretto (2007: Table 3-17).

### Comparative CEO Total Compensation and Pay Gap with Average Worker, 2003–2005*

| Country | CEO total compensation | Gap between CEO and average industrial worker salary |
|---|---|---|
| United States | $11 million | 400 to 1 |
| Switzerland | 4 million | 11 to 1 |
| Germany | 2.6 million | 11 to 1 |
| France | 2 million | 16 to 1 |
| Great Britain | 1.7 million | 25 to 1 |
| The Netherlands | 1.5 million | 22 to 1 |

*European data based on a survey of top 300 corporations in 2003; U.S. data based on a survey of top 200 corporations in 2005. Total compensation includes basic salary, stock options, and bonuses.

*SOURCES*: Pearl, Meyer, and Partners (2006); *New York Times*, June 15, 2006; data from Towers Perrin in www.finfacts.com (March 7, 2007); www.swissinfo.org (July 26, 2004).

where data were available for total CEO compensation, which includes stock options and bonuses, as well as basic salary. Most other industrial nations either strictly limit compensation through stock options or ban such compensation altogether. Most striking, though, is the wage gap between American CEOs and the average industrial worker compared to that gap in Europe in these 300 largest corporations. Though difficult to compare precisely because different numbers of top corporations are used to measure CEO income averages in European countries and the United States, these ratios give a rough idea of income inequality for top managers in big corporations and the average pay of their employees. While the gap in pay between CEOs and the average industrial worker in Europe ranges from 11 to 1 in Switzerland and Germany, to 25 to 1 in Great Britain, the gap is an amazing 400 to 1 in the United States, with some estimates going up to 500 to 1 (*New York Times,* June 15, 2006; data from Towers Perrin in www.finfacts. com [March 7, 2007]; www.swissinfo.org [July 26, 2004]; also see Mishel, Bernstein, and Allegretto 2007: Figure 3z). Back in 1980 this gap between CEOs and average industrial workers in the United States was estimated to be 40 to 1. Even more striking today is the U.S. ratio of 821 to 1 for CEOs and people working at minimum wage.

## Wealth Inequality

Despite the importance of income inequality in the United States, in some ways wealth inequality is more significant. Most people use income for day-to-day necessities. Substantial wealth, however, often brings income, power, and independence. On one hand, wealth in significant quantities relieves individuals from dependence on others for an income. As we will see, the authority structure associated with occupational differentiation is one of the most important aspects of the stratification system in the United States, and the impact of this authority structure is reduced when people have substantial wealth. On the other hand, if wealth is used to purchase significant ownership of the means of production in the society (most important, stock ownership in major corporations), it can bring authority to the holder of such wealth (depending on the amount of ownership). Substantial wealth is also important because it can be transferred from generation to generation more easily than income, producing greater inheritance of position and opportunity within the stratification system. This has been especially true since 1982, when one of President Reagan's tax bills substantially reduced inheritance taxes in this country. This inheritance tax was further reduced in 2001, with more reductions scheduled in coming years.

Estimates of wealth holdings and wealth are difficult to come by in any society, including the United States. This is so not only because much wealth can be and is hidden from those trying to make an estimate but also because most countries, including the United States, seldom try to collect the figures annually, as is more often done with income figures. Table 2-7 reports wealth inequality data that exist for 1989 and 2004. Wealth holdings are estimated by fifths of the population, as were shown for income inequality, and are presented with figures on income inequality for the same year for comparison purposes. Although income is highly unequal in the United States, these data show wealth to be even more unequally distributed. As Table 2-7 indicates, whereas the top 20 percent of Americans got just over 50 percent of the income in 2004, the wealthiest 20 percent of Americans held over 84 percent of the wealth in 2004. This means only 16 percent of the wealth was left over for the remaining 80 percent of Americans. The bottom 20 percent of Americans in terms of wealth, in fact, were in the red: Considering debts, their share of the wealth was –0.5. The next 20 percent of Americans were not much better off, with only 0.7 percent of the wealth. The top

## T A B L E   2 - 7

### Distribution of Wealth and Income by Family Fifths, Top 1 Percent and Top 10 Percent, 1989–2004

| Family fifths | Percentage of total wealth | | Percentage of total income | |
|---|---|---|---|---|
| | 1989 | 2004 | 1989 | 2004 |
| Highest fifth | 78.7% | 84.4% | 42.7% | 50.1% |
| Fourth fifth | 14.5 | 11.3 | 24.4 | 23.2 |
| Middle fifth | 6.2 | 3.8 | 17.1 | 14.7 |
| Second fifth | 1.1 | 0.7 | 11.1 | 8.7 |
| Lowest fifth | −0.4 | −0.5 | 4.7 | 3.4 |
| | 100.0% | 100.0% | 100.0% | 100.0% |

| Percentage of population (1989 and 2004) | Percentage of all wealth | |
|---|---|---|
| | 1989 | 2004 |
| Top 1 percent | 38.3% | 34.3% |
| Top 10 percent | 71.2 | 71.2 |

SOURCES: U.S. Bureau of the Census, 1989, *Current Population Reports,* series P–60, no. 146; Mishel and Bernstein (1993:254); Mishel, Bernstein, and Shierholz (2009: Chapter 5).

1 percent of people in the United States alone held over 34 percent of the wealth in 2004, with the top 10 percent holding over 71 percent. In contrast to income inequality, however, we do find a small reduction in the amount of wealth held at the very top between 1995 and 2004. The amount of wealth held by the top 1 percent of Americans dropped from 38.5 percent in 1995 to 34.3 percent in 2004. As we will consider in the next section, though, this shift was contained exclusively within the top 20 percent, with the remaining 80 percent of families losing shares of wealth by 2004.

One of the most interesting questions that Keister's (2000) analysis of wealth inequality data was able to answer with confidence for the first time is the degree of wealth mobility in the United States. For example, we want to know if the top 1 percent or top 10 percent of wealth holders in 1975 or 1980 and 1995 are mostly the same people or different people. Keister's (2000:79) analysis was able to show that between 1975 and 1995, 54 percent of the top 5 percent of wealth holders were the same people. The vast majority of the people who dropped out of the top 5 percent of wealth holders between 1975 and 1995, however, dropped down only to the top 10 percent group. The picture was rather similar at the other end of the wealth scale: 60 percent of those at the bottom 25 percent of wealth holders in 1975 were still there in 1995, with 21 percent moving up to the next 25 percent, and 12 percent of those people moving up to the next 25 percent group (50 to 74 percent group with respect to wealth).

## TABLE 2-8

### Top Wealth Holders by Type of Wealth, 1989 to 2004

|  | % of all stock | | | | % of all bonds | | |
|---|---|---|---|---|---|---|---|
| **Richest** | **1989** | **1995** | **1998** | **2004** | **1989** | **1995** | **2004** |
| 1 percent | 46.7% | 51.4% | 53.2% | 39.2% | 72.9% | 65.9% | 49.1% |
| 10 percent | 83.8 | 88.4 | 91.7 | 81.6 | 94.0 | 89.8 | 81.5 |

*SOURCE:* Mishel and Bernstein (1993:256); Mishel, Bernstein, and Schmitt (1999:260); Mishel, Bernstein, and Allegretto (2007: Table 5.7).

Another way to look at wealth inequality, of course, is by examining the super rich. The 1990s were a fine climate for the super rich (Hacker 1997:89); the number of billionaires tripled during the decade. Although not at the same rate, this increase continued for most years of the 2000s, with a slight drop in the dot-com stock values in 2001, until the large drop in the stock market during the financial crisis of 2008 and 2009. During this time the world's billionaires dropped from 1,125 to 793. But the United States continued to account for more than any other country, with 45 percent of these 793 billionaires (www.forbes.com). Bill Gates, founder of Microsoft, and Warren Buffett remained the first and second richest in the United States in 2009, with $50 billion and $40 billion, respectively. Lawrence Ellison of Oracle was third, with fourth through seventh held by members of the Walton family, who inherited their wealth from the founder of Wal-Mart. In total there were 371 billionaires in the United States in 2009.

Another important question pertains to the source of wealth for the top wealth holders in the United States. As indicated in Table 2-8, in 1998 the top 1 percent of the population (in terms of wealth) held 53.2 percent of all personally owned corporate stock in the United States. Then, we see that the top 10 percent of people owned over 90 percent (91.7) of all personally held stock in the United States. (For a more detailed breakdown of types of wealth held, see Keister 2000:92–95.) However, as we see from Table 2-8, by 2004 the shares of stock held by the top 1 percent of American families had dropped from 53.2 percent in 1998 to 39.2 percent in 2004. Likewise, the percentage of stock held by the top 10 percent of Americans dropped from 91.7 percent to 81.6 percent. The bottom 80 percent of Americans, however, have made no gains in stock ownership for many years (Mishel, Bernstein, and Allegretto 2007: Figure 5F). Thus, as we saw with the shift in net wealth at the top in Table 2-7, the shift in stock ownership since 1998 has been among the top 20 percent of Americans only. The last three decades have been ones of significant gains in income and wealth for the top 20 percent of Americans, and losses for the bottom 80 percent of Americans.

### Historical Trends in Wealth Inequality

As with income inequality, a major question pertains to the historical trends in wealth inequality in the United States. Table 2-9 shows that the proportion of wealth held by the top 1 percent of the population had mostly been going down slowly between World

### TABLE 2-9

### Percentage of Total Wealth Held by Top 1 percent, 1922–2004

| Year | Percentage of wealth held by top 1 percent |
|------|-------------------------------------------|
| 1922 | 31.6% |
| 1929 | 36.3 |
| 1933 | 28.3 |
| 1939 | 30.6 |
| 1945 | 23.3 |
| 1949 | 20.8 |
| 1953 | 24.3 |
| 1954 | 24.0 |
| 1956 | 26.0 |
| 1958 | 23.8 |
| 1962 | 22.0 |
| 1965 | 23.4 |
| 1969 | 20.1 |
| 1972 | 20.7 |
| 1989 | 38.3 |
| 1995 | 38.5 |
| 1998 | 38.1 |
| 2004 | 34.3 |

*SOURCE:* U.S. Bureau of the Census, 1980, *Statistical Abstracts of the United States,* Table 785, p. 471; Mishel and Bernstein (1993:254); Mishel, Bernstein, and Schmitt (1999:258); Mishel, Bernstein, and Shierholz (2009:267).

War II (1945) and 1972, only to jump again dramatically in the 1980s. We do find a significant increase and then a drop in the wealth holdings of the top 1 percent between 1922 and 1945, which (along with the change in income distribution) is no doubt related to the major changes in this country brought about by the Great Depression of the 1930s and World War II. But despite these changes since 1922, we have other evidence that the amount of wealth held by the most wealthy 1 percent did not change much between 1810 and 1945 (see Gallman 1969:6). By 1998, therefore, the wealth held by the richest 1 percent of Americans had reached its highest level in probably 200 years. The sharp "dot-com crash" in the stock market in 2000 was no doubt a reason for the decline in percentage of wealth held by the richest 1 percent and 10 percent of Americans by 2004 (see Table 2-7). But the wider distribution of corporate stock among the top 20 percent of Americans in the last decade shown in Table 2-8 has also reduced the amount of wealth held by the top 1 percent and 10 percent of Americans. Again, we must stress, this wealth redistribution has been confined to the top 20 percent of Americans only, with no gains made by the other 80 percent of Americans.

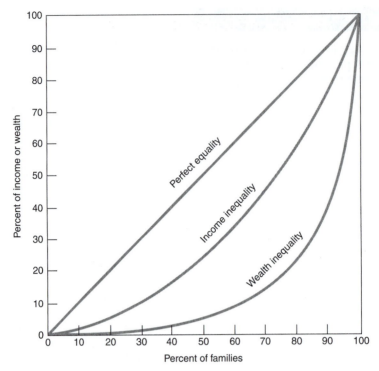

**FIGURE 2-6**    *Lorenz Curves on Wealth and Income Inequality; These Curves are Estimates from Data Presented in Table 2-7*

As noted previously, while both wealth and income are distributed very unequally in the United States, wealth is distributed even more unequally. A comparison of wealth and income inequality can be made most strikingly with what is known as a **Lorenz curve,** which is constructed by indicating how much wealth or income is held by various percentages of the total population. As shown in Figure 2-6, a condition of equality would show a straight diagonal line across the graph. In other words, 20 percent of the population would receive 20 percent of the wealth or income, 40 percent of the population would receive 40 percent of the wealth or income, and so on. On the other hand, the farther the curve is from the diagonal, the greater the inequality. Using 2004 data, Figure 2-6 graphically shows the magnitude of both income and wealth inequality in the United States.

## *Comparative Wealth Inequality*
For the first time in history we have a fairly comprehensive data set of wealth inequality among several nations in the world. Undertaken by a United Nations research institute (see Davis et al. 2006), the estimates of wealth inequality within 38 nations around the world were impossible to make with precision, as these researchers admit. But these estimates are reasonably accurate, especially for the 18 richest nations.

## TABLE 2-10

### Comparative Wealth Inequality, 2000

| Country | Share of wealth held by top 10 percent of families |
|---|---|
| Australia | 45% |
| Canada | 53 |
| Germany | 44 |
| Ireland | 42 |
| Italy | 48 |
| Japan | 39 |
| Norway | 50 |
| Spain | 42 |
| Sweden | 59 |
| Switzerland | 71 |
| Great Britain | 56 |
| United States | 70 |

*SOURCE*: Davis et al. (2006).

Table 2-10 shows that wealth inequality among 12 of the richest nations follows approximately the lineup of income inequality among these nations we have seen in Table 2-5. The amount of wealth held by the top 10 percent of people in these nations ranges from a low of 39 percent in Japan to a high of 71 percent for Switzerland, with the United States the second highest at 70 percent of wealth held by the top 10 percent of Americans. Both the United States and Switzerland are substantially ahead of the other countries, which have percentages in the 40s and 50s for wealth held by their richest 10 percent of families. But in all of these countries the distribution of wealth is more unequal than the distribution of income. The high rate of wealth inequality for Switzerland is no doubt related to their low tax rate on wealth and income, as well as the concentration of big banks in the country (Benini 2000). As we see in Chapter 15 on social stratification in Japan, their low concentration of wealth is related to the dramatic redistribution of wealth in the country soon after World War II.

## ✖ Inequality in Basic Necessities

With the extent of income and wealth inequality reviewed here, it would seem quite obvious that other material goods are distributed unequally in the United States. However, other issues must be noted with respect to the distribution of basic necessities. An unequal distribution of income is not always an accurate indication of how basic necessities such as food, housing, and medical care are distributed. There are two reasons for this: First, we must consider the possibility of state subsidies of necessities; second, we must consider the relative cost of basic necessities.

In considering state subsidies for basic necessities, we need only mention at this point that contrary to political rhetoric, the United States spends less on subsidies for low-income people than almost any other industrial nation. As we see in more detail in our chapter on poverty, the American government also has the lowest record of action to reduce poverty of all industrial nations (also see Mishel, Bernstein, and Shierholz 2009: Chapter 8; de Beer, Vrooman, and Schut 2001; Kim 2000; Behrendt 2000). The United States is the only industrial nation that does not have a basic guaranteed income program for all families below the poverty level or a comprehensive national health program meeting the medical needs of all families (Mishel, Bernstein, and Shierholz 2009), though the United States has moved closer to this with Obama's health legislation.

Even with a highly unequal distribution of income, the distribution of basic necessities may be less unequal if the cost of such basic items is relatively low. If this is the case, luxuries and savings, not basic necessities, become most unequal. But to the extent that this has ever been the case in the United States, it is rapidly becoming less so. Inflation has been rather low from the late 1980s to 2007, but the decade of the 1970s was one of rapid inflation; between 1967 and 1978 the consumer price index almost doubled. More important, the cost of basic necessities rose 44 percent *faster* than the cost of nonnecessities between 1970 and 1976 (Blumberg 1980:182), which means that those toward the bottom of the income scale find it even harder to maintain an adequate standard of living. We do not have studies such as these since the 1970s, but all of the poverty, income, and cost-of-living statistics indicate the standard of living has gone down for low-income people. We do, however, have estimates of income to cost-of-living ratios that indicate that the cost of living is somewhat less in the United States compared to Europe and Japan, but not different enough to overcome the greater level of inequality in the United States (Mishel, Bernstein, and Shierholz 2009).

## ⚔ Health Inequalities

Good health is an important human condition, but unfortunately for those toward the bottom of the stratification system, good health is to some degree unequally distributed through the stratification system. There are two basic reasons for this: First, adequate health care is unequally distributed, and second, conditions promoting better health are unequally distributed.

Much like income and wealth, health care is in constant demand. People seldom have enough health care; there are often new aches, new procedures, brighter and straighter teeth to attain, and preventive medicine. Thus, because health care is a scarce quantity, as with any scarce quantity, there must be a method of distribution. With health care there are two opposing methods of distribution. On one hand, health care can be distributed through a pricing mechanism. Those who can afford to pay for it get it; those who cannot afford to pay do without. On the other hand, health care distribution can be based on some principle of need. Those in greatest need get it first; those with less need must wait. Between these opposing methods of distribution, the distribution of health care in the United States is based more on the ability to pay, whereas in virtually all other industrialized nations distribution is based more on need (although no society today is at either extreme).

Since 1915 there have been attempts in the United States to enact legislation establishing a national health care system that would help distribute health care on the basis of need (Morris 1979:77). It was not until 1965 that a small achievement in this direction was gained with the Medicare and Medicaid programs. But the way these programs were designed, especially with Medicaid for the poor, it was only a small achievement. In all states in this country Medicaid does not pay for all kinds of medical needs, and what is paid for is done at a reduced level. Hospitals and doctors accepting Medicaid patients must accept a lower fee (usually 80 percent of standard fees). Studies have shown that with this program the poor now get more medical care than in the past, but it is care of lower quality than that received by the more affluent (Dutton 1978). As even the American Medical Association (AMA) has admitted, health care quality continues to be unequally distributed in the United States through the ability to pay (Schneider et al. 2002; Fiscella et al. 2000; Marmot 2004).

For the first time, in 2000 the World Health Organization ranked the health care systems of 191 nations in the world in terms of such things as the overall health of the population, extent of health coverage among the population, and "fairness in financial costs" among the population. As can be seen in Table 2-11, France and Italy ranked highest. Spain, Austria, and Japan were also in the top 10. The United States was ranked 37th—among countries such as Costa Rica, Chile, and Cuba—primarily because the United States is the only major nation that does not ensure health care for all its citizens (World Health Organization 2000: Annex Table 1). It is primarily the cost of medical care in the United States and the inability of many people to pay for this health care that accounts for the low rank for the United States, not the quality of health care when Americans have enough money to pay for it. The United States as a whole pays over 15 percent of GDP for health care, of which government expenditures account for 7 percent of total spending. In France the percent of GDP going to health care is 11 percent, of which the government pays almost 9 percent. The costs of health care as a percent of GDP are even lower, and the percentage paid by national health care systems are even higher, in Japan and all the other European countries (U.S. Bureau of the Census 2010a: Table 1310). As of 2008, over 15 percent of Americans had no health care coverage, an unprecedented number compared to all other wealthy nations and many less developed nations, and a percentage that no doubt increased in 2009 with rapidly rising unemployment rates (U.S. Bureau of the Census 2009a: Table 7). This means that people who have no health care insurance through employment or a national health care system in the United States must pay for it out of their own limited income, which usually means they don't get health care. At the end of 2009 the U.S. Congress finally passed something like a national health care insurance system for most Americans, which all other wealthy nations have had for many decades. There is promise that this more complete health care coverage will bring the health of Americans up to the level of these other wealthy nations.

A second reason good health is unequally distributed in the United States is that a low income often means poor nutrition, less sanitary living conditions, and (less important) less knowledge about how to maintain better health (Korenman and Miller 1997). But also, as we are increasingly finding, a lower position in the stratification system means a more unhealthy work environment. With more and more dangerous machines and industrial chemicals, the working class must put its life and health on the line for

## TABLE 2-11

**World Health Organization Ranking of National Health Care Systems, 2000, Select Listing**

| Country | Rank |
| --- | --- |
| France | 1 |
| Italy | 2 |
| Singapore | 6 |
| Spain | 7 |
| Austria | 9 |
| Japan | 10 |
| Norway | 11 |
| Portugal | 12 |
| Greece | 14 |
| The Netherlands | 17 |
| Great Britain | 18 |
| Switzerland | 20 |
| Belgium | 21 |
| Sweden | 23 |
| Germany | 25 |
| Morocco | 29 |
| Chile | 33 |
| Costa Rica | 36 |
| **United States** | **37** |
| Cuba | 39 |
| Thailand | 47 |
| Afghanistan | 173 |
| Central Africa Republic | 189 |
| Burma (Myanmar) | 190 |
| Sierra Leone | 191 |

*SOURCE:* World Health Organization (2000: Annex Table 1).

corporate profits. For reasons such as these, Muennig et al. (2010) found poverty to be the biggest risk to health and life expectancy in the United States. Using a large nationwide survey, this study found that living with an income below 200 percent of the poverty line (about $40,000 for a family of four) was the number-one health risk, above smoking, obesity, and binge drinking. Being an African American was ranked sixth for health and life expectancy.

The outcome of these two sources for an unequal distribution of good health can be found in a number of statistics. For example, infant mortality is an often-used indicator because it is a condition that can be reduced with better medical care. Consistently, data indicate that the lower the income, the higher the infant mortality rate in the United

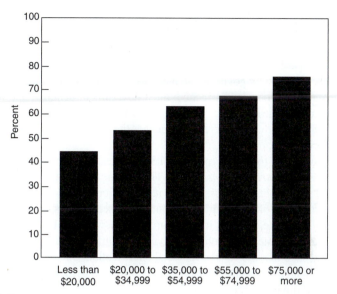

**FIGURE 2-7**    *Personal Assessment of Excellent or Very Good Health by Income Level*

*SOURCE:* U.S. Department of Health and Human Services, *Summary of Health Statistics for U.S. Adults Survey, 2002* (2004: Table 21).

States. A prime reason for this may be that the distribution of medical care is based more on the ability to pay than on need. Studies have shown that it *is* the lack of adequate medical care that explains much of the higher infant mortality rate among the poor in this country (Korenman and Miller 1997; Gortmaker 1979).

All of the above can help us understand why in the United States death rates and rates of serious illnesses are strongly related to family income. Study after study by U.S. health agencies find that death rates from all kinds of serious illness such as cancer and heart disease are about twice the rate for lower-income individuals. (For one of the most recent studies, see U.S. Department of Health and Human Services, *Health, United States, 2008: With Socioeconomic Status and Health Chart Book*) The same is found for depression and several other types of mental illness. Figure 2-7 provides a summary of these findings. When people of various income levels are asked to simply judge the state of their health, higher-income people are much more likely to rate their overall health as excellent or very good.

---

# ⚔ Unequal Political Outputs

By unequal political outputs, or simply political inequalities, we refer to outcomes of the political process that favor some class interests more than others. In this section our focus is not on inequalities of political power per se but rather on the outcomes of differing amounts of political power—or the benefits flowing from the attainment of political power. This subject, as one may suspect, is rather broad when we consider the extent of government outputs today. But our goal at this point is simply to indicate a pattern using a few basic examples.

When examining political inequalities, we find that the pattern that emerges is one in which those toward the top of the stratification system receive more of the services or general outputs provided by government agencies. Despite the common misconception of a welfare state, the poor do not receive most government benefits, and the benefits going to those toward the bottom of the stratification system are the ones most likely to be cut back in times of government retrenchment as the extensive welfare cuts beginning in 1996 clearly indicate.

At this point, and for our purpose (which is to describe inequality), the state can be considered as a *redistributive institution*. That is, one function of the state is to take from some and redistribute to others. In this regard, of course, the state is an important mechanism in a system of social stratification. It is based in class conflict to the extent that one class wants to be sure that it gets from the state what has been taken from other classes, while at the same time having to give up as little as possible. There are other functions of the state that are related to social stratification, one of the most important being the maintenance of the class system. Again, however, our focus at present is on the inequality in government outputs.

## Taxes

One very important type of political inequality pertains to government tax policies. Government services and functions must be paid for by someone. The question becomes, who pays? Because most states in industrialized nations emerged when the old aristocratic privileges of the Middle Ages were under attack, new ideas of democracy and equality (or equality of opportunity) were built into these new states. With respect to government tax policies, this often meant that those most able to pay would pay more in taxes—that there would be **progressive taxation.** In reality, however, this philosophy is often subverted.

We can begin by noting the sources of total federal tax revenue in the United States. As shown in Table 2-12, money from individuals and families accounts for over 80 percent of tax revenues in the form of individual income taxes and Social Security deductions (called employment taxes). These sources of tax revenue have been increasing most since 1960, while corporate income taxes have decreased.

If we look back further than 1960, this pattern becomes even clearer. In 1916, individual and employment taxes made up only 9.4 percent of tax revenues; in 1930, 31.6 percent; and in 1950, 43.6 percent. In contrast, corporate income taxes accounted for 34.8 percent of federal tax revenues in 1930; 27.6 percent in 1950; 12.5 percent in 1980; and, as shown in Table 2-12, only 12.9 percent in 2008 (U.S. Bureau of the Census, *Statistical Abstracts of the United States,* 2010b:468; U.S. Bureau of the Census, *Historical Statistics of the United States,* 1960:713).

When we turn more directly to individual and family income taxes, a major question, of course, is who pays? One way we can approach this question is by looking at how the distribution of income is affected by the tax system. If we have a truly progressive income tax, one in which the rich are taxed at a higher rate than the poor and the not so

## TABLE 2-12

**Internal Revenue Collections by Selected Sources, 1960–2008**

| Source of revenue | Percentage of total | | | | | |
| --- | --- | --- | --- | --- | --- | --- |
| | 1960 | 1970 | 1980 | 1993 | 2004 | 2008 |
| Individual income taxes | 49.0% | 53.0% | 47.2% | 45.0% | 49.1% | 52.0% |
| Employment taxes such as old-age and disability insurance, unemployment insurance | 12.2 | 19.1 | 30.5 | 37.3 | 35.5 | 32.2 |
| Corporation income taxes | 24.2 | 17.9 | 12.5 | 9.3 | 11.4 | 12.9 |
| Estate and gift taxes | 1.8 | 1.9 | 1.1 | 1.2 | 1.3 | 1.1 |
| Excise taxes | 12.9 | 8.1 | 4.7 | 4.2 | 2.7 | 1.9 |

*SOURCES:* U.S. Bureau of the Census, 1980, *Statistical Abstracts of the United States,* Table 446, p. 268; U.S. Bureau of the Census, 2010b, *Statistical Abstracts of the United States,* Table 468.

rich, then the after-tax income distribution should be less unequal than the before-tax income distribution. This question is addressed in Table 2-13. Unfortunately the most recent data the U.S. Census Bureau has given us is for the year 2000.

This table shows five income distributions by 20 percent population segments, from the poorest 20 percent of the population to the richest 20 percent of the population. The first line in Table 2-13 shows the distribution of income before taxes, but after government transfers (such as welfare and Social Security payments) are added to income. Thus, the first line shows that the poorest 20 percent of the population receives 3.6 percent of the income, while the richest 20 percent of the population receives 49.7 percent of the income. The next line shows what the distribution of income would look like without the government transfer payments. As would be expected, in this case

## TABLE 2-13

**The Effects of Taxes and Welfare Payments on the Distribution of Household Income by Income Quintiles, 2000**

| Definition of income | Lowest quintile | Second quintile | Third quintile | Fourth quintile | Highest quintile |
| --- | --- | --- | --- | --- | --- |
| Income before taxes: | | | | | |
| Money income | 3.6 | 9.0 | 14.8 | 23.0 | 49.7 |
| Less government money transfers, capital gains | 1.1 | 7.1 | 13.9 | 22.8 | 55.1 |
| Income after taxes | 1.4 | 8.3 | 15.1 | 24.0 | 51.2 |
| After taxes plus welfare income | 4.6 | 10.3 | 15.7 | 22.7 | 46.2 |

*SOURCE:* U.S. Bureau of the Census, *Money Income in the United States, 2000* (2001:13).

the income share of the poorest 20 percent is reduced sharply to 1.1 percent, which then leaves more of the total income to go to other groups, with the upper 20 percent group gaining. The third line shows the distribution of income after taxes have been taken out of people's income. We find that this brings the distribution going to the bottom 20 percent of people up slightly from 1.1 percent of all income to 1.4 percent of all income, while the top 20 percent have their amount reduced from 55.1 percent to 51.2 percent. (This means that the share of all income in the nation going to the bottom people goes up because that share for the more affluent is reduced by taxes.) Then, adding in people's income from welfare, Social Security, and other types of government payments, we find a much bigger change on the top and bottom; the bottom 20 percent goes from a 1.4 share of income to 4.8 percent, while the top 20 percent of people have their share reduced from 51.2 percent to 46.2 percent. (This means the incomes of the richest 20 percent are less of the total for the nation when the "pie" is increased through government transfers going to the bottom.) In short, government taxes and welfare spending affect the distribution of income slightly, but it is transfer payments that have a far bigger effect than tax policies on reducing income inequality. However, most of the transfers are to retired people under the Social Security system. Welfare to the poor has a very small effect because so few people get any of this money, and not very much goes to each person.

We must look further into the effects of taxes on the distribution of income, however, because Table 2-13 includes only income taxes in the analysis. Another form of taxation is a sales tax, which is regressive rather than being even close to progressive, as with income taxes in the United States. Sales taxes are called **regressive** because the less affluent pay more as a percentage of their income than do the more affluent. (For example, if a person with an income of $10,000 and a person with $100,000 both pay a total of $300 in sales taxes in a year, this represents a much greater share of the first person's income.) A study of the effects of all forms of taxes on the distribution of income has found that all forms of taxation taken together actually increase the level of income inequality in the United States (Devine 1983).

As can be seen in Table 2-14, the personal income tax in the United States is somewhat progressive. The effective tax rate refers to what people actually pay in income taxes after all tax breaks. In 2005, for example, the bottom 20 percent of Americans actually averaged –6.2 percent of their pay to personal income taxes while the top 20 percent of Americans averaged 14.1 percent of their income going to personal income taxes. (The negative percentage averaged by the bottom 20 percent of Americans is due to income tax credits paid to families with the lowest incomes; that is, you get a "tax credit" check from the federal government like a tax return if your income is very low. These income "tax credits" were expanded during the Clinton presidency.) But in contrast to the much higher income tax required on highest incomes in Europe, the top 1 percent of Americans only paid 19.4 percent of their personal income to taxes in 2005. (Of course there are other taxes that high-income people pay on such things as capital gains.)

The regressive nature of the U.S. income tax system comes with what is referred to as "payroll taxes" such as tax deductions for Social Security and Medicare. Because there is a ceiling on how much one must pay per year in these payroll taxes, people at the top 20 percent income category and higher pay less in payroll taxes as a percentage of their overall income than do people in the lower income categories.

## TABLE 2-14

### Effective Tax Rates for Personal Income Tax and Payroll Taxes by Income Segments, 1979–2005

| Income category | Personal income tax | | | | Payroll tax | | | |
|---|---|---|---|---|---|---|---|---|
| | 1979 | 1989 | 2000 | 2005 | 1979 | 1989 | 2000 | 2005 |
| **Bottom four-fifths** | | | | | | | | |
| First | 0.0% | −1.6% | −4.6% | −6.5% | 5.3% | 7.1% | 8.2% | 8.3% |
| Second | 4.1 | 2.9 | 1.5 | −1.0 | 7.7 | 8.9 | 9.4 | 9.2 |
| Third | 7.5 | 6.0 | 5.0 | 3.0 | 8.6 | 9.8 | 9.6 | 9.5 |
| Fourth | 10.1 | 8.3 | 8.1 | 6.0 | 8.5 | 10.0 | 10.4 | 9.7 |
| **Top fifth** | 15.7% | 14.6% | 17.5% | 14.1% | 5.4% | 6.6% | 6.3% | 6.0% |
| Top 10% | 17.4 | 16.3 | 19.7 | 16.0 | 4.2 | 5.1 | 5.0 | 4.8 |
| Top 5% | 19.0 | 17.7 | 21.6 | 17.6 | 2.8 | 3.7 | 3.8 | 3.4 |
| Top 1% | 21.8 | 19.9 | 24.2 | 19.4 | 0.9 | 1.4 | 1.9 | 1.7 |

*SOURCE*: Table constructed from Congressional Budget Office data presented in Mishel, Bernstein, and Shierholz (2009: Table 1-11).

Much was said about the tax law changes during the Reagan administration because these changes purposely reduced the tax rates for the wealthy early in the 1980s. Reagan's tax bill certainly did that, but what also happened due to increases in other more regressive income taxes, such as the Social Security payroll tax, is that the overall tax rates for the less affluent and poor actually went up in the 1980s (Harrison and Bluestone 1988).

During the Clinton administration in the mid-1990s, again there were important tax changes. For whatever reason (perhaps embarrassment over tax rates for the poor going up before), there were finally tax reductions to lower-income groups and slight increases to top-income groups. For example, the bottom 20 percent of people had an effective federal income tax rate reduced from 8 percent to 4.6 percent, while the top 20 percent had their effective federal tax rate increased from 26.2 percent to 29.1 percent of their income (Mishel, Bernstein, and Schmitt 1999:99).

It is not surprising that the election of George W. Bush in 2000 resumed the tax rate cuts for the highest-income Americans. By 2001 George W. Bush had signed a law lowering the top tax rate by 30 percent, with further cuts reducing the top rate by 8 percent in 2006. When it is completed and totaled, George W. Bush will go down in history as reducing taxes even more than did President Reagan during the 1980s (*Los Angeles Times,* March 9 and May 11, 2003). George W. Bush will achieve this distinction of cutting taxes more than any other president not only for his reductions in personal income taxes especially for the most wealthy, but because of corporate tax cuts. In 2004 Bush signed a bill giving corporations $136 billion in tax cuts, the biggest in history (*Los Angeles Times,* October 23, 2004). We must remember that these figures involve only federal income taxes; other taxes such as Social Security deductions and sales taxes take a bigger percentage of the wages of middle- and low-income Americans, and these taxes have gone up for these groups in recent decades.

According to a recent report by the U.S. Government Accountability Office (*New York Times*, August 13, 2008), nearly two out of every three U.S. corporations paid no federal income taxes from 1998 through 2005. Most of these 1.3 million corporations were small and had low or no profits in the period. However, of the largest 1,000 corporations in the United States in 2005 (certainly no recession year), 25 percent paid no federal income tax. As suggested by Table 2-12, the biggest beneficiaries of tax breaks in recent decades have been large U.S. corporations.

## Government Services

In this final section on inequalities we approach a vast subject that can be treated at this point with only a brief description and a few examples. When the subject of government services is raised, welfare for the poor most often comes to mind. But such an image of government services is highly misleading. There is another side of government services often called **wealthfare.** Most of what government does, it does *not* for the poor but for the nonpoor. And among the nonpoor, it is often the wealthy and corporations that benefit most. This is yet another aspect of how the stratification system and unequal power affect the state as a redistributive mechanism.

In addition to providing welfare for the poor, consider what else the federal government does. The federal government provides subsidies to many industries such as agriculture and research and development that directly benefit major corporations, tariff protection for many industries, regulatory agencies that protect major industries, and other direct services that industries would otherwise have to pay for out of their own profits (such as the Federal Aviation Administration's maintenance of air guidance systems, airport landing systems, and research and development for new airline technology).

Let us look at a few examples. Currently, over one-half of all 2009 federal spending goes for various programs that provide money or services (such as health care) for individuals. On one hand, most of these programs and money transfers do not go to poor people; on the other hand, most of these transfers are paid for through specific or additional regressive withholding taxes that operate much like pension programs or insurance programs.

The largest example of federal money going to the nonpoor as well as the poor is Social Security. The Social Security program operates much like a pension or insurance program (that is, workers pay for the system by contributing to a special fund), and it accounted for almost $678 billion, or about 20 percent of the federal budget in 2009 (U.S Bureau of the Census 2010b).

As we will see when considering the subject of poverty in Chapter 9, this means the poor are mostly left out of this system because they did not have enough income in their working lives to pay into the system so they can receive support when they are elderly or disabled. Although the amount of money spent on Social Security for the nonpoor has been going up dramatically in recent decades, government spending for the poor has been dropping dramatically. (This is certainly not because the number of poor people has been dropping in the United States.) Other government spending for the nonpoor during 2009 included such things as $94 billion for transportation programs and $20 billion to support farmers.

The main point in presenting these examples of federal spending is to demonstrate the expanse of government programs and services going to the nonpoor. But the actual benefit these services provided to the wealthy cannot be judged solely in government outlays. A relatively inexpensive government program for price supports, business regulation, or protection from foreign and domestic business competition can result in billions of dollars in greater profits or in transfers from consumers to business.

It can be argued that many of these government services that directly help the wealthy and corporations also help the general public, hence the working class and poor. The question becomes one of who is helped most, and by how much. If we find that the wealthy and corporate classes have more resources that are used to influence government policies and programs, we must recognize that it is their interests that are probably most directly served. Information supporting such a conclusion is central to the study of social stratification and will be considered in coming chapters. We can conclude this discussion by simply noting again that the wealthfare system is more importantly an aspect of the state than is welfare for the poor. Along with the many other inequalities described in this chapter, inequalities in government services must be added.

## ✖ Dimensions of Inequality: A Conclusion

This chapter was designed to present descriptive information on the extent of inequality in the contemporary United States. Toward this end, inequalities in income and wealth, standards of living and health, and taxation and government services were examined. These primarily material inequalities are among the most important, but they are by no means the only important ones.

We have said nothing about educational opportunities and inequalities in the actual attainment of education. Educational attainment, as might be expected, is in many ways linked to divisions in the stratification system—as both an outcome of this system and a means of its maintenance. This subject receives considerable attention later.

Neither have we said anything substantial about inequalities in power and authority. Authority divisions (or institutionalized power) are obvious outcomes of social organization in complex societies with an expanded division of labor. Some people give orders, while others only take orders. And power inequalities per se, or the ability to influence others whether such power is institutionalized or not, are difficult to measure in the absence of a specific context. We have no simple scales with which to rank people in terms of power as people can be ranked in terms of income or wealth. We consider the importance of inequalities in both power and authority in later chapters.

In addition to the inequalities already outlined, it should now be evident that any material good, condition, or service that people come to value, for whatever reason, may be unequally distributed by or through a stratification system. One such valued condition, of course, is life itself. Those lower in the stratification system, however, are more likely to be victims of domestic violent crimes and find they must fight and die for their country, as shown in studies of the Korean War (Mayer and Hoult 1955) and the Vietnam War (Zeitlin, Lutterman, and Russel 1973). But there are other inequalities that require brief mention.

Along with various material goods and services, the stratification system also provides an unequal distribution of status or honor, self-esteem or self-evaluations, and social deference. As briefly noted in the previous chapter, because human beings tend to evaluate things, conditions, behavior, and people differently, a status hierarchy will emerge that tends to correspond with hierarchical divisions within a stratification system. Thus, people and groups are ranked by others in terms of status, prestige, or honor. They usually receive social deference from those of lower-status rank in ritual interactions, and they tend to rank or evaluate themselves unequally in terms of their positions in a system of social stratification.

Many sociologists, have argued that this status dimension of social stratification is of primary importance. Among functional theorists (such as Parsons 1951, 1970) there is the view that status inequality produces an unequal distribution of material goods and services as rewards for attaining high status. There is, as we will see, extensive research on the distribution of status within the occupational structure.

For several reasons outlined in subsequent chapters, however, more sociologists now reject the causal logic of this functional argument. Especially in complex societies, status is considered more a product than a cause of unequal power and wealth. In other words, power and material wealth usually bring status or prestige, not the other way around (see Lenski 1984). But none of this rejection of the functional view of status inequality is to deny its existence or its secondary importance for understanding social stratification.

Status divisions are of considerable importance in understanding the *maintenance* of social stratification. For example, individuals of a particular class often establish status boundaries (based on lifestyle) to protect their privilege by excluding people from lower-class divisions. Also, there is everyday social interaction that requires prescribed deference rituals among members of unequal status. These deference rituals give everyday meaning and reinforcement to the stratification system (Collins 1975:161–215). Finally, such status divisions can lead to differing amounts of self-esteem and differing self-evaluations that lead people to accept their place in the stratification system and to accept the system's legitimacy (Della Fave 1980). These nonmaterial inequalities will be discussed more fully when we have occasion to explain their use in maintaining a system of social stratification.

The point that inequalities of many kinds are shaped and produced by a system of social stratification has been made. It is time to consider why and how such inequality is produced. We will first explore how stratification systems have evolved throughout the history of human societies. That is the task of our next chapter.

## Summary

The main objective of this chapter has been to describe the exact details of inequality in the contemporary United States. We found that income inequality is growing in the United States and is now the highest among the major industrial nations, with European nations such as Sweden and Germany having among the lowest levels of income inequality. Wealth inequality is more difficult to measure than is income inequality, but data indicate that wealth is much more unequally distributed compared with income, with wealth inequality also growing. We then examined a number of other types of inequality that are also very important but often more difficult to measure such as health inequalities, government services, and tax rates.

# Social Stratification in Human Societies: The History of Inequality

The top photo shows young girls leaving a textile "sweatshop" in Phnom Penh in 2007. Conditions in this Cambodian sweatshop include pay averaging around $2 per day, long working hours, and dangerous, unsafe, and unhealthy conditions. Young girls I have interviewed here, living far away from their village families, tell me they are fearful of being kidnapped and forced into prostitution. The bottom photo shows another sweatshop about 100 years earlier, in New York City. Conditions and pay for these American workers were equally bad, if not worse, and certainly unsafe. In a tragic incident, for example, 146 young girls at the Triangle Waist Factory in New York City were trapped inside during a fire and burned to death. People in rich countries today tend to assume that only poor countries have sweatshops, not realizing that their own countries have had sweatshops often worse than those that exist in less-developed countries today.

*SOURCES:* © Harold Kerbo, Library of Congress, Prints and Photographs Division [LC-DIG-nclc-04454]

## Chapter Outline

❖ Varieties of Human Stratification Systems

❖ The Emergence of Inequality and Social Stratification

❖ The Reduction of Inequality with Industrial and Postindustrial Societies

❖ Conclusion: The History of Inequality

❖ Summary

❖ Notes

I began the first chapter with an example of the impact of social stratification on individual life chances. Before proceeding in this chapter on the history of social stratification, it is useful to begin with a brief macrolevel example of how the rise and fall of whole nations and their standard of living can depend on their system of social stratification.

Like most Westerners, until several years ago I hadn't realized the extent to which China was ahead of Western countries in math, science, almost all technologies, and commerce in 1400. As I traveled throughout Southeast Asia, I kept finding evidence of that advanced Chinese civilization here and there, such as monuments to Admiral Zheng He (who commanded the Chinese Navy at the time) in Malaysia, Indonesia, and southern Thailand. In particular, China was centuries ahead of the West in shipbuilding and navigation technology, and had the largest navy the world has ever seen (Levathes, 1994; Needham 1983; Menzies 2002). They had 3,000 ships that could sail the world's oceans, and huge Chinese "treasure ships" that dwarfed the small and less technically advanced ships the Europeans used to sail to the Americas almost 100 years later. The evidence is clear that China was sailing to Africa, the Middle East, and South Asia as well as all through East and Southeast Asia long before the Europeans could do so. There is even some weak evidence that these Chinese ships sailed to the Americas 100 years before the Europeans (Menzies 2002). The Chinese were on top of something like a world system based on trade and commerce long before the Europeans began to slowly establish a similar world system in the 1500s. By the 1800s China was in a long decline and the Europeans passed them by. By the late 1800s China was cut up into areas of European dominance, which the Chinese could not prevent. What happened?

There are many aspects to the long Chinese decline from the early 1400s, but their system of social stratification played a major part. As the Chinese "treasure ships" were sailing around half the world in the early 1400s for trade and commerce, the Chinese merchant class was rapidly gaining wealth and power. This brought them into conflict with the old Chinese feudal elites and the bureaucratic mandarin class who ran the government. The old feudal elites and emperor system were threatened by the power of this new merchant class. This conflict came to a head in 1424 when a new Chinese emperor came to power who was less sympathetic to merchant-class interests. The internal conflict between the old imperial elites and the merchant class was won by the old elites. The new emperor ordered the country closed off, and the huge navy of "treasure ships" were destroyed or confined to harbor where they were to rot, never again sailing the high seas. This new emperor and the mandarin class also forbid Chinese to travel outside of China, and communities were moved inland from the seacoast to enforce these closure rules. The wealth and influence of the new merchant class rapidly fell. China remained in a "time warp" while the Europeans passed them by in science, technology, and commerce. By 1911 the Chinese social order collapsed into chaos and revolution, not to recover until well into the second half of the 20th century.

As we will see in this chapter and others, it is not the power of any particular class—such as kings or emperors, a merchant class, or corporate class—that matters. What matters is when current elites (perhaps a state communist elite or an old corporate class) are so powerful, and their class opponents so weak (such as a new middle class or working class), that change needed to be more competitive in the world system is prevented. The shortsighted and selfish interests of this powerful elite can prevent needed changes that would advance the long-term interests of all in the society. The power of these elites is based on a particular kind of stratification system, or a type of political economy, that we consider in more detail in this chapter.

We live in a society and a world with extensive inequality. In recent years these inequalities in the United States and in the world have been growing rather dramatically. We have already seen the extent to which inequalities of many kinds have been growing in the United States. As for worldwide inequalities, World Bank figures indicate the gap is far greater: "As late as 1820 per capita incomes were quite similar around the world— and very low, ranging from around $500 in China and South Asia to $1,000–1,500 in the richest countries of Europe" (World Bank 2000:45, 274–275). At the begining of the 21st century, while the annual per capita income of people in rich countries like the United States was $30,600, there were poor countries such as Sierra Leone, Tanzania, and Ethiopia where the per capita annual income was in the $500 range. As we will see in more detail in the final chapter, some 20 percent of the world's people now live on less than $1 a day, while the gap between the incomes and living standards of the world's richest 20 percent of people and the world's poorest 20 percent of people is huge (Korzeniewicz and Moran 1997). One of the most important new trends is the rapid growth of inequalities between the small group of rich and increasing mass of poor across the world's least-developed countries (Firebaugh 2003; Goesling 2001). Have these inequalities always been so great? Is our society more unequal than others? Will it always be so? The last question, no doubt, is among the most difficult to answer. No one is very good at predicting the future with any degree of accuracy, but the first two questions can be answered with some confidence.

In this chapter we are concerned with the first question along with an examination of types of stratification systems. Our subject is the history of inequality and social stratification in human societies. The age in which we find ourselves has been shaped in large measure by the historical hand of many human solutions to the question of who gets what, and why. Thus, in addition to comparing our age with previous ages, we can gain some insight into how we got where we are today. The insight gained will prove invaluable in our later attempts to understand the nature and causes of inequality and social stratification.

At the outset the relative brevity of what we think of as society must be recognized. What can be called *hominids* (our closest ancestors) have lived on this earth for at least 4 million years (see Leakey and Lewin 1977). Human beings began settling down in more or less stable agricultural communities, forming what we can call *societies,* only about 10,000 years ago. Thus, even from that time (10,000 years ago) to the present represents less than 1 percent of human existence.

What, in general, do we know about the extent of inequality throughout this long history of human existence? In comparison with our present society, we can say that inequality most often was less, but sometimes (in the more recent past with fully developed agrarian societies) it was greater. It has been noted (see van den Berghe 1978) that human beings are unique among animals in the systematic coercion of nonkin, in cooperative efforts to exploit others of the species, and in the degree of inequality among our own kind.

All of this can be found to vary greatly in the history of human societies, and for the most part it is relatively recent. The best evidence, some of which is examined in the following pages, suggests that throughout most of their existence human beings have lived in a state of near equality, in vast contrast to the inequality that is prevalent today.

About 10,000 or so years ago, however, after many more thousands of years of life in small hunting and gathering societies, something revolutionary began happening. During what may be called the **Neolithic revolution,** our ancestors began settling down to an agricultural life, a life of planting crops and herding food animals that increased their output of basic necessities.

In a few thousand years large cities began emerging and, a few thousand years after that, civilizations and empires. No longer was everyone required to work the fields to feed the population. The division of labor increased, and some people were able to pursue science, religion, arts, or military technology. Soon, in relative terms, a cycle of technical innovation producing higher crop yields freed still more people from the land for other occupations (producing even greater technical innovation) and propelled us into the industrial age.

Most people paid a price for this advance. As one observer put it, with only some exaggeration, the process of civilization was also one of enslavement (see Wells 1971:193). When human beings ceased their nomadic ways during the Neolithic revolution, the history of stratification, inequality, elites, and exploitation began (see Pfeiffer 1977:20; Higham 2002). The history of civilization *is,* in fact, the history of social stratification. Only in recent times, with advanced industrial or postindustrial societies, has the level of inequality been relatively reduced compared with that of previous civilizations (Lenski 1984, 2005; Nielsen 1994). But we are getting too far ahead of our story. We must first consider the major types of stratification systems that have existed throughout history, then see how they developed through time, and why.

# ⚔ Varieties of Human Stratification Systems

Social scientists are not in complete agreement on the most useful typology or method of comparing types of social stratification systems that have existed throughout history, but five general types are most commonly described: *primitive communal, slavery, caste, estate or feudal,* and *class systems.* (For a discussion similar to what follows, see Heller 1987.) Each of these five general types can be compared on five basic characteristics of stratification systems: normatively closed versus open divisions, the actual method of status or class placement, the major method of legitimation, the predominant form of inequality, and the comparative level of inequality in each type of stratification system.[1]

With respect to the first main characteristic, these societies vary according to the degree of normative closure or openness between the hierarchical divisions or ranks within the stratification system. We say *normative* because we are referring to norms or values prescribing relatively open versus closed rankings. For example, social norms may stress that individuals are free, following certain rules, to leave their present rank (or rank at birth) by moving into a higher or lower rank. Conversely, in other societies such vertical mobility may be prohibited.

Closely following the first characteristic, we find differing methods by which people are *actually* placed within ranks in the stratification system. These methods range along a continuum from *ascription* to *achievement.* As noted earlier, **ascription** refers to placement beyond the control of the individual. Placement is determined by such characteristics as the rank of one's parents, gender, or race. **Achievement** refers to placement based on individual merit or, as the name suggests, achievement. Few societies can be located at either extreme end of the ascription–achievement continuum (the caste system is one exception); most have a varying mixture of ascription and achievement.

Each society must, at least to a degree, employ some method for justifying the existence of inequality among its population. This method typically follows a process referred to as **legitimation.** Such a process is of primary importance in societies maintaining a high degree of inequality among their members (which is to say most societies in the past 10,000 years or so). For example, those at the bottom of the stratification system must in some way be convinced that their low position is "right and proper." Otherwise social order and structured inequalities can be maintained only through the use of physical force—a method that can be very costly in lives and resources, and that in the long run is often unsuccessful. Most societies, in fact, rely upon a number of methods of legitimation, although one or two tend to predominate.

Tradition or *custom* as a method of legitimation forces attention to the past. People may be taught that this is how things have always been, thus closing their minds to any possible alternatives to a present distribution of valued goods and services. A more systematic *ideological* justification may also be used. Although such an ideological justification may rely in part on tradition, here we are speaking of a more systematic belief system, often pointing to the superior qualities of those at the top of the stratification system and/or to their "important" contribution to the overall social well-being as justification for their greater share of valued goods and services.

Often similar to more secular ideological justifications are religious beliefs. Here the "superior qualifications" of those on top of the stratification system are not as important. Rather, the existing system of stratification is deemed legitimate because a deity or supernatural force wills it so. Accompanying a religious justification, we typically find promised rewards (usually in the next life or in heaven) for those who obey the rules and obligations of their present class or caste position. Finally, there are varying methods of *legal* justification. These are based either on laws enforcing the rights, privileges, and duties of existing ranks backed up by the authority of the state or on legal procedures that claim to ensure a fair set of rules in assigning ranks and rewards.

Three major dimensions or kinds of inequality can be found in most human societies. These three are (1) inequalities of honor, *status,* or prestige; (2) inequalities of *economic* influence and material rewards; and (3) inequalities based on military, political, or bureaucratic *power.* In most societies all three types of inequality are present and are usually interrelated. For example, when a person is favored with respect to one type of inequality, he or she is usually well off with respect to others as well. But in different types of stratification systems one of the three tends to be most important. In other words, a high position within one dimension of inequality can be used to obtain a high position in the others. Remembering that all three dimensions of inequality are present in most societies, we will indicate the dimension that is most important in each type of stratification system.

We can provide a rough estimate of the overall degree of inequality in these differing ideal types of stratification systems. Our estimate is based primarily on the range of inequality between elites and the common people in each society. This estimate is made with respect to economic and power values, which are more easily represented across societies. Considering the five types of stratification systems, overall inequality ranges from a very low level in primitive communal societies to a high level in slave, caste, and estate societies and a medium level in class or industrial societies. The reasons for this range in the level of inequality are of major importance for an overall understanding of social stratification, and because they are so important, we focus on them later in this chapter.

## Primitive Communal Societies

**Primitive communal societies** represent the earliest forms of social organization. Their economy is based on simple hunting and gathering methods of killing or trapping animals, with little use of agricultural methods of food production. Because hunting and gathering methods of food production usually result in a depletion of resources in the immediate environment (how rapidly depends on the size of the tribe and climatic conditions), these people tend to be nomadic or seminomadic. Also, because of their primitive methods of food production and nomadic lifestyle, an accumulation of material possessions generally is impossible. What goods and food they have are usually divided more or less equally among all members of the tribe.

Primitive communal societies may have chiefs, respected leaders, medicine men, or shamans who have more influence or power within the tribe. However, their influence over others is relatively limited and restricted to their ability to perform valuable functions for the tribe as a whole. Thus, positions such as chief are achieved positions with an open method of placement. The predominant form of inequality—in fact, often the only major form of inequality—is status or honor. Because of some important function served by a particular individual, such as in providing food, a higher-status position may be obtained, with few if any material rewards above the general level found among other tribal members. No legal, religious, or systematic ideological justifications are offered for the existence of inequalities of status. Most important, with the overall level of inequality very low, none is needed. The inequalities of status that are found are simply explained by tradition. That is, the best hunter is customarily awarded greater status or honor.[2]

# Slavery

One of the most persistent historical forms of inequality has been **slavery.** This form of domination emerged soon after human beings settled down in established agricultural communities, reaching its high point with early agrarian civilizations. It can be found in different parts of the world in slightly altered forms, but with a few major characteristics dominating. First of all, it is an economic relationship, the ownership of human beings, and an economic form of inequality dominates. Throughout history the position of slave has been acquired in many ways—through birth, military defeat, falling into debt, or, as with slaves in the United States, through capture and then commercial trade. Likewise, throughout history the level of hardship and misery for slaves has varied, as has their hope of freedom.

Contrary to the American experience, slavery has not always been a hereditary condition, nor has it always been a normatively closed system. Especially in ancient slave societies, freedom could be purchased or otherwise acquired by the slave. Thus, although slavery was often an ascribed status, achievement out of slave status could be attained. Slavery in the United States was compounded by what will be described later as caste. Only in a few societies such as the United States did racial caste produce a more closed, hereditary slave status.

The level of inequality between the slave and the owner, as well as between the common people and elites, in agrarian slave societies was great. But, again, the level of inequality varied greatly. In some societies slaves did have legal rights and were treated fairly well, in contrast to the U.S. experience. In some ancient societies, slaves were sometimes highly rewarded and even placed in positions of high authority. Elites sometimes believed that slaves could be controlled and trusted with power more than could nonslaves, who might aspire to the kingship.

The two primary means of legitimation in slave societies were legal and ideological. Slave status was usually a legal property relation sanctioned by state authority. Ideological justification varied from racist beliefs "explaining" the inferior qualities of slaves (thus making them "fit" for slavery) to nonracial ideologies. The latter type of ideology was more common throughout history because the combination of racial caste and slavery was less common. The more usual type of ideological justification for slavery can be found in ancient Greek civilization, where Aristotle wrote that "it is clear that some men are by nature free, and others slaves, and that for these latter slavery is both expedient and right."

# Caste

Nowhere has the **caste system** approximated the ideal type as closely as in India. In fact, some authors (see Dumont 1970) maintain that a caste system in the full sense of the term has existed only in India. Although our focus at this point is India, we note caste characteristics found in other localities, even in preindustrial Japan. With respect to the Indian caste system, there is no clear information about its origins. It seems to have grown from a system of domination by nomadic Aryan invaders about 4,000 years ago (Wells 1971:203; Pfeiffer 1977:213).

In the Indian caste system four main divisions or castes *(varnas),* with priests (Brahmans) and a warrior caste (Kshatriyas) on top of this highly rigid hierarchy, developed. In addition to the four main castes there are *many* subcastes *(jatis),* with much local variation based on occupational specialization (Ghurye 1969; Bougle 1958). But not everyone in the population is located in a particular caste or subcaste. A large number of people are literally "outcastes," that is, outside of the caste system. These people, commonly referred to as *untouchables,* are considered by others to be so lowly and unclean as to have no place within this system of stratification.

Most important among the distinguishing characteristics of a caste system are its high degree of normative closure and rigid ranks. Unlike a class system, for example, there are no ambiguous gray areas in which one class or rank shades into another; rather, the divisions are well defined and clear. Along with this, normative closure specifies that no one born into one caste can be socially mobile, either up or down. Although there have been some cases of marriage across caste lines (Dumont 1970), and in special cases a whole subcaste has moved up in rank, this system represents extreme ascription. However, we must add that more recent historical research on small villages in India has indicated that the caste system was not always quite as rigid as earlier scholars have claimed, nor as completely accepted by people in lower caste positions (Sekhon 2000; Fuller 1996; Srinivas 1996; Gupta 1991; Beteille 1996). It seems that with British rule after 1750 the Brahmanic ruling class was able to increase its power over people in local areas to make the system more rigid. Also, in the late 1800s the British colonial rulers began taking a census of the Indian population outside the big cities, accepting, and in a sense legitimizing, the Brahmanic interpretation of the almost completely rigid caste system. Even with these modifications of the older interpretation of a much more rigid caste system in India, it must be said that this Indian caste system was no doubt the most complete caste system found in history.

Another important aspect of a caste system is the very high degree of institutionalization and acceptance of rigid ranks, as well as the rights and duties of each caste. It is a highly ritualistic system, meaning that strict rules must be observed whenever people from differing castes come into contact with each other. For example, untouchables are considered so unclean as to be required to hide whenever anyone from a higher caste (or, more accurately, anyone with a caste position) is in the area, or, if this is not possible, they are required to bow with their faces to the earth.

The relative acceptance of such ritual and caste inequality in India, especially among the lowest castes and untouchables (until this century), seems quite remarkable. It is this acceptance that has led some, as noted earlier, to suggest that a caste system has existed in its fullest sense only in India. As evidence of this acceptance, in an "extensive search" through the historical literature, Moore (1978:62) claims he could find no report of revolts by untouchables in India before this century. Again, however, we must note that recent historical research on less urbanized areas of India indicate the caste system was not *always* completely accepted by untouchables (Dube 1998), and there were some religious social movements based on Bhakti, Buddhism, Jainism, and Sikhism that challenged the legitimacy of the caste system in early Indian history (Sekhon 2000; Fuller 1996; Srinivas 1996; Gupta 1991). Rather than accept the caste system and Brahmanic rule, these social movements explained the lower status of most Indians as a result of the economic and political power and greed of the upper castes. Such new research confirms our view that systems of social stratification work to stabilize and create acceptance of high degrees of inequality in human societies, or in other words, answer the question of "who gets what, and why," but only for a time.

An immediate question arises: What accounts for this general acceptance (especially by those toward the bottom of the stratification system)? The best answer, it seems, can be found with the method of justification or legitimation of caste inequalities. In India the Hindu religion has provided such a justification through an elaborate code spelling out the obligations, rights, and overall workings of the caste system. If accepted (which no doubt they generally were), these religious beliefs provided the sanctions necessary for enforcement of caste duties and obligations.

The Hindu religion maintains a belief in reincarnation—that souls are reborn after death. For enforcement of caste duties the key is that individuals are believed to experience reincarnation upward or downward within the caste system, depending on how well they respect their caste duties and obligations. Thus, depending on the acceptance of this religious belief, and the evidence suggests that such acceptance was typical (Dumont 1970), we find an incredibly strong mechanism for maintaining the stratification system. No one wants to be reborn as an untouchable—least of all the untouchables, who best know the miseries of this position. Furthermore, we can understand the contempt received by untouchables; they are those believed to have sinned most in a previous life.

As might be expected with such closure and ascribed rankings, the degree of inequality within the Indian caste system has been high. Incumbents of top caste positions maintain vast amounts of wealth and power, while those below remain very poor. But economic and power differences are not the most prominent forms of inequality. Rather, as the Indian caste system has operated, it is status inequality that dominates. The caste rankings are primarily status ranks, while inequalities of wealth and power flow from, or are traditionally attached to, the inequalities in status.

As mentioned previously, at least some characteristics of caste can be found outside India. For example, some Asian countries, such as Japan and Thailand, have had stratification systems roughly similar to the caste system for at least a relatively brief period of time (Reischauer and Craig 1978; Hane 1982; Kerbo and McKinstry 1998; Slagter and Kerbo 2000; Eisenstadt 1996; Neary 1997). As we will see later, in Japan from the early 1600s to the middle 1800s, during what is called the Tokugawa period in Japan, the shogun rulers established a very rigid system of closed caste ranks to maintain strict control as European countries threatened Japan with colonization.

It is common to hear any form of inequality based on ascription referred to as a caste ranking. For example, race and gender inequalities are often referred to as caste divisions, and so is the ascriptive status maintained by old upper-class families in countries such as the United States. Most of the controversy over the existence of caste outside India, however, has been focused on black racial inequality in the United States (see Cox 1948; Sio 1969; Dumont 1970).

We do, of course, find racial ascription maintained by a racist ideology. But, it is argued, the most important aspect of a highly institutionalized system of caste inequality is lacking with respect to black–white divisions in the United States. Most significant is that there has never been a high degree of acceptance of racial ascription in the United States, especially among blacks. We can conclude by noting only that there are at least some caste characteristics found with race and gender ascription in modern societies like the United States.

## Estate

There is also a controversy over whether feudalism, or the **estate system,** is primarily a relationship based on military power or economic dominance (see Heller 1969:57). Marc Bloch disputed the economic view by describing the origins of feudalism in military power held by some families during Europe's early Middle Ages (Bloch 1961). Marx, stressed the relation of economic dominance whereby one class owned the major means of production (in this case land) while others lived at its mercy. We may enter this debate only by suggesting that in the early European age of feudalism the military power aspect was dominant, while an economic form of control (enforced by the state) increased in importance later. But, to be completely accurate, in the final stage of European feudalism bureaucratic state power also became an important element, as in late 18th-century France and Germany (Kerbo and Strasser 2000).

A form of feudalism existed in many, if not most, agrarian societies, but it was in Europe during the Middle Ages that a form of feudalism developed that most conformed to the described ideal type. By the 12th century in Europe the feudal system was firmly established. This system centered on the landholdings of an originally military class termed a *nobility.* There were ties of obedience, agrarian labor, and protection between the nobility and subjects (mostly peasants or serfs) called a *vassalage.* Peasants were required to supply labor and military service to their lords (nobility) when needed, in exchange for the necessities of life and protection from external threats.

During the early period of feudalism, Europe was a continent of overlapping and fragmented areas of authority (Davies 1996). Land was dominated primarily by rather independent noble kinship groups, but with shifting alliances to other noble families in an area. As these ties among noble families became more extensive, more dominant noble families emerged, forming kingdoms. Later, what we know of as modern states further institutionalized the authority of the more dominant nobility.

It was with the consolidation of early feudal states around the 12th century that the true form of an *estate system* fully emerged. For it was with state sanction that estate ranks, similar to classes, were formalized and given justification or legitimation through law. Three estates were defined by law—the priestly class (the first estate); the nobility (the second estate); and commoners (or everyone else, including artisans, merchants, and peasants), who accounted for the lowest rank (or third estate). Thus, in the early stages of feudalism custom or tradition justified the structured social inequalities. But with the growth of the state, legal sanction became of greater importance.

However, religion always played a justifying role. The church, primarily the Roman Catholic church, was a hierarchical institution that through its teachings supported the tradition of worldly inequality. And later, with the emergence of the state, the higher church officials were given legal sanction as the first estate. In this later stage of feudalism, the church usually gave supporting religious sanction to the secular rulers through an ideology of divine right of kings.

With respect to normatively closed versus open ranks or estates, closure represented the primary form. However, the degree of closure varied. Especially in early feudalism, when estates were not yet given formal legal sanction, there was some chance of social mobility. For example, an exceptionally bright peasant could achieve a high religious position, or an exceptionally skilled warrior could achieve a position among nobility. But in the later stages of feudalism the ranks became more rigid. Hereditary placement became more strictly the rule—ascription predominated. Marriage across estate or class lines was forbidden, ensuring hereditary closure.

The span of inequality between the elites (in this case, the first and second estates) and the masses (or the third estate) was high. In fact, as we will see, it was in this type of society that relative inequality reached its highest level (see Lenski 1966, 1984; Nolan and Lenski 1998). With the technological superiority of this type of agrarian society there was a much greater output of material goods and, for the most part, the surplus of material goods went to the elites.

## Class

The industrial revolution ultimately shaped a new system of stratification we call a **class system.** Some characteristics of a class system have existed before—during the Roman Empire, for example—but it was not until the emergence of industrial societies that this kind of stratification system could survive and spread around the world. This is not to say that class systems throughout the world are identical. Many differences can be found, although industrial societies tend to have the broadly similar characteristics of stratification outlined in the following paragraphs. In other words, although we can identify an ideal type of class system, there is more variation in this type than in some others (such as caste and feudal systems).

One of the most important aspects of class societies is their industrial (in contrast to agrarian) economic base. With the changing economic substructure during the late feudal period in Europe, the old nobility lost its position of economic and political dominance. At the same time, the ascriptive inequalities and rigid estate divisions gave way. The new industrial societies required a different system of stratification if they were to expand and prosper—that is, if the new dominant economic class was to expand and prosper.

A stratification system was required that could respond to the need for an educated, more skilled workforce to operate in the more complex industrial economy. And it had to be a stratification system that would, at least to some degree, allow for class placement in terms of ability or merit, rather than in terms of the ascriptive criteria of previous stratification systems. Thus, we find normatively open ranks based to a greater degree on achievement rather than ascription. We say "to a greater degree" based on achievement because, as is considered more fully in later chapters, ascription is still a significant method of placement.

With a stress on open ranks and achievement in class societies, however, it does *not* follow that there is also a normative stress on equality. The normative stress (never a complete reality) is on inequality resulting from the existence of equality of opportunity or free competition. The belief is that those with the greatest ability will be rewarded most highly. The actual level of inequality between elites and the general population, however, is reduced in comparison with previous ideal types of stratification systems (Nolan and Lenski 1998). Elites in class societies do not have fewer material benefits than their counterparts in feudal, caste, or slave societies, but most of the general population is better off, at least materially (that is, the separation between elites and the masses has been reduced), though inequality is on the upswing again in many industrial societies with changes in the world system (or world economy), which must be considered in some detail later.

The preceding comments have hinted at how the important legitimation process operates in class societies. We must now outline this process more specifically. The same problem exists for class societies as for the others: Those less advantaged in the society must be convinced, at least to some degree, that their low position is somehow right or fair. In class societies inequalities are justified in large measure by an ideology of equality of opportunity (see Huber and Form 1973; Feagin 1975; Ladd and Bowman 1998). Thus, the normative stress on open ranks and achievement itself becomes part of the legitimation process.

To some degree this ideology has been institutionalized through the legal system. Gone are the legal sanctions *overtly* supporting ascriptive inequalities found in feudal or estate societies. In their place are laws intended to promote free competition or equality of opportunity (laws intended to prevent monopolistic business practices, promote equal access to education and job opportunities, and so on). But as will be evident upon a more detailed analysis of the U.S. class system, these laws are in part an aspect of the legitimation of inequality and are often circumvented in actual application.

In early class systems the most prominent form of inequality was economic. Either the ownership (or control) of the means of production (that is, industrial capital) or occupational skill brought high economic reward that influenced status and political power. However, as is described in later chapters, today the dominance of economic inequalities is weakened. Some argue that what can be called modern, advanced, or postindustrial societies are replacing early industrial societies. In these societies most aspects of the class system have remained. But the most prominent form or base of inequality is said to differ.

Generally, the view is that economically based inequalities are not as important now as inequalities in bureaucratic power. With the ownership of the means of production (capital or factories) no longer securely in the hands of wealthy families and with the growth of corporate and government bureaucratic institutions, it is said that top positions in these bureaucratic institutions are the most prominent forms of class superiority in advanced industrial societies.

Table 3-1 has been included to summarize our discussion of the major types of stratification systems throughout history. Across the top of Table 3-1 are the defining characteristics of each type of stratification system, with the five major types of stratification systems listed down the left side of the table.

## TABLE 3-1

### Characteristics of Stratification Systems

| Type of system | Rank | Placement | Form of legitimation | Primary basis of ranking |
|---|---|---|---|---|
| Primitive communal | Open | Achievement | Tradition | Status-honor |
| Slave system | Generally closed | Usually ascription | Legal ideology | Economic |
| Caste system | Closed | Ascription | Religious ideology | Status-honor |
| Estate, feudal | Primarily closed | Primarily ascription | Legal ideology | Economic |
| Class | Primarily open | Mix of ascription, achievement | Legal ideology | Economic, bureaucratic authority |

# ❈ The Emergence of Inequality and Social Stratification

It is time to add a more detailed historical dimension to our examination of inequality and human stratification systems. At the outset it must be clear that what follows is only a general outline of this history of inequality. In reality we find no unaltered linear progression from primitive communal societies to industrial class system, only a general tendency in this direction over the centuries.

Also, it must be clear that what follows is a review of the development of human societies as well as systems of social stratification. Thus, we will be referring mostly to *types of societies* in terms of their levels of technology in contrast to *types of stratification systems* in the above material. For example, in what follows we will be describing hunting and gathering societies, early agrarian empires, and so on. In the case of hunting and gathering societies, primitive communal stratification systems existed. But in some cases, as in early agrarian empires, the type of stratification system varied, with only some having what could best be called slave systems. Table 3-2 is provided as a summary of the relationship between the type of society and type of social stratification system.

## Early Human Groups

The most conclusive evidence of early human beings *(Homo habilis)* was located decades ago by Louis Leakey in the Olduvai Gorge in East Africa. These remains (primarily skull fragments) date back some 3 to 4 million years (Leakey and Lewin 1977:86). From what were the original sites of human existence in Africa, DNA evidence shows steady but slow movement of *Homo sapiens* (our closest ancestors) across the earth, beginning about 50,000 years ago, (Pfeiffer 1977:53).

## TABLE 3-2

### Evolution of Human Societies and Types of Stratification Systems

| Type of society | Period | Type of stratification system |
|---|---|---|
| Hunting and gathering societies | Changed from 10,000 yrs. ago | Primitive communal |
| Early agrarian societies | From 6,000 yrs. ago | Slave systems, feudal, or caste systems |
| Late agrarian societies | From approximately 2,000–3,000 yrs. ago | Feudal/estate, caste, Asia mode |
| Industrial societies | From about 300 yrs. ago | Class systems |

*SOURCE:* From Lenski (1966, 1984); Nolan and Lenski (1998).

By 15,000 years ago *Homo sapiens* had reached the North American continent, spreading southward from their crossing over the then existing land bridge from what is now Russia (Chanda 2007). This movement across the earth was not what we would consider a planned migration but movement in search of food. In these very early times, much before the important changes some 10,000 years ago, if food became scarce in one area (because of increased population or poor climate), there was space to move on.

The general type of social organization of these early humans was described earlier as primitive communalism. Although geographic and environmental variations helped produce many differences among these primitive communal tribes (such as differences in beliefs about the supernatural, family structure, food sources, and degree of male dominance; see Lenski 1966:101, 1984; Nolan and Lenski 1998), one characteristic appears quite common—near equality. By our definition of social stratification—structured inequalities—it was seldom if ever found.

Several living examples of this type of human existence—such as the Andaman Islanders (Radcliffe-Brown 1948) and the Bambuti Pygmies of Zaire (Turnbull 1961)—have been found to meet this characteristic of equality most fully. Whatever tools and other artifacts they have, the food they find is either considered common property or divided equally among all members of the tribe. Inequalities of power and influence over others in the tribe have been found at times, but the level of these inequalities tends to be very low. When inequalities of power are found, they usually are based on the experience of age or the status of being the best provider of food. Most common is a decision-making method involving free group discussion by all adult members of the tribe (in some tribes only males are included, however); thus, a form of democracy or equality of influence exists.

Because of their level of technology—that is, their methods of providing the necessities of life—these tribes are generally nomadic or seminomadic. Because they lack knowledge of or at least the use of agriculture or animal husbandry, the food sources in their environment are usually depleted through time, and they must move on. This also prevents the accumulation of many personal possessions; they must travel light. The maximum size of the tribe is also strongly related to its level of technology; its method of food production can support only a few people in one area. An examination of living hunting and gathering tribes shows they average only about 50 members (Murdock 1949:81), and that about 90 percent are nomadic or seminomadic (Murdock 1957; see also Lenski 1966:98).

Along with the relationship between their level of technology, tribal size, and nomadic lifestyle, we generally find other characteristics that affect the degree and type of social equality among these people. With respect to the first of these, cooperation versus conflict, the general evidence would suggest that the French philosopher Rousseau was more accurate (though not completely) in his view of early human beings than was Thomas Hobbes (who assumed their life to be "solitary, poor, nasty, brutish, and short"). Hunting, especially, is much more efficient as a cooperative enterprise. From cooperative food gathering comes the necessity of sharing (Pfeiffer 1977:50). What is gained through cooperation must generally be shared among others in the tribe. If such sharing was not practiced, the incentive to continue the cooperative exchange relationship was probably weakened; thus, all could starve. Moreover, with weapons no more sophisticated than a club or spear, no member of the tribe had the power to forcefully prevent a majority of others from attaining their share of the prey. It simply made sense to work and share together, for, in the long run, all were better off for it.

Thus far we have neglected an important biological trait in the long process of human evolution. This biological trait combined with the mode of production among early human beings to produce a sexual division of labor. Because of infant dependency, mothers were required to stay closer to the home base and could not pursue wild game as easily. As we consider in more detail in Chapter 10 on gender inequalities, a division of labor based on sex developed, with men doing the hunting and women taking care of infants and gathering food that could more easily be collected around the home base (Chafetz 1984, 1988; Sanday 1981). A division of labor alone does not necessarily require social inequality. But, in the absence of economic or power concentration, when one occupation comes to be of major importance for the survival of the group, those who are most skilled in this occupation will usually come to be more highly rewarded.[3] In hunting and gathering societies, most goods were in short supply, but status or honor was not. Thus, the skilled hunter came to be more highly honored, and it is here that we find the most important form of inequality in primitive communal societies.

The development of this form of gender inequality is demonstrated most clearly through an examination of living tribes that vary in their dependence on meat. For example, the Hadza of Tanzania and the Palliyans of southwest India eat little meat. Here the level of status inequality between the sexes is low. However, the Eskimos, the !Kung, and the Bambuti of Africa have a high dependence on meat, and the level of sexual inequality among them is greater (see Leakey and Lewin 1977:235; 1978:247). Women don't always have low status, nor has biology always placed women in an inferior status. But when physical strength is demanded for tasks very important to group survival (a condition seldom found in modern societies), men usually perform this work and receive more status.

We must note two further aspects of status inequality based on skill. Age ranking is also quite common among primitive communal tribes. Again, this status ranking is based primarily on skill in hunting. The young to middle-aged male is favored. But there is also skill, or rather knowledge, that comes with age. The older tribal members may through experience know where and how best to find food, or their knowledge of tradition, mythology, or any other set of knowledge may be superior. Thus, we may find both age and sexual status inequality.

Last, many primitive communal tribes do have leaders in the form of chiefs or medicine men. However, these are part-time leaders (Lenski 1966:100). They cannot accumulate material riches, for there are few. They cannot demand that all others work for their benefit, for there is seldom enough food to relieve people from their daily food-gathering duties. Their part-time leadership status is based on skill: skill in storytelling, skill in performing religious rituals, or, again, skill in providing food. Thus, it is based on status gained through function. The advantaged position cannot bring an accumulation of power and wealth to create hereditary inequalities or a system of social stratification. Unlike in most later societies, the offspring are not assured their parents' higher place in a stratification system.

## *Early Social Change*

The thousands, if not millions, of years between the emergence of human beings and a change away from hunting and gathering or primitive communal tribes is not what is most incredible. What is incredible is that change occurred at all. A cycle existed in which primitive methods of food production required most of the daily energy and attention of every tribal member (Lenski 1966:97). There was no time, energy, or incentive for advancement. And contrary to what is often thought, life for these early human beings was not always "solitary, poor, nasty, brutish, and short." From our evidence of present-day hunting and gathering tribes, tribes isolated from the technical progress of modern society, we often find rather content and happy people. Not all prehistoric people were so secure and content, of course. But it took a significant change that affected the lives of many such primitive people to propel our ancestors into a cycle of increasing technological advancement.

The change came for an increasing number of hunting and gathering people about 10,000 to 15,000 years ago. Most archaeologists agree that a primary stimulus for the change was a steady increase in population in many areas, in the face of declining food resources (see Cohen 1977; Harris 1977; Redman 1978:88–112). Population had increased before, but by this time it was more difficult to find new territory not already claimed by others. In addition, some argue that "there was less land as well as more people. Land had been decreasing ever since the height of the last ice age 20,000 or so years ago, when so much water was locked up in polar ice caps and glaciers that the ocean levels stood 250 to 500 feet lower than they stand today" (Pfeiffer 1977:69).

In what were the more populated areas of the world at the time, such as northern Africa and the Near East, the ever-increasing scarcity of food and land produced more intertribal conflicts (Pfeiffer 1977:33). Change and disruption of some kind seem to account for the violent behavior and high inequality reported in a few living primitive communal tribes (see Skinner 1973). We have some archaeological evidence of this increase in violent conflict. Sites dating to about 15,000 years ago show human remains with arrowheads and other stone projectiles piercing the bones (Pfeiffer 1977:246).

The pressure of less land and more people provided the necessity for change. We will never know with certainty *exactly* where and when human beings found that through settled agricultural methods of food production more people could be fed, but the current evidence seems to show that this happened in the Near East about 10,000 years ago. It is unlikely that someone suddenly discovered that plants could be cultivated—the eureka theory. It is more likely that the knowledge was already present.

What happened was that it became necessary for more and more people to apply agricultural methods. Every member of the tribe was required to participate in agriculture to survive. The pattern of nomadic hunting and gathering was altered for more and more people. Those who did not change failed to survive in these highly populated areas. The Neolithic revolution had arrived.

## The Neolithic Revolution

Most social scientists regard the Neolithic revolution as the earliest, most important event in the evolution of human societies (see Lenski 2005; Childe 1952). Not only do we find a change in the technology of food production, we find change in almost every aspect of human organization. The changes, of course, did not come as rapidly as did those during the industrial revolution. Human settlements at this time were more isolated, and transportation and communication were still undeveloped. It took about 5,000 years for agricultural methods to be established firmly with farming villages and irrigation (Pfeiffer 1977:144).

At first, people remained in small tribes, mixing farming with their old hunting and gathering ways. Their first agricultural tools were simple digging sticks. Consequently, their level of food production remained relatively low. But, because of the new agricultural methods, there was at least some surplus of food, a surplus that freed some people from full-time labor producing food.

With the release from food production for some (at least part-time) there emerged artisans, craft workers, a small commercial class, and, most important, political and religious leaders. But as yet we find no great distinctions in wealth and power. These leaders are not placed far above common members of the farming tribe. More often we find only a "nominal leader who acts to redistribute food and perform a few minor ceremonial activities" (Wenke 1980:343). As with earlier hunting and gathering tribes, status is the main form of inequality. In the earliest farming tribes the status distinctions may have been greater than before but were not yet attached to hereditary wealth and power (Flannery 1972).

Through time, however, especially in the more populated areas such as the Near East, hunting and gathering methods increasingly gave way to full-time agriculture. And our ancestors became better at it. In fact, the population increase that provided part of the stimulus for agriculture was given an even greater boost. It is estimated that during the first 8,000 years of agriculture (beginning about 10,000 years ago, remember) the total human population rose from 10 million to 300 million people (Leakey and Lewin 1977:176). Through hunting and gathering methods of food production it had taken human beings more than a million years to reach a population of 10 million. This relatively rapid population growth, itself an aspect of new agricultural methods, produced further change in human societies.

It is useful at this point to examine some of the data from the first few thousand years of agricultural development that relate to our specific topic of social stratification. We have no written records from these early agricultural tribes and later agricultural settlements, but we do have archaeological data. And what we have shows *increasing social inequality.*

The two main types of archaeological evidence that concern us are burial practices and housing structures. It became common practice to bury personal possessions with the dead: "There were numerous reasons for including valuable goods with burials . . . but in general it indicated a person's wealth or status" (Redman 1978:197). What these burial sites show is increasing inequality with the development of agriculture (Redman 1978:277). Some archaeologists also conclude from the evidence that these inequalities of wealth and power finally emerged as hereditary inequalities. This conclusion is based on findings of children buried in graves rich with material possessions (see Redman 1978:277; Wenke 1980:349). In summarizing the general findings on burial practices, Wenke (1980:349) writes: "Some ancient cemeteries have three or four distinct classes of burials. Some types are well constructed of stone, have rich grave goods, and are centrally located, while others are simple graves with little in them except the corpse. And it is a reasonable inference that these divisions correspond to different economic and social classes."

In addition to the burial data there are indications of growing inequality reflected in housing (see Redman 1978:277; Wenke 1980:346). With the advancement in agriculture we find villages with many simple common houses, but toward the center are often larger, better-constructed family dwellings (Pfeiffer 1977:94–95).

Again, as with burial sites, we find increasing material inequality. But evidence of inequality is also found in large religious monuments. An example of such monuments is Stonehenge on England's Salisbury Plain. It is estimated that 30 million hours of human labor were required to construct this monument. A reasonable conclusion is that such an investment in human labor required inequalities of power and sufficient power over others to mobilize such a work effort (Pfeiffer 1977:95).

Having noted the importance of religious monuments, we should also note the overall importance of religion in these early agricultural societies. Religion generally became the most important base of structured inequalities in these early agricultural societies (Lenski 1984). It is hard to say which came first, wealth and power inequalities or high status as a religious leader. The two, however, reinforced one another. Religion has often been a useful means of justifying and maintaining power and wealth inequalities (Pfeiffer 1977:104). But this religious base for inequality, as we will see, slowly gave way to more powerful secular political elites with advanced agricultural societies.

The digging stick and hoe gave way to the plow and irrigation about 5,000 years ago. At this time we find evidence of more stable agricultural settlements able to support greater numbers of people. And with these more advanced methods of agriculture more people were freed to pursue other occupations in the arts, crafts, religion, and warfare. Accompanying these changes were further increases in hereditary inequalities of all types.

While many cities were emerging independently at this time, the first known city was Uruk. This city was in southern Mesopotamia, located between the Tigris and Euphrates rivers, about 5,500 years ago, with an estimated population of 20,000 people.

Here again, as in the early village in Jordan reported earlier, excavations have shown that over the years there were increasing levels of inequality among its inhabitants (Pfeiffer 1977:159). An important base of inequality was slavery, although religion was clearly the most important. Impressive religious temples that contained much of the riches of the city have been uncovered. However, "although the evidence is slight, it is likely that individual families or groups of families rose to positions of wealth and power on the basis of success in agriculture" (Redman 1978:278). Wealthy families independent of religious elites may have emerged at this time, but religious elites often remained primary. However, top religious leaders alone could not command such a growing population. Armies and administrative officials developed to tend to the business of social order, construction projects, and taxation (Higham 2001, 2002; Hall 1999).

With respect to the more complex form of agricultural production and the emergence of secular elites, it should be noted that with some agricultural settlements we find the early beginning of what Marx called the "Asiatic mode of production" (see Mandel 1971:116–129; Krader 1975). The development of this Asiatic mode of production is found especially in regions such as China, India, and the Middle East, where agriculture required irrigation (Hall 1999). Because irrigation required a higher form of social organization, even though land was often common property, something like a state elite emerged in charge of common projects like irrigation systems. Through time, in places like China and India, this state elite grew to dominate the society in a form of social organization distinct from feudalism (where power was based on land ownership rather than on the political elite positions with the Asiatic mode of production). It was the power of the Chinese state made possible by this Asiatic mode of production that enabled the Chinese emperor and Mandarin class in 1424 to suppress an emerging merchant class and shut down the huge "treasure fleet" described at the beginning of this chapter.

Agricultural methods of production alone do not explain the rise of these new cities. There were forces pulling more people into cities, as well as other forces pushing them toward cities. The pull came with city elites looking for more personnel to work on construction projects and to pay taxes. The push came with threats to the security of rural people from armies of other cities (Pfeiffer 1977:165). Throughout this period of urban development, an increasing number of city elites often competed for people, land, and other resources. Military conflict thus increased, as is suggested by the often large walls built around these early cities (Redman 1978:266).

As military conflict increased, a new type of inequality slowly took hold. For the first time among human societies we find human beings owning other human beings. Slavery did not represent a widespread form of inequality in early agricultural cities, in contrast with later civilizations, but it was almost nonexistent in hunting and gathering societies. The reason for the absence of slavery in hunting and gathering societies is related to their methods of food production. It simply did not make sense to hold slaves when every individual could produce only enough food to feed one person. Slaves, therefore, could not improve economic output for the tribe.

When food production methods advanced to the point where one person could produce a surplus, slavery did develop. And when more and more people were freed from food production, slaves could be used in construction projects more cheaply and efficiently than free labor. The final factor of importance in the development of slavery was, of course, military power. Military power was necessary to hold slaves as well as to attain them.

One other form of inequality deserves mention. We last found women in a lower-status position in some hunting and gathering societies (especially in those most dependent on hunting). Lenski (1984), through an examination of living agricultural tribes, finds the status of women in most of these tribes unimproved. Others, however, argue that women's status was probably worse in most agricultural tribes (see Pfeiffer 1977:463). For one thing, with simple agriculture and a decline in the importance of hunting, there was more work that could be done by women tending small children (Sanderson, Heckert, and Dubrow 2005). A related and probably more important factor was the emergence of organized warfare. The high status of the hunter shifted to the high status of the warrior. Again, women, who more often than today were with small children, were at a disadvantage.

It should be clear that agricultural settlements and early cities existed at varying times throughout much of the world. And, of course, in the more undeveloped regions of the world they exist to this day. Their development and existence depended on a particular method of food production that left a food surplus and a growing population. In the Americas these conditions emerged later, about 3,000 years ago, primarily in Central America. The first large city of about 125,000 people at its high point, Teotihuacán, did not emerge until about A.D. 100 around what is now Mexico City (Pfeiffer 1977:369). Others, for example, in the Aztec and Mayan civilizations, followed even later and were still in existence during the Spanish conquest. In Southwest Asia these agricultural civilizations emerged even later, with large cities some 2,000 years ago, culminating in the huge Angkor Wat civilization that reached its high point about 1,000 years ago (Higham 2001, 2002; Hall 1999).

What is important to note about these early American cities is that extensive archaeological investigation has found the existence and forms of inequality roughly similar to those of early cities in other parts of the world. There were powerful religious leaders, vast material inequalities, and early slavery, and all of these inequalities became hereditary. At this stage of economic development the archaeological data, as well as studies of living human societies, show the first big jump in the level of human inequality (Lenski 1984; Higham 2001, 2002). As we will see, inequality did continue to expand in more advanced agrarian societies, but the *magnitude of the increase* was never as large.

## Early Agrarian Empires

Among the developments discussed here, the emergence of a distinct military class and state organization proved crucial for further inequalities of power and privilege. Out of these new means of power agrarian empires developed. The agricultural economic base of these societies expanded, and became more complex and more technologically advanced. But it was state organization and military power, along with more rapid transportation and communication (with the use of the wheel and the sail) that could spread this power over wider areas, that produced empires: "For the first time in history, technologically based differences in military might become a basic reality within human societies, and the opportunities for exploitation were correspondingly enlarged" (Lenski 1966:194).

These early agrarian empires began some 5,000 years ago, in places such as Egypt and China, although the height of their development came much later. Of these, the Roman Empire was one of the most powerful, and one of the last in a series. This empire began its ascent around 300 B.C. and its final decline at the hands of invaders (such as Attila the Hun) 1,500 years ago (A.D. 500). What followed was a period of stagnation and decline through much of the advanced world (China's advance was less broken, and the Islamic empire did emerge at this time), until new feudal states emerged during the Middle Ages in Europe (the subject of our next section).

Before their decline, there were internal variations in the Roman and Egyptian empires; for example, they experienced early periods of less inequality and some democracy, especially in Rome (Antonio 1979; MacMullen 1974; Brunt 1971). All these societies suffered from chronic warfare, and slavery tended to be very important in their economies. These empires were usually conquest states; thus, the ruling class was often in a position of power because of such conquests. And more than anything else these empires approximate slave stratification systems.

Despite the differences in these empires, we find other common characteristics. They generally had centralized governments with political and religious ruling elites who had vast economic as well as political control. The state function was to enforce laws, draft soldiers, levy taxes, and extract tribute from conquered territories. The empires had large populations and wide territories that contained many settlements and cities of various sizes and often distinct economic functions. There was a complex division of labor, with full-time craft workers, artisans, and merchants, plus the usual religious, military, and agricultural people. The agricultural production that supported these more complex societies had to be more technologically efficient. There were metal plows with animal power to pull them, irrigation, and more high-yield strains of cereal crops.

Human societies had the first major increase in inequality during this period. At the top of the hierarchy of wealth and power was a small ruling class. In earlier societies (before agrarian empires) the ruler was considered more the trustee of communal property (Lenski 1984). Now, however, the property belonged to the ruler. With this property and surplus production the ruler could buy the loyalty of functionaries who worked to maintain this system of high inequality.

The structured inequalities and hierarchical divisions were not always completely rigid. Although most inequalities of wealth and power were hereditary, there was at least some chance of social mobility. And while there was not a total separation between those on top of the stratification system and the masses, the masses for the most part lived at or close to a subsistence level. Only a small group owned a little land or possessed a skilled trade, placing it between the masses and the ruling class in the stratification system.

## Late Agrarian Societies

With the increase of nomadic conquests around A.D. 500, most of the early agrarian empires were in decline. The Western world regressed toward what is known as the Dark Ages. It is true that Attila the Hun and Genghis Khan (who appeared a few centuries later) received bad press; Western historians have written much about the atrocities of these nomadic invaders, while more often neglecting those of early agrarian empires (Wells 1971). But these societies did enter a period in which art, literature, science, technological innovation, and social institutions in general were in decline. Especially in what was once the northern part of the Roman Empire, and in Europe more generally, people banded together for protection, forming small settlements much like those of earlier agricultural people. For centuries this was the form of social organization in what we call the West.

In the East, China, for example, was able to absorb the nomadic invaders with less social disorganization. And in the Middle East, North Africa, and Spain, the Islamic empire emerged with the fall of the Roman Empire to bring advance and social order. But not until about A.D. 1000 to 1200 were technological advancement and widespread sociopolitical organization on the advance in the West again. It was in these years that the classical period of feudal or estate societies emerged in Europe. And with these new societies, extreme inequalities reemerged.

Our description of the ideal type of estate or feudal system of stratification should be remembered at this point. We need not present a detailed description again. But Bloch's (1961) argument that the feudal period in Europe should be divided into two stages is worth repeating. In the earlier stage, before A.D. 1200, social stratification was less institutionalized; inequalities of power and wealth were supported by tradition and custom. Out of the disintegration of previous civilizations, people had grouped together to live and work under the protection of a military nobility. In return for protection the common people followed a new tradition of providing tribute to the nobility in the form of service (such as military duty) and turning over much of their economic surplus. By about A.D. 1200, however, inequality had grown, and the more informal system of social stratification was threatened, both by rebellion from the lower orders and by the gradual emergence of a new class of merchants whose wealth at times equaled that of the nobility.

In a very interesting work, Hechter and Brustein (1980) have provided more detail on the growth of the feudal system and on how the more rigid inequalities of this system later developed. Before A.D. 1200 in Europe there were at least three differing modes of agricultural production and corresponding forms of social organization. Among these, the sedentary pastoral mode involved self-sufficient households linked through kinship. In contrast to the feudal mode, there was much more independence and equality. Around the Mediterranean and southern Germany a petty commodity mode of production dominated. Here land was worked in small independent units, with production oriented toward trade to the more numerous towns in the area. There was a higher level of social mobility, with less-rigid class divisions.

In other areas around Europe the feudal mode dominated; there was a manor system, with tenants and a landlord. Agricultural production was a more collective and more organized operation. Moreover, in contrast to the other modes of production, land remained in large units over the years because it was not subdivided with each new generation. A result was greater production under the feudal mode, and thus a greater surplus. In part, this was because collective labor on larger units of land was more efficient, especially with new advances in agricultural technology at the time. Because of its greater efficiency, the feudal mode finally came to dominate all of Europe.

At first the feudal system represented many fairly independent manors, with a local nobility dominating each. But as the power and wealth of some landowners grew, they began dominating other landowners. A wealthier and more powerful nobility emerged, producing even greater levels of inequality between the nobility and the common people. To further solidify these inequalities, by A.D. 1300 "modern" states emerged.

Hechter and Brustein (1980) are primarily concerned with why these states developed when and where they did. We saw that during the Roman Empire a strong bureaucracy supported by the upper class developed in response to a rebellious lower class. Something similar occurred in later feudal Europe, but this time it was in response to a two-pronged threat to the upper class (Hechter and Brustein 1980:1085). By the 14th century in Europe, peasant revolts were perhaps more widespread throughout Europe than at any other time. At the same time, in the cities, a wealthy merchant class began challenging the power and wealth of the nobility. In response to both challenges, the nobility united in support of new state systems with the power to maintain their positions of privilege.

The key to Hechter and Brustein's argument is in data showing that the feudal zones in Europe, where threats to the privileges of nobility were experienced, were where the modern state grew. With the development of these states across the face of Europe, a rigid system of inequality, lost with previous agrarian empires, was restored. For a time there was another period of order until, as we will see, change again disrupted the rigid inequalities enjoyed by an agrarian-based upper class.

Before turning from the feudal period, we should briefly consider the inequalities and lifestyle differences of the three major estates, or divisions, in this type of society. In the first estate, is the higher clergy; the second belongs to the nobility. However, one must not get the idea that the clergy was always most prominent in the estate system. The underlying ideology that God was first in the affairs of people and the divine sanction given secular rulers by the church accounted for the clergy's position (and throughout most of feudal history in Europe, Catholic clergy made up the first estate). Although the church and nobility often coexisted in a somewhat uneasy relationship, they tended to work together to strengthen and reinforce the position of each other above the third estate (or commoners). This uneasy relationship is nowhere better symbolized than at the crowning of Charlemagne, the first king in early feudal Europe, by Pope Leo III. Although the ceremony did not call for it, the pope placed the crown on Charlemagne's head (to the surprise of the new king). With this act the pope sought to signify what he saw as the authority of the church over the affairs of secular leaders.

Despite vows to be the humble servants of God, the priestly class was extremely wealthy. Priests received much of the surplus produced by laboring classes, and lived in comfort exceeded only by that of the higher nobility. The most important source of wealth during this period was land ownership. From land ownership came rents, taxes, and other forms of tribute and services. In 14th-century England, for example, the church owned about one-third of all land; the situation was similar in France.

The clergy itself was highly stratified. During this time the main division was between the upper and lower clergy, a division similar to that between the nobility and peasants. The upper clergy was most often recruited from the nobility or governing class and enjoyed a similar lifestyle. The lower clergy, in contrast, was recruited from the common people. It was the job of the lower clergy to serve the common people, to watch over them for the church and nobility, as parish priests living not much better than commoners (see Lenski 1984). They were to watch over commoners because, for most of these common people in small villages and the countryside, the upper clergy and nobility were far away. But the parish priest was always there. It was the parish priest who could be counted on to follow the dictates of the church hierarchy and make sure the common people followed (Le Roy Ladurie 1979:11).

The principal center of wealth and power was found with the nobility, the governing class, and, as more powerful states emerged, most importantly with the king. The lifestyle and riches of this feudal aristocracy are legendary, and this wealthy and powerful group was very small. In 19th-century Russia (which was still a feudal society at the time), this group accounted for 1.25 percent of the population; in 17th-century England it was roughly 1 percent (Lenski 1966:219); and in 17th-century France it was about 1.5 percent (Soboul 1974:35).

Despite its small numbers, the nobility did hold most of the wealth. For example, during the 13th century, the King of England had an income about 24,000 times greater than that of the average peasant (Lenski 1966:212). In France during the 16th century it is estimated that the nobility—accounting for 1.5 percent of the population, remember—owned 20 percent of the land (Soboul 1974:35). Overall, from his review of many agrarian societies, Lenski (1966:228) estimates that the ruler and his or her governing class usually accounted for about 2 percent of the population but received about one-half of all income.

In contrast with the great wealth of the first and second estates, commoners most often lived in extreme poverty. There were merchants and artisans who did well, and sometimes equaled the nobility in wealth. But for the vast majority life was harsh. Lenski presents the following description (1966:271):

> [T]he diet of the average peasant consisted of little more than the following: a hunk of bread and a mug of ale in the morning; a lump of cheese and bread with perhaps an onion or two to flavor it, and more ale at noon; a thick soup or pottage followed by bread and cheese at the main meal in the evening. Meat was rare, and the ale was usually thin. Household furniture consisted of a few stools, a table, and a chest to hold the best clothes and other treasured possessions. Beds were uncommon and most peasants simply slept on earthen floors covered with straw. Other household possessions were apparently limited to cooking utensils.

## The Fall of Feudalism and the Rise of Industrial Societies

The feudal system's fall throughout most of the world has been one of the most intensely studied subjects in the social sciences. Many books by early sociologists were devoted to the subject, and many others were concerned with what was emerging out of the ruins of feudal systems. Interest remains at a high level today. With all that has been written on the subject, we know that it was a complex process of change that varied somewhat from nation to nation. Simply put, we also know that the timing of the shift in each nation and the outcome of the fall of feudalism were related to international competition in the world system and previous class alignments in each nation, as will be considered later (Skocpol 1979).

The forces of change that were stimulated when human beings first settled down to more stable agricultural villages between 5,000 and 10,000 years ago gradually reached another stage—first in Europe, in about the 15th and 16th centuries. The cycle of better agricultural methods producing an ever-greater surplus, freeing more and more people from the land to expand the level of technology further, had continued (Chirot 1984, 1986). By the 16th century in Europe a new industrial system of production was taking root that was to change the nature of society perhaps more rapidly than ever before.

Three principal actors were thrown into conflict by these changes: (1) the old nobility or aristocracy whose profit and influence ultimately depended on land owner-ship, (2) the political elite whose position came with the large state bureaucracy that (as we have seen) originally developed to protect the interests of the nobility, and (3) a new and increasingly powerful merchant class that depended on the emerging industrial system of production (Davies 1996; Bendix 1978). The common people—the craft workers, peasants, bakers, and so on—also played a part in this drama of change. But their role was usually that of pawns: people who, because of their misery in the face of change, rioted, rebelled, or in other ways contributed to a national crisis that was then played out by the three principal actors seeking to turn the crisis to their advantage.

In places like China and India the change came more slowly. As we have seen, a principal reason for this lack of change (until later), it is argued, is that in China and India the form of agricultural production was not exactly feudalism but an Asiatic mode of production (Mandel 1971; Krader 1975). As with late feudalism, a state structure with powerful political elites developed. However, with the Asiatic mode of production these political elites developed much earlier (with the greater importance of a political elite to oversee irrigation projects and other collective agricultural needs) and grew more powerful.

Also, because land was less often privately owned, and new urban merchants were more dominated by political elites, the power of political elites was not challenged by wealthy landowners or a new merchant class. Thus, the Asiatic mode of production was more stable, lasted longer, and retarded industrialization. But the Asiatic mode of produc-tion was eventually forced into change through international conflict with new industrial societies. We have seen that China was far ahead of European nations in technological and scientific knowledge in 1400. But China's domination by an old imperial system opposed to the merchant class prevented change that could have easily led to a Chinese-dominated world economy by 1500 (Levathes 1994; Needham 1983; Menzies 2002).

The story of these changes is not complete unless we recognize that by the 16th century a European-dominated world economic system was developing that increas-ingly brought the more powerful nations into conflict, often over the question of which powerful nation would exploit which of the less-developed nations or regions as colo-nies (Kennedy 1987; Wallerstein 1974, 1980, 1989; Chirot 1986). As we will see in more detail later, Portugal and then Spain were the first European nations to send many ships all over the world to exploit the riches, cheap labor, and resources of these other world regions. But Spain and Portugal were not able to become capitalist industrial powers because of their outdated political systems.

The Netherlands was the first country to become a dominant nation in this modern world system, in large part because the Dutch were the first to have a bourgeois revolution in the 1560s that overthrew the outdated state. It was the old political system dominated by the old landed nobility that prevented the new merchant class from becoming stronger through commerce. England also came to be a dominant nation in the modern world system after the decline of the Dutch because the British landed nobility lost political power as well. In England, however, it was more of a gradual process of a shift from dominance by the landed nobility to dominance by the new merchant class. This occurred because the nobility in England was weaker, unable to prevent the expansion of industrial commerce at its expense, and also sometimes joined the merchant activity.

In other nations, such as France, the old nobility was stronger for a longer period of time (Bendix 1978; Schama 1989). Here, feudal interests of the landed nobility were protected by the state—until an economic crisis provoked by international competition became extreme. The economic and political crisis resulted in violent revolution and the emergence of a merchant class (or bourgeoisie) as the class of dominance.

In societies that advanced less rapidly, such as China (with an Asiatic mode of production) and Russia, the economic and political crisis, when it came, followed a somewhat different line. In these nations the state and the merchant class were both too weak in the face of dominance from the nations (in the world economic system) that had moved to the industrial stage earlier. What happened in these more slowly developing nations was that authoritarian state bureaucracies emerged out of violent revolution, leading to state socialism. (See Moore 1966, and Skocpol 1979, for the best descriptions of this process of change.)

Of most concern for us is that new industrial societies developed, ranging from capitalist to socialist, with all kinds of mixtures in between. In all these societies, new elites emerged with new bases of power. The differences among these new societies should not be overstressed. Despite differences in political ideology, degrees of democracy, and (to some extent) levels of inequality and social mobility, the new industrial technology and social organization that emerged placed general limits on the type of stratification system that could exist.

## ❧ The Reduction of Inequality with Industrial and Postindustrial Societies

The history of human societies has been shown to be one of increasing inequalities. We moved from relative equality in hunting and gathering societies, or primitive communalism, to very high levels of inequality in advanced agrarian societies. The life of the common people throughout this progression to advanced agrarian societies improved only slightly, if at all, whereas the wealth and power of elites multiplied rapidly.

With mature industrial societies the trend has been altered. After an initial period of increase in inequalities at the beginning of industrialization for most countries (Nielsen 1994), inequalities have been reduced. As we have seen in Chapter 2, a high level of inequality of all types remains. And as we have also seen in Chapter 2, there is significant variation in inequality among industrial societies, with growing inequality in the

United States, where there is already the highest level of inequality. However, the general population has finally achieved some benefits from revolution connected to the expanding output of ever more advanced systems of economic production. Research indicates that generally the same can be said for countries that have been developing economically in recent times (Firebaugh 2003; Firebaugh and Beck 1994). Although elites in relatively democratic industrial societies may have lost some of the commanding political power once held by elites in earlier societies, the material advances of the general population have *not* come at the expense of the elites. In other words, as is roughly indicated in Figure 3-1, in industrial societies the lot of the masses has generally improved, but so has that of elites. In fact, it can be said that the economic position of elites in industrial societies has improved in part because that of the masses has also improved.

Again we must stress that this is not to say that all industrial societies have equally low levels of inequality. Nor is this to say that inequality will not again increase, as it has been doing in the United States in recent years. In recent decades we have heard much about **postindustrial societies** with the most advanced economies. In essence, these societies have less heavy industrial production (as the name implies) and more of the economy based on services and high-tech industries. Knowledge and education, it is said, have become more important than ownership of property or wealth per se in determining a person's life chances (Thurow 1991; Galbraith 1971; Bell 1976). There is a corresponding shift in occupations from working-class industrial labor to middle-class or white-collar jobs requiring more education in postindustrial societies. This change has certainly been going on in the United States. However, what these theories of a "postindustrial society" did not account for years ago is greater variation in inequality among these societies: Because there is increasingly a large population at the bottom unable to make the shift to higher-skill jobs requiring more education in some of the postindustrial societies such as the United States, in contrast to others such as Germany and Japan with a much higher level of education in the population, the postindustrial change has brought greater differences among these nations with respect to levels of inequality. Added to this is a change in the competitive position of nations in the modern world economy,

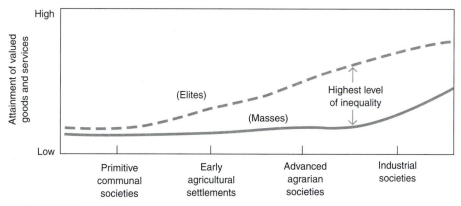

**FIGURE 3-1**    *The Progression of Inequality in Human Societies*

bringing greater variation in inequality among these nations. However, our basic point for now is that compared with preindustrial societies, inequality is generally much lower in industrial societies and postindustrial societies (Breedlove and Nolan 1988; Nielsen 1994). This growing variation in inequality among the postindustrial societies is the subject of much discussion in later chapters.

For now, we can list some of the reasons for this change in the historical trend of growing inequality. All these factors may not be of equal importance, and, no doubt, there can be disagreement on which are more important. But all have clearly had a significant impact on the level of inequality in industrial societies (see Lenski 1966:313–318).

**1.** One of the major characteristics of industrial societies is the complexity of the machine and organizational technology. Elites have found themselves in a position of ignorance about much of this technology. This is because no individual or even small group of individuals can possess the knowledge needed to run the vast industrial enterprise. Thus, elites have had to make concessions to their authority for the sake of efficiency, and these concessions have resulted in greater rewards for subordinates. Elites in the economy do have final authority, but they have had to delegate at least part of that authority with respect to technical details.

**2.** Allowing lower classes more of the economic surplus has increased productivity. This is partly because a working class that is less hostile due to increasing personal benefits from the expanding industrial output will be less likely to strike, to stage slowdowns, and to indulge in industrial sabotage. Also, with a rapidly expanding industrial output, if wages were kept on a subsistence level, there would be no market for the increase in industrial goods. In short, with a general population having no money to buy goods above the basic necessities of life, increased profits for elites would be difficult to achieve.

**3.** A rapid increase in wealth and material goods soon reaches a level of marginal utility. With an income of several million dollars, another million brings less value. As Lenski (1966:315) writes, "Because elites have multiple goals, and are not concerned with maximizing material rewards alone, they may be willing to make certain economic concessions in a highly productive and expanding economy." These concessions may reduce the dangers of revolution and win some measure of respect from the lower classes.

**4.** Also important is the reduced rate of population growth in industrial societies, especially for the lower classes. In previous societies, as production increased, so did the population. With the population growing at a rate that closely equaled the increase in production, there was only enough produced to support this growing population without reducing the proportion going to elites. But with production increasing along with a more stable population, there is much more to divide between both the elites and the masses.

**5.** In the first point it was noted that the increasing complexity of industry has forced elites into a greater reliance on technical experts. But throughout the industrial system much more knowledge and skill is required. A poor and ignorant class of peasants would not be useful in today's industrial society. Again, concessions must be made to ensure a more skilled workforce.

**6.** The spread of a more egalitarian ideology and democratic systems have generally followed industrialization and revolution. In large part this occurred because the new class of merchants that replaced the powerful agrarian nobility at the end of feudalism did so only with the help of the masses. In order to ensure the support of the masses in these revolutions, it was necessary to make democratic political concessions. And with at least some voice in the new industrial state, the general population has been able to receive other concessions in the level of inequality.

**7.** With increasing international conflict and the development of total war, elites could not afford to lose the allegiance of the population. To place one's life in jeopardy for a nation requires a belief that the nation is worth fighting for. Slaves may go to battle, but they may also flee if the chance arises. We have seen how the general population in the late Roman Empire put up little or no resistance to nomadic invaders. The Roman Empire had lost the allegiance of its people in the face of extreme inequalities and exploitation. So concessions had to be made in order for industrial societies to survive in growing international conflicts that often resulted in total war.

**8.** Finally, while the level of inequality within industrial nations is lower, worldwide inequality is growing rapidly (Wilderdink and Potharst 2001; Korzeniewicz and Moran 1997; World Bank 2000; Nolan 1983a, 1983b; Chirot 1986; Breedlove and Nolan 1988). It may well be that the two are, in fact, related. The division of labor is becoming world-wide, with more of the lowest-paying jobs occurring in the less-developed nations, while advanced industrial societies benefit from more high-tech and higher-paying jobs, and a higher standard of living made possible by the exploitation of cheap third world labor and resources (Wright and Martin 1987).

**9.** More recently it has become clear that much of the reduction in inequality during the 20th century has been due to increases in democracy in Europe and the United States. As the middle class, working class, and at times even the poor have become politically more active, the state and political elites have responded with programs and policies that help nonelite interests. As we will see in coming chapters, however, the increasing inequality in the United States compared to Europe stems from changes in government policies. European governments are still more likely to maintain policies reducing inequality, whereas the United States government is not (Esping-Anderson 1990; Goodin et al. 1999; Mahler 2001, 2002).

---

# ⚔ Conclusion: The History of Inequality

The primary task of this chapter has been to provide the reader with a general idea of what existed before with respect to inequality and social stratification. Of course, our outline of history has been more than descriptive. As with *any* historical presentation, ours has been guided by some general theoretical assumptions. With the outline of history behind us, we can now consider more fully the conflict perspective that has guided our review of history.

The theoretical perspective in this chapter follows to some degree that of Gerhard Lenski (1966, 1984, 2005; Lenski, Lenski, and Nolan 1991; Nolan and Lenski 1998), who has reviewed the history of stratification in much more detail than space allows here. What Lenski generally found is that the level of inequality in a society is related to (1) the *level of technology* and (2) the *amount of surplus goods* produced by that society. These two factors are usually interrelated. The higher the level of technology, the greater the amount of surplus goods and services produced. From these interrelated factors Lenski (1966:46) predicts that "in the simplest societies, or those which are technologically most primitive, the goods and services available will be distributed wholly, or largely, on the basis of need," whereas "with technological advance, an increasing proportion of the goods and services available to a society will be distributed on the basis of power."

With a low level of technology, and, thus, little or no surplus, no one will have the power to dominate the resources of the society. A general level of equality will exist. As technology advances and more surplus is produced, the elites, freed from everyday production, will find ways of dominating the surplus of goods, giving them power over others as well as a greater share of the surplus. The level of inequality generally increases with the advance of technology.[4]

Our review of history has more or less conformed to Lenski's general findings. In early hunting and gathering societies the surplus production of food and other goods was generally low. Along with this, the degree of inequality was also low. With the emergence of agricultural methods of food production, the stage was set for ever-increasing levels of inequality. A significant degree of inequality first became widespread in early agricultural settlements about 10,000 years ago. The expansion and growth of these settlements into large civilizations occurred about 6,000 years ago. With more advanced methods of food production we found a further jump in the level of inequality. The highest levels of inequality were then attained with more advanced agrarian societies a few thousand years later (Ziltener and Mueller 2007). Only since the industrial revolution has the trend reversed somewhat (for the reasons listed at the close of the last section). Recent empirical research with data from 56 nations has strongly confirmed Lenski's explanations of changes in income inequality through history (Nielsen 1994).

A further point about Lenski's perspective and the historical outline presented here is in order. There is no simple path of social evolution that all societies have followed or will follow. There is only a very rough tendency toward ever more complex and technologically advanced societies. Along the way, because of a particular physical, social, and cultural environment, some societies change (or advance) while others do not.[5] This goes almost without saying, given the diversity of cultures in the world today.

Also, when societies change, they do not change according to one established pattern because of a particular physical, social, and cultural environment in which they find themselves. A simple linear model of social evolution, one that sees all societies following a similar path of development, must be rejected (Portes 1976). This is especially true with respect to economic development. For example, as we will see in the chapters on world stratification, unlike the already developed nations, undeveloped and developing nations today must contend with an international system of economic power that often negatively affects their chances of becoming more advanced economically.

The outline of history presented here does provide a general picture of how inequality came to be a pervasive aspect of most human societies. With it we can understand the conflict that usually lies behind systems of social stratification. In fact, *the existence of inequality and conflict over scarce resources is what makes social stratification necessary.* Without a system of social stratification, we would find perpetual overt conflict and aggression over the question of how scarce resources are to be distributed. Once a system of social stratification is firmly established, however, "little contest need take place concerning the sharing of resources. The contest has already taken place and has been settled—at least for a time" (van den Berghe 1978:54). In other words, the questions of who gets what, and why, have been answered. But, as our historical review of inequality suggests, and even new research on the Indian caste system shows, we must add—"at least for a time."

## Summary

This brief examination of the history of inequality began with a description of major types of systems of social stratification found around the world and through history. The earliest types of stratification systems were found in primitive communal societies, where there was generally very little inequality, especially in societies with more food gathering than hunting. Later there emerged slave societies, then caste and feudal systems of social stratification, before the modern class systems with industrial societies. Through this history of social stratification we have found that inequality has not always been as high as it is in modern societies today. In the past 10,000 years, however, since primitive communal societies were no longer the standard, inequality usually has been much higher than it is in the advanced societies today. Inequality first emerged significantly in what Lenski calls horticulture societies and reached a high point in advanced agrarian societies, before being reduced in modern industrial class systems. Lenski has shown that the level of inequality in a society is related to the level of technology and the level of surplus. With a surplus beginning in horticulture societies, an elite emerged that was able to control the surplus and thus control others in the society. With modern industrial societies, however, we outlined a number of changes that have occurred that reduce the level of inequality compared with what it was with advanced agrarian societies.

## Notes

1.  However, it should be noted that, given our definition of social stratification stressing structured inequalities in the first chapter, it is somewhat inaccurate to suggest that all primitive communal societies have a *system* of social stratification. As we will see, the inequalities in many of these societies are relatively minor, unstructured, and informal. But for the sake of comparison, this type of society can be included in the typology as long as the above point is recognized.

2.  We should note that this ideal type is very general (as are the others) and includes primitive societies with slightly differing levels and forms of inequality. One important distinction can be made between what has been called *bands,* which are nonranked and nonstratified, and *tribes,* which are ranked but nonstratified (see Sahlins and Service 1960; Fried 1973). In the band we find unlimited higher-status positions based exclusively on individual abilities. Higher status is given to some,

such as the best hunter, and if there are 10 or 15 good hunters there are 10 or 15 higher-status positions (that is, higher status is given to all who achieve it).

In the tribe, however, while still nonstratified, the higher-status positions are more formalized, with a specific number of higher-status positions. Those with the higher-status positions perform specific tribal functions, such as presiding over rituals or overseeing the distribution of goods and resources. Thus, in contrast to the band, in the tribe higher status is not an unlimited commodity, and elementary rules of succession have developed.

3.  Following Lenski's (1984) description of hunting and gathering societies, we are saying that rewards (in this case status) are distributed on the basis of functional contribution to the group. In later types of societies, the concentration of power and wealth in the hands of a few can result in ever-greater rewards going to this small group irrespective of its contribution to the common good. As for the lower status of women in hunting and gathering or primitive communal societies, it is *not* being argued that the child rearing and food gathering done by women were not functional for group survival. But two factors led to lower status with these tasks: (1) They were not tasks that generally required scarce abilities, and (2) although one mother may have been especially skilled at caring for children, the payoff would not be seen until the children grew up. With hunting, a rare ability in bringing back meat was more obvious.

4.  It should be clear that the term *technology* is being used in a very broad sense. By technology we mean everything from stone tools to modern machines, and even the knowledge of various methods of food gathering and other types of production.

5.  The review of the history of inequality presented in this chapter has stressed material variables (such as technology) over culture or values in shaping the basic nature of societies and social change. We are not suggesting that these material variables explain everything, or that they fail to combine with culture and values for specific outcomes. The level of inequality, the power of elites, how inequality is maintained, among many other aspects of society, are all influenced by political ideology, religion, family systems, or, more generally, culture. But in such a general review of human societies as the one presented here, the important factors that affect social organization most widely must be the dominant focus. In a study of 330 existing societies of varying types, Heise, Lenski, and Wardwell (1976) have found that material variables (such as level and type of technology) explain much more of the other characteristics of these societies than do values or cultural differences.

# Explanations of Social Stratification: Stratification Theories

# Social Stratification Theory: Early Statements

One of the greatest sociologists of the late 19th century
and early 20th century, the German Max Weber perhaps
contributed more to our understanding of social
stratification than any other individual.

*SOURCE:* © AKG London.

## Chapter Outline

❖ Competing Paradigms in the Study of Social Stratification

❖ The Marxian Heritage in Social Stratification: The Development of a Critical-Conflict
 Paradigm

❖ Social Change

❖ The Marxian View of Class

❖ Max Weber: An Alternative Conflict Paradigm

❖ An Uncritical-Order Paradigm Matures: The Functional Theory of Émile Durkheim

❖ The Classical Period of Sociological Theory: A Summary

❖ Summary

❖ Notes

From the earliest writings on the human condition we find an interest in inequality and social divisions. Whatever the reason—guilt, curiosity, anger, or justification—the topic has often been one of lively concern. "Some of the earliest records of thought on this subject are found in the writings of the early Hebrew prophets who lived approximately 800 years before Christ. In the writings of such men as Amos, Micah, and Isaiah we find repeated denunciations of the rich and powerful members of society" (Lenski 1966:3). Aristotle as well had much to say about inequality; but for him there was no criticism of this "natural condition." As he wrote in *Politics,* about 350 B.C. (see Dahrendorf 1968:153), "It is thus clear that there are *by nature* free men and slaves, and that servitude is agreeable and just for the latter. . . . Equally, the relation of the male to the female is *by nature* such that one is superior and the other is dominated."

During the 17th and especially the 18th century the nature and causes of social inequality were the subject of even more lively debate. It was during the Age of Enlightenment that the old inequalities of the feudal period were attacked by such philosophers as Locke, Rousseau, and Montesquieu. Somewhat later, after revolutionary movements had taken their toll on many feudal inequalities, 19th-century philosophers such as Bonald, Maistre, and Saint-Simon further developed systematic theories of society, theories in which the nature of human inequalities played a central role (see Zeitlin 1968; Strasser 1976). A science of society emerged from the work of these philosophers. As with these earlier philosophers, the nature of human inequalities provided the central question for the new science called sociology (Dahrendorf 1968:152).

In this chapter we examine some of the earliest sociological thought on social stratification. For our purpose—which is to understand the foundations of modern thinking on the subject—the works of Karl Marx and Max Weber are most important. The works of Émile Durkheim will be briefly considered to show the neglect of social stratification with the other major sociological perspective. Beginning with Marx, we examine the major assumptions behind these theories, as well as show the roots of major contemporary theories of social stratification to be explored in Chapter 5.

# ✥ Competing Paradigms in the Study of Social Stratification

Contrary to the idealized view of scientific methods and theory, a scientist's view of the subject matter and the construction of theory are not based only and completely on a cold calculation of available empirical data. Rather, scientists must, to some degree, work from a set of prescientific and untested assumptions about the phenomena under study. This is true for physical science no less than for social science. As Albert Einstein put it, "For the creation of a theory the mere collection of recorded phenomena never suffices—there must always be added a free invention of the human mind that attacks the heart of the matter" (quoted in Dukas and Hoffman 1979:24–25). At times Einstein went further by *rejecting* the idea that "facts by themselves can and should yield scientific knowledge without the free conceptual construction" (quoted in Clark 1971:63). We can call the general images of reality (which shape more specific theories) **paradigms,** and the assumptions about reality within paradigms can be called paradigm assumptions.[1]

Before we consider the most important theories of social stratification in this chapter and the next, it is useful to begin with a brief examination of conflicting paradigms in the study of social stratification. But two points of caution must first be made:

**1.** Although we will see that values and politically related assumptions at times have shaped or influenced theories of social stratification, we do *not* find only political debates in the study of social stratification. There is a reality out there, however complex and many-sided it may be, that these theories are struggling to understand. Just as the physical scientist must attempt to understand his or her subject matter by making certain untested or even untestable assumptions, as Kuhn's (1970) work clearly shows, so must the social scientist.[2]

**2.** Related to this, at the level of general theory or paradigms, we cannot ask whether a paradigm is right or wrong, true or false. Rather, we must ask whether a paradigm is useful or less useful in answering specific questions about the subject matter. All of the paradigms and general theories outlined in the following lead us to some important insights about the nature of social stratification. But, depending on the questions asked, some may be more useful than others. As will be seen throughout the remainder of this book, if in the study of social stratification we are most concerned with the questions of who gets what, and why, it is increasingly recognized in sociology that some type of conflict theory will supply the most useful answers.

Since the earliest years of sociology there have been two main macrolevel general theories or paradigms that have influenced the development of theories of social stratification. In comparing these two general theories of society, we must begin by recognizing the main task of what can be called **functional** and **conflict theories** of society. They are both attempts at answering the most basic question in sociology—How is society possible? In other words, with a mass of people in large industrial societies, how is it that most people obey the rules most of the time? How is it that we can have orderly interaction without perpetual disruptive conflict between differing interest groups? From the works of several sociologists (see Dahrendorf 1959; van den Berghe 1963; Horton 1966;

Cohen 1968), we can select three main model assumptions found to diverge between functional and conflict paradigms (also see Wallace and Wolf 1999:11).

**1.** Functional theorists maintain that society is held together primarily by a general consensus over the major values and norms in the society. People tend to obey the rules because through a long socialization process they have come to accept these rules, so for the most part they live by them. Conflict theorists, on the other hand, maintain that society is held together in the face of conflicting interests because either (*a*) one group in the society has the power to enforce the rules (and thus make subordinate groups follow rules that may primarily serve the interests of the superordinate group) or (*b*) there are so many overlapping and divided interest groups that individuals or groups must learn to cooperate. The overall argument made by conflict theorists, however, is that through the structure of conflict in society, order can be maintained in one of these two ways.

**2.** One reason for these divergent model assumptions between functional and conflict theorists is that whereas functional theorists tend to focus more on societies as holistic systems (much like biological organisms), conflict theorists tend to focus on parts and processes within what we call societies.

**3.** It follows from this organic analogy that functional theorists tend to view societies as social systems with specific needs of their own that must be met if the societies are to function properly, and thus survive. Conflict theorists, on the other hand, view societies as settings within which various groups with differing interests interact and compete.

These three sets of divergent assumptions represent two competing models of society that attempt to answer the most basic question of how social order is possible. They are, as we defined paradigms, differing images of the subject matter (society), just as the physicist has an image of his or her subject matter (for example, an Einsteinian image of the universe). These images are not right or wrong, but simply more or less useful in answering specific questions about the subject matter.

Our typology of stratification paradigms is constructed by combining two divergent sets of paradigm assumptions. One set of assumptions comes from those discussed earlier separating functional and conflict images or models of society. The other set of three assumptions is taken from Lenski's (1984) discussion of conserva-tive and radical value assumptions on social stratification, using more politically neutral terms—what we will refer to as *critical* and *uncritical* value assumptions. Table 4-1 summarizes these two sets of model and value assumptions. Combining these gives us a four-cell typology (Table 4-2) similar to one suggested by Strasser (1976). In the first cell we have what can be called a *critical-order* paradigm; in the second, an *uncritical-order* paradigm; in the third, a *critical-conflict* paradigm; and in the fourth, an *uncritical-conflict* paradigm.

The payoff in constructing such a typology as presented in Table 4-2 is in the understanding or clarification it provides. With this typology we can group specific theories of social stratification having similar properties or explanations. The reason for these similarities is that they share some basic paradigm assumptions about the nature of society and social inequality. The use of such a typology is *not* an excuse for ignoring

## TABLE 4-1

### Value and Model Assumptions in Social Stratification Paradigms

#### Value assumptions

| Critical | Uncritical |
|---|---|
| 1. Inequality not inevitable (at least to present degrees) | 1. Inequality inevitable (little or no criticism) |
| 2. Optimistic view of human nature | 2. Distrust of human nature |
| 3. Better, more just, societies the goal of social science | 3. Sociology should be value-free |

#### Model assumptions

| Conflict | Order |
|---|---|
| 1. Society held together by conflict and unequal power | 1. Society held together by consensus (norms and values) |
| 2. Focus on parts and processes within the society | 2. Holistic view of society |
| 3. Society a setting for struggles between classes or interest groups | 3. Focus on a social system with needs of its own |

the finer points of each theory (as they will be presented in this chapter and the next) but a method for furthering a better understanding. Let us now proceed by examining the logic of the paradigms in explaining the nature of social stratification.

We must begin by noting that the first cell of our typology (Table 4-2) remains empty with respect to *recent* theories of social stratification (see Strasser 1976). Although

## TABLE 4-2

### A Typology of Social Stratification Paradigms

| | | Value assumptions | |
|---|---|---|---|
| | | **Critical** | **Uncritical** |
| | Order | Critical-order paradigm | Uncritical-order paradigm Functional theory (Durkheim)* |
| Model of society | Conflict | Critical-conflict paradigm | Uncritical-conflict paradigm |
| | | Ruling class theory (Marx) | Power conflict theory (Weber) |

*The placement of specific theorists will be discussed later in this chapter.

*SOURCE:* Adapted from Strasser (1976).

a number of 18th- and 19th-century theorists can be described as working from a *critical-order* paradigm (such as de Bonald and de Maistre; see Strasser 1976), the most prominent contemporary theories are grouped around the three remaining cells.[3]

In the second cell of the typology we can describe a general *uncritical-order* paradigm. This label indicates a combination of uncritical value assumptions (little or no criticism of the status quo) and an order model of society (Table 4-1). With respect to social stratification, the logic of the assumptions within this paradigm suggests that present inequalities are inevitable because (1) human nature is basically selfish and/or (2) the social system requires inequalities to meet some of its basic needs.

The second point is to suggest that social inequality or social stratification serves some function for the health and well-being of the total society—such as ensuring that the most talented people are motivated to fill the most important positions in the society. Another major tenet of this uncritical-order paradigm is that because human nature is not to be trusted, the needs of society, if it is to survive, require some restraining mechanisms. These mechanisms are usually found with a socialization process and an ongoing legitimation process that maintain consensus around major norms and values in the society. These norms and values justify the existing inequalities as necessary for a society's health and survival, thus preventing those with fewer rewards from threatening the system. The elites must also be restrained, lest they use their favored positions for individual greed.

Last, theorists working within this paradigm tend to view the task of social science as that of making a value-free analysis of society, rather than of attempting to understand how societies can be changed for the better. However, there is a tendency to be at least *relatively* supportive of the status quo, because given selfish human nature and the needs of society, a more equal society (in their view) is unlikely. As we will discuss later, what is commonly called a *functional* theory of social stratification is located within this cell of our typology.

In the bottom right cell of our typology we find an *uncritical-conflict* paradigm of social stratification. This paradigm shares with the uncritical-order paradigm a distrust of human nature and an assumption that inequalities are in large measure inevitable. In one major variant of this paradigm, because society is assumed to be a setting for conflicting interests, it is the power of one group over others that maintains social order. Given the view of human nature inherent in this paradigm, when one group is able to achieve a dominant position in the society, this group will tend to use that position to serve selfish interests.[4]

In addition, as with the uncritical-order paradigm, theorists in an uncritical-conflict paradigm tend to view the task of social science as that of making a value-free analysis of society in order to uncover basic social laws, rather than of attempting to promote social change. From their perspective, a society without some form of class conflict is viewed as impossible, and a more equal or just society is rejected. As will be discussed later, specific theories within this uncritical-conflict paradigm can most commonly be referred to as power conflict theories, although other varieties will be examined.

In the lower left cell of our typology we find what can be called a *critical-conflict* paradigm. This paradigm shares with the uncritical-conflict paradigm an image or model of society that considers conflict and power as the key to social order (at least in present societies). The power of one group—such as an upper class or a power elite—leads to social order. A powerful group is usually able to coerce or manipulate subordinate classes (through force, threat of force, withholding of jobs, or other means) because of the dominant group's influence over basic institutions in the society (such as the economy, government, courts, and police).

But the critical-conflict paradigm combines this conflict model of society with critical value assumptions. Although theorists working under an uncritical-conflict paradigm view power, conflict, and exploitation in much the same way, they are less critical of this perceived status quo. Theorists from an uncritical-conflict paradigm are more accepting of these conditions, not necessarily because they are unsympathetic toward the lower class but because, given their assumptions about human nature and the inevitability of inequalities, they fail to foresee that more just and equitable societies are possible.

Critical-conflict theorists, on the other hand, are more optimistic. Because they view human nature as more altruistic, cooperative, and unselfish, or perhaps simply more flexible (meaning that human beings can be either selfish or unselfish, depending on factors outside themselves), they believe that more equal and humane societies are possible. But if they agree with power conflict or critical-conflict theorists about present social conditions of inequality and exploitation, how do they explain these conditions?

Uncritical-conflict theorists are distrustful of human nature, whereas critical-conflict theorists are distrustful of *restraining social institutions.* According to them, the historical development of present social institutions shapes human behavior in such a way as to lead to exploitation by the powerful. In other words, the role people must play under a particular set of social institutions requires the exploitation. If this historical stage of social development is altered, the new set of social institutions can lead to basically different social relations.

Critical-conflict theorists are, as the label implies, more critical of the status quo because their value assumptions lead them to be more optimistic about future social conditions. It follows that they are more likely to maintain that the task of social science is to understand present society in order to be able to alter it. Their work is often more historically oriented than that of other theorists. They believe that by examining the historical progression or evaluation of human societies we can better understand how we arrived at our present predicament, and thus how we can change the status quo.

Within the critical-conflict paradigm we have just outlined, the most prominent group of theorists can be described as Marxists. For them it is the capitalist *system* and its characteristics that shape present conditions of exploitation and inequality. Clearly, not all theorists working within this critical-conflict paradigm can be described as Marxists. Theorists like C. Wright Mills (1956) and G. William Domhoff (1967, 2010) are equally critical of present social, political, and economic institutions, but their explanations of present social arrangements are not based on Marxian terms; nor do they see a social ideal in a communist state.

We stress that this typology is a simplification. Theories can never be placed into neat either-or categories represented by a dichotomy. For example, with respect to the critical versus uncritical value assumptions described in the typology (Table 4-1), we are not suggesting that all theories are *totally* critical or uncritical of such conditions as inequality. We can speak more accurately of *degrees* of criticism. Many theorists within the uncritical side of the typology may believe that poverty or the extent of inequality found in the society is deplorable. But their criticisms of this situation are less extensive and/or their suggested solutions are less drastic than those of theorists on the critical side of the typology. In essence, this dimension of critical versus uncritical may be viewed as a continuum, with theories most accurately located at different points along the continuum.

---

# ⚔ The Marxian Heritage in Social Stratification: The Development of a Critical-Conflict Paradigm

With the fall of the Berlin Wall, and indeed even the Soviet Union itself, the death of Marxism has been declared by many. Marxian theory and many of the basic ideas behind it, however, are far from dead. Cold war–era communism and Marxian theory are generally unrelated; in fact, Marxian theory did not provide support for basic Soviet policies. We might even say that Marxian ideas have been freed from the ideological interpretation of Marxist governments since the fall of communism. None of this is to say, however, that Marxian theory is correct in every aspect.

Marx's ideas were most influential in early European social science, where, as we will see, both Weber and Durkheim, in part, constructed their theories in reaction to Marx's earlier works. But Marx's influence has been increasingly felt in the United States as well (see Mullins 1973:273), where his general perspective and predictions about some aspects of advanced capitalist societies are becoming more respected today.

Several historians of social thought (see Zeitlin 1968; Gouldner 1970; Giddens 1973; Strasser 1976) have traced the development of modern sociological theory from Saint-Simon, whose ideas date back to the early 1800s. The seeds for both conflict and functional theories were contained in Saint-Simon's works. Durkheim was a principal figure who transferred Saint-Simon's ideas into Western academic sociology in the form of an uncritical-order paradigm. But it was Marx who transferred these ideas into a critical-conflict paradigm. Like perhaps all great theories, Marx's ideas had many predecessors (see Berlin 1963:129). And, clearly, Saint-Simon's view of class conflict and exploitation influenced Marx (Berlin 1963:74–75). With Marx, however, these ideas matured into a complex, critical explanation of class and of class domination as a historical force in the development of human societies.

We need comment only briefly on some of the underlying paradigm assumptions in Marx's work, for these will be evident in the more detailed exploration of his theory that follows. Any examination of Marx's many writings shows that at the base of human societies (at least until the "final" stage of communism) he saw class conflict and domination. Marx's perspective was one of dynamics and change, in contrast to the static and holistic perspective of early functionalists such as Durkheim. In Marx's view, social order exists because one class (the dominant class) is favored by a specific stage of economic development and is thus able to maintain social order through its power over the lower classes.

With respect to Marx's value assumptions, he saw the tasks of social science as not only to understand society but also to change it. He was critical of existing inequalities, conflicts, and exploitation, and he believed these conditions could, or more strongly *would,* be changed. Unlike an uncritical-conflict theorist like Weber, Marx was an optimist. He saw the root of these conditions of inequality and exploitation in social structures that had been, and would continue to be, subject to change. These conditions were *not,* according to Marx, explained by "selfish human nature": "A positive image of man, of what man might come to be, lies under every line of his analysis of what he held to be an inhuman society" (Mills 1962:25). Thus, Marx anticipated more humane social conditions, and saw his task as furthering social change and an objective understanding of the present (see Strasser 1976:108).

Karl Marx was born in Trier, Germany, in 1818. His family lived in relatively comfortable economic conditions, in contrast to Marx's later years in London. His father, Heinrich Marx, was a respected lawyer and government servant who was "closely connected with the Rhineland liberal movement" (McLellan 1973:7; for another interesting biography of Marx, see Berlin 1963). Karl Marx attended the universities of Bonn and Berlin (beginning in 1835), and finished a doctorate of philosophy in 1841. After completing a PhD, however, Marx could not find employment in a university, so he turned to journalism, editing several newspapers, first in Cologne and later in Paris.

During the 1840s most of Europe was in political turmoil. Many socialist movements were active, especially in Germany and France, where Marx spent these years. Although not exactly a political activist in the physical sense of participating in street battles of the times, Marx nonetheless supported many of these movements through his journalism. His vocal editorship of newspapers in Germany and France led to trouble with political authorities. He was first deported from Germany to France. Then, after the massive rebellion in 1848 in Paris, he was forced by political authorities back to Germany. But again he was not welcome in Germany, and in 1849 he finally found a home in London.

Marx spent most of his remaining years in London, in desperate poverty because of his inability to find stable work. His family survived through his part-time employment as a newspaper correspondent (he wrote many articles for the *New York Herald Tribune*) and many contributions from his friend and collaborator, Friedrich Engels (a wealthy capitalist). Still, his family lived in extreme poverty, often without adequate food, clothing, or medical care. (The death of one of his children is attributed to the family's lack of money to pay a doctor.) The poverty he saw around him and the general conditions of poverty and worker exploitation in England at the time no doubt contributed to his view of capitalism.

Despite his poverty, or perhaps because of it, Marx found time in London to research and write his most important works. He spent most of his days, usually from 9 A.M. to 7 P.M., reading and writing in the British Museum. It was during this time that he completed his three-volume *Capital* and notes for another work that was more than 1,000 pages long, *The Grundrisse,* as well as many other books. During this time Marx also helped establish the Communist International, an organization important in bringing together many communist and socialist leaders throughout the world and shaping the future of communism.

## On Understanding Marx

Before turning to some of the key components of Marxian theory, it is necessary to consider a few points of caution. At first glance the main ideas behind Marx's theory of society and social stratification are deceptively simple. And, of course, in the brief summary of his theory that follows, the simplicity may seem overemphasized. But Marxian theory is at the same time both simple *and* very complex. Marx began or built his theory of society from a set of very basic concepts. From this base he then expanded with many elaborations, qualifiers, and amendments, thus producing a complex theory contained in many volumes of work written over a period of about 40 years. It is important to understand these basic concepts of Marxian theory first, but its richness and complexity should not be overlooked.

In a related point, it should be recognized that there are to this day many confusing debates over what Marx really said. A good deal of this debate can be traced to the complexity of Marxian theory, but there are other reasons as well. As noted in the brief description of Marx's life, he was at the same time a political activist *and* a social scientist. This dual role is found in Marx's works. Some of his works reflect the political activist role; they were written in a simplified form to make their ideas more accessible to the general population. His motive here was to stimulate social action. Included in this category is the famous *Communist Manifesto,* written with Engels during the many socialist revolts in Europe around 1848. To a large degree, it has been argued, *Capital* must be included among his more political works as well (see Bottomore 1973:23; McLellan 1973). Therefore, a problem with understanding the richness of Marxian theory fully is created when the essence of his ideas is taken only from these more politically motivated writings. To do so is tempting because his more political writings are brief and require less intellectual investment (such as his preface to *Critique of Political Economy,* written in 1859; see Marx 1971:14; Harrington 1976:37; Miliband 1977:7). But this problem in understanding his work is compounded by another.

The limited access Western social theorists have had to Marx's complete works provides another obstacle to a full understanding. The works that have been most accessible, until recently, more often reflect the political side of Marx. It was only in 1953 that a German edition of what has been described as the most complete of Marx's works *(The Grundrisse)* was published; and only in 1971 was part of this work published in the United States (Marx 1971). Research now suggests that Marx himself viewed *Capital* as a more political statement taken from the more general work published later as *The Grundrisse* (McLellan 1973).

The main point is that, for several reasons, social scientists are just beginning to understand the complexity and richness of Marxian theory. This is not to say that most are now convinced Marx was the most accurate social theorist of his time, or that all of his ideas remain useful today. But the old "vulgar" interpretations of Marxian theory must now be rejected. In what follows, we attempt to respect the complexity of Marxian theory, at the same time trying to be brief.

## Basic Foundations of Marxian Theory

As an introduction to the basics of Marxian theory, and to make the preceding comments about political interpretations of Marx more concrete, it is useful to consider first what has been described (somewhat inaccurately) as the overall *historical-materialist* and *deterministic* thrust of Marxian theory. Marx (Marx and Engels 1965:27–31) began by stressing the following:

> The first premise of all human history is, of course, the existence of living human beings. Thus the first fact to be established is the physical organization of these individuals and their consequent relation to the rest of nature. . . . Man can be distinguished from animals by consciousness, by religion or anything else you like. They themselves begin to distinguish themselves from animals as soon as they begin to *produce* their means of subsistence, a step which is conditioned by their physical organizations. By producing their means of subsistence men are indirectly producing their actual material life. The way in which men produce their means of subsistence depends first of all on the nature of the actual means of subsistence they find in existence and have to produce. . . . The nature of individuals thus depends on the material conditions determining their production.

In short, Marx believed that to understand human societies the theorist must begin with the *material* conditions of human subsistence, or the economics of producing the necessities of life. And to understand human societies most fully, the key is the *historical* progression or development of these material conditions of production. Thus, we find the concept of **historical materialism.** All other aspects of human societies—from political organization and family structures to religion and ideologies—are generally (though not always) secondary phenomena. The nature or variety of political organization, political ideologies, religion, family organization, and other factors in specific human societies are typically *shaped* by the particular means of production or economic base in that society. This Marxian or materialist perspective is usually contrasted with that of Weber, who argued, for example, that cultural factors such as religious beliefs could have an equal hand in shaping the economic structure (see Weber's *The Protestant Ethic and the Spirit of Capitalism,* 1958).

This, then, is a key or foundation of Marxian sociology. However, it must be stressed that the rigid historical-materialist and deterministic strain is found only in Marx's more political works (those until recently most accessible to Western social theorists). In *The Grundrisse,* for example, this relationship between the material (or economic) and the cultural and ideological aspects of society is viewed as less rigid and less deterministic (see Bottomore 1973:18; Harrington 1976:41; Appelbaum 1978a:78). While understanding that the relationship between what Marx labeled the **substructure** and the **superstructure** of society is a key in Marxian theory, one must not overstress a deterministic relationship. Marx clearly recognized that *ideas* or other aspects of the superstructure can at times be of independent importance in shaping the nature of human societies (a view that places Marx much closer to Weber than heretofore recognized).

We must be more specific about what Marx meant by *substructure* and *superstructure.* Following this idea that the nature of human society "depends on the material conditions determining . . . production," he referred to this material and economic base as the substructure. Human beings may go about producing what they need for survival simply by gathering what can be found in the forest, hunting, herding animals, planting crops, or working at the most complex method of industrial production. Because of the importance of economic tasks and the amount of time people invest in these activities, each of these differing modes of production tends to influence (or shape within

**FIGURE 4-1**    *The Marxian Model of Social Organization* The solid arrow indicates a primary causal relation, and the broken arrows indicate a secondary causal relation.

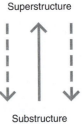

(Political organization, ideology, religion, etc.)

Superstructure

Substructure

(Means and relations of production)

certain limits) other aspects of life in these societies. Thus, the substructure shapes the superstructure.

Following Marxian theory, in agrarian societies or feudalism, for example, we would be surprised to find a democratic political system, a nuclear democratic family structure, the absence of strong authoritarian religious traditions, or an individualistic ideology because the substructure (or mode of production) found in this type of society would not fit well with such a superstructure (see Figure 4-1).

To make our point clear, we must further specify what Marx included within the substructure. Within the **mode of production** that makes up this substructure Marx also distinguished between the means of production and the relations of production. The **means of production** refers most directly to the type of technology used to produce goods (such as hunting and gathering, agrarian methods of varying sophistication, machine technology). As we saw with Lenski's work in Chapter 3, the level of technology has many important consequences for the general nature of the society and the stratification system. But in understanding class divisions Marx also distinguished level of technology or the means of production from the relations of production. This was seen as necessary because differing relations of production can be found within a given level of technology or means of production.

By **relations of production** Marx meant the human relationships within a given means of production. Under capitalism these relationships include (1) the relationships between workers as dictated by the type of production (whether they work together and can interact in a mass-production setting or work in smaller settings or in isolation from other workers), (2) the dominance–submission relationships among workers and authorities, and (3) the ownership and distribution of valued goods in the society. (For a discussion of all of this, see Giddens 1973:85–88.)

Thus, the relations of production are a part of the substructure that can influence the superstructure. For example, how workers relate to machines and other workers can influence their outlook on life or their belief systems. The predominant type of authority relation within the economy or production system can shape authority relations within the wider society. Also, how workers are related to machines and each other can affect their family relations, leisure activities, child-rearing practices, and self-esteem. (All of this is discussed more fully in Chapter 8 on the middle and working classes in the United States.)

Perhaps most important for Marxian theory, however, is the way ownership patterns can shape the superstructure. When one group in the society is able to own and/or control the most important means of production within the society, the power this gives the owner–controller class allows it to shape or maintain aspects of the superstructure favoring its class interests. In a famous phrase Marx (Marx and Engels 1965:61) wrote, "The ideas of the ruling class are in every epoch the ruling ideas: i.e., the class which is the ruling material force of society, is at the same time its ruling intellectual force."

Marx meant that the dominant normative system or ideology in a society is shaped and maintained by this powerful group because it serves its interests. An example can be found in the extent to which owners or controllers of the means of production in capitalist nations sponsor programs to "educate the public" about the lack of alternatives to capitalism, how capitalism works, and the importance of private property for the "health and well-being of society."

But we must also consider how the political system is shaped by ownership relations. A political system that gives voting rights only to those who own land, for example, may be supported successfully by landowners in an agrarian society, but this political system is likely to be destroyed when the power of factory owners is increased.

Again we must caution that the superstructure is not completely determined, but only influenced or shaped, by the substructure or general mode of production. Marx recognized that in many places the political system or cultural traditions could at times shape or influence the means and relations of production (more generally the substructure) (see Giddens 1973:87; Harrington 1976:43). In the long run, however, the influence of the substructure over the superstructure was seen as primary in Marx's writings.

# ✖ Social Change

Marxian theory is one of dynamics, social change, and conflict, rather than one of social equilibrium and order, as with functional theory. The historical progression of human societies has a major place in the Marxian view of the world. With the stimulus of class conflict and "internal contradictions" within societies "based on the exploitation of one class by another," human societies are seen to evolve through a series of stages to the final communist society. We can now build upon the basic concepts discussed earlier to understand the Marxian view of social change.

If it is the substructure of society that primarily shapes the superstructure (rather than vice versa), then, from the perspective of Marxian theory, change in the substructure leads to more total or revolutionary social change (see the simplified diagram in Figure 4-2). It is useful to consider first some of the major types of societies described in various places in Marx's writings. Five are given primary attention: primitive communism, ancient society (slavery), feudalism, capitalism, and communism (with another, Asian systems, or the Asiatic mode of production, given less attention).

Each of these types of societies is characterized by a particular substructure or mode of production. In primitive communism (similar to what Lenski described in hunting and gathering societies), most property that exists is held collectively and production of necessities is achieved collectively. There are few, if any, inequalities of power and material goods. Ancient society is based on slave labor, or a mode of production that

**FIGURE 4-2** *The Marxian Model of Social Change*

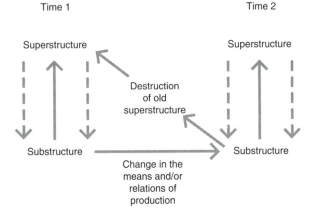

involves slaves performing much of the necessary labor but receiving only enough to stay alive. In feudalism the most important means of production is land, owned primarily by the nobility, with serfs working the land and turning over the surplus to landowners.[5] Capitalist society is based on a new substructure; the means of production are primarily industrial, with relations of production characterized primarily by private ownership of the major means of production. Finally, in communist society the means of production remain industrial, but the relations of production have changed to collective (rather than private) ownership of the means of production.

In tracing Marx's logic of social change, we can focus briefly on feudal and capitalist societies. The breakup of feudal society is located primarily in the emergence of a new means of production—from production based on land to production based in industry—and relations of production based on new market forces and labor power as commodity (see Giddens 1973:84–85). By the end of the Middle Ages in Europe (around the 1600s and 1700s), factory production was beginning to challenge agrarian production as the most important form of commerce. With this developing change in the overall mode of production, conflict surfaced between two classes with differing interests in these two competing modes of production. The old superstructure (the political, ideological, and religious components) had been shaped by the old feudal substructure, and thus continued to favor the interests of landowners over those of the emerging factory owners. Tax laws, the method of political representation, and foreign policy, for example, were all structured to meet the needs of the dominant class under feudalism.

In this situation, one of two extreme outcomes was possible. As was more the case in England, various compromises were achieved with relatively less violence to transform the superstructure to one more in line with the new substructure. This process began as far back as the Magna Carta in 1215, increased with Cromwell's revolution in the mid-1600s, and continued through the 19th century (Davies 1996). This less violent change was due in part to the fact that many of the old landowners moved to capitalist forms of trade and agrarian production and invested in industrial production. In essence, the two powerful classes were not always confronted with such mutually exclusive interests.

At the other end of the spectrum, as in France, the strongly opposed powerful classes did not make for such a relatively nonviolent transition. Compromise could not be satisfactorily achieved, and the contradictions between the old feudal superstructure and the emerging industrial, capitalist substructure led to a violent break with the French Revolution of 1789. (For a discussion of the French Revolution, see Soboul 1974.) With this break a radically new social order was created; in short order there was a drastic transformation of the state and religious hierarchy that had previously supported the old substructure.

The triumph of capitalism, however, would not resolve forever the conflicts and contradictions between the substructure and the superstructure, Marx believed. With time he saw further change in the mode of production that would lead to the eventual emergence of communism. Change would result not so much from a radical alteration in the technical means of production, as it did with agrarian to industrial production, but from a radical change in the relations of production. Of primary importance would be a change from small-scale, individual production to **monopoly capitalism.**

Under monopoly capitalism production is performed collectively in large factories by a mass of industrial workers, while private ownership of the means of production continues. This occurs because industrial firms grow in size, with a few large firms accounting for more and more of the production. At the same time many former factory owners are "thrown down" to the level of workers (that is, lose their place as industrial owners), and with these large factories workers become more numerous.

A contradiction in the relations of production emerges. Although production capacity expands, with many workers *collectively* producing goods (that is, working together in large factories), private ownership of the means of production remains. Also, the extreme unequal distribution of the fruits of this production (wealth and income) remains. In time, the numerically powerful workers, Marx believed, will recognize that their interests are in opposition to the private ownership of the means of production and the unequal distribution of rewards (profits or surplus). Revolution is inevitable, placing workers in power and resolving the contradiction between *private* ownership of the means of production and *collective* production in favor of collective ownership.[6]

This description of social change from a Marxian perspective has been brief, and many details have been omitted. In many ways, the materialistic, deterministic side of Marxian theory has been overemphasized. Thus, the full richness of the theory has not come through. However, Marx began from the basic ideas presented here, refining and amending as he shaped his theory. For an understanding of the fundamentals of Marxian theory, we have only his more specific view of class and class exploitation.

## ✵ The Marxian View of Class

Marx and Engels began their most famous work, *The Communist Manifesto,* in 1848, by writing,

> The history of all hitherto existing society is the history of class struggles. Free man and slave, patrician and plebeian, lord and serf, guild-master and journeyman, in a word, oppressor and oppressed, stood in constant opposition to one another, carried on an uninterrupted, now hidden, now open fight, a fight that each time ended, either in a revolutionary reconstitution of society at large, or in the common ruin of the contending classes.

This statement is powerful and to the point, but, as we have noted, it is more of a political statement than a cautious, scientific one. However, it is clear that class and class conflict run throughout Marxian theory as *the* basic concepts in understanding human societies.

With class divisions maintaining such a central role in Marxian theory, one would expect Marx to have spent much time on a specific definition of the concept. But he did not. Through the many volumes of Marx's writings, class is used in differing, and at times contradictory, ways. When he was finally about to undertake a more detailed and systematic discussion of class at the end of the third volume of *Capital,* he died (see Dahrendorf 1959:8). It was as if Marx saw the concept of class as so basic and important he assumed until the end of his life that it needed no systematic discussion. Although he used the word in different ways and wrote of several different classes in many of his works, his most important general and abstract view of class is relatively clear.[7] It is here that we will begin.

The key in understanding human societies for Marx was "the material conditions determining their production," that is, the mode of production. It is with *private ownership of the means of production* that class and class conflict begin. In feudal societies based on land and agricultural production, the two great classes are the lord and the serf, or the landed aristocracy and the peasant. The lord or the aristocracy owned the land (the means of production), while the serf and peasant owned little but their labor power.

In capitalist societies based on industrial production the two great classes are the **bourgeoisie** (the owners of the means of production or capital) and the **proletariat** (or working class). Marx recognized the existence of the bourgeoisie in the later stages of feudal societies and the continued presence of the aristocracy in capitalist societies. But as noted in the discussion of Marx's theory of social change, when the dominant means of production shifted from land to industry, it was the bourgeoisie that came to dominate in capitalist society.

Having considered Marx's most general definition of class, it is next important to understand what he saw as the moving force in history—that is, "the history of all hitherto existing society is the history of class struggles," or *class conflict.* The root of class conflict is differing class interests. In class societies, which include, in Marx's view, all existing societies except "primitive communism" and the "future mature communist society," one class owns or controls the means of production. This class dominates and controls the surplus goods produced in that society for its own needs. There is exploitation by one class over another.

Marx was most concerned with capitalist societies, and it was here that he devoted most attention to the details of this exploitative class relation. He proposed a **labor theory of value** to explain the value of all goods produced in a society. As he wrote, "The magnitude of the value of any article is the amount of labor socially necessary, or the labor-time socially necessary for its production" (see Anderson 1974:16).

The exploitative nature of capitalism, for Marx, is found in the fact that the capitalists (owners of the means of production or the factories) pay workers only a living or subliving wage, a wage below the value workers actually produce. The remainder is "surplus value" that is taken by the capitalist for his or her own profit; "surplus value is nothing but the difference between the value created by the worker and the cost of maintaining him" (see Anderson 1974:18).

The exploitative relationship of capitalism is extended by the production of capital itself. By capital is meant the factories, machines, or any goods used as a means to produce more goods. Thus, "capital is stored-up, accumulated labor" (Anderson 1974:18). This stored-up labor or capital from past workers is used to produce even more surplus value for the capitalists' own profit, taking more and more profit from fewer and fewer workers.

With a reduced need for workers as capitalism advances, more workers are reduced to an **industrial reserve army** living in poverty and able to work only in times of boom or periods of economic expansion. In Marx's poetic terms, "Capital is dead labor, that vampire-like, only lives by sucking living labor, and lives the more, the more labor it sucks" (Marx 1906:257).

For Marx, then, class and class conflict were the moving forces in history. There is a dominant class that owns the means of production and exploits other classes. But in the face of this exploitation, these other classes find it in their interest to overthrow the dominant class and establish a social order more favorable to their interests when the historical progression of the mode of production allows. With feudalism, as we have seen, the dominant class was overthrown by the bourgeoisie; with capitalism, the dominant class would be overthrown by the proletariat.

This would happen, in part, when the proletariat *recognized* its true interests—moving from a class in itself that has only objective interests in common but does not yet recognize its common interests or act upon them, to a class for itself that does. With the proletariat in power, however, Marx believed that class struggle would end because he saw the proletariat as the final class in the history of class struggles, with no class below it to exploit. This is why he believed that with the coming of a workers' state in advanced communism, class conflict would end where human society began (with "primitive communism"). But at the end of this class struggle would be an industrial society of plenty so that all could live in comfort.

## Concluding Notes

We can conclude our discussion of Marx by again noting the importance of his ideas in the development of social stratification theory. His image of society, or the critical-conflict paradigm he helped develop, is most important. Many of his specific predictions about the future of capitalism we now know are incorrect. The nations that have experienced "communist revolution" (Russia, China, Cuba, Vietnam), contrary to Marxian ideas, were less-industrialized, principally agrarian societies. In the most advanced capitalist nations, where he saw communist revolution as most likely, the working class has been less than revolutionary. (Some of the reasons will be taken up in later chapters.)

Marx failed to see how a state coming to power in the name of his ideas could develop into a society far from what he envisioned, as did the states of the failed communist societies. He also failed to see how a welfare state could develop in capitalist societies to manage some of the conflicts, exploitation, and internal contradictions that he believed would lead to the demise of capitalism. (This is considered in Chapter 9.)

But Marx did see better than most in his time the expansion of "monopoly capitalism." And with the elaboration of Marxian ideas by Lenin, the expansion of capitalism into a worldwide network of class conflict and exploitation was foreseen (to be considered most fully in the last chapters of this book). Overall, although not accurate in many details, the Marxian view of society has been valuable to our present understanding of inequality, class, and social stratification in human societies.

# ⚔ Max Weber: An Alternative Conflict Paradigm

In comparison with those of Marx, Max Weber's specific contributions to stratification theory were relatively brief—but no less powerful. Two sets of ideas developed and expanded by Weber have had a particular impact on our understanding of advanced industrial societies. The first, his expansion of Marx's single class or economic dimension of social stratification into a *multidimensional view* (class, status, and party), has provided us with a very useful tool in understanding the complex nature of social stratification. Perhaps most important, however, Weber's writings on the development and growth of large *bureaucratic institutions* has enabled us to understand the nature of power and dominance within advanced industrial societies of all types (whether capitalist or communist) better than any other single idea by a social theorist.

Therefore, Weber's insights into the multidimensional nature of social stratification and the power of bureaucratic institutions will concern us most in this discussion. However, as we have done with Marx, we must look more broadly into the development of Weber's general sociological perspective. In contrast to Marx's critical-conflict assumptions, we find with Weber a set of paradigm assumptions we have labeled uncritical-conflict.

Like Marx, Weber was most consistent in stressing conflict as the human relationship most important in shaping the nature of society although, as we will see, Weber's view of conflict was more encompassing. But even more important, with Weber we find a far different perspective with regard to what we have called value assumptions. While it can be said that Marx was basically an optimist—for he believed that conflict, inequality, alienation, and exploitation could eventually be reduced or eliminated in future societies—Weber had no such hope. As we will see, he was truly a pessimist in his estimate of the potential for more just and humane societies. Especially in his view of the legal-rational mode of social organization (that is, bureaucracies), Weber was pessimistic and even fearful of what he saw as an expanding "iron cage."

At the outset it should be noted that Weber's ideas, much like Marx's, have been misunderstood until recently by many social scientists. Weber's work was most often described as primarily a "debate with Marx's ghost." Weber *was* aware of the limitations of a *strict* historical-materialist view of society; thus, he showed (1) how a new value system was also behind the development of capitalism in *The Protestant Ethic and the Spirit of Capitalism* (1958) and (2) that there are dimensions of social stratification other than just the material or economic.

But his work was much more than simply an alternative to that of Marx. Rather, in many cases it was an expansion of Marx's ideas. As with Marx, American social scientists have only recently had the benefit of translations (from the German) of most of Weber's work. In addition, the most extensive early interpretations of Weber's work (see Parsons 1937) came from theorists who read into Weber many functional (or, in our terms, uncritical-order) assumptions that were found to be inaccurate upon a more complete analysis (see Cohen, Hazelrigg, and Pope 1975). Thus, overall, we find more agreement between Weber and Marx than was heretofore recognized.

Max Weber was born in Erfurt, Germany, in 1864 and died in 1920. (For very useful biographies of Weber and his times see Marianne Weber 1975; Mitzman 1969; see also Gerth and Mills 1946; Bendix 1960.) His life, therefore, spanned an exciting and challenging period of change and conflict in his homeland. And unlike Marx, it can be said that Weber had a homeland; for he was a patriotic citizen of Germany who sought to understand his society so that it could be strengthened and humanized (much like Durkheim, discussed later). In fact, his earliest professional work was an attempt to shed light on the problems of land ownership and utilization in this country, with special emphasis on the power of the old backward-oriented upper class in Germany at the time (the Junker class).

For brief periods Weber left his academic studies for service to his country—as a hospital administrator during World War I, as a delegate to the peace conference after World War I, and as a voice and consultant on many issues confronting the new German government during reconstruction. But over the years Weber grew more pessimistic about the prospect of reform, especially after the recurring bouts with extreme mental depressions that began with his father's death in 1897. For many years Weber was unable to lecture or write, but his greatest works were completed after his recovery.

Like Marx, Weber grew up in an upper-middle-class family. His father was a lawyer who held several political positions. But unlike Marx, Max Weber primarily pursued the life of a scholar and teacher within the academic hall. He held positions in a number of major German universities and was a central figure in the establishment of sociology as a respected academic discipline.

Also in contrast to Marx, Weber was an early advocate of a value-free orientation in the study of society. That is, Weber maintained that the social scientist's task is to understand human societies without the interference of political objectives. However, as we have discussed in the preceding chapter, very *general* paradigm assumptions about human nature and social organization make a completely value-free analysis impossible.

Although it seems Weber was advocating this value-free stance in order to shelter the new discipline of sociology from the political debates on both the left and the right (see Gouldner 1973:3–26), this value-free perspective guided his work by making him more concerned with *what exists,* rather than attempting to understand what *could be* (in contrast with Marx's attempt to understand how society will change for the better). We can now examine how a particular set of paradigm assumptions we have called uncritical-conflict assumptions informed Weber's work and through him influenced the development of many modern theories of social stratification.

## Weber's Paradigm Assumptions

As with Marx, but not Durkheim, the image or model of society that guided Weber's perspective on social stratification was one of conflict. He did *not,* however, view conflict between the owners of the means of production (the bourgeoisie in capitalist societies) and the workers (the proletariat) as the only, or even at times the most important, conflict relationship in the society. For Weber, many varied and differing group or individual interests could form the basis of conflict relationships in human societies. As we will see, he believed these varied conflicting interests could be merged with more specific economic interests, although this is not always so.

Weber's conflict perspective can be understood in contrast with that of functional (order) theorists such as Durkheim. For example, "Weber did not suggest that dominant persons act to integrate collectivities in the interest of effective functioning. Rather, he treated such individuals as acting in terms of their own ideal and material interests as they perceive them" (Cohen, Hazelrigg, and Pope 1975:238). Furthermore, Weber did not neglect the divisions and separate elements of human societies by focusing exclusively on the integration and functioning of the whole. In fact, "A correct understanding of Weber's general sociology is impossible unless founded on a faithful reading of his theory of domination" (Cohen, Hazelrigg, and Pope 1975:237).

As we have suggested, unlike Marx, Weber did not focus only on conflict flowing from the economic relations within society. In Weber's view, the base of conflict relations could be located in many differing types of interests (social, material, political, and so on). But, if any of these can be said to be more important in his interpretations of society, it is political or organizational conflict and dominance; "Weber . . . came very close to what amounted to a transposition of Marx's monistic explanation from the economic to the political realm. One sees this most graphically where Weber describes the ongoing process of centralization of power in all fields of human activity: war, education, economics, religion, and most crucial of all, politics" (Mitzman 1969:183–184).

With respect to what we have described as value assumptions, Weber's view of conflict and domination in human societies converged with his pessimistic view toward the possibility of a more equal and just society. The result was a perspective that saw no end to conflict and domination, only changing forms or bases of conflict.

Much like Pareto, Mosca, and Michels, who also contributed much toward an uncritical-conflict paradigm, Weber saw a society always divided between those who ruled and those who were ruled. But Weber differs from these theorists by providing a more complex and robust theory of social conflict. The interests behind this conflict and domination are viewed as more diverse, and he recognized that the *means* of domination must be distinguished from the interests or goals of domination.

Finally, Weber was not explicit in charging that continued domination was due to anything like selfish human nature. Whether or not human nature was part of the cause, Weber saw that increasing population density and diversity resulted in the need for organization and coordination. The most efficient means of achieving this organization was bureaucratic administration. It was for this reason that Weber came to view programs for radical alternatives to the present inequality and domination as hopeless (Mitzman 1969:185).

## Multidimensional View of Stratification

Having discussed some of the more general aspects of Weber's work, we are prepared to examine the two aspects of his work that are most important for modern theories of social stratification. We can begin with his **multidimensional view of social stratification.** Marx, as we have seen, believed the key to social stratification in capitalist societies was the division between those who owned and controlled the important means of production (capitalists, or the bourgeoisie) and those who have only their labor to sell (the proletariat). For Marx, these two groups and their conflicting interests formed the two major classes in capitalist societies (that is, Marx stressed this single dimension of social stratification).

Weber, however, argued that this view of class was overly simplistic for two reasons. First, Weber demonstrated that this class or economic dimension of stratification was in itself too simple. In addition to ownership versus nonownership of the means of production, the social scientist must consider a person's more general *relationship to the marketplace.* Thus, we find Weber's expanded view of economic or class divisions. Second, he maintained that other important divisions exist within society, divisions that are at times independent of this class division. Weber, then, came to stress a *multidimensional* aspect of social stratification; more specifically, the dimensions of **class, status,** and **party** (or **power**).

With respect to *class,* Weber wrote (see Gerth and Mills 1946:181), "We may speak of a class when (1) a number of people have in common a specific causal component of their life chances, insofar as, (2) this component is represented exclusively by economic interests in the possession of goods and opportunities for income, and (3) is represented under the conditions of the commodity or labor markets."

Again, we can see that Weber saw more than ownership behind class divisions, although this ownership of productive forces was primary (see Gerth and Mills 1946:182). There is also the important aspect of opportunities for income. By opportunities for income, Weber meant the skill level possessed by a worker (such as a scientist, lab technician, or skilled blue-collar worker). The higher the skill level, other things being equal, the more return (income or wealth) a worker was able to obtain for his or her labor (also see Wright's [2002a] analysis of Weber's view of class).

Most sociologists today agree that this is an important expansion of Marx's view of class, given the growth of technology—and thus needed skills—in advanced industrial societies (capitalist and communist). Furthermore, this expanded dimension of class stratification, most sociologists stress, is needed in understanding the place of the new middle class in industrial societies. In Weber's view, therefore, in addition to the dichotomy between owners and nonowners of the means of production, there is a dimension of class stratification based on skill level that is more continuous (that is, contains many ranks or levels, rather than only two).

In understanding divisions and inequalities in human societies (or even small social groups), Weber also stressed status honor or prestige. "In content, status honor is normally expressed by the fact that above all else a specific style of life can be expected from all those who wish to belong to the circle. Linked with this expectation are restrictions on 'social' intercourse" (Gerth and Mills 1946:187).

Divisions based on status honor flow from the ability of someone to live up to some set of ideals or principles held important by the society or some social group within it. As people, we tend to judge and evaluate others in terms of a set of ideals or values. Thus, we commonly find rankings based on these evaluations. Examples may be an old family of wealth able to pursue a life of high culture, interacting with movie stars, famous athletes, or famous scientists. This, then, is a more subjective dimension of social stratification, one that has been stressed most often by functional theorists.

Important also within the status dimension are the restrictions on social intercourse. By this Weber wanted to emphasize that status groups tend to draw lines around themselves, restricting intimate social interaction, marriage, and other relations within the status group. Thus, "where the consequences have been realized to their full extent, the status group evolves into a closed 'caste'" (Gerth and Mills 1946:188). Here we find much of the ascriptive nature of class systems, often (but by no means always) based on racial or ethnic divisions. In our discussion of the upper class in the United States, we will find how useful this status dimension of stratification is in understanding how powerful upper-class families have been able to keep wealth and power within their own group by status distinctions that hold the new rich at a distance. When we examine social stratification in Japan, we will see how the status dimension of stratification can be very important in a homogeneous society with extensive value consensus (or agreement on major values).

Finally, there is the dimension of *party* or power. Weber (Gerth and Mills 1946:194) wrote,

> Whereas the genuine place of "classes" is within the economic order, the place of "status groups" is within the social order, that is, within the sphere of the distribution of "honor." . . . But "parties" live in a house of "power." Their action is oriented toward the acquisition of social "power," that is to say, toward influencing a communal action no matter what its content may be.

The most important aspect of this party (or power) dimension of stratification is organization, or "rational order," and a staff with which to dominate or influence others for whatever goal. Thus, it is the political party or the bureaucratic form of organization that most typifies this dimension of stratification. Where one stands with respect to the organized forms of dominance or power within the society defines one's position in this dimension of stratification. Weber came to stress this dimension as increasingly important in advanced industrial societies.

Weber, then, saw all three dimensions as important hierarchies leading to the ranking of individuals or groups in human societies. However, they were not all of equal importance throughout the history of human societies. In the early stages of capitalism the class dimension was viewed as more important. In caste societies, the status dimension remained supreme. And, as we have said, Weber saw that in modern societies the party or power dimension gained importance.

But—and this must be stressed—Weber considered all societies to have divisions based on all three dimensions of class, status, and party. Equally important, Weber saw that normally there would be a *large degree of overlap* among all three dimensions. A person high in one dimension, such as class, would typically achieve a high position on the dimensions of status and party as well. For those on top, of course, this overlap adds to their overall strength within the stratification system (as we will discuss with the upper class in America). It is primarily in times of social change that these three dimensions can diverge most widely, leading to differing arenas (for class, status, and party) in which conflicts for advantage may be brought to the forefront.

With respect to Weber's more general model of society, we can see that he viewed conflict and domination as more pervasive and enduring than did Marx. For Weber, even if one aspect of conflict and inequality could ever be eliminated, others would remain, and perhaps become an even more important basis for inequality and conflict. In short, Weber's view of conflict was broader than that of Marx. It was partly for this reason that Weber was less hopeful than critical-conflict theorists that inequality, conflict, and domination could ever be substantially overcome.

# The Rise of Bureaucratic Dominance

It may be that sociologists will soon come to recognize (if they have not already) that Weber's ideas on the bureaucratic form of organization and power have contributed most to our understanding of advanced industrial societies. Currently, we find politicians, business leaders, and the general public from all political perspectives denouncing the growing influence bureaucracies have over our lives. Large bureaucratic organizations are seen as dehumanizing, alienating, inefficient, and encroaching upon valued human freedoms. But in spite of all the denunciations, complaints, and political rhetoric, no one has been able to do much toward solving the problem.

Everyone seems to want less government, but a wide collection of interest groups also wants a strong military, better economic planning, protection for business in the face of foreign competition, better prices for farmers, less crime, protection from pollution and unsafe consumer products, and so on. The sum total of all these interest group demands is more government and bureaucratic regulation. It must be recognized that the many problems flowing from large and complex societies such as ours require some means of corrective action; this invariably results in expanded bureaucracies.

Max Weber, at the turn of the century, clearly recognized the future growth and increasing influence of rational-legal forms of social organization—that is, bureaucracies. By the later 1800s, Weber could already see how the state bureaucracy was growing in response to interest group demands for protection, primarily from powerful capitalists (DiMaggio and Powell 1983). And Max Weber recognized the human costs of this condition. Weber foresaw what he called a growing iron cage that people were building for themselves; but he foresaw no solution to this situation (see Marianne Weber 1975:415; Mitzman 1969:177).

Weber (1947:328) wrote of three principal ideal types of legitimate authority: **rational-legal authority,** "resting on a belief in the 'legality' of patterns of normative rules and the right of those elevated to authority under such rules to issue commands"; **traditional authority,** "resting on an established belief in the sanctity of immemorial traditions and the legitimacy of the status of those exercising authority under them"; and **charismatic authority,** "resting on devotion to the specific and exceptional sanctity, heroism, or exemplary character of an individual person, and of the normative patterns or order revealed or ordained by him."

Traditional authority was primarily of earlier times and began falling with the breakdown of feudalism in the face of rising industrialization. Charismatic authority is only temporary; it comes with a revolt against the old status quo led by an influential personality (such as Jesus, Lenin, or the Ayatollah Khomeini). Once a new authority structure is established after successful revolt, charismatic authority gives way to one of the other, more stable, types. Of the three, Weber saw rational-legal authority as the most efficient for modern societies.

We must be specific on what this form of authority and organization entails. Weber (Gerth and Mills 1946:196–198) wrote of six main characteristics of **bureaucracy:**

**1.** There is the principle of fixed and official jurisdictional areas, which are generally ordered by rules: that is, by laws or administrative regulations.

**2.** The principles of office hierarchy and of levels of graded authority mean a firmly ordered system of superordination and subordination in which there is a supervision of the lower offices by the higher ones.

**3.** The management of the modern office is based on written documents.

**4.** Office management . . . usually presupposes thorough and expert training.

**5.** When the office is fully developed, official activity demands the full working capacity of the official. Formerly, official business was discharged as a secondary activity.

**6.** The management of the office follows general rules, which are more or less stable and more or less exhaustive, and which can be learned.

Weber believed this form of social organization was far superior to any other (in terms of a rational means to goals), and would therefore come to exclude all others. "The fully developed bureaucratic mechanism compares with other organizations exactly as does the machine with the non-mechanical modes of production" (Gerth and Mills 1946:214). The "precision, speed, unambiguity, knowledge of the files, continuity, discretion, unity, strict subordination, reduction of friction and of material and personal costs, and calculatable rules" are all among the reasons cited by Weber for the superiority of the bureaucratic form of organization.

It can be argued that Weber was overstating the efficiency of bureaucratic organizations in these descriptions; no doubt he was. But we must recognize what preceded this form of organization to understand Weber's point. The list of states that fell to revolutions because of their inability or unwillingness to embrace this more efficient form of organization is a long one (see Skocpol 1979). And it must also be recognized that Weber is referring to the superiority of bureaucracy as a rational *means* of organization. The *goals* for which this means is applied, of course, may be (and often are) irrational with respect to differing interests within the society (see Marcuse 1971).

One final characteristic of bureaucracy described by Weber is important for our consideration: "Once it is fully established, bureaucracy is among those social structures which are the hardest to destroy. . . . And where the bureaucratization of administration has been completely carried through, a form of power relation is established that is practically unshatterable" (Gerth and Mills 1946:228). This "permanence" of bureaucracy, once established, does not mean, however, that it will always be used to serve the same goals or interests. The key, again, is that bureaucratic organization is a *means* of domination; it "is easily made to work for anybody who knows how to gain control over it" (Gerth and Mills 1946:229). The large bureaucratic structures that expanded rapidly in Bismarck's Germany, for example, served liberal governments and Hitler equally well.

Herein lies the primary importance of Weber's view of bureaucratic organization for understanding social stratification. Because bureaucratic organization is a form, or means, of control, it implies the existence of conflict (see Collins 1975:289). If one group, such as an economic class, fascist party, or small communist organization, is able to gain control or influence over established bureaucratic organization, the power of this group is *greatly* increased.

Theorists concerned with political and economic power in advanced industrial societies (that is, the power of those at the top of the stratification system) have all benefited from Weber's ideas. As we will see in Chapters 6 and 7 on the top of the stratification system in the United States, major theorists such as C. Wright Mills (1956), G. William Domhoff (2010), and Thomas Dye (1990), as well as recent Marxian theorists, have come to recognize that the system of stratification in advanced industrial societies cannot be understood adequately without a recognition of this new dimension of power.

It may be useful in concluding our discussion of Weber's work to summarize the important influence he has had on modern thought on social stratification. Functional theorists (or those within what we have called an uncritical-order paradigm) have tended to stress the status dimension of Weber's multidimensional view. Strata or class divisions, they maintain, flow from the need people have to evaluate and rank others in terms of a dominant value system (see especially Parsons 1951, 1970). In addition, functional theorists (among many others) have tended to stress a *continuous* class ranking rather than more rigid class divisions. This means that functionalists have emphasized occupational *status*.

Further, Weber's work has provided a base for the study of status consistency or **status inconsistency.** From the functional view of an integrated social system, if the social system is to be healthy, the various dimensions of social stratification should show at least a minimum of convergence. It is believed that if some degree of convergence between stratification dimensions (such as occupational status, education, income) is not achieved, tensions, conflicts, and confusion will be the result—for the general society as well as for individuals within it.

Conflict theorists as well have benefited from Weber's work. For example, theories within what we have called a critical-conflict paradigm have benefited from Weber's critique and expansion of Marx's ideas. While often continuing to stress the importance of class divisions as Marx originally described them and Weber continued to stress as important, these theorists have come to recognize the significance of bureaucratic means of domination.

Thus, we find many contemporary Marxian theorists writing of the importance of the state and other bureaucratic forms of dominance in providing the upper class (in Marxian terms the owners of the means of production) with an added means to maintain their position (for example, see Miliband 1969, 1977; Harrington 1976; Therborn 1978; Wright 1997).

Finally, theorists working from what we have called an uncritical-conflict paradigm have benefited from Weber's ideas. Many, if not most, of the current theorists within this paradigm have built their theories around the dimension of stratification Weber came to stress in his later years—that is, party, power, or domination by centralized bureaucratic organizations (see Dahrendorf 1959; Collins 1975). While it may be argued that Weber's work is more useful than that of others of his time in understanding the contemporary United States because of his recognition of our particular traditions and values (see Tiryakian 1975), it can equally be argued that Weber's work is most valuable in its recognition of a primary aspect of all advanced industrial societies—the bureaucratic mode of organization.

---

# ⚹ An Uncritical-Order Paradigm Matures: The Functional Theory of Émile Durkheim

From the conflict perspectives of Marx and Weber, we turn briefly to the functional perspective of Émile Durkheim. Durkheim's work provided fertile ground for later functional theorists of social stratification. But unlike Marx or Weber, Durkheim himself gave only passing attention to class divisions, class conflict, and even social stratification. His relative neglect of class and his writing on the subject when it was forced on his attention, however, are most instructive in themselves. The brief treatment given class and social stratification by Durkheim shows how the more holistic perspective taken by functional theorists leads to a worldview in which the needs of a social system overshadow those of interest groups or classes within this social system.

In tracing the development of functional theory (or, more broadly, an uncritical-order paradigm), most historians of social thought draw a direct line from Saint-Simon and Auguste Comte, through Émile Durkheim, to modern functional theorists such as Talcott Parsons (see Gouldner 1970; Giddens 1973; Strasser 1976). Saint-Simon, a French philosopher and social scientist, made some of the first contributions to functional theory in the early 1800s (Zeitlin 1968:58). But it was with Comte that this perspective was carried into the academic hall; and it was with Durkheim that it grew to maturity. It was with both Comte and Durkheim that this perspective was "relieved of its critical potential" (Strasser 1976:5).

Durkheim called for bolstering the status quo (uncritical value assumptions) around a moral integration of society (order model). For Durkheim, the problems of his era were moral, not material; problems of alienation, exploitation, structured inequalities, or class conflict were due "not to the state of our economy, but rather the state of our morality" (Durkheim 1962:247). But even the solution to this problem of morality should not be in terms of a new morality; this reform "has for its object, not to make an ethic completely different from the prevailing one, but to correct the latter, or partially to improve it" (Durkheim 1964:35–36).[8]

A key to understanding Durkheim's sociological perspective, and thus his view of social stratification, is his **organic analogy.** From this perspective, society is considered as similar to a biological organism. There are various organs or parts within this social system that serve different functions for the health and maintenance of the total society—much like the functions served by organs within the human body.

It is easy to see that this organic analogy could lead a social theorist to focus on the social system as a whole (holistic perspective) and on the interrelation of its parts rather than on divisions and opposed interests among groups within the society. For example, one does not usually think in terms of a differing set of "interests" between the heart and lungs, and although we may think in terms of a hierarchy of biological organs—for example, the heart and brain are more critical for the overall survival of the organism than are the eyes—all are considered as contributing to the maintenance of the whole. Hence, this organic analogy leads to a perspective on social stratification far different from that of Marx and Weber.

Within the social system, it must be added, Durkheim considered morality to be the major factor contributing to social order and integration. For Durkheim, it has been said, "morality was the centre and the end of his work" (see Lukes 1973a:95). The importance of morality in maintaining social order is related to his view of human nature, as well as his view of the needs of the social system. Much like Weber, Durkheim was distrustful of human nature. Left to themselves, he thought, people would be in continuous conflict, selfishly dominating and exploiting fellow human beings for their own narrow interests. In order to save people from social chaos and even individual destruction (that is, suicide), a strong moral order is necessary (Strasser 1976:120).

Unlike Weber, however, Durkheim was optimistic about the ability of new social institutions to continue regulating selfish conflict for the common good. Various social institutions are important in maintaining this strong moral integration—such as religion, the family, occupational associations, and, above all, education. A continuing socialization process is needed so that people can internalize a moral order that could reduce selfish behavior for the collective good.

## The Division of Labor and Organic Solidarity

The maintenance of social order (that is, moral integration) was relatively simple in small-scale preindustrial communities. In the idealized view of these preindustrial societies held by Durkheim, Ferdinand Tönnies, and other early sociologists, it was in large part the closeness of interpersonal relations that helped maintain moral integration. But with a change toward large industrial societies, with many social divisions resulting from an expanding division of labor, moral integration was recognized to be increasingly problematic. Thus, the question of social order in industrial societies became central to the work of early sociologists such as Durkheim.

As Durkheim viewed the problem, societies must move from **mechanical solidarity** (the moral order in preindustrial societies) to **organic solidarity** in industrial societies. This organic solidarity was possible, he believed, through occupational organizations or guilds. It was reasoned that within each of the many occupational guilds, moral principles could be established regarding the rights and duties of workers and employers. As with preindustrial societies, this new type of moral order could restrain the selfish interests for the good of the larger society (see Durkheim 1964). Thus, in industrial societies there was need for more social differentiation, but this social differentiation did not have to result in social disorganization.

In the context of Durkheim's thought in *The Division of Labor in Society* (1964), we can gain some insight into his more specific views on inequality and social stratification. But for the most part, as noted earlier, Durkheim had relatively little to say on the subject. His concern, his model of society, was so dominated by a holistic image that the divisions (such as classes) that may exist within this society were easily neglected. And when they were not neglected, they were given only minor consideration.

The functional theory Durkheim helped establish was to wait almost 50 years before a systematic analysis of the functions of inequality "for the good of the social system" was undertaken (see the discussion of the Davis and Moore theory in the next chapter). However, the early ideas behind this systematic theory of the function of inequality can be found in Durkheim's work.

Principally, Durkheim saw two types of inequality, what he called *external* and *internal inequality*. As he described them in *The Division of Labor,* external inequalities are those imposed upon the individual by the social circumstances of birth, what we have referred to earlier as ascribed status. It was in mechanical solidarity, or preindustrial societies, that these external inequalities predominated. In industrial society, on the other hand, there was a need for internal inequality: "All external inequalities compromise organic solidarity" (Durkheim 1964:371); that is, threaten social order and the proper functioning of the division of labor in industrial societies. Internal inequalities were seen as inequalities based on individual talent, what we earlier called achieved status. For the proper functioning of the industrial system, Durkheim implied, the people with the proper talents must be allowed to move into positions for which their talents are best suited.

What Durkheim anticipated was a "meritocracy" based on equality of opportunity. Inequality there would be, but he believed an inequality based on merit was needed. Although Durkheim's ideas paralleled somewhat those of many modern functionalists, given his overriding concern with solidarity and moral integration in society, his stress was different. The dominance of internal over external inequality, he believed, was most important for the maintenance of social solidarity. If external inequalities were forced upon individuals, "constraint alone, more or less violent and more or less direct, binds them to their functions; in consequence, only an imperfect and troubled solidarity is possible" (see Lukes 1973a:175). Thus, in contrast to Davis and Moore (1945, considered in Chapter 5), Durkheim was more concerned with moral integration and cooperation than he was with the efficient staffing of "important" positions in industrial society.

The outcome of this functional perspective was that Durkheim dealt with the existence of class and class conflict by dismissing them as unnatural: "If the division of labor produces conflict, it is either because society is in a transitional state of development, or because of the existence of a pathological condition of social order" (Giddens 1978:114). This pathological condition of conflict existed, in Durkheim's view, because the occupational guilds were not performing their proper function of providing moral order and society was being threatened by selfish individual or group interests. But it never occurred to Durkheim that the whole system of a division of labor in industrial society could be a power structure for the domination of one class by another (as conflict theorists maintain).

# ⚔ The Classical Period of Sociological Theory: A Summary

To summarize the key ideas from the three theorists considered in this chapter, we must remember that Marx began with the assumption that people's material needs are basic. From Marx's perspective, those aspects of society located in the *superstructure* are also important in understanding the nature of society and social stratification; but the *substructure* is primary and, more often than not, shapes the aspects of society he located within the superstructure.

In understanding class divisions and social change, two elements of the substructure must be considered: The *means of production* refer to how people go about producing the necessities of life, and the *relations of production* refer to such things as how the fruits of this labor are distributed, how people are related to each other in the production process, and what the authority and ownership relations are within the production process. A change in some aspect of the substructure (means or relations of production) will force changes in aspects of the superstructure. This change may be gradual or violent and revolutionary; but from Marx's perspective, a change in the substructure is the key to moving human societies from primitive communism through feudalism and capitalism to the "final" communist society.

Most important for the study of social stratification, Marx saw all societies (except in the first and last stages) divided between those who ruled and those who were ruled. The key to this division was again the substructure. Those who owned or controlled the major means of production in the society were able to dominate the other classes because the owners of the means of production are able to control the necessities of life. Thus, they can require others to follow their rules to obtain these necessities. Also, the owners' favored position in relation to the superstructure must be considered. The various components of the superstructure (ideologies, political organization, the legal system, and so on) generally help reinforce ruling-class dominance.

Finally, Marx viewed the class system as loaded with conflict and exploitation because the favored position of the ruling class, or the bourgeoisie in capitalist society, allows it to extract surplus value from the working class. Marx's labor theory of value considered the value of all things produced to be found in the amount of labor time necessary to produce these goods. But in a class society workers are not given (or paid) the full value of their labor. Rather, they are given only a living wage, with the surplus going to enrich the ruling class. With Marx, therefore, we find the essence of a critical-conflict paradigm.

With the work of Max Weber we do not find such a systematic set of concepts used to construct a basic framework of the total structure of society. But Weber's view of society was no less guided by the overall existence of social conflict. However, because Weber saw conflict as more pervasive and at the very heart of all complex social organization, unlike Marx he held no hope that this human conflict could ever be completely eliminated.

For the study of social stratification, Weber made two most important contributions. *First,* he expanded Marx's class dimension of stratification and added the dimensions of status and party (or power). In addition to ownership of the means of production, he saw a person's relation to the market (or level of skill that could bring a greater or lesser return) as leading to a particular class position.

*Second,* Weber recognized most fully in these early years of sociology the importance of the legal-rational mode of social organization for the nature of social stratification. In fact, it is here that Weber came to stress the party or power dimension of social stratification over the other two. The bureaucratic form of organization made necessary by large, complex industrial societies provided the means of dominance of one group over others. It is also here that we find the essence of Weber's uncritical-conflict paradigm.

Finally, with Émile Durkheim we examined the basic paradigm that was to shape modern functional theories of social stratification. Durkheim himself had little to say about class, conflict, or even social stratification. But his holistic view and organic analogy led to a stress on the needs of a social system, requiring social stratification for the good of the whole. Class divisions and conflicting class interests were neglected from this perspective. When Durkheim was forced to recognize the existence of such divisions and conflicts, he explained them as unnatural and only temporary conditions. In time, he believed, such conditions would be eliminated or reduced when morality was strengthened in new industrialized societies. With Durkheim we find the essence of an uncritical-order paradigm of social stratification.

Having considered briefly some of the major ideas about the nature of social stratification from three major theorists during the early years of sociology's development, it is time to reemphasize some central points. We have chosen to focus on the works of Marx, Weber, and Durkheim not only because they are among the most respected classical sociological theorists but also because their ideas helped form the basis of three competing schools or paradigms in the study of social stratification today. By focusing on these three theorists we hope to enable the reader to have a better grasp of the major contemporary theories of social stratification to be considered in more detail in the next chapter.

## Summary

This chapter began with a discussion of paradigms of social stratification theories. Following some of the paradigm assumptions behind major theories of social stratification, we outlined one typology that distinguishes among functional theories, critical-conflict theories, and uncritical-conflict theories. The primary goal of this chapter has been to describe the works of the three main classical theorists of social stratification—Marx, Weber, and Durkheim. Karl Marx, both a political activist and a social scientist, is primarily responsible for establishing a critical-conflict paradigm of social stratification. We outlined the historical-materialist perspective behind his theory of social change to capitalist industrial societies and what he believed would be the future communist societies. Directly opposed to Marx on many points, Max Weber is recognized as one of the main founders of an uncritical-conflict paradigm of social stratification. Most important among his contributions are the multidimensional view of social stratification and his description of types of authority, especially the rational bureaucratic authority structures that were to become most important in modern societies. Finally, we considered the works of Émile Durkheim, who is most noted for the development of the functional paradigm. This early functional paradigm, however, had little to say about social stratification and inequality, and considered class conflict to be only a temporary and unnatural consequence of change to modern societies.

# Notes

1. "A paradigm is a fundamental image of the subject matter within a science. It serves to define what should be studied, what questions should be asked, how they should be asked, and what rules should be followed in interpreting the answers obtained" (Ritzer 1980:7). Similar to a paradigm, but more specific as to images and assumptions about the subject matter contained within a paradigm, are what Gouldner (1970:31) calls *domain assumptions,* or what we may also call *paradigm assumptions.* Examples of domain assumptions relevant to the study of society are assumptions of human nature as rational or irrational or as selfish or altruistic and assumptions of whether society is fundamentally stable or changing and based on unity or conflict.

    At the outset, it must be noted that the idea of paradigms behind sociological theory is relatively controversial. Most sociologists do not reject the view that paradigms exist; rather, they disagree about what is contained within paradigms and about the exact number of paradigms that can be located behind competing sociological theories. Since Kuhn's (1962) first work on the subject of paradigms in the physical sciences, there have been a number of works applying the idea of a paradigm to sociological theory (for example, see Friedrichs 1970; Effrat 1972; Ritzer 1975, 1980). These works have defined a differing number of paradigms, with differing sets of paradigm assumptions and slightly differing views on what constitutes a paradigm.

2. In a fundamental respect, social scientific paradigms must be related to our experience of social phenomena. With respect to social inequality in particular, we can assume that as inequality emerged as an important aspect of society when human beings turned from hunting and gathering or primitive communal societies, people began a struggle to understand and act on this new experience. Since human beings first learned to express themselves in written records that could be preserved, they left evidence of competing assumptions about the nature of inequality that are in some ways similar to current competing assumptions (see Lenski 1966:3–17).

    But this story of the development of assumptions about the nature of social stratification requires us to recognize a difference in the nature of social scientific paradigms when compared with physical science paradigms. The struggle to understand social phenomena such as inequality is not only a scientific endeavor; it also has a basis in class or group interests. The advantaged classes, and especially elites, have had (and continue to have) an interest in shaping the understanding of social stratification so that this understanding does not threaten their interests in the status quo.

    Elites prefer to think that inequality rests on the superior qualities of those on top, that it is beneficial for all, and that it is inevitable or necessary. The lower classes, especially when their conditions become unbearable, struggle to understand the exploitative and negative nature of structured inequality so that it can be altered. Because the upper classes have usually had the means to make their view of social phenomena the accepted view (because of their free time to speculate and write, because of their influence over religion and education, and because of their ability to reward or punish social thinkers), the upper-class view of inequality has usually (although by no means always) been the dominant view.

3.  It can be argued, however, that Marx's view of the future communist society would fit in this critical-order cell in our typology (see Strasser 1976). With an optimistic view of human nature and a belief that inequality is not inevitable, Marx was critical of capitalist society because he believed that the future mature communist society would be based on cooperation and a lack of major class conflicts. This is in contrast to his view of capitalist societies as based on class conflict and exploitation, thus placing his theory of capitalist societies in the critical-conflict cell of our typology (to be discussed in detail later).

4.  There is, however, another major variant within this uncritical-conflict paradigm, one that has been especially predominant in the study of the distribution of political power. This variant of the paradigm differs primarily in one respect from that discussed earlier. It is assumed in this variant that conflicting interests can be *structured* in such a way as to limit the extremes of conflict and exploitation. If, for example, conflicting interest groups are overlapping rather than superimposed, the society will not represent two exclusive groups in conflict (the haves and have-nots, for example). With overlapping conflict groups it is argued that a "web of conflicting interests" reduces extreme conflict (see Coser 1956, 1967). It is generally held, however, that the overlapping web of conflict can work only to limit to *some degree* the inevitable inequalities. This perspective is discussed in more detail in our chapter on the corporate class.

5.  It should be noted that although Marx had less to say about an Asiatic mode of production, many sociologists are recognizing the utility of considering this mode of production as distinct from feudalism (Mandel 1971; Krader 1975). As we saw in Chapter 3, with this Asiatic mode of production as a relatively distinct form of production and social stratification, we are better able to understand the agriculturally based differences in China and India as contrasted with those in Japan and European feudal societies (Eisenstadt 1996; Collins 1997). With an Asiatic mode of production there is less private ownership of land and a stronger political elite that developed with need for collective management of irrigation projects. In time this political elite came to control the surplus production much as the landowners did under feudalism. As with feudalism, the dominant means of production was agriculture, but the relations of production differed. In the Asiatic mode of production the relations of production involved political elite control of production (rather than private ownership of the means of production), with the surplus going to this political elite.

6.  In his later years Marx came to believe that violent revolution may *not* be necessary to transform capitalist societies to communism (see Berlin 1963:207; McLellan 1973:444). In one of those contradictions in Marx's writings Marxian theorists today would like to forget, Marx came to recognize that workers may gradually gain power through unions and working-class political parties to transform the state, and through it the economic structure of society to communism.

7. Marx did have a more complex view of class divisions than will be stressed here. For example, Marx did foresee the rapid growth of a middle class in advanced capitalism because of the increased need for technical skills and bureaucratic organization (see Giddens 1973:177). Most Marxian theorists, however, continue to stress that this middle class is an extension of the working class or proletariat (see Anderson 1974:52–56). Also, Marx described the *lumpenproletariat* as an extremely poor urban class that had no function in industrial society. But for the most part, in capitalist societies the bourgeoisie (or capitalists) and the proletariat (working class) were the primary class divisions in Marx's views.

8. Karl Mannheim (see Wolff 1971:161) best conceptualized this aspect of "conservative thought": "Thus progressive reform tends to tackle the system as a whole, while conservative reformism tackles particular details." In other words, for Durkheim no basic change is needed in the status quo; only small changes are needed to make it work better. This is in contrast to the position of a critical theorist like Marx, who called for a more basic or radical change of the status quo. Using common political descriptions, we can say that Durkheim would be described as conservative, or even liberal, while Marx would be described as a radical.

# Modern Theories of Social Stratification

Shown here in his office, C. Wright Mills was ahead of his time in explaining how America's political and economic institutions increasingly allowed a power elite to dominate the nation and the world.

*SOURCE:* © Getty Images

## Chapter Outline

# ❈ Views of Social Stratification in America: Early Years

Though today most sociologists consider social stratification one of the most important areas of study, this has not always been the case. In fact, the importance of this subject in understanding society and human behavior has been widely recognized by American sociologists only in the past 50 years, at most. The contrast to European social thought is clear. As we noted in the previous chapter, Marx, Weber, and even those before them such as Comte and Saint-Simon began their studies of society with the nature of class divisions and inequality as central questions (see Strasser 1976). What accounts for this contrast to American sociology? Our answer to this question can, in part, help us understand the state of stratification theory today.

Sociology as a separate discipline of study in the United States dates back only to about the early 1900s. But in the works of the founders of American sociology (men such as William Graham Sumner, Albion Small, and Edward Ross), we find a rather classless view of American society (Pease, Form, and Huber 1970; for a summary of these works see Gordon 1963; Page 1969). The relative neglect of social stratification is not surprising, however. Unlike in European nations, the old rigid class and estate inequalities were less in evidence. The value system stressed equality of opportunity for all, and at least an appearance of opportunity and democracy was in greater evidence. Not until the Great Depression of the 1930s was this classless image seriously reexamined, and then only by a few social scientists. Even then, many years passed before the study of social stratification was able to make a significant break with American classless mythology.

The first detailed American study in social stratification appeared in 1929 with Robert and Helen Lynd's *Middletown,* followed later by *Middletown in Transition* (1937). This first work was to establish a long tradition of stratification studies of small community life in the United States. But the general conflict perspective of this study was only much later a part of this tradition. The Lynds' focus was on power and economic inequalities, and the overpowering image of equality of opportunity in American society was exposed as a myth (see Gordon 1963:66). With the depression over, their view of American society was placed on the shelf and all but forgotten.

Of the social stratification research stimulated by the Great Depression, Lloyd Warner's work (in the 1930s and 1940s) had the most significant impact, at least for the next 20 to 30 years. Like the Lynds' research, Warner's many-volume *Yankee City* study (as well as others by his students) was centered on social stratification in small communities. Using various methods of study, from survey research to detailed participant observation, these works sought to examine the extent of inequality and social mobility, as well as the meaning of social stratification for the people involved.

But the Warner school differed from the Lynd tradition in three important ways. Most important, the Warner school came to define social stratification in terms of *status* (Weber's second dimension of social stratification). As Warner (and Lunt 1941:82) wrote: "By class is meant two or more orders of people who are believed to be, and are accordingly ranked by the members of the community, in superior and inferior positions." With such a view, inequalities of power and economic dominance were easily ignored, and the dynamics of conflict related to these stratification dimensions were dismissed.

Second, the Warner school failed to examine the actual extent of equality of opportunity critically. In the face of contrary experience highlighted by the depression, this research tradition continued to stress a "reality" of social mobility for all who had the talent and ambition to succeed, a finding now disputed in a reanalysis of *Yankee City* (Thernstrom 1964).

Finally, we find in the Warner school an emphasis on social stratification as *functional* and necessary for complex societies like our own. The conflict, the structured and hereditary nature of inequalities, the harsh conditions for workers, and the extensive poverty all too often found in the expansion of American capitalism were all but ignored.

The primary points are these:

**1.** During the earliest stage of American sociology the subject of social stratification was generally ignored. With very few exceptions, such as in the work of Thorstein Veblen, it was as if "nasty" conditions of class conflict, hereditary wealth, and race and class exploitation did not exist in the "classless" American society.

**2.** It took the experience of this country's most severe economic crisis to bring many social scientists to face the reality of rigid class inequalities. But even when this happened, the sobering reality forced upon us by this economic crisis was for most social scientists short-lived.

**3.** When the study of social stratification was increasingly taken up by American social scientists, the more palatable subject of *status* inequality dominated their work. The praise of America as the most classless of all industrial societies would continue for some time.

However flawed, a tradition of stratification theory and research was at least begun. The Warner school stimulated many students, and there was soon a wide variety of research on subjects such as differing class values and lifestyles, occupational prestige (if not occupational power), and the degree and causes of social mobility (Pease et al. 1970). One review of the early stratification literature found at least 333 research articles and books on the subject published between 1945 and 1953 (Pfautz 1953). By 1954 the first American textbook on the subject was published (Cuber and Kenkel 1954).

By the 1950s, however, the study of social stratification was clearly dominated by a *functional* perspective. It was a perspective more in line with that of Durkheim than Marx or even Weber. Such dominance could not last. As social scientists looked more deeply, the American values of equality of opportunity and free enterprise began to appear as questionable guides to the reality of social stratification in this country.

The break with functional theory came first with Floyd Hunter's (1953) study of community power, then most dramatically with C. Wright Mills's (1956) description of a power elite on the national level. Before Watergate, Vietnam, the energy crisis, and our discovery of poverty and discrimination in the 1960s, these works were ahead of their time. And though they were initially attacked by social scientists (see Domhoff and Ballard 1968), just as Einstein's paradigm-breaking work was originally attacked, they could not long be ignored.

More recently some sociologists have again begun questioning the extent to which economic class conflicts are important in the most advanced industrial or postindustrial societies. There is evidence that Americans are less likely to think about common economic class interests and associate with others on the basis of nonclass lifestyle or subcultural preferences rather than within their own economic class (Kingston 2000). There is also evidence that voting in national elections is now more likely based on "moral" or value issues rather than economic class issues (Clark and Lipset 2001; Evans 1999; LeDuc, Niemi, and Norris, 1996). However, there is plenty of research showing that class broadly defined, as well as narrowly defined through occupational position, helps us understand people's life chances, standards of living, as well as lifestyles and political ideologies (for example, see the new research by Weeden and Grusky 2005). We will also see in later chapters that this decline in class voting is occurring to the greatest extent in the United States only, and the United States is most unique in *lower class nonvoting*. In other words, something in the United States (abandonment by the two major political parties, for example) has led to the neglect of issues important to the less affluent (Kerbo and Gonzalez 2003; Kerbo 2002). When the interests of the less affluent are being ignored in the political system, this in itself suggests an element of class conflict.

Before we proceed to contemporary debates of class conflict, though, it is time to consider the utility of functional views of social stratification. Like other perspectives we have considered in the book, functional theories do have some value, though this value may be limited compared to other theories of social stratification.

# ❈ Functional Theories of Social Stratification

Within the functional or uncritical-order paradigm described in Chapter 4, and following the Warner tradition described here, we find two most prominent modern functional theories of social stratification. The first of these was published by Kingsley Davis and Wilbert Moore in 1945, somewhat amended by Kingsley Davis in 1948, and has come to be known simply as the Davis and Moore theory of social stratification. The theory was "logically" constructed to show why social stratification and inequality are positively functional, and therefore necessary in all but the simplest human societies. The second theory is from the more abstract and general functional perspective of Talcott Parsons.

This theory does not contradict that of Davis and Moore, but its focus is on social order more generally and the function of social stratification for the overall maintenance of social order.

## The Davis and Moore Theory

The Davis and Moore theory clearly and simply outlined the functional view of social stratification as necessary to meet the needs of complex social systems. In other words, from a perspective that considers society as something like an organism, the theory argued that this organism has needs that must be met if it is to remain healthy. Among these needs is for the most important positions or jobs in the society to be staffed by the most qualified and competent people. Social stratification is considered a mechanism that ensures that the need is met.

The following seven points provide a basic summary of the theory (Tumin 1953):

**1.** Certain positions in any society are functionally more important than others, and require special skills to fill them.

**2.** Only a limited number of people in any society have the talents that can be trained into the skills appropriate to these positions.

**3.** The conversion of talents into skills involves a training period during which sacrifices of one kind or another are made by those undergoing the training.

**4.** In order to induce the talented people to undergo these sacrifices and acquire the training, their future positions must carry an inducement value in the form of a differential—that is, privileged and disproportionate access to the scarce and desired rewards the society has to offer.

**5.** These scarce and desired goods consist of the rights and prerequisites attached to, or built into, the positions, and can be classified into those things that contribute to (a) sustenance and comfort, (b) humor and diversion, and (c) self-respect and ego expansion.

**6.** This differential access to the basic rewards of the society has as a consequence the differentiation of the prestige and esteem various strata acquire. It may be said to constitute, along with the rights and prerequisites, institutionalized social inequality: that is, stratification.

**7.** Therefore, social inequality among different strata in the amounts of scarce and desired goods and the amounts of prestige and esteem they receive is both positively functional and inevitable in any society.

At face value the Davis and Moore theory of stratification appears a simple, clear, and valid explanation of inequality and social stratification in industrial, if not all, societies. In a sense it is a labor market model analyzing the supply and demand of labor as it relates to rewards for labor. In short, when the supply of skilled labor is low in relation to the amount of labor needed, the employer (in Davis and Moore's perspective, the society) will be required to pay more for this labor. *But* the Davis and Moore view of this labor market model is flawed. And several social scientists have revealed other problems of logic and omission over the years. The Davis and Moore theory doesn't have to be rejected on every point, but it does need to be amended in several respects. Let us turn first to some of the criticisms of the Davis and Moore theory, then go on to some empirical research.

## *Critiques of Davis and Moore*

We may begin with one of the most far-reaching criticisms of the implied labor market model behind the Davis and Moore theory. As Collins (1975:420) argues: "Following through the pure market model leads us to a startling conclusion: The system must tend toward perfect equality in the distribution of wealth." This is the opposite of what Davis and Moore suggest with their theory to explain why an unequal distribution of rewards must exist.

One problem with the theory is that Davis and Moore neglect restraints on the labor market in the form of unequal power and influence: that is, conflict assumptions. Without such market restraints there would be a tendency toward equality because where labor is free to move to higher-paying jobs, the jobs that pay high wages will attract a surplus of workers, leading to a decline in the income for these jobs. Jobs paying low wages would tend to attract fewer workers. Without market restraints, "wherever jobs pay above or below the average, processes are set in motion through labor mobility which eventually bring wages back into line with all the others" (Collins 1975:120).

If we consider other rewards attached to positions, such as a good working environment or the prestige that comes with greater skill, we might find another result opposite from that predicted by Davis and Moore. Again assuming a free-market model, we might find that, for example, a physician would be paid *less* (in income) than a garbage collector because of the other rewards (such as prestige and working environment) attached to the position of physician.

Davis and Moore have two lines of defense to this criticism. Both, however, are weak. On one hand, Davis (1948) amended the theory shortly after it was published to say that the family structure will create a restraint on equal access to occupations. This occurs because those families higher in the stratification system will be able to secure better access to education and jobs for their children. Davis argues that their original theory was abstract theoretical reasoning, and in real life other factors will influence the process they described. But, of course, this is the point of critiques from conflict theorists! The question is, how much does the theory part from real life? The critics argue that real life is far different from the theory.

Davis and Moore, on the other hand, argue in the original theory that not everyone is equally talented or capable of performing the tasks of some very important positions. In this sense they do not acknowledge free labor competition. Many people could collect garbage, but only a few have the talent to become physicians. But again we find a weakness in the theory. Are there really so few people with the talent to make it through medical school and become physicians? The critics' response is no. Many people have the talent to become physicians, but in reality there are limitations on who and how many people can become physicians because of the ability of the medical profession to restrict and limit access to training for the occupation.

There is also the question of what, in fact, the most important positions in the society are. The critics' response is that those with power are able to influence which positions are defined as most important (see Tumin 1963; Cohen 1968:60; Kerbo 1976a). And some criticism questions the *degree* of inequality necessary among positions in our society. One may grant the assumption that a physician is more important than a garbage collector, or at least that the position of physician requires more training and skill. But, for example, if we find that the physician earns 50 to 100 times more income than the garbage collector, can we say that the physician is 50 to 100 times more important than the garbage collector? Or do some occupations provide greater control and influence that allow them to demand greater pay?

Finally, among other criticisms of the functional theory of Davis and Moore is Tumin's (1953:393), pointing out how social stratification and high inequality can at times be dysfunctional for the society. For example, "Social stratification systems function to limit the possibility of discovery of the full range of talent available in a society because of unequal access to appropriate motivation, channels of recruitment, and centers of training." Thus, social stratification systems can function to set limits on the possibility of expanding the productive resources of the society. Also, "To the extent that inequalities in social rewards cannot be made fully acceptable to the less privileged in a society, social stratification systems function to encourage hostility, suspicion, and distrust among the various segments of a society and thus to limit the possibilities of extensive social integration." The result of this, as other theories and research tell us, is a higher level of social problems such as crime.

## Empirical Research on the Davis and Moore Theory

Although it is often difficult to examine general theories of social stratification empirically, the Davis and Moore theory does make some specific predictions that can be tested. But even here, it is most difficult to measure and test all important propositions suggested by the theory.

Abrahamson (1973) has empirically examined the proposition that the most important positions in a society will be more highly rewarded. To measure functional importance, Abrahamson reasoned, periods in which some needs of the society have undergone change can be considered. One such change may be during times of war. In this case, it is suggested, positions in the military would be functionally more important than during peacetime. Comparing three military positions and three similar occupations in the private sector over a period from 1939 to 1967, which included three wars, Abrahamson was able to find adequate data on only about one-half of the comparisons. The Davis and Moore thesis appears supported in 11 out of the 12 comparisons.

Abrahamson's test of the Davis and Moore theory, however, has received extensive criticism. For example, in addition to neglecting the potential effects of scarcity of qualified workers, the study does not show that more qualified personnel were attracted to these positions when pay increased (a key point in the Davis and Moore thesis). But most important, as Leavy (1974) suggests, many of the industrial workers during the three war periods included in the study were involved in military production, a fact making the comparisons less meaningful.

In other research, Abrahamson (1979) found that scarcity and importance of differing positions on major-league baseball teams are related to the pay of these positions, as Davis and Moore would predict. But in a study of corporate executive income, Broom and Cushing (1977) found that the functional importance of a corporate executive (measured by how many other workers depend on the executive role) and the performance of an executive (corporate profits and growth) were not related to income. Further, Broom and Cushing found that corporations that could be assumed to be more important for a society (producing products such as steel, food, drugs, and clothing) did *not* pay their executives more than executives were paid in less functional corporations (such as those producing tobacco, cosmetics, and soft drinks). More recently, Weeden (2002) examined a number of job-related characteristics that might explain why some occupations pay more than do others. The most important factor seemed to be "social closure," the extent to which access to the occupation is relatively closed, thus creating an artificial shortage of people in the occupation. Again, the Davis and Moore theory is not supported. More recently, Jonsson et al. (2009) examined data from Sweden, Japan, Germany, and the United States and found that the inheritance of occupational positions from parents was even higher than income or educational level inheritance from parents to their adult children.

A number of empirical studies have shown that the general population in this nation, as well as in others, tends to believe that inequality and social stratification *should* operate in a manner generally suggested by the Davis and Moore theory (for example, Grandjean and Bean 1975; Jasso and Rossi 1977; Alves and Rossi 1978; see also Verba and Orren 1985; Coxon, Davies, and Jones 1986; Vanneman and Cannon 1987). Opinion polls show that compared to people in England, Germany, Japan, Hungary, and Poland, Americans are much more likely to think that there is equality of opportunity in America, thus indicating they tend to think the stratification system in America operates in a manner suggested by the functional theory of stratification (Ladd and Bowman 1998:118). But, of course, this does not mean that the theory fits reality. One of the most obvious conflicts with reality for the functional theory of social stratification came with the economic crisis in the United States during 2008 and 2009. The functional theory of stratification predicts that the best performing CEOs of big corporations should be the highest paid whereas those running corporations that are failing should not be highly paid. As we saw in Chapter 2 and will see again in Chapters 6 and 7, such certainly was not the case in the financial sector in the United States. We have examined some of the limited empirical research on this question, and the overall findings are at best mixed. As we will see in a coming chapter, the United States in fact *does not* have more equality of opportunity than other industrial nations.

## Parsons's Functional Theory of Social Stratification

Compared with the Davis and Moore theory, Talcott Parsons's work is much more general and abstract. One of the central figures in modern American sociology, Parsons developed a theory that is often considered the most important functional statement on all aspects of society ever made. But, as stated, his work is so abstract and highly theoretical that few precise empirical predictions can be made or tested from it (as Parsons admitted, 1977). Nonetheless, Parsons's work has been highly influential in carrying on the tradition of Durkheim and the Warner school of social stratification in American sociology. In this section we consider briefly the major components of Parsons's theory, then criticisms of this theory, and finally some research attempting to test the validity of some of his ideas.

Parsons argued that two sets of concepts are most important in helping us understand social stratification. In his first article on social stratification in 1940, Parsons (see 1964:70) wrote that "central for the purposes of this discussion is the differential evaluation in the moral sense of individuals as units." In his subsequent works on social stratification in 1949, 1953, and 1970, this theme was continued (see Parsons 1964, 1970). What Parsons meant by this, as in the Warner school, is that *status* or honor is the most important dimension of social stratification. People are evaluated and ranked by others in terms of how well they live up to the dominant values in the society, whatever these values may be. This means that there will always be a hierarchy of status honor in every society.

Parsons recognized wealth and power differences, of course, but for him these are by definition *secondary*. Writing of wealth, Parsons (1964:83) stated, "In spite of much opinion to the contrary, it is not a primary criterion, seen in terms of the common value system. . . . its primary significance is a symbol of achievement." Parsons arrived at the same conclusion as Davis and Moore. But for Parsons the common value system helps ensure that the functionally most important roles are filled by competent people through their status striving.

It will be helpful at this point to recall our earlier discussion of the organic analogy of society. Like body organs, each of these types of institutions is said to be serving a function for the health of the total organism—that is, society. For example, it is the task of economic institutions to extract resources from the environment and produce needed goods and services. The task of the state or polity is to define goals and provide direction toward these collective goals. Institutions such as law and religion help provide integration of the social system through rules or moral standards. Finally, the family and institutions such as education perform pattern maintenance through training and socializing individual members of the society and serving their personal needs so that they can be functioning members of the society.

The importance of the preceding in understanding social stratification, Parsons claimed, is twofold: (1) The differing tasks of these various institutions lead them to stress differing values (or pattern variables). (2) Societies differ with respect to which of the four sets of institutions (adaptive, goal attainment, integration, or latent pattern maintenance) is primary. In a society where one set of institutions is primary (say, goal attainment or the polity), the common value system will be more heavily weighted toward the values most consistent with this institutional stress. Thus, the individuals who best live up to the values shaped by the primary institution or institutions will receive more status, as well as the secondary rewards that are tied to high status, like wealth.

Let us summarize these very abstract ideas:

**1.** A person's place in the status hierarchy (stratification system) is determined by the moral evaluation of others.

**2.** This moral evaluation is made in terms of a common value system.

**3.** The common value system is shaped by the institution that is given primary stress in the society (the institutional stress coming from the particular historical and environmental circumstances of the society).

**4.** Thus, people who best live up to these values or ideas will receive, in addition to high status, other rewards, such as a high income and wealth.

Parsons's view does not contradict that of Davis and Moore. Only the stress on moral evaluation is different. Parsons still maintains that the most important positions in the society will be most highly rewarded, with status first, and wealth as a secondary reward. What Parsons has done, however, is specify more clearly what the most important positions will be, given a particular institutional stress in the society.

## Critiques of Parsons

One does not need an empirical study to test Parsons's prediction that top business executives are most highly rewarded in the United States. But one can certainly disagree with Parsons over *why* these people are on top of the stratification system in these countries. In other words, what Parsons leaves out of his analysis, or reduces to secondary importance, is a key to the critics' responses. And because Parsons clearly follows the functional tradition of Durkheim, most criticisms of Durkheim's view noted in the previous chapter apply equally to Parsons.

One of the most prominent criticisms of Parsons's work involves his assumption of a society with needs of its own. From this perspective, people in top institutional positions are doing what they do for the interests and needs of the total society. For Parsons, the interests of individuals and groups within the society are secondary. Like Durkheim, Parsons recognized class divisions, but again, these were seen as less important (Burger 1977).

Take the example of power. Parsons preferred the term *authority* because he viewed power and influence over others as something given to occupants of top institutional positions so that the interests and needs of the total society would be furthered (see Parsons 1960:181; 1964:327). Parsons rejected the notion that power is often used to promote the interests of particular individuals or groups over others. One need only remember our review of history in Chapter 3 to see the problem with Parsons's assumptions about power.

Most enlightening in this respect was Parsons's reactions to C. Wright Mills's famous work *The Power Elite*. Parsons (1968:61) began his criticism of Mills's thesis (that there is a power elite that dominates the country in its own interests) by saying he had very few criticisms of fact, only of theoretical interpretation. In Parsons's (1968:82) view, "The essential point at present is that, to Mills, power is not a facility for the performance of function in, and on the behalf of, the society as a system, but is interpreted exclusively as a facility for getting what one group, the holders of power, wants by preventing another group, the 'outs,' from getting what it wants."

In other words, if you take away Parsons's assumptions that there is a social system with needs of its own and that actors in this system are working to fulfill society's needs rather than their own, Parsons's description of the U.S. stratification system is close to that in C. Wright Mills's *The Power Elite* (Atkinson 1972:33). This also means that "what was a nightmare to C. Wright Mills, it seems, constitutes perfection of the social system to Talcott Parsons" (Strasser 1976:179).

This view of a society with needs of its own also helps us understand Parsons's conceptual trick in defining wealth and high income as secondary rewards. Parsons could do this because he believed that people primarily seek status, therefore striving to live up to dominant values. By striving to live up to the dominant values—remembering that Parsons saw the values as shaped by the needs of society—people are serving the needs of society. Parsons did not see people as striving primarily for power and material wealth for *personal interests*. But even if status striving is primary, also neglected by Parsons is the idea that a common value system may be shaped by the interest of those in powerful, wealthy positions in the society.

Conflict theorists like Tumin (1953:393) point out that "social stratification systems function to provide the elite with the political power necessary to procure acceptance and dominance of an ideology which rationalizes the status quo, whatever this may be, as 'logical,' 'natural,' and 'morally right.'" An elite may legitimize its own high status through its influence over people's perspectives of what is to be valued. To the extent that this is the case, people may be given status and other rewards not because they meet the needs of the overall society but because they *serve the interests of elites in the society*. More detail on this process is given in Chapter 13 on legitimation.

## Studies of Occupational Prestige

The vast majority of people in industrial societies depend on income from a job to meet their needs. That often makes the occupational structure the most visible form of stratification, in contrast to property relations or power differences. Functional theorists suggest that this visibility leads to extensive agreement among the population on relative ranks in the occupational structure, what they claim are ranks based on status or prestige. Let us examine the evidence.

In 1947 (North and Hatt 1947), 1963 (Hodge, Siegel, and Rossi 1964), 1971 (Siegel 1971), and then again in 1989 (Nakao and Treas 1990, 1994), similar studies were conducted to access occupational prestige rankings in the United States.[1] In the 1989 study a total of 740 occupations were ranked by subjects in a national sample, with a focus on a core of 40 well-known occupations. The responses given by the national sample for each occupation were transformed into a ranking for each occupation that ranged from a possible high of 100 (all excellent responses) to a low of 0 (all poor responses).

What is rather remarkable is that all three occupational prestige studies found very similar rankings by national samples. For example, there was a correlation of 0.96 to 0.97 (1.00 being a perfect correlation) between the 1963 and 1989 occupational rankings (Nakao and Treas 1994). There have been a few differences; for example, in 1947 only 49 percent of the respondents claimed to know what a nuclear physicist was, and it was ranked below 17 other occupations. By 1963, 90 percent claimed to know what a nuclear physicist was, and only 2 occupations received a higher rating. In the 1989 study, service occupations in general had a relative increase in ranking, with professional positions remaining about the same compared with 1964. Again, however, the differences in order of rank were minor in all three studies.

There is other evidence of strong agreement on occupational rankings. Hodge et al. (1966) also compared the 1947 and 1963 national studies with more limited studies done in the United States in 1925 and 1940. Again strong consensus was found, with correlations of $r = 0.93$ and $r = 0.97$ to the 1963 study. Furthermore, Hodge, Treiman, and Rossi (1966) compared the 1963 national ranking with similar studies conducted in 24 other nations. Correlations to the 1963 U.S. study ranged from a low of $r = 0.62$ with Poland to a high of $r = 0.95$ with New Zealand. Another study has found similar occupational prestige rankings in urban China (Lin and Xie 1988). The most comprehensive comparison, however, was made by Treiman (1977), who was able to find extensive agreement on occupational prestige in 60 nations around the world. A reasonable conclusion from these various studies is that people do, in fact, agree widely on the relative standing of occupational positions in this society, as well as across most industrial nations. But we can question the reasons for such wide agreement on occupational ranks, and will do so after considering the development of stratification scales.

## Socioeconomic Status Scales

Given the importance of social stratification in understanding much of human behavior, and given functional theorists' stress on the occupational status dimension of social stratification, there was a clear need to devise simple and useful **socioeconomic status scales** for empirical research. Since the early history of American sociology, class position or socioeconomic status has been measured in a number of ways. One of the first measurements was developed by people from the ecological school. Focusing much of their research on the population of Chicago (the ecological school was dominated by sociologists at the University of Chicago), they employed a *residential approach,* with the assumption that people from different social classes live in different parts or zones of the city. Thus, a person's class position could be indicated by area of residence (see, for example, Zorbaugh 1929; Frazier 1932). There were obvious limitations to this approach. The correspondence between class and area of residence is not always close, and severe restrictions are placed on research conducted across several cities.

A new trend in class measurement began with Lloyd Warner's *Yankee City* studies. Focusing on small communities and using extensive observational techniques, Warner developed a *reputational method* of class identification. This method relied primarily on the *status* judgments of people made by others in the community (see Warner 1953). From this method Warner concluded that there are six distinct class positions based on status.

The upper upper class included rich and old, well-established families in the community. The lower upper class included the new rich who did not yet have the respect and lifestyle of older rich families. The upper middle class represented successful (but not rich) families in business and the professions. The lower middle class was made up of the small business families and what we would call lower white-collar occupations (such as sales clerks and teachers). Those in the upper lower class were strong, "moral" members of the community but were not economically well off. Finally, the lower lower class included the poor and unemployed, with "low moral standards," who were looked down on by those in the community.

Besides the fact that this technique of class measurement employed by Warner is time-consuming and would be difficult to use with studies examining stratification in more than one small community, there are other problems. One of the most critical is that studies of other communities using the same technique have found differing numbers of class positions (see Lynd and Lynd 1929, 1937; West 1945; Hollingshead 1949). Of course, there is also the problem of basing class position exclusively on status judgments as described in the preceding chapter.

A breakthrough in class or prestige measurement came with the first study of occupational prestige in 1947. However, a problem remained: Rankings were obtained for only 90 occupations. If this ranking was to be widely useful for studies of social stratification, it had to be extended. The problem was solved in part with the development of *Duncan's Socioeconomic Index* (see Reiss et al. 1961). This SEI scale was constructed by weighting a person's educational level and income so that a ranking of occupations could be made resembling that found in the 1947 occupational prestige study. The method was then able to expand the original 90 occupations ranked in 1947 to a set of 425 occupations.

An even simpler method of measuring socioeconomic status (though with less direct relation to the occupational prestige studies) was developed by Hollingshead (see Hollingshead and Redlich 1958; Miller 1977:230). Referred to as *Hollingshead's Two Factor Index of Social Position,* this scale gives differing weight to a respondent's type of occupation (from a simpler listing of occupations) and educational level to indicate a respondent's class position.

## Critique of Occupation as a Status Hierarchy

Studies of occupational prestige demonstrate a high rate of agreement in this country and in others on the relative rankings of different occupations. But do these studies show that the agreement is based on status or prestige rather than on other factors related to an occupation? One study (Balkwell, Bates, and Garbin 1980) showed that people carry in their minds similar concepts of occupational ranks, although there is no doubt that people judge many factors about an occupation when ranking occupations (see Baker 1977).

Conflict theorists claim these rankings are made by people in terms of the income and power of the occupation ranked, with status factors secondary (see Gusfield and Schwartz 1963; Lenski 1966:431). Functional theorists seem to have ignored the fact that when respondents in the original 1947 study were asked why they rated an occupation high, the most important reason listed was that "the job pays well" (see Heller 1969:120).

Studies have indicated that occupational status research has not adequately recognized the class differences in ranking occupations (Guppy 1982; Coxon et al. 1986). One study has shown that there is significant disagreement when people of different classes, races, and educational levels are asked to rank occupations (Guppy and Goyder 1984). It seems that education is one of the most important factors leading raters to agree or disagree on the level of status for particular occupations. The higher the level of education of the raters, the greater their agreement, indicating that learning is perhaps leading to similar ratings. Finally, Hope (1982) has presented data indicating that the economic rewards of the occupation are as important as the social importance of the occupation in the minds of raters when they rate an occupation as high or low in status.

Other conflict theorists argue that even to the extent that prestige or status is a factor in making such occupational rankings, a person's concept of which jobs are more important and honorable can be influenced by inequalities of power. For example, status judgments can be shaped by (1) the ability of those high in the stratification system to obtain higher income because of their power, and reward with higher income those occupations serving elite interests (income is related to prestige judgments, remember); and (2) the ability of elites to influence what we think about different occupations through their influence over the dominant values in the society (see Kerbo 1976a). There is some support for both arguments in the cross-national prestige comparisons. It was noted earlier that Hodge, Treiman, and Rossi (1966) found much agreement on cross-national studies of occupational prestige. But there was some variation, with least agreement found between Poland (then a communist country) and the United States (see endnote 1).

Other occupational/class categories have been constructed that rely on the common economic class characteristics of groups of occupations. Erikson and Goldthorpe's (1992) 12-class scheme, for example, includes categories such as self-employed professionals, employed professionals, employed managers, self-employed managers, sales workers, clerical workers, craft workers, operatives, service workers, laborers, farmers, and farm laborers. Erik Olin Wright (1997), as we will see in more detail later, has created a class scheme that includes a person's position in a bureaucracy as well as ownership of property and occupational skill level. Both of these class schemes make much more sense in terms of economic position and power, and both help us distinguish differing standards of living and social mobility opportunities. But even these more preferable class schemes share a basic problem with the old occupational status scales; compared to other countries, particularly in Europe, these class categories are not strongly related to such things as differing lifestyles and political attitudes (Kingston 2000). Weeden and Grusky (2005) have shown that these older occupation rankings/class rankings are not strongly related to 55 measures of lifestyle differences, value orientations, and political attitudes. Their work does not imply these "big class schemes" have no value in understanding life chances and rewards like income, but it does show lifestyles and attitudes are shaped by a much more complex set of factors working within similar occupations than has been heretofore realized. Weeden and Grusky are in the process of producing an occupational class scheme that does explain more about many aspects of people's lives, which looks promising.

We can conclude that continuous occupational divisions do exist in industrial societies, and that people in these societies have a remarkably similar conception of these occupational rankings. We must question, however, the degree to which these occupational divisions are based on status or prestige, rather than on economic market forces (many of them not free-market competition). The status dimension can be very important in small communities (as we saw with Warner's studies, and studies of the kibbutzim and monasteries). But the information we have examined and will examine later suggests that with the occupational structure, occupational skill level, income, and power in the marketplace (as Weber described) are most important in affecting life chances.

# ⚔ Conflict Theories of Social Stratification

The main tasks of this section are to (1) outline briefly recent additions to Marxian theory, (2) examine some uncritical-conflict theories (primarily that of Dahrendorf), and (3) provide a general description of the main components of conflict theories (of all types) most useful for understanding the nature of inequality and social stratification in the advanced industrial societies. We can begin by noting some of the main differences between the two conflict paradigms (and the functional paradigm as well), along with the dimension of social stratification stressed by each. From Weber's influential description of stratification systems we recognize the primary dimensions of class, status, and party (or power).

What is interesting about theories of stratification is that there has been a tendency for theorists to stress one of these dimensions most heavily (see Table 5-1). Theories from the uncritical-conflict paradigm have tended to stress *power* or party as the main dimension of social stratification. For example, these theories focus attention on political power or formalized bureaucratic power and authority (as did Weber) in explaining the nature of inequality and social stratification in industrial societies.

Theories from the critical-conflict paradigm have tended to stress Marx's view of economic or property relations, that is, *class* as the most important dimension. Following our discussion of functional theories, we can see that these theorists have stressed Weber's *status* dimension.

Although functional theorists have also stressed the importance of an occupational structure (the other part of Weber's class dimension) in the nature of inequality and social stratification (especially the Davis and Moore theory), at the base of this occupational structure they stress *status* divisions (as we saw especially with Parsons's theory).

In part, a reason for this difference in stress on the various dimensions of stratification can be found in the divergent paradigm assumptions outlined in Chapter 4. Critical-conflict theorists assume that inequality can be significantly reduced and that the major source of inequality in our society is related to the historical development of

## TABLE 5-1

### Class, Status, and Power Dimensions Stressed in Stratification Paradigms

|  |  | Value assumptions | |
|---|---|---|---|
|  |  | **Critical** | **Uncritical** |
|  | Order | Empty with modern theories | Functional theory **Status-honor** (and occupational status) |
| **Model assumptions** | Conflict | Ruling-class theory **Class** | Power-conflict theory **Power** |

property relations. If inequality is to be reduced, it must be based on changing property or class relations, rather than on a more general conflict of interests "always found" among human beings.

Uncritical-conflict theorists, in contrast, tend to view inequality and social stratification as based on differing human and group interests in a more general sense. Although not always explicitly stressing this conflict of interests as related to selfish human nature, they assume that some kinds of interests will always be in conflict. In complex societies, therefore, these differing group interests will be reflected in organized power structures (or bureaucratic or political organizations) that are generalized means of furthering group interests of any type.

Uncritical-order or functional theorists maintain that inequality will always be present, but they tend to stress the needs of complex human organizations as the reason for this inequality. Thus, it is the status structure that helps provide social order and results in unequal status ranking in relation to the functional division of labor (or occupational structure necessary in complex societies) that explains social stratification and inequality.

## Modern Marxian Theory

We can begin by stating that modern Marxian theorists continue to accept Marx's basic view of social stratification outlined in Chapter 4. We need not repeat that basic outline. The primary concern of modern Marxian theorists has been to apply this Marxian view of society to industrial societies that have experienced change since Marx's time, while also using new methods of social science research to validate some of the principal Marxian concepts. We will consider first the changes in industrial societies that produce apparent problems for Marxian theory. We can approach these changes by focusing on some of the main problems faced by Marxian analysis today.

Among these problems, by far the most serious is the absence of socialist revolutions in any of the advanced capitalist nations. In fact, the working class that was seen by Marx as making such a revolution has become, it seems, less class-conscious and less critical of capitalism since Marx's time. Related to this, capitalist nations have not experienced the crisis periods Marx saw as leading to revolution, or, to the extent that they have experienced such crisis periods, the crisis has so far been managed with less than revolutionary results.

It will be remembered that Marx predicted increasing monopoly capitalism with a more powerful upper class in control of the economy and nation. Something like monopoly capitalism has certainly developed, as we will see in chapters on the upper classes that follow. But many argue, with some convincing evidence, that an upper class in the traditional sense of wealthy families with ownership of the major means of production in the society no longer exists, or, if it does, it has much less ownership and power.

In addition, we find a relative reduction in traditional working-class occupations in advanced capitalist societies and the emergence of a new middle class (especially what we call an upper middle class) to an extent Marx did not predict (Wright 1997; Wright and Martin 1987). Finally, there is a serious problem with respect to the reality of communism in nations that once claimed to be communist. Part of the problem is that nations like Russia and China did not develop "communism" from the breakdown of advanced capitalist nations as Marx predicted. Furthermore, we should add, the communist nations that have existed were far from the ideal that Marx envisioned, even after Gorbachev's reforms and democracy in the old Soviet Union.

In the face of these problems, many theorists point out that Marx cannot be held responsible for failure to predict the future in every respect. They also note, with some validity, that Marx was not concerned with formulating exact universal laws, only historical tendencies (see Wright 1997; Appelbaum 1978a, 1978b). The basic Marxian view of society, they claim, must not be considered a deterministic model of society but a guide to our thinking. As we noted in our earlier discussion of Marx, recent Marxian theorists are correct in stating that the political and deterministic–materialistic Marx has been overly stressed in the past. Nevertheless, some specific predictions in Marxian theory have been shown to be incorrect. How are these incorrect predictions dealt with?

With respect to the first major problem, that of no socialist revolution in advanced capitalist nations and little revolutionary consciousness among the working class, some argue that Marx was simply inaccurate in timing. The revolution will come, sooner or later. But even if this is true, it begs the question of why it has taken so long. The Marxian response to this question can be combined with the response to the second question noted previously: Why has there been no major crisis in capitalist societies, or why have such crisis periods been managed without revolutionary changes? Two general factors are presented to account for these original inaccuracies in Marxian theory: (1) *the growth and strength of the state* and (2) *unforeseen influences on the working class.*

There has been much recent work by Marxian theorists to correct Marx's neglect of the function of the state in capitalist societies by adding Weber's insights (Miliband 1969, 1977; Harrington 1976; Therborn 1978; Wright 1997). Another group of structural Marxists even argues that a strong state has developed in capitalist societies with *some* autonomy from upper-class interests (Skocpol 1979, 1992; Althusser 1969, 1977; Poulantzas 1973, 1975; Domhoff 2002). This strong state so far has been able to manage the *collective* interests of the bourgeoisie (upper class) to prevent crisis, and has managed crisis periods to prevent revolutionary changes. This is done through (1) economic planning and control of conditions (such as a failing profit rate, inflation, reduced demand for goods produced) that could produce crisis, (2) welfare spending to control and appease the poor and unemployed during hard times, and (3) the management of conflicts within the bourgeoisie that could result in economic crisis (such as government regulation preventing competition from getting out of hand and destroying some corporations or regulating the unsound practices of big financial institutions). In other words, rather than being almost a captive of upper-class capitalists, the state is now viewed by recent Marxian theorists as somewhat autonomous and managing the economy for overall upper-class interests.

In addition to describing how the working class has been pacified by welfare state reforms, modern Marxians cite other factors as reducing revolutionary class consciousness among the working class (see primarily Herman and Chomsky 1988; Marcuse 1964; Miliband 1969; Aronowitz 1974; Piven and Cloward 1971, 1982, 1988). First of all, labor unions are seen as making some material gains for the workers, but at the expense of controlling the working class for long-term capitalist interests. In what is called *institutionalization of class conflict,* elites in big labor unions are seen as working for capitalist interests by controlling strikes and preventing workers from considering more threatening issues such as worker influence over corporate decision making.

Second, with respect to material gains, the high standard of living achieved by the working class in advanced capitalist nations is seen as co-opting labor. A consumption orientation among workers, promoted by the higher standard of living and mass advertising, was never foreseen by Marx. An outcome has been a willingness on the part of workers to support the basic capitalist system and tolerate alienating working conditions as long as they can share in the material fruits of capitalism (such as cars, boats, campers, and motorcycles).

A third factor often cited for the absence of revolutionary class consciousness is the strength of the legitimation process in advanced capitalist nations (Habermas 1975, 1984; Herman and Chomsky 1988). As noted previously, every stratification system must convince those toward the bottom of this system that their low position is somehow justified. The effects of a mass media unimagined in Marx's day, among other factors such as education (to be described in our later chapter on this process), are cited by Marxian theorists as helping to produce acceptance of the capitalist system by the general population (Kellner 1990).

The expansion of the white-collar class of technical, sales, clerical, service, and bureaucratic workers is also acknowledged by many as unforeseen by Marx. But some Marxian theorists see no serious problem for Marxian theory: This middle class is simply defined as part of the working class, although serving a different role in the capitalist system (Anderson 1974). More recently, however, the prediction that the growing middle-class jobs have been "deskilled," making them like working-class jobs (Wright et al. 1982), has been refuted empirically (Wright 1997; Wright and Martin 1987). There are, in fact, more middle-class jobs that cannot truly be defined as working-class jobs. Wright and Martin (1987) argue that this goes against Marxian predictions but can still be explained in a Marxian framework. What Marx failed to see was that capitalism has become more international, with working-class labor growing and conditions for the working class becoming worse as these types of jobs are exported by the rich capitalist nations to poor countries.

The growth of the middle class and upper middle class in advanced capitalist nations is also seen as posing another problem for the Marxian prediction of increasing criticism and opposition to the capitalist class in the population. This new middle class is usually rather conservative politically (see Mills 1953 for an excellent analysis), promoting divisions among nonowners below the rank of capitalist class. The divisions are produced because (1) white-collar workers generally have higher status (if not more pay), leading to status divisions; (2) white-collar workers (because of more interaction with capitalists and their managers) tend to identify more with capitalist interests; and (3) the expansion of the occupational structure (more ranks from top to bottom) has promoted more social mobility. In addition to creating more divisions in the working class, the expansion of the occupational structure and the hope of social mobility have reduced class consciousness because of the possibility of escape from "alienating" and low-status blue-collar work.

Finally, more Marxian theorists now agree that the Soviet Union had created a form of state communism (some say state capitalism) far from what Marx predicted.

A new class of party bureaucrats took power in the name of the working class, but rather than working for the working class, this new class was "exploitative in the exact sense that Marx gave the term—the workers and peasants were forced to surrender a surplus to the bureaucracy" (Harrington 1976:50).

Generally, the problem with Marxian theory in this respect is that Marx failed to understand the state as a generalized power structure, a power structure that can serve the particular interests of capitalists as well as the narrow interests of some other type of elite (as Weber understood; see Wright 1978a:213). Some argue that a new class of party bureaucrats emerged in the Soviet Union because that country experienced a premature communist revolution. (In 1917 Russia was not an advanced capitalist nation with a strong working class that had sufficient power to maintain its class interests.) But most also agree that Marxian theorists must understand political structures better to prevent the type of bureaucratic dominance that developed in the old Soviet Union (Wright 1978a:219).

In conclusion, it must be stressed that the preceding is not exhaustive of all the problems recent theorists have recognized in Marx's original work, nor do all Marxian theorists today agree on all the points we have described. But this is a fair sampling of some of the main problems found in Marx's work and of how recent Marxian writers have attempted to deal with these problems. For our concern, the main point is this: Marxian theorists continue to follow the basic guidelines of Marx's theoretical work. With some revision, they find this general theory useful in understanding most aspects of contemporary stratification systems.

## Some Empirical Work and Wright's Class Categories

Of course, one may well disagree that current Marxian theory is a useful guide to understanding most aspects of modern stratification systems. A clear problem remains: Marx's writings were at times ambiguous and contradictory. Even today there is much disagreement over what Marx really meant, and almost any criticism can be deflected by Marxists with one or another interpretation of the "true" Marx (a situation not unlike that in functionalism). Until more aspects of Marxian theory are examined empirically and the theory is further refined, problems will remain.

However, some interesting empirical research from a Marxian perspective has been attempted with success. The most impressive of these attempts has been Erik O. Wright's empirical work on Marxian class categories (1978a, 1978b, 1997; Wright and Perrone 1977; Wright et al. 1982; Wright and Martin 1987). By following Marx's idea that class must be defined in relation to the productive system in the society (that is, by one's relation to the means of production), rather than simply occupational status levels, as functionalists suggest, Wright has developed a four-class model. With this four-class model Wright is able to show the usefulness of the Marxian view of class and to explain some of the problems found with functional views of occupational categories.

Defining class in relation to the productive system, we have what Wright calls capitalists, managers, workers, and the petty bourgeoisie. Capitalists own the means of production (factories, banks, and so on), purchase the labor of others, and control the labor of others. Managers merely control the labor of others for capitalists and sell their labor to capitalists (such as managers of corporations). Workers, of course, have only their labor to sell to capitalists, while the petty bourgeoisie own some small means of production but employ very few or no workers. (This includes, for example, small shop or store owners.) What does this Marxian concept of class help us understand?

Most previous empirical research in social stratification has been done from the functional perspective. Class positions or, more accurately, occupational status positions, are viewed by functionalists as skill and status rankings on a continuum from lowest to highest. Pay, status, and educational levels are all assumed to roughly follow this continuum. In other words, functionalists do not consider class divisions, but rather rankings, as on a ladder. However, these previous functional studies have many problems. For one, research shows no simple relation between these occupational grades and income. Another problem is that education level does not predict income very well (see Jencks et al. 1972 on these problems).

Research by Wright and Perrone (1977) and Wright (1978b, 1997) has produced some interesting findings using the Marxian class categories. With national samples of people in the labor force, Wright's research found class position (the four categories described earlier) to be about as good in explaining differences in income between people as are occupational status and educational level. It is also interesting that capitalists have higher incomes, even controlling for (or eliminating) the effects on income from educational level, occupational skill, age, and job tenure. In other words, being a capitalist, and especially a big capitalist, irrespective of other factors such as education and occupational skill, brings more income (see also Aldrich and Weiss 1981).

There are other interesting findings. For example, education does *not* on average help workers attain a higher income, but more education does bring more income for the managerial class. Examining people *within* class categories, there is not much difference between males and females, and blacks and whites on income. The male–female and black–white overall income differences (males and whites have higher incomes) are due primarily to *class position*. That is, females and blacks have lower average incomes because they are proportionately more often than white males to be in the *working class* (as defined by Wright).

A study by Robinson and Kelley (1979) attained similar results using national samples from the United States and England. These researchers also found separate mobility patterns in terms of class position and occupational status. To attain a capitalist class position, it is best to be born of capitalist parents; to attain a high occupational position, it is best to be born of parents with high education and high occupational position.

What all this means is that a person's relation to the productive system, or means of production, does make a difference that has been ignored by most social scientists in the past. Considered another way, however, this research shows that class position defined in Marxian terms does not explain everything about social mobility and income attainment and that Marxian theory alone does not tell us all we need to know about social stratification. We will return to this theme at the end of this chapter.

Let us conclude our discussion by noting a final criticism that brings us to the next group of conflict theories. Perhaps the most important weakness of Marxian theory is the assumption that class or economic conflicts are the only conflicts of interest among people or groups, or at least the most important conflicts. It is because of this assumption that Marxian theorists can foresee equality and harmony (no conflict) when the private ownership of productive forces (capital, factories, and so on) is eliminated. History, at least so far, and except for small, exceptional human groups, suggests this assumption is incorrect. Inequality may be reduced to a degree with the elimination of private ownership of productive forces, but there are other interests in conflict and other conflict groups in modern societies.

# Power Conflict Theories

Other conflict theories of social stratification follow what we have described as an uncritical-conflict paradigm. Most important, these theories view conflict as a more pervasive aspect of human beings and human societies, a condition not restricted to economic relations. As Dahrendorf (1959:208) puts it, "It appears that not only in social life, but wherever there is life, there is conflict." Or as Collins (1975:59) tells us, "For conflict theory, the basic insight is that human beings are sociable but conflict-prone animals."

The label "uncritical-conflict theorist" is a bit unfair. We are *not* saying that these theorists are often uncritical of exploitation and inequality, or unsympathetic toward those at the bottom of the stratification system. But these theorists agree that conflict and exploitation, in one form or another and to some degree, will always be found among human beings and in human societies. It is only from this understanding of the conflict in all societies, they argue, that we can ever learn to deal with, and perhaps reduce, inequality and exploitation. Like Weber, however, they tend to be pessimistic about this possibility.

Aside from telling us about the conflict nature of human beings and human societies, what, specifically, does this type of conflict theory have to say about social stratification? Beginning from the assumption that people have conflicting interests of many types, they suggest that a more general view of power and conflict is needed to understand social stratification. Power may be defined in many ways, but most broadly it means the ability to compel (through force, rewards, or other means) another individual to do what you want, or to give you what you want, even when it is against the other person's interests to do so. Whatever the means of power (economic, political, military, and so on), it is a generalized commodity that can serve many interests or goals. Furthermore, if one wants to understand a widespread social arrangement such as social stratification, it must be recognized that collectives of individuals can have common interests and work together to meet these common interests. Thus, to understand a *system* of social stratification, we must understand organized class or group interests, rather than random individual conflicts.

## *Dahrendorf's Conflict Theory*

One of the most influential conflict theories of social stratification is that of Ralf Dahrendorf (1959). He begins his theory by describing the strong and weak points of Marxian theory, then adds to Marx's strong points what he sees as the strong points of Weber's work. In his review of Marx, Dahrendorf agrees that societies must be viewed from the perspective of conflict and differing interests. Furthermore, he believes that Marx was correct to focus on both organized (or manifest) and unorganized (or latent) *group* interests to understand the more fundamental aspects of social stratification.

In other words, the social scientist must understand not just the organized and manifest group conflicts but also the manner in which group or class interests are distributed in a society and whether or not a particular group or class recognizes its latent group interests and acts upon these interests. The potential for these latent group interests to become manifest is always present. Finally, Dahrendorf accepts Marx's primary *two-class model.* There are always, from his perspective, superordinate and subordinate classes.

Unlike Marx, Dahrendorf recognizes all kinds of individual or group interests. There are interests in obtaining more material rewards, freedom, status recognition, leisure, all kinds of services from others, and so on. But the main point is that the *means* to attaining these interests are related to authority positions within. In other words, the *haves* get what they want because they are on top in the political and economic bureaucracies, while the *have-nots* find it in their interests to challenge the status quo that assigns them low positions and low rewards (Dahrendorf 1959:176).

## Summary and Critiques of Power Conflict Theories

Although attention has been focused on Dahrendorf's theory of social stratification, there are other theories that generally fit within the uncritical-conflict paradigm. In most respects, Lenski's (1966, 1984) theory, discussed briefly in Chapter 3, is in this category. We say "in most respects" because with hunting and gathering societies and industrial societies Lenski reverts to a few functional assumptions in explaining social stratification.

Randall Collins (1975) has also constructed a conflict theory based on various conflicting interests. Especially interesting and useful with Collins's theory is that he combines microlevel (individual or small-group level) analysis from social interaction theorists such as Goffman (1959) and Garfinkel (1967) with macrolevel analysis. More than other theories, Collins's work is devoted to explaining all types of human behavior (such as family relations, social interaction, and conversation) that is influenced by a system of social stratification.

Another important theorist to mention is Pierre Bourdieu, a French sociologist who became respected in the United States in the 1990s as he had been in France for some time. (His death in 2002 made the front pages of most respected French newspapers.) Bourdieu's style of conflict theory has similarities to that of Collins in that Bourdieu tried to combine the macro- and microlevels of analysis, especially in how individuals make sense of the world in which they live (Bourdieu 1993). But from a French structuralist tradition, Bourdieu also recognized how these meanings people have of the world are shaped or limited from objective structures in the society. In social stratification, for example, Bourdieu recognized that economic class positions that individuals hold shape their worldviews and also what is usually called culture. Thus, Bourdieu's work is very useful in helping us understand how "class subcultures" are shaped and thus how people in different class positions can have different tastes, lifestyles, and even value preferences (1984, 1996). Through differing class subcultures people of different classes tend to draw lines around their class "in-group" and the "out-group" of people in other class positions. Thus, people in higher-class positions come to define those of lower-class positions as different and perhaps not as capable of fitting into higher positions in the class system. One can say that from this perspective, "people compete about culture and they compete with it" (Jenkins 1992:128). As we see in Chapter 12 on social mobility, this perspective has contributed much to our understanding of how social mobility might be restricted or enhanced by how people in higher-class positions (as teachers with lower-class children) evaluate others in terms of their knowledge of "higher culture."

While Bourdieu's theories of class cultural distinctions, or tastes, certainly help us understand many aspects of modern stratification systems and "class cultures," there are questions about how widely the concept applies outside of Europe and even among countries within Europe. Chan and Goldthorpe (2007a, 2007b) have found Bourdieu's concept of class cultures to have validity in explaining some worldviews and things like newspaper readership in Great Britain. However, others question the extent to which the concept of class cultures fits other countries, especially the United States (Daloz 2010; Calhoun, Lipuma, and Postone 1993; Wacquant 1993). Without old aristocratic traditions, and with more of a mass middle-class culture in the United States, we seem to find fewer class cultural taste differences compared to Europe.

We do not have the space to consider all the differences and particular character-istics of the various power conflict theories, but we should summarize their common principles. They all begin from the assumptions that (1) theories of social stratification must be grounded in differing individual and group interests, (2) these interests are var-ied, and (3) they form the basis of class conflict. Most important is how groups come together within organized social structures that form systems of social stratification.

Most criticisms of this general type of conflict theory are related to the assump-tions held by other theorists. For example, functionalists charge that individuals primar-ily seek status in terms of a common value system, which in turn leads people to ensure that needs of the social system are met. Critical-conflict theorists, of course, tend to stress economic relations as primary.

But focusing on Dahrendorf's theory reveals more serious criticisms involving his very general treatment of bureaucratic organizations. It may be agreed that these are all structures of hierarchical authority relations, with some people having more authority than others. But considering cross-national and cross-historical comparisons, surely some imperatively coordinated associations are at times more important within a nation than others (Giddens 1973:73). This is not the same as the Marxist critique because it may be that in some nations economic associations are primary, while in others political, religious, military, or other associations may be more important in the overall stratification system.

Also, with Dahrendorf's theory, how do we decide who is in which of the two classes? At times this is a simple matter. At General Motors the board of directors belongs to the superordinate class, while a worker on the assembly line is in the sub-ordinate class. But what about engineers, lesser managers, line supervisors? In other words, where do we draw the line between the two classes? Dahrendorf could respond that it depends on the particular interests that are in conflict. This response, however, is too arbitrary. There are degrees of authority, but recognizing this makes the theory much more complex and at times confusing.

Before concluding, let us consider some relevant and interesting empirical studies on this issue. Robinson and Kelley's (1979) study was mentioned earlier in relation to

Marxian class categories, but it also attempted to measure and test some of Dahrendorf's views of class (see also Robinson and Garnier 1985). The capitalist class (in a Marxian sense) was defined and measured as those who own or control the means of production, while Dahrendorf's class categories were measured in terms of *degrees* of authority (noting the earlier criticism). Robinson and Kelley measured degrees of authority by how many levels of employees were above and below the individual. As a third definition of ranking, they measured the usual occupational status or skill levels. Their data consisted of national samples of employed people in England and the United States.

Robinson and Kelley correlated these differing measures of class and occupational status with three main dependent variables. They found (1) that all three class/occupational measures did about equally well in explaining income differences among individuals in their sample; (2) that all three class/occupational measures helped explain differing class identification in the sample (for example, whether people saw themselves in the upper class, middle class, or working class); and (3) that all three class/occupational measures were related to differing political party voting (that is, voting Democrat or Republican in the United States), except for class position (in Dahrendorf's terms) in the United States.

Finally, as discussed in part earlier, their findings show that there are distinct lines of class and occupational attainment. For example, having a father with a high class position, in either Marx's or Dahrendorf's definition of class, will provide a better chance for the son to attain the high class position also. At the same time, having a father with a high occupational position as defined by status and skill level will provide a better chance for the son to attain the high occupational position also. But the processes are not strongly related. That is, having a father with a high *occupational* status position will not be of much help for the son in attaining a high *class* position (defined in either of the two ways), and vice versa.

Kalleberg and Griffin (1980) examined the effects of bureaucratic power divisions on income and job fulfillment. In this study they were concerned with bureaucratic authority divisions in both capitalist sector organizations (corporations) and noncapitalist organizations (such as government agencies and educational and civic organizations). To measure bureaucratic authority divisions Kalleberg and Griffin (1980:737) asked two questions of respondents in their sample: (1) Are they self-employed? (2) Do they supervise anyone as part of their job? "Individuals who responded 'yes' to both were defined as *employers*. Individuals who responded 'no' to both were defined as *workers*. *Managers* were those who responded 'no' to the first and 'yes' to the second."

The researchers admit that this is a very rough measurement of authority divisions, and their findings are probably weaker than if more precise measures were possible. It may also be added that degrees of authority are missed in these measures. But the findings are significant; there were clear income differences between these divisions, even after controlling for the influence on income from job tenure, work experience, educational level, occupational skill level, and mental ability. And although the income of people in capitalist sector organizations was greater, the income differences in relation to authority divisions were significant in both capitalist and noncapitalist sectors examined separately. Finally, the higher the position in the authority structure, the greater the job fulfillment claimed.

Thus, in addition to having some analytic value, Dahrendorf's class theory receives some empirical support. But as we noted in our discussion of recent Marxian theorists, Dahrendorf's theory does not tell us all we need to know about social stratification. We will return to this theme in our concluding section after we examine some relevant information from sociobiology.

### Modern World System Theory

Over the last couple of decades it has become clear that one of the most important new theories related to social stratification comes under the general title of the **modern world system** theory. As we have seen to some extent already in the previous pages of this book, and as we will see to a much greater extent in coming pages, no clear understanding of social stratification in the United States or any other country can now be achieved without reference to the effects of the modern world system. The growing income inequality in the United States, the growing class conflict in Europe over changes in class relations and rewards, to name just a few topics, must be considered in relation to changes in the modern world system. We must also include major world events, such as colonialism, World War I, World War II, and the cold war, along with all of the events and conditions these world-shaping events caused, as related to changes in the modern world system.

Because of its importance, we will examine world system theory more extensively in the beginning of Chapter 14 on the world stratification system and at that point consider the works of people such as Wallerstein (1974, 1977, 1980, 1989, 1999), Frank (1969, 1975, 1978, 1998), Bornschier (1995), Chase-Dunn (1989), and Chirot (1986). In summary, the basic point of the modern world system theory is that from about A.D. 1500 when the new modern world system began, nations have been in competition with each other for dominance over other nations, especially with respect to economic domination. **Core nations** are the richer nations on top of the modern world system, with **semiperiphery** and **periphery nations** in lower ranks in this system, much like middle class, working class, and the poor in an internal stratification system. As the previous description suggests, modern world system theory is a form of conflict theory, often considered to be a variety of neo-Marxian theory (Ritzer 2004), though as we see in Chapter 14, not all theorists in this area could be considered Marxist. But it is certainly a form of conflict theory that has many parallels to conflict theories that help us understand class conflicts and inequalities within countries such as the United States.

## The Bases of Class Stratification and Class Location

Considering the theoretical controversies in the study of social stratification, a controversy might be anticipated over how class can be defined most meaningfully as well. In large measure the controversy follows the theoretical debates (functional versus conflict theories) over which dimension of social stratification is most important (Weber's class, status, or power). Other assumptions, however, also are involved in the debate over the most useful conceptualization of class.

Dennis Wrong (1959, 1964), for example, outlines what he calls **realist** versus **nominalist** definitions of class. As Kingston's (2000) recent attempt at revival shows, the realist places emphasis on clear class boundaries—people identifying themselves as members of a particular class and interacting most with others in the same class; in other words, forming distinct social groupings based on class divisions. For the nominalist, most important are the common characteristics groups of people may have that influence their life chances and share of valued rewards in the society, such as education level, occupational position, or bureaucratic power position. People are then placed in class categories in terms of these common characteristics, whether or not they are aware of these characteristics and associate with others in the same class.

Similar to the preceding are **subjective** versus **objective** definitions of class. With the subjective view the emphasis is on whether class has meaning to the people said to be in a particular class, while the objective view stresses particular life chances or economic characteristics people may have in common. Some theorists use the term *class* to cover both views, reserving subdefinitions of class for the objective and subjective aspects. Examples would be Marx and Dahrendorf, who refer to a class in itself and latent interest groups on the objective or nominalist side of the debate, while using the term class for itself and manifest interest groups on the subjective or realist side.

Another definitional issue is whether **continuous** or **discontinuous class rankings** are most evident. The continuous view is that class or strata should be considered as ranks on a scale; there are positions from high to low, with numerous grades in between. From the continuous view it therefore becomes difficult, or even meaningless, to determine specific class boundaries. The discontinuous view, in contrast, is that there are fewer class divisions, that we can find class divisions with distinct boundaries, and that the divisions between classes are more important than differences within class divisions. Conflict theorists tend to favor the discontinuous and objective views, while functionalists tend to favor the continuous and subjective views (the second leading a few functionalists to suggest that the concept of class only weakly applies to the United States; see Nisbet 1959).

We will to some degree take sides in these debates by referring again to what may be considered the most important question in the study of social stratification, Who gets what, and why? When attempting to answer this question, we are directed to *objective class divisions* that people may commonly share. Class in a subjective sense (whether people recognize these conditions, interact with others having similar objective interests, and collectively act upon these interests) is important but may or may not exist, depending on conditions that must be explored later.

To identify some of the most important objective factors behind class location, we must consider the *occupational structure,* the *bureaucratic authority structure,* and the *capitalist property structure.* We must understand how people's life chances are affected by these structures, separately and in combination, and, for our present purpose, how people are ranked in each. When we do this, we will also find that the debate over how class should be viewed (continuous versus discontinuous, objective versus subjective) differs to some extent with respect to which of the three structures is seen as shaping class interests. After examining the divisions created by these three structures, we can discuss how these divisions converge on what is commonly referred to as the upper, middle, working, and lower classes in the advanced or postindustrial societies.

# Occupational Structure

By position in the occupational structure we are referring to one's relation to the market, as Weber, in part, referred to economic class. (The other economic class ranking Weber used was similar to Marx's ownership of the means of production.) In other words, within the occupational structure, people are ranked in terms of skill level and tend to receive greater rewards (such as income) with higher skills. (The exact relationship between rewards and skill level will be examined later.) Thus, with the occupational structure we are stressing objective class factors and a continuous ranking. We are not saying that these rankings are determined and rewards given because of the contribution to the needs of society made by a person in his or her occupation, or that status is received primarily because a certain occupation or skill level meets society's needs (the functionalist position). Rather, we are suggesting that rewards are given because the jobs are more or less important to the people (economic or bureaucratic elites) who are more in control of the rewards to be given. This, of course, is the conflict position.

# Bureaucratic Authority Divisions

With bureaucratic organizations we are concerned with organized authority or power structures. As Weber (1947:325) observed, "the imperative coordination of the action of a considerable number of men requires control of a staff of persons"; that is, divisions formed in relation to bureaucratic authority (formalized, legitimated power).

The number of staff and their exact function vary across different organizations, but there are usually top positions such as president, chairman of the board, chief executive officer, and vice president. Below this level we may find many staff positions in charge of more specific functions or departments within the organization, such as assistant secretaries in the federal government or deans within a university. Below these typically many-layered authority positions, and closer to the low skilled employees employees at the bottom, we usually find supervisory positions. These include such positions as plant foreperson, department chair in a university, and employee supervisors in a state agency. Finally, at the very bottom are employees performing various types of labor within the organization—assembling cars, sending bills to customers, watching over welfare recipients and determining eligibility for public assistance, and so on.

# Divisions within the Property Structure

In a Marxian sense it is the property structure that creates a primary division between those who own the major means of production and control both the use of this property and the profits derived from it, and those who fit none of these conditions. In reality, of course, the advance of industrialization under capitalism has created a property structure that is in no way simple.

However, neither was it simple when Marx produced his major works; and, as previously noted (in Chapter 4), many differing levels and descriptions of what he called class can be found in these works. But central to the concept of class for Marx was how people are tied to the productive forces (the means of production) in the society—in other words, the relations of production.

A primary question remains: What is the most useful means of defining property relations or divisions for our present purpose? Following the main idea that class (in this sense) must be defined in the context of people's relation to the means of production in a society, Erik O. Wright (see Wright 1997; Wright and Perrone 1977; Wright 1978a) defined *capitalists* as those who own the means of production and employ many others; *managers* as those who work for capitalists and control the labor of others; *workers* as those who simply sell their labor to capitalists; and the *petty bourgeoisie* as those who own their means of production but employ few workers. With these definitions Wright was able to show significant income differences between class categories and differing effects of education in obtaining more income (such as managers receiving a greater return from more education).

# The Convergence of Occupation, Power, and Property on Class Stratification

Thus far we have examined divisions or ranks in what many consider three of the most important institutional structures in our society. Not only do these three hierarchical structures help shape the interests of major divisions or classes within the population, for the most part they also provide the setting in which conflicts (sometimes overt, sometimes hidden) over valued rewards take place.

## *A Working Definition of Class*

It is time to provide the working definition of *class* that will guide the remainder of our examination of class stratification in contemporary societies. One goal of this chapter has been to demonstrate why we must reject any definition of *class* based on a single dimension of inequality (whether this is occupational status, bureaucratic power, property relations, or anything else). However, in the face of such complexity, how can class be defined in order to capture the many divisions and rankings we have outlined? As noted in beginning this work, we can define a class as a group of people who share common objective interests in the system of social stratification.

A second goal of this chapter has been to specify these important objective interests. We are *not* suggesting that there are three (or more) separate class systems (occupational class, bureaucratic class, and property class systems). Rather, these three structures tend to converge, producing groups or classes that have common interests with respect to all three structures. In contemporary societies, more often than not the *interaction* or *convergence* of all three influences life chances and rewards, or who gets what, and why.

In identifying classes in relation to the convergence of the three institutional structures we have thus far examined, we will use the rather standard labels *upper class, middle class, working class,* and *lower class* (or the poor). In addition, we have inserted between the upper and middle classes a group that will be called the *corporate class.* As is suggested in Table 5-2, members of the upper class tend to have high positions in the occupational structure and bureaucratic authority structure and are primary owners of the means of production. Those in the corporate class are high in both the

## TABLE 5-2

### The Convergence of Occupational, Bureaucratic, and Property Divisions on Class Categories

| Class categories | Positions in three main types of institutional structures | | |
| --- | --- | --- | --- |
| | Occupation | Bureaucratic authority | Property relation |
| Upper class | High | High | Owner |
| Corporate class | High | High | Nonowner/low |
| Middle class | High to mid-level | Mid-level | Nonowner/low |
| Working class | Mid-level to low | Low | Nonowner/low |
| Lower class | Low | Low | Nonowner |

occupational and bureaucratic authority structures but lack significant ownership of the means of production. Those in the middle class are high- to mid-level in occupation, mid-level in specific bureaucratic structures (when not self-employed professionals), and nonowners. However, while the percentage of the American population who are self-employed or are small business owners who hire a few workers (the "petty bourgeoisie") has been declining during the 20th century in the United States (and other industrial nations), during the 1980s and especially 1990s there has been a slight rise in self employed people (Wright 1997:114–145). By the 1990s, in fact, 16 percent of the labor force said they had been self employed sometime in their life, rising to around 20 percent in the 2000s. Thus, we must recognize that some in the middle class (and even working class) can own some small means of production (their own tools, shop, etc.), be self employed, or even hire a few workers and be included among the "petty bourgeoisie." This is indicated in Table 5-2 to show that some among the middle class and even working class could be described as having low amounts of property. Those in the working class are mid-level to low in occupation, low in specific bureaucratic organizations, and usually nonowners. Finally, those in the lower class are low in occupation and bureaucratic authority and, of course, are nonowners.

The class divisions outlined in Table 5-2 represent something of a synthesis of the three main paradigms of social stratification described in Chapter 4 and the present chapter. Remembering that functional theorists focus on occupational status, power conflict theorists focus on authority divisions, and Marxists or ruling-class theorists focus on property class divisions, all three sets of divisions have been included in Table 5-2. However, two points must be stressed: First, we have rejected the functional view of occupational status ranks in favor of Weber's view of occupational competition through skill or relation to the marketplace; and second, we have stressed the convergence of the occupational structure, authority structure, and property structure.

This typology of objective class positions is not all-inclusive. There are people or even categories of people that provide problems of placement in the typology. However, it is the function of a typology, as with a theory, to provide some understanding in the face of apparent complexity. The value of understanding class with respect to positions in the three main institutional structures we have examined should be evident in coming chapters.

# A Note on Sociobiology

As described previously, stratification theorists in this uncritical-conflict category maintain that conflict and inequality (of some kind, to some degree) will always be found in human societies. While most of these theorists suggest only implicitly that conflict and inequality are related to selfish human nature, others are quite clear in their arguments that selfish human nature is behind much of the inequality and aggression found in human societies (see van den Berghe 1974, 1978). To the extent that this is true, we find further support for at least some aspects of this type of stratification theory. Let us examine some of the evidence.

Sociobiology is a new and rather controversial area of study in sociology. Some of the most important works in this area were published by Wilson (1975) and were soon followed by many critical (see Barash 1977; Lenski 1977; Quadagno 1979; Lewontin, Rose, and Kamin 1984) and supportive publications (see van den Berghe 1977, 1978; Ellis 1977; Bolin and Bolin 1980; Maryanski 1994; Maryanski and Turner 1992; Crippen 1994). The main argument for sociobiology is that by relating our studies of society and human behavior to certain biological tendencies within human beings we can increase our understanding of some aspects of this behavior. The counterargument is that although biology can help us understand the behavior of other animals, human behavior is much more complex and almost completely shaped by learning, culture, the social environment, and other nonbiological factors.

A basic assumption of sociobiology in that what Charles Darwin described as the process of natural selection has resulted in the survival of only those human beings most genetically fit for the environment in which they existed. Those who were best equipped genetically to survive in their environment in turn passed their genes on to the next generation of human beings. The process has continued into the present generation. Most important is that (1) it takes many generations for a gene pool to be altered significantly; and (2) because over 99 percent of human existence has been in an environment far different from the one that exists in modern societies, the earliest human environment shaped much of our biologically influenced behavior.

What was it about this early environment that shaped the genetically influenced behavior in people? In contrast to advanced industrial societies, it is argued, basic necessities such as food were seldom secure for early human beings. Competition for the resources that did exist was usually great, and more often than not the competition was from other animals as well (see van den Berghe 1978:30). If this is true—and the description does seem reasonable—over the few million years that human beings were developing in this environment, the most aggressive and selfish people were the ones who survived (van den Berghe 1978:46).

If all this is true, however, how do we explain the frequent altruistic, generous, and cooperative behavior also found among human beings? Sociobiologists offer two additional arguments. As for the first, it is pointed out that survival of a gene pool requires altruistic behavior toward kin (Wilson 1975:117; Bolin and Bolin 1980). That is, if a particular set of genes is to survive, there must be protection or even sacrifice for close kin (especially children). Second, it is argued that more general cooperation was also required for survival. This cooperative behavior is especially related to hunting: "For early hominids, solitary hunting or even scavenging was not a realistic possibility" (van den Berghe 1978:46). Human beings with a tendency toward this cooperative small-group behavior, sociobiologists conclude, were more likely to survive (Leakey and Lewin 1977:149; Pfeiffer 1977:48).

Sociobiology is a relatively new area of study, and very little of what we can judge to be well-established explanations of human behavior can be found in the literature yet. There is evidence of genetic factors behind *some* cases and *some* types of human behavior, such as extensive violence, alcoholism, and homosexuality. There is also evidence that many of the biological effects on human behavior come in the form of emotions located in brain function. Yet, even many who support this area of study admit that some writers have been overly ambitious in trying to set biological foundations for human behavior (see Bolin and Bolin 1980). Clearly, even if there are some biologically based tendencies in human behavior, the wide variety of behavior among human societies tells us that most of what we do is shaped by nonbiological factors. But the preceding description of a biological tendency toward both selfish and altruistic or cooperative behavior does seem reasonable.

What do these selfish and cooperative tendencies in human behavior help us understand about social stratification? Probably not much. It is absurd to think that a set of genes leads us to establish feudal systems or caste systems rather than join the Peace Corps. But biologically influenced selfish behavior may lead us to maximizing our rewards under certain conditions. Combined with a tendency toward cooperative behavior, people do tend to share with others, at the same time they are cooperating to exploit others. All of these types of behavior are common in human stratification systems.

Under conditions of scarcity, people tend to become more aggressive. In an earlier chapter we examined archaeological evidence for this type of aggressive behavior during the scarcity that led to early agrarian settlements about 10,000 to 15,000 years ago. Under conditions of adequate resources but no surplus, we found there was evidence of more cooperative and sharing behavior. Under conditions of surplus goods, people tend to be more selfish, while cooperating with a few to control the surplus. This is precisely the behavior that many sociobiologists predict (see van den Berghe 1974:785).

But this tells us very little of what we need to know about systems of social stratification. It does tell us that we must recognize a selfish tendency among people, and a tendency to cooperate to exploit others under certain conditions. The task for theories of social stratification is to recognize these tendencies and specify how and when this selfish behavior will be maximized or minimized. Perhaps most important, stratification theories must specify how the social structure in a particular society determines which interests (attaining ownership of factories, political power, positions in imperatively coordinated associations, or others) are most important.

# ⚹ Theories of Social Stratification: A Conclusion

In this chapter and the preceding one we examined some of the leading theories of social stratification. We have noted some of the value in functional theories but for the most part found them quite limited. We have noted more value in various conflict theories but again found some weakness. Theories, as Einstein put it, are attempts at simplification. The general task of a theory—any theory—is to evaluate the many factors influencing a phenomenon such as social stratification in order to detect which of the factors or set of factors provides the clearest explanation. It is then the task of social scientists to examine the logic of each theory, balance and weigh the evidence put forth as support for each theory, and make a decision as to which of the competing theories or group of theories is most useful. However, the task is even more complex when we find that some theories answer some questions best while other theories answer other questions.

In the study of social stratification, we mainly want to know who gets what, and why. Related to this question are others. How are inequalities maintained? Why are inequalities and the groups that receive the most rewards in the society often quite stable over long periods of time? Why do stratification systems change? Upon balancing and weighing the evidence presented in this chapter, in those that follow, and in our review of history, we have concluded that conflict theories are better able to answer more questions about social stratification.

A main assumption is that *stratification systems are attempts to reduce overt conflict over the distribution of valued goods and services in a society.* Once a system of social stratification is established, the manner in which valued goods and services are distributed requires less conflict and aggression, at least for a time. All of this means, of course, that at the base of social stratification we find individual and, most important, group conflicts. These conflicts may be more hidden at times, the distribution of rewards may be less contested, the power of those at the top less challenged. But this only shows that the stratification system has, for a time at least, succeeded in regulating and controlling the conflicts of interest. As our review of history has shown, however, the conflicts regulated by a system of social stratification are brought to the forefront again and again.

With the various factors helping to shape the nature of stratification systems in mind, we can begin by focusing on stratification systems in advanced industrial societies, especially the United States. We will begin with the structures of social stratification, that is, the class and caste positions and their characteristics, and then move to what can be called processes of social stratification, which involve changes and movements in the stratification system.

## Summary

Following the introduction of the three major paradigms of social stratification in the previous chapter, we have examined the modern varieties of functional theory, critical-conflict theory, and uncritical-conflict theory. After a brief review of the history of sociology and views of social stratification in the United States, we considered the functional theories of Davis and Moore and then Talcott Parsons. Because of the importance placed on the status dimension of social stratification by functional theory, we also examined the nature of occupational status ranking in modern societies and scales to measure occupational status ranks in sociological research. Modern critical-conflict theories of social stratification were introduced by examining some of the problem aspects of Marxian theory. Modern Marxian theories today are primarily divided among those who focus on different problems with the original Marxian theory and how difficulties with the original theory can be corrected. Some of the best modern Marxian theories have combined Marxian insights on economic class divisions with Weber's view of the state and bureaucratic power in capitalist industrial societies. We then examined more recent uncritical-conflict theories that generally can be called power conflict theories. Finally, with our discussion of theory completed, we presented a more detailed analysis of the occupational, bureaucratic authority, and property dimensions behind the class divisions in modern industrial societies such as the United States.

## Note

1. It is interesting to look more closely at studies conducted in the United States and in former communist countries. Yanowitch (1977:105) describes similar occupational prestige studies conducted in Russia, and Parkin (1971) describes such studies conducted in Poland and Yugoslavia. These studies from communist countries show a consistent difference from those from the United States; working-class or manual labor occupations in communist nations are ranked significantly *higher* than in the United States (higher even than many white-collar or nonmanual occupations).

   A conclusion is that a communist ideology that praises the working class, an ideology maintained in part to justify elite dominance, has had an influence on the population's concept of occupational prestige. This conclusion is further supported when we find that occupations in *industries* (such as heavy production) that are given more recognition by the communist elite (by stressing rapid economic development) receive more occupational prestige, even compared with the same occupation in less favored industries (Yanowitch 1977:107).

   In addition, the income influence on occupational prestige is shown, because working-class or manual jobs receive more pay than most low-level white-collar or nonmanual jobs in Russia (Yanowitch 1977:30). Furthermore, manual jobs in industrial sectors stressed by the communist elite receive more pay than the same manual jobs in industrial sectors that are not stressed (Yanowitch 1977:32).

# The American Class Structure

# The Upper Class

During the late 1800s and early 1900s there was an explosion of new wealth in the United States. Many of the people who originally made great fortunes were not acceptable to the U.S. upper class. Only the future generations of these wealthy families could make it into the social upper class. William Randolf Hearst was certainly one of these. Despite his wealth and political power, he was rejected by the upper class. Flaunting wealth, as Hearst did with his California "castle" pool area shown above and his lavish parties for Hollywood movie stars, is not typical of the American upper class.

*SOURCE:* © CORBIS; ALL RIGHTS RESERVED

## Chapter Outline

The upper class in the United States and in other Western industrial nations is no longer as powerful as that found during the early 20th century. Still, there are certainly powerful people and institutions they dominate. No industrial nation today can be fully understood without reference to these people and institutions, their interests and motives. In this chapter and the next we examine the top of the stratification system, particularly in the United States. We begin by considering the nature and means of influence held by an upper class of interrelated families. Then, in Chapter 7, we consider the nature and means of influence held by what we have called a corporate class. To be sure, there is some overlap or interrelationship between the upper class and the corporate class. But as the size and complexity of major corporations increase in capitalist societies, some argue that the corporate class is emerging out of the old upper class of family wealth to maintain dominance. Still, even to the extent that this corporate class is emerging with greater power, the upper class continues to share the top of the stratification system, and the base of power created by upper-class wealth was what made a corporate class possible.

# ⚔ Locating the Upper Class

Probably one of the most used, and abused, terms referring to the people in a position of superiority in the society is the **upper class.** In everyday language the term can be found describing a wealthy small-town merchant, higher professional people such as physicians, celebrities, and movie stars, or anyone with wealth or income substantially above the average. Most likely, however, none of these categories would qualify as truly upper class.

The "true" upper class is so removed from the experience of most people that for them local physicians or current movie stars become the only candidates for the position of upper class. But wealth, power, education, or fame by themselves (or in combination, for that matter) will not assure one of upper-class status. So exclusive is this group that only from 0.5 percent to 1 percent of the population in this country would qualify.

Names such as Du Pont, Mellon, Rockefeller, Vanderbilt, and Carnegie may come to mind as signifying the upper class. Most of those who are members today, however, are unknown outside this exclusive social circle. In fact, many of the names identified with upper-class membership were at one time excluded from this social circle. The "original" Rockefeller, John D. Rockefeller, who made the family millions (later billions) in oil during the late 1800s, was rejected by some in this social circle as a gangster (see Lundberg 1968:343). Even former presidents of the United States are usually of questionable material for upper-class membership.

Clearly, such criteria as wealth, fame, and power do not ensure upper-class status. More important is the kind of wealth and how old it is, a certain lifestyle rather than celebrity recognition, and the source of power rather than power per se. Remember that Max Weber described three dimensions of stratification as class, status, and party (or power). These three typically converge, with upper-class families usually at the top on all three dimensions. Simply effecting a certain lifestyle, however, would not be enough. Being involved in the social institutions of the upper class—such as social clubs, expensive private schools, exclusive summer resorts, debutante balls, high-status charities, and cultural events that promote a certain lifestyle—is most important.

The United States has never had an aristocracy in the true sense of the word. As a new nation, born in an age of revolt against European traditions of aristocratic rule, the United States proved to be less than fertile ground for a well-developed royalty. A 19th-century French diplomat and author, Alexis de Tocqueville (1969), marveled at the spirit of equality that seemed to thrive in this new nation at the time of his visit in the early 1800s. But old cultural traditions, even when transmitted from abroad, die hard. Before the wounds of the Revolutionary War had healed, the founders of this new nation were considering whether or not the position of president should be hereditary and what the proper title should be. (Should it be "His Highness the President of the United States," "His Serene Highness the President of the United States," or, thought Washington himself, "High Mightiness"? See Amory 1960:61.)

The urge to establish some kind of aristocratic tradition, even if it lacked legal support, as in Europe, did not stop with the nation's leadership positions. Attempts to establish exclusive societies signifying a family pedigree and hereditary social status emerged quickly. First there was the Society of Cincinnati (having nothing to do with the city), founded in 1783, which originally included Washington, Hamilton, and Knox as members (Amory 1960:41). There was also the First Families of Virginia (Amory 1960:43), mentioned by Max Weber as an example of a status group established to restrict social intercourse within a circle of acceptable hereditary families. But this nation was to wait about 100 years before anything resembling a national aristocracy could emerge.

It is time to offer a concise definition of *upper class*. E. Digby Baltzell (1958:7), one of the most quoted researchers in this area of study (a sociologist, and himself a member of the Philadelphia upper class), offers the following:

> The *upper class concept* . . . refers to a group of families, whose members are descendants of successful individuals (elite members) of one, two, three, or more generations ago. These families are at the top of the *social class* hierarchy; they are brought up together, are friends, and are intermarried one with another; and finally, they maintain a distinctive style of life and a kind of primary group solidarity which sets them apart from the rest of the population.

There are several components of the concept of upper class as defined here that need further explanation and detail. First, we find a stress on families who have *descended* from successful people (usually successful in terms of making a great fortune). New money is always suspect. It is assumed (and at times it is a well-founded assumption) that great wealth generated over a short period of time is somehow dirty money. Members of the upper class often view the new rich as gangsters who have acquired great wealth through illegal or immoral means (forgetting, of course, that their inherited wealth originally sprang from similar methods). For example, the Kennedy family has only recently become secure in its upper-class status because the father (Joseph Kennedy) of John, Robert, and Teddy Kennedy was believed to have acquired the family millions in illegal whiskey deals during Prohibition. A logical conclusion from this requirement of "descendants of success and wealth" for upper-class membership is that from the beginning all who were not white Anglo-Saxon Protestants were excluded. Perhaps as much as being a bootlegger during the Prohibition era, Joseph Kennedy was rejected because he was from Catholic descendants. The history of the American upper class has been one of British (and to a much lesser extent, German) domination. Studies show that in many industries the upper class and corporate elite are still dominated by people of British ancestry (Ingham 1978), and extensive studies of the corporate elite find the vast majority to be white Anglo-Saxon Protestants (Alba and Moore 1982; Mintz 1975). All other minorities have been almost completely or completely excluded from the beginning of upper-class circles in the United States, which includes people of Jewish background, in contrast to some common myths in America.

Tied to the requirement of descendants of success and wealth, upper-class members must cultivate a "distinctive style of life." This cultivation takes time, and few of the new rich are able to make it. One must be involved with the arts and the right charities, and must acquire a whole host of proper manners and traits to be displayed among high society. The crude Texas millionaire, though he or she may try, will usually find that his or her efforts in cultivating the proper style of life are judged unacceptable.

There are also the women who must attach themselves to their husbands' success if they are to break into the upper class. The wife is an equal partner in displaying the proper lifestyle to gain acceptance. She must be involved in the right charity work and community organizations to enhance the status and power of the upper class in general, as well as the position of her husband (Ostrander 1984). Many years ago Thorstein Veblen (1899), in his famous work *The Theory of the Leisure Class,* also noted the importance of women in displaying a lifestyle that would make one an acceptable upper-class member.

The men, of course, must display a lifestyle that only great wealth can bring. But this display requires much time and effort—time and effort that men busy managing their wealth may not have to spare. Also, there is the display of wealth in the style of dress that business dress codes often (especially in earlier days) prohibited. Thus, it falls to the women to involve themselves in activities that only great wealth (and servants at home) will allow, and to show their great wealth through expensive dress and jewelry.

We also find that, according to Baltzell's definition, the upper class tends to be "brought up together, are friends, and are intermarried one with another." Among other things, this suggests that there is a *class consciousness* or group unity among the upper class. Several social scientists (such as Mills 1956; Baltzell 1958; Domhoff 1970, 1974, 1998, 2010) argue that the upper class shows a higher degree of class consciousness and unity of action with respect to common political and economic interests than any other class in the United States. An important reason for this is that the upper class, due to its close interaction in early school years and later in life, has created a strong "we" feeling.

This social solidarity is furthered by several important social institutions of the upper class. As Domhoff (1967:16) describes it, "Underlying the American upper class are a set of social institutions which are its backbone—private schools, elite universities, the 'right' fraternities and sororities, gentlemen's clubs, debutante balls, summer resorts, charitable and cultural organizations, and such recreational activities as foxhunts, polo matches, and yachting." Through the life cycle from childhood to adulthood, the upper class experiences these social institutions, which help promote class consciousness and unity.

In the earliest years, the young child is brought into an advantaged world of the upper class that provides many unique learning experiences and an early socialization into the world outlook and values of this class. But the formal upper-class institutions begin with the prep schools or private boarding schools. These schools are most important in transmitting the traditions and values of the upper class, as well as in forming the early friendship ties that remain in later years (Mills 1956:65; Lundberg 1968:338; Cookson and Persell 1985). Not all children of upper-class, or prospective upper-class, parents attend these boarding schools, and more recently these schools have opened their doors to a few bright students who are not upper class.

A small number of highly exclusive schools (such as Groton, Choate, and St. Andrew's) are commonly listed as most important (see Domhoff 1983:44–46; Cookson and Persell 1985:43), and old school ties formed at such schools seem more important as an identification of upper-class status than those formed at the elite universities attended in later life. The girls of the upper class have their elite prep schools as well. These girls' schools have not been given equal importance, and the standard list is somewhat larger, but they serve the same basic functions for the transmission of upper-class traditions and social ties later in life. (It should be noted, however, that some of these schools have become co-ed or have merged with other schools to become co-ed in recent years.)

The next stage in the life cycle, especially for the upper class, leads to college. With a high degree of regularity the graduates of exclusive prep schools attend a handful of rather exclusive Ivy League colleges, such as Harvard, Yale, and Princeton (see Domhoff 1983:27). But here there is an increasing problem of upper-class identification; more and more, these institutions have opened their doors to "commoners." This is one reason that the prep school ties have become more important. The problem is not great, however, because within these Ivy League colleges, most important for upper-class identification, are exclusive fraternities, sororities, and eating clubs, which become the most important badges of upper-class standing. For example, as C. Wright Mills (1956:67) noted, there are actually "two Harvards":

> The clubs and cliques of college are usually composed of carry-overs of association and name made in the lower levels at the proper schools; one's friends at Harvard are friends made at prep school. That is why in the upper social classes, it does not by itself mean much merely to have a degree from an Ivy League college. That is assumed: the point is not Harvard, but which Harvard? By Harvard, one means Porcellian, Fly, or A.D.: by Yale, one means Zeta Psi or Fence or Delta Kappa Epsilon: by Princeton, Cottage, Tiger, Cap and Gown, or Ivy.

By the college years the exclusive social circles maintained by fraternities and sororities are important not only for their influence on later social and business ties but also for regulating the marriage market. Debutante balls serve this function earlier; however, the college years remain critical. Each of the exclusive fraternities for men has its counterpart in an equally exclusive sorority for young women of the upper class. Dating ties are maintained between upper-class fraternities and sororities, and criticism is often brought to bear on someone from one of these exclusive clubs dating outside this network. In this way the marriage market is restricted, and it becomes more certain that someone from the upper class will marry within the upper class—preventing "tragedies" such as the one depicted by Erich Segal in *Love Story*. As Baltzell (1958:26) puts it, "The democratic whims of romantic love often play havoc with class solidarity." It is always well received when, for example, a Mellon marries a Du Pont, for tremendous fortunes are merged and the unity of upper-class interests is increased. Increasingly, however, this intermarriage has become more difficult and occurs less often (Domhoff 1983:34–36).

The next set of upper-class institutions said to promote unity and class consciousness are the exclusive men's social clubs. According to Dye (1979:184) and Domhoff (1970:22–26; 2002:209–210), the most important upper-class male social clubs are the following:

Arlington (Portland)
Bohemian Club (San Francisco)
Boston (New Orleans)
Brook (New York)
Burlingame Country Club (San Francisco)
California (Los Angeles)
Casino (Chicago)
Century Association (New York)
Chagrin Valley Hunt (Cleveland)
Charleston (Charleston)
Chicago (Chicago)
Cuyamuca (San Diego)
Denver (Denver)
Detroit (Detroit)
Eagle Lake (Houston)
Everglades (Palm Beach)
Hartford (Hartford)
Hope (Providence)
Idlewild (Dallas)
Knickerbocker (New York)
Links (New York)
Maryland (Baltimore)
Milwaukee (Milwaukee)
Minneapolis (Minneapolis)
New Haven Lawn Club (New Haven)
Pacific Union (San Francisco)
Philadelphia (Philadelphia)

Piedmont Driving (Atlanta)
Piping Rock (New York)
Racquet Club (St. Louis)
Rainier (Seattle)
Richmond German (Richmond)
Rittenhouse (Philadelphia)
River (New York)
Rolling Rock (Pittsburgh)
Saturn (Buffalo)
Somerset (Boston)
St. Cecelia (Charleston)
St. Louis Country Club (St. Louis)
Union (Cleveland)
Woodhill Country Club (Minneapolis)

These clubs provide a social setting within which their typically upper-class members can share their ideas about common political and economic concerns and maintain social and business ties. Also important are the multiple-club memberships of upper-class people that help transform the upper-class network into national proportions (Mills 1956:61). Becoming a regular member of one of these clubs is no easy task. They pride themselves on being exclusive, and to a large degree view their task as gatekeepers of the upper class.

In his research on San Francisco's Bohemian Club, Domhoff (2002:51–54) reports the following membership procedures:

1. Membership is by invitation only.

2. The potential member must be nominated by at least two regular members.

3. The prospective member must then fill out application forms and list at least five club members as references.

4. Personal interviews are conducted by a membership committee.

5. A list of prospective members is then given to all regular members of the club for their opinions.

6. Finally, the prospective member must pass a vote of the membership committee.

On top of all the socializing, drinking, sporting events, and other types of recreational activities, club participation is a serious matter. As would be suspected, many business deals are made. And as Amory (1960:212) reports through one of his informants, the more important the club, the bigger the business deals: "At the Metropolitan or the Union League or the University . . . you might do a $10,000 deal, but you'd use the Knickerbocker or the Union or Racquet for $100,000 and then, for $1,000,000 you move on to the Brook or Links."

Mingling with and hearing politicians is no less important. Beside the usual discussion of various political and economic issues facing big business and the upper class, at clubs like the Bohemian Domhoff found that noonday speeches brought together top business leaders and high government officials. (See Domhoff's excellent and frequently updated Web site on all aspects of upper-class power and privilege, including often amusing information about the Bohemian Club; http://sociology.ucsc.edu/whorulesamerica/power/index.html.) For example, at one summer meeting of the Bohemian Club in 1991, Phillips (1994; also see Domhoff 2002:53) found there were seven board members from Bank of America present, four from AT&T, three from Ford, and three from General Motors, to name only a few. As with Domhoff, in gathering some of his information about the Bohemian Club, I also had an inside informant among one of my recent California students. Not all of these people were in attendance at the summer retreat, but among the hundreds of individuals on the 1994 membership list of the Bohemian Club were key corporate figures with familiar names such as David Rockefeller, James Classen, Leonard Firestone, and some male members of the Ford family. Important political figures on the membership list included Ronald Reagan, Donald Rumsfeld, George Bush, Gerald R. Ford, Henry Kissinger, Caspar Weinberger, and George P. Shultz.

Finally, we move to an "institution" that has a most interesting place in the history of the upper class in this country. In the second half of the 19th century, with new wealth emerging quite rapidly, it became increasingly difficult to determine who was in and who was still out of respectability among the upper class. A scorecard was needed—a list that could be referred to when giving a party or deciding who should be invited to any type of social event. In a rather informal way, the *Social Register* was brought into existence.

Founded in 1887, and dominated by Mrs. Edward Barry for many years, the *Social Register* is nothing more than a listing of families who are acceptable members of high society or the upper class (Amory 1960:3–7). Much of the responsibility for deciding who was listed (or dropped) was retained by Mrs. Barry (and later the other "secretaries"). To become listed, a prospective family must submit five reference letters from families already included in the *Social Register.*

The listings are still controlled by a few people, and there is always much speculation among the upper class as to why someone is dropped or included. For example, as Domhoff (1983:23) found, names are dropped for such reasons as "scandal, divorce, marrying outside of one's social class, marrying a movie star, and so forth." Perhaps for this reason, the *Social Register* has lost some of its authority today as a gatekeeper of upper-class membership. Still, several studies have shown that these volumes remain rather reliable lists of the old families that make up the center of the upper class (see Domhoff 1983:21). At its high point in 1925, the *Social Register* was published in 25 cities, but then that number was reduced to 12. Since 1976 (when publication was taken over by the Malcolm Forbes family), however, the *Social Register* has been consolidated into one large book (Domhoff 1983:20–21).

To the extent that the upper class exists today, it is at the summit of all three dimensions of social stratification (class, status, and party) described by Weber. In the preceding discussion we have focused most on the dimension of social status or esteem. This dimension is by no means the most important in determining the place of the upper class in the overall stratification system in this country, for in the final analysis wealth and political power are primary. But the social esteem dimension is important in maintaining the upper-class unity and class consciousness that in the long run affect the dimensions of economic and political power.

# ⚔ Upper-Class Dominance Today?

Most social scientists agree that the power of wealthy upper-class families was extensive at the beginning of the 20th century in this country. No one believes that the upper class completely dominated the country economically and politically; there were conflicts within this group (as there are today), and there have always been other economic and political contenders who were able to prevent complete dominance by one group. But compared with that of other groups in the country, the economic and political dominance of the upper class was most pervasive. We find much less agreement today on the current place of an upper class in the overall stratification system.

Several changes, some say, reduced the power of wealthy upper-class families in the second half of the 20th century. Most important, the large industrial and financial corporations once under the control of these wealthy families are now mostly controlled by a new group of corporate managers. In addition, it is said, the federal government has grown more independently powerful since the Great Depression of the 1930s, thus reducing upper-class power. And, it is charged, the upper class is no longer playing as important a role within government as it once did. Finally, some argue, the upper class is no longer as unified as it once was.

We begin here with an examination of information suggesting continued upper-class dominance. In the next chapter we consider evidence of the emergence of new contenders for power.

# ⚔ The Upper Class as a Governing Class

G. William Domhoff is among those most actively attempting to demonstrate that an upper class of wealth continues to have extensive dominance in the United States. He recognizes that something like what we have called here a corporate class also has extensive dominance today. Domhoff argues that it is an overlap between the upper class and the corporate class that forms the "power elite" that has most influence in both the economy and government today (see Domhoff 2010). Two major steps are involved in Domhoff's research approach: (1) He attempts to show that the upper class continues to exist and that there is enough unity among the members of this class, and (2) he presents evidence showing that this class is a governing class through its various means of influence over the economy and the political system.

In part, the second step relies on what Domhoff calls a *sociology of leadership method* to indicate that people from the upper class (measured in the first step) hold important positions within the major economic and political institutions in the country. Domhoff (1990, 2006a) has also focused on how the policy-forming process in the government and economy is shaped by upper-class influence, whether from the direct involvement of the upper class in institutional positions of power or from other, more indirect, means of influence.

In his first works (*Who Rules America?,* 1967; updated again in 1998, 2002, and 2010, and *The Higher Circles,* 1970) Domhoff included information on both the unity among the upper class and how it is able to dominate economic and political institutions.

In a subsequent work (*The Bohemian Grove,* 1974) Domhoff provided some very interesting inside information on upper-class unity and consensus-forming processes in social clubs and retreats. In still other works (*The Powers That Be,* 1979, and *The Power Elite and the State,* 1990) he provided more detail on various processes employed by the wealthy in influencing government policy.

At the outset, however, it must be stressed that, much like C. Wright Mills (1956) and even more Marxian-oriented theorists, Domhoff does *not* argue that this upper class or governing class completely dominates or rules the country politically and economically. Given the many interest groups that exist and the complexity of advanced industrial societies such as ours, no one group can be completely dominant. But when important decisions are made (involving such things as how to deal with inflation, foreign trade problems, and becoming involved in foreign conflicts), and especially when these decisions may affect the interests and well-being of the upper class, Domhoff believes that this class has more influence than any other group. Researchers in this area of study are concerned with relative *degrees* of dominance by one group or another. Reality, especially with the present subject matter, never fits nicely into clear-cut categories. For this reason, as should be evident in what follows, researchers in such an important area of study remain divided over many conclusions.

## Indicators of Upper-Class Membership

To begin, Domhoff must show that an upper class does continue to exist, and that this class maintains sufficient unity and interaction to act on common interests. Indivuduals or small groups may try to influence events on a national (or local) level. But it is most unlikely that these people will have much impact until they are united in such numbers that their power outweighs that of other groups. The wealthy, of course, have vast political and economic resources that can be mobilized to influence national events. But even the resources of these wealthy people are usually not enough, operating alone. Thus, unity and consensus are critical if they are to have an impact on major events.

As previously discussed, there are several types of upper-class institutions (ranging from elite prep schools and social clubs to listings of upper-class status in such books as the *Social Register*). Having participated in these institutions and/or being listed in the *Social Register* would seem to indicate upper-class membership. Possessing great wealth is also considered a criterion of upper-class membership, but if you are a member of a social club or listed in the *Social Register,* for example, you are assumed to be wealthy. To be specific, Domhoff (1970:21–27) originally listed five major indicators of upper-class membership (see also Domhoff 1983:44–49):

**1.** A listing in one of the various blue books or the *Social Register*

**2.** Any male member of the family attending one of the exclusive prep schools (such as those listed in Domhoff 1970)

**3.** Any male member of the family belonging to one of the exclusive social clubs (see Domhoff 1970)

**4.** Any female member of the family belonging to an exclusive club or attending an exclusive prep school or,

**5.** Upper-class membership is assumed if the "father was a millionaire entrepreneur or $100,000-a-year corporation executive or corporation lawyer" *and* the person attended an elite prep school or belonged to an exclusive club on a *more inclusive* list of these schools and clubs.

Obviously, with the top management of big corporations today averaging more than $10 million a year in compensation (see Chapter 2), category five is outdated today. But Domhoff's original research showed that these five indicators have a high degree of overlap, meaning if a person fits one they usually also fit within others as well.

## Upper-Class Unity

Some historical case studies of the upper class indicate extensive upper-class unity in some parts of the country. E. Digby Baltzell (1958), for example, has studied the Philadelphia upper class and found that the tendency of the upper class to attend the same schools, belong to the same clubs, and frequent the same resort areas leads to much unity, class consciousness, and organized political and economic activity. (For similar findings in five other cities, see Ingham 1978. For an interesting study of the community upper-class institutions and status ranking in New Orleans, see Raabe 1973.) We find major limitations with this type of research, however, the most obvious being that these are only local examinations of the upper class. If it is a national upper class and this class is able to maintain some level of unity and concerted action on a national level, the type of research done by Baltzell is not adequate. To date, Domhoff is one of the few who have attempted to demonstrate the existence of upper-class consensus and unity on a national level.

Domhoff's most interesting study of upper-class unity is contained in his book *The Bohemian Grove* (1974; also see Domhoff 2010:64–68). The Bohemian Grove is a summer retreat north of San Francisco, primarily for members of one of San Francisco's most exclusive social clubs, the Bohemian Club. For 2 weeks every summer these members (still all male at the Bohemian Club, which is fighting laws requiring it to open its doors to women) come together for relaxation, drinking, and amateur theatrical performances, among other things. Aside from the serious subject matter of the book, Domhoff paints an interesting picture of an upper-class lifestyle, which, despite the wealth and power, is not far removed from that of the middle class.

In some ways the retreat is like a Boy Scout summer camp. This image comes across most directly in the annual opening ceremony, called the *Cremation of Care* (Domhoff 1974:1–7; see also Domhoff 2002:51–54). But of course, these men are not Boy Scouts. Rather, they are people from wealthy and powerful families, major corporate executives, and political leaders. And despite what is suggested in the Cremation of Care ceremony, these men do not forget their worldly business while at the 2-week retreat. Through inside informants, a study of guest and membership lists, and a list of the actual activities during this retreat, Domhoff found that much serious work is accomplished.

In examining this retreat it is important to be specific about who is involved. Reviewing the membership list of the Bohemian Club, Domhoff (1974:30) found that 27 percent of the members are also members of the exclusive Pacific Union Club of

San Francisco. In addition, he found 45 percent of the 411 nonresident regular members (members living outside California) listed in various upper-class blue books such as the *Social Register.*

Finally, Domhoff (1974:31) interprets as a tie to the corporate elite figures showing "that at least one officer or director from forty of the fifty largest industrial corporations in America were present" at the Bohemian Grove retreat in 1970, along with directors of 20 of the top 25 banks, 12 of the top 25 life insurance companies, 10 of the top 25 in transportation, and 8 of the 25 top utilities. In total, 29 percent of the top 797 corporations in the United States were represented at just *one* 2-week retreat by at least one officer or director! Domhoff (1983:70) again examined the list of those attending the 1980 Bohemian Grove retreat and found very similar figures on corporate elite participation. Another study of those attending the 1991 retreat of the Bohemian Grove found 24 percent of the largest 1,144 corporations in the United States had at least one of their executives present, with 42 percent of the top 100 corporations outside California represented by at least one of their executives (Phillips 1994; Domhoff 2002:53).

Other important research on upper-class unity is focused on more quantitative indicators; for example, measures of association between various clubs and other policy-forming organizations to which the upper class often belongs. This type of research attempts to show that upper-class members interact extensively with one another, creating a network for cooperative political and economic activity, along with upper-class unity. In one study Domhoff (1975) was able to show that 673 of the top 797 corporations in America have at least one corporate executive represented in *just 15 clubs and policy organizations* (such as Links, Bohemian Club, and Council on Foreign Relations, and the Business Council). In Domhoff's words (1975:179), "This finding is even more impressive when we consider only the top 25 corporations in each category. Here we see that 25 of 25 industrials, 25 of 25 banks, 23 of 25 insurance companies, 24 of 25 transportation, 24 of 25 utilities, 19 of 25 retails, and 18 of 25 conglomerates are connected" by these 15 clubs and organizations. (Again, see Domhoff's excellent and frequently updated Web site on all aspects of upper-class power and privilege, including more data on corporate-class and upper-class connections; http://sociology.ucsc.edu/whorulesamerica/power/index.html.)

## Upper-Class Economic Power

If we have an upper class in this country that, because of its power, can be described as a governing class, by what means does it govern or dominate? As noted, theorists such as Domhoff consider the upper class to be dominant in both the economy and politics. But precisely how is this dominance achieved? We first examine how the upper class is said to have extensive influence over the economy through stock ownership, then turn to the question of economic power through extensive representation in major corporate offices.

### Stock Ownership

As some argue, the most important means of upper-class economic power lies in its ownership of the primary means of production. The upper class has power over our economy because of its control of the biggest corporations through stock ownership. (We discuss in more detail in the next chapter the importance of the tremendous size and concentration of major corporations today, which make such ownership even more significant.)

Legally, the ultimate control of corporations is found not with top corporate executives but with major stockholders. In a sense, top corporate executives and boards of directors are charged with managing these corporations for the real owners—the stockholders. Stockholders have the authority to elect corporate directors who are to represent stockholder interests. These directors are then responsible for general corporate policy, including the task of filling top executive positions. The day-to-day management of the corporation is in turn the responsibility of the executive officers, who must generally answer to stockholders and their representatives on the board of directors.

Assuming for now that corporate authority actually operates in this way (questions about this ideal power arrangement will be considered later), the largest stockholder or stockholders in a corporation should be in control. Thus, if we find that upper-class families have extensive stock ownership and that this stock is in major corporations, we can say that upper-class families dominate the American economy.

It is clear, as described in Chapter 2, that wealth is very unequally distributed in this country—more so even than family or personal income. One of the most important categories of wealth (because of its usual high return on investment) is corporate stock. We have seen that 1 percent of the people in this country owned almost 40 percent of the privately held corporate stock in 2004 (also see Keister 2000:92–95). Thus, from 1 to 0.5 percent of the people in this country (roughly equal to the number Domhoff believes is in the upper class) hold the largest block of the privately owned corporate stock.

This concentration of private stock ownership is even more striking when we find that most of the remaining stock is controlled by large financial corporations (see Blair 1995; Domhoff 2002:33; U.S. Senate Committee on Governmental Affairs 1978a, 1980; Kerbo and Della Fave 1983, 1984). To the degree that the upper class also has a lot of influence over these financial corporations (such as banks with large amounts of stock control in other big corporations), the actual stock control of the upper class is much greater (for example, see Figure 6-1, showing upper-class stock ownership in corporation B plus ownership in corporation A, which also controls stock in corporation B).

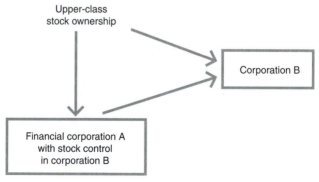

**FIGURE 6-1** *Upper-Class Economic Power through Stock Ownership and Control*

In the early stages of industrialization in this country, the control of corporations was fairly easy to estimate. Most corporations were owned, and thus controlled, by specific families. We knew, for example, that the Rockefeller family controlled Standard Oil, the McCormick family controlled International Harvester, the Mellon family controlled the Aluminum Company of America, and the Morgan family controlled Morgan Bank by virtue of their extensive stock ownership of these companies. But this concentration of stock ownership by specific families in one or a few corporations has changed greatly in recent decades. Few clearly family-controlled corporations such as the Ford Motor Company (with the Ford family owning 40 percent of the stock) are found today.

Because of the wide distribution of stockholders in most corporations, government agencies and researchers agree that 5 to 10 percent ownership in a particular company by a family will often result in control of that company by the family.

Several studies, however, have concluded that very few corporations today are controlled by particular families. Indeed, only 10 to 15 percent of the corporate stock in the largest corporations in the United States today are owned and controlled by individuals at all (Blair 1995; Domhoff 2002:32–35). The most accurate and detailed study of corporate ownership was done in the 1970s when the U.S. Senate passed legislation requiring cooperation with the investigation. Only 13 of the largest 122 corporations in the United States at the time, the focus of the Senate study, were controlled by families or private individuals through significant stock ownership (U.S. Senate Committee on Governmental Affairs 1978a:252). One of the problems in determining control, however, is that the ownership of stock in specific corporations is often hidden. For example, the owner of stock may be listed under meaningless names (such as street names) or under trusts and foundations (Zeitlin 1974). To make the situation even more complex, corporations (especially banks) control stock in other corporations.

Consider the following situation: A family owns about 2 percent of the stock in corporation A, with other families also owning about 2 percent each. In turn, this original family owns, say, 5 percent of the stock in corporation B (a bank) and 6 percent in corporation C (an insurance company). We find upon further investigation that company B (the bank) controls 4 percent of the stock in corporation A, and corporation C (the insurance company) controls 7 percent of the stock in corporation A. Who controls corporation A?

It *may* be that our original family does, through its stock in corporation A, as well as in B and C. But other families own stock in A who in addition have much stock in corporations D and E. And (you are probably ahead of me), corporations D and E also control stock in corporation A! This example is not an exaggeration, as anyone will see in examining the data on stock ownership published in a Senate study (U.S. Senate Committee on Governmental Affairs 1978a, 1980). In the face of this complexity of wide stockholdings, many researchers simply conclude that top managers of a corporation control by default (for example, Berle 1959; Galbraith 1971; Bell 1976). But, as we will see in the following sections, this generalization also has many drawbacks.

## Upper-Class Backgrounds of Economic Elites

Aside from actual stock ownership, there is another possible means of upper-class leverage over the economy. After the authority of stockholders in a corporation, we find the

board of directors and top executive officers. We will call these people *economic elites.*
The family backgrounds of these economic elites may be important in how they think,
whom they trust, and what group interests they serve while making decisions in their
positions of authority in the corporate world. Ruling-class theorists such as Domhoff
believe that these economic elites often come from, or have backgrounds in, upper-class
families. Thus, even if upper-class families may not own enough stock to control many
corporations, their people are there in important positions of authority.

Using the indicators of upper-class membership outlined earlier, Domhoff's
(2002, 2006a) work examined the directors from many top corporations. He found (see
Table 6-1) that of the top 20 industrial corporations, 54 percent of the board members
were from the upper class; of the top 15 banks, 62 percent were upper-class members;
of the top 15 insurance companies, 44 percent were upper-class members; of the top
15 transportation companies, 53 percent were upper-class members; and of the top
15 utility corporations, 30 percent were upper-class members. Clearly we find much
overrepresentation by the upper class on these boards of directors when it is noted that
the upper class accounts for only about 0.5 percent of the population.

In another study, Soref (1976) took a random sample of board members from the
top 121 corporations in the United States. Using Domhoff's definition of upper class, he
found upper-class board members had more board positions in other companies (average of 3.49 for upper-class directors, 2.0 for others) and were more often members of
board subcommittees that made important long-range decisions in the company. In a
similar study of corporate directors who were also college trustees (thus the sample is
somewhat limited), Useem (1978, 1984) found that the directors who were wealthier
and also members of elite social clubs (indicating upper-class membership) had more
directorship positions in corporations than did directors who were not upper class.

Finally, in a massive study of institutional elites, Thomas Dye (1995) obtained
background information on the boards of directors *and* top executive officers of the top

## TABLE 6-1

### Upper-Class Family Backgrounds of Corporate Elites

| Domhoff's study (corporate directors) | |
|---|---|
| **Type of corporation** | **Upper class, %** |
| Top 20 industrials | 54% |
| Top 15 banks | 62 |
| Top 15 insurance | 44 |
| Top 15 transportation | 53 |
| Top 15 utilities | 30 |
| **Dye's study (upper-class membership indicated by exclusive club membership)** | |
| Top 201 corporations (all types, directors and top officers) | 44% |

*SOURCES:* Domhoff (2006a); Dye (1995).

201 corporations (those corporations controlling 50 percent of the assets in each type of corporation—industrial, financial, insurance, and utilities). This sample included 3,572 people who by our definition were economic elites. Using a list of 37 upper-class social clubs from Domhoff's work, Dye found that *44 percent* of these 3,572 economic elites were members of one or more of these upper-class clubs (see Table 6-1). Thus, by Domhoff's definition, 44 percent of these people were members of the upper class.

In conclusion, we find some evidence supporting the argument that the upper class is able to dominate the economy through positions of authority in major corporations. But this evidence is far from conclusive. A primary reservation raised by Dye (1995) pertains to the validity of upper-class indicators such as elite social clubs. It may be that many economic elites gain club memberships only after they become economic elites. To the extent that this is true, we cannot always say club membership indicates upper-class background or upper-class membership.

There is also the question of whether upper-class members act exclusively to protect the interests of the upper class when in positions of corporate authority. In part, this second reservation pertains to the strength of upper-class unity and consciousness discussed earlier. It is clear that corporate elite membership in social clubs and interlocking directorates through multiple board memberships help unify the structure of large corporations today. However, the question of whose interests (an upper class or corporate elites themselves) are served by this unified corporate structure remains inadequately answered.

# Upper-Class Political Power

The next questions of importance for ruling-class or governing-class theorists are the degree and means of political power exercised by the upper class. The significance of the state, and especially the federal government, on domestic affairs in this nation has increased rapidly since the 1930s. We find today a federal government with an annual budget of about $4 trillion, with programs designed for such purposes as regulating the economy as well as its traditional job of managing foreign affairs.

The potential impact of the federal government on upper-class interests is clear. If the upper class is to maintain a position of dominance in the nation, it is imperative that it have influence over the state as well as the economy. In this section we consider evidence suggesting upper-class influence over the government through (1) direct participation by the upper class in politics, (2) the selection of government leaders, (3) the activities of lobby organizations, and (4) organizations established to shape the development of government policy.

## *Upper-Class Participation in Government*

Research on direct participation by the upper class in government is focused heavily on the president's cabinet. Cabinet members are under the direction of the president, but because of the president's many concerns and lack of time in gathering all the needed information in making policy, the president must rely heavily on cabinet members for advice and information. If these cabinet members represent the interests of the upper class, they can provide the president with information to guide his policy decisions in a way that will ensure that upper-class interests are maintained.

Shortly, we will consider research that directly attempts to measure the upper-class membership of cabinet members. But at this point it will be interesting to examine briefly how cabinet members may be selected. Jimmy Carter's cabinet is of special interest. As the first president *elected* after Watergate, Carter presented himself as a political outsider who would represent the people, in contrast to previous presidents, who were among the inner circle of old-guard politicians and big business.

However, even before Carter became a candidate for the presidency he was associated with upper-class circles. He was recommended by J. Paul Austin (chair of the board of Atlanta-based Coca-Cola) for membership in a new upper-class organization called the Trilateral Commission. The Trilateral Commission was established in 1972 by David Rockefeller, with the assistance of the Council on Foreign Relations and the Rockefeller Foundation. "The Trilateral Commission is a group of corporate officials of multinational corporations and government officials of several industrialized nations who meet periodically to coordinate economic policy between the United States, Western Europe, and Japan" (Dye 1995:227).

The Trilateral Commission is today a rather weak arm of the Council on Foreign Relations (an upper-class organization, by Domhoff's definition; over one-half of its members have upper-class backgrounds; Domhoff 1998). But in its early days there were big plans for the Trilateral Commission to be a mechanism for coordinating the economic activity of multinational corporations.

All cabinet members do not have upper-class family backgrounds. But even where upper-class background is lacking, cabinet membership may be attained through the sponsorship of upper-class circles. Henry Kissinger's rise from Harvard professor to Nixon's cabinet was strongly influenced by the Council on Foreign Relations (and the Rockefeller family), as was Zbigniew Brzezinski's rise to Carter's cabinet (Dye 1979).

In contrast to Carter, who was supported by the liberal wing of the upper class and corporate class, Reagan was seen as the president of the very conservative new rich. When we look at Reagan's early supporters from California, there is strong evidence for this description (Brownstein and Easton 1983). And, like Carter, before being elected to the presidency Reagan was associated with an organization sponsored by the corporate elite (Committee on the Present Danger), though in this case, of course, it was a right-wing political organization devoted to reviving the cold war against the Soviet Union (see Domhoff 1983:140). But, again like Carter, Reagan selected 32 members of this organization to serve in his new administration.

At the beginning of the Reagan administration there was the idea that the old upper class had been thrown out of power by Reagan's right-wing new-rich supporters. However, when we examine Reagan's top political appointees we get a somewhat different picture. The rich were certainly there: Reagan's top five political appointees (vice president, attorney general, secretary of state, secretary of defense, and secretary of the treasury) were all multimillionaires, and over 25 percent of the top 100 appointments that Reagan made were of millionaires (Brownstein and Easton 1983:xv). But there was a mixture of the old establishment rich and the new rich. Of his 90 top appointees, 31 were members of the upper-class Council on Foreign Relations and 12 were members of the Trilateral Commission (Domhoff 1983:140). As for his most important selections, the cabinet, 10 had elite Ivy League university degrees, 11 had been executives or directors of major corporations, and 8 were members of the Council on Foreign Relations (Dye 1983:74).

Then Reagan's vice president became president himself. But unlike any president since John F. Kennedy, Bush (the first Bush president) not only selected top advisers from the corporate class and establishment upper class, but he *was* old-line upper class. Bush's parents were members of the New England upper class, where Bush attended an elite prep school (Phillips Andover Academy) and then graduated from Yale (where he was a member of one of the most elite fraternities). After college and World War II, Bush took some of his father's support and money to Texas (where new money at the time was being made in oil) to start his own company in the oil industry and make his own fortune (Dye 1983:74). But during this time he kept his upper-class ties through membership in the Bohemian Club, the Council on Foreign Relations, and the Trilateral Commission, among other organizations.

When Bill Clinton was elected to the presidency in 1992, he at first selected far fewer corporate elites for his cabinet than previous presidents. The majority of his cabinet was made up of previously elected politicians, Washington lawyers, and lobbyists (Dye 1995:84–94). Still, almost half had degrees from prestigious universities—Harvard, Yale, and Stanford. However, through time many of his original cabinet members left to be replaced by members of the corporate elite. Indeed, when Bill Clinton began his run for the presidency in 1991, he was examined by the corporate elite, as were all the main candidates, to make sure his policies "were correct" before he could receive their support and funding. At the time the top executives of big financial institutions were worried about losing business in the rapidly growing Asian market, and they wanted to impress upon the candidates that new policies were needed if their support was to be forthcoming. In what one organizer of the selection process called "an elegant cattle show," Bill Clinton was "invited" to the "21" Club in New York City (as were other top presidential candidates) where the corporate elite impressed upon Mr. Clinton "the need for the Democratic Party to have a new and much more forward-looking economic policy" (*International Herald Tribune,* February 16, 1999). It was from this meeting that we find the origins of the U.S. government push to open financial markets in Asia (and roots of the Asian economic crisis of 1997), and Bill Clinton's friendship with Robert Rubin, then head of Goldman Sachs and Company, and later Clinton's treasury secretary from 1995 until 1999.

Then, there was the cabinet of George W. Bush (2001–2009), which has been described as one of the most connected to major corporations in U.S. history (see for example, *International Herald Tribune,* December 26, 2000). Like George W. Bush himself, Vice President Richard Cheney had been an oil company executive after leaving the cabinet of George Bush Sr. 8 years before. He was also a corporate board member at Procter & Gamble, Electronic Data Systems, and Union Pacific, and served as a director of the Council on Foreign Relations and was vice-chair of the American Enterprise Institute. George W. Bush's first treasury secretary, Paul O'Neill, was the CEO of Alcoa and International Paper; White House chief of staff Andrew Card was a Washington lobbyist for General Motors; domestic policy chief Josh Bolten is from Goldman Sachs;

Commerce Secretary Donald Evans was an oil executive; director of the Office of Management and Budget Mitchell Daniels was an executive of the leading pharmaceutical company Eli Lilly & Co; Donald Rumsfeld, as well as being in and out of government for many years, was a CEO of General Instruments and sat on the boards of directors of Kellogg, Sears Roebuck, and Gulfstream Aerospace; and even Bush's secretary of labor, Elaine Chao, held top management positions at Bank of America and Citicorp before joining the president's cabinet (see for example, Domhoff 2002:153–157).

Finally, there is the cabinet of President Obama. After his analysis of the Obama cabinet, Domhoff (2010: 188) wrote: "the Obama Administration appointees are different from past appointees in major respects as far as a class-dominance theory is concerned. First, they are far more likely to have spent most of their careers in government service than business. . . . Second, they are less likely to have served on corporate boards than appointees in previous administrations." Several have held elective office as governors, senators, or House members. Others have been college professors or held administrative positions in government agencies, such as Treasury Secretary Timothy Geithner who came directly to the cabinet from the U.S. Federal Reserve. The secretary of energy, Steven Chu, is a Nobel Prize–winning physicist from the University of California, Berkeley. President Obama's cabinet members are certainly from an elite group, several with PhDs from leading universities. Soon after this cabinet was formed in early 2009, the joke was that if the United States were to be attacked by a foreign power, the worst time would be during the Harvard-Yale football game. Obama's cabinet is a different elite group compared to presidential cabinet members of at least the past 100 years (as we will see below). Very few have any ties with the corporate class or the upper class.

It is time to present some evidence of the upper-class and corporate backgrounds of cabinet members in general. Using his definition of upper-class membership outlined earlier, Domhoff (1967:97–99; see also Kerbo and Della Fave 1979:7) examined the backgrounds of secretaries of state, the treasury, and defense between 1932 and 1964. He found that 63 percent of the secretaries of state, 62 percent of the secretaries of defense, and 63 percent of the secretaries of the treasury could be classified as members of the upper class before assuming office (see Table 6-2). As Domhoff admits, the preceding represents only a small part of the cabinet for a period of a little more than 30 years. But with these positions we find the upper class represented in proportions far greater than its 0.5 percent of the population would suggest.

Since Domhoff's earlier work, an extensive study of cabinet members has been conducted by Beth Mintz (1975). Using Domhoff's indicators of upper-class membership, Mintz (1975, along with Peter Freitag, 1975) undertook the massive job of examining the backgrounds of all cabinet members (205 people) serving between 1897 and 1973. Her most interesting finding at this point was that *66 percent* of these cabinet members could be classified as members of the upper class before obtaining their cabinet positions (see Table 6-2). Also interesting was that the number of cabinet members coming from the upper class was fairly consistent between 1897 and 1973, suggesting that Baltzell (1964) was incorrect in his belief that the upper class is not participating in government as much as it once did. And in case anyone believes that the wealthy and upper class strongly favor Republicans over Democrats, Mintz's data showed that Republican

## TABLE 6-2

### Upper-Class Origins of Government Elite

| Domhoff study | |
|---|---|
| **Position in government** | **Upper class, %** |
| Cabinet (1932–1964) | |
| Secretaries of state | 63% |
| Secretaries of defense | 62 |
| Secretaries of the treasury | 63 |
| **Mintz study** | |
| All cabinet (1897–1973) | 66% |
| Democratic cabinet (1897–1973) | 60 |
| Republican cabinet (1897–1973) | 71 |

*SOURCES:* Domhoff (1998); Mintz (1975).

presidents chose more than 71 percent of their cabinet members from the upper class, while Democratic presidents chose more than 60 percent from the upper class.

In her background research on these cabinet members, Mintz also included information pertaining to the previous occupations of these people. Along with Freitag (1975), she reported that more than 76 percent of the cabinet members were associated with big corporations before or after their cabinet position, 54 percent were from *both* the upper class and top corporate positions, and *90 percent* either came from the upper class or were associated with big corporations. Focusing on corporate ties of cabinet members, Freitag (1975) showed that these ties have not changed much over the years, and vary only slightly by particular cabinet position. In fact, even most secretaries of labor have been associated with big corporations in the capacity of top executives, board members, or corporate lawyers.

In a massive three-volume work by Burch (1981) examining elites throughout American history, we find that the rich and corporate elite have always dominated the top federal government positions. From 1789 to 1861, 96 percent of the cabinet and diplomatic appointees "were members of the economic elite, with a great many landowners, lawyers, and merchants in the group" (Domhoff 1983:142). Then from 1861 to 1933 the proportion was 84 percent, with more of these people now coming from major corporations that did not exist before 1861.

The United States is truly unique with respect to where the top executive officials such as the U.S. president's cabinet come from. In other Western industrial nations these people almost always are elected government officials from the country's parliament (Putnam 1976:48–49). And few executive officials below cabinet level are appointed by political leaders at all in other countries. Most are career civil servants who have worked their way up the ladder in government agencies like the Ministry of Finance, Foreign

Affairs, and so forth. Japan provides the biggest contrast. When a new U.S. president is elected, he or she appoints some 4,000 people to top staff positions in the Treasury Department, State Department, Commerce Department, and so on. These people are seldom career civil servants. In Japan, a new prime minister appoints about 20 people (Kerbo and McKinstry 1995). That is it. All of the other people in top positions in government agencies are career civil servants who moved up the ranks of their agencies after graduating from top universities some 30 or more years previously. The U.S. political system is very different in this respect. The Obama appointments have been at least somewhat less unique compared to all other industrial nations, however, because most have not come from big corporations.

## *Political Campaign Contributions*
Today it costs money, lots of money, to obtain a major elective office. In 1972, for example, Richard Nixon spent $60 million to win reelection, while his opponent spent $30 million. In the 1978 U.S. congressional elections, special-interest groups alone contributed $35 million to candidates. This figure increased to $55 million in 1980, and to $150 million in 1988. The average Senate campaign in 1988 cost $4 million. By 2006 campaign spending (which began in 2005) had reached $179 million for Republicans and $206 million for Democrats, compared to $130 million for Republicans and only $82 million for Democrats in 1991–1992. In 1960, the average cost of running for the U.S. Congress was about $25,000, but by the 2006 elections the average race for the House of Representatives cost over $600,000, and $5.6 million for the Senate. About $1 billion was spent on elections by all candidates during the 2006 elections (www.fec.gov). In 2008 candidates running for seats in the House of Representatives collectively spent over $1 billion, and those running for the Senate almost half a billion dollars. The amounts spent by Democrats and Republicans were about even (U.S. Bureau of the Census 2010b: Table 414).

In his famous work on the power elite over 50 years ago, C. Wright Mills had relatively little to say about campaign contributions. But the subject can no longer be neglected. Especially in an age when political campaigns are won more through presenting images than through issues, the image-creating mass media are extremely important and costly. Most presidents and congressional officeholders are wealthy, but they are not superrich. With a few rare exceptions, they cannot afford to finance their own political campaigns. Who, then, pays for these campaigns? Thousands of contributors send $25 or $50 to favored candidates. For the most part, however, the money comes from corporations and the wealthy.

With the nationwide reaction against Watergate and the many illegal campaign contributions to Nixon's reelection committee in 1972, some election reforms were undertaken by Congress in 1974. Among these reforms was the creation of a voluntary $1-per-person campaign contribution from individual income tax reports. A Presidential Election Campaign Fund was established to distribute this money to the major parties and candidates during an election year. In addition, a Federal Election Commission was established to watch over campaign spending, and people were limited to a $1,000 contribution in any single presidential election, with organizations limited to $5,000.

Perhaps these reforms contributed to less spending in the 1976 presidential election (Dye 1979:90); Carter and Ford spent a combined total of about $50 million in 1976, compared with Nixon and McGovern's $90 million in 1972. But $50 million continues to be a substantial investment and requires large contributions.

An interesting outcome of the campaign reform law of 1974 is that much of the illegal activity in Nixon's 1972 campaign was *made legal* as long as correct procedures are followed. For example, organizations are limited to $5,000 in political contributions per election. However, if there are more organizations, more money can be contributed. This is precisely what happened by 1976. There was an explosion in the number of political action committees (PACs) established by large corporations and their executives, an increase far outnumbering those established by any other group, such as labor unions (Domhoff 2002). In 2005 there were 638 corporate PACs and 912 trade/health industry PACs, compared to 296 labor union PACs. In the 1980 congressional elections, corporate, health industry, and other business PACs contributed $36 million to candidates, while $1.3 million was contributed by labor union PACs. By the 2006 elections, corporate, health industry, and other business PACs contributed $191 million directly to candidates, compared to $51.6 million by labor union PACs (U.S. Bureau of the Census 2007b:259). In the 2008 elections the corporate PACs contributed about $250 million to candidates while labor union PACs contributed about $60 million (U.S. Bureau of the Census 2010b:Table 415).

Campaign contributions, therefore, continue to be an important means of political influence. The wealthy are not assured that their interests will be protected by those they help place in office, but they obviously consider the gamble worth taking. Usually, it is hoped that these campaign contributions are placing people in office who hold political views that lead to the defense of privilege when unforeseen challenges to upper-class interests occur along the way.

For example, in 1996 the millions of corporate contributions from the health care industry paid off well when the "health care reform" bill that would have limited health care costs and provided wider health care coverage to all Americans was completely defeated in Congress and an alternative health care reform bill was not even brought up after this sound defeat. More recently corporate political action has helped pass laws allowing corporations to more freely set up offshore operations to save taxes. One study of 9,669 U.S. corporations suggested corporations have reduced their tax bill from around 35 percent of profits to 21 percent through this favorable legislation (*New York Times,* April 17, 2002). The Enron Corporation was able to avoid taxes completely in 4 of the last 5 years before it went bankrupt, plus it received a $382 million tax refund by setting up over 800 offshore subsidiaries. The investigation of illegality at Enron later showed another big tax break U.S. corporations obtained for awarding CEOs stock options. Of the largest 500 U.S. corporations, 24 paid no taxes at all in 1998 partly because of this tax break (*New York Times,* January 18, 2002). Remember that Chapter 2 discussed how the CEOs of America's largest corporations average about $11 million in annual income. Most comes in the form of stock options, which are completely tax deductible, leaving the rest of Americans to make up the lost tax revenues from their own pockets.

With respect to presidential campaign contributions, Obama again broke the pattern. Obama did receive money from wealthy individuals and corporate PACs. As Domhoff has argued since the 1960s and showed again with his analysis of contributions to Obama's presidential campaign, to become President of the United States one must get the backing of at least part of the upper class and corporate class (Domhoff 2010:163–166). However, a smaller percentage of contributions to Obama's campaign were from corporate PACs, with most coming in small contributions from a large number of people throughout the United States. For example, Obama received over $650 million from private individuals, and almost $250 million of this came from people who contributed $200 or less. McCain, in contrast, received less than $200 million from private individuals, with only $63 million coming from people contributing $200 or less (www.fec.gov).

The future of campaign contributions will be different, however. In a 5 to 4 deci-sion in 2010, the U.S. Supreme Court ruled that most of the restrictions on campaign contributions put in effect during the 1970s are unconstitutional, ruling that freedom of speech allows the rich and corporations to contribute as much as they want to campaign advertisements for political candidates. In future elections the amounts of money from corporations and the rich will likely explode, favoring candidates who will protect their interests. Money contributed by average individuals and unions will become insignificant in comparison.

## Congressional Lobbying

If the interests of the wealthy are not ensured by their direct participation in government, and if those the wealthy helped put in office seem to be forgetting their debtors, a third force can be brought into action. The basic job of a lobbyist is to make friends among congressional leaders; provide them with favors such as trips, small gifts, and parties; and, most important, provide these leaders with information and arguments favoring their employers' interests and needs. All of this requires a large staff and lots of money.

In one of the first empirical studies of the effects of certain characteristics of corporations on government policies toward these corporations (such as tax policies), Salamon and Siegfried (1977) found that the size of the corporation showed a strong inverse relation to the amount of taxes paid by the corporation. This inverse relation between size of the corporation and the corporation's tax rate was especially upheld when examining the oil companies and including their state as well as federal taxes paid (Salamon and Siegfried 1977:1039). Thus, the bigger the corporation, the less it tends to pay in corporate taxes.

Later studies have confirmed this relationship between size (and power) and corporate tax rates. Jacobs (1988), however, measured the concentration of powerful corporations within each type of industry. The findings were similar: The more corporate concentration (meaning the size of the firms in the industry and their dominance in the industry), the lower the taxes for the corporations in that industry. In examining how this is done in the oil industry and health care industry, Laumann, Knoke, and Kim (1985) studied 166 government policy decisions relating to these industries and interviewed 458 lobbyists for these industries. They found that there are leading corporations in these industries that have a reputation for being most politically active in influencing government for the overall industry, and that this reputation is very accurate when measuring their lobbying activity. Finally, in a historical study of industrial corporations between

1886 and 1905, Roy (1981) reached similar conclusions. He found that the size of the corporation, the volume of its exports, and its political activity were related to the extent of favorable treatment it received in government policy decisions. This is a major reason 25 percent of the largest 1,000 corporations in the United States in 2005 paid no federal income tax (see Chapter 2). They were most successful during the George W. Bush years. The effective tax rate on the largest corporations in the United States fell from 21.7 percent during the last years of the 1990s to 17.2 percent in 2003, a time when corporate profits were relatively high (Domhoff 2010:177).

Campaign contributions, of course, are something of a gamble. Money does not always win elections. But once candidates gain high political office, there is no question about the potential influence they have over government policy and legislation. This is one reason corporations pay more money to lobbyists than to political action committees (PACs) by a margin of 10 to 1 (Domhoff 2010:176).

Lobby organizations, therefore, can be of major importance in ensuring that the special interests of a wealthy upper-class and corporate elite are served. If special favors are not completely ensured through direct participation in the cabinet and campaign contributions, the powerful lobby organizations may then move into action. The upper class and big business are not the only groups that maintain lobby organizations in Washington. The American Medical Association, the National Rifle Association, the Milk Producers Association, and many others have maintained successful lobby organizations. But when considering the big issues such as how to deal with inflation, tax policy, unemployment, foreign affairs, and many others that broadly affect the lives of people in this country, the corporate and upper-class lobbies are most important. Of the lobby process, Domhoff (2006a) writes, "The effects of lobbying are hard to assess, for the process is more subtle than it supposedly used to be. However, it is certain that various business groups and their Washington lawyers are the most prominent lobbyists, even when they do not bother to register as such."

## Shaping Government Policy

Of the various means of upper-class and corporate political influence, the type least recognized by the general public is referred to as the *policy-forming process* (see Domhoff 1979:61–128; 2010:85–115; Dye 1995:219–239). In the long run this means of political influence is perhaps one of the most important. The basic argument is this: The federal government is faced with many national problems for which there are many possible alternative solutions. For example, consider the problem of unemployment. The possible government means of dealing with this problem are varied, and a key is that different solutions to the problem may favor different class interests. Some possible solutions (such as stimulating the economy with low interest rates and restricting imports) are believed to favor the working class and help create new jobs, and thus are pushed by labor unions. Other possible solutions (such as the "Reagonomics" idea of cutting taxes for the rich and corporations) favor the interests of corporations and the upper class. A contemporary example is "outsourcing" of jobs. In the past decade the United States lost some 2 million jobs as corporations moved operations to countries with extremely low wages, such as China. The critical question is, how has this affected the long-term interests of the U.S. economy? The corporate elite like to tell Americans that outsourcing actually helps us because it leads to more U.S. jobs as we focus more on higher-tech industries. Is this true, or is it only a story to keep Americans from trying to force politicians to make outsourcing more difficult, as it is in countries like Germany? (In Chapter 8 we examine data showing this is a questionable argument.) One important means of ensuring that the federal government follows a policy that is favorable to your class interests is to convince the government through various types of research data that one line of policy is the overall best policy. Generating the needed information and spelling out the exact policy required take a lot of planning, organization, personnel, and resources. There also must be avenues for getting this policy information to the attention of government leaders. It is no surprise, ruling-class theorists argue, that the upper class and its corporations are able to achieve this and guide government policy in their interests.

Far from the eyes of the general public, there is a little-known policy-formation process that goes on in the United States and most other capitalist industrial nations. The federal government cannot always use its massive resources to generate the information needed in developing policy alternatives with respect to many issues. A mostly private network has developed over the years, supported with upper-class and corporate money and personnel to provide government input when important decisions are to be made. Domhoff (1979:63, 2002:72; see also Dye 1995:221) has charted this process, as shown in Figure 6-2.

At the heart of this process are upper-class and corporate *money and personnel* that fund and guide *research* on important questions through foundations and universities, then process the information through *policy-planning groups* sponsored by the upper class that make *direct recommendations* to government and influence the opinion-making centers, such as the media and government commissions, which in turn influence the population and government leaders in favoring specific policy alternatives. Much of this "knowledge" is generated through upper-class sponsorship, and thus favors its class interests. Increasingly, knowledge needed by corporations and government is generated through research conducted at major universities. Scientific research requires time, money, and personnel. The upper class and corporations, it is argued, influence the research process through funding and authority positions in major research-oriented universities.

The Ford Foundation, one of the largest, included among its top officials people who are on the boards of directors of Citicorp, CBS, Aluminum Company of America, Allied Stores, AT&T, Chase Manhattan Bank, Levi Strauss Co., General Electric, Massachusetts Mutual Life, International Paper, Coca-Cola, Smith-Kline Beecham, American Stock Exchange, American Express, Bankers Trust, Union Carbide, JC Penney, Xerox, Corning Glass, and Dow Jones. Another of the largest foundations, the Rockefeller Foundation, has top officials who are (or have been) on the boards of directors of Equitable Life, the American Stock Exchange, Manufacturers Hanover Trust Bank, Walt Disney, CBS, and IBM (Domhoff 2010:90–96, Dye 1995:135–137).

Also important in the research process are the major universities in which much of this research is conducted. Among these universities, for example, are Harvard, Yale, Chicago, Stanford, the Massachusetts Institute of Technology, and the California Institute of Technology. In these universities faculty are often released from their

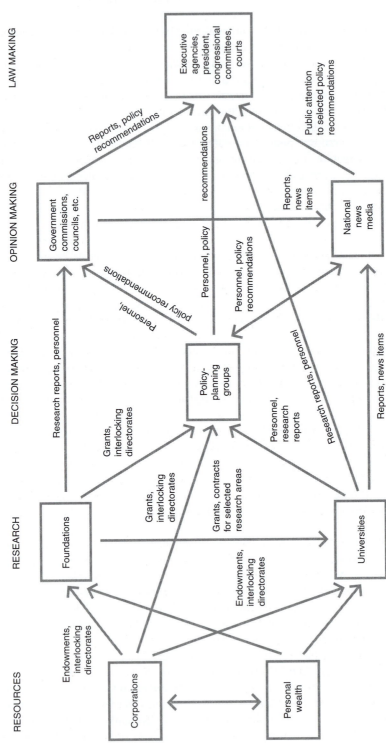

**FIGURE 6-2** *The Policy-Formation Process*

*SOURCES:* Domhoff (1979:63); Dye (1995:221).

teaching responsibilities to devote most of their time to conducting research sponsored by large corporations and foundations, as well as the federal government. One means of upper-class and corporate influence, therefore, is through guiding what type of research is conducted by the faculty.

We have only a few studies of the exact impact of funding sources on this research, but what we do have is enlightening. For example, Useem, Hoops, and Moore (1976) have found that there is a relationship between members from the upper class on a university's board of trustees and obtaining more funds from corporations and foundations. As to the effect of these funds on the direction of research conducted, Useem (1976a, 1976b) obtained answers to questionnaires from 1,079 professors in anthropology, economics, political science, and psychology. A majority of these professors admitted that their research plans (what type of research they could do) were influenced by the policies of funding agencies (in this case, the federal government). In other words, they were doing the research the funding agency thought was most important, not what they or their scientific disciplines thought most important. This study by Useem involved only social science research. But it can be suggested that the influence of these funding agencies is even more extensive in other branches of science, where corporate and foundation funding is more extensive.

Finally, there is the more general influence over university policy that may be exercised by corporations and the upper class. Most universities are governed much like a corporation. Above the executive officers (such as presidents and vice presidents) is the board of trustees (resembling a board of directors in a corporation). This board of trustees has broad authority in governing the university and its general policies. Thus, it is often deemed important to understand the outside interests of the university board of trustees.

In Dye's (1995) study of elites he examined the backgrounds of presidents and trustees of the top 12 private universities (such as Harvard, Princeton, and MIT). He found that *62 percent* of these university trustees were members of just 37 exclusive upper-class clubs. Much of the research sponsored by corporations and the upper class is in state-sponsored universities not included in Dye's sample. But other research indicates that the trustees of these universities are also dominated by corporations and the upper class.

In this policy-forming process the next important link is through what has been called *policy-planning groups*. The corporate elites and upper class come together in these groups, discuss policy, publish and disseminate research, and, according to Dye and Domhoff, arrive at some consensus about what should be done in the nation. The most important of the policy groups are sponsored directly by the upper class for the purpose of linking the research information discussed earlier to specific policy alternatives and making certain these policy alternatives find their way to government circles.

Perhaps the most has been written about the Council on Foreign Relations (CFR) and the Committee on Economic Development (CED) (Domhoff 2010:104–115). The CFR was established shortly after World War I by upper-class members with the direct intent of influencing the U.S. government with respect to their business interests overseas (see Shoup 1975). Among the CFR's early successes were to have the government define Japan as an economic threat by 1940, to establish some of the ideas behind the development of the World Bank and the United Nations, and to motivate the government to define certain parts of the world as important areas of economic interest (multinational corporation interests). Membership in the CFR is limited to 1,400 people, half of whom are members of the upper class (Domhoff 1983). The CED emerged out of the Business Advisory Council in 1942 to continue the input into government by the upper class that began with this earlier organization in the 1930s (Domhoff 1970:123–128, 1979:67–69; Collins 1977).

Using network analysis of personal ties of board members of leading "think tanks" and policy discussion groups, Burris (2008; also see Domhoff 2010:104) found the Business Roundtable, Business Council, American Enterprise Institute, Council on Foreign Relations, and U.S. Chamber of Commerce to be among the most important. Figure 6-3 also provides an example of the extent to which managers and directors of the largest U.S. corporations are linked to these nonprofit organizations such as major

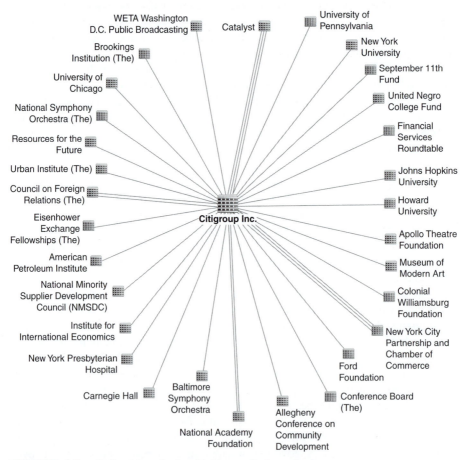

**FIGURE 6-3**    *Citibank Interlocks with Nonprofit Organizations*

*SOURCES:* Domhoff (2007) (http://sociology.ucsc.edu/whorulesamerica/power/corporate_community.html).

universities, foundations, and "think tanks." Citigroup, the parent company of CitiBank, we will see in the next chapter, was ranked as the top corporation in the United States in 2007 by *Forbes*. Figure 6-3 shows that managers or board members of CitiBank were also directors or regents at five major universities and nine of the most important "think tanks" and foundations in the United States.

Finally, we have to mention briefly the other parts of the policy-forming process described in Figure 6-2. Various government commissions are established from time to time to make recommendations on such issues as civil disorders, the conduct of the CIA, and energy (to list some recent examples). These commissions make public the recommendations of these upper-class policy groups and provide their members with a semiofficial position in the government.

Finally, we will see data in Chapter 13 indicating the extent to which the news media in the United States are dominated by a few giants owned primarily by big corporations. Few theorists writing in this area (on the upper class or, more specifically, on upper-class influence in the mass media) suggest that the upper-class or corporate elites completely control the mass media in the country. Neither do most writers in this area believe that there is some kind of upper-class secret conspiracy to control the mass media—or anything else in the country, for that matter. Rather, they are trying to call attention to an economic structure that allows more influence (in the many ways outlined previously) to fall into the hands of groups like the upper-class and corporate elites. Each class or economic interest group tends to have a worldview or way of perceiving reality that has been shaped by its own economic and political interests. When one group has more influence over the major means of conveying information, its view of reality often comes to be accepted by more people.

# ✂ The Upper Class: A Conclusion

In this chapter we have outlined the main arguments of the ruling-class thesis, along with bits of data often used to support their case. We began by considering the evidence relating to the existence and unity of the upper class, then approached the question of how this class is able to dominate the economy and the political system.

We have found some support for the existence of upper-class unity through interaction patterns in prep schools, social clubs, policy-formation organizations, and multiple corporate board positions. We have also found evidence of upper-class influence in the economy through stock ownership and membership on corporate boards. And we have found evidence of upper-class political influence through direct participation in government, campaign contributions, lobby organizations, and a policy-formation process. Upper-class interests are said to be maintained through these means of influence in the economy and the political system.

We have seen a few of the criticisms directed toward the ruling-class thesis along the way, but we have yet to look at these criticisms and others in a more systematic manner. The basic task of this chapter has been to present the ruling-class view for what it has to offer in understanding our current system of stratification. But along with other theories attempting to explain this most difficult area of research in social stratification, the ruling-class view leaves many questions unanswered or answered less than adequately. Much information needed to resolve the many debates about the power of an upper class is simply lacking. The wealthy and powerful closely guard much of this information because of the legal, political, or economic interests they have at stake. In Chapter 7 we critique the ruling-class arguments more systematically, then present some alternative perspectives, with a focus on what can be called a corporate class.

## Summary

This chapter began with a description of the upper class, its primary characteristics, and how this upper class can be located in capitalist societies today. This description has relied heavily on Domhoff's view of the upper class as a governing class with extensive unity through various upper-class institutions. The chapter then turned to how the upper class has economic power through corporate stock ownership, corporate board positions, and interlocking directorates, and how upper-class political power is achieved through positions in government (especially in the president's cabinet), campaign contributions, lobbying organizations, and the policy-formation process.

# The Corporate Class

Irresponsible and illegal behavior by large corporations again caused a U.S. economic crisis in 2008, with consequences such as mass mortgage defaults and unemployment shooting up to 10 percent. Multibillion-dollar government bailouts of banks sent their profits rapidly climbing back to their normal high levels during 2009, while unemployment for nonelites remained around 10 percent as of late 2010. In the right photo is the old head office of Bank of America in San Francisco, which helped start the financial crash of 2008. Bank of America received $45 billion in government bailout money in late 2008, then paid their top four executives a total of more than $64 million in bonuses in 2009. The photo on the left shows the main branch office of Citibank in Moscow, the largest bank in the United States in 2008, with more branches worldwide than any other bank. Citibank also receive $45 billion in government bailout money in 2008, but their top four executives received a total of only $37 million in bonuses in 2009.

*SOURCES:* Left: © Harold Kerbo; right: © The McGraw-Hill Companies, Inc./Christopher Kerrigan, photographer

# Chapter Outline

❖ The Upper Class as Ruling Class: A Critique
❖ The Structure of Corporate Concentration: Foundation for a Corporate Class
❖ Competing Capitalisms: A Conclusion
❖ Summary

Upper-class families such as the Rockefellers, Mellons, and Vanderbilts have nowhere near the power over the American economy and politics they did in the beginning of the 20th century. This is not to say that these families and the corporate institutions they helped build fail to remain extremely powerful in the nation or that they are unable to shape the economy and political events to fit their interests. In some ways, in fact, there is even more power in the hands of individuals who sit at the top of the American stratification system. In the words of C. Wright Mills (1956:28), who in his time understood better than most the potent new forces developing (Domhoff 2006b), "given the enlargement and the centralization of the means of power now available, the decisions that [the power elite] make and fail to make carry more consequences for more people than has ever been the case in the world history of mankind." This is particularly so in the United States where the prevailing conservative ideology is one in which any U.S. government regulation or restraint of the corporate class is seen as an evil that will bring down the capitalist system, cut jobs for all employees, and lead to "socialism."

We constantly hear that the most respected theorist of capitalism, Adam Smith, in his famous book *The Wealth of Nations* published in 1776, told us that government regulation of corporations will lead to the fall of the U.S. economy. One must only assume that these people never really read *The Wealth of Nations*. To understand how these ideas of Adam Smith and others of his time developed, we must for a moment consider the historical period. Industrial technology was emerging in the 1700s, but the political and economic systems of Europe continued to operate under rules and policies that evolved under feudalism. As we saw in Chapter 3, the old, wealthy elites dominated, and there was little free competition in the "marketplace." The state, which was primarily controlled by the feudal elites, was heavily involved in influencing economic activity, and mostly protecting the agricultural interests of the landed aristocracy. The emerging merchants and capitalists were restrained. This was especially so in France until the French economy crashed, leading to revolution in 1789 during the French competition with Great Britain, whose government put fewer restrictions on the emerging British capitalists (Skocpol 1979; Gershoy 1964; Soboul 1974). Thus, social scientists like Adam Smith were reacting against the old social structures that were impeding economic growth.

It is often forgotten today, however, that Adam Smith did not trust big business any more than he trusted the government. On this subject, Smith (1950, vol. 1:144) wrote, "people of the same trade seldom meet together, even for merriment and diversion, but the conversation ends in a conspiracy against the public, or in some contrivance to raise prices." And neither did Adam Smith favor large corporations, commonly called "joint stock companies" at the time. He saw the stockholders as unable to understand what is best for the company, and corporate directors as inefficient: "being the managers rather of other people's money than of their own, it cannot well be expected that they should watch over it with the same anxious vigilance with which the partners in a private copartnery [company] frequently watch over their own" (Smith 1950, vol. II:264).

In what follows we build upon ruling-class views of today, amending weak points and retaining those judged stronger. In brief, we examine arguments suggesting that a somewhat different class can now be described as at the top of the stratification system in this country.

The *corporate class,* as it will be called, retains many of the same characteristics as the upper class; however, its basis of power lies not so much with ownership of the means of production, but rather with *control* of the major means of production (large corporations) in this advanced capitalist society. The analysis of corporate-class power presented here does *not* rest with a conspiracy theory that sees evil forces or evil people at work in the world. What must be understood is a social structure that provides a group of otherwise normal people with the power to protect and maintain its particular economic and political interests, even when these interests are in conflict with others in the society. Before we examine this social structure, however, we need to review some weak points of the ruling-class view outlined in the previous chapter.

## ⚔ The Upper Class as Ruling Class: A Critique

The ruling-class view has been attacked on many points, although most recently the criticisms have centered on two fundamental themes. The first is directed toward the question of whether or not the upper class even exists as an identifiable group with unity and class consciousness; the second is directed toward the extent of its ownership and control of corporations.

This first question is of major importance because only if this class identifies itself as a class with common interests can it work together to achieve the tremendous power claimed by ruling-class theorists. There is no question as to the existence of wealthy families who tend to belong to elite social clubs, frequent the same resorts, are listed year after year in blue books such as the *Social Register,* and send their children to exclusive prep schools. But do they form a united class? If they do not, then the findings indicating upper-class dominance of corporate positions and the cabinet, for example, have less significance.

One charge is that too many people are considered to be members of the upper class for it to have much overall unity and organization (see Dye 1995; Hacker 1975; McNall 1977). Related to this is the charge that ruling-class theorists have not shown enough overlap among the indicators of upper-class membership. Are people who attend the prep schools also listed in the *Social Register,* and do they belong to the same exclusive social clubs? Last, there is the question of whether membership in elite social clubs and/or a listing in the *Social Register* indicates upper-class family background or simply represents high institutional position (in the economy, government, foundations, and so on). In other words, does one have to be from an old, wealthy family to belong to exclusive clubs and obtain a listing in the *Social Register* today? As far back as the 1960s one study has suggested that intraclass marriage is less frequent among the upper class and that listings in the *Social Register* are less restrictive today (Rosen and Bell 1966).

The significance of all these criticisms is that there is not enough unity among the upper class to claim that it is a ruling class. The question of how much unity is enough, however, cannot be answered with any degree of confidence. We are speaking of matters of degree; other things being equal (such as the amount of wealth), the greater the unity and cooperation to meet common interests, the greater the dominance of this class will be. But the point at which an upper class ceases to be a ruling class because of disunity cannot be specified.

The second fundamental set of criticisms directed toward the ruling-class view pertains to upper-class ownership and control of the means of production: that is, major corporations. This is perhaps the central criticism because ruling-class theorists claim that the basis of upper-class power lies with its ownership and/or control of corporations. Wealth alone brings little power. One could have $1 billion but remain relatively powerless if this $1 billion were in a blind trust or simply sitting in a bank.

It is how money is used in influencing people and institutions that is a key to great power. If this $1 billion is used to buy stock, and through this stock controlling interest in a major corporation, then in addition to the $1 billion there is control over vast assets of the corporation. This massive corporate institution and its resources are now more or less at one's command to influence other corporations, the U.S. government, consumers, and even foreign governments. Given the size of our major institutions today (discussed in more detail in the following sections), no one is really powerful without a command position that is attached to one of those institutions. The wealth of individuals or families is dwarfed alongside the assets of these institutions.

We have already considered the difficulty, in contrast to that during previous decades, in determining the ownership and control of major corporations today. While such studies are rare due to opposition by the corporate rich and conservative politicians, in the 1970s Congress (U.S. Senate Committee on Governmental Affairs 1978a, 1980) concluded that only 13 of the top 122 corporations were family-controlled. Ruling-class theorists counter, and will no doubt continue to do so for some time, that there is much hidden stock control that if uncovered would show that families continue to control most corporations. For most corporations, however, any evidence for this is lacking.

Who, then, controls corporations in most capitalist societies today where such family control is weak? Since the early writings of Berle and Means (1932), the concept of a managerial revolution has gained popularity. Until recently this view had come to dominate the thinking on the subject in the social sciences (Zeitlin 1974). The managerial-revolution or managerial-control thesis claims that today the control of each corporation is found with the top corporate executives. The old wealthy families, it claims, have lost their control of corporations because of the wide distribution of stock ownership in most corporations. In fact, it is believed, the stock ownership in most corporations is distributed among so many people that they cannot effectively unite in confronting the authority of corporate management. The top executive officers of the corporation are thus free to run the corporation as they see fit. The basic perspective presented by most who accept the managerial-control thesis is one of many separate corporations, each with its management in control, competing among themselves for a share of the market in the economy. But there are several weaknesses in this managerial-control view.

For one, the evidence strongly favors a conclusion that major corporations are not separate and competitive economic units. We live in a period of a few corporate giants who among themselves account for a majority of the corporate assets in the present economy. In addition, various interests tie these corporations together, reducing competition (though seldom completely) and magnifying their collective means of dominating the economy.

There is also a problem with the view of managers in control of each corporation *without* major interests from outside the corporation looking over their shoulders as they run the corporation. Although the board of directors, the body that legally has authority over management, may not represent the interests of major stockholders as much as it once did (because of the wide distribution of stockholders), there are new interests represented on the board. These interests are from other corporations that may have business interests at stake or banks with financial interests at stake.

These ties and outside interests will be described in more detail in this chapter. For now it must be pointed out that a new thesis has emerged. In this view a group that can be referred to as a *corporate class* (see Useem 1978, 1979b, 1984) is considered at the top of the present stratification system in the United States. The group is called a *class* because it has economic interests in common, possesses enough unity and intraclass organization to recognize these common class interests, and has the means to dominate the economy and political system.

In essence, this corporate class is in many ways similar to an upper class. Its power, however, lies not with the ownership of the means of production but with *control* of the collective means of production. This corporate class is also similar in some ways to the managerial elite described by those accepting the managerial revolution view. But this corporate class is above the interests of separate, competing corporations; rather, it unites them into a complex of interrelated corporate bodies. Finally, this corporate-class perspective forces us to *retain many of the arguments from the ruling-class theory* about the overall dominance of the economy and political system by one class.

In what follows we briefly consider the evidence showing the economic concentration within our society today. We then outline the place of the corporate class within this structure of economic concentration, along with its means of influence over the political system.

## The Structure of Corporate Concentration: Foundation for a Corporate Class

We may define a **corporate class** as a group of people holding key positions of authority in major corporations. They form a network of associations, much like old upper-class families, that crisscross these major corporate institutions, creating an interpersonal web of relations at the top of these institutions. Their influence is not found in personal wealth, although many are wealthy, but in *control* of corporate resources.

These people are chief executive officers or board members of a major corporation, and at the same time board members in other corporations. And they are not unfamiliar in the halls of government, with many in the corporate class having moved in and out of government in various capacities such as advisers, cabinet secretaries, or special committee members. Their personal as well as class interests lie not just with one corporation but with the structure of corporate concentration as a whole. Again, much like the old upper class, they are often members of exclusive social clubs, frequent many of the same resorts, and send their children to exclusive prep schools. But unlike the old upper class, their ranks are permeable. There is at least some room at the top for those who win the recognition of members of this corporate class (Zweigenhaft and Domhoff 2006, 2008; Alba and Moore 1982).

While corporate concentration due to huge conglomerate firms is less than it used to be in the United States before the 1980s (Davis, Diekmann, and Tinsley 1994), the economic concentration that sets the stage for a corporate class to exist continues to be based on the following:

**1.** The size of major corporations and their ability to dominate the market for their particular industrial products or services.

**2.** The concentrated control of stock in major corporations by other corporations (mostly large banks and insurance companies).

**3.** The network of interlocking directorates that ties top corporate personnel together, distributing their loyalties from individual corporations to the corporate structure as a whole and making possible coordinated activities, more influence in government, and planning.

## Corporate Size and Concentration

One of the most important characteristics of our economy is the increasing size and market control of major corporations (see Table 7-1). There are more than 200,000 industrial corporations operating in the economy today. Most of the 200,000 are small local enterprises that come and go from year to year. For these lesser firms the old capitalist ideal of competition is alive and deadly. But in the upper ranks the old capitalist ideal is more dogma than reality. Their size and market concentration have largely reduced the ordeal of competition *within national boundaries* for these corporations. Corporations are usually grouped by function into several categories. Among these are industrial corporations (producing or mining a product); transportation, utilities, and communication corporations; commercial banks; and insurance companies. As an indication of growth, we may consider the share of industrial assets held by the top 100 corporations since 1950. In 1950 it was 39.8 percent; in 1955, 44.3 percent; in 1960, 46.4 percent; in 1965, 46.5 percent; in 1970, 52.3 percent; in 1980, 55 percent; and by 1993, about 75 percent (Dye 1995:16–17). Commercial banks represent another sector of corporate concentration. Here we find the largest grouping of corporate assets overall. There were 12,345 commercial banks in the 1990s, and just 30 banks accounted for over half of all banking assets (Dye 1995:19). With the deregulation wave of the 1990s (especially 1999), financial mergers increased rapidly. Mergers increased even more with the financial crisis of 2008–2009, and today the top 10 financial institutions control 70 percent of the business

## TABLE 7-1

### Top 25 U.S. Corporations, 2009*

| Rank | Company | Industry | Sales ($bil) | Profits ($bil) | Assets ($bil) | Market value ($bil) |
|------|---------|----------|--------------|----------------|---------------|---------------------|
| 1 | General Electric | Conglomerates | 182.52 | 17.41 | 797.77 | 89.87 |
| 2 | ExxonMobil | Oil and gas operations | 425.70 | 45.22 | 228.05 | 335.54 |
| 3 | AT&T | Telecommunications services | 124.03 | 12.87 | 265.25 | 140.08 |
| 4 | Wal-Mart Stores | Retailing | 405.61 | 13.40 | 163.43 | 193.15 |
| 5 | Chevron | Oil and gas operations | 255.11 | 23.93 | 161.17 | 121.70 |
| 6 | JP Morgan Chase | Banking | 101.49 | 3.70 | 2,175.05 | 85.87 |
| 7 | Berkshire Hathaway | Diversified financials | 107.79 | 4.99 | 267.40 | 122.11 |
| 8 | Procter & Gamble | Household and personal products | 83.68 | 14.08 | 138.26 | 141.18 |
| 9 | Verizon Communications | Telecommunications services | 97.35 | 6.43 | 202.35 | 81.04 |
| 10 | IBM | Software and services | 103.63 | 12.34 | 109.53 | 123.47 |
| 11 | Hewlett-Packard | Technology hardware and equipment | 118.70 | 8.05 | 109.63 | 69.57 |
| 12 | Bank of America | Banking | 113.11 | 4.01 | 1,817.94 | 25.29 |
| 13 | Johnson & Johnson | Drugs and biotechnology | 63.75 | 12.95 | 84.91 | 138.29 |
| 14 | Microsoft | Software and services | 61.98 | 17.23 | 65.79 | 143.58 |
| 15 | Pfizer | Drugs and biotechnology | 48.30 | 8.10 | 111.15 | 83.03 |
| 16 | Wells Fargo | Banking | 51.65 | 2.66 | 1,309.64 | 51.28 |
| 17 | Goldman Sachs Group | Diversified financials | 53.58 | 2.32 | 884.55 | 42.06 |
| 18 | Cisco Systems | Technology hardware & equipment | 39.58 | 7.49 | 61.36 | 85.05 |
| 19 | CVS Caremark | Retailing | 87.47 | 3.21 | 60.96 | 37.46 |
| 20 | United Technologies | Conglomerates | 58.68 | 4.69 | 56.47 | 38.53 |
| 21 | MetLife | Insurance | 50.99 | 3.21 | 501.68 | 15.10 |
| 22 | Morgan Stanley | Diversified financials | 62.26 | 1.71 | 658.81 | 21.00 |
| 23 | Intel | Semiconductors | 37.59 | 5.29 | 50.72 | 70.86 |
| 24 | Comcast | Media | 34.26 | 2.55 | 113.02 | 37.62 |
| 25 | Walt Disney | Media | 36.99 | 4.02 | 64.90 | 31.13 |

*Forbes ranks these corporations using a composite of sales, profits, market value, and assets.

SOURCE: Forbes (www.forbes.com).

in the United States. The term "too big to fail" was commonly used during the financial crisis to justify government bailouts of these large financial corporations. There is no doubt their failure would have brought down the whole economy. Congressional legislation was introduced in 2010 to reverse this radical deregulation of financial institutions, which began in the 1990s.

Table 7–1 lists the top 25 corporations in the United States for 2009 using the *Forbes* ranking scale, which combines sales, profits, assets, and market value of the corporation. The list is headed by then Exon Mobil, General Electric, AT&T, and Wal-Mart. Three oil companies that recently expanded their size through mergers are in the top 10, but the once mighty American car companies have fallen out of the top 25.

The size of major corporations in our society is only one aspect of economic concentration, though a very important aspect. What this size indicates is that the overall economy is dominated by a mere handful of corporations. This gives these corporations the ability to have an enormous effect on the economy (as well as politics) by the decisions they make or fail to make. Their performance as corporations, their profits, losses, and layoffs, affect the lives and well-being of millions of people.

## *The Power of Wal-Mart*

With more that $400 billion in sales in 2009, Wal-Mart was the second largest corporation in the United States, and third in the world. But with over 2 million employees, Wal-Mart was the world's largest employer in 2009 as it has been for several years. The five children of Sam Walton, the founder of Wal-Mart, have an estimated wealth of about $18 billion each, making them the 4th through the 7th richest people in the United States. Not surprisingly, because of its size Wal-Mart establishes trends in American labor relations and shapes the production of goods all over the world. These trends in American labor relations are toward lower wages, fewer benefits, longer working hours, and the extermination of labor unions. The company admits that you cannot raise a family on the average $8 per hour that it pays new employees, but adds that "working for Wal-Mart is maybe not right for everyone." (Information in this section comes primarily from a series of investigative reports appearing in the *Los Angeles Times,* November 23, 24, and 25, 2003). In the state of California, Wal-Mart's 44,000 employees averaged $9.70 an hour in 2003. At that level each employee was eligible for $1,952 in various types of welfare benefits. This led California to subsidize Wal-Mart's low-wage labor force by $86 million in 2003. At a time when the poverty line was about $20,000 per year for a family of four, Wal-Mart employees averaged $17,500 a year in 2005. Also in 2005, with only 45 percent of Wal-Mart employees getting any health benefits at all, the *New York Times* obtained a secret memo from top management at Wal-Mart discussing how the company could reduce these health benefits even further, even though 46 percent of the children of Wal-Mart employees were uninsured or receiving state welfare benefits for health care (*New York Times,* October 26, 2005).

During the mid-20th century the largest U.S. employer was General Motors, where unions were strong, benefits were good, and wages were high enough to allow its families to live above the poverty line. Now the trend is for more employers to be like Wal-Mart. And for the first time since the U.S. Census Bureau began measuring poverty in 1959, we will see in Chapter 9 that by 2000 almost 50 percent of all people who lived below the poverty line in the United States had a full-time worker living in the household.

Knowing that labor unions could help raise the wages and benefits of its employees, Wal-Mart has a strict policy of no union activity among its employees. If employees so much as talk with a union representative, they can be fired or denied any promotions. All new workers are required to watch a film depicting unions as corrupt and only out to take members' money. Managers of Wal-Mart branch stores are required to quickly report any union activity so the head office can rush out an "antiunion" SWAT team to make sure there is no further contact with a union.

Wal-Mart's impact on working Americans, however, is not confined to its low wages, disappearing benefits, or union busting. Wal-Mart is a leader in helping move jobs from the United States to poor countries with low-wage labor. In the early days of Wal-Mart, only 5 percent of goods bought in its stores were made in other countries. In 1985, founder Sam Walton launched his Bring It Home to the USA program. "Wal-Mart believes American workers can make a difference," he told suppliers, offering to pay as much as 5 percent more for U.S.-made products. By 2002 around 60 percent of merchandise sold in Wal-Mart stores was made in other countries. So fierce is the cost-cutting pressure of Wal-Mart on its suppliers that companies who wish to remain suppliers to Wal-Mart are often forced to locate new factories in poor developing countries around the world. Wal-Mart now has more than 3,000 supplier factories in China alone, with many more moving to other poor countries, contributing a considerable portion of all factories moving from American shores.

Even in food retailing Wal-Mart has established new records in price cutting, largely through very low wages and benefits for its employees. A cart of groceries at one of Wal-Mart's superstores, for example, costs 17 to 39 percent less than in grocery stores paying workers wages keeping them above the poverty line and allowing union membership. In order to compete with Wal-Mart superstores, large corporations selling groceries, such as Safeway and Vons, attempted to impose new cost-cutting measures on employees in late 2003. These corporations wanted to cut health care benefits for current employees and offer no salary increases. Most important, the big companies wanted a new contract allowing lower entry wages for all future employees, severely reduced benefits, and the prohibition of any future union membership. This would bring the hourly wage and benefit cost for the supermarket chains down from $19 per hour to the current $9 per hour for Wal-Mart employees. Employees of the big supermarket chains went on strike for 3½ months in an attempt to stop these demands. In the end the employees lost. Future employees will be offered pay and benefits close to those of current Wal-Mart employees and will be forbidden to join unions. With no union pressure or U.S. government laws restricting any of the actions of Wal-Mart described above, and now big supermarket chains as well, all other U.S. retailers must follow Wal-Mart's lead if they are to stay in business.

## Concentration of Stock Control

One of the most important means of influence within a corporation is the ownership or control of a large amount of stock in that corporation. Stock ownership usually brings votes in the affairs of that corporation in direct proportion to the amount of stock owned. The individual or family ownership of stock in major corporations today has become dispersed rather than concentrated. Fewer individuals or families own large amounts of stock in *particular* corporations.

But a new form of stock control is emerging. With growing funds from pension programs for workers and other large trust holdings, large *institutional investors* have increasing control over stock in major corporations (O'Sullivan 2000:156). These institutional investors, such as banks and insurance companies, do not own these massive concentrations of stock but do *control* them (Blair 1995). Again, the last time such a study was allowed in the U.S. Congress, the U.S. Senate Committee on Governmental Affairs (1978a) found that the institutional investors are most often given the voting and selling rights to this stock by the true owners. The result is control of the stock by large institutional investors.

The previously mentioned Senate study examined the stock control patterns in the nation's top 122 corporations. As an indication of the size of these corporations, their stock accounted for 41 percent of all the common stock issued in the United States at the end of 1976. The study was most concerned with investors who held one of the *top five* stock-voting positions in these 122 corporations. The study attempted to identify the investor controlling the most stock (or stock votes) in each corporation, the investor controlling the second-highest amount of stock (or stock votes), and so on. It should be noted that while some changes in the *exact* stock control figures for *particular* companies have occurred since 1976, the overall structure of corporate stock control has not changed significantly.

With 122 top corporations in the study there are 610 top-five stock-voting positions (5 × 122 corporations = 610). The most interesting finding from this study is that just *21 investors* accounted for more than *half* of all these top five stock-voting positions (325 of the total 610 top five positions). These 21 investors include 11 banks, 5 investment companies, 4 insurance companies, and 1 family group (the Kirby family). The most important investor was Morgan Bank, with one of the top five stock-voting positions in almost *half* of these top 122 corporations. Morgan Bank was the number one stock voter in 27 of these corporations, the number two stock voter in 11, number three in 8, number four in 7, and number five in 3 (see Table 7-2).

Large banks make up the most important group of stock voters in these 122 top corporations. Who controls the stock in these banks? In the U.S. Senate Committee's words (1978a:260), "the principal stockvoters in large banks are—large banks" (see Table 7-3). Of the top five banks in the nation (Bank of America, Citibank of New York, Chase Manhattan, Manufacturers Hanover, and Morgan) in 1976, Morgan was the number one stock voter in Bank of America, Citibank, and Manufacturers Hanover. Morgan was also the top stock voter in Chemical Bank (the sixth-largest in 1976) and Bankers Trust (the seventh-largest in 1976). Chase Manhattan was the only one that varied from this pattern; the Rockefeller family was the number one stock voter in Chase Manhattan. Given the prominence of Morgan Bank among these other banks, we need to know who dominates Morgan Bank. In short, the other banks dominate. The top stock voters in Morgan Bank were Citibank, Chase Manhattan, Manufacturers Hanover, and Bankers Trust.

The proportion of total corporate stock held by individuals or families in this country is declining steadily. At present, personal or family-owned and family-controlled

## TABLE 7-2

### Morgan Bank's Stock-Voting Position in 56 Large Corporations

| Company in which Morgan has stock control | Morgan Bank's stock-voting rank among all stockholders in listed corporation* | Percentage of total stock controlled in each corporation by Morgan Bank |
|---|---|---|
| 1. American Airlines | 1 | 6.05% |
| 2. American Express Company | 1 | 5.22 |
| 3. BankAmerica Corp. | 1 | 2.88 |
| 4. Bankers Trust New York Corp. | 1 | 1.67 |
| 5. Burlington Northern | 1 | 4.03 |
| 6. Chemical New York Corp. | 1 | 3.72 |
| 7. Citibank | 1 | 3.26 |
| 8. Connecticut General Insurance | 1 | 7.25 |
| 9. Consolidated Freightways Inc. | 1 | 5.27 |
| 10. Federated Department Stores Inc. | 1 | 3.45 |
| 11. General Electric Company | 1 | 1.30 |
| 12. Goodyear Tire and Rubber Company | 1 | 5.94 |
| 13. International Business Machines (IBM) | 1 | 2.53 |
| 14. International Telephone & Telegraph (IT&T) | 1 | 2.13 |
| 15. Kmart Corp. (Kresge Co., S. S.) | 1 | 4.63 |
| 16. Manufacturers Hanover Corp. | 1 | 3.88 |
| 17. Mobil Corporation | 1 | 2.46 |
| 18. Norfolk and Western Railroad Company | 1 | 1.62 |
| 19. Pepsico Inc. | 1 | 6.59 |
| 20. Santa Fe Industries Inc. | 1 | 2.87 |
| 21. Sears Roebuck and Company | 1 | 2.02 |
| 22. Southern Co. | 1 | 0.58 |
| 23. Southern Railway Co. | 1 | 4.38 |
| 24. UAL Inc. (United Air Lines) | 1 | 6.73 |
| 25. Union Carbide Corp. | 1 | 2.46 |
| 26. U.S. Steel Corp. | 1 | 2.40 |
| 27. Westinghouse Electric Corp. | 1 | 1.62 |
| 28. Caterpillar Tractor Co. | 2 | 1.66 |
| 29. Continental Illinois Corp. | 2 | 3.35 |
| 30. Exxon Corp. | 2 | 1.09 |
| 31. Eastman Kodak Co. | 2 | 1.55 |
| 32. General Motors Co. | 2 | 1.13 |
| 33. General Public Utilities Corp. | 2 | 0.30 |
| 34. Mellon National Corp. | 2 | 1.86 |
| 35. Missouri Pacific Corp. | 2 | 2.02 |
| 36. Penney Inc., JC | 2 | 3.06 |

*(Continued)*

## TABLE 7-2 (continued)

### Morgan Bank's Stock-Voting Position in 56 Large Corporations

| Company in which Morgan has stock control | Morgan Bank's stock-voting rank among all stockholders in listed corporation* | Percentage of total stock controlled in each corporation by Morgan Bank |
|---|---|---|
| 37. Procter & Gamble Co. | 2 | 2.41 |
| 38. Travelers Corp. | 2 | 3.36 |
| 39. American Broadcasting Companies Inc. | 3 | 2.65 |
| 40. Bethlehem Steel Corporation | 3 | 1.89 |
| 41. Coca-Cola Co. | 3 | 2.84 |
| 42. Du Pont de Nemours Co. | 3 | 1.02 |
| 43. Ford Motor Co. | 3 | 1.74 |
| 44. Rio Grande Industries Inc. | 3 | 4.39 |
| 45. Standard Oil Co. of California | 3 | 1.27 |
| 46. Union Oil Co. of California | 3 | 1.63 |
| 47. Continental Corp. | 4 | 1.14 |
| 48. Gulf Oil | 4 | 0.93 |
| 49. Middle South Utilities Inc. | 4 | 1.78 |
| 50. Northwest Airlines Inc. | 4 | 3.74 |
| 51. Northwest Bancorporation | 4 | 2.61 |
| 52. Reynolds Industries Inc., R. J. | 4 | 1.49 |
| 53. Texaco Inc. | 4 | 0.92 |
| 54. Consumers Power Co. | 5 | 0.37 |
| 55. Public Service Electric & Gas Co. | 5 | 0.59 |
| 56. Southern Pacific Co. | 5 | 0.90 |

*A rank of 1 means that Morgan Bank controls the most stock and stock votes of all the stockholders in the particular corporation. For example, Morgan Bank is the number one stock voter in American Airlines with 6.05 percent of the total stock votes in American Airlines.

SOURCE: U.S. Senate Committee on Governmental Affairs, *Voting Rights in Major Corporations* (1978a:280–281).

corporate stock accounts for about 50 percent of the total. In 1956 institutional investors controlled about 25 percent of the total stock; in 1976 their control was more than 40 percent; and by 1986 institutional investors controlled 50 percent of the total stock in the United States (U.S. Senate Committee on Governmental Affairs 1978a:593). Thus, the importance of family-controlled stock is declining both in proportion to the total U.S. stock and in proportion to the stock held in particular corporations. Corresponding to this decrease is the increase in stock controlled by the institutional investor both in proportion to the total U.S. stock and in proportion to the stock held in particular corporations.

The precise meaning of this shift is in dispute. On one hand, it is charged that institutional investors are not actively involved in using their mass of stock votes to influence the behavior or practices of corporations whose stock they control

(Domhoff 2002:32–35; Herman 1975). On the other hand, there is more evidence to suggest that these institutional investors do use their power from stock control to influence these corporations from time to time in various ways.

These corporations communicate frequently with the institutional investors, ask their advice, and consult with them before major issues (such as the election of board members) come before the stockholders (see the study by Julius Allen in U.S. Senate Committee on Governmental Affairs 1978a:559–799). The exact amount of influence these institutional investors (such as banks) exert over corporations whose stock they control is unclear. But the potential for influence is present and recognized by the corporations. This in itself can lead to a relationship in which corporate management is in contact with large institutional investors to make sure it has their confidence—and votes.

One major implication of the increasing importance of institutional investors in top corporations is the additional concentration of economic power in our society. Using Morgan Bank as an example, we find that American Express, Bank of America, Bankers Trust, Chemical Bank, Citibank, and Manufacturers Hanover have a relationship through Morgan as their number one stock voter. With industrial corporations, we find that General Electric, Westinghouse Electric, Mobil, Exxon, Standard of California, Union Oil, Gulf, and Texaco (to name only a few) are all related because Morgan is one of their top five stock voters (see Table 7-3). Through this mass of corporate relations

## TABLE 7-3

### Stock-Voting Positions in Top Five Banks Held by Other Top Banks

| Rank of bank by bank assets | Name | Stock-voting rank held in the bank by other top banks* | Percentage of total stock votes held by other banks |
|---|---|---|---|
| 1 | BankAmerica Corp. | 1 Morgan Bank | 2.88% |
| | | 2 Citibank | 2.47 |
| | | 4 First National, Chicago | 1.08 |
| 2 | Citibank | 1 Morgan Bank | 3.26 |
| | | 2 First National, Boston | 2.65 |
| | | 3 Harris Trust & Savings | 1.59 |
| 3 | Chase Manhattan Corp. | 1 Rockefeller Family | 1.85 |
| 4 | Manufacturers Hanover | 1 Morgan Bank | 3.88 |
| | | 3 Hartford National Bank | 1.09 |
| | | 4 Bankers Trust | 0.80 |
| 5 | Morgan Bank | 1 Citibank | 2.63 |
| | (J. P. Morgan & Co.) | 2 Chase Manhattan | 1.43 |
| | | 3 Manufacturers Hanover | 1.42 |
| | | 4 Bankers Trust | 1.10 |

*List of stock-voting positions held by other banks only; for example, stock voter number 3 in BankAmerica Corp. is not a bank and thus is not listed. The exception is that the Rockefeller family is listed as the number one stock voter in Chase Manhattan Corp.

SOURCE: U.S. Senate Committee on Governmental Affairs, *Voting Rights in Major Corporations* (1978a:260).

due to stock votes we find one common denominator: The banks have a lot of influence, but it is not independent influence by a particular bank because they all have stock-voting influence over each other. And if this were not enough to create a concentrated web of corporate connections, there is another web—interlocking directorates.

## Interlocking Directorates and Economic Concentration

The highest position of authority within a corporate hierarchy is represented by the board of directors. As a body averaging about 25 people per corporation, this group has the authority to hire and fire management and set broad policy. Its members come from both inside the corporation's management (its top managers, such as president and vice presidents) and outside the corporation. Most of the board members in big corporations are top executive officers (management) from other top corporations (Mizruchi 1992; Allen 1978; Mintz and Schwartz 1985).

The board members are charged with representing the interests of stockholders in the corporation, but, as we have shown earlier, the controllers of stock are often other corporations. Also, most individual stockholders are widely dispersed throughout the nation and have relatively minor amounts of stock. The result often is that interests within the corporation and other large corporations that have interests in the corporation (through control of stock, business deals, and financial holdings) gain representation on the board of directors.

Because the position of board member is not a full-time job, these people are free to participate in other activities, such as memberships in other corporate boards and positions as executives of other corporations. **Interlocking directorates** can be defined as the linking of two or more corporations through at least one of their board members. For example, a member of the board of directors of corporation A is also a member of the board of directors of corporation B. Corporations A and B are said to be linked through their boards of directors. Though not exactly within this definition, corporate interlocks through a corporate executive (such as a president) who is a board member of another corporation are considered equally important by most researchers. Another relationship has received increasing attention by researchers and government agencies. This relationship of **indirect interlocks** is defined as two corporations tied by their board members through a third corporation. Two corporations are indirectly interlocked when a board member from corporation A is linked to a board member from corporation B because both board members come together on the board of directors of corporation C. The relationship between corporations A and B in this case is less than with a direct interlock, but because some of the same outcomes may be achieved (discussed later), it is also considered important. We may add that indirect interlocks have received increasing attention because direct interlocking directorates between competing corporations (such as General Motors and Ford) are illegal. But such competing companies often are found with extensive indirect interlocking directorates, which as yet have not been made illegal (although this has been suggested; see U.S. Senate Committee on Governmental Affairs 1978b).

It is generally assumed that corporate interlocks are important because they (1) reduce competition among corporations in general, (2) represent outside influences over the corporation, (3) provide a means of sharing information about corporate plans and operations, (4) help provide unity among top corporate officials in the economy (much like social clubs), and (5) thus help provide unity in corporate dealings with the government.

In his detailed study of the corporate class in the United States and England, Useem (1984) found that the most important reason for interlocking directorates was to gain information from other corporate leaders that could be used for economic advantage, what he called "business scan." Galaskiewicz et al. (1985) found that interlocks were more common with chief executive officers from the biggest corporations and that high-status people who would likely have more information were sought out for these interlocks, thus seeming to confirm Useem's (1984) idea. But others have found additional reasons for these interlocks. For example, Galaskiewicz and Wasserman (1981) found that corporations often seek out directors from financial institutions to secure good relations with possible sources of capital. Burt, Christman, and Kilburn (1980) compiled data on interlocks that suggest many interlocks are for the purpose of maintaining or creating market relations with other firms. Burris (2005) examined over 700 corporate board members in more than 1,000 of the largest U.S. corporations to assess the extent to which these networks tend to form cohesion and common political attitudes and behavior such as making political contributions to the same candidates. He found that being in the same corporate network of interlocked directorates was more important than other factors such as type of industry in shaping this political behavior and cohesion.

Perhaps most important, however, these interlocks create another layer of *economic concentration* in addition to those already discussed through corporate size and stock control. With respect to the second point above, some researchers argue that interlocking directorates provide another means (in addition to stock control and credit) for board influence by large banks over other corporations (Mintz and Schwartz 1985; Mintz 1989; Mizruchi 1992; Scott 1991a, 1991b).

Having discussed why interlocking directorates can be important sources of corporate concentration and power, it is time to consider some of the evidence indicating the extent and patterns of such interlocks. We can begin by describing the overall magnitude of interlocking directorates among top corporations. In a study of interlocks among the top 250 corporations in 1970, Allen (1974) found these corporations to have an average of 10.41 interlocking directorates each. Among these corporations, financial institutions (primarily banks) had the highest number, with an average of 16.92 interlocking directorates.

Another study of interlocking directorates comes from Senate investigations (U.S. Senate Committee on Governmental Affairs 1978b, 1980). In this study the Senate committee included information on 130 top corporations in the United States (115 of the 122 corporations included in the previous Senate study on the control of stock, 1978a). Overall, each of 123 corporations (excluding 7 investment corporations) was directly or indirectly interlocked at least once with an average of 62 of the other 122 corporations (1978b:280). Nine of these corporations had from 90 to 99 direct or indirect interlocks with the other 122 corporations, 22 had from 80 to 89 interlocks, and 22 others had from 70 to 79 such interlocks.

Special attention was given by this Senate committee to the 13 largest corporations. These had ties with *70 percent* of the other 117 corporations through 240 direct and 5,547 indirect interlocking directorates. Among themselves, with the exception of BankAmerica, these 13 corporations were all directly or indirectly interlocked. Morgan Bank (previously found to have the most stock control in the top corporations) had the most interlocking directorates of all 130 corporations. The most heavily interlocked group among these 130 corporations included Citibank, Chase Manhattan Bank, Manufacturers Hanover, Morgan Bank, Prudential Life Insurance, Metropolitan Life, AT&T, Exxon, and General Motors. The financial corporations in this group were, of course, among the most important institutional investors listed in the previous section on stock control.

We may cite one final aspect of the Senate study of interlocking directorates. As noted earlier, direct interlocking directorates between competing companies are illegal. But the Senate was interested in the extent of *indirect* locking directorates among competitors. Each type of industry (such as auto producers, banks, and energy corporations) was examined and found to contain extensive indirect interlocks.

We will take the example of banks due to their importance in the economy (Mizruchi 1992; Mintz 1989; Mintz and Schwartz 1985). With the exception of BankAmerica to Bankers Trust and Western Bancorp to Chase Manhattan Bank, all top 10 banks in the country were indirectly interlocked. These indirect interlocks ranged from a low of only 1 between Western Bancorp and Bankers Trust to a high of 42 between First Chicago Bank and Continental Illinois. Others of importance include 30 indirect interlocks between Morgan and Citibank, 25 between Morgan and Manufacturers Hanover, 27 between Manufacturers Hanover and Chase Manhattan, and 26 between Manufacturers Hanover and Citibank. If indirect interlocks have the potential for restraining competition, increasing economic concentration, and increasing influence over the government, as suggested by the Senate committee, we certainly have the potential for financial corporate dominance in our society.

In one of the most recent studies of 1,029 larger corporations in the United States, the mass of connections among them was again shown. Of the largest, 28 had 28 to 45 ties to the other corporations in the group, 65 had 20 to 27 ties to other corporations, with 248 of these companies having from 10 to 19 ties with the others (Domhoff 2002:20). Table 7-4 lists the 28 corporations with the highest number of interlocks among the 1,029 corporations in the study.

Finally, we need to note how the reality of the massive number of direct and indirect interlocks is often difficult to imagine. Figure 7-1 may be of some help in this regard. In Figure 7-1 we find only the four largest New York banks and *some* of their interlocks with the corporations included in the U.S. Senate studies (1978, 1980) discussed earlier. These lines in the figure represent one direct interlock each to the corporations listed on the right side of the figure. Also remember, however, that these lines are multiplied numerous times as they result in indirect interlocks among all of the corporations listed in Figure 7-1. Figure 7-2 also shows the magnitude of interlocking directorates by graphically depicting the large corporations that are linked to the top-ranked corporation, Citigroup, parent of Citibank.

# The Inner Group of the Corporate Class

We began our discussion of this corporate class by suggesting that it was made up of people holding positions of authority in major corporations. But among these board members and top corporate officers there is a group that some suggest represents an even more elite group—the **inner group of the corporate class.** What are the characteristics of this inner group and of the people who are in it? What function does this inner group serve for the overall dominance of large economic institutions? A good place to begin

## TABLE 7-4

### The 28 Most Interlocked Corporations of 1,029 in 1996

| Company | Number of interlocks with others |
| --- | --- |
| Chase Manhattan Bank | 45 |
| Wells Fargo Bank | 41 |
| American Express | 40 |
| Prudential Insurance | 39 |
| Sara Lee Foods | 39 |
| Minnesota Mining and Manufacturing | 37 |
| General Motors | 33 |
| Kroger Stores | 33 |
| Ashland Oil | 32 |
| Bank of America | 32 |
| CSX (railroad) | 32 |
| Bell Atlantic | 31 |
| Coca-Cola | 31 |
| Procter and Gamble | 31 |
| Spring Industries | 31 |
| AMR | 30 |
| Mobil Oil | 30 |
| TRW | 30 |
| Xerox | 30 |
| Ameritech | 29 |
| Bell South | 29 |
| Union Pacific | 29 |
| Westinghouse Electric | 29 |
| Burlington Northern | 28 |
| Cummins Engine | 28 |
| Kellogg | 28 |
| Kmart | 28 |
| AOL Time Warner | 28 |

*SOURCE:* Domhoff (2002:22).

our search for this group is among the mass of interlocking directorates already identi-fied at the top of these corporate structures. Much research remains to be done, but we do have some information that proves very interesting.

At the outset it is important to recognize that of the mass of interlocking director-ates previously discussed, most interlocks are accounted for by a relatively small num-ber of people. For example, in a study of the biggest 797 corporations in 1969, Mariolis (1975) found that of 8,623 board members of these corporations, 7,051 had only one board position (that is, were not interlocked with another corporation). The interlocks were therefore accounted for by the 1,572 remaining board members.

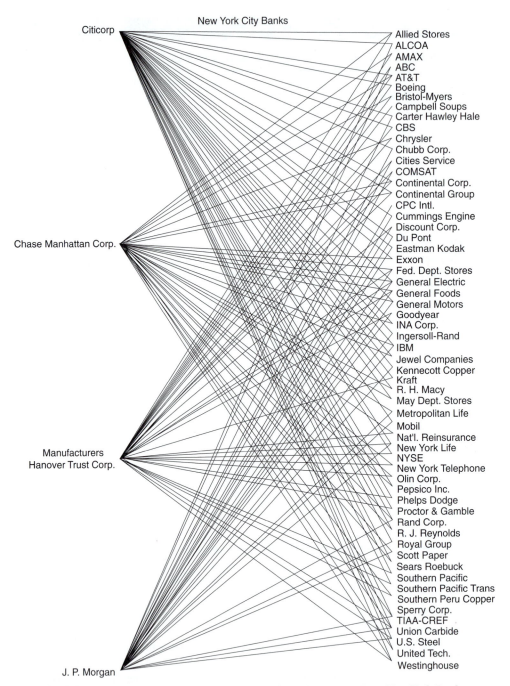

**FIGURE 7-1**   *Some of the Corporate Interlocks from the Largest Four New York Banks*

*SOURCE:* U.S. Senate Committee on Governmental Affairs (1980).

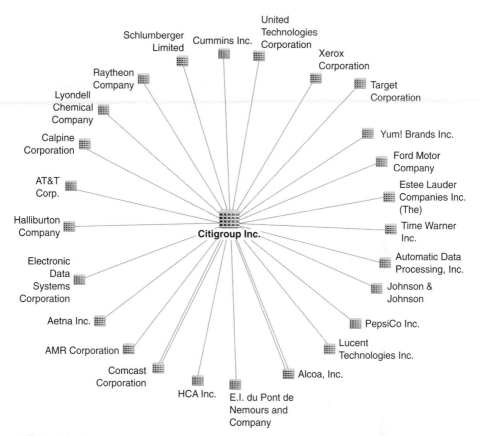

**FIGURE 7-2** *Interlocks from the Parent Company of Citibank to Other Major U.S. Corporations*

*SOURCE:* Domhoff (2009) (http://sociology.ucsc.edu/whorulesamerica/power/corporate_community.html).

Extensive research by several social scientists indicates this inner group of the corporate class (see Burris 2005; Useem 1976b, 1978, 1984; Soref 1976; Allen 1978; Mariolis 1975; Mizruchi 1992):

Tend to have more positions on corporate boards

Are more likely to be board members of larger corporations

Often represent large banks on corporate boards

More often belong to elite social clubs

Have worked their way up the corporate ladder to top positions rather than started at the top from wealthy family backgrounds

Represent general corporate interests in other institutions such as foundations, universities, and the government

Within the corporate class (as defined earlier), therefore, we find an elite group that makes up an inner circle having more corporate contacts. But is there any special significance in this inner group of the corporate class, or does it simply represent the most respected members of the corporate class? Useem (1978, 1979b, 1984), for one, argues that this inner group has an important function for the structure of corporate concentration today. Most important, this inner group functions to tie the large corporations more closely together. To the extent that these large corporations have common economic interests, the inner group of the corporate class helps unite these corporations so they may act upon their common interests.

One set of common interests, of course, is the political environment. When members of this inner group find their way into positions of political authority (such as the president's cabinet or advisory agencies), they are more able to speak for the interests of large corporations as a whole, rather than for the separate interests of one corporation. Also, this inner group may be able to coordinate corporate activities in combating challenges to the common interests of large corporations.

For example, Burris (2005) examined the unity and coordinated political activity among corporate board members that had the most extensive corporate interlocks. He found that no matter what kind of industry these board members were from, they tended to promote unity within the corporate class, have similar political attitudes, and took political action (such as making campaign contributions) to defend common corporate interests.

The unity and coordinating functions of social clubs and business organizations must also be considered. In our earlier discussion of these social clubs and business organizations, the views of Domhoff and others were presented on the importance of these organizations for upper-class unity and coordination. But whether or not Domhoff is correct about the continued existence of a powerful upper class, it should be recognized that these social clubs and business organizations are able to perform the same coordinating functions for a corporate class as well. As we have found with studies of the inner group of this corporate class, they, too, are frequent members of these organizations.

In fact, as Domhoff's (1974) study of the Bohemian Grove indicates, the participants at the retreat were more often corporate leaders than upper-class members. Thus, no matter whether an upper class or corporate class is seen as more important in the economy, these social clubs and business organizations (such as the Council on Foreign Relations and the Committee for Economic Development) may perform the same functions of unity and coordination for either group.

---

# ✳ Competing Capitalisms: A Conclusion

Back in 1776 Adam Smith probably had no idea of the various forms and directions capitalism would take by the end of the 20th century. Indeed, before the fall of the Berlin wall, the end of the cold war, and the end of almost all communist political economies around the world, most people in advanced industrial democracies thought only capitalism and communism were competing for world dominance. We know now that such assumptions were incorrect because there are clearly different forms, or modes, of capitalism around the world today. The political and economic systems in the United States, Continental Europe, and Asian nations are significantly different, with the American system the most unique in the 21st century. Each of these forms of capitalism allows differing economic classes advantages or disadvantages in pushing through agendas favoring their interests relative to those in other class positions.

There are what some refer to as competing models of "welfare capitalism," or simply different types of capitalist systems, with different relations between the government, the capitalist class or corporate class, and the middle and working class (Esping-Andersen 1990; Goodin et. al. 1999). The United States, and to a lesser degree Britain and Canada, have what some refer to as a neo-liberal system or corporate-dominated political economy in which the government stays relatively uninvolved in the economy (with little economic planning and almost no government ownership of industry), resulting in more freedom for a corporate class to run the economy as they see fit (Kerbo 2006: Chapter 3). Government in this form of capitalism is similar to what is described by the "instrumentalist" view of the state noted in Chapter 5. Implied in this description of a corporate-dominated political economy is a relatively weak working class, and especially a working class lacking influence in the government and in obtaining government protection (with labor laws, income protection, social benefits).

A significantly different capitalist system, found in varying degrees in Continental European countries (especially Germany and France), can be called "cooperative capitalism" or a corporatist system. As shown in Table 7-5, in a cooperative capitalist

## TABLE 7-5

### Competing Forms of Capitalism

|  | Corporate-Dominated Capitalism | Cooperative Capitalism | State Development Capitalism |
|---|---|---|---|
| **Countries** | USA<br>Canada<br>United Kingdom | Western European Union countries | Japan<br>Developing countries in East and Southeast Asia |
| **Characteristics** | Small state<br>Little government regulation<br>Weak unions<br>Low labor costs | Large welfare state<br>State regulation of the economy<br>Economic planning<br>Strong unions | Strong state intervention<br>Extensive regulation/planning<br>Weak unions |
| **Outcomes** | Cheap production costs<br>High inequality<br>Low benefits to workers<br>Less job security<br>Low unemployment<br>High poverty<br>Low taxes | High production costs<br>Low inequality<br>High worker benefits<br>High job security<br>High unemployment<br>Low poverty<br>High taxes | Medium production costs<br>Low inequality<br>Medium worker benefits<br>Medium job security<br>Low unemployment<br>Low poverty<br>Low taxes |

system the corporate class and working class, in alliance with government, have arrived at a power-sharing agreement in which the government helps to organize the economy and protect the interests of all parties. Central components of cooperative capitalism, in contrast to the U.S. corporate-dominated system, are strong labor unions and labor laws restricting what corporate elites can do in the economy and political system. As we will see in Chapter 15, perhaps the most striking contrast to the American form of corporate-dominated capitalism is Germany, where about 50 percent of corporate board members must be elected by the employees of the company, with the other half elected by stock-holders. In addition to this, a powerful "works council" is mandated by labor laws. This works council is also elected by employees and has the strong potential of blocking most management decisions that affect workers, such as hiring and firing employees, chang-ing working hours, or organizing work operations.

The most rapidly growing economies of the world today, primarily in Asia, have what can generally be called "state development capitalism" (Johnson 1982; Kerbo and McKinstry 1995; Vogel 1991; Fallows 1994). In this model of capitalism the state has more independent, or autonomous, political power, as well as more control over the economy. As in the case of the second largest economy in the world, Japan, there is little government ownership of industry, but the private sector is rigidly guided and restricted by bureaucratic government elites. Indeed, these bureaucratic government elites are not elected officials and are thus less subject to influence by either the corporate class or working class through the political process. The argument from this perspective has been that a government ministry can have the freedom to plan the economy and look to long-term national interests without having their economic policies disrupted by either corporate class or working class short-term and narrow interests, close to the "state autonomy" view we saw in Chapter 5. We especially consider these other two forms of capitalism in more detail in Chapter 15 when we outline the different stratification systems in Germany and Japan today.

The global economic competition of the 21st century will be played out under these differing forms of capitalism. The American elites have been betting that more deregulation of corporations (especially financial institutions), lower wages, fewer benefits, lower taxes, and less welfare will make the United States more competi-tive in the global economy. The Europeans have been betting that more government restrictions on corporations, more influence by employees of these corporations, more spending on social programs and human and physical infrastructure, and more government coordination of the economy will make them more competitive. They believe the U.S. model of less government regulation, fewer employee benefits, less pay, longer working hours for employees, and lower taxes will lead the U.S. economy to eventually self-destruct. Most Asian nations are betting that a much stronger state with less democracy guiding the economy will make them more dominant by the end of the 21st century.

These issues are examined in more detail in Chapters 14 and 15. For now it is time to turn to the middle and working classes in the United States to examine their position in the stratification system, their changing fortunes in recent decades, and how their comparatively low political influence in the political system contrasts with their counterparts in European countries.

## Summary

This chapter began with a critique of upper-class theory and information showing that the upper class is neither as united nor as powerful as it was in the earlier stages of capitalist societies. We then outlined why a new corporate class is more important and more powerful in advanced industrial societies as stock control has moved away from rich upper-class families to institutional investors made up of large banks and investment firms not so dominated by the old upper class. The power of this corporate class today is based on its control of corporations that are bigger and more concentrated, with an extensive network of interlocking directorates. The other means of upper-class influence, such as positions on the president's cabinet and lobbying organizations, are today held just as effectively by this newly dominant corporate class. At the center of this corporate class is what has been called the "inner group of the corporate class," made up of corporate executives with extensive director positions, as well as government and civic positions. We concluded the chapter with a discussion of several competing forms of capitalism and the advantages and disadvantages each form may have in the 21st century world of developing nations.

**8**

# The Middle and Working Classes

While America's corporate elite continued to far surpass the corporate elite of other industrial nations in income and stock options, working-class Americans such as these on an auto assembly line saw their wages stagnate and benefits decline in recent decades.

*SOURCE:* © ColorBlind Images/Getty Images.

# Chapter Outline

❖ The Middle and Working Classes in the System of Social Stratification

❖ The Middle Class and Working Class: Recent Historical Changes

❖ Some Consequences of Class Position

❖ Middle-Class and Working-Class Positions in the Structures of Economic and Political Power

❖ Summary

In the eyes of 19th-century Europeans, the founding and survival of the United States of America seemed one of the most radical developments in the history of human societies. True, some nations, like France, had embarked on their road to "equality and fraternity" with revolution. But by the early 1800s the French Revolution of 1789 had grown cold. The new dictatorship of Napoleon Bonaparte was in many ways a major reversal for these egalitarian principles—a reversal that would last for many years.

So it was that the French writer Alexis de Tocqueville was "startled" by what he saw as a condition of "equality" in this new country of America. From his travels throughout the United States in the 1830s he wrote the famous work *Democracy in America,* which began with the words "No novelty in the United States struck me more vividly during my stay there than the equality of conditions" (1969:9). Somewhat later in this work he wrote, "Men there are nearer equality in wealth and mental endowments, or, in other words, more nearly equally powerful, than in any other country of the world or in any other age of recorded history" (1969:56).

In two senses, de Tocqueville's observations were quite correct. Then, as now, the United States had a level of informality of personal interaction, a presumption of status equality, not found in Europe, or in Asia for that matter. But also, though it might seem ironic today with income inequality among industrial nations highest in the United States, compared with Europe at the time, inequality in America was lower. The United States was among the industrializing nations in which the level of inequality found in feudal societies was being rapidly reduced. Furthermore, in the United States this process of industrialization was proceeding without the strong tradition of aristocratic inequality found throughout Europe. One purpose of de Tocqueville's writing was to warn his European contemporaries of the "hidden dangers" of this new "equality"; that is, of the "tyranny of the majority" and the "restlessness in the midst of prosperity." This theme of the "excesses of equality and democracy" led some writers, such as Baltzell (1958), to defend upper-class traditions and power once they were established in this country.

In another sense, de Tocqueville's observations were misleading. These observations of equality and democracy were made through the eyes of a man accustomed to rigid and still quite pronounced class inequalities in Europe. Although there was a greater *degree* of equality and democracy in this new country, the inequalities of wealth and power were still there. The wealth of our country's founders is well known, and, as many have argued, our federal government and Constitution were constructed in such a way as to protect the economic interests of wealthy planters, financiers, and merchants (see Zinn 1995: Chapter 5; Morgan 1956 for a summary of this argument). Perhaps most important, as we saw in Chapter 6, by the later 1800s a national upper class emerged in this country that in many ways resembled the European upper class based in aristocratic traditions.

In direct contrast to de Tocqueville's observations is a Marxian perspective on the growth of capitalism in the United States. As we have seen, a wealthy and powerful upper class did develop based on ownership of the most important means of production—quite in line with Marxian analysis. The stark contrast between the living conditions of this relatively small group of propertied families and those of the rapidly growing industrial proletariat was all too clear, as it continues to be today.

However, neither is this historical analysis of the United States without inaccuracies. It is true that ownership and power became more concentrated through time, but the industrial proletariat (or working class) did not grow to the point of including the vast majority of people in this country, nor did their material conditions always grow steadily worse. There was another process at work, one that led to a large new middle class of white-collar workers as a buffer between the two main classes in Marxian theory. With what is called the shrinkage of the middle class today, however, this buffer is breaking down.

The past 30 years indeed have been bad ones for people in the bottom half of America's income distribution. As we will see in more detail in this chapter, in the last three decades, the American middle class and working class have been working longer hours, for less money and fewer benefits, and have less secure employment. (See Mishel, Bernstein, and Allegretto, 2007, Chapters 3 and 4, for more detailed figures like these below.) The percentage of people in the middle of the income scale has been shrinking. Those who remain in the middle have seen slight improvements in real income since 1970, but their situation is less secure. Using data from the Panel Study of Income Dynamics at the University of Michigan—a panel study that has tracked a sample of 5,000 American families for almost 40 years—a *Los Angeles Times* investigative report found their incomes to vary by an average of $13,500 from year to year in 2004 compared to $6,500 in the 1970s (*Los Angeles Times,* October 10, 2004). When unemployed, these families could expect only 6 months of unemployment benefits, at reduced levels, compared to 15 months in the mid-1970s. In 2003, only 2.9 million of the more than 8 million unemployed in the United States received any unemployment benefits. During the 1970s the federal government kicked in $27.3 billion annually to help retrain those unemployed; in 2004 it contributed only $4.4 billion. Also, 25 years ago more than 40 percent of these middle-class employees had full pension coverage from their jobs. Currently only 20 percent have such coverage, with the rate falling fast. As recently as 1987 about 80 percent of these middle-income workers had good health benefits. Today that figure is 63 percent and falling fast. Just since 2000 these employers have raised the cost their employees must pay for health benefits by 50 percent. In 1978 a middle-aged man could expect to stay with a job for an average of 11 years. Today that is down to 7.5 years. In addition, the average length of time a person remains unemployed is 50 percent greater than in 1978. In the same time period, as discussed in earlier chapters, CEO salaries have soared. So has their security; 300 of the top 500 corporations in the United States today guarantee their CEOs full pay for 2 years even if they leave their job on their own initiative. Some give $2 million in base pay for up to 5 years. And this does not include the stock options. These CEOs have also been handsomely rewarded for increasing profits by outsourcing, sending millions of American jobs overseas, thus helping to create this greater insecurity for middle-income Americans. A 2004 study by the Institute for Policy Studies found that U.S. corporations outsourcing American jobs received pay increases during 2003 averaging 46 percent, compared to only 9 percent pay increases for CEOs who did not export American jobs (Institute for Policy Studies; www.ips-dc.org).

The major economic crisis that began in 2008 was one of the sharpest, and probably the worst, since the Great Depression of the 1930s. As of 2010, almost all economists agreed that quick government action to stimulate the economy from late 2008 and through 2009 kept this major recession from turning into another great depression (for example, see Wessel 2009). By late 2009 the stock market was moving back up at a strong pace. Top management at the biggest financial firms that helped cause the financial crisis had no cuts in their annual multimillion dollar pay checks and bonuses. But the middle and working classes took a big hit. While the stock market and corporate profits were moving back up sharply by the end of 2009, unemployment remained in the 10 percent range in 2010. People continued to lose their homes because they couldn't make mortgage payments. Unemployment benefits were extended for a few months, but for most of the unemployed these benefits were running out by mid-2010. As with the last two recessions since 1990, it appears it will take much longer for unemployment to go back down compared to previous decades in the United States. And it also appears likely that, like recessions since 1990, many of the better paying jobs lost in 2008 and 2009 will never return.

This chapter examines the place and life conditions of the two *numerically* dominant classes in the United States system of stratification. As is typical in writings on the American class system, much of this chapter is devoted to the standard of living, lifestyle, attitudes, and social behavior of these two classes. Equally important is our task to locate and describe the position of these two great classes in the more general system of power and social stratification in this country. By doing so we will be able to better understand the forces producing differences in lifestyle, attitudes, and social behavior.

## ✻ The Middle and Working Classes in the System of Social Stratification

In Chapter 5 (see Table 5-2) the place of the middle and working classes in the overall system of stratification was outlined with reference to the occupational, bureaucratic authority, and property structures in this society. At this point we must expand this outline, as well as note the diversity within these two classes. We can begin with the middle class.

With respect to the *occupational structure,* the *middle class* is located within a range of occupations ranked (in terms of complexity and skill) from the highest (such as the traditional professions of doctor and lawyer, accountants, architects, higher-level scientists, and engineers) to mid-level (such as public school teachers, insurance agents, sales clerks, and office workers). There is a wide range of income and education levels within this grouping of occupations, but they do have some important common characteristics.

One of these is the general type of work performed, which can be described as *non-manual,* in contrast to manual or physical labor. These people are typically involved in less strenuous or less physically demanding labor, labor that involves working with symbols or abstract ideas or talking with people. Because it is not "dirty work"—that is, working with oily machines, digging ditches, or constructing buildings—it is often labeled *white-collar* work. White-collar labor does have a higher status. In part, most people feel they have higher status when they leave for work wearing a suit rather than overalls or "work clothes."

Another common characteristic of white-collar labor is a requirement of average to above-average education (that is, from high school to college-level education). To perform white-collar labor means using abstract ideas or numbers or writing reports—in short, using skills that must usually be obtained through a formal educational system (in contrast to physical skills, which may often be learned in short periods of time).

A wide range of skill levels is used in white-collar labor, and some manual-labor tasks demand a skill and knowledge higher than those demanded by lower-level white-collar occupations (for example, compare office jobs involving nothing more than adding a few simple numbers with manual jobs requiring an extensive knowledge of electricity; Wright 1997; Wright et al. 1982). But despite the wide range in job complexity and a small overlap with some manual-labor occupations in terms of skill level, the nonmanual versus manual distinction remains useful.

Before turning to working-class positions in the occupational structure, let us note the useful distinction commonly made between *upper-middle-class* and *lower-middle-class* occupations. The upper middle class is at the very top of the occupational structure, with jobs bringing high rewards and requiring higher levels of education (such as a postgraduate college degree). In one sense the distinction between upper- and lower-middle-class occupations is a matter of degree, but the boundary (though somewhat arbitrary and often difficult to specify) is useful.

As we will see below, characteristics other than income and education level tend to differentiate upper-middle-class and lower-middle-class people. What was called the corporate class in the previous chapter may also be located toward the top of the occupational structure. However, the corporate class can be distinguished from the upper middle class in terms of position in the bureaucratic authority structure (with the corporate class on top) and control of the most important means of production.

*Working-class* or *blue-collar* people occupy mid-level to low positions within the occupational structure. Working-class occupations are typically characterized by relatively low skill level, lower education, and a lower degree of complexity, as well as manual instead of nonmanual labor. Working-class people are factory workers, truck drivers, plumbers, gas station attendants, welders, and so on. Their jobs are for the most part lower paying, less secure, and more physically demanding and dangerous.

As with the middle class, a further distinction is often made within the working class, dividing it about equally between skilled and unskilled working-class occupations. The more skilled jobs require more training (usually on the job or as an apprentice), are usually better paying and (until recent years) much more secure, and provide higher job satisfaction. In contrast, unskilled jobs are less complex, require little training, are less secure, and are less rewarding both materially and psychologically. Of those who work in our society, the unskilled laborer is on the bottom of the occupational structure.

Clearly, the occupational structure represents a system of continuous rankings (in terms of skill and job complexity) in which it is difficult to draw firm lines around upper-middle-class, lower-middle-class, and skilled and unskilled working-class occupations. The manual versus nonmanual distinction is less difficult to make, although even here there are a few relatively ambiguous occupational roles (such as computer repair). But we do find it useful to identify class positions, in part, through positioning in the occupational structure.

For most people, occupation influences much about what happens in their lives, how others view them, and how they come to view themselves. However, there is another predominant social structure that produces social divisions and shapes the general nature of the stratification system in this country. People are also divided with respect to positions within *bureaucratic authority* structures.

The middle class, when not self-employed, usually occupies positions toward the middle of authority structures. Its members receive orders from above while giving orders to those below. In the large corporation they are the mid-level to lower-level managers who receive orders from the corporate elite, then pass along orders to lesser managers or workers on the shop floor. In government agencies they are the bureaucrats who receive orders from political elites and pass along orders to lesser bureaucrats or whatever type of low-level worker is associated with the government agency.

There is no simple congruence between position in the occupational structure and position in authority structures. Some workers are self-employed, and the nature of some authority structures leaves mid-level workers (in terms of occupation) on or close to the bottom of the authority structure. Examples of the latter would be legal secretaries in a law firm, caseworkers in a state welfare department (if we choose to assume that welfare recipients are not part of the work-oriented aspect of this authority structure), and teachers (again, if we choose to assume students are in some ways not part of this authority structure).

The working class usually occupies positions toward the bottom of all authority structures. Its members receive orders from many layers above and are seldom in a position to give orders to others. Typically, they are told what work to do, how it should be done, when, and how fast. (Though, as we will see in Chapter 15 on social stratification in Germany, nowhere among industrial nations can this last statement be made in such an extreme fashion as in the United States.)

---

# ✴ The Middle Class and Working Class: Recent Historical Changes

Class relations are seldom static. If nothing else, a historical analysis of inequality can make this observation obvious. From the vantage point of the present we find striking differences when looking back to, say, the Roman Empire or European feudalism. The overall nature of social stratification may be quite similar—that is, those on top receive more rewards and maintain their advantaged positions in some familiar ways and those on the bottom are viewed as inferior, lazy, immoral, and deserving of their status. But we often find a differing number of classes, laboring under diverse conditions, with an upper class holding its position for different reasons (such as ownership of land, ownership of industrial capital, control of the organized means of violence, or control of religious hierarchies).

When comparing the present with more recent history, however, differences are often less obvious. Except for periods of violent upheaval, as in revolution, class systems normally change slowly. But they do change. The past 100 years or so of U.S. history has shown some significant, though not often obvious, changes with respect to class distribution. And as already noted, big changes are again taking shape in the middle of the class structure.

At the outset we can examine how the occupational composition of the class system has changed. As is indicated in Table 8-1, in terms of occupation, the civilian labor force in this country has become substantially more middle class since 1900. Whereas 18 percent of the labor force was in white-collar occupations and 83 percent in blue-collar occupations in 1900, by the 1970s this distribution had changed to about 50 percent white-collar and 50 percent blue-collar. Table 8-1 shows that by 2002 white-collar occupations had expanded to almost 60 percent of the total. (After 2002 the U.S. Census Bureau and Labor Department changed the way jobs are categorized and thus we cannot make as precise comparisons after 2002. But as we will see below, there has been a continued shrinking of skilled blue-collar jobs, but with an increase in low-paying and less-skilled service jobs in recent decades.) The continued decline in blue-collar jobs is related to changes in the U.S. economy as well as the export of these jobs to cheaper labor in other countries. While the percentage of working-class jobs has been declining

## TABLE 8-1

### Occupational Distribution of Civilian Labor Force, 1900–2002

| Occupation | 1900 | 1920 | 1940 | 1960 | 1979 | 1990 | 2002 |
|---|---|---|---|---|---|---|---|
| Professionals | 4% | 5% | 7% | 11% | 15% | 13% | 16% |
| Managers | 6 | 7 | 7 | 11 | 11 | 11 | 15 |
| Sales/tech | 5 | 5 | 7 | 6 | 6 | 15 | 15 |
| Clerical | 3 | 8 | 10 | 15 | 18 | 15 | 13 |
| Total white-collar | 18% | 25% | 31% | 43% | 50% | 54% | 59% |
| Crafts | 11 | 13 | 13 | 13 | 13 | 11 | 11 |
| Operatives | 13 | 16 | 18 | 18 | 15 | 11 } | 13 |
| Laborers | 12 | 12 | 9 | 5 | 5 | 4 } | |
| Service | 9 | 8 | 12 | 12 | 14 | 18 | 14 |
| Farmers* | 38 | 27 | 17 | 8 | 3 | 3 | 3 |
| Total blue-collar | 83% | 76% | 68% | 56% | 50% | 47% | 41% |

*Because some farmers own extensive farm property, it is somewhat misleading to place all farmers among blue-collar workers. However, as all farmers accounted for only 3 percent of the civilian labor force in 1990, the overall conclusions of this table are not altered.

*SOURCES:* U.S. Bureau of the Census, *Historical Statistics of the United States, Colonial Times to 1970* (1972:139); U.S. Bureau of Labor Statistics, *Handbook of Labor Statistics* (1990: Table 17, p. 78); and calculated from U.S. Bureau of the Census, *Statistical Abstracts of the U.S., 2003* (2004: Table 615).

overall (Wright 1997; Wright and Martin 1987), there are important changes *within* the working-class category. There has been a substantial decrease in the higher-skilled working-class positions and an increase in the lower-paying working-class positions not adequately represented in Table 8-1 (Tilly and Tilly 1998; Thurow 1987), but that will be considered in more detail later.

Table 8-1 also does not indicate change with respect to authority positions, though the expansion of bureaucratic organizations and the positive relationship between occupational position and authority position (shown earlier) lead us to conclude that there has been an accompanying increase in mid-level authority positions since 1900. That is, with more bureaucratization, there were more people watching over and giving orders to others. We do have detailed studies showing that the percentage of the workforce holding managerial and supervisory positions has grown steadily since 1960 (Wright 1997; Wright and Martin 1987), and, in fact, the United States now has a higher number of managers per worker than any other industrial nation (Tilly and Tilly 1998:205).

## Stability and Change in the Working Class

Although the rise of the new middle class came late in the process of industrialization, the industrial proletariat or working class was born with the industrial revolution. "The modern working class is the product of the machine. . . . It is the creation of the machine—to be exact, of the mechanical tool. No machines would mean no working class" (Kuczynski 1967:51).

The rise of the industrial working class was the product of a dual process: the spread of agrarian capitalism, which pushed peasants off the land, and the growth of urban industry, which brought work to some of the landless peasants. This dual process, as it began in Western Europe, first brought work mostly to women and children. The novels of Charles Dickens, such as *Oliver Twist,* are all too accurate on this point. For example, in the British cotton industry in 1835, 74 percent of the labor was made up of women and children below the age of 18 (13 percent of the labor force was younger than 13).

Comparable figures are found for the United States in 1831: 60 percent of all laborers in the cotton industry were women (Kuczynski 1967:62–63). Factory owners preferred the labor of women and children because they were considered more docile and easily controlled. But as the pool of unemployed males increased, as child labor laws were enacted, and as industrialization spread to other types of production, the industrial labor force became predominantly male.

Since the early stages of capitalism in the United States, as we have seen, the percentage of working-class jobs has been slowly shrinking (Tilly and Tilly 1998). Since the 1970s, an important change has been the reduction in skilled working-class jobs while the number of low-skilled working-class jobs has increased. But one of the most important changes not yet discussed has been in the percentage of the labor force represented by a labor union. With the increase in skilled working-class jobs and large corporations in this century, the percentage of the labor force in unions was increasing. But in the United States there has been a rather dramatic change downward in the percentage of the labor force represented by unions in the last two decades, which requires more analysis later in this chapter.

Another change deserves more extensive comment at this point. The growth of major corporations, their control over the market, and the concentration of workers in these big corporations are relatively recent phenomena. Such concentration remains unequally distributed throughout industrial sectors. What can be called a **dual economy,** or, from the worker's perspective, a *dual labor market,* exists. In brief, the dual economy means that industries (groups of corporations with the same economic functions, such as producing steel, producing electrical power, or merchandising) are divided between **core** and **periphery industries** (see Beck et al. 1978; Tolbert et al. 1980).

Some characteristics of core industries include (1) a high concentration of corporate assets within the industry (a few large corporations do most of the business), (2) higher productivity, (3) higher profits, (4) more capital-intensive production, and (5) less economic competition (that is, the industry is more like a monopoly). The periphery industries fall toward the opposite of all *five* of these characteristics. (In reality, we can look at the core and periphery characteristics as opposite poles of a continuum.) Examples of core industries are petroleum, auto production, and primary metal production (such as steel). Examples of periphery industries are general merchandising (department stores), service stations, and restaurants (see Tolbert et al. 1980:1109).

Most important for our present discussion are the differing outcomes for workers employed in either core or periphery industries in the dual economy. In the core industries in the United States, as well as in other advanced capitalist industrial societies such as Japan (Kalleberg and Lincoln 1988), we find (1) higher wages, (2) better-than-average working conditions, and (3) more fringe benefits. Core industries are in a better position to provide higher wages and better benefits because they have less competition and more profits, and are able to pass higher labor costs to consumers. Also, workers in core industries are somewhat more unionized, and thus are more successful in pressing their demands. We must note that with more foreign competition affecting especially core industries, and "downsizing," the income advantage of U.S. core workers compared with periphery workers has been significantly reduced since the 1960s (Tigges 1988; Tilly and Tilly 1998:202–227).

## The Changing Occupational Structure: The Shrinking Middle

The "shrinking middle class" has become one of the hottest topics of discussion in the mass media in recent years. Newspapers are full of stories about the loss of jobs to foreign competition, factories closing in the United States while corporations open new factories in other countries such as China, and "outsourcing" of jobs to other countries. (By "outsourcing" of jobs we mean foreign workers hired to do jobs in their own countries that were previously done by Americans working inside the United States.) Many of these jobs are low skilled manufacturing jobs going to places like China. In the last 25 years the percentage of U.S. jobs in manufacturing has dropped from 23 percent to 11 percent of total U.S. jobs (Prestowitz 2005:200). Wal-Mart in China provides a good example. As noted earlier, when Wal-Mart founder Sam Walton was alive, he made sure less than 10 percent of goods sold in Wal-Mart were made in other countries. Foreign-made goods sold in Wal-Mart is now 60 percent, with Wal-Mart alone responsible for about 10 percent of the huge trade deficit the United States has with China. For another example, 60 percent of the new Boeing "Dream Liner" 787 that is coming out in 2011 is being made in Japan (Prestowitz 2005:68, 128). U.S. jobs are also flowing to India. Since 2002 the number of jobs from U.S. *Fortune* 500 companies moving to India has tripled. And these jobs are more traditional middle-class service jobs and high-tech jobs. India produces more engineering graduates than the United States, and by all accounts they are as well trained as Americans, and often better. Many high-tech electronics firms in California's famous Silicon Valley are hiring a large percentage of Indian engineers, both in California and India. I know of many cases where an American engineer does his or her work during the day, then communicates with a work partner in India who takes over the work assignment on their shared computer while the American sleeps. The engineer in India works for 30 percent of the wage paid that American engineer. Former U.S. trade negotiator Clyde Prestowitz likes to tell the story of his MIT engineering graduate son who ask his father to invest in a Colorado snow removal company he was starting. Asked why a young man with an engineering degree from MIT would want to do that, his son replied, "they can't remove snow from India" (Prestowitz 2005).

As we have seen, there was shrinkage in the middle through the 1980s, with slight growth at the top and much growth in the bottom in terms of the income of jobs. In the first half of the 1990s the shrinking middle-paying jobs continued as in the 1980s, with these jobs primarily being lost from manufacturing, mining, and construction. For example, from just 1988 to 1993 there was a loss of almost 2 million skilled and semiskilled jobs in these areas, while there was a net increase of 1.3 million service jobs paying an average of $215 per week according to U.S. Census data (see, for example, the *New York Times,* October 17, 1994). This is a primary reason that, as of 1993, the U.S. Bureau of the Census, in its publication *The Earnings Ladder,* reported 18 percent of all fully employed workers in the United States were making wages *below the poverty line.* This represents a 50 percent increase in full-time workers below the poverty line since 1979. Another way of viewing this shift is to simply compare production jobs versus service jobs. The percentage of U.S. jobs producing things dropped from about 30 percent in 1979 to 19 percent in 2001. The percentage of U.S. jobs involving service to other people increased from 70 percent in 1979 to 81 percent in 2001 (Mishel, Bernstein, and Boushey 2003:179). Some of these service jobs are well paid, but most are not.

This shift from good-paying industrial jobs to low-paying, low-skilled service jobs continued unabated through the George W. Bush presidency. By then, though, the new buzzword was *outsourcing,* the process of sending good American jobs to low-wage countries to increase U.S. corporate profits. The concern over outsourcing was stimulated when a curious thing happened during the slow economic recovery from late 2001. The United States had gone through the longest economic boom in history through the 1990s. Unemployment remained very low during this period, though for the first time in history wages failed to increase through this long economic boom. But when the new recovery started in late 2001 we had another historical record: Almost 3 years into the economic recovery, by the winter of 2004 unemployment and poverty continued to increase. It was the longest period of economic recovery in American history without a drop in unemployment. There was a loss of over 3 million American jobs while corporate profits surged, and an additional one and a half million Americans fell into poverty. It was not until later in 2004 that the number of jobs started to increase with the economic recovery. However, doing the math on the job losses shows that even with the small gains, a net loss of jobs still occurred in the first 4 years of economic recovery. By all indications, the sharp recession that began in 2008, with unemployment still in the 10 percent range in mid-2010, will repeat this pattern.

This situation was simply a continuation of trends that sped up during the long economic boom. In previous economic recessions corporations cut back production, laid off workers, and cut inventory to save profits as they rode out the recession. When the recession was over, corporations started rehiring workers to increase production to take advantage of the new demand for goods. Now it is different. With more freedom to move around the world, more U.S. industrial corporations figure they can beat a recession by cutting costs with low-wage third world labor. The recessions, in other words, further drive U.S. corporations to close operations in America and move overseas.

The United States was not alone among major industrial nations with a shrinking middle class. However, the shrinking of the middle class (defined as being between 75 percent and 125 percent of median income in each nation) was largest in the United States between 1980 and 1995, and several European Union nations actually had increases in their middle class (Pressman 2001). By 1995 the United States had the smallest middle class of all these nations, with its 27.3 percent of all households in the middle class in stark contrast to most other nations, such as Germany's 43.9 percent and Sweden's 52.7 percent.

Recent research indicates that there is increasing income variation within occupational categories today (Kim and Sakamoto 2008). In other words, when considering a shrinking middle class we can no longer look just at changes in occupational types in the United States. A better understanding of the shrinking middle class can be estimated by the percentage of jobs paying middle-class wages, below middle-class wages, or above middle-class wages. In new job data supplied by Erik Olin Wright (some unpublished, but see Wright and Dwyer 2003), we find more details of why there is this shrinking middle class in terms of middle-paying jobs in the United States. With detailed job data from the Bureau of Labor Statistics, Wright ranked a large sample of jobs in terms of their average pay. He divided these jobs into 20 percent segments from lowest-paid to highest-paid jobs to track the changes from the 1960s to the early 2000s. Figure 8-1 shows clearly what has been occurring. From 1963 to 1970 there were more higher-paying jobs being produced in the United States. Middle-paying jobs also show healthy growth, while the lowest-paying jobs grew the least. This is one reason for the reduction in inequality during this period we found in Chapter 2. However, the pattern is far different during the 1990s. From 1992 to 2000 we find that the number of middle-paying jobs grew far less, while the lowest-paid and highest-paid 20 percent of jobs increased more, with the highest-paid 20 percent of jobs increasing most. Then in Figure 8-2 we find a continuation of the pattern; between 2003 and 2006 the middle-paying jobs increased least, but this time the lowest-paid jobs increased even more than the highest-paying jobs. At first, during the 1980s, Wright and Dwyer (2003) found the drop in new middle-paying jobs to be due to productivity increases in manufacturing, meaning few workers were needed in these industries. However, there is now evidence that the reduced growth of middle-paying jobs is due to imports, factories moving overseas, and outsourcing, with a large dose of low-paying jobs coming in services industries and places like Wal-Mart.

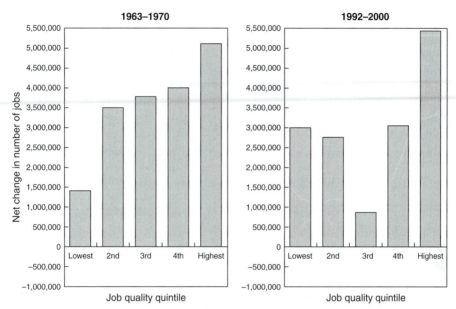

**FIGURE 8-1**     *Changes in Jobs by Lowest to Highest Paid, 1963–1970 and 1992–2000*

*SOURCE:* Wright and Dwyer (2003).

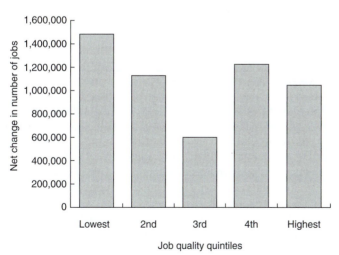

**FIGURE 8-2**     *Changes in Jobs by Lowest to Highest Paid, 2003–2006*

*SOURCE:* Erik Olin Wright, unpublished data using Bureau of Labor Statistics data.

There are a combination of factors responsible for this shrinking middle class, or middle-paying jobs, in the United States in recent decades. As Wright and Dwyer (2003) have shown, much of the loss is due to increased productivity in manufacturing firms in response to increased foreign competition (machines and higher-tech production methods mean fewer workers are needed in the industries). But in the 1990s through 2007 we also know that many jobs have been sent abroad to produce goods and services for U.S. corporations that were once produced at home. As noted in the previous chapter, Wal-Mart provides a leading example.

Finally, there have been changes in the United States related to political policies and the greater power of the corporate elite, noted earlier. Recent research by Weeden and Grusky (some still unpublished, but see Weeden et al. 2007) has shown that increasing income for higher-paying occupations has been due to the continued ability to organize within the occupational category to keep wages up and to limit the numbers of people entering these jobs through educational credentials and other means. The reduction in wages for middle- and lower-skilled occupations is related to less bargaining power and organization within their occupations, to a large degree related to the huge drop in union membership in the United States since the 1950s.

To fully explain this historic shift in the American occupational structure, we must consider the changed U.S. position in the modern world system in our latter chapters. But the basic reasons for the shift are generally well known: (1) The United States has lost manufacturing to several countries such as China, Japan, South Korea, and Germany. (2) At the same time, the United States is winning in competition with these countries in the higher-income service and high-tech industries (such as computers). (3) To try to regain some of the competitive edge in manufacturing and keep its competitive edge in service industries of all kinds, American corporations began aggressively downsizing and following new ideas of "lean production" and "lean management," which means the loss of middle-income jobs. Then outsourcing middle-paying American jobs to low-wage countries became the trend as the 1990s progressed into the new century.

# ✠ Some Consequences of Class Position

Whether or not they recognize precise class divisions or even the general nature of social stratification, most people in industrial societies are at least vaguely aware of many class differences. They may know, for example, that working-class people tend to live in neighborhoods that are different from those of the middle class, or that U.S. working-class people tend to favor country-and-western music, or that political candidates often appeal to different classes. Various class differences are presented every night on the television news, and we read about them in our newspapers.

We have a great deal to understand about human behavior and social organization, but the relatively short history of empirical research in the social sciences has at least demonstrated the importance of social stratification in much of this understanding. We can't always predict individual behavior or attitudes from class position alone, but the research is consistent in showing that many differences in behavior, attitudes, and other individual characteristics are often associated with positions in the stratification system. Let us consider some specific examples.

Even the most intimate kinds of human behavior can be influenced by place in the stratification system. Using level of education as an indicator of class position, Weinberg and Williams (1980) examined extensive data on many types of sexual behavior from separate studies conducted between 1938 and 1970. They conclude from their examination that throughout this period clear differences are evident between social classes in many types of sexual behavior. For example, among their findings in the 1970 data is that people with less education generally had earlier sexual experiences of various types (from necking to sexual intercourse). However, females with a college education more often responded positively to their initial experience with sexual intercourse, masturbation (by self and opposite sex), and oral sex (Weinberg and Williams 1980:43).

Very general psychological conditions such as happiness and self-respect also have been found to have a significant relationship to social class. For example, Bradburn and Caplovitz (1965) discovered that those higher in the class system were more likely to report being happy. Similarly, Andrews and Withey (1976) have shown that there is a positive relationship between social class and a general sense of well-being. The important condition of self-worth or self-esteem, which itself has many implications for behavior, has been found to be positively related to social class among adults (Rosenberg and Pearlin 1978).

Even when these class differences are recognized, however, they are not always accurately perceived; nor is the range of the differences fully appreciated. Perhaps most important, the *reasons* for these differences are seldom understood. In this section our task will be to examine some of the consequences of class position for the middle and working classes. While the topic is perhaps mundane compared with sex differences, we will begin with income differences, then consider differences related to working conditions and attitudes toward work. Last, general cultural and lifestyle differences between the middle and working classes will be explored.

## Income Distribution by Class

The most commonly recognized class inequality is income. The usual assumption is that working-class people receive below-average incomes, the middle class receives average incomes, and the upper-middle-class professionals and managers receive above-average to high incomes. These traditional assumptions about class income inequality are becoming much more of a reality today with the growing inequality and ever lower pay for working-class positions.

With a drop in middle-paying jobs and a huge growth in lower-paying jobs in the last two decades indicated in the previous section, one would wonder why the average standard of living has not dropped in the United States. We saw in Chapter 2, for example, that the median wage has gone up and down only slightly from the 1980s to the present. Figure 8-3 helps us understand what is happening for the American middle class especially: We see at the top of Figure 8-3 that median household income has been going up slightly in the last two decades, though with a drop since the late 1990s and of course a drop from 2008 at the beginning of the "great recession." But the bottom part

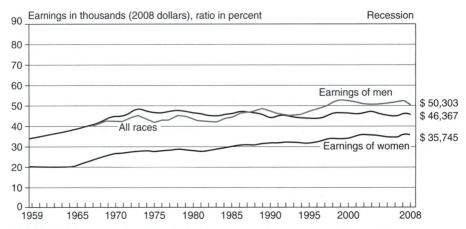

**FIGURE 8-3** *Rise of Household Income Compared to Income of Men and Women,*
*1959–2008*

*SOURCE:* U.S. Bureau of the Census. *Income, Poverty, and Health Insurance Coverage, 2008* (2009: Figures 1, 2).

of Figure 8-3 shows another pattern: Women's wages have been generally catching up
to men's median wages since 1980 mostly because men's wages have been flat during
this period. Curiously, median household income went up slightly in 2002 and 2007
while the median wages of both men and women went down. What is obvious when
comparing Figure 8-3 with figures on the increase in women employed in the labor
force, an increase from 40 percent of married women in the full-time labor force in
1970 to 60 percent in 2007 (U.S. Bureau of the Census, 2010b), is that we can see that
the median household income has not dropped because there are more two-wage-earner
families. Both husband and wife have had to work more hours just to keep their household income from falling.

In addition, we must recognize, however, that there is no simple relationship between income
and class position because of the many variables that help determine income attainment. One problem has been that, in the past, occupational status or occupational
skill level alone was assumed to indicate class position. But as we have already seen,
bureaucratic authority and ownership and control of the means of production must also
be considered in locating class. Also, in recent years there has been much more income
variation within occupational categories (Kim and Sakamoto 2008). The standard U.S.
Census data, such as that presented in Chapter 2, is based on standard occupational
divisions. This type of data consistently shows middle-class occupations (or white-
collar laborers) with higher income than working-class occupations (or blue-collar
laborers). But this type of data, while useful, masks important income differences
*within* occupational categories.

Studies such as those by Wright (1978a, 1979, 1997; Wright and Perrone 1977),
Robinson and Kelley (1979), and Kalleberg and Griffin (1980) have examined income
inequalities produced by the property and authority structures (as well as occupation) in
the stratification system. For example, Wright and Perrone (1977:48) found an average

### TABLE 8-2

## Mean Wealth by 20 Percent Population Groups, 1962–2004*

|            | 1962       | 1998        | 2004        |
|------------|-----------|-------------|-------------|
| Top 20%    | $680,800  | $1,305,800  | $1,822,600  |
| Second 20% | 112,700   | 186,900     | 243,600     |
| Third 20%  | 45,700    | 70,700      | 81,900      |
| Fourth 20% | 8,000     | 12,900      | 14,400      |
| Bottom 20% | −6,000    | −10,300     | −11,400     |

*Average wealth of 20 percent group in constant 2004 dollars.

SOURCE: Mishel, Bernstein, and Allegretto (2007: Table 5-4).

income (in 1969 dollars) for big employers (those owning their means of production and hiring 10 or more employees) of $19,188, an average income for small employers (with less than 10 employees) of $12,915, an average income for managers of $9,226, and an average income for workers (those with no ownership of the means of production and no subordinates) of $6,145. As Robinson and Kelley (1979) found, significant income differences between these class categories (defined by ownership and authority position) remain when controlling for the effects of occupational skill level.

As one would expect from what we have already seen in Chapter 2, the accumulation of wealth is also related to class position and is much more unequally distributed than is income. As can be seen in Table 8-2, the average wealth (in constant 2004 dollars) has been going up for all 20 percent wealth groups between 1962 and 2004 (except the bottom 20 percent). However, while the average wealth of the top 20 percent of Americans increased from $680,800 in 1962 to $1,822,600 in 2004, all other 20 percent wealth groups had much more modest gains, except for the bottom 20 percent. The bottom 20 percent went from −$6,100 in 1962 to −$11,400 in 2004.

Another source of unequal income related to the nature of the stratification system is worth discussion. Remember that the development of a *dual economy* has direct bearing on middle- and working-class income. But in this case, the major effect of interest to us is how the dual economy produces income inequality *within* class and occupational divisions.

Earlier studies by Beck et al. (1978; also Tolbert et al. 1980; Bloomquist and Summer 1982; Jacobs 1982, 1985; Kaufman 1983), among others, had shown that workers in core industries receive higher wages than those in periphery industries, even when controlling for the effects on income from occupational level, education, age, hours worked, job tenure, and union membership in the industry. It was estimated by Beck et al. (1978:716) that in dollar terms (for 1976 income), males who are employed full-time in periphery industries have an annual income loss of $4,097.51 because of periphery rather than core employment. Moreover, Parcel (1979) has found that the positive income effect of core industries extends to the wider geographic area in which core corporations are located. That is, even the wages of workers in periphery corporations are higher when periphery corporations are located near core industries.

However, we must again point out changes due to the continued globalization of the U.S. economy and the wave of downsizing through the 1990s in the United States (Brady and Denniston 2006; Brady 2006; Brady, Beckfield, and Seeleib-Kaiser 2005; Sorenson and Sorenson 2007). Downsizing, making jobs more temporary with fewer benefits, has been most dramatic in the core firms increasingly brought into more international competition. Thus, the differences in income as well as promotions between workers in core versus periphery firms in the United States has been significantly reduced (Hollister 2004; Tilly and Tilly 1998:200–227; Kim and Sakamoto 2008).

## Conditions of Work

For the big capitalist and the corporate class, the conditions of work could seldom be better. As we saw in Chapter 2, in no other country in the world do top executives make as much money as in the United States. But in addition to their greater financial resources, the upper and corporate classes have more interest, respect, and diversion in their jobs; they have a sense of doing something important, of controlling their own lives; and they have the resources of the institutions they head—the private jet, vacation resorts, expense accounts, and the services of many people. What is more, they have a lot of occupational freedom. If their job is a burden, they can move on to another. If they prefer to leave their private-sector job for a top government job (like a cabinet position), they can do so with the knowledge that suitable work (if work is even needed) will be found after the cabinet post is gone.

As with income, the conditions of work are stratified (Tilly and Tilly 1998; Kalleberg 2009). Those on top are generally better off, while those in the middle can look down upon those at the bottom with a feeling that their own condition could be worse. In this section we examine two important aspects of the conditions of work. The first is the satisfaction or fulfillment that work may or may not bring. The second has to do with the physical conditions of work—its safety and physical demands.

### Work Satisfaction and Alienation

In Marx's view (see Marx 1964:124–125), the alienation of labor comes when work becomes "external to the worker," when "it is not his own work but work for someone else," or when work is "only a *means* for satisfying other needs." There is an underlying assumption in Marx's view that human nature requires us to have meaningful work, work that can be identified as an extension of ourselves, to fulfill psychological needs. When the conditions of labor remove this identity with work, when the worker has no control over the work process, the result is unfulfillment and alienation.

C. Wright Mills (1953:215) had a different assumption about the meaning of work but arrived at a similar conclusion about the contemporary conditions of work for most workers: "Neither love nor hatred of work is inherent in man, or inherent in any given line of work. For work has no intrinsic meaning." Because, in Mills's view, work has no intrinsic meaning, the meaning it has comes from our beliefs about work. For today's worker, an ideology placing value on the type of work most people do is lacking.

What we have is a view of work inherited from a previous age—the age of the old middle class and independent artisan. The kind of work that is most valued is work that results in an identification with what is produced or accomplished, work that is an extension or expression of the self, work that is controlled by the worker. This low value of most contemporary work, Mills (1953:227) believed, holds for both blue-collar and white-collar work.

For many, an important outcome of this alienation from work is the segmentation of their lives. There are hours of work, and there are the hours away from work. It is often difficult for us to understand that in the past work more often provided an identity, a meaningful life in what was accomplished, and that one's life was so much a part of work that lives were less segmented between working hours and leisure hours.

Given the chance, most people today prefer the latter hours, or work of a different type. But given that a different type of work is usually not attainable, work is something that must be tolerated; for there is also an important new longing for consumption and expensive leisure activities that must be paid for by work. In Mills's (1953:237) descriptive words, "Each day men sell little pieces of themselves in order to try to buy them back each night and weekend with the coin of 'fun.'"

There are many detailed examinations of the lives of individual workers with varied occupations. Most of these examinations attest to the alienation from work described by Mills. Such studies include Studs Terkel's (1972) *Working,* Sennett and Cobb's (1973) *The Hidden Injuries of Class,* and Lasson's (1971) *The Workers.* There are also the social scientists who have temporarily left their university jobs to understand the meaning of work by working in a factory themselves (for example, Pfeffer, 1979, *Working for Capitalism;* Kamata, 1982, *Japan in the Passing Lane*). Books with the theme of worker alienation and degradation continue to this day. But given what we have seen about the sharp decline in American wages and benefits, there are added themes of working full time without getting out of poverty in books such as Barbara Ehrenreich's *Nickel and Dimed: On (Not) Getting By in America* (2001), Beth Shulman's *The Betrayal of Work* (2003), David Shipler's *The Working Poor: Invisible in America* (2004), or of losing jobs altogether (such as Ellen Rosen's *Making Sweatshops: The Globalization of the U.S. Apparel Industry* [2002]).

We can start with the rather simplistic concept of satisfaction with work. Studies of this type generally begin by asking workers some variation of the following questions: "Do you find your work satisfying?" "Would you get into this line of work again if you had to do it over?" "Would you recommend the type of work you do to friends or relatives?" Others may use some variation of questions to get at the feeling of finding work fulfilling.

In summary (see Jencks et al. 1972:247–252), several studies have found that work satisfaction is positively related to occupational status, income, education level, and general occupational categories (such as manager, professional, clerical worker, skilled laborer, unskilled laborer, service worker). The relationship between occupational divisions and work satisfaction found in these studies is not especially strong, however, because other dimensions of class have not been directly measured.

Kalleberg and Griffin (1980) examined the relationship between other dimensions of class and job satisfaction (or, rather, feeling fulfillment with work). Following our perspective of the most important structures or divisions that determine class position— occupational skill level (rather than occupational status), authority position (following and/or giving orders), and ownership—these researchers were able to specify more exactly how class position influences job satisfaction (or fulfillment).

We note first that Kalleberg and Griffin found only a weak relationship between job fulfillment and the functional view of occupational status in their national sample of 1,569 workers. But when class position was defined in terms of ownership and control over the work of others (employers), control over the work of others without ownership (managers), and having no ownership and no control over the work of others (workers), they found significant differences in job fulfillment. Employers felt the most fulfillment in work, then managers, and workers felt the least fulfillment.

The positive correlation between class and fulfillment was maintained even when controlling for the effects of occupational census titles (such as clerk, professional, or sales worker), and when considering separately capitalist (private business) and non-capitalist (such as government) employment sectors (with the manager and worker-class positions). Finally, by defining ranks in the occupational structure in terms of skill level and job complexity (as we have done), they found a greater relationship to job fulfillment than with occupational ranking defined in terms of status (that is, the greater the skill needed and the complexity of the job, the greater the fulfillment).

We have yet to consider empirical research on the complex concept of alienation. Marx wrote of two aspects of alienation—loss of control over the *products* of one's labor and loss of control over the *process* of labor. Most research has been concerned with the loss of control over the process of labor in highly industrial societies.

To empirically test the relation between alienation and class position, Kohn (1976) examined a national sample of 3,101 people in the civilian labor force. Kohn examined alienation in relation to ownership or lack of ownership of the means of production, position in the authority structure, and degree of occupational self-direction (that is, closeness of supervision, routinization of work, and complexity of work). He found that the lack of occupational self-direction was most strongly related to four psychological measures of alienation (see Kohn 1976:119). This suggests that alienation is mostly the product of work that provides little control over the process of work, as Marx in part defined alienation. Work performed most by the lower middle class (clerks, clerical workers, lower sales positions) and the working class is most conducive to alienation.

Comparative studies on Japan and Japanese management techniques support these conclusions. However, in contrast to the image of Japanese workers often held by Americans, not all Japanese are content, unalienated, and happy workers. Alienation is produced by the machine pace and how workers are treated by management in Japan, just as in the United States (Kamata 1982; Naoi and Schooler 1985). Workers in Japan tend to adjust to this alienation or learn to live with it as they get older, just as in the United States (Loscocco and Kalleberg 1988). However, an important difference is that, more often in Japan than in the United States, management does try to implement policies and management styles that allow for more worker input and more human contact between management and workers. This to some extent reduces the alienation of work (Dore 1987).

## *The Physical Conditions of Work*

By the physical conditions of work we refer to the work environment in terms of its safety, health, or physical stress. Along with the psychological aspects of work, these physical aspects of work are influenced by one's position in the stratification system.

## T A B L E   8 - 3

### Accidental Deaths by Industry, 2007

**Total Accidental Deaths in Private Industry
per 100,000 Workers by Industry**

| | |
|---|---|
| Agriculture | 26.3 |
| Mining | 24.4 |
| Construction | 10.0 |
| Manufacturing | 2.2 |
| Transportation | 14.5 |
| Services | 1.6 |
| Total number of fatal accidents in private industry in 2007 = 4,689 | |

*SOURCE:* U.S. Bureau of the Census, *Statistical Abstracts of the United States, 2010*
(2010: Table 641).

When we consider physical safety and health conditions of work, the dichotomy of manual versus nonmanual labor becomes most important.

White-collar workers may suffer alienating psychological conditions or lack of job satisfaction in common with blue-collar workers. But white-collar work is generally safe in a physical sense. Few white-collar workers are subject to health hazards, injury, or death in the workplace. For blue-collar workers, the work is sometimes dangerous. They often do the dirty work, the dangerous work, the work that few people want, the work the blue-collar worker may be unable to avoid if food is to be kept on the table.

Table 8-3 shows the number of fatal industrial accidents by industry per 100,000 workers for 2007. As one would expect, the industries with a high concentration of blue-collar jobs, such as agriculture, mining, and construction, have the highest rates. Overall during 2007 there were 4,689 fatal accidents in U.S. private industries.

## Class Subcultures and Lifestyles

Income inequalities, job satisfaction, conditions of work, and differing amounts of political and economic power (discussed in the next section) are clearly among the most important consequences of class in the United States. But they are not the only consequences of class, nor always the only ones of considerable importance. There are other sometimes obvious, sometimes subtle, sometimes very important differences between classes that must also be understood as consequences of class position.

Under the general concept of **class subcultures** we may consider beliefs, world-views, values, and behavior associated with these attitudes that may differ with class position. We use the term *subculture* rather than *culture* to suggest that whatever differences found are usually variations within a more dominant culture that most members of a society tend to share.

Under the concept of a *lifestyle* we include tastes, preferences, and general styles of living that are more superficial in nature—that is, not necessarily related to important value differences or having important consequences in and of themselves. Various life-style differences, however, can also often be traced to experiences and problems that vary by class. These lifestyle differences can have very important consequences, as we will see, when they lead to differential treatment by class.

Almost any casual observation of people in different sections of a city can turn up differences of class lifestyle. Some of these differences may reflect variations in economic resources, while others reflect differing tastes. For example, let us imagine that an upper-middle-class person goes shopping in an unfamiliar working-class section of a city. As this person looks around the stores, he or she may soon have a sense that the people are somehow different. The clothing or hairstyles may stand out as different from those of people in the more familiar upper-middle-class milieu. Closer observation may reveal speech differences or differences in body language.

Consider another example—say, of driving through different class neighborhoods of a city. Some differences are striking. The sizes of houses and the amount of space between them may differ considerably between upper-middle-class and working-class neighborhoods. But other differences may become apparent as well. The style of the homes may be noticeably different. In upper-middle-class areas we may find more modern, stylish-looking homes or very old, well-preserved homes (in an old city like New Orleans). In working-class areas we may find simple frame or stucco homes of box shape. A closer look may reveal differences in landscaping, fewer cars, more of which are foreign, in upper-middle-class areas, or more children playing in the street in working-class areas. (In upper-middle-class areas the children are usually off to piano, dancing, or some other kind of lessons.)

Some of the differences between classes may seem trivial or unimportant, although interesting at times. These differences may simply *reflect* the particular daily routines, concerns, or life choices available to class members. For example, the country music that is more often preferred by working-class people tends to stress themes of everyday problems (family stability, unemployment, relations on the job).

Other class differences may not only reflect particular class experiences but also *reinforce* class inequalities and class boundaries in complex ways. For example, research by Ellis (1967) found that subjects selected for the study were often able to correctly identify the class position of unseen people simply by listening to short recordings of standard sentences. This suggests that there are some class differences in speech patterns and pronunciation. But what is equally interesting is that subjects in a similar research project (see Harms 1961) rated higher-class speakers as more credible, and in Ellis's (1967) study as more likable. As Ellis suggests, these findings have strong implications for hiring practices and employee performance ratings, and for how lower-class people are respected. In a similar manner, as we will see in more detail when we cover the subject of "status attainment," class subcultures and lifestyles can have important consequences in the process of educational attainment. Whether they realize it or not, teachers are often influenced by class background clues of their students. Those who seem to fit the upper-middle-class mold are more likely treated positively by teachers, and consequently more likely to do better in school (Aschaffenburg and Mass 1997; DiMaggio 1982).

Class differences in lifestyle, attitudes, and behavior are only tendencies. Wide variations are sometimes found *within* class categories, and the mass media have greatly homogenized modern people to an ever-increasing extent. This homogenizing by the mass media, as we will see, seems to have occurred more in the United States than in Europe, especially with political attitudes. However, there are still these tendencies for different lifestyles, beliefs, and other behavioral differences by class in the United States despite claims to the contrary (such as by Kingston 2000). One of the key problems in previous research has been the simple measures of class using broad occupational categories. For example, assuming all university professors and lawyers are in the same socioeconomic class and therefore should have the same attitudes, lifestyles, and political beliefs can be highly misleading. Sociology professors can have different political attitudes and lifestyles compared to professors in agricultural areas, and judges or trial lawyers may have different political attitudes and lifestyles compared to corporate lawyers or lawyers defending the poor such as legal aid lawyers. Weeden and Grusky (2005; also see Jonsson et al. 2009) have shown that even within the same suboccupation (such as lawyer or college professor) there are factors related to who is attracted to a more specific occupation (sociology professor or soil science professor), the exact training for each occupation, and the long-term interaction with others in that subprofession that also shape lifestyles and values. Weeden and Grusky's (2005) beginning attempt to create a more specific "class map" related to how specific working conditions and training for suboccupations affect lifestyles and attitudes has been highly promising. Their categorization of 126 suboccupations has been found highly related to 55 different measures of lifestyles and attitudes, such as importance of the family, views toward the death penalty, spending time with people in the neighborhood, and different sports and hobbies. They note that the broader class categories (such as working class, upper middle class, etc.) are still important in understanding people's life chances and other aspects of their lives. But there are many influences people encounter within broad occupational categories, such as bank clerk compared to postal clerk (for example, job security, working hours, etc.), that affect their lives and thinking as well. It is time to consider some of these class subcultural and lifestyle differences.

## *Sociability and Community Participation*

The early concern in sociology with community organization and social networks has resulted in a wealth of research on class differences in community involvement, neighboring, and friendship ties outside the nuclear family. Such research has shown that the middle class is generally more involved in the community and less tied to extended family relations than the working class. For example, there is a direct relationship between class position and joining voluntary associations (for example, the PTA, VFW, Lions Club, or sewing clubs; see Hodge and Treiman 1968a; Hyman and Wright 1971). More recently, however, research has shown that working-class community participation is as high as that of the middle class when considering only older working-class neighborhoods that are racially homogeneous (Eckstein 2001).

In contrast, members of the working class, when they are involved in relationships outside the home, are more likely than the middle class to be involved with their extended family (visiting with parents, grandparents, and more distant relatives; see Komarovsky 1962; Cohen and Hodges 1963). Also, among the working class, husband

and wife tend to have separate friendship patterns. The husband goes out with his friends (usually from work) and the wife with hers (usually from the neighborhood). And when people in both the middle and working classes are involved in associations or with friends outside the home, they are class-specific relationships; that is, they tend to associate with people of similar class backgrounds.

What is it about the class system that produces these differing tendencies among the middle class and the working class? First, members of the middle class are more mobile. Their jobs require them to relocate more often, and they commonly live in communities other than the ones in which they lived as children. In contrast to members of the working class, they are more often away from extended family members. Second, as described earlier, middle-class occupations tend to produce less alienation. And with less alienation there is a greater sense of being a part of the larger community, and thus there is more participation in it. Third, "the greater resources of the higher classes help account for their wider social participation" (Collins 1975:80). It is easy to forget that it takes money and time to become involved outside the home. Fourth, there is a differing worldview that is shaped by the occupational structure. What can be called *cosmopolitanism* is the product of a greater variety of interactions and more communications with people from diverse backgrounds. It creates the sense of a wider social environment that affects one's life.

Conversely, the less the cosmopolitan orientation, and "the less the variety of communications, the more one thinks in terms of particular persons and things, short-term contingencies, and an alien and uncontrollable world surrounding familiar local circles" (Collins 1975:75–76). This sense of a wider community or cosmopolitanism is related to the occupational structure because the higher the occupation, the more interaction there is with diverse people; the working-class person "regularly deals with few besides his boss and a little-changing circle of friends and family" (Collins 1975:64).

## *Childhood Socialization*

Of all the contrasting class characteristics, childhood socialization or child-rearing practices have received the most attention from social scientists. One reason for this attention is the importance of child rearing for the future of children *and* the maintenance of class boundaries. To the extent that childhood socialization varies by class, these class differences may in some way help retard intergenerational mobility in the class system. That is, it may be that *to some degree* working-class children are raised to be working-class, while middle-class children are raised to be middle-class.

As we will see in Chapter 12 (where the subject of social mobility will be considered in more detail), child-rearing differences alone cannot explain the pattern of social mobility whereby most working-class children remain working-class in their adult life. Rather, there is a cycle of variables operating, and childhood socialization is only one link, although an important one, in this cycle.

A number of specific child socialization experiences have received extensive empirical examination. Most important, the research shows that middle-class children experience child-rearing methods that stress initiative, self-reliance, an emphasis on ideas and people, achievement of higher occupation, and more deferred gratification.

Working-class socialization tends to stress external conformity to rules, less self-reliance and creativity, and working with things rather than ideas (see Kohn 1969).

Most of the research has been directed toward the important contrast between socialization for self-reliance in middle-class families and conformity to external rules in working-class families. For example, when middle-class children are punished, there is usually greater stress on why rules should be followed or why some rules are important, rather than simple conformity to all external rules. It is argued that the former type of punishment leads to more self-reliance and a personal code of what is right or wrong rather than to a simple conformity to rules, whatever they may be.

The most comprehensive study of this type showed that middle-class fathers do stress self-reliance for their children, whereas working-class fathers stress conformity to external rules (Kohn 1969). A replication of this study by Wright and Wright (1976) supports Kohn's findings (for both fathers and mothers), although it found somewhat less difference between the middle and working class on this aspect of child rearing. This research has also been replicated in several countries (see Pearlin 1971; Olsen 1973; Slomczynski, Miller, and Kohn 1981; Naoi and Schooler 1985; Schooler and Naoi 1988) with very similar results.

Studies showing different socialization patterns by class do not suggest that working-class parents have less concern for their children or are harder on their children. For example, it was often thought that middle-class parents are less likely to use corporal punishment (Erlanger 1974). Also, one should not get the idea that working-class parents are less concerned about their children's future. What the studies do indicate is that middle-class parents are more concerned with higher-level occupational attainment for their children, while working-class parents are concerned with their children's well-being without reference to occupational level per se (see Keller and Zavalloni 1964; Turner 1970). But we must also recognize there are often simply different levels of material and social resources held by working-class compared to middle-class parents with which to socialize their children. Devine (2004) has given us valuable research showing the complexity of how parents learn to skillfully use the resources they have as working-class or middle-class parents to best improve the educational and occupational chances of their children through ethnographic studies with working-class and middle-class parents in the United States and Britain. Upper-middle-class parents, for example, are much more likely to have gone to a university and know how to motivate their children to aspire to a university education, advise them on how to be accepted at a university, spend money on extra education, and simply get their children to believe they can be successful at a university.

As with other characteristics found to differ by class, it is important that we understand why these differences exist. We can conclude by examining a key class difference in child socialization—the differing stress on self-reliance and conformity. Most researchers refer to the importance of parents' occupational status and position in authority structures as producing these child-rearing differences (Kohn and Schooler 1982). For example, working-class parents are lower in authority structures and have occupations that require greater conformity to external rules and unquestioned obedience. This experience is reflected in how they treat their children (Kohn 1969). This conclusion has received support from an interesting study by Ellis, Lee, and Peterson (1978) with data from 122 cultures. In this cross-national study they found that the greater the supervision over parents in important aspects of life (like work), the greater the stress on conformity in child socialization.

# ⚔ Middle-Class and Working-Class Positions in the Structures of Economic and Political Power

We turn to one of the most important issues in the study of social stratification: the extent and potential of political and economic power among the middle class and working class today. As noted in the previous chapter, the corporate class will be much more powerful to the extent it can keep others relatively powerless. This section begins with a discussion on a topic that could *potentially* make the more numerous middle and working class quite powerful in the United States and other relatively democratic countries—voting.

## Political Values and Behavior

A number of generalizations can be made with respect to class and political values. To begin with, around the world we find the upper middle class tends to be the most pro-capitalist, with the lower working class expressing least support for capitalism (Wright 1997:417–430). Most generalizations, however, must be qualified, given the complex relationship between political values and class position. We may begin with the relationship between class and party voting. In party voting in the United States, the usual assumption is that voting Democratic means a more liberal political orientation, while voting Republican means a more conservative political orientation. As shown later, there are problems with this assumption, but party voting does give us some indication of liberal versus conservative political values.

The research was quite consistent in showing a strong relationship between class and party vote in earlier decades of the 20th century in the United States (Hamilton 1972; Knoke and Hout 1974; Levinson 1975). Compared to the working class, the upper middle class has been most conservative and most likely to vote Republican. As we move down the class system from the lower middle class through skilled blue-collar workers to unskilled blue-collar workers, there was a greater tendency to vote Democratic. This relation between lower-class position and voting for liberal parties has been found in most Western industrial societies (see Szymanski 1978; Tufte 1978), and usually more so than in the United States (Clark and Lipset 2001).

However, the relationship between class and party voting is only a tendency and may vary under certain conditions (Brooks and Manza 1997a, 1997b; Hout, Brooks, and Manza 1995). And there is increasing evidence that in the United States the relationship between class and voting behavior is becoming more complicated. At the time of the longest economic boom in American history, the 2000 presidential and congressional elections in the United States were more than most based on issues other than class issues. Evidence of this was shown on election night when the middle of the United States, the South, and Southwest went almost exclusively Republican, while the upper Midwest, West Coast, and Northeast were in the Democratic camp (U.S. Bureau of the Census, 2002c:235). Further, analysis of election results shows that in the $50,000-plus income category, the spread in voting for Democrats versus Republicans was only 7 percent compared to 25 percent back in 1988. People in working-class occupations were about equally split between voting for Democrats or Republicans, though members of labor unions, African Americans, and Hispanic Americans were still much more likely to vote for Democrats. Rather than class membership, the best predictor for voting Republican in 2000 was church membership

(*International Herald Tribune,* March 27, 2001). Among whites who attend church regularly, almost 80 percent voted for George W. Bush over Al Gore. For Bush voters the number one issue was "moral values," meaning Christian fundamentalist values in most cases (*New York Times,* November 3, 2004; *Los Angeles Times,* November 3, 2004). It is far too early to tell if class voting in the United States is in a continuing decline. Several specialists in the area argue that class voting is still most common in the United States and other countries (Hout, Brooks, and Manza 2001; Goldthorpe 2001; Weakliem 2001), while others disagree (Clark, Lipset, and Rempel 2001). But even if there is a decline in the relationship between class and the party voted for in the United States, one relationship remains very strong—class and voter participation.

In reference to actual voter participation in the United States, which is lower than in other industrial democracies, we also find class influences (Kerbo and Gonzalez 2003). The lower we go in the stratification system, the lower the percentage of eligible voters who participate in elections. Research shows, for example, that between 1952 and 1988 there was a steady increase in voter participation among minorities. Voter participation by class, however, has changed less throughout this period (Rosenstone and Hansen 1993:236–248). It is important to stress that voter participation by class varies very little in other industrial democracies—the middle-class to lower-working-class vote at about the same rate (Kerbo and Gonzalez 2003; Zipp, Landerman, and Luebke 1982).

Table 8-4 lists the percentage of voting from 1984 to 2008. In 1984 only 37.5 percent of those with less than $5,000 annual income voted, compared with 75.6 percent of those with $50,000 annual income or higher. In 1992 the percentage of low-income people voting was even lower, 32.4 percent. Then, in the 1996 presidential election there was a small increase in voting rates for lower-income groups, with a small decrease in voting participation among upper-income groups. In one of the most important presidential elections in many decades, only 28 percent of the lowest-income people voted compared to 71.5 percent for those with incomes of $75,000 or more. The same steady increase in voting occurs as we move up the income scale in 2000 as occurred in elections going back for three decades. In one of the most critical elections in decades, during a time of the most serious polarization in American history (Osberg and Smeeding 2006:466–467), in 2004 the overall voter turnout rose to 55.5 percent, though income differences in voting rates continued.

There was a significant change in 2008. The old "rule of thumb" was again shown to be accurate: The higher the voter turnout, the greater the percentage of votes for Democrats. With 59.7 percent of U.S. citizens voting, it was the highest in decades (U.S. Bureau of Census 2009). At 44.6 percent, the turnout for younger voters (18 to 24) was at its highest level, as was the voting percentage for African Americans. Table 8-4 shows there was still a major difference in the voting rate by income, but there was a significant increase in the percentage of lower-income people voting, with less change in voting percentages for upper-income Americans. Although still low compared to European nations, it is obvious that class issues became more important in 2008. In contrast to 2008, during the November elections of 2010 in the United States, Republicans made big gains, and retook a majority in the House. As the Pew polling firm indicated, the percentage of lower income people voting in the United States dropped significantly compared to 2008 (pewresearch.org, November 2010).

An interesting question becomes: What would have happened if all income groups voted at about 60 to 75 percent in the United States as they do in European countries?

## TABLE 8-4

### Voting Rates by Income, USA: 1984–2000*

| Family income | Percentage who voted | | | | | | |
|---|---|---|---|---|---|---|---|
| | **1984** | **1988** | **1992** | **1996** | **1998** | **2000** | **2008\*\*** |
| Under $5,000 | 37.5% | 34.7% | 32.4% | 37.9% | 21.1% | 28.2% } | 41.3 |
| $5,000–9,999 | 46.2 | 41.3 | 39.5 | 38.3 | 23.9 | 34.7 | |
| $10,000–14,999 | 53.5 | 47.7 | 46.8 | 46.7 | 30.4 | 37.7 | 41.2 |
| $15,000–19,999 | 57.1 | 53.5 | 55.7 | 52.8 } | 34.6 | 43.4 | 44.3 |
| $20,000–24,999 | 61.1 | 57.8 | 62.5 | 52.8 | | | |
| $25,000–34,999 | 67.0 | 64.0 | 69.5 | 56.6 | 40.2 | 51.0 } | 54.4 |
| $35,000–49,999 | 72.9 | 70.3 | 75.7 | 62.6 | 44.0 | 57.5 | |
| $50,000 and over | 76.0 | 75.6 | 79.9 | 72.8 | | | |
| $50,000–74,999 | | | | | 49.9 | 65.2 | 65.9 |
| $75,000 and over | | | | | 57.3 | 71.5 | 76.9 |
| $100,000 and over | | | | | | | 91.8 |

*Figures are for U.S. citizens voting, not total population (see Casper and Bass 1998).

**Some figures averaged for broader income categories.

*SOURCES:* U.S. Bureau of the Census, *Current Population Reports,* "Voting and Registration in the Election of November 1988" (1989: Series P–20, no. 440, p. 4); U.S. Bureau of the Census, *Current Population Reports,* "Voting and Registration in the Election of November 1992" (1993: Series P–20, no. 466, p. 55); Web site http://www.census.gov (voting in the 1996 election); U.S. Bureau of the Census, *Current Population Reports,* "Voting and Registration in the Election of November 1998" (2000: Table C); U.S. Bureau of the Census, Internet release, February 27, 2002, Table 8 for 2008 data, see 2010; www.census.gov/voting/ detailed tables.

There is substantial evidence suggesting that low-income people in the United States would more likely vote for Democrats and others supporting policies more favorable to the working class and poor if they did vote (Kerbo and Gonzalez 2003). In other words, in 2000, George W. Bush would very likely have lost the presidential race and Al Gore would have been president. There is other evidence suggesting the United States would be quite different if class differences in voting did not exist. Table 8-5 indicates the extent to which governments in Europe and North America reduce poverty through welfare benefits, unemployment benefits, and minimum-wage laws. The right column in Table 8-5 ranks the countries on how important class issues are in elections (on a scale of 1 to 4, 4 showing a higher rate of voting on class issues). There is no perfect lineup, but it is clear that governments are more likely to reduce poverty when such issues are made significant with more lower-class voter action (Kerbo and Gonzalez 2003).

With the exception of works by Piven and Cloward (1988, 2000) and Teixeira (1987), very little research has been done on why there are such large differences in voter turnout by income in the United States. Piven and Cloward (1988:96) divide the explanations into two groups: those that "blame" the nonvoters themselves and suggest that "nonvoting results from one or another of the characteristics of the nonvoters," and those that focus on political institutions. From a long historical perspective, Piven and Cloward's

## TABLE 8-5

### Class Voting and Comparative Impact of Welfare Benefits on Reducing Poverty*

| Country | Percentage of poverty reduction through government action | Rank on class** issues in national voting |
|---|---|---|
| Sweden | −80.4% | 4 |
| Denmark | −72.1 | 4 |
| England | −50.0 | 4 |
| Belgium | −80.6 | 3 |
| Germany | −65.5 | 3 |
| Australia | −50.0 | 3 |
| The Netherlands | −70.6 | 2 |
| France | −65.3 | 2 |
| Italy | −64.7 | 2 |
| Spain | −63.1 | 2 |
| Canada | −50.0 | 1 |
| United States | −28.5 | 1 |

*Poverty is measured by income below 50 percent of median income in the nation. Data are available from 1989 to 1994.

**Ranking of class voting from lowest (1) to highest (4), from Nieuwbeerta (2001). The lowest class voting was found in the United States and Canada (around 0.5 on the Thomsen Index for most years), with relatively low levels in France, Italy, Netherlands, and Spain (Thomsen Index scores of around 1.0); intermediate levels in Australia, Austria, and Germany (Thomsen Index of around 1.5); and higher levels (Thomsen Index of around 2.0) in Scandinavian countries and Britain (Nieuwbeerta 2001:125).

SOURCES: Constructed from data presented by Smeeding (1997); Mishel, Bernstein, and Schmitt (1999:377); Nieuwbeerta (2001).

work is among the second group and has focused on how political factors have reduced voting among the lowest-income groups, and even how politicians have purposely written off low-income groups. In summary, Piven and Cloward (1988, 2000) attempt to show how upper-class interests have slowly captured the major political parties and moved them away from issues that would attract lower-class interests and have initiated barriers making it more difficult for lower-income groups to vote. With this perspective, Piven and Cloward were among the most active in promoting the "Motor-Voter" legislation that finally passed in 1993 making it easier to get low-income people registered to vote. But as the 1996 and 2000 voter turnouts suggest, and Piven and Cloward (2000) admit, the Motor-Voter bill, although increasing voter registration, had almost no effect on increasing actual voter turnout among lower-income groups in the United States.

Other explanations for nonvoting among the lower classes in the United States, still from an institutional perspective, cite how the American political system leads the two major parties to lack strong differences on class issues in order to attract the mass of voters from all class, religious, and regional groups (Vanneman and Cannon 1987; Verba, Nie, and Kim 1978; Teixeira 1987; Franklin 1996; Jackman and Miller 1995).

Under the American presidential system of winner take all, it is the "middle mass" that is most important. If a major party went after the working-class vote too overtly, it might alienate some of the middle-mass voters, and alienate more than would be gained through attempting to attract low-income and working-class voters. This is in contrast to parliamentary systems of government in most other democratic nations. In a parliamentary system the prime minister is elected from within the parliament through a coalition of parties. Thus, a working-class political party could become quite powerful with only 10 or 20 percent of the vote if it were able to form a governing coalition with another nonconservative party or two to create a 50 percent majority in the parliament.

Moving away from an institutional perspective, still others cite less political knowledge among the lower classes and less educated, and thus less interest in politics. It is also suggested that working-class turnout is low because of less organization among the lower classes to motivate voting (Lipset 1981; Houtman 2001; Winders 1999). Others cite the more extreme individualism in the United States leading to detachment from broader institutions (Inglehart 1990; Rose and McAllister 1986). It is the institutional perspective, however, that seems to have more support when we consider that class voting and union organization to vote has been stronger in early American history despite the constant influence of individualism.

## Labor Unions

A central premise in the conflict perspective of social stratification is that groups with strong common interests will, when these interests are recognized and when possible, work together to ensure that they are attained and maintained. This is no less true for those groups on the bottom than for those on the top. But this is true only to the extent that a group is able to recognize its common interests, and has resources (such as money, numbers, organization, and time) with which to attain its common interests.

As should be evident from our discussion of the upper class and the corporate class, those at the top of the stratification system are usually favored in both respects. However, those below the top are not totally powerless, passive, or nonparticipants in the conflict process of reward distribution in the society. Too many theories and too much research on power elites (see Domhoff 2010; Mintz et al. 1976; Whitt 1979) have assumed that they are. But there is clear evidence that inequality has been reduced and working conditions improved by past union activity in many industrial societies (Cornfield 1991).

If we had to select one major difference of the working class in the United States compared with other industrial nations, it must be the lack of union membership, union influence, and worker influence in the workplace. The contrast to Germany, as we will see in more detail in a later chapter, is most striking. While union membership is not as high in Germany compared with some other European countries (in the 40 percent range compared with 13.5 percent in the United States in 2000), unions are very strong in Germany because of cooperation with elected "works councils" in almost every company, workplace, and office (Kerbo and Strasser 2000; U.S. Bureau of the Census 2002c:411). But an even bigger contrast involves the participation of employees in almost every major decision in the workplace. By German law, every company

## TABLE 8-6

### Union Wage and Benefit Premium, March 2005 (2005 dollars)

| | Hourly pay | | | |
| | Wages | Insurance | Pension | Compensation |
|---|---|---|---|---|
| **All workers** | | | | |
| Union | $24.10 | $3.63 | $2.39 | $33.17 |
| Nonunion | 18.81 | 1.54 | 0.72 | 23.09 |
| *Union premium* | | | | |
| Dollars | $5.29 | $2.09 | $1.67 | $10.08 |
| Percent | 28.1% | 135.7% | 231.9% | 43.7% |

*SOURCE:* Mishel, Bernstein, and Allegretto (2007: Table 3-33).

must allow the workers to elect a works council made up of their fellow workers, then management must consult with this works council to get its approval before any major changes are carried out or workers are fired or laid off (Thelen 1991; Turner 1991).

This lack of labor organization in the United States is somewhat surprising when we consider that workers who are unionized have considerably better working conditions, pay, and benefits. As Table 8-6 suggests, the differences between union and nonunion workers on basic wages, insurance coverage by employers, pension coverage, and total compensation are substantial. The question then becomes, why do so few American workers join unions?

We may begin by noting that the history of union activity in the United States has three primary lessons for understanding the place of workers in the economic power structure. First, gains were seldom made by workers until they were able to organize effectively. This is the essence of power or *party* as defined by Weber. Before effective union organization, workers were low in all three of Weber's dimensions of social stratification—class, status, and party.

Second, the greater power of capitalists (in class, status, and party) enabled them to prevent the more extensive change sought by labor (Tilly and Tilly 1998:249). In other words, although changes were made (such as higher wages and shorter working hours), these changes represented only relatively small concessions that kept the more important issues—such as corporate control of profits, economic decision making, and control of the workplace—from successful challenge. In effect, it is argued, the recognition of labor unions strengthened corporate capitalism (Aronowitz 1974).

Third, and perhaps most important in showing the conflict relationship between capitalists and labor, we find that workers are able to win some demands primarily when political or economic conditions are such that the bargaining position of labor is strengthened. For example, although workers had been struggling for years, legal rights for collective bargaining were not won until 1935 (Tilly and Tilly 1998:249–253; Griffin, Wallace, and Rubin 1986; Cornfield 1991). It took a major economic crisis to

(1) provide more worker unity of action, (2) make the political and (some) economic elites realize that major reforms were needed, and (3) present Franklin Roosevelt with the need for working-class support to achieve economic reforms. All of these factors led to the successful push for union recognition.

Since the routinization (legalization) of labor conflict, we find a similar pattern of some successful labor demands when political or economic conditions provide labor with a better bargaining position. It is commonly thought that strikes occur when conditions are worse for workers. Rather, when unemployment is low and the economy is generally healthy (for example, output is higher), workers can better afford to strike, and capitalists are more hurt by strikes (Snyder 1975).

Furthermore, while reduced in its effects in the 1990s, as the dual-economy research shows, the working class gets better wages in core industries, where union organizing is made easier (Beck et al. 1978; Form 1985; Rubin 1986), and in larger factories and cities in which workers are more concentrated and more easily organized (Lincoln 1978). Finally, research on farm laborers shows that after years of struggle they were able to achieve union recognition and improved wages in the 1960s, when they obtained outside support from liberal organizations and politicians (Jenkins and Perrow 1977).

Thus far our discussion has been concerned only with working-class unionization, primarily because middle-class unionization remains even more limited in the United States. A brief explanation of this limitation is in order. It is understandable that the upper middle class is not inclined toward unionization—for the most part, it is part of management or consists of free professionals. As Collins (1975) notes, the more one gives orders in the name of the organization and the closer one is to upper management (or can realistically face the possibility of moving into top management), the more one identifies with the organization and its ideology. Upper-middle-class people working in large organizations have on occasion participated in strikes (take, for example, doctors in large hospitals). But the lower middle class often works under conditions similar to those of blue-collar workers, whom we expect to be more unionized. Still, white-collar unionization remains, in this country at least (Giddens 1973:188), quite limited.

There seem to be several reasons for this limited and uneven white-collar, or lower-middle-class, participation in unions. As Mills (1953:305–308) pointed out more than 40 years ago, white-collar unionization is limited because white-collar employees often feel they have a greater chance to move into higher occupational positions, are closer to and identify more with management, and are less exposed to union organizing, which is usually directed toward blue-collar workers. One reason union organizing is less often directed toward white-collar employees is that these employees are more often women, who are seen as being in the labor force temporarily (Aronowitz 1974:297). Also, white-collar workers are less often employed in concentrated, homogeneous work settings where labor organization is less difficult (Giddens 1973:191).

The bigger question, however, pertains to the shrinking level of unionization for all levels of workers, especially the working class. From a level of about one-half after World War II, by 1975 only 28 percent of workers were union members (U.S. Bureau of the Census, 2010b). At the end of the 1980s the level of union membership had fallen to about 18 percent, and to just over 13 percent by 1994, where it remained as of 2009. We see in Table 8-7 that this rate of union membership is much lower than for any other

| TABLE 8-7 |
|---|

### Comparative Rates of Union Membership

| Country | Rate of union membership, % |
|---|---|
| United States | 13.5% |
| Japan | 27 |
| England | 42 |
| West Germany | 34 |

*SOURCES:* United Nations, *Human Development Report 1994* (1994:194);
U.S. Bureau of the Census (2010b: Table 648).

capitalist nation (Tilly and Tilly 1998:249). But even this unionization rate of 13 percent for U.S. employees is misleading (Mishel et al. 2009). When we exclude government employees such as teachers whose union is more like a professional association, we find only 7 percent of private sector employees were members of unions in 2008 (U.S. Bureau of the Census 2010b: Table 648).

Among the most important reasons for this recent reduction is the change in the occupational structure; again, it is that shrinking of middle-paying jobs in this country. It is the workers in precisely these jobs who have had the highest rates of union membership. The big increase in low-paying and temporary jobs, on the other hand, is found in those periphery industries that are the most difficult for labor unions to organize.

Even before this change occurred in the occupational structure, the level of union membership in this country was low compared with other nations. Political elites in the United States have never been as tolerant of unions as have other industrial nations (Form 1985). We must remember that it was not until 1935 that workers were even given the legal right to call for a vote of workers to establish a union without being fired from their jobs, or being subjected to other forms of repression. An impressive research project has shown that it was primarily organized efforts by corporate and political elites that were successful in keeping unions from organizing and establishing themselves in the United States (Griffin et al. 1986). More recent research has shown that this trend increased during the Reagan administration (Tope and Jacobs 2009). Since 1980 there have been far fewer elections in the workplace to decide if workers want to be represented by a union. No doubt related to this, Kalleberg (2009) shows that job security for American workers is less than it was before.

## Middle-Class and Working-Class Political Influence: A Conclusion

The extent and means of political influence by the upper class and the corporate class have been examined in detail in Chapters 6 and 7. In light of our previous discussion, we need only a brief examination of middle- and working-class political influence here. One means of political influence is voting. But, as we have noted, this means of influence is limited because (1) those candidates who are more acceptable to the people who provide campaign funds (most often the wealthy) usually have a greater chance of being elected, and (2) once a candidate is elected, his or her behavior in office is often strongly influenced by those able to afford extensive lobby organizations. Also, as we have noted, the lower the class position, the less likely one is to vote. Perhaps one reason for this lack of voter participation by the lower classes is a recognition of the political influence of the wealthy, but more likely it is related to the greater alienation from society found among the lower classes.

However, voting is not meaningless, and some influence is gained by the middle and working classes through voting. In 1932, 1980, and 2008, for example, the United States experienced voter shifts by the middle and working classes that put a new party in office. In 1932 it was the Great Depression that led to voter rebellion; in 1980 it was primarily inflation and unemployment. In 1932 significant reforms were forthcoming that helped the middle and working classes. The effects of the 1980 election, however, were not what the middle and working class expected and brought increased inequality, tax breaks for the rich, welfare cuts, and policies attempting to reduce union influence. Then again in 2008, with a serious economic crisis and two wars not going well, there was a voter shift, with one of the biggest voter turnouts in recent decades to elect President Obama. At present it is too early to tell whether this voter shift will create significant change in government policies because of resistance in the U.S. Congress.

What happens is that on occasion, when economic or other conditions that widely affect middle- and working-class people are worsening, these conditions are politicized by elites of the other party so as to win an election. Another faction of the political elite achieves power (with the backing of another faction of the business elite). The political rhetoric used to gain popular support in the election may lead to some reforms in the interests of lower classes, but such reforms are usually limited, and at times harmful to lower-class interests, as in the 1980s and 1990s.

Besides political influence through electing candidates believed to favor particular class interests (by voting and/or campaign contributions), there is the possibility of political pressure on government officials already in office, a possibility greater in the United States than in other industrial nations (Lipset 1996:44). We need not review again the most consistent form of this type of political pressure, but we do need to note how those below the upper and corporate classes may be able to use this form of influence.

Most important, this form of political influence requires a strong central organization that can pool resources and keep track of the decisions that are being made and need to be made that affect the interests of those represented by the organization. In order to get resources for effective political pressure, a strong organization is needed to convince or even coerce those who would benefit from the political pressure to contribute resources for doing so.

Most broad-based interest groups (such as those with common class interests) usually find it very difficult to form effective political lobbying organizations. For members of the working class or middle class who are unionized, labor unions do represent a form of organization that may be able to pool resources and overcome the free-rider problem for effective political pressure. Unions have been active with political action committees (PACs) in making campaign contributions (though much less so than corporations).

Also, unions have been active in lobbying activities of various kinds. Evidence of this is found in interesting research by Hicks, Friedland, and Johnson (1978). Noting that the lower classes (whether working class or poor) have common interests in greater government redistribution policies to the lower classes, these researchers examined the differing power bases of the corporate class versus the working class in individual states to see if there was a tie between the relative strength of these class power bases and state government redistribution policies. They found that the more big corporations are headquartered in a state, the less a state's redistribution policy helps the lower classes (in such things as welfare spending). In contrast, the more union headquarters, union locals, and union membership found in the state, the greater the state government redistribution to the lower classes. They interpret these findings to mean that the relative strength of corporate to union elites leads to government policies that favor the class interests of the stronger. But with labor unions in rapid decline in the United States, the same must be said for working-class political influence (Tilly and Tilly 1998).

A curious thing happened during the longest economic boom in American history—there was never any serious threat of inflation throughout the 1990s. A basic law of capitalist economies has been in inverse relationship between unemployment and inflation: When unemployment is low inflation tends to go up, and vice versa (Piven and Cloward 1982). Unemployment usually goes down with economic expansion because companies hire more workers to keep up with the increasing demand for goods. With more people employed and spending money, prices increase for the now more limited goods. More important, however, is the upward pressure on wages as corporations compete for workers. More people are already employed, and there are fewer poor people, so workers are in a better position to ask for higher wages. The cycle reverses itself once an economic recession sets in: There are fewer people working, there is less money chasing goods, and those who manage to keep their jobs know they can be easily replaced if they demand higher wages.

Known as the Phillips Curve, this inverse relation between unemployment and inflation has been a basic law of capitalist societies throughout history. A primary task of the American Federal Reserve chair and the head of the European Central Bank is to track these trends to keep the balance of inflation versus unemployment at manageable levels. The Federal Reserve or European Central Bank will push up interest rates when the economy shows signs of growing inflation, or cut interest rates when unemployment becomes a major problem. Though unstated, their actions are aimed at increasing or decreasing levels of unemployment to manage inflation.

During the longest economic boom in American history, however, with unemployment as low as 4 percent, *the Phillips Curve never kicked in.* The United States had a rare period of low unemployment and extremely low inflation at the same time. Federal Reserve chair Alan Greenspan became something of a folk hero among American corporate leaders—his skill at managing and fine-tuning the American economy was seen as masterful. But few people considered another unique situation in the American economy during this long economic boom: Relatively high rates of poverty continued throughout the 1990s, real wages for American workers remained almost unchanged, and inequality increased steadily year after year. This condition of low unemployment and low inflation continued through 2007, and until the financial crisis and "great recession" of late 2008.

Alan Greenspan's job was actually quite easy. In contrast to European countries, from the early 1980s, the United States has made drastic cuts in welfare programs, and U.S. corporate and political elites promoted a situation in which *American workers were in more direct competition with low-wage labor throughout the world*. Except for the few workers in new high-tech industries, even with a booming U.S. economy the majority of American workers could no longer demand higher wages. Nor would employers have to offer higher wages to keep and attract good employees, because the whole world became their labor pool. If American workers demanded higher wages or a continuation of their health care benefits the company had the easy option of closing the factory and moving it to any number of poor countries. Or it could simply import what it needed from other corporations operating in these poor countries. For upper-income Americans and corporate managers this meant their incomes and profits could continue to increase far longer than ever before with no hint of inflation messing things up. For lower-skilled American workers there were lower levels of unemployment and a record creation of new jobs through the 1990s, but at a price—the new jobs were often "junk jobs" with very low wages, longer worker hours, and fewer benefits. No longer did lower-skilled American workers need to become unemployed to fall into poverty; they could now do so working 40 hours a week, 52 weeks a year. Years ago Herbert Gans wrote about the "positive functions" of poverty for the more affluent (Gans 1972). We can now add that world poverty may have some of the same effect on the world's rich. To understand the situation of working-class people today we must also understand the situation of the world's poor as well as the American poor. We turn now to poverty in the United States in Chapter 9, and take up the issue of world poverty in Chapter 16.

## Summary

The focus of this chapter has been the middle and working classes in modern industrial societies such as the United States. We began with some of the major characteristics of the middle and working classes in the United States, and how the position of these classes has been changing in recent history. The major consequences of class position were described, especially income inequality, conditions of work, class subcultures, and the political influences of the middle and working classes.

# Poverty and the Political Economy of Welfare

 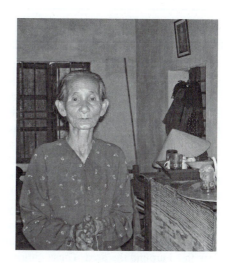

The life of a homeless America Vietnam War veteran (left) contrasted with that of an older woman I met in central Vietnam who lost her husband and all four sons fighting alongside U.S. troops in the war. If her husband and sons had fought with the North Vietnam communist government back then, she would be honored in the "multistar mother's" room in the War Museum in Hanoi and receive a nice pension in her old age. Because this lady's husband and sons were fighting with the Americans and South Vietnamese government, she has no pension nor any government benefits. However, unlike many poor in America, she is taken care of by all of the families in her village near Danang. For example, they bring her food every day (with an elaborate dinner laid out for the Tete New Year when I visited her in 2007), repair her house after typhoons roll in, and take her to a clinic when she is sick.

*SOURCES:* Left: © The McGraw-Hill Companies, Inc./John Flournoy, photographer; right: © Harold Kerbo.

## Chapter Outline

❖ **A Brief History of Poverty in America**

❖ **Counting the Poor**

❖ **The Extent of Poverty in the United States**

❖ **Theories of Poverty**

❖ **Class Conflict and the Welfare State**

❖ **Summary**

In the south of Bangkok, within a seaport area along the Chao Parya River, is a neighborhood called Klong Toey. Perhaps "neighborhood" is not the best description, because Klong Toey is one of the largest slum areas in Thailand. Thai relief workers tell me there are some 1,000 such slum areas in Bangkok alone, containing approximately 1.5 million people (see also Pornchokchai 1992). When I last visited Klong Toey in April of 2008, some 100,000 poor squatters lived in the three- to four-square-mile section of the Port Authority land that has been left undeveloped. Walking through the narrow pathways among the shacks, one sees families of four, five, or more living in makeshift huts of cardboard, plywood, and tin measuring no more than 10 to 15 feet in each direction. Each hut is built with the common walls and roofs of the neighboring shack, one after the other, throughout this settlement of 100,000 people. Located in a low-lying river bank, the area is usually pocketed with large stagnant pools of green, slimy water, filled with all sorts of trash and a dead animal here and there. Among all of this are thousands of children playing, quite happy to see *farang* (Westerners) and follow them around the area. These children generally look healthy, though thinning hair and bad teeth sometimes suggest malnutrition at least at some time in their young lives.

Across Bangkok from Klong Toey, and in another slum area along train tracks, I was invited to dinner one evening by some of the residents of a scrap wood and metal shack whose relatives I had spent some time with a couple of weeks earlier in a small village. The shacks were quite similar to those in Klong Toey, though the slimy water didn't seem to surround everything. My dinner hosts that evening lived in a much smaller slum area when compared to Klong Toey, but again it was on unused land, in this case so close to the train tracks I could have reached out to touch a train going by as we ate dinner on a makeshift table of wood that evening. As with the larger slum area of Klong Toey, most of the people in this slum area are unskilled laborers seeking work in Bangkok, or are street venders who get up at 2:30 a.m. to visit the night markets for fruits and vegetables they can sell on street corners in Bangkok during the morning rush hour. It was easy to see that life was often quite difficult for these people, but they were working hard to survive.

When walking through squatters' slums such as those in Bangkok, people from rich countries usually find it almost impossible to believe other humans could live in such a way. The residents of Klong Toey and the slum of my dinner hosts are actually comparatively lucky. As third world slums go, *it can get much worse.* The thousands of homeless people in Manila living in massive garbage dumps scavenging to stay alive come to mind. Many die when mountains of garbage explode or collapse from time to time and bury them. For these people, Klong Toey would be a definite step up in the world. Compared to the poor of most other developing countries, the 100,000 or so people crammed into Klong Toey are lucky in other ways as well. Even when economic crisis hits as it did in 1997, most have family in the countryside to move back in with when things become hopeless in the city. In other regions of the world, the urban homeless have nowhere else to go because the vast majority of land is in the hands of just a few wealthy people.

When walking through squatters' slums such as those in Bangkok, people from rich countries also assume that the poor in industrial nations such as the United States must be far better off. Their assumptions, however, are not always accurate. Poverty, of course, must be considered in a *relative sense*. There is certainly absolute poverty in the United States—poverty due to lack of basic necessities that is life-threatening. The homeless in the United States dying in a cold winter are just as dead as the people starving to death in third world countries. But many (though certainly not all) who are considered poor by the material standards of the United States would not be considered poor if living under the same conditions in nations such as Chad, Haiti, Uganda, Laos, the Philippines, or India.

A beginning point is that poverty cannot simply be considered relative to the material existence of people throughout the world; in many important ways it is *relative to the society in which the poor find themselves*. In large part this is because the self-worth, the aspirations, and the expectations of people are shaped by the relative position of others in the society. While the poor in rural India may feel no shame or deprivation living in a poverty that has existed throughout the centuries, poverty in the United States will create more psychological damage, shame, and discontent in the context of the affluence of many others in the country. This is not to say that poverty is less "bad" or less harmful in India; absolute deprivation, hunger, and homelessness hurt the same anywhere. But there is a psychological aspect of poverty amid plenty. This difference between *poverty* per se and *inequality* (that is, the gap between the rich, middle class, and poor in a community) is indicated by studies of the statistical relationships among poverty, inequality, and crime or political violence. Studies of inequality and poverty in American cities show that poverty alone is not related to more crime in the city (Blau and Blau 1982; Williams 1984); the level of inequality usually shows a stronger relationship to crimes like murder. Recent research, for example, has found that falling wages since the early 1980s has caused as much as 15 to 25 percent of the increased prison population in the United States (Western, Kleykamp, and Rosenfeld 2006). In a similar manner, studies have found that the number of police (per population) hired by a community is related to the level of inequality in the community, not simply the rate of poverty in the community (Jacobs 1979). The same can be said internationally. The murder rate in a country and the level of political violence (such as riots, terrorist activity, and violent protests) are more related to the level of inequality in the country than simply the rate of poverty (Messner 1982; Muller 1985).

But there are other factors when comparing the situations of poor people around the world. While visiting poor villages in Thailand and Vietnam for my current research comparing poverty in these two countries (as well as Cambodia), I found less of the despair one sees in the faces of other poor people, even the poor of the United States. A reason for this in Thailand and Vietnam is that (1) there is some hope in their lives today, and (2) they are less likely to feel there is no place to turn if things get worse. As we will see in more detail in the final chapter of this book, Thailand and Vietnam have made considerable progress in improving conditions for their poor. It took a couple of decades in Thailand, while more recently Vietnam has cut poverty in half during the past decade. Both countries are now cited by the World Bank (2006a) as world leaders in reducing poverty. In late 2006 and early 2007, I randomly selected villages in poor areas in Vietnam for interviews. I was often met by village leaders showing me new irrigation projects that were dramatically increasing their rice yield, or new pig farms they were able to set up with micro loans from the government or international agencies. As I walked through the villages talking with individual families, they proudly showed me new motorbikes and other household goods they have been able to buy in recent years. Many seemed most proud that their children were now able to get much more education than they had when young. Soon after beginning one interview I will never forget how a proud mother and father started pulling out award after award their daughter was getting for her good marks in school. During the Tet New Year holiday one mother proudly introduced me to her son and daughter who had just received junior college degrees in the city of Da Nang about 50 miles away. They both now had good jobs in the city and were visiting for the holidays. Their father had died 15 years ago, but relatives had helped out this mother in the rice fields so she could keep food on the table, while at the same time making sure her son and daughter kept up with their schoolwork.

Equally important is that the poor in places like Southeast Asia have a strong family network that can be called on if they become desperate. Even the poor of Cambodia more often have this advantage than many poor in the United States. The poverty I have seen in Cambodia is much worse than in Thailand and Vietnam, and there is less hope for much improvement in coming decades for village people of Cambodia. I almost never saw villages with running water or electricity. They mostly live in small bamboo huts and use ox carts for transportation, much as they did 1,000 years ago. But relatives throughout the village were there to help others in crisis—help with the rice crop when parents are ill, take in children who become orphaned, or give the old people food and mend their houses when they are unable to take care of themselves. While the material conditions of many U.S. poor might be better than those of people living in the big slum Klong Toey in Bangkok, I found that these poor of Bangkok have relatives in villages with houses, plenty of food, and other help whenever it is needed. Soon after the tragedy in New Orleans when Hurricane Katrina destroyed much of the city, I realized that most of the poor of Bangkok would probably be better off much more quickly. The poor of New Orleans were less likely to have extended families around the United States who would help them out. Thousands were in shelters for months, some even years. After such a disaster in Bangkok the poor would quickly stream back to the countryside to be taken into the homes of relatives who would feed them and give them work in the fields. The relative breakdown of the extended family in the United States, and the absence of welfare system protection compared to other industrial nations (as we will see), can make poverty in America much more frightening.

In this chapter our examination of the bottom of the stratification system in the United States focuses on the following questions:

**1.** Who are the poor? We examine the methods used to estimate the existence of poverty in this country and then examine the distribution of poverty among subgroups in the society.

**2.** What are the causes of poverty? In this section we review some of the most noted theories of poverty, examine some of the empirical evidence related to these theories, and offer conclusions on the value of each theory.

**3.** What has been done about poverty in this country? We examine the various welfare programs designed to meet the needs of the poor or reduce poverty, the history of these poverty programs, some of their outcomes, and how these programs are related to assumptions about poverty contained in the theories previously reviewed.

**4.** What is the nature of the welfare state, and what is the position of the poor in the power structure of this country? As we will see, these two questions are of necessity related. We want to know the main functions of the welfare state (as it relates to the lower class), the degree to which the United States has a welfare state, and why and when it was developed. Finally, as we have done with our examination of other classes, we examine the position of the poor in relation to the overall power structure in our society. In contrast to what is often stated, the poor are not completely powerless, for although the traditional means of influence in the society are often closed to the poor, they have at times gone outside these traditional means of influence to effect social change.

Before we begin all of this, however, it is useful to take a brief tour of the history of poverty in the United States with a comparison to other countries.

## ⚔ A Brief History of Poverty in America

When looking around at the affluence of cities in North America and Europe today, it is easy to forget how relatively recent it all is. Just a couple of centuries back a large percentage of the populations in the rich countries of today lived more like the people in poor countries today. It also took a long time for the urban environment to reach even minimal standards of sanitation and cleanliness. Waterways through European cities were often polluted, and rarely did people make distinctions between sewers and water mains. In England during the 1800s "ditches in cities were everywhere used as latrines. Dead animals were left to rot where they lay. The decomposing bodies of the poor in common graves stank" (Thomas 1979:417). Visiting Venice in the 1800s, the German literary giant Goethe complained that rubbish and human excrement were simply pushed into piles in the street to be carried away, but carried away infrequently. With rapid growth, cities had a most serious problem with sewage. In 1850, London dealt with the problem by collecting human waste in "privy buckets" to be dumped in one of 250,000 open cesspools around the city, which of course created further problems, owing to the city's dependence on well water.

In the United States as well, we often do not realize how recent is our affluence. Most of our grandparents or great-grandparents lived in rural areas without electricity, running water, or of course indoor plumbing. And then there was the Great Depression: More than 30 percent of the labor force was unemployed, and those who kept their jobs usually did so with huge wage reductions. It was during World War II that America moved most of its people out of poverty, and U.S. economic dominance in the world made Americans much more prosperous. Still, poverty was high, some 22 percent of the population, until the "War on Poverty" during the 1960s brought that rate down to 11 percent by the 1970s, mainly (as we will see) with expanded welfare aid (Danziger and Haveman 2001). Poverty was up again during the 1980s and early 1990s, this time because of changes in the position of the United States in the world economy resulting in job losses for Americans and lower wages. But poverty was also going up during this time because of cutbacks in America's welfare system during the Reagan years. After the first years of the 1990s, however, the United States entered a period of economic expansion that by 2001 turned out to be the longest in history. With unemployment dropping to the 4 percent range for the first time in decades, poverty finally started coming down by the end of the 1990s (Freeman 2001), *but not by much.* By the end of the 1990s the poverty rate was still in the 11 percent range. As expected, with the end to the longest boom in American history in 2001, poverty quickly went back up above 13 percent of the American population. But unexpectedly, in spite of the economic recovery in 2002 *poverty did not go down* and, in fact, kept going up as the economy improved. There was no downturn in poverty through 2004, then finally only a 0.4 percent drop in 2006. The cause is twofold: continued welfare cuts and the "jobless recovery" described in the previous chapter. As we will see, with fewer welfare and unemployment benefits, poverty was already increasing again in 2007. And as we would expect, the poverty rate began shooting up in 2008 and 2009 with the "great recession." An investigative report by the *New York Times* (January 4, 2010) found that 1 in 50 Americans had no income at all and existed only on food stamps, which do not have time limitations like the cash welfare and unemployment programs. These people live homeless, or are given a roof to live under by friends and relatives.

Perhaps even more troubling is the continuing high rate of poverty among children and female-headed households with children. Again, *finally* the poverty rate for this group came down slightly by 1997, but it was still 31.6 percent for all female-headed households and 19.9 percent for children under 18 in the United States in 1997. In 2006 the poverty rate for children under 18 years old was still 17.4 percent. This growth in poverty among children and their mothers is especially troubling because of the clear physical and psychological effects of poverty on children that are likely to remain with them for life, and perhaps even be passed on to the next generation (Duncan et al. 1998; Duncan and Brooks-Gunn 1997; McLeod and Shanahan 1993; Duncan and Rodgers 1991; Corcoran 2001).

The poor have been getting poorer. As can be seen in Figure 9-1, the percentage of the poor living in "extreme poverty," that is, below 50 percent of the poverty line, has gone up substantially since 1975. With increases in the number of poor people in the 1980s and early 1990s, we might expect an increase in hunger in the United States. Hunger was brought down in the late 1960s and 1970s, but it was back up in the 1980s. U.S. Department of Agriculture (USDA) figures for 1993–1994 indicated there were perhaps 30 million Americans defined as hungry (skipping meals each month due to

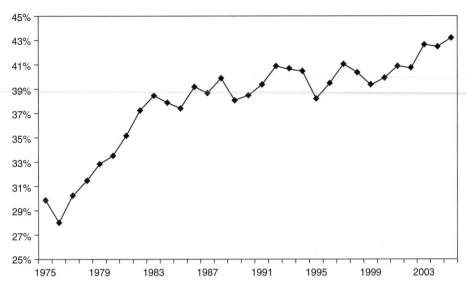

**FIGURE 9-1**    *Percentage of the Poor below 50 Percent of the Poverty Line, 1975–2005*

*SOURCE:* Mishel, Bernstein, and Allegretto (2007: Figure 6D).

lack of money). A study of hunger by the Department of Agriculture released in 2000 is perhaps most striking because it came at the high point of the U.S. economic boom that had gone on for almost 8 years. During 1999 it was estimated that more than 10 percent of Americans faced hunger at some time that year or were worried that their food would run out. The study estimated that approximately 17 percent of America's children, about 12 million young people, did not get enough to eat. Female-headed households had the highest rate of hunger (at around 30 percent), followed by African American families (21 percent), and Hispanic families (20.8 percent). Most people will find it surprising that during this long U.S. economic boom, this USDA study found an overall increase in rates of hunger for people below the poverty line and as high as $6,000 *above* the poverty line between 1995 and 1999 (U.S. Department of Agriculture 2000). The most recent survey of hunger in America by the USDA found that almost 15 percent of Americans lacked an adequate amount of food for at least some part of 2008. Even before the "great recession" began, the percent of Americans with "food insecurity" had already gone up in 2007, reaching the highest level since the USDA began their annual study, *Household Food Security in the United States* (www.ers. usda.gov/Publications/). The reports for 2009 and 2010 will certainly show even more dramatic increases in hunger as the "great recession" continues and other welfare and unemployment benefits run out.

　　Strangely, though, we have no consensus on the number of homeless people in the United States. The U.S. Census Bureau does an excellent job measuring poverty and inequality, but it can't get the numbers correct on the amount of homelessness in America. It is not for lack of trying. During the 2000 Census it announced that for the first time there would be a concerted effort at getting the numbers right on homelessness by hiring thousands of census takers to go through the streets on the same night to make an accurate count. The methodology was fairly straightforward: Like estimating millions of trees in a forest, there are statistical techniques that allow researchers to make random selections of certain areas for a detailed count. But after it was all over, the U.S. Census Bureau declared it had no confidence in its estimate and refused to even release the figures demanded by some cities (see the *Los Angeles Times,* June 8, 2003). Other agencies offer widely varying estimates. The National Alliance to End Homelessness, for example, estimated almost 700,000 Americans were homeless on any one night in 2007 (www.endhomelessness.org). The National Coalition for the Homeless estimated 1.5 million children were homeless some time during 2008, with over 200,000 children homeless on any given night. Other agencies estimated over 1.6 million people of all ages were homeless some time during 2007, while others estimate over 3 million were homeless (www.nationalhomeless.org). Whichever is the most accurate estimate, no one disagrees this is a very high rate for one of the richest countries in the world.

## ✖ Counting the Poor

As most people recognize, the poor in this country are primarily those with limited job skills, inadequate diet, substandard housing, low education, inadequate medical care, a shorter life expectancy—the list goes on. All of these things, of course, are important outcomes of living at the bottom of the stratification system. However, our major task is not to describe all the negative consequences of poverty; rather, it is to understand the existence of poverty in highly industrialized and affluent countries like the United States. We begin by describing briefly who the poor are.

Counting and identifying the poor are typically accomplished by establishing a **poverty line**—that is, an *economic definition* of poverty. Living at the bottom of the stratification system and the primary dimensions that make up this stratification system mean having limited economic resources to meet family needs. The Census Bureau arrives at its estimate of poverty through a determination of what it costs a family (of a certain size, age composition, and place of residence) to buy food, housing, and other necessities.

Using these estimates, in 2009 the U.S. Census Bureau considered a family of four, with no children under 18 years of age, to be poor living below $22,128 a year. A family of three with no children under 18 years of age was considered poor living with less than $16,781, while a family of two was poor under $14,366, and a single person was considered poor living on less than $11,161. The presence of people over 65 or under 18 years of age in the family changes the poverty threshold by $200 to $300 per year for each family size (U.S. Bureau of the Census, *Income, Poverty, and Health Insurance Coverage in the United States,* 2009, 2010:55).

### Criticisms of the Poverty Line

As might be expected, much controversy is created when attempting such an estimate, and most social scientists argue that the poverty line is established too low (Iceland 2003:10–37; Brady 2003b). The government estimate does not consider poverty to exist when a barely adequate standard of living is maintained; the standard of living has to be considerably less than adequate. With respect to food, for example, the official definition of living in poverty means spending less than one dollar (in 1990 dollars) per meal per person and having a diet that is not adequate to maintain long-term health (see Miller 1971:119; Rein 1971; Blumberg 1980:94).

It is also important to note that the official measure of poverty considers only pretax income. That is, when the Census Bureau determines whether or not a family is considered to be living in poverty, all of its cash income is totaled to see if the family is above or below the poverty line without subtracting how much of that cash income is taken away by taxes.

Criticisms of official poverty statistics, therefore, include the obvious charge that poverty is underestimated in this country. But also, the critics charge, a poverty line should consider the *relative* aspects of poverty—that is, because poverty is not only a material condition, we should consider poverty to exist when people are far below the average standard of living in the country. Some suggest that a relative poverty line could be drawn at about half of the average income of the population. If this were done and used as the official poverty rate, the level of poverty would be over 19 percent.

By the late 1970s, and especially during the early years of the Reagan administration, a different critique of the official Census Bureau's estimate of poverty emerged. In this case it was argued that the amount of poverty is overestimated in the United States. This argument was not so much that the poverty line itself is determined inaccurately, but that the measures of income used by the Census Bureau should be expanded. With the standard Census Bureau definition of poverty, all cash income is considered when placing a family above or below the poverty line. Cash income includes all money from any source—a job, investments, rent, royalties, welfare payments, pension benefits, and so on. However, since the 1960s, there has been relatively more government welfare aid in the form of "income-in-kind" benefits, such as food stamps and health care (Medicaid). Thus, the argument is that the value of these kinds of aid should be added to a family's cash income when determining the rate of poverty.

The rate of poverty is somewhat lower when considering income-in-kind as well as cash income, while using the same definition of poverty (the poverty line). For example, in 1997 the standard income definition (U.S. Bureau of the Census definition) showed the poverty rate at 13.3 percent, whereas the adjusted income definition (including income-in-kind) showed poverty at 11.9 percent of the population. However, with cuts in "income-in-kind" benefits increasing in the 1990s and 2000s the poverty rates using the Census income definition and adjusted income definition of poverty moved closer and closer together, prompting the Census Bureau to finally drop the separate estimate of "adjusted income definition of poverty."

There are, however, several problems with establishing the value of income-in-kind benefits and using this to estimate the rate of poverty (*Focus* 1982). For example, how do we value the medical benefits from the Medicaid program for the poor? If we simply total the dollar amount of the medical care the poor have been given, one could become nonpoor simply by becoming very ill and receiving much medical aid from the government. We could attempt to determine what the poor would pay for medical care through a private insurance program (which is what the Census Bureau has done), but this remains misleading in many ways (Mishel et al. 2003:319–329; Iceland 2003; see Harrington 1984:85–86). About 17 percent of the people just above them in terms of income cannot afford health care at all.

There is the additional problem that all the poor do not receive equal benefits from the income-in-kind aid programs, and many of the poor actually receive nothing. For example, to receive money from welfare programs and therefore qualify for many of the income-in-kind benefits as well, most states require a person to have an income much lower than the poverty line.

In response to many of these criticisms, the U.S. government created a panel of poverty experts under the National Research Council to study the problem and make recommendations. It released its report and recommendations in 1995. These recommendations were implemented by the Census Bureau and an alternate poverty line was established that takes into consideration such things as tax changes for the poor, the value of various government benefits as income, employment expenses (such as child care), and out-of-pocket medical costs (Mishel et al. 2003:319–324; Iceland 2003:20–37). In 1999, for example, while the traditional measure of poverty (official still) showed 11.8 percent of the American population living in poverty, the alternate measure showed 15 percent of the American population living in poverty. The "experimental measures" of poverty were reported every year by the Census Bureau until the 2003 poverty report that came out in 2004. Curiously, for the first time in decades, in 2004 the Census Bureau combined its annual reports on both income and poverty in the United States, along with a report on health care coverage for Americans. The combined report provided much less information on income and poverty, and dropped the experimental measures of poverty, which were higher estimates. Also dropped in the 2003 report were such things as measures of "extreme poverty" (how many of the poor are below 50 percent of the poverty line) and the extent to which the poor lived in families with a full-time worker. Most curious, the annual poverty reports have always been released in October. But the 2003 shortened, combined report, showing a significant increase in poverty, was released in August 2004, further away from election time.

### Poverty in Comparative Perspective

Before we move to a more detailed analysis of poverty in the United States, it is useful to put the level of poverty in the United States into perspective by comparing rates of poverty in other countries. There is something of a surprise in the newest comparative figures on poverty because one of the new measures of poverty indicates that for the first time in decades the United States does not have the highest rate of absolute poverty in the industrialized world. As can be seen in Table 9-1, during the mid-1990s, Australia and the United Kingdom had higher rates of absolute poverty than the United States. To understand this we must first consider the new Purchasing Power Parity (PPP) method of comparing what currencies in countries around the world will purchase. To create this new measure, economists estimated what a set amount of basic necessities would cost in each country around the world so we can make better comparisons across countries with differing costs of living. (For more details see the World Bank, Technical Notes, 2000:320.) This helps overcome the problem of shifting currency exchange rates that

## TABLE 9-1

### Percentage of People Living in Poverty, Absolute and Relative Poverty Rates, 1990s

| Country | Relative poverty* | Absolute poverty (PPP estimate)** | Children in relative poverty |
|---|---|---|---|
| United States | 19.1% | 13.6% | 24.9% |
| United Kingdom | 14.6 | 15.7 | 18.5 |
| Australia | 12.9 | 17.6 | 15.4 |
| Japan | 11.8 | — | 15.3 |
| Canada | 11.7 | 7.4 | 15.3 |
| Germany (West) | 7.6 | 7.3 | 8.6 |
| France | 7.5 | — | 7.4 |
| The Netherlands | 6.7 | 7.1 | 8.3 |
| Norway | 6.6 | 4.3 | 4.9 |
| Italy | 6.5 | — | 10.5 |
| Finland | 6.2 | 4.8 | 2.7 |

*Relative poverty measure is percent of people living below 50 percent of the median income.

**Estimate of poverty based on the U.S. definition of an absolute poverty line, using the new *Purchasing Power Parity* (PPP) estimate of the actual purchasing power compared to U.S. dollars of each nation's currency.

*SOURCES:* Data from Smeeding (1997); Mishel et al. (1999:375); Smeeding, Rainwater, and Burtless (2001:51).

often do not realistically represent actual cost-of-living differences. As we will see in the last chapter, this new PPP measure has been useful in comparing rates of poverty in poor countries around the world with the World Bank's new definition of extreme poverty as living on less than $1 a day. To make this estimate economists consider first what $1 would buy in the United States (say, one sandwich). They then consider what it costs to buy the same goods, like our sandwich example, in each country around the world to establish this poverty rate of less than $1 per day. One further example might help to explain this measure: In 2007 the exchange rate between the Thai currency (baht) and the U.S. dollar was $1 = 36 baht. However, because the cost of living in Thailand is much lower than in the United States, my experience is that about 25 baht would buy a sandwich in Thailand. Thus, with the new PPP estimate, the poverty rate of less than $1 per day is set at around 25 baht in Thailand rather than at 36 baht.

Returning to the figures in Table 9-1, "absolute poverty" is measured in the same way as the economic definition of poverty established by the U.S. Census Bureau described above. With the new statistical tool of Purchasing Power Parity (PPP) to measure the real incomes of people across nations, the rates of poverty now appear higher in the United Kingdom and Australia than in the United States (Smeeding, Rainwater, and Burtless 2001). With this new absolute definition of poverty using PPP income estimates, the United States had the third-highest rate of poverty among industrial nations, though with poverty substantially higher than that of the other industrial nations for which we have absolute rates of poverty.

Using a measure of "relative poverty" that all other industrial nations use more consistently to indicate poverty levels (below 50 percent of median income in the country), however, the United States still has a much higher rate of poverty than other industrial nations. This is especially the case for American children. Putting these two measures together—absolute poverty using PPP and relative poverty—we see in Table 9-1 that while the poor in Britain and Australia might be a bit worse off compared to the U.S. poor, when we consider poverty in relation to the level of income inequality in the society, the rate for the United States continues to be higher.

While recognizing the utility of this new absolute measure of poverty using PPP, when this measure becomes more critically examined it is likely some flaws will be discovered. For example, while the cost of living is higher in many other industrial nations, almost all of these other nations provide more welfare benefits in terms of income-in-kind than does the United States. Thus, subsidized housing, medical care, education, food aid, and other benefits are likely to improve the standards of living for the poor in European countries compared to those in the United States. These benefits are not adequately estimated in the "absolute" measure of poverty in Table 9-1, suggesting the rate of absolute poverty may in fact still be higher in the United States.

## ❊ The Extent of Poverty in the United States

In estimating the level of poverty in the United States for 2009, the U.S. Bureau of the Census (2010a) considered a nonfarm family of four to be poor if its yearly income fell below $ 22,128. Using this estimate, we find that 14.3 percent of the U.S. population was considered poor in 2009, as shown in Table 9-2. Comparing the estimated amount of poverty in this country over the past few years, Figure 9-2 shows that the percentage of poor dropped during the 1960s (from about 22 percent in 1959 when the poverty figures were first estimated), then leveled off in the 1970s to about 11 or 12 percent. During the 1980s, however, the rate of poverty went up again, reaching a high point of 15.2 percent in 1983, before slowly moving down again to the 13 percent range by 1989. From 1989, poverty was increasing again, to 13.5 percent in 1990, 14.2 percent in 1991, and 14.8 percent in 1992, before going over the 15 percent line in 1993. We must note again that the rather puzzling part is that 1992 and especially 1993 were years when the country was already into an economic boom. Poverty, according to past trends, should have been going down. Finally, from 1995 to 1997 the rate of poverty did drop slightly as the economic boom in the United States continued and unemployment dropped to around 5 percent. While the drop in poverty to 11.3 percent of the population by 2000 compared to 13.7 percent in 1996 and 15 percent for 1993 was not especially large, a few categories of Americans did benefit more. In the case of black Americans, for example, the rate of poverty went from 33.3 percent in 1992 to 26.5 percent in 1997, and 22.1 percent by 2000. For female-headed households the rate of poverty went from over 48 percent in 1992 to 31.6 percent in 1997 and 24.7 percent in 2000. And for black female-headed households, in particular, the rate of poverty dropped from over 60 percent in 1992 to 39.8 percent in 1997 and 34.6 percent in 2000. These rates, of course, are still very high, but it can be said that with unemployment finally down to 5 percent or less in the United States, it seems that the people hired last are finally finding employment. Although employment alone may not

## TABLE 9-2

### Extent of Poverty for Select Categories of the Population in 1997, 2000, and 2009

| | Percentage of group at poverty level | | |
| --- | --- | --- | --- |
| | 1997 | 2000 | 2009 |
| Total U.S. population | 13.3% | 11.3% | 14.3% |
| Whites | 11.0 | 7.5 | 9.4 |
| Blacks | 26.5 | 22.1 | 25.8 |
| Hispanic origin | 27.1 | 21.2 | 25.3 |
| Aged (65+) | 10.5 | 10.2 | 8.9 |
| Under 18 | 19.9 | 16.2 | 20.7 |
| Female-headed households with children | 31.6% | 24.7% | 29.9% |
| White | 27.7 | 16.9 | 23.8 |
| Black | 39.8 | 34.6 | 39.7 |
| Hispanic origin | 47.6 | 34.2 | 40.6 |
| Residence | | | |
| Inside metropolitan areas | 12.6% | 10.8% | 13.9% |
| In central cities | 18.8 | 16.1 | 18.7 |
| Outside central cities | 9.0 | 7.8 | 11.0 |
| Outside metropolitan areas | 15.9 | 13.4 | 16.6 |
| Region | | | |
| Northeast | 12.6% | 10.3% | 12.2% |
| Midwest | 10.4 | 9.5 | 13.3 |
| South | 14.6 | 12.5 | 15.7 |
| West | 14.6 | 11.9 | 14.8 |

*SOURCES:* U.S. Bureau of the Census, *Money Income and Poverty Status of Families and Persons in the United States: 1997,* Current Population Reports (1998: series P-60); U.S. Bureau of the Census, *Poverty in the United States, 2000* (2001: Table A); U.S. Bureau of the Census, *Income, Poverty, and Health Insurance Coverage in the United States, 2009* (2010: Table 4).

remove many of these people from poverty, low-wage employment in addition to some aid such as food stamps does move some out of poverty.

With the longest economic boom in American history over in 2001, poverty quickly increased again. We will see that this was especially so because, unlike in the decades before the 1980s, there was now much less government aid in the form of welfare and unemployment benefits to help people who lost their jobs or had their working hours reduced. By 2009 the poverty rate was back up to 14.3 percent of the population, and the figure will likely be higher when the 2010 poverty figures are released. Interestingly too, the people who were helped briefly at the end of the longest boom in American history were hurt most by the downturn beginning in 2001 and the jobless recovery that followed through 2004. Table 9-2, for example, shows that the rate of poverty for female-headed households shot back up from 24.7 percent in 2000 to 29.9 percent in 2009.

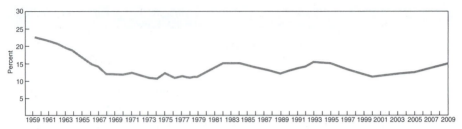

**FIGURE 9-2**     *Percentage of Population Living in Poverty According to Official Government Statistics, 1959–2009*

SOURCES: U.S. Bureau of the Census, *Money Income and Poverty Status of Families and Persons in the U.S.: 1978,* Current Population Reports (1979: series P-60, no. 120); U.S. Bureau of the Census, *Population Profile of the United States: 1993,* Current Population Reports (1993: series P-20, no. 363); U.S. Bureau of the Census 1998; U.S. Bureau of the Census, *Poverty in the United States, 2000* (2001: Table A); U.S. Bureau of the Census, *Income, Poverty, and Health Insurance Coverage in the United States, 2009* (2010: Table 4).

Finally, one of the most important new trends in American poverty must be considered—the working poor. In the past one could more likely assume that a full-time job would mean a person and his or her family would not be poor. This is no longer always the case. With increasingly lower wages for American workers described in Chapter 2, more and more people find they are still in poverty even working 40 hours a week, 52 weeks a year. Table 9-3 shows that in 1993, 36 percent of the poor in America lived in a family that had a full-time worker. By 2000 that figure had increased to 44.5 percent of the poor.

## Changes in the Rate of Poverty

With reference to Figure 9-2, we should consider some of the reasons why the rate of poverty moved up and down as it did between 1959 and 1997. The drop in the poverty level between 1959 and 1970, and the continued lower level of poverty through the 1970s, was *primarily the result of expanded welfare benefits* beginning in the second half of the 1960s (Blumberg 1980:100). It must be stressed that welfare benefits alone

## TABLE 9-3

### The Work History of Families in Poverty, 1993–2000

| Work history | All poor in families | |
|---|---|---|
| | **1993** | **2000** |
| No full-time worker in the family | 55.0% | 46.1% |
| One full-time worker in the family | 36.0 | 44.5 |
| Two or more full-time workers in the family | 9.0 | 9.4 |
| | 100% | 100% |

SOURCE: U.S. Bureau of the Census, *Poverty in the United States, 2000* (2001: Table C).

would very seldom bring a person or family out of poverty. For example, in 1983 only 3.4 percent of the poor were removed from poverty by welfare benefits in cash (such as Aid to Families with Dependent Children, or AFDC) and another 9.1 percent were removed by the income-in-kind benefits (Danziger, Haveman, and Plotnick 1986:65). What happened in this time period was that more of the working poor were allowed to receive some welfare benefits, which, combined with their job income, brought them above the poverty line. Thus, poverty was reduced mainly by government aid in this period, *not* by more jobs or by better-paying jobs. This also helps us understand why poverty stayed down in the 1970s despite the fact that the United States had a higher level of unemployment. The sharp increase in poverty from 2008 is, of course, due to the "great recession" at a time when cash welfare programs are more limited, with time limits placed on them by the "welfare reform" legislation of 1996 (as we will see in more detail later in this chapter).

Looking at Table 9-4, we see that while federal and state governments in the United States reduced the level of poverty with welfare benefits, it was done to a much smaller degree than all other major nations around the world. Using the relative definition of poverty all other governments use to measure poverty (below 50 percent of median income in the country), we see the results of welfare policies on the level of poverty. In the early 1990s, for the United States before welfare payments 26.7 percent of the people were considered poor by this definition. After considering the effects of welfare payments, the U.S. poverty rate went down to 19.1 percent of the population, for a 28.5 percent reduction in what poverty would have been otherwise. However, as

## TABLE 9-4

### The Comparative Impact of Welfare Benefits on Reducing Poverty*

| Country | Poverty (before welfare payments) | Poverty (after welfare payments) | Poverty reduction |
|---|---|---|---|
| United States | 26.7% | 19.1% | −28.5% |
| Germany | 22.0 | 7.6 | −65.5 |
| France | 21.6 | 7.5 | −65.3 |
| Italy | 18.4 | 6.5 | −64.7 |
| England | 29.2 | 14.6 | −50.0 |
| Canada | 23.4 | 11.7 | −50.0 |
| Australia | 23.2 | 12.9 | −50.0 |
| Belgium | 28.4 | 5.5 | −80.6 |
| Denmark | 26.9 | 7.5 | −72.1 |
| The Netherlands | 22.8 | 6.7 | −70.6 |
| Spain | 28.2 | 10.4 | −63.1 |
| Sweden | 34.1 | 6.7 | −80.4 |

*Poverty measured by income below 50 percent of median income in the nation. Data are available from 1989 to 1994.

SOURCES: Constructed from data presented by Smeeding (1997); Mishel et al. (1999:377).

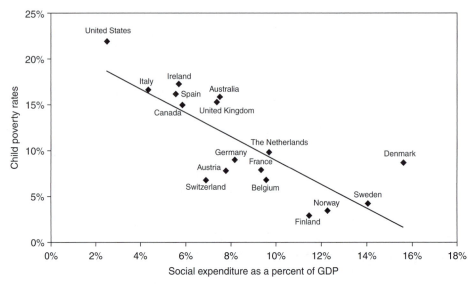

**FIGURE 9-3**     *Social Welfare Expenditures per GDP and Child Poverty Rates*

*SOURCE:* Mishel, Bernstein, and Allegretto (2007: Figure 8H).

we look down the list of other nations, we find that poverty is *much lower primarily because of much more extensive welfare aid* (also see Kim 2000). For example, consider Germany; poverty would have been 21.6 percent without welfare benefits, instead of actually 7.6 percent. In other words, the German government brought the rate of poverty down by more than 65 percent due to its efforts, while the U.S. government brought poverty down by only 28.5 percent (also see Gangl 2004). Recent research has shown clearly that it is primarily cuts in U.S. government spending on social welfare programs that are most responsible for the higher level of poverty in the United States (Lobao and Hooks 2003; Brady 2006, 2005, 2003a; Brady, Beckfield, and Seeleib-Kaiser 2005; also see Moran 2006). The same relationship between government efforts to reduce poverty and actual poverty reduction can also be seen in Figure 9-3. There is a very strong relationship between government spending for social programs as a percentage of the country's gross domestic product (GDP) and rates of poverty among children. At the top left of Figure 9-3 we see that the United States has the highest level of poverty among children for rich industrial nations and spends the least on social welfare programs as a percentage of its GDP.

Now that welfare and unemployment benefits are less likely obtainable for the American poor, the poverty rate is more responsive to economic changes. Freeman (2001:110–111) examined all factors influencing poverty rates in recent years and concluded that unemployment, real wages, and increasing income inequality create most changes in the U.S. poverty rate today. Real wages deserve more consideration at this point. One of the factors pushing up poverty rates and keeping them up even when unemployment is low is the minimum wage. In real income (what a dollar will buy at the time), compared to the federal minimum wage of $5.15 today, in 1974 the minimum wage was $7.99 (U.S. Bureau of the Census, *Statistical Abstracts of the United States, 2003* [2004:425]). A few states such as California have state minimum wage laws slightly higher. But since 1974 the wage of low-income, low-skilled workers has been dropping. If the minimum wage was actually $7.99 today poverty would be lower. When the 2008 recession is over and unemployment goes down, we can assume that congressional legislation increasing the national minimum wage to $7.25 in 2009 will have a positive effect on reducing poverty. It is far too soon to tell how much the reduction in poverty might be, however (Mishel, Bernstein, and Shierholz 2009:209).

## Movement into and out of Poverty

Until there was more extensive research on the subject of poverty, it was commonly assumed that once a person falls into poverty, or especially if he or she is born into poverty, the chance of moving out of poverty was very low. We now know that this assumption was inaccurate for many of the poor. From a series of studies (see Corcoran 2001; Evanson 1981; Wilson 1987:174–178), the more optimistic conclusion is that there is movement out of poverty. But there is also the less pleasant finding that more people in this country experience poverty at least some time in their life than was previously thought. Also, the first set of findings must not be seen as totally positive, because those who do move out of poverty seldom move very far above it, with a tendency to fall back into poverty some time in their life.

In the study covering the longest period of time, Blank (1997; also see Corcoran 2001) found that almost 33 percent of Americans had been below the poverty line for at least 1 year between 1979 and 1991. Over 10 percent of Americans had been below the poverty line for 7 or more years in this time period. Danziger and Gottschalk (1995) found more than half of all Americans in the bottom 20 percent income category in 1968 were still there in 1991. Also, 72 percent of nonwhites and 78 percent of welfare recipients who were in the bottom 20 percent income category in 1968 were still there 20 years later. Recent studies also show that groups of 10-year-olds with identical social characteristics have very different high school dropout rates when the groups are later divided into those growing up in poor neighborhoods and those growing up in more affluent neighborhoods (Harding 2003). Simply put, growing up in a poor neighborhood makes you more likely to be poor in later life. In earlier studies, Levy (1977), for example, found that only 43 percent of those who were poor continued to be poor for 5 of the next 7 years, and that only 5 percent of the U.S. population was poor for at least 5 of the 7 years (compared with 12 percent of the population poor in any 1 year). Coe (1978) found that only 1 percent of the U.S. population was poor 9 out of the 9 years included in his study. And Hill (1981) found only 0.7 percent of the U.S. population to be poor for the full 10 years in her study. However, Hill found that 24 percent of the U.S. population was poor at least 1 year of the 10 years under study, and Coe (1978) found that 25 percent of Americans were poor at least 1 year in a 9-year period. Thus, while there is movement into and out of poverty, (1) from 43 percent to 60 percent of the poor do not move out (*Focus* 1984:8; Wilson 1987:176); (2) when they do move out, they do not move very far above poverty or stay out; and (3) about one-fourth of the U.S. population experiences poverty for at least 1 year during any given 10-year period.

In contrast to other major industrial nations, however, we must note that the United States has a less conducive political and economic system for moving out of poverty. Again using data from European governments and measuring poverty with their relative definition, we find that in The Netherlands about 45 percent of families in poverty are able to escape after 1 year. In the United States the rate is only about 15 percent able to escape after 1 year. As for other countries, the rate of escaping poverty after 1 year is between 25 and 28 percent for France, Germany, and Ireland (Mishel et al. 1999:379; Mishel et al. 2003:416). As we will see in Chapter 12, though, it is not just less movement out of poverty in the United States compared to European countries today. Moving up to higher income levels for the bottom 20 percent and 40 percent of Americans is less than what it used to be in the United States, and less today than in European countries (see, for example, Mishel, Bernstein, and Shierholz 2009: Chapter 2).

# ✁ Theories of Poverty

When, toward the middle of this century, it finally became apparent to most social scientists that poverty was a pervasive and continuing feature of our society, poverty was singled out as an important social problem worthy of special study. One outcome of this recognition has been special theories devoted to understanding this particular condition.

The separate status of poverty theories are worth noting because they tell us something rather curious about how the subject matter of poverty has been treated by social scientists. It suggests that although one set of processes was believed to help explain "normal" inequality and class divisions, the existence of poverty in our affluent society is somehow different. Some of the special theories of poverty examined here provide valuable insights, but we can best understand the existence of poverty as we have class divisions in general—that is, with a conflict (or structural) theory of social stratification.

## Blaming the Poor

Before turning to the various theories of poverty, it is helpful to discuss the belief in the social value of *individualism* in this country. By doing so we can better understand (1) how the general population tends to view the poor in our society, (2) what some of the particular problems faced by the poor are, (3) how our present welfare system is designed, and (4) what some of the main points of the first group of theories examined here mean.

**Individualism** may be defined broadly as the belief that the individual is more important than the social group (see Lukes 1973b). For those who are a product of the American culture this may seem an unquestionable statement, but in many non-Western cultures it is not. In other cultures the individual is often of secondary importance; the collective is given precedence over the needs and particular interests of the individual (see Dumont 1970 and Sekhon 2000 for discussions of India and individualism, Kerbo and McKinstry 1998 for Japan, and Slagter and Kerbo 2000 for a discussion of Thailand). Several studies, including Hofstede's (1991) massive study of people's attitudes in more than 50 nations around the world, have shown that the highest rate of individualism is found in the United States.

This general value of individualism has very wide implications for the society. It usually means, for example, that government should not infringe upon the rights of individuals—giving us our value of *freedom*. Individualism suggests the importance of free competition in business affairs and of having government not interfere in "free" economic pursuits (that is, a laissez faire view of government). Individualism also conveys the ideal of equality of opportunity (not equality per se), whereby people should have the opportunity to better themselves, or to be upwardly mobile and prosper as their talents and motivation allow.

Most important for the present discussion, individualism can mean that people are held responsible for their lot in life. For many, the logic of this value is that because equality of opportunity is supposed to exist, those who are poor have only themselves to blame for their poverty. There are special circumstances in which a person is relieved of responsibility for his or her poverty; to some degree our society has been willing to recognize the unique problems of poverty for the elderly, the disabled, and children. These people make up the "deserving poor." But for the most part, the poor without such "excuses" for their poverty are held in contempt by the general population.

This description and implications of a strong belief in individualism are somewhat overstated. General social values are never completely accepted by all in the society; nor are they always interpreted in exactly the same way by everyone. Historical change, the realities of a new age, must erode the original strength and meaning of traditional social values.

To the degree that our individualistic tradition was shaped by our frontier era, early Protestant beliefs, and the view of this country as a place where immigrants of the 18th and 19th centuries could find a new, prosperous life, we might expect this traditional value of individualism to have lost some of its strength. The evidence confirms this, but only to a small degree (Bellah et al. 1985). The continued effect of this value is in part reflected in the operation of our social welfare system and in the beliefs held about the cause of poverty in this society. Let us examine the latter in more detail.

Many studies have examined popular beliefs about poverty in the United States. For example, Feagin (1972, 1975) found that over 50 percent of a national sample of Americans felt "lack of thrift," "lack of effort," and "lack of ability" by the poor were very *important* causes of poverty; a near majority (48 percent) thought "loose morals and drunkenness" were very important. A more recent national poll conducted in 2001 showed much the same attitude toward the causes of poverty, but with more contradictions among people. For example, 48 percent of Americans said that "lack of effort" was the main cause of poverty, while 45 percent cited "circumstances" (things beyond the control of the poor) as more important (*Demos* 2002). But it seems that Americans have become ambivalent in their views with growing inequality and continuing high rates of poverty after the longest economic boom in American history. When asked to agree or disagree with the statement "most people who don't get ahead should not blame the system, they only have themselves to blame," 72 percent of Americans voice agreement. But when asked to agree or disagree with the statement "if people were treated more equally in this country we would have fewer problems," 79 percent agreed. It seems Americans still voice the old ideology, while at the same time they are starting to be concerned about the rising inequality and continuing poverty in America (*Demos* 2002:7).

Other studies of the poor and welfare recipients (Cole and Lejeune 1972; Kerbo 1976b) concur in showing that even the poor themselves are often likely to hold the poor responsible for poverty. These findings clearly attest to the strength of individualistic explanations of poverty when even some poor can be convinced the poor are to blame (Ryan 1971). These beliefs about poverty held by the poor themselves have important implications for social stability, the self-concepts of the poor, and the perpetuation of poverty.

Every society has some negative views toward the poor as a category of people, as Georg Simmel was among the first to clearly explain in his 1908 essay "The Poor" (Simmel 1971). But few other countries go to such an extreme with these negative views as does the United States. This negative view of the poor in the United States is, of course, related to the extreme level of individualism in this country and can also be seen in the degree of acceptance of higher inequality compared with other nations, as well as a lack of support for government intervention to reduce inequality. For example, in their study of attitudes about equality held by elites in the United States, Sweden, and Japan, Verba et al. (1987) found much more support for income equality in Sweden and Japan than in the United States. In other studies by Simkus and Robert (1989) and Ladd and Bowman (1998) of popular attitudes about issues related to an individualistic ideology, again we see the United States is rather different. Table 9-5 indicates much less popular support in the United States for government action to reduce unemployment and income inequality compared with other industrial nations in the sample. Though the evidence does not support the existence of more equality of opportunity in the United States than any other industrial nation (as we will see in Chapter 12), Americans are much more likely to believe equality of opportunity exists in the United States and more likely to believe that hard work will "pay off." However, as noted above, a 2001 poll indicates some of these attitudes may be changing in the United States. The American faith that equality of opportunity will make everything better remains, with 90 percent in 2001 agreeing that "our society should do what is necessary to make sure that everyone has an equal opportunity to succeed" (*Demos* 2002:7). But 48 percent of Americans think that compared to 10 years ago it is more difficult to move out of poverty because equal opportunity is lacking. As much as 44 percent of Americans today view society as divided between the "haves" and the "have-nots" compared with only 26 percent of Americans who felt that way in 1988 (*Demos* 2002:10). Using a large sample of respondents from Europe and the United States, Di Tella and MacCulloch (2001) found that Europeans were much more disturbed over high levels of inequality than were Americans, and Americans (incorrectly) believe their society is more open with more social mobility than are societies in other nations. More recently, data indicate the biggest difference between attitudes on equality between Europeans and Americans has to do with poverty. Both Europeans and Americans believe top salaries should not be as high as they are today, but only Americans are less concerned about poverty (Osberg and Smeeding 2006; also see Somers and Block 2006, and Birchfield 2008, for a comparison of value differences in the United States and Europe).

## Four Categories of Poverty Theories

Research remains quite clear: Being born into poverty and growing up in poverty make a person much more likely to be poor as an adult (Duncan et al. 1998; Duncan and

# TABLE 9-5

## Comparative Attitudes toward Inequality and Government Involvement in the Economy to Reduce Inequality

| Question | Hungary | Austria | Italy | West Germany | Switzerland | The Netherlands | Great Britain | Australia | United States |
|---|---|---|---|---|---|---|---|---|---|
| 1. The government should provide everyone with a guaranteed basic income. | 77.8% | 53.6% | 66.9% | 50.1% | 41.6% | 47.9% | 59.4% | 38.1% | 17.6% |
| 2. The government should provide a job for everyone who wants one. | 90.0 | 76.9 | 82.0 | 74.3 | 48.4 | 73.8 | 57.9 | 39.7 | 44.0 |
| 3. The government should provide support for children from poor families to attend college. | 71.6 | 78.3 | 89.8 | 84.8 | 80.7 | 84.1 | 82.6 | 74.0 | 75.2 |
| 4. It is the responsibility of government to reduce the differences in income between people with high incomes and those with low incomes. | 76.9 | 76.7 | 81.0 | 55.9 | 41.1 | 63.9 | 62.9 | 43.8 | 28.3 |
| 5. People have equal opportunities to get ahead in this country. | 18.0 | NA | NA | 55.0 | NA | NA | 42.0 | NA | 66.0 |
| 6. Upper limits should be placed on incomes. | 58.0 | NA | NA | 32.0 | NA | NA | 39.0 | NA | 17.0 |
| 7. Hard work brings a better life in this country. | NA | NA | NA | 43.0 | NA | NA | 38.0 | NA | 59.0 |

SOURCES: Simkus and Robert (1989); Ladd and Bowman (1998).

Brooks-Gunn 1997). But there are still questions about exactly why this occurs. With this in mind, it is time to take a closer look at some of the theories developed to explain poverty. Four types of theories are examined. The first goes back to the early history in sociology but was never accepted by many social scientists even at the time. This theory, however, which we refer to as the *popular view,* follows much popular sentiment of blaming the poor by suggesting that the characteristics of the poor are the cause of poverty. The second theory does suggest that the characteristics of the poor help maintain poverty but do so indirectly and shows how social conditions were originally behind these characteristics of the poor. Although a *culture-of-poverty theory* is inadequate in many respects in explaining most poverty in industrial societies, we will see that it has limited value and must be examined to understand why it is inaccurate (as well as why the common myths about poverty are wrong). The third group of theories are *situational theories,* and the fourth is the *structural* or *conflict perspective.*

At the outset, Figure 9-4 may be helpful in summarizing some of the most important differences among the four types of poverty theories. Beginning with Figure 9-4A, we find a representation of the common view of the causes of poverty, and one reinvigorated recently by Herrnstein and Murray (1994). In short, the poor and their characteristics, including biological characteristics such as IQ, are said to be the cause of poverty.

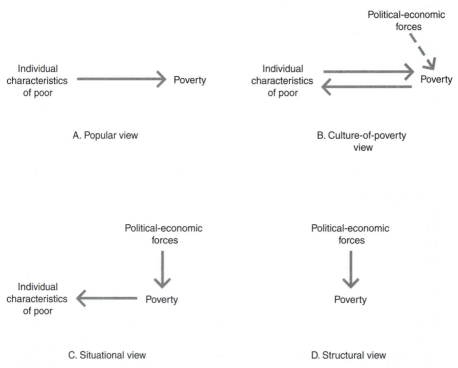

**FIGURE 9-4**     *Causes of Poverty Assumed by Theories of Poverty and the General Population*

Figure 9-4B represents the main points of the culture-of-poverty view. This theory (weakly) suggests that social conditions originally helped produce poverty (the broken line in Figure 9-4B); but, most important, this theory argues that poverty produces people with unique personal characteristics that in turn help ensure that the poor—and their children—remain poor.

Situational theories of poverty, as represented in Figure 9-4C, place more stress on social conditions as causing poverty. However, they do suggest that poverty produces people with particular characteristics, although these characteristics are not viewed as a compounding cause of poverty. Finally, Figure 9-4D represents a structural or conflict view of poverty. There is almost complete stress on the political and economic forces in the society that produce and maintain poverty.

## Blaming the Poor: Social Darwinism

Most generally, the popular view of blaming the poor for their own poverty has focused on the "moral character" of the poor. As we saw earlier, many people think the poor are poor because they are lazy, waste their time and money, and simply do not have the self-control to succeed. As Simmel (1908) pointed out long ago, and Gans (1972) more recently, this view of the poor is popular because it provides the nonpoor with a justification for poverty and a category of people they can look down on to make themselves feel better. And as Piven and Cloward (1971) have shown, this "blaming the victim" perspective can also be a means of controlling the poor when the poor themselves come to believe it, at least to some extent. The poor who blame themselves are not likely to disrupt the society or make demands for improved conditions.

Going back to the earlier years of social science, however, various theories suggest the poor, criminals, and others at the bottom of society are in fact either biologically inferior or inferior due to character, and these defects are the cause of their behavior. This was much the position taken by one of the early social Darwinists, British sociologist Herbert Spencer, who died in 1903, and by the American sociologist William Graham Sumner, who died in 1910. Following the Darwinist idea of "survival of the fittest," the basic argument of **social Darwinism** is that these people are on the bottom because they are unfit to survive the competition, and conversely, the rich and powerful are on top because they are the fittest. This situation, therefore, is as it should be according to social Darwinists, and any attempt at social engineering to change the situation will be only harmful to the society by allowing the "unfit" to survive, multiply, and weaken the society. As we might expect, Herbert Spencer in particular was greatly admired by the rich at the time, and was even supported by none other than Andrew Carnegie (Ritzer 2004).

Somewhat like Herbert Spencer, more recently two writers have found great favor among the rich, primarily the new right political conservatives in the United States since the late 1970s. In his most popular book, *Wealth and Poverty,* George Gilder (1981) provided a rather useful argument for the "superiority" of the rich and powerful, and gave justification for the ideas of Reaganomics that were being pushed in political circles at the time. Soon after these ideas took hold, along came the ideas of Charles Murray. He first became well known for a book, *Losing Ground* (Murray 1984), which claimed that the welfare system in the United States should be eliminated because it supports the immorality and deviant behavior of the poor, much as Herbert Spencer had suggested over 100 years ago. But in 1994 his book *The Bell Curve,* written with Richard Herrnstein (Herrnstein and Murray 1994), argued more directly that the poor are on the bottom for biological reasons—in particular because of low mental ability as shown in below-average IQ scores. The argument that intelligence and education are ever more important for occupational success in modern societies is obvious and needs no further comment. But the argument that most of the poor (as well as a disproportionate number of blacks) are on the bottom because they are biologically inferior in mental ability attempts to reinvigorate old ideas that simply have no empirical basis. Nor does their argument that the overall IQ of the population is going down because of higher fertility rates among the poor have empirical validity (Preston and Campbell 1993).

There are data showing that the poor, on average, score lower on tests of mental ability, such as IQ exams, as Herrnstein and Murray (1994) indicate. Anyone who works with welfare recipients knows that some of their clients—but certainly not even close to a majority—seem to have problems coping with many aspects of everyday life. These are individuals who must be helped in an industrial society that has less family support and fewer low-skilled jobs. But it must be stressed that only a slightly higher number of poor and welfare recipients than the general population can be described as such. Even the data presented by Herrnstein and Murray indicate this by showing much more overlap than separation in IQ scores among the poor and the American population in general.

There is considerable evidence in the studies of status attainment, or studies of what factors lead some people to get ahead and others to end up in low positions in the class system, that mental ability is only very weakly involved in the process, and in fact secondary to many social factors. In other words, many factors other than IQ are found to be more important in explaining why those at the top as well as the bottom of the occupational ladder are there. These studies are considered in detail in Chapter 12 on social mobility.

The biggest problem with the thesis that the poor and blacks are on average lower in IQ, however, involves the causal direction of the reasoning. The abundance of evidence, much of it also discussed in our chapter on social mobility and status attainment, indicates the causal direction is the reverse of the Herrnstein and Murray thesis (Feldman, Otto, and Christiansen 2000; Flynn 2000): Many of the poor (including poor minorities) have lower IQs *because they are poor,* not the other way around. We know that much in the social and physical environment of poor children harms their intellectual development (Jencks et al. 1972, 1979; Mercy and Steelman 1982). Such harm starts with a fetus that is not given proper nutrition and perhaps is even exposed to drugs and excessive alcohol. After birth there can be continuing poor nutrition and poor health, as well as a lack of mental stimulation, causing retarded brain development. Recent studies, for example, indicate that poor children with anemia and iron deficiency due to hunger are on average 25 percent behind other children in mental development. Another study of 1,023 elementary school children at the Tufts University Center on Hunger, Poverty and Nutrition Policy (see also *Los Angeles Times,* November 20, 1994) found that test scores of these hungry children rose dramatically, especially in math, after they were provided with a breakfast at school. And research by McLeod and Shanahan (1993) has shown the persistent mental and psychological damage caused by poverty among children for all racial groups.

We also know that class oppression among people from the same gene pool, such as Protestants and Catholics in Northern Ireland, can produce the same IQ score gap, as can the disruptive effects of immigration by poor ethnic groups (Sowell 1978, 1981, 1994). Irish Americans, for example, also had IQ scores about 15 points below average soon after they migrated to the United States during the second half of the 19th century. But after the poverty and disruption of their earlier generations in the United States, their IQ scores have come to match the average for the rest of the population.

Because of such weaknesses in the thesis suggesting the poor are poor *because* of low mental ability rather than the other way around, the Herrnstein and Murray argument has been soundly rejected by biological and social scientists, as was the earlier thesis that blacks have low IQs due to biology put forth in the 1970s by William Shockley and Arthur Jensen. Among a panel of top scientists who have rejected the book as unscientific and simply wrong, Harvard's Stephen Jay Gould put it most clearly: "They have bamboozled everybody" (*Los Angeles Times,* December 14, 1994, p. A-25). But such scientific rejection does not always result in a popular rejection of a thesis that people may find useful in blaming victims of social situations other people would prefer to ignore. It didn't help that the book was covered on the front pages of leading newspapers and on the covers of news magazines in the fall of 1994, while the rejections by scientists were generally found later on the back pages of the newspapers.

# A Culture of Poverty?

The study of poverty, unfortunately, has been dominated by three questions: (1) Are the poor different from other people? (2) If so, how different are the poor? (3) How deep are these differences? The dominance of these questions is unfortunate not because they lack any significance but because they have deflected interest from more important questions about the nature of societies and a world system that helps produce poverty. For example, despite the abundance of research showing that the vast majority of poor, like anyone else, would rather have a decent job than receive welfare, research funding continues to go to studies that find (surprise!) that the poor prefer jobs over welfare. The abundance of such research tells us more about our social myths than about the poor.

The most noted **culture-of-poverty theory** is that of Oscar Lewis. A social anthropologist, Oscar Lewis conducted his research through detailed and lengthy personal observations of families living in poverty. His books, such as *Five Families* (1959), *La Vida* (1966), and *The Children of Sanchez* (1961), make interesting reading—full of sex, violence, and drama—and are more like novels than scientific reports. In these works Lewis attempted to show the existence of a culture of poverty that produces personality and value differences among the poor. There are five major points in this theory:

1. Because of the conditions of poverty, the poor are presented with unique problems in living (compared with the nonpoor).

2. In order to cope with these problems, the poor follow a unique lifestyle.

**3.** Through collective interaction and in the face of relative isolation from the nonpoor, this unique lifestyle becomes a common characteristic of the poor, producing common values, attitudes, and behavior. A common culture (or, more accurately, a subculture) is developed.

**4.** Once this common subculture of poverty has become, in a sense, institutionalized, it is self-perpetuating. In other words, it becomes relatively *independent* of the social conditions of poverty that helped produce the subculture. The values, attitudes, and behavior that are a part of this subculture are passed on to the children of the poor—that is, *the children are socialized into this subculture of poverty.*

**5.** Because this subculture is believed to shape the basic character and personality of people raised in poverty, even if opportunities to become nonpoor arise, the poor will retain the traits that allowed them to adjust to the original conditions of poverty. Thus, the poor will *not be able to adjust to the new situation* through values and behavior that will allow them to take advantage of new opportunities to become nonpoor.

Many characteristics of a culture of poverty have been listed by social scientists (see Lewis 1966:xlv–xlviii). For example, on a community level, there is a lack of participation in the institutions of the wider society (except for contact with the criminal justice system and welfare institutions). On a family level, there is the absence of a long childhood, "early initiation into sex, free unions or consensual marriages, a relatively high incidence of the abandonment of wives and children," and female-centered families. On an individual level, the poor are believed to have "strong feelings of marginality, of helplessness, of dependence, and of inferiority." Other individual characteristics are believed to be a weak ego, lack of impulse control, "a present-time orientation with relatively little ability to defer gratification and to plan for the future," a sense of fatalism, a value stress on male superiority, and "a high tolerance for psychological pathology of all sorts."

Social scientists have paid considerable attention to the "trait" of a present-time orientation, or an inability to delay gratification. This trait is said to be a coping mechanism, for example, because it would be psychologically damaging to continually worry about and plan for a future that holds no promise of a better life or more opportunities. In short, the poor must learn to live for today.

This cultural trait is also seen as important in perpetuating poverty and preventing upward mobility out of poverty because the poor "learn not to delay gratification or plan for the future" and are unable to take advantage of new opportunities. More specifically, the existence of this trait is taken to mean that if new educational or job-training opportunities become available, the poor would be unable to make the sacrifice in time and energy needed to get the job training.

The theory is logical, clear, and, perhaps most important, fits nicely with most of the common stereotypes of the poor held by the dominant society. But at the same time this explanation holds some sympathy for the poor, while also not contradicting stereotypes, and maintains the liberal tradition of ultimately seeing society as part of the problem. However, this theory is not overly critical of social institutions because even when some small (nonradical) reforms have been made in the society (as reformers may claim have been made), the poor inevitably continue to exist, with their poverty now seen as their own fault. The goal then becomes one of changing the poor (rather than aspects of the society) so the poor can become "more like us."

## The Culture of Poverty: A Critique

Despite this theory's wide appeal and logic, it contains serious shortcomings, especially when applied to the United States (Wilson 1987:182–183). In the first place, Oscar Lewis himself never suggested that the theory had wide relevance in the United States (see Valentine 1971:215). As he made clear in one of his most noted works (Lewis 1966:li),

> Because of the advanced technology, high level of literacy, the development of mass media and the relatively high aspiration level of all sectors of the population, especially when compared with underdeveloped nations, I believe that although there is still a great deal of poverty in the United States . . . there is relatively little of what I would call the culture of poverty.

Many people, however, have chosen to ignore Oscar Lewis on this point. Accepting this theory is difficult to resist, given our cultural assumptions about the poor.

More specifically, the culture-of-poverty theory can be questioned on several grounds. First, even to the extent that we do find behavioral differences among the poor, this does *not* mean that the *values* of the poor differ. As other evidence suggests, because of their conditions of poverty, the poor may not be able to live up to an ideal they value equally with the nonpoor (see Rainwater 1969; Gans 1969). The point can be made clearly with respect to the higher rate of single-parent families among poor whites and poor minorities. This rate has been growing rapidly among the poor, especially poor minorities, in the United States. With respect to women on welfare (AFDC), while 31 percent of the women recipients with children were never married in 1980, by 1992 the rate was 52 percent. Although changing attitudes may in part be involved, data show that young women living in poverty are in one sense acting as they must because prison rates, death rates, and the inability of young poor men to get jobs suggest their chances of staying with a man who has fathered their children are not comparatively high (Lichter, LeClere, and McLaughlin 1991; Wilson 1987; Jencks 1991; Duncan and Hoffman 1991; Mare and Winship 1991). To the extent value preferences are a cause of female-headed families, it must be noted the increase has grown rapidly among the middle class as well, though not as rapidly, suggesting the added effects of poverty described earlier.

Second, in common with functional theory in general, the culture-of-poverty theory assumes an overly uniform view of culture and values in industrial societies like the United States (Gans 1969; Wilson 1987). We can assume the existence of some very abstract ideals, such as the individualism discussed earlier, but even these abstract ideals are viewed and applied differently by different segments of the society. When we focus on more specific values and actual behavior, like deferred gratification and child rearing, we find wide variance among many groups in the society. The poor may differ in some respects, but so do many other people. If we can speak of a subculture of the poor, we can also speak of a subculture of college students, professors, salespeople, politicians, and so on. With many relatively minor differences among many segments of the population, any differences that may exist among the poor must not be overemphasized.

Third, in the previous chapter we saw that various classes may have differing tendencies with respect to such things as political attitudes and community participation. However, these differences *reflect* rather than cause class position. For the most part, this line of reasoning in the culture-of-poverty theory is incorrectly reversed—value and lifestyle differences are said to help cause lower-class placement.

Fourth, direct attempts to measure significant value differences among the poor have for the most part not supported the culture-of-poverty theory (see Ryan 1971; Miller, Riessman, and Seagull 1971). With respect to work values, many have long assumed, following a culture-of-poverty perspective, that the poor value work less than other people do. Several empirical studies of work attitudes have soundly rejected this idea (Goodwin 1972; Kaplan and Travsky 1972). In research on actual behavior, income-maintenance experiments, offering the poor government aid only slightly below what they could receive by working, have shown that the poor continue to seek and accept employment (Wright 1975; Rossi and Lyall 1976). And now, of course, with almost 45 percent of the heads of poor families working full-time in 2000, it is very difficult to charge that many of the poor do not value work (U.S. Bureau of the Census, *Poverty in the United States 2000* [2001: Table C]).

Fifth, and perhaps most important, contrary to the culture-of-poverty view, the poor do not constitute a homogeneous group. More directly to the point of a culture of poverty that is said to keep people in poverty, we have already seen that there is rather extensive movement out of poverty. Remember that only about 1 percent of the population in the United States has been found to stay in poverty for 9 years in a row. The culture-of-poverty theory, of course, stresses that it is the children who have grown up in poverty who are most likely to have this culture of poverty that keeps them there. But again, the studies do not show much support for this idea. For example, Levy (1977) found that "only three of every ten young adults reared in poverty homes, compared to one of ten reared in nonpoverty homes, set up poverty households on their own" (Wilson 1987:175). Even when blacks are reared in a poverty, welfare-supported, female-headed household, the probability of a young woman setting up her own poverty home was found to be only about one in three.

None of the preceding, however, is meant to suggest that the culture-of-poverty theory is useless in helping us understand anything about poverty. Sociologists have begun to use the terms "the underclass" (Auletta 1983), the "hard core poor," or "the truly disadvantaged" (Wilson 1987) to describe a relatively small percentage of the poor whose values, lifestyles, and personality problems make them seem close to those said to be affected by a culture of poverty. This group may include only 20 percent of all the poor (or perhaps only 2 percent of the U.S. population), but they make up a larger percentage of the persistent poor (Auletta 1983:37; Wilson 1987:176).

## The Situational View of Poverty

As a group the poor do differ from the middle class on some characteristics, such as family stability and work history, and other studies have found the poor to have somewhat lower aspirations for education, occupation, and income (Della Fave 1974a). If these characteristics and behavior are not due to significant value differences, how are they to be explained? What can be called a **situational view of poverty** offers a realistic explanation.

The situational view argues that the poor may sometimes behave differently or have different lifestyles and preferences *because* they are poor, lack secure jobs, or simply lack opportunities to live up to values held by most in the society. In other words, the poor may be reacting realistically to their situation. Thus, although the situational view of poverty may agree with proponents of the culture-of-poverty theory that the poor may at times differ in behavior when compared with the middle class, the situational view *rejects* the idea (1) that the poor would not prefer to live up to most values held by a majority in the society or (2) that the differences found result from deeply held values.

Let us look at some examples. The suggested importance of an inability by the poor to delay gratification has been noted. Even to the extent that this does exist among some of the poor, it may simply stem from a realistic estimation that delaying gratification may not be rewarded. Valentine (1968) uses the example of "free unions and consensual marriages," found to be more prevalent among the poor and said to reflect value differences by the culture-of-poverty theory. In contrast to the culture-of-poverty view, Valentine (1968:132) suggests that "consensual unions provide a flexible adaptation that is functional under conditions in which fluctuating economic circumstances, actual or threatened incarceration, and other external conditions often make it advisable for cohabiting pairs to separate either temporarily or permanently and contract alternative unions, again either temporary or lasting." As already noted, Wilson (1987) has provided extensive data supporting this statement.

Hyman Rodman (1963) has introduced the concept of "lower-class value stretch" to explain how, although the poor may recognize and accept dominant values of the society, they learn to accept behavior that does not meet these ideal values. As Rodman (1963:213) writes, "Lower-class persons . . . do not maintain a strong commitment to middle-class values that they cannot attain, and they do not continue to respond to others in a rewarding or punishing way simply on the basis of whether these others are living up to middle-class values." They have learned they must tolerate deviations from middle-class ideals. "The result is a stretched value system."

Following the idea of a lower-class value stretch, Della Fave (1974b) adds the concepts of value preferences, expectations, and "tolerance." He argues that although the poor may prefer to live up to certain values, when their own expectations of being able to do so are low because of their poverty, they learn to tolerate less than preferred behavior. We can use the example of educational aspirations. The idea of a lower-class value stretch suggests realistic expectations may be that (given their circumstances) a college education is unlikely. Thus, they may come to tolerate or strive for less—say, completing high school or a trade school.

Differences between the culture-of-poverty theory and the situational view of poverty may seem trivial, but they are not; they view the causes of poverty in a very different light. For the culture-of-poverty theory the characteristics of the poor are part of the problem; for the situational view of poverty, although the poor may have some differences from the middle class, the differences are not part of the causes of poverty— only a reflection of their situation. And where the culture-of-poverty theory suggests that the poor must be changed if we are to reduce poverty, the situational view suggests that if the situation of poverty is changed, if there are opportunities and jobs, any differing characteristics of the poor will not prevent them from taking advantage of new opportunities. For example, when a present-time orientation or lack of delayed gratification is no longer a functional response to poverty, the poor will respond to new opportunities by investing time and energy for future rewards.

Both theories do have one similarity: They are primarily concerned with the individual characteristics of the poor. The culture-of-poverty theory is concerned with these characteristics because it sees them as part of the problem of poverty, while the situational view is concerned with these individual characteristics more to show that the culture-of-poverty theory is incorrect.

Though theorists following the situational view of poverty recognize that structural conditions, or political and economic forces, are the most important causes of poverty, they have been less concerned with these structural conditions than with showing why the culture-of-poverty theory is wrong. If we want to understand the causes of poverty for most people in the United States and the world, we must focus on these structural conditions. That is our next goal.

## A Structural View of Poverty

Considering the inadequacies of the culture-of-poverty theory and the incomplete nature of situational views of poverty, Rossi and Lyall (1976) question the existence of a satisfactory theory of poverty. The absence of such a *specific* theory of poverty, however, is perhaps as it should be. If a focus on group conflict and unequal resources of political and economic power can help us understand social stratification and inequality in general, it can also help us understand poverty. We need not neglect the characteristics of the poor (the preoccupation of the preceding theories), but this is a secondary question, as it was with the individual characteristics of the working class, middle class, and upper class. Thus, we need to take a **structural view of poverty,** which argues that poverty can be understood and explained only with reference to political and economic characteristics of the society rather than any characteristics of the poor.

### *Poverty and the Occupational Structure*

We can begin a structural-level conflict view of poverty by considering the position of the poor in the *occupational structure.* As noted in earlier chapters, Weber viewed the occupational structure as a situation of conflict and competition in the marketplace. Those with greater skills—skills that are in demand and are relatively scarce—can demand and receive higher wages for their labor and maintain more secure jobs. The poor, of course, are at the bottom of the occupational structure. They have few skills, or skills that can be easily learned by almost anyone (such as how to pick tomatoes or grapes or assemble a part on a gadget moving along an assembly line). The large number of people competing for such jobs reduces their chances for secure jobs as well as their wage levels even when jobs are found.

One of the biggest pools of poor and unemployed people in our society is made up of former agricultural workers and their sons and daughters (Piven and Cloward 1971). We have seen the figures on the reduction of farm labor in the previous chapter. Many people were needed to work the fields 30 or 40 years ago, but, increasingly, machines are doing the work. Since World War II about 20 million people have left farm employment in the United States (Piven and Cloward 1971:214). Some of the former farm laborers and their offspring have moved into well-paying blue-collar and white-collar jobs, but many have been unable to do so.

This brings us to the story we have seen many times already. The once-growing, well-paid blue-collar jobs that Americans could reasonably expect to get even if they did not have a good education are shrinking. As we saw in Chapter 8, taking the place of these well-paid blue-collar jobs increasingly are the low-skilled jobs paying poverty wages.

It is not just the reduction in middle-paying jobs and the loss of income that have the effect of producing more poverty. There are also social effects, especially, it has been found, in the black community. Research by Wilson (1987, 1991, 1996) has shown that the reduction of skilled blue-collar workers in the inner cities has meant a growing concentration of poor young people without stable working men who can provide role models (see also Jencks 1991; Jargowsky and Bane 1991). In addition to providing a role model showing the young poor what can be possible with hard work and a stable lifestyle, the blue-collar workers provided the young with connections and other tangible aid in locating jobs. The changing occupational structure has severely reduced all of this, making the very poor more isolated socially and psychologically, and with less help in the community.

A structural feature of capitalist industrial societies that helps produce and maintain poverty is related to the "necessity" of business cycles. No one has yet found a way of preventing the cyclic movements between economic expansion and retraction, or economic boom and bust, in a capitalist economy; it is probable that no such prevention exists short of a rigid state-regulated economy. In the United States, unemployment is therefore increased in times of a business downturn, then somewhat reduced in times of business expansion. (Of course, there are many hard-core unemployed who are not directly affected by either economic shift.)

It is important to recognize that the cyclic changes in unemployment are *not* always an unintended effect of the business cycles of boom and bust. Inflation can in part be produced by a boom that lasts too long. Thus, unemployment is often *consciously* produced by government economic policies as a by-product of a planned economic slowdown intended to reduce inflation. Inflation, of course, is most harmful to higher classes not much worried about unemployment themselves.

A result of the above is the existence of what Marx called an **industrial reserve army** that is functional for the well-being of the corporate economy (or at least functional for the elites and the more affluent in this economy). The industrial reserve army consists of those people on the bottom of the occupational structure who can be laid off to protect corporate profits in times of economic stagnation, then rehired when needed for increased profits in times of economic expansion.

## Class Conflict and the Welfare State

The term **welfare state** is often used to describe a society in which the state has taken rather broad responsibility for social problems and the general social welfare of the population through direct provision of goods and services. However, as noted in many places earlier, what can be called the welfare state (or *wealthfare state*) usually does much more than provide necessities to the poor and disabled; it often helps the rich and middle class in many more ways than it does the poor. But in varying degrees among advanced industrial nations the poor, sick, young, and elderly were provided with extensive benefits and services in the second half of the 20th century.

Throughout the history of the United States, with the slight exception of the last 70 years, help for the poor was not considered a proper function of the state. Some poor were seen as "deserving" of aid, such as children, the sick, the blind, and perhaps the aged; but aid even to these categories of people was usually seen as the task of private charity agencies (such as religious groups and other private aid societies) and local communities. It was not until the 1930s that resistance to government welfare programs for the poor was broken, at least in a limited way. As we will see, another historical change occurred in the mid-1990s in the United States. The major change that got the federal government into the business of providing welfare benefits to all "deserving poor" was extensively reversed during the mid-1990s, giving control and most funding for welfare to individual states. Also, the limited amount of money the federal government continues to transfer to states for welfare benefits comes with the rule that most people will not be allowed to receive benefits for more than 2 years.

## Welfare in the United States

In the face of widespread turmoil and unemployment coming out of the Great Depression of the 1930s, Franklin Roosevelt established many reform programs to regulate the economy and help the unemployed (see Patterson 1986; Piven and Cloward 1971, 1982; Domhoff 1990; Jenkins and Brents 1989). Most welfare programs for the unemployed did not survive, and were cut back or eliminated before unemployment was substantially reduced. Those that did survive, however, were to establish the basic welfare system that existed in the United States from 1935 until 1996.

The most important foundation of this welfare system was contained in the Social Security Act of 1935. This law created what is commonly called Social Security, which is a program that collects money from workers and employers primarily to pay benefits to those workers (who pay into this system) who retire or become disabled. However, because the Social Security system was not to begin paying benefits until the 1940s, and because people must work for an employer from whom Social Security deductions are withheld to be eligible for Social Security benefits (this program is primarily for the nonpoor), the Social Security Act of 1935 established another aid program for the poor.

What is commonly called *public assistance, categorical assistance,* or just *welfare* was also established by the Social Security Act of 1935. The original (1935) categories of people considered deserving of public assistance were children under Aid to Dependent Children (ADC), the blind and disabled under Aid to the Blind and Aid to the Disabled (AB and AD), and the aged (those over 65 and not eligible for Social Security) under Aid to the Aged (AA). In the 1950s it was recognized that aid to children could not be achieved unless an adult could survive to help the children, so ADC was expanded to Aid to Families with Dependent Children (AFDC). However, "families" meant children and *one* adult (usually the mother) who was judged not able to work. If the family was intact—that is, the mother and father were both present—even if such a family was poor, *it was not eligible for AFDC* as long as the "man of the house" was not disabled and therefore should be working. (Despite their "family values" argument, it might be added, the welfare system was moved back in this direction during the Reagan alterations of the reforms of the 1960s.)

In the 1960s AFDC-UP (AFDC-unemployed parent) was added in about half the states (see Piven and Cloward 1971; Steiner 1971:35), although even in many of these states AFDC-UP remains very limited. Under AFDC-UP some families could receive welfare aid when the father was present but unemployed, as long as he was looking for work, was in a job-training program, or was disabled. In 1972 there was also a change in the welfare system that combined AA, AD, and AB into Supplementary Security Income (SSI) under more direct control of the federal government (with the states left with shared federal–state control of AFDC). Also, shortly before this the federal government created the food stamp program, providing low-income families with some material aid to buy food and therefore add to the AFDC cash payments that come from the states and the federal government.

Finally, there was another aid category called General Assistance (GA) that was controlled by the states and local governments. This program sometimes amounted to a catchall category for people in need of assistance who did not fall within the other categories. However, because funding of GA was the responsibility of individual states and local government, coverage was uneven across the United States and the aid the poor could receive under GA was usually very limited.

In addition to the categorical restrictions defining who could receive welfare described earlier, there were many eligibility rules that further limited who could receive welfare. And because individual states had primary authority to establish these eligibility rules (under AFDC and GA), there was much diversity across the United States as to who could receive welfare and how much they could receive. The most important eligibility rules pertained to income and property. For example, "earned" and "unearned" income was considered in determining eligibility and assistance levels (how much a person can receive in aid), as was the ownership of any kind of property (such as a home, a car, or a boat).

In the United States, states continue to go to great lengths to make sure only the "deserving poor" receive welfare aid. Most welfare recipients are children, with only about 1 percent of welfare recipients considered "able-bodied males." There are other types of aid programs (such as food stamps and Medicaid), but these programs also have many eligibility rules (although somewhat less restrictive) that limit assistance to the deserving poor, and these other aid programs were extensively reduced under the Reagan administration. A person must be *very* poor (significantly below the poverty line) to receive welfare in the United States, and even many of the very poor do not receive welfare because they do not fit into the aid categories that define the deserving poor.

It was recognized that welfare in the United States only keeps recipients alive and does nothing to reduce poverty or get those who are poor out of poverty. Increasing concern about poverty in the 1960s (for reasons considered later) resulted in President Johnson's Great Society program, or War on Poverty. Working from assumptions about the causes of poverty in the culture-of-poverty theory, the War on Poverty programs attempted to reduce poverty by making the poor upwardly mobile (Patterson 1986).

There were many specific programs designed to change the characteristics of the poor—to provide motivation, better educational opportunities, and job training, to make welfare mothers "better mothers," and so on.

But the stress on rehabilitation of the poor proved less than effective in reducing poverty, in part because the nature of poverty was misunderstood. The culture-of-poverty view led to a war on the characteristics of the poor rather than a war on the structural conditions producing poverty in the United States. Many War on Poverty programs were of value, for they did provide additional aid to those living in poverty. But even to the extent that poverty was reduced during the 1960s and 1970s, the reduction was primarily due to additional aid, not employment as we saw in Figure 9-2. After President Nixon was elected in 1968, many of Johnson's War on Poverty programs were reduced or eliminated, with even more extensive reductions and eliminations under the Reagan administration.

During the 1980s, Ronald Reagan's approach to fighting poverty was to provide big tax cuts for corporations and the wealthy. With more profits for business and with more money in the hands of the rich for investments (tax breaks to the less wealthy "would only be spent, not invested"), there is supposed to be a trickle-down effect to the poor in the form of more jobs. But there is no guarantee that the increased corporate profits and tax cuts for the rich will result in job-producing investments. And if there is greater investment in industry, it is most likely to be in more profitable capital-intensive industries, producing fewer jobs than promised, and jobs only for higher-skilled workers who do not represent the long-term unemployed. Miller (1976:136) predicted that the "free-enterprise" approach to creating jobs (what could now be called the Reaganomics approach) will only create more inequality. As we have already seen, he was correct. Inequality grew in the 1980s because of a small increase in high-tech, high-paying jobs, a significant decrease in middle-paying jobs, and a big increase in jobs paying poverty wages with no future of advancement (Treas 1983). But, as we have already seen in Chapter 2, inequality and poverty were also increased by the welfare benefit and welfare eligibility cuts made by the Reagan administration and Congress in the 1980s.

## The 1996 "Welfare Reform"

The welfare system put in place in the United States with the Social Security Act of 1935 came to an abrupt end in August of 1996 when President Clinton signed the "welfare reform bill." The categories of welfare aid that existed in the past, especially AFDC, have not necessarily been eliminated, but drastically altered. Most important, what has been changed is that each individual state has now been set free to design its own welfare system without significant federal government guidelines that had existed since 1935. In essence, there are now 50 different welfare systems in the United States, and the variance in who can receive aid, how much, and for how long is extensive (Pavetti 2001). But it is actually even more complicated than this because in many states, like California, *each county* has been given the task of designing its own welfare system with few state government guidelines (*Los Angeles Times,* February 2, 1998).

Under this 1996 welfare reform the federal government did make a few small stipulations before allowing individual states to receive some federal money. There had been work requirements for able-bodied recipients for many years, but these have been made more strict, such as requiring even mothers with babies just a few months old to find work or be cut off welfare. Most important of these is *time limits* on how long people can receive welfare. The basic American philosophy (and one found in *all* other industrial nations) of support for the needy has been eliminated: No longer will all deserving people who are hungry and poor be guaranteed some aid. According to federal rules, the time limits are 2 years, though many states have taken up the option to make these limits shorter. What this means is that after the time limit, if the person is still poor and unemployed, it doesn't matter; they will be prevented from receiving further aid (though children may still receive some aid). Some forms of aid may remain in limited amounts, such as food stamps, but the primary aid that has existed in the United States since 1935 is gone.

In 1998 these time limits started to become a reality across the United States. There are reports of increasing numbers of people asking for emergency food as reported in the beginning of this chapter. Most likely, the future for the U.S. poor will be disastrous. First, in a sense the U.S. government "got lucky" when the time limits on receiving welfare became a reality in 1998. The country was in the longest economic boom in the 20th century with unemployment about 5 percent nationally, and under 4 percent in some states. The major question is, what happens now that the longest economic boom in American history ended in 2001? What will happen to people with no more welfare eligibility and no job? We are now finding an answer to this question. One year after the great recession began in 2008, the percentage of the poor receiving no income at all, and no cash assistance from unemployment benefits or welfare, was the highest in decades, highest since records have been kept (*New York Times,* January 4, 2010). Some *6 million Americans* in 2009 existed only on the small monthly amount given by the food stamp program.

There is, however, another clear result of the new limits on welfare assistance: The hundreds of thousands of people who have been and will be kicked off the welfare rolls will push down wages for low-skilled workers in the United States. Surveys have already shown that this is happening in many states (*Los Angeles Times,* February 8 and February 9, 1998). People desperate for food and shelter are working for lower wages than the currently employed, who often are then losing their jobs to people recently kicked off welfare. As we will see, in their classic work on the *functions of public welfare,* Piven and Cloward (1971) argued that one function of welfare was to keep benefits low and restrict them to the "able bodied poor" so that low wages would be provided to business owners. It seems clear that in 1996 the welfare systems given to each individual state will now serve this function much more efficiently than in the recent past.

To be fair to the Clinton administration, we must recognize many positive accomplishments to support the working poor, such as more child care benefits and tax credits paid to match earned income for those below the poverty line. But the fact remains, the more complete safety net for the poor and unemployed is gone.

# A Cross-National Perspective on Welfare

From the political rhetoric one gets the idea that the United States has had the most extensive and costly welfare system in the world—with the exception of England, which is always used as a negative example of how the United States may end up if the spread of the welfare state is not stopped. But comparative data show that this idea is, in fact, only political rhetoric. Nothing could be further from the truth. To begin with, of the 63 most industrialized nations in the world, *only one nation* does not have some form of guaranteed income program for all families in need. That exception is the United States. as of 2009 the United States was also the only one of these 63 industrialized nations without some form of comprehensive national health system for all citizens (World Health Organization 2000). During the 1990s President Clinton tried to change this but failed.

Comparative statistics on government spending show roughly the same picture. As indicated in Table 9-6, among major industrial nations supplying complete data for 1998, the United States had the lowest rate of government spending as a percentage of GNP. Further, even with this small amount of government spending (in relation to the size of the country and economy) compared to other nations, a smaller percentage of what the U.S. government does spend goes to social programs. The vast majority of this spending on social programs goes not to the poor but to Social Security for the aged who had been affluent enough in their earlier lives to pay into and thus qualify for Social Security (U.S. Federal Government 2001:2). For example, while the U.S. government spent over $433 billion on Social Security in 2001, it spent just over $50 billion for unemployment benefits and food programs for the poor (U.S. Bureau of the Census, 2002c:307). Earlier in this chapter, Table 9-4 indicated that the U.S. government

## TABLE 9-6

### Total Government Expenditures as Percent of GNP, and Percent of Government Expenditures Going to Social Programs, 1998

| Country | Government spending as percent of GNP | Percent of government spending going to social programs |
|---|---|---|
| Australia | 23.3% | 66.3% |
| Austria | 37.9 | 68.2 |
| Belgium | 44.4 | — |
| Denmark | 37.7 | — |
| Finland | 34.2 | 55.3 |
| France | 44.6 | — |
| Germany | 36.1 | 69.8 |
| The Netherlands | 46.0 | 63.9 |
| New Zealand | 32.5 | 71.0 |
| Spain | 34.2 | 46.3 |
| Sweden | 41.7 | 53.2 |
| Switzerland | 22.1 | 72.9 |
| United Kingdom | 36.3 | 57.5 |
| United States | 20.4 | 53.8 |

*SOURCE:* World Bank, *World Bank Development Report 2000/2001* (2000:300).

**TABLE 9-7**

**Top and Bottom Five Rankings on the United Nations' Human Poverty Index-2 for the 17 Most Developed Nations, 2006**

| Highest ranked nations | Lowest ranked nations |
| --- | --- |
| 1. Sweden | 13. Spain |
| 2. Norway | 14. Australia |
| 3. The Netherlands | 15. United Kingdom |
| 4. Finland | 16. United States |
| 5. Denmark | 17. Ireland |

*SOURCE:* United Nations, *Human Development Report, 2006* (2006:295).

had a smaller impact on reducing poverty than any other major industrial nation—a 28.5 percent reduction for the United States compared to a 50–80 percent reduction of poverty for all other nations. Table 9-6 helps us understand one of the reasons (less government spending on the poor) this is the case.

A final comparative table is useful in bringing together the above points about inequality and lack of human welfare protection. For years the United Nations has published its famous *Human Development Index,* which rates all countries in the world with respect to the health, education, and material welfare of their people. More recently the United Nations has developed an index called the *Human Poverty Index-2* to evaluate the 17 richest nations on overall conditions associated with health, poverty, and the state of educational and job opportunities among people within these nations. As can be seen from Table 9-7, which lists the top-ranked and bottom-ranked countries in 2006, the United States was 16th.

The major question at this point is why the United States lags far behind so many nations in welfare spending. But a question that must be answered first is, what accounts for changes in the level of welfare-type spending in the United States? As we have already noted, U.S. welfare spending showed major increases during the 1930s and 1960s. To help answer these questions, we must return to some of the characteristics of class conflict in our system of social stratification.

# The Welfare State as Conflict Management and the Lower Class in the Power Structure

The first assumption is that the following two factors are most important in explaining differing welfare commitments among industrial nations. First, it is often assumed that mutual aid is a "human drive" (see Friedlander 1968:9); that is, people have a noble side to their character that produces a desire to help less fortunate members of society. Such an assumption is speculative; but, as noted in our review of the history of inequality, we do find some evidence for this drive. However, the evidence also suggests that such a human tendency toward sharing is found primarily in very small human collectives with close social relations. A human drive toward mutual aid seems much more difficult to maintain over a large, diverse population in complex societies, especially when it means giving up relatively scarce resources to strangers.

Second, following the first assumption, it is usually believed that when the resources of the society are greater, more will be devoted to the welfare of the less advantaged. (This can be referred to as the *state modernization* thesis; see Isaac and Kelly 1981.) Our earlier review of history suggests that this assumption is faulty. As Lenski's (1984) research shows, when societies are able to produce a greater economic surplus, this surplus most often goes to the more affluent. More specifically, with data from 22 nations Wilensky (1975) found that the level of economic resources of a society is not directly related to differing levels of welfare spending.

We must return to the conflict perspective that has guided our understanding of social stratification more generally if we are to understand the nature of welfare state development. We can suggest again that the question of who gets what in a society is related to political or economic power. This in turn leads us to suggest that since welfare spending in the United States increased substantially (compared with other years) during the 1930s and 1960s, something must have happened to increase the influence of the poor. How can this be when the poor are so powerless in the society? The poor are generally at the very bottom of the occupational, authority, and property structures in the society. In the political arena, where welfare questions are decided, they are less likely to vote, less likely to make political contributions, and less likely to have any kind of lobby organization.

As we found in our review of history, however, when the traditional avenues of power and influence in a society are less accessible to the lower classes, they have at times gone outside these traditional avenues. This usually means using the disruptive tactics of social movements and collective behavior in obtaining influence. If the lower classes are strong enough, or, in other words, if the lower classes can cause enough disruption in the society, the elites and more affluent may be willing to give them concessions in order to remove this threat to the overall status quo.

In reality, political elites usually employ two tactics in managing disruption by the lower class. These tactics are often referred to as a *two-war strategy* (see Miliband 1969; Oppenheimer 1969:164). On one hand, force is used to arrest, imprison, or kill primary participants in rebellious activities. On the other hand, this tactic is usually accompanied by reforms to convince less rebellious factions of the lower classes not to join the rebellion. Reforms are intended to show that things will be better, and that therefore there is no need to join the rebellion.

What this is meant to suggest is that, like the working class, the poor are not completely powerless. Power, of course, is unequally distributed, and the poor have less of it than other segments of the society. When social order is strong and when the poor are relatively weak in number, a rebellious call for more jobs, social justice, and a decent standard of living is answered (if at all) by welfare. Gains may be made, but welfare, as should be evident, is not the most ideal gain.

Our remarks thus far have been speculative in nature. It is time to add data to these ideas about the conflict nature of the welfare state. We turn first to the influential work of Piven and Cloward (1971), then to more empirical tests of their thesis of welfare development and growth.

## *The Functions of Public Welfare*

Piven and Cloward (1971) maintain that public welfare serves two primary functions in industrial societies such as the United States. First, during periods of social stability, the welfare system functions to *enforce work norms* and *maintain low-wage labor.* As industrial societies become more affluent, it becomes more and more difficult to keep the lowest-paid workers content doing the dirty, dangerous, and low-paying jobs. But when welfare (the other alternative besides starvation) is rendered highly degrading and recipients are stigmatized, the near-poor are more willing to maintain employment in the worst jobs in the society.

As Piven and Cloward (1971:3) put it, "Some of the aged, the disabled, the insane, and others who are of no use as workers are left on the relief rolls, and their treatment is so degrading and punitive as to instill in the laboring masses a fear of the fate that awaits them should they relax into beggary and pauperism." For the most part, the attitudes we hold toward the poor, and especially toward welfare recipients, help maintain the stigma of welfare status. The strength of this stigma directed toward welfare recipients is shown when even the poor themselves (Feagin 1975), and welfare recipients in particular, tend to hold these views (for research on these views held by welfare recipients see Briar 1966; Handler and Hollingsworth 1971; Cole and Lejeune 1972; Kerbo 1976b). Though it should be added that in the new era that the United States has moved into since the late 1990s with *no* welfare possible for most people after time limits have been met, the stigma of welfare is not such a significant tool to enforce low-wage labor simply compared to hunger.

Second, Piven and Cloward maintain, during periods of social disruption and turmoil created by the poor and unemployed, the welfare system functions to *restore social order.* Social order is restored in part by expansion of the welfare system to take care of some of the basic needs of the poor. Also, however, social order is furthered because once on welfare the poor can be controlled better and watched over, and the threat of withholding benefits can be used to keep them in line. When social order has been restored, Piven and Cloward argue, the welfare system is again restricted, pushing as many of the poor as possible off the welfare rolls.

The view of welfare put forth by Piven and Cloward may seem depressing and pessimistic to those concerned with the well-being of the poor, but it is supported by much empirical evidence (reviewed later). This view of the functions of public welfare may also seem to contain a conspiracy view of history, wherein elites are working behind the scenes to exploit the poor, to keep them poor and in low-wage work to benefit the rich (see the critical debate in Trattner 1983). That may be the outcome of welfare, but it is less a conscious conspiracy than a result of the system of power stratification in the society.

We can focus on our major concern at present, the welfare function of restoring social order (the second function mentioned earlier), to show that Piven and Cloward's thesis does not rest on a conspiracy view of history. Consider the position of a U.S. senator. From what we have already reviewed about the influence of the stratification system on the political process in this country, we can understand some of the pressures on this senator. Federal government funds are always restricted because demands for funding and services by various interest groups are always greater than the amount of funds available to the government. Thus, the groups who have contributed (and most likely will contribute) to this senator's campaign for election, the groups that can pay for lobbying activities to influence this senator, and the groups that are more likely to vote in elections are the groups most likely to get the government attention and support they are seeking.

The poor have few of these traditional means of political influence, so their needs are ignored more often than the needs of more influential groups. But when the poor revolt, when they threaten social order, the situation changes somewhat. This senator may now recognize that there is a problem in the country. Some of the demands by other groups are resisted by this senator, who is now more willing to vote for bills in the Senate designed to help the poor.

When social order is restored, when the poor stop rioting, it is back to business as usual. The order of priorities in the political system is shifted back to the more influential interest groups in the country. As Piven and Cloward (1971:338) end their book, "A placid poor get nothing, but a turbulent poor sometimes get something."

The attack on the poor and welfare during the 1980s and 1990s, of course, fits quite well with the basic thesis of Piven and Cloward (Block et al. 1987). But there is a new twist to it in recent years. As the social climate of America continues to deteriorate, with accompanying social problems such as crime, gang activity, drug addiction, an explosion of single-parent families, fathers not providing for their children, not to mention ever more poverty, the new theme in the attack on welfare and the poor is that the welfare system is the root cause of all these problems. These problems are, in fact, worse in the United States than in all of the other industrial societies. However, as we have just seen, the United States has the least generous of welfare states. In short, it does not fit. Frances Fox Piven's response to such charges by Charles Murray and William F. Buckley in a national PBS debate in 1994 was, simply, these people "don't have a clue" as to what is happening.

## *Protest Movements and Welfare: Empirical Evidence*

A brief review of welfare changes in the United States gives concrete meaning to the earlier thesis. It must first be recognized that the United States has had many periods of very high unemployment. But during these periods when the poor and unemployed needed help, the welfare system was seldom expanded. For example, although there were periods of relatively high unemployment in 1893–1894, 1914, and 1921, welfare aid was not substantially institutionalized and expanded until the Great Depression of the 1930s.

True, the depression of the 1930s was worse than the others. However, as Piven and Cloward show with historical evidence: (1) the depression of the 1930s per se did not force welfare expansion; rather, it was the rebellion that followed; and (2) welfare has also expanded in times of lower-class rebellion when there was no change in the level of poverty and unemployment (as in the 1960s).

Figure 9-5 presents data that tend to confirm the Piven and Cloward thesis of welfare expansion due to protest by the poor rather than because of increasing need for welfare benefits. Three variables are plotted in Figure 9-5: the rate of unemployment, the

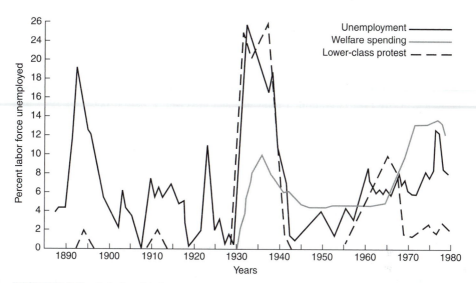

**FIGURE 9-5**    *Relationship between Unemployment, Protest, and Welfare Expansion, 1890–1980*

*SOURCE:* Adapted from Shaffer and Kerbo (1987).

amount of protest by the unemployed, and a rough indicator of welfare spending by the federal and state governments (for more details on how these variables were measured and sources of data, see Kerbo and Shaffer 1986a, 1986b; Shaffer and Kerbo 1987). We can see that though unemployment was high several times before the 1930s (reaching a level almost as high as the 1930s in 1894), welfare spending did not increase significantly until the 1930s. And, of course, protest by the unemployed was very low until the 1930s, when massive protest occurred with the first year of rising unemployment in 1930, creating a political crisis that helped convince political elites to support welfare expansion (see Jenkins and Brents 1989).

We also see in Figure 9-5 that welfare spending went down with falling protest in the late 1930s and during World War II, but many of the welfare programs begun in the 1930s continued to operate, though at lower levels of support. Welfare spending went up dramatically again in the 1960s—this time, however, without the huge increase in unemployment as in the 1930s. But consistent with the 1930s, the 1960s brought high levels of protest in the streets by the poor and minorities.

More extensive empirical research attempting to assess the validity of the Piven and Cloward thesis has focused on the post–World War II period of United States history. In the 1950s the welfare rolls in the United States increased by only 17 percent. But during the 1960s the welfare rolls increased by 225 percent, with most of the increase coming after the major urban riots that began in 1964 (Piven and Cloward 1971:341). These urban riots did not end until 1968, after more than 300 major urban riots had occurred in this 5-year period, with 220 people killed and more than 8,000 injured

(Downes 1970; Salert and Sprague 1980). Betz (1974) has examined changes in the welfare rolls of major cities that experienced riots compared with changes in cities that did not experience riots. This study showed a significant increase in the welfare rolls of riot cities about 1 year after a major riot.

In the most extensive empirical examination of the Piven and Cloward thesis, Isaac and Kelly (1981) compiled relevant data covering a period between 1947 and 1976. Most important, Isaac and Kelly found that the frequency and severity of riots were directly related to welfare expansion after controlling for (or ruling out the significance of) many other variables that may have been factors in producing the welfare expansion. For example, neither changes in the unemployment rate nor an increase in the number of female-headed families (which could make more people eligible for welfare) was found to be related significantly to an increase in the number of people receiving welfare. Since this major study by Isaac and Kelly, several others have strongly confirmed their conclusions for the 1960s (see Schram and Turbett 1983; Jennings 1983; but for a critique of the Piven and Cloward thesis as it applies to the earlier 1900s, suggesting these authors neglected the importance of state modernization, see Orloff and Skocpol 1984; Quadagno 1984; Skocpol and Amenta 1985; as well as the research more supportive of Piven and Cloward by Jenkins and Brents 1989).

As described previously, welfare is a means of placating a rebellious poor that is cheaper and less threatening to the status quo. In other words, little is given up by the more affluent in granting the poor welfare—it is the line of least resistance. Providing jobs and other opportunities for the poor will be most difficult because unless a substantial increase in the number of jobs is forthcoming, it will mean jobs must be taken from the more advantaged.

Research by Kelly and Snyder (1980) supports this view. Using national-level data, they found that the frequency and severity of riots in the 1960s did *not* create (1) changes in the black–white income ratio, (2) black gains in occupational status, or (3) a reduction in the black unemployment level. Also, Isaac and Kelly (1981) did *not* find that the frequency and severity of riots in the 1960s produced increased benefits from welfare. That is, the riots did not increase the amount of money going to each welfare family; they only produced an increase in the *number of people* receiving welfare benefits.

We can conclude this discussion of historical trends in welfare spending in the United States by noting the welfare cutbacks in the 1980s under the Reagan administration and the 1996 welfare reform bill. Piven and Cloward (1971) ended their book by predicting welfare cuts in coming years with a downturn in protest by the poor and minorities (however, see Piven and Cloward 1982 for their view of why the cuts in welfare were not as much as Reagan had hoped for). Cutbacks in welfare programs of various kinds were not immediate, but the accuracy of their prediction is no longer in question. The 1980s and 1990s went back to the work-enforcing function of welfare through degrading welfare recipients and outcries against those who seek welfare who are not "truly needy."

Turning to cross-national comparisons, we find a much more complex situation with many possible national differences potentially related to varying welfare commitments. However, with a focus on the low welfare commitment in the United States compared with that in most Western European nations and given what we have learned about welfare development in this country, we can suggest the importance of other variables producing cross-national differences in welfare spending.

**1.** Given the relation between lower-class protest and welfare expansion in this country, we can suggest that a longer history of more intense class conflict in the nations of Western Europe is in part responsible for greater welfare spending in these nations.

**2.** As Wilensky (1975:65) and Pampel and Williamson (1985, 1988) suggest, a longer history of more extensive political organization among the lower classes and union activity in some industrialized nations may produce higher levels of welfare spending (also see Kropi 1989). As we will see in more detail later, this is clearly the case in countries such as Germany.

**3.** The lower classes in most Western European countries are more likely to participate in elections (Piven and Cloward 1988; Kerbo and Gonzalez 2003). A multiparty political system, in contrast to our two-party system, seems in part responsible. Thus, politicians may be more likely to work for lower-class votes by providing more benefits for the lower classes (Tufte 1978; Pampel and Williamson 1988). We have similar research showing that cross-state differences in welfare benefits in the United States are related to conditions of political competition that make the votes of the poor more important in some states (Tompkins 1975).

**4.** Social services are more widely distributed among various classes in many industrialized nations (Kahn and Kamerman 1977). In contrast to the United States, a number of countries provide various state social services such as medical assistance, housing programs, and child care centers that benefit many above the level of poverty (including the working and middle classes). Because those above the poverty line are more politically active, they are more likely to defend and support these programs. Only with this situation can we understand what has been happening in European Union nations in the late 1990s. In what seems unbelievable to most Americans, no doubt, Germans voted out their old government in 1998 because it was trying to *lower their taxes and cut welfare programs.* In reaction to new European Union rules attempting to unite monetary policies with the new Euro currency, many European nations have been trying to cut social welfare benefits. But all over Europe socialist governments have been elected by the population in large part to prevent cuts in welfare and social services.

**5.** Despite Wilensky's (1975) findings, it remains likely that differences in the political ideology and political systems of nations help produce differing levels of welfare spending. For example, other studies (see Hewitt 1977; Rubinson and Quinlan 1977; Tufte 1978) have shown that more support for democratic socialist parties and greater political democracy in general are related to less inequality in a nation. Less inequality does not always mean more social welfare spending in industrial nations, but it is likely that less inequality is usually achieved through an expanded welfare state. More recently, Brooks and Manza (2006) found that government policies in North America and Europe to a large extent respond to value preferences of people in the nation. Thus, with less concern about poverty in the United States compared to Europe, shown earlier in this chapter, we can expect less welfare spending in the United States.

Although much more research is needed, it can be suggested that cross-national differences in welfare spending are related to the nature of class conflict. When the poor and lower classes are better organized to further their common class interests, when the poor and lower classes have a longer history of political protest and rebellion, welfare benefits are expanded. The lower classes have not always been passive in the United States (Garner 1977), but the more turbulent class conflicts in the history of most Western European nations throughout the past 200 years certainly overshadow lower-class rebellion in the United States.

## Class Conflict and the Welfare State: A Conclusion

The development of the welfare state, like the existence of the poor it is meant to control, can be understood most fully with reference to the nature of class conflict. The state has become a central institution with the task of redistribution. Resources are taken from some and redistributed to others. Those classes with more power are able to ensure that they receive more from the state than is taken by the state. Such a result should be evident from our discussion of the upper class and corporate class in earlier chapters.

But contrary to usual assumptions, the poor are not totally powerless. When the poor achieve some influence, when the poor become turbulent and demanding, they may get government redistribution in the form of welfare. The upper classes, of course, continue to receive the greater benefits of state redistribution policies, although in the interest of maintaining social stability, concessions to the poor are made. Such a result rests not upon any conscious organized conspiracy by the upper classes but upon a multitude of contested policy decisions (the long-range implications of which are seldom fully recognized at the time) that add up to government policy that expands aid to the poor primarily when the poor become disruptive.

It would be more noble, of course, if the existence of welfare programs were mainly the result of our humanistic desire to help those in need. But the evidence, unfortunately, does not support such a view. Many people do have a humanistic desire to help those in need. But when people are able to act on their humanistic values to provide the poor with goods and services made available by the society, they are able to do so most often because of social forces they are unable to control. The social worker, the humanistic government bureaucrat, the person volunteering time to work for a welfare agency are all participating in attempts to aid the poor set in motion by political forces that have led to the development and expansion of the welfare state.

## Summary

This chapter began with definitions of poverty and how poverty can be measured. Using the official economic definition of poverty, or the poverty line, developed by the Census Bureau of the United States, we described who is poor and how poverty has changed in recent years. After a drop in the percentage of the population living in poverty from the 1960s through the 1970s, poverty began to increase in the 1980s, and especially in the first half of the 1990s, decreasing (but only slightly) with the prolonged economic boom of the late 1990s. Between 2001 and 2005 there was again an increase in poverty. We examined information showing this increase in poverty has been due to political changes such as cuts in welfare benefits and higher taxes for low-income families, and economic changes such as lower wages and fewer middle-paying jobs due to the relative decline of the U.S. economy in the modern world system.

The chapter then turned to an analysis of the tendency to blame the poor for their poverty in this society, and four main types of poverty theories—social Darwinism, culture-of-poverty theory, situational theories of poverty, and structural theories of poverty. Finally, the American welfare system was examined to explain how this system is a means of maintaining low wages and controlling the poor when they become disruptive.

# Gender Stratification and Inequalities: The Persistence of Ascription

With Joti Sekhon

These two photos display a striking contrast between the United States and Japan today. Although discrimination against women continues in the American workplace, as we will see in this chapter, few countries in the world have a higher percentage of women in management positions. At the other extreme is Japan; my attempt to find a photo of a corporate boardroom in Japan with any women sitting at the table rather than serving tea failed.

*SOURCES:* Left: © Roy McMahon/Corbis; right: © Ryan McVay/Getty lmages.

# Chapter Outline

❖ Sex and Gender

❖ Gender Inequalities

❖ Educational Attainment and Gender

❖ A History of Gender Stratification

❖ Theories of Gender Stratification

❖ Class Effects on Gender Income Inequality

❖ Summary

In previous chapters we have seen that class placement due to achievement factors becomes more common as a nation reaches industrialization. Still, we must again stress that the influence of ascription—those factors related to class of birth, gender, race, and ethnicity that influence a person's life chances—has certainly not disappeared in modern societies. Even today the importance of these factors, in advanced industrial as well as less-developed countries, varies widely. Consider the following examples.

In one of the most modern industrialized societies, Japan, it was only during the 1970s that it became illegal to fire a woman from her job when she married or had children. Though illegal, it is still common practice today. Only recently have women had some equal rights in the case of divorce in Japan, or even an equal chance of gaining custody of children after a divorce. With respect to many indicators of women's status, such as income inequality with men, legal rights, and educational and occupational attainment, Japan is lowest among the advanced industrial nations. Japanese women have the lowest level of political power among all major industrial nations. Using their "gender empowerment measure" (an index measuring female members of the legislature and other public positions, as well as private sector positions), the United Nations ranked Japan 57th out of almost 180 countries in the world in 2009 (United Nations, *Human Development Report, 2009*).

The low status of women is well known in less-developed nations, especially in some Arab countries where "honor killings" are still commonplace. (When a woman "dishonors her family" in some way, such as by having sexual relations outside marriage, the tradition is for her to be killed by one of the male family members.) But while industrial nations vary with respect to the rights and equality of women, as the contrast between Japan and most Western industrial nations suggests, so too is there variation among less-developed and developing countries. Sometimes the variation even within a particular nation can be complex.

I was in the southern Thai city of Hat Yai a few days after a young girl was found dead of an apparent suicide in a police jail. Upon further investigation it was discovered that twice previously the Hat Yai police had arrested the girl and returned her to a brothel from which she had escaped. In response to the public outcry over the death, the Thai government closed the Hat Yai brothels, which are particularly popular with Muslim tourists from Malaysia and Indonesia. Somewhat later, friends at Prince of Songkla University in the city told me the brothels remained closed—for about 2 weeks.

Prostitution, often involving very young girls, has existed for centuries in the Thai society, though it has become much more prevalent in recent years, with sex tourists coming especially from Japan, Germany, Switzerland, and a few other industrial nations (Pasuk, Sungsidh, and Nualnoi 1998). It is commonly assumed that Thai prostitution and the low position of women in countries such as Japan are due mainly to some common Asian cultural characteristics. The assumptions, however, are dead wrong. There is wide variation in the status of Asian women (Brinton, Lee, and Parish 1995)—even more variation than can be found in Western societies. In fact, it is inaccurate to say that the status and influence of Japanese and Thai women are low in every respect. In Japan, women in each household generally make all financial decisions independently, from what household goods to buy to when to save and where to invest. Men turn over their paychecks to wives and are given a weekly allowance (Kerbo and McKinstry 1998). In Thailand, the overall status of women is actually comparatively high despite the depressing prevalence of child prostitution (Slagter and Kerbo 2000; Wyatt 1984:4). In most professions, in universities, and in the corporate sector, the occupational attainment of Thai women is higher than in most Western industrial nations, including the United States (Kulick and Wilson 1996:77–79; Pasuk and Baker 1996:111). For example, women hold 53 percent of all the professional and technical jobs in Thailand, a figure higher than in most advanced industrial nations (United Nations, *Human Development Report, 2009*).

To a large degree, the relatively high position of Thai women is rooted in old agricultural traditions. Central, lowland Thais for centuries have lived with a *matrilocal* family system, which means that daughters are most likely to inherit the family's land and their husbands must come to work and live on the family lands of their wives (Slagter and Kerbo 2000). This also means the family line is not traced through the male line, and in the case of most Southeast Asian countries they did not even have family names until the 20th century. Even today it remains common for Thais to use only first names, which is why I am often addressed as "Dr. Harold" when in Thailand. But this matrilocal family system also means that daughters can have a stronger sense of obligation toward the extended family compared to sons. Thus, if times are hard economically, there is pressure on young women to go to the cities to somehow make money to take care of the family. Sometimes this means working in factories, but sometimes it can mean getting involved in the more highly paid sex industry in places like Thailand. In 2002, for example, the *Bangkok Post* estimated that some $300 million was sent back to poor families in the northeastern part of Thailand, and some 20,000 girls from the region were working in just one of the infamous bar districts of Bangkok. Very few of these girls, however, are held as virtual sex slaves like the young lady described above who committed suicide in a Hat Yai jail. It is the poorest of the poor women and girls in Southeast Asian countries such as Laos, Cambodia, and Burma who end up in the worst situations.

The most important point about the apparent contradiction between the young Thai, Cambodian, Laotian, and Burmese women working as prostitutes and the comparatively high occupational status of Thai women involves the class system. There are, for example, no middle-class or upper-class Thai women found in the famous Patpong and Soi Cowboy brothels and bars in Bangkok. The young middle-class Thai women, if away from their families at all in the evening, are more likely found in a trendy jazz club such as the Brown Sugar, where the cost of a single drink almost equals the daily wage of Thais in the northeast.

The purpose of this chapter is not to attempt an examination of everything there is to know about gender discrimination and inequality. Rather, our purpose is to consider how, and to what extent, this discrimination and inequality are related to systems of social stratification. Some of this task has been started in previous chapters. Here our goal is to add to this previous material and to focus discussion on the ascriptive aspects of gender inequalities. We will do so, much like the plan of this book in general, by first exploring additional empirical and historical data on gender inequalities. We will then consider theoretical explanations of the persistence of gender discrimination and inequalities in modern times, as well as efforts to reduce gender inequalities.

# ✖ Sex and Gender

We may speak of gender stratification when social, material, and political resources in a society are hierarchically distributed by gender, which usually translates into males having disproportionate access to these valued resources compared with females. To understand gender stratification and inequalities, however, we must first distinguish between the terms **sex** and **gender.** When sociologists talk of sex differences between females and males, they usually refer to the biological characteristics, such as hormonal, anatomical, and physiological differences that define them. Gender differences, however, refer to the socially and culturally constructed definitions of what it means to be female and male. These meanings, then, shape norms and expectations for appropriate behaviors, roles, and appearance for males and females in society. Most sociologists argue that the life chances of women and men are significantly influenced by gender differences, and are suspicious of the often disproportionate attention given to biological differences as the basis for gender inequalities.

The notion that gender is socially constructed rather than a biological given is evident when we acknowledge that what it means to be male and female varies within a culture as well as from one culture to another. Moreover, the appropriate roles, behaviors, and expectations for males and females have modified considerably over time. For instance, men are stereotypically considered to be more aggressive and action-oriented while women are thought to be more capable of nurturant and caring behavior that makes them better able to take care of family and household needs. In a now classic study, however, Margaret Mead (1935, 1950, 1963) noted that among the Arapesh, the Mundugumor, and the Tchambuli tribes in the South Pacific, masculinity and femininity were constructed differently in each. Among the Arapesh, women as well as men displayed unaggressive, cooperative, and caring behavior, while among the Mundugumor both sexes exhibited aggressive behavior. Among the Tchambuli, the men displayed more passive and dependent behavior than women, quite different from the expectations in North America. Among the Aka, a hunting and gathering tribe in central Africa, Hewlett (1991) notes the close bond between infants and fathers, and the open display of affection and nurturing behavior by men, quite distinct from the "rough-and-tumble" play characteristic of interaction between American fathers and infants. Recent studies also show varied definitions of masculinity and femininity in America, and variations in behavior among women and men. For example, when men have taken on the primary parenting role and share in household responsibilities, they display close emotional and nurturing ties to their children and are capable of developing "maternal thinking" (Coltrane 1989). It is also quite evident that women and men are now taking on roles and responsibilities that were considered quite inappropriate one or two generations ago, thereby adding to the varied experiences of males and females.

This does not suggest that gender is not an important element in shaping human lives and that biological sex is insignificant. However, in order to understand gender stratification, we need to explain how gender structures social life. In most human societies gender is assigned to biological males and females who are then treated differently through differential socialization and behavioral expectations. From birth, females and males are treated differently, made to dress differently, play with different toys, and are exposed to different experiences at home and elsewhere. This leads to the development of gendered identities and self-concept, and often influences choices women and men make. Gender is also reproduced through interactions between individuals in contexts that are gendered. For example, even when women and men are geared toward playing nontraditional roles in the home or the workplace, parenting expectations differ for males and females, and even when in identical professional positions, males and females are expected to behave differently. Gender identities are therefore reproduced and modified in key social institutions, such as the family, the workplace, and schools. As Kimmel (2000:107) notes, these institutions "create gender difference and reproduce gender inequality." This happens when behaviors, expectations, and qualities associated with traditionally male characteristics are valued more highly in society. For example, success and status in modern American society is defined in terms of material wealth and occupational status. Traditionally, however, it is men who are expected to be the primary breadwinners while women are expected to take on the primary parenting and homemaker role. This makes women economically more dependent on men, and when women are in the paid labor force, they are often in lower-paid and lower-status occupations as we shall see in the next section.

In order to gain a higher status in society women are then expected to compete with men for higher-paid and higher-status jobs, and have to meet male standards and expectations in order to succeed. This leaves a gap in terms of household and parenting tasks, for which women get blamed, and the task of "balancing work and family" is still considered primarily a woman's responsibility rather than a man's. This is easily understood when we realize that many magazines are oriented to "working mothers" and "working women," and most parenting magazines are also oriented toward mothers.

## ⚒ Gender Inequalities

We have examined basic indicators of gender inequalities in earlier chapters, especially Chapter 2. In this section, however, we explore in greater detail the various dimensions of gender inequality and the institutions through which it is perpetuated.

# Gender and Work

The work that women and men do has the most significant impact on their status in society. Who does what, and how that work is defined and valued, is closely linked to access to economic and social resources. In all known human societies, gender is a key variable affecting the nature of work. Activities that are viewed as "productive" and contributing to the survival of groups and communities are valued as work. In the modern Western concept, productive work is defined primarily as work for which a wage or salary is paid. The income derived from paid work is then a key indicator of a person's economic and social worth. We therefore take a look at the distribution of income by gender in order to understand gender stratification. Before we do that, however, we need to look at an alternative definition of work that helps explain gender stratification.

Feminist scholars note that gender inequalities result also from all kinds of work, including unpaid work, done by women and men (Ward 1999; Ammott and Matthaei 1996). A broader definition of productive work would include the production and distribution of goods and services in exchange for payment in cash or kind. Worldwide, however, much of the work that gets noted in economic statistics is work for which people are paid formally. Many people, particularly women, are engaged in home-based production and work in the informal sector that is often not recorded in official statistics. Thus, a significant amount of productive work that women do remains invisible. Many argue that a broader definition of work would include acknowledging the work of reproduction that is done mainly by women. This work involves bearing and taking care of children, a variety of household tasks, as well as caring for the sick and elderly. Moreover, women do most of the work of "status enhancement" through voluntary work and leisure activities that enhance the prestige of high-status males. Much of the "emotional labor" and "kin work" associated with meeting the needs of family members, connecting with kin and community, and maintaining family and friendship networks is also a woman's responsibility. All of these forms of work, as we know, are not considered productive work, but as we shall soon see, have a crucial impact on the status and worth of women in relation to men. With these considerations in mind, we can turn to empirical evidence relating to women's labor force participation, income, and occupational distribution in the United States.

# Labor Force Participation and Income Inequalities by Gender

It is well known that there has been a dramatic increase in the participation of women in the paid labor force in the United States over the last 60 years. In 1948, for instance, 32.7 percent of women over age 16 were in paid employment compared with 86.6 percent of males. By 1970, this figure had risen to 43.3 percent for women and declined to 79.7 percent for men. By the year 2005, almost 60 percent of women over age 16 were employed compared to 77 percent of men. By early 2010, slightly more women were in the labor force than men because the great recession from 2008 created higher unemployment in jobs normally held by men (U.S. Bureau of Labor Statistics, 2010). For both males and females, participation rates are higher for those with more education. For college graduates over the age of 24, 83 percent of males and 73 percent of females are in paid employment, compared to 73 percent and 54 percent, respectively, for male and female high school graduates. For men and women over age 24 with less than a high school diploma, the participation rate is 59 percent and 33 percent, respectively (U.S. Bureau of the Census 2010b). A more significant trend in the last 35 years has been the rise in labor force participation rates for single and married women with children age 17 and below. In 1970, for instance, 39.7 percent of married women with children were employed, and the figure rose to almost 68 percent by 2005. In 1980, 52 percent of single women with children were employed, while in 2005 it reached 73 percent. The change is particularly dramatic for women with children under age 6. For single women the percentage rose from 44.1 percent in 1980 (figures for 1970 are not available) to 68 percent in 2005, while for married women the percentage increased from 30.3 percent in 1970 to 60 percent in 2005.

Turning now to income inequalities, the good news is that the income gap between women and men is narrowing, though it still remains quite wide, and there was a slight setback in 2003. Table 10-1 shows women's and men's median hourly earnings and income ratios (percent earned by women compared to men) by race and ethnic origin from 1989 to 2007. The annual income ratio between men and women (the ratio most often reported) was 0.69 in 1989 and 0.77 in 2008. (Also see Figure 10-1 for the longer time period.) Table 10-1 also shows that white women pulled ahead of black men by 2000. The gap between black and Hispanic men and women is much lower than that between white and Asian men and women, reflecting the much higher incomes of both white and Asian men.

## TABLE 10-1

### Women's and Men's Median Hourly Earnings by Race/Ethnic Origin, and Male/Female Earnings Ratio, 1989–2007

| Demographic group | Hourly wage | | | |
|---|---|---|---|---|
| | **1989** | **1995** | **2000** | **2007** |
| **Men** | | | | |
| *Medians* | | | | |
| White | $16.51 | $15.88 | $17.28 | $18.75 |
| Black | 11.94 | 11.61 | 12.64 | 13.47 |
| Hispanic | 11.10 | 10.12 | 11.09 | 12.20 |
| Asian | 15.42 | 15.29 | 17.18 | 20.73 |
| **Women** | | | | |
| *Medians* | | | | |
| White | $11.56 | $11.84 | $12.96 | $14.71 |
| Black | 10.30 | 10.18 | 11.33 | 12.23 |
| Hispanic | 9.19 | 9.00 | 9.58 | 10.74 |
| Asian | 11.96 | 12.18 | 13.81 | 15.73 |

*SOURCES:* Mishel, Bernstein, and Shierholz (2009: Table 3.22).

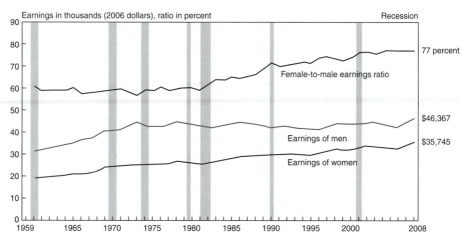

**FIGURE 10-1**   *Female-to-Male Earnings Ratio and Median Earnings of Full-Time,*
*Year-Round Workers 15 Years Old and Over by Sex: 1960–2008*

SOURCE: U.S. Bureau of the Census, *Income, Poverty, and Health Insurance Coverage in the United States, 2008* (2009: Figure 2).

One important feature related to the narrowing of the wage gap between women and men, however, is that much of the reduction is due to the decline or stagnation in men's wages rather than increases in women's earnings. Figure 10-1 shows that from 1979 to 2000 men's wages declined or remained about the same when adjusted for inflation, while white women's earnings rose by 22.9 percent. Black women's earnings, though, rose by only 14.7 percent, and Hispanic women's incomes increased 4.6 percent. In the future, there is some expectation that the wage gaps will decline further. Some evidence of this is found in the fact that the wage gap is narrower in the younger age groups. For instance, in 2000 the earnings ratio for females age 16–24 was 91 percent and for workers age 25–34 the earnings ratio was 81.9 percent. Part of the differential in earnings can be clarified by looking at the occupational distribution and educational attainment by gender, and it is to this task that we now turn.

## Occupational Segregation and Income

A review of the occupational distribution of the paid labor force in the United States reveals that women and men are primarily placed in different occupations. Gender segregation refers to the fact that women mostly work in jobs where most of the other workers are also women. The jobs that are most likely to be held by women are for the most part also more likely to be lower paid and less prestigious (Kaufman 2002). In keeping with the trend toward increased labor force participation by women, the percentage of women in most occupational categories has also increased, thereby increasing somewhat their percentage in male-dominated occupations. For example, women have increased their share of the managerial and professional specialty workforce from 40.9 percent in 1983 to 49.8 percent in 2000.

According to the most recent United Nations *Human Development Report* (2009), American women hold 56 percent of all professional and technical positions in this country, a percentage only exceed by Australia at 57 percent. As we will see in Table 10-8 toward the end of this chapter, more American women are now in top-management positions compared to any other industrial nation. Some are certainly among the corporate elite. *Fortune* magazine's 2010 list of the top 10 women CEOs in U.S. corporations (according to the size of the corporation) is a good example:

Indra Nooyi, CEO and chairperson, Pepisco
Irene Rosenfeld, CEO and chairperson, Kraft Foods
Pat Woertz, CEO, chairperson, and president, Archer Daniels Midland
Angela Braly, CEO and president, Wellpoint Corporation
Andrea Jung, CEO and chairperson, Avon Products
Oprah Winfrey, chairperson, Harpo
Ellen Kullman, CEO, Dupont
Carol Bartz, CEO, Yahoo
Ursula Burns, CEO, Xerox
Brenda Barnes, CEO and chairperson, Sara Lee

But the fact remains that women are still heavily underrepresented at the very top of the corporate ladder, and even though occupational gains have been made by American women in recent years, the gender pay gap continues.

As can be seen in Figure 10-1, the average pay of women relative to men has been increasing slowly in recent years. Figure 10-1 shows that on average, across all occupations, women received about 77 percent of the income that men received in 2008. According to the United Nations, though, of the 21 most industrialized nations, only 8 countries have a higher income gap between men and women than the United States, though these data are from earlier years and do not reflect the narrowing gap in the United States (United Nations, *Human Development Report, 2009*). Also important, the income of American women still lags behind the male counterparts in the same occupations. As can be seen in Table 10-2, for even full-time employees, women lag behind men considerably. For example, the average annual income of men in executive, administrative, and managerial business and professional positions was 70,008 in 2007 compared to just over $50,303 for women. The same kind of pay gap can be seen down all of the broad occupational categories. We will see later in this chapter that tenure and authority rank within each of these broad occupational positions help account for a large part of the pay disparity.

As we will consider more specifically in our section on theories of gender inequality, several factors contribute to sex segregation in the paid workforce with consequences for gender stratification. While there is some outright wage discrimination, perhaps more damaging are subtle and overt attitudes about appropriate occupations for women, and the worth of jobs done primarily by women (Cohen and Huffman 2003). Women are considered to be more suited to tasks involving caring for and teaching young children, or other caring professions such as nursing, social work, secretarial support, and meeting personal needs. Moreover, women's paid work is considered to be supplementary and secondary, as their primary responsibility is to bear and care for

## TABLE 10-2

### Median Annual Earnings for Men and Women by Occupation, 2007

| | Full-time, year-round median earnings | |
| --- | --- | --- |
| | Women | Men |
| **Major occupation of longest job held in 2004** | | |
| **Total** | **$35,102** | **$45,113** |
| Management, business, and financial occupations | 50,303 | 70,008 |
| Professional and related occupations | 45,842 | 62,426 |
| Service occupations | 22,023 | 29,657 |
| Sales and office occupations | 30,950 | 42,033 |
| Natural resources, construction, and maintenance | 36,246 | 36,590 |
| Production, transportation, and material moving occupations | 26,014 | 36,017 |
| Armed Forces | | |

SOURCE: U.S. Bureau of the Census, *Statistical Abstracts of the United States, 2010* (2010b: Table 634).

children and families. Males, meanwhile, are viewed as the primary breadwinners, and as more suited to leadership roles in public life, roles that require more aggression and assertiveness, the stereotypically masculine traits. These gender stereotypes channel females and males into differential socialization experiences, as well as differential educational experiences and occupational choices.

Even when women and men are in nontraditional jobs, they face different expectations and have different experiences. Because women are still the numerical minority in traditionally male-dominated jobs, in order to succeed in these jobs, they have to play by the rules designed by men. Men have often actively resisted the entry of women by isolating and segregating women, and shutting them out of informal networks, mentoring opportunities, and referrals for new jobs. These barriers are frequently invisible, but limit women from moving out of middle-management positions into higher management jobs, and constitute "a glass ceiling" (Reskin 1988; Lorber 1994). The qualities deemed valuable in managers are stereotypically masculine such as assertiveness, independence, and aggressiveness. Men, on the other hand, find that they are welcomed into traditionally female-dominated occupations such as nursing and elementary school teaching. They are often placed on a "glass escalator" and encouraged to move quickly through the ranks to supervisory and managerial positions (Williams 1992). Women, therefore, often find themselves as tokens within male-dominated work environments. In order to succeed women have to strike a delicate balance between femininity and assertiveness, by distancing themselves from male coworkers as well as other women in the workplace. Studies suggest that in order to succeed in corporate leadership positions women report having to do more than their male counterparts, taking on high-risk tasks that others are unwilling to assume, acquiring unique skills and expertise, seeking networking and mentoring opportunities, learning to play the "male game," and maintaining a sharp distinction between private and professional life (Wellington and Giscombe 2001). While it helps to have some commitment and support for family needs from upper management, women have to continuously fight assumptions and stereotypes about their abilities and commitment. Women are more likely to be offered to go on the "mommy track" that on one level offers an opportunity to balance work and family, but at another level keeps them from moving into higher management positions, and reinforces the assumption that family responsibilities are primarily female responsibilities (Budig and England 2001). In fact, a key factor in maintaining gender stereotypes and gender inequality in the paid labor force is the fact that family responsibilities and child care continue to be disproportionately assigned to women even when they are in paid employment. As noted earlier, much of the family work is invisible and not viewed as work, even though it has significant consequences for gender stratification.

Given these barriers to women's employment and earnings, **pay equity** and **comparable worth** measures have limited impact. Pay equity legislation makes it illegal to pay different wages to women and men doing similar tasks. However, as we have seen, women and men are mostly in different occupations. Another measure to improve women's earnings is through assigning the same value to work requiring similar skill and complexity level, also known as comparable worth. While this has helped in some specific cases, women and men are trained for different kinds of jobs that are valued differently, and even with similar levels of education, women's and men's incomes are not equal. Because of this it is important to consider educational attainment in order to gain further insight into gender stratification and inequality later in this chapter.

## Political Authority

As we have seen with the U.S. corporate class, a primary way to improve one's position in modern industrial societies, or protect advantages already secured, is to attain political influence. Political influence can come in the form of political action committees (PACs) that funnel campaign funds to candidates running for political office, funding lobby organizations to influence those already in political office, or through holding political offices themselves. For nonelites with large numbers of people in the society, a highly organized group able to vote in a united manner also brings political power. In none of these have American women achieved significant political despite occupational gains in recent years.

Table 10-3 tells much of the story. The United Nations annually ranks countries in terms of its "human development index" created from figures on economic standards of living, health, and education. In 2009 the United States was ranked 13th in the world on this index. The top 22 industrial nations are also ranked in terms of conditions for women. In the overall "gender empowerment measure" the United States slipped in rank from 8th in 2004 to 18th in 2009 (United Nations, *Human Development Report, 2009,* 2010b:Table 10-3). This index has four indicators: female members of the legislature, female participation in selected positions in the public and private sector, female participation in academic and technical work, and estimated income. If it were not for

## TABLE 10-3

### United Nations' Rankings of Gender Empowerment, 2009

| HDI rank | Gender empowerment measure (GEM) Rank | Gender empowerment measure (GEM) Value | Seats in parliament held by women (% of total) | Female legislators, senior officials, and managers (% of total) | Female professional and technical workers (% of total) | Ratio of estimated female to male earned income |
|---|---|---|---|---|---|---|
| **Very High Human Development** | | | | | | |
| 1. Norway | 2 | 0.906 | 36 | 31 | 51 | 0.77 |
| 2. Australia | 7 | 0.870 | 30 | 37 | 57 | 0.70 |
| 3. Iceland | 8 | 0.859 | 33 | 30 | 56 | 0.62 |
| 4. Canada | 12 | 0.830 | 25 | 37 | 56 | 0.65 |
| 5. Ireland | 22 | 0.722 | 15 | 31 | 53 | 0.56 |
| 6. The Netherlands | 5 | 0.882 | 39 | 28 | 50 | 0.67 |
| 7. Sweden | 1 | 0.909 | 47 | 32 | 51 | 0.67 |
| 8. France | 17 | 0.779 | 20 | 38 | 48 | 0.61 |
| 9. Switzerland | 13 | 0.822 | 27 | 30 | 46 | 0.62 |
| 10. Japan | 57 | 0.567 | 12 | 9 | 46 | 0.45 |
| 11. Luxembourg | | | 23 | | | 0.57 |
| 12. Finland | 3 | 0.902 | 42 | 29 | 55 | 0.73 |
| 13. United States | 18 | 0.767 | 17 | 43 | 56 | 0.62 |
| 14. Austria | 20 | 0.744 | 27 | 27 | 48 | 0.40 |
| 15. Spain | 11 | 0.835 | 34 | 32 | 49 | 0.52 |
| 16. Denmark | 4 | 0.896 | 38 | 28 | 52 | 0.74 |
| 17. Belgium | 6 | 0.874 | 36 | 32 | 49 | 0.64 |
| 18. Italy | 21 | 0.741 | 20 | 34 | 47 | 0.49 |
| 19. Liechtenstein | | | 24 | | | |
| 20. New Zealand | 10 | 0.841 | 34 | 40 | 54 | 0.69 |
| 21. United Kingdom | 15 | 0.790 | 20 | 34 | 47 | 0.67 |
| 22. Germany | 9 | 0.852 | 31 | 38 | 50 | 0.59 |

*SOURCE:* United Nations, *Human Development Report, 2009* (2009: Table 25).

a relatively respectable ranking for American women in higher occupational positions compared to other advanced industrial nations, the U.S. ranking would be much lower. While the women's movement in the last century has led to an increase in women holding political office around the world, this has not happened as much in the United States (Paxton, Hughes, and Green 2006). As shown in Table 10-3, only 17 percent of congressional seats in the national government are held by women in the United States. That figure is lower than all other major industrial nations except Japan and Ireland, with most countries having about 30 percent of congressional seats held by women, and Sweden with 47 percent.

This is no doubt one of the reasons the United States has fewer government programs devoted to women's needs. As can be seen in Table 10-4, the United States is far behind almost all other industrial nations in mandating child care leave with pay. In addition, most of these countries have laws guaranteeing that the mother can return to her same position without loss of job tenure. A few states in the United States, such as

## TABLE 10-4

### State-Mandated Maternity/Child Care Leave Provisions in Comparative Perspective

| Country | Duration of maternity leave (weeks) | Maternity benefits (% of average wages) | Total weeks of maternity/child care leave |
|---|---|---|---|
| United States | 0 | 0% | 12 |
| Japan | 14 | 60 | 58 |
| Germany | 14 | 100 | 162 |
| France | 16 | 100 | 162 |
| Italy | 21.5 | 80 | 64.5 |
| United Kingdom | 18 | 44 | 44 |
| Canada | 15 | 55 | 50 |
| Australia | 0 | 0 | 52 |
| Austria | 16 | 100 | 112 |
| Belgium | 15 | 77 | 67 |
| Denmark | 30 | 100 | 82 |
| Finland | 52 | 70 | 164 |
| Iceland | 14 | 70 | 42 |
| The Netherlands | 16 | 100 | 68 |
| New Zealand | 0 | 0 | 52 |
| Norway | 42 | 100 | 116 |
| Portugal | 24.3 | 100 | 128.3 |
| Spain | 16 | 100 | 164 |
| Sweden | 64 | 63 | 85 |

*SOURCE:* Mishel, Bernstein, and Boushey (2003:420–421).

California, have some mandated period for maternity leave, but not with guaranteed pay. We will see later that this is one of the factors helping women hold on to higher incomes compared to men in these other countries.

# ✳ Educational Attainment and Gender

Gender ideologies and structural constraints females face in relation to work are also affected by, and affect, educational opportunities and educational attainment by gender. Formal education in the United States emerged and grew alongside European settlement and later industrialization, urbanization, and immigration. During the 18th and 19th centuries formal instruction was almost exclusively limited to upper-class boys, but gradually expanded to include girls and women. However, there was a widespread belief that the rigors of formal education, especially higher education, were detrimental to the physical and mental well-being of females. If women were to be educated, it was primarily to prepare them to raise and nurture their children for successful living in an industrializing society. This was particularly considered important for middle- and upper-class wives and mothers, and as a result was geared to limiting their influence to the private sphere of home and family. Gradually, however, restrictions to women's education were lifted, with women finally making enormous strides during the 20th century, especially since 1970.

Table 10-5 shows that the overall gap in educational attainment has narrowed considerably between males and females, especially in higher education. The college completion rates have more than quadrupled for women, and tripled for men. There has been improvement for all sexes, races, and ethnic groups, though the rate of improvement has been much smaller for Hispanic men and women due to the large influx of less educated immigrants from Latin American countries.

Figure 10-2 shows more clearly the continuation of educational trends between men and women in the United States. Men have had higher educational attainment at the college levels in the past. In 2003, however, in the age categories of 25 years old and older and 25 to 29 years of age, women were ahead of men. It is only recently (in the 25 to 29 years age group) that women have overtaken men with some college and completion of a BA degree. This gap in college completion has been widening in recent years.

In spite of great strides in women's education, males and females continue to be concentrated in different specialties leading to differential occupational placement and income earning potential as detailed in the previous section (Charles and Bradley 2002). Women continue to be overrepresented in education, health, psychology, and English, for instance. Also, males and females have different experiences in the classroom, with teachers' perceptions about boys and girls affecting their interactions. For example, boys are perceived to be more aggressive and expressing anger, while girls are perceived to be more gentle, obedient, and affectionate. Boys, therefore, tend to attract more attention, and get called on more frequently to answer questions. Curricular materials also are heavily biased to reflect male images and male-oriented information, while males and females are presented in stereotypical roles and activities. These patterns are reflected in research that shows girls experience a loss of self-esteem and self-confidence especially

# TABLE 10-5

## Educational Attainment by Race, Ethnic Origin, and Gender, 1960–2008

| Year | All races Male | All races Female | White Male | White Female | Black Male | Black Female | Asian and Pacific Islander Male | Asian and Pacific Islander Female | Hispanic Male | Hispanic Female |
|---|---|---|---|---|---|---|---|---|---|---|
| **High School Graduate Or More** | | | | | | | | | | |
| 1960 | 39.5% | 42.5% | 41.6% | 44.7% | 18.2% | 21.8% | (NA) | (NA) | (NA) | (NA) |
| 1970 | 51.9 | 52.8 | 54.0 | 55.0 | 30.1 | 32.5 | (NA) | (NA) | 37.9% | 34.2% |
| 1980 | 67.3 | 65.8 | 69.6 | 68.1 | 50.8 | 51.5 | (NA) | (NA) | 67.3 | 65.8 |
| 1990 | 77.7 | 77.5 | 79.1 | 79.0 | 65.8 | 66.5 | 84.0% | 77.2% | 50.3 | 51.3 |
| 1995 | 81.7 | 81.6 | 83.0 | 83.0 | 73.4 | 74.1 | (NA) | (NA) | 52.9 | 53.8 |
| 2000 | 84.2 | 84.0 | 84.8 | 85.0 | 78.7 | 78.3 | 88.2 | 83.4 | 56.6 | 57.5 |
| 2008 | 85.9 | 87.2 | 86.3 | 87.8 | 81.8 | 84.0 | 90.8 | 86.9 | 60.9 | 63.7 |
| **College Graduate Or More** | | | | | | | | | | |
| 1960 | 9.7 | 5.8 | 10.3 | 6.0 | 2.8 | 3.3 | (NA) | (NA) | (NA) | (NA) |
| 1970 | 13.5 | 8.1 | 14.4 | 8.4 | 4.2 | 4.6 | (NA) | (NA) | 7.8 | 4.3 |
| 1980 | 20.1 | 12.8 | 21.3 | 13.3 | 8.4 | 8.3 | (NA) | (NA) | 9.4 | 6.0 |
| 1990 | 24.4 | 18.4 | 25.3 | 19.0 | 11.9 | 10.8 | 44.9 | 35.4 | 9.8 | 8.7 |
| 1995 | 26.0 | 20.2 | 27.2 | 21.0 | 13.6 | 12.9 | (NA) | (NA) | 10.1 | 8.4 |
| 2000 | 27.8 | 23.6 | 28.5 | 23.9 | 16.3 | 16.7 | 47.6 | 40.7 | 10.7 | 10.6 |
| 2008 | 30.1 | 28.8 | 30.5 | 29.1 | 18.7 | 20.4 | 55.8 | 49.8 | 12.6 | 14.1 |

*SOURCE:* U.S. Bureau of the Census, *Statistical Abstracts of the United States, 2010* (2010b: Table 225).

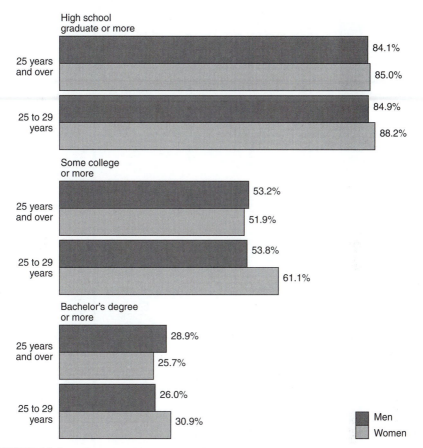

**FIGURE 10-2**    *Educational Attainment of the Population 25 Years and Over by Sex and Age, 2003*

*SOURCE:* U.S. Bureau of the Census, *Educational Attainment in the United States, 2003* (2004:4).

in their adolescent years, and often behave in ways that are less likely to lead to successful and independent career choices (Correll 2001, 2004; Sadker and Sadker 1994).

There is, however, evidence that inequalities in gender occupational attainment through education will be further reduced in the future because of the slight shift in what women are now studying in universities. For example, in 1983, only 5.8 percent of engineering majors were women compared to 11.1 percent in 1998. For other professional areas, the 1983 to 1998 difference was 12 percent to 17 percent of women majoring in architecture, 15 percent to 26 percent studying to be physicians, and 36 percent to 42 percent of people seeking PhDs to become university professors (U.S. Bureau of the Census, *Statistical Abstracts of the United States, 1999,* 2000:424). And, as can be seen in Table 10-6, by 2007 women had almost reached parity with men in professional degrees in medicine (MDs), dentistry, and law.

## TABLE 10-6

### First Professional Degrees Earned in Selected Professions, 1970–2007

| Type of degree and sex of recipient | 1970 | 1980 | 1985 | 1990 | 1995 | 2000 | 2004 | 2005 | 2006 | 2007 |
|---|---|---|---|---|---|---|---|---|---|---|
| Medicine (MD): | | | | | | | | | | |
| Institutions conferring degrees | 86 | 112 | 120 | 124 | 119 | 118 | 118 | 120 | 119 | 120 |
| Degrees conferred, total | 8,314 | 14,902 | 16,041 | 15,075 | 15,537 | 15,286 | 15,442 | 15,461 | 15,455 | 15,730 |
| percent of women | 8.4 | 23.4 | 30.4 | 34.2 | 38.8 | 42.7 | 46.4 | 47.3 | 48.9 | 49.2 |
| Dentistry (DDS or DMD): | | | | | | | | | | |
| Institutions conferring degrees | 48 | 58 | 59 | 57 | 53 | 54 | 53 | 53 | 54 | 55 |
| Degrees conferred, total | 3,718 | 5,258 | 5,339 | 4,100 | 3,897 | 4,250 | 4,335 | 4,454 | 4,389 | 4,596 |
| percent to women | 0.9 | 13.3 | 20.7 | 30.9 | 36.4 | 40.1 | 41.6 | 43.8 | 44.5 | 44.6 |
| Law (LLB or JD): | | | | | | | | | | |
| Institutions conferring degrees | 145 | 179 | 181 | 182 | 183 | 190 | 195 | 198 | 197 | 200 |
| Degrees conferred, total | 14,916 | 35,647 | 37,491 | 36,485 | 39,349 | 38,152 | 40,209 | 43,423 | 43,440 | 43,486 |
| percent to women | 5.4 | 30.2 | 38.5 | 42.2 | 42.6 | 45.9 | 49.4 | 48.7 | 48.0 | 47.6 |

First professional degrees include degrees which require at least 6 years of college work for completion (including at least 2 years of preprofessional training).

*SOURCE:* U.S. Bureau of the Census, *Statistical Abstracts of the United States, 2010* (2010b: Table 293).

# ⚔ A History of Gender Stratification

As in the contemporary world, historically gender roles and gender inequality have varied considerably in different societies and within the same society. To a significant degree, the relative real or perceived contribution of males and females to meeting the key survival needs and productive functions of food, shelter, and clothing influenced the status and importance of women and men. As noted in Chapter 3, before the Neolithic revolution about 10,000 years ago, the level of male–female inequality among hunting and gathering tribes depended on the mixture of hunting versus gathering. In hunting tribes, primarily for biological reasons, males were usually dominant and held more status: Tribes less dependent on hunting (which most were) had more equality between males and females. There is at least one exception to this rule—among the Dobi !Kung tribe of hunters there is a belief that the skill in making arrows is most important in bringing back the food. Men do the hunting, but both men and women make the arrows, with equal skill it seems, for the level of male–female inequality is more in line with that of tribes that depend primarily on gathering for their food (Lee 1985).

With a movement away from hunting and gathering to simple horticulture about 10,000 years ago, the level of male–female inequality grew progressively higher, though there is considerable variation and complexity in reality. In a few societies, for example, there is evidence of women also hunting alongside gathering of food. Anthropological research on some groups that still exist reveals that in some instances there is a coexistence of hunting and gathering tasks with simple horticulture. Among the Agta in the Philippines, for example, many women hunt in addition to trading, fishing, and gathering forest products for food (Estioko-Griffin and Griffin 1981). In some cases women hunt using bows and arrows, and also grow food. There is a high degree of gender equality, and women have equal authority in decision making in productive tasks as well as in issues such as marriage and family relationships. Among the Vanatinai in the South Pacific, there is considerable gender equality alongside flexibility and overlap of activities among females and males (Lepowsky 1993). Most of the work involves simple horticulture along with some hunting. Women are mainly responsible for planting and maintaining the garden, while men do the weeding and harvesting. But both women and men collect food and hunt, and both engage in various status-enhancing activities such as exchanging goods based on individual interests and abilities.

In many seminomadic herding societies men perform the primary economic functions, but women also do some cultivation, and there is considerable variability and flexibility in gender roles and status (Rasmussen 2001). Much depends on the local culture and history. Among the Tuareg, a seminomadic tribe in the African Sahara and Sahel dispersed in parts of Niger, Mali, Burkina Faso, and Algeria, women overall enjoy considerable privileges and rights. There is little sex segregation in public. However, those Tuareg groups that are more nomadic and less influenced by official Islamic prescriptions exhibit greater gender equality and flexibility in male–female roles and relationships. Even when there is more Islamic influence, women are not veiled or secluded and own considerable property rights.

There is increasing loss of status and autonomy for women with the pressure to move to a more sedentary lifestyle, as well as the transition to a modern nation-state and greater urbanization (Sanderson, Heckert, and Dubrow 2005). In rural areas, though, women continue to do much of the subsistence work, and maintain considerable freedom and autonomy. Economic crisis in many countries, however, presents a significant threat to both subsistence and gender equality. Some anthropologists believe that women were in fact responsible for the first step toward simple horticulture. Still, we must recognize that even in agricultural societies there has been some variance around the world, and there remains variation in preindustrial societies. For example, in our beginning comments on gender relations we considered the relatively greater gender equality in Thailand. Perhaps due to climate, more favorable land-to-population ratios, and relatively less warfare over the centuries, males in Thailand have been less dominant, and a bilateral system of family descent (and to some extent a matrilineal system of family descent) has existed. And in many parts of Thailand and Southeast Asia more generally, the tradition has been that daughters inherit the land and their husbands move into the woman's household and work her land, thus helping women attain higher status even today (Slagter and Kerbo 2000; Pasuk and Baker 1998).

Some variation on gender roles and status is also linked to the nature of tasks women perform. In India, for example, both women and men perform agricultural tasks, especially on the small family farms. But much of what women do, such as maintaining dairy cattle, remains invisible to outsiders, especially in the wheat-growing regions in northern India. However, among the middle- and lower-status families the further south and east one goes, and where there is more rice cultivation, women work openly in the fields as agricultural laborers (Sekhon 2000). This gives women a little more autonomy and flexibility. In colonial and preindustrial America also, women performed a variety of productive tasks, and the labor of women and men was interdependent. In most preindustrial societies, however, the men attained power from political organization and warfare.

With early industrialization the position of women generally became even worse. For the average woman there was usually no improvement in standard of living or status and authority compared with men. Early industrialization forced people to leave rural areas for big cities, where families were commonly torn apart, with women sometimes left to begging, prostitution, or exploitation in low-paid factory jobs. Recent empirical evidence indicates that women and small children did not make up as much of the low-paid factory labor as previously thought. Still, during the early period of industrialization, rural immigrants, along with women and children from the new working class, were sought after as workers because they were more easily controlled, and therefore less likely to strike over low wages and poor working conditions. Irving Howe's (1976) descriptions of working conditions for immigrant women in the New York City garment industry are not atypical. Women and children were forced to work in very crowded, dangerous little workshops for many hours, day after day. They had few breaks from work, and there was seldom clean air to breathe or sanitary rest rooms. Many injuries and deaths resulted from the unsafe conditions, as during the 1911 Triangle Shirt Factory fire in New York City, which killed 146 young women in a matter of minutes. Similar situations are found in most of the rapidly industrializing countries today. Even in Thailand, where the status of women is generally higher, poor peasant girls, especially from the northeast, crowd into Bangkok and are exploited for their docile, low-wage labor. There are repetitions of the Triangle Shirt Factory fire, such as the fire in Bangkok killing many young girls in a doll factory in 1993. As noted earlier, women's work in factories around the world is often done in very poor and unsafe working conditions, and workers are in a very powerless position.

With advanced industrial societies, however, we find the status of women changing. There are still many forms of inequality between men and women, and, as we have seen, there is still much variety among the advanced industrial societies. But in advanced industrial societies gender inequalities are lower than in preindustrial societies. To cite only a few examples, which may seem commonplace to women today but did not to their great-grandmothers, women are entitled to vote and hold office in all advanced industrial societies; labor laws have benefited women in the workplace; women may now obtain credit from financial institutions; women have more rights in divorce cases, and in the legal system generally; and women are not as restricted to certain jobs, though they are certainly underrepresented in many jobs. Describing all of this is in no way meant to imply that few inequalities remain, or that we are approaching equality. The point is to put gender inequality into a historical perspective and to recognize the changes that have occurred.

Much of the improved position of women is associated with a shift in attitudes among both men and women. For example, as late as 1938 in the United States, only about 20 percent of the population approved of married women working outside the home, compared with about 80 percent by the 1980s. But other developments are behind changes in today's attitudes. We must recognize that the improved position of women, as with any minority group, is related to underlying changes in the basic nature of a society. As we saw in our more general history of inequality in human societies, improvements do not come simply because the dominant group suddenly has a change of heart. The improved status of women in advanced industrial societies, as well as improvements yet to come, are related to basic economic and political changes, and to the push given by women's movements.

Economic changes that have helped the position of women are in some cases obvious. Women may sometimes be unable to compete with men in jobs requiring heavy physical labor, though even here the abilities of women have been extremely underestimated in the past. With the vast majority of jobs now primarily requiring brain power and skills with people, women at times are even at an advantage when sexual barriers are removed. And very importantly women are not unqualified for the highest-status jobs in the professions, science, and management.

Less obvious changes also occur when economic opportunities for women are improved. One of the most important is related to the general dependency of women. In the past, women were more often dependent on men for economic security. With the ability to enter the labor force on their own, however, women gained an important freedom or option. If necessary and desired, women can now survive independently of men, which over time usually creates adjustments in the thinking and behavior of men. Another overlooked technological change underlies the relatively improved position of women in advanced industrial societies' reproductive control. In previous ages women usually had dependent children until late in life and gave birth to many more children than in modern societies today. Although most of these children died before reaching adulthood, their existence still meant that women were less free to enter the labor force even when jobs existed for them. The advent of birth control, in short, has meant the freedom to control the number of children they have so that women can focus more attention on educational and occupational attainment.

Again, none of the preceding is meant to suggest that few gender inequalities remain. At best, the status of women relative to men varies within and between societies. These variations relate to factors such as class differences, racial or ethnic diversities, different levels of industrial and technological development, and simultaneous coexistence in many societies of subsistence and semisubsistence economies along with commercial trading and industrial production. It is important, however, to understand where we have come from, perhaps where we are going, and, in view of what follows, why gender inequalities have emerged and evolved.

## Theories of Gender Stratification

It is useful to consider theories of gender inequality in some detail as they not only attempt to explain the reasons for the inequalities we have considered in this chapter, but also offer up visions for more egalitarian gender relations. As such, they provide a framework for considering some key aspects of women's movements in the United States and elsewhere.

As we will see with the subject of racial and ethnic inequalities in the next chapter, there are many types of theories on the subject of gender inequalities and sex discrimination. In fact, there has been a virtual explosion of new works on feminist sociology and feminist theory (see, for example, Chafetz 1988, 1990; Nielsen 1990; Connell 1987). It will be useful to first consider briefly something of the variety of these theories.

Lengermann and Niebrugge-Brantley (1992), as well as Andersen (1997:317–381), categorize theories of gender inequalities into three types: *theories of difference, theories of inequality,* and *theories of oppression.* The first group includes theories that stress that women's location in, and experience of, most situations is different from that of men in the situation. These theories can have biosocial explanations, institutional explanations, or sociopsychological explanations. Theories of inequality stress that women's location in most situations is not only different from but less privileged than or unequal to that of men. As we will see later in this section, these theories range from liberal feminist explanations of inequality to Marxian explanations. Finally, theories of oppression stress that women are oppressed, not just different from or unequal to, but actively restrained, subordinated, molded, and used and abused by men (Lengermann and Niebrugge-Brantley 1992:458). These theories of oppression range from psychoanalytic and radical feminist/socialist to "third-wave feminist theory." The second type of theories, as the name suggests, will be most useful for our subject matter. Other theories, however, such as those of the gender oppression variety, which are more politically oriented and focus on the active maintenance of gender inequalities, will certainly be of value in considering how gender stratification is maintained.

In another survey of feminist theories, Nielsen (1990) groups them into those that focus on biology, social learning, social structure, and material conditions in the society. As will be seen shortly, the materialist theories are favored here in explaining the broad movement of history and the position of women in systems of stratification, but combinations of others are useful for our subject matter. As for the biological theories, we note that there are important biological differences, and it seems that new ones involving the brain are being suggested almost daily. However, the usefulness of these theories and empirical findings for our subject matter of gender stratification in modern societies remains in question. This statement will be more fully explained as we reconsider the evolution of human societies.

Theories of gender stratification that focus on socialization and learning have been most popular in recent decades. And there is plenty of evidence that girls are taught to accept their subordinate roles in societies all over the world. One of the most respected of these types of theories today, Chodorow's (1978) interesting combination of feminist and Freudian theory in *The Reproduction of Mothering,* is quite useful in understanding how from a very early age boys and girls are taught in subtle ways to accept different, unequal positions in the society. For example, a key part of this theory suggests that because women almost always do the mothering, both girls and boys first identify with a female view of the self. But because boys come to reject this self, and focus on its opposite, they come to devalue everything that is feminine. While valuable, this type of theory begs several questions that can better be answered by material conflict theories. Why, we must ask, has there been variation in the level of sex inequality throughout the history of human societies, and why do we find much variation even in modern industrial societies today? Other factors must be in operation. Too often explanations of gender inequality simply stop with a learning theory, as if a structural level did not exist or social institutions do not shape the nature of gender inequalities. It is time to consider some structural-level theories.

## Structural Functional Theories

Most social scientists would probably agree that traditional functional theories have not been very kind to women, or at least not kind in the sense of leaving open the possibility of substantial social change, much less gender inequality. According to Parsons's (1964:423) theory of social stratification in modern societies, women must have less status than men. The family is the central institution in all societies, according to Parsons, and strict sex divisions of labor in the family are required. This institutional prerequisite requires women to play expressive, caring roles within the family rather than the instrumental roles outside of the family played by men. Further, if men and women came to play too similar a role, the competition would drive the family apart (see especially Parsons 1964:422–423).

In Chapter 5 we considered the basic problems with functional theories of social stratification. Their strict focus on societies as holistic systems, and institutions within the society as only functioning for the good of the whole, has led them to neglect conflicting interest groups, and how power differences explain much about the opera-tion of societies, especially social stratification. The same must be said for their view of the family and sex roles. That power differences in the traditional family described by Parsons could be used to the advantage of one person in the family at the expense of other family members does not occur in his theory. Nor could Parsons ever address the big differences found between societies such as Sweden, Germany, and Japan with respect to gender inequalities because of this neglect.

## Conflict Theories

Earlier in this chapter we reviewed and added to the history of social stratification in human societies that we began to consider in Chapter 3. In this first review of the his-tory of human societies you will remember that we relied heavily on the work of Lenski (1966, 1984), who himself relied heavily on historical materialists among anthropolo-gists to explain the evolution of social stratification in human societies. Some of the most respected theories of gender inequalities in recent years follow the same historical-materialist perspective quite closely.

Among the best of these theories is that of Chafetz (1984, 1988). To understand the position of women throughout history, Chafetz argues that three things must be consid-ered: how work is organized, the type of kinship system that exists, and the degrees of ideological support for sex inequality. The first of these points follows our examination of the evolution of types of societies through history. As we have seen, the organization of work in gathering societies favored more gender equality than did work in hunting societies. The move to simple horticulture and then to more advanced agriculture led to an increased subordination of women in history. Only with advanced industrial societies has the nature of work organization allowed for more gender equality. *Allowed* for more gender equality is the key word because the other two forces can still operate to reduce gender equalities. One must look at the tradition of kinship and how this tradition has lin-gered in a society to also understand gender inequalities, past and present. For example, Thailand's matrilocal (married men coming to live in the female's household) and uni-lineal (not tracing the family line exclusively to the male or female ancestors) traditions must be considered in understanding why in some respects Thailand has much more gender equality than does another Asian society such as Korea. Likewise, the compara-tively lower gender inequality in the United States and other industrial nations in Europe in contrast to Japan can be understood with reference to both the kinship systems and ideologies affecting the position of women (Casper, McLanahan, and Garfinkel 1994).

A somewhat similar theory with supporting data from more than 150 societies comes from the work of Sanday (1981). With a focus on the environment, Sanday found that when there is more risk in the environment (social and geographic environment), and when resources are less secure, there tends to be more dominance by men. In other words, as we have seen, in societies focused on hunting and in those with extensive warfare, men tend to have greater dominance. From the basic environment in which the society finds itself, in addition to economic institutions that develop to deal with the environment, the traditions, kinship systems, and ideologies evolve that reinforce the level of gender inequality in the society. In fact, much of Sanday's (1981) work involves an analysis of creation stories in the 150 societies studied that reflect both the environment and the relative place of men and women in the society.

Under the category of conflict theories we should further consider various types of feminist theorists that share a general conflict perspective. First of all, liberal feminist theorists locate gender inequality in sex role socialization and sexism. The emphasis is on limits on individual rights and freedoms for women as compared to men. Women are, according proponents of this approach, expected to be confined mainly to the private sphere of the family and domestic responsibilities, and are socialized for these roles. Women, therefore, lack equal opportunities in education, work outside the home, and in public political participation. Since real power in the modern world resides in activities in the public sphere, gender equality can be enhanced, in this theory, through advancing to women equal rights and opportunities through legal and political channels. This would also require changes in gender role socialization as well as changing traditional gender role stereotypes. The liberal feminist perspective has been criticized for assuming that equal opportunities and greater individual rights for women alone would lead to greater equality. Critics argue that in the absence of structural changes in the way in which institutions, such as work, education, and politics, are organized, gender equality would be limited. For instance, if all adult women and men are well educated and working long hours in order to be successful in the modern industrial world, then how will all the care work and domestic work be done?

Radical feminists locate women's subordination in a patriarchal system rooted in male domination and control of all institutions in public and private life, such as economic power and privilege as well as control over female sexuality and reproduction. They argue that women and men are taught to internalize female subordination and devaluation of women's roles and contributions. Gender equality, in this view, would require a radical reworking of institutional structures that privilege men, as well as consciousness raising that would value women as well as men, and reconstruct male and female relationships in a more egalitarian and flexible way. Some radical feminists reject any connection with men if women are to have any power in society.

For Marxist feminists, gender inequality is rooted in class oppression under capitalism, a system based on private ownership of property. Effective control over property, in this view, leads to a stress on monogamous patrilineal and patriarchal nuclear family structure, and consequent control over wives and children by the husband/father, the owner of individual property rights. Women, according to Marxist feminists, provide private household labor and service thereby making it possible for capitalists to extract more work from wage laborers. Many women also provide the reserve labor that capitalists can call on when needed. Some recent Marxist feminists also note that women of different social classes are incorporated differently into the capitalist system, as formal and informal workers. If class oppression is overcome, in this view, then gender oppression and inequality would also not be necessary.

More recently, a broader socialist feminist perspective has emerged among feminists who argue that gender oppression predates capitalism, and that women's oppression is likened to both patriarchy and class oppression under capitalism. Moreover, gender oppression is, in this view, linked to multiple forms of oppression in society, such as those based on race, ethnicity, nationality, sexual orientation, disability, and so on. Greater gender equality, then, would be possible only as part of the struggle for overcoming all forms of oppression in society. Both knowledge and consciousness, as well as social institutions, would need to be transformed to enable more balanced and humane lives for all people. These recent developments in feminist theory are connected to increased awareness of the plurality of women's lives both in the United States and globally. Women's lives, for instance, are not just determined by their gender, but are also closely connected to economic, social, cultural, and environmental issues affecting local communities. Gender equality, therefore, requires action not just on the part of women, but also at many different levels in defense of communities and cultures facing threats from corporate globalization, ecological disasters, imperialism, and racism, for instance.

---

# ✖ Class Effects on Gender Income Inequality

It is time to leave specialized theories of gender discrimination and inequality. As described in the previous chapter on poverty, despite the specialized theories of the causes of poverty, the fact remains that much of why people are poor can be understood through the standard operation of the class system in the country. Likewise, no matter which theory of gender discrimination or oppression described earlier is most accurate or useful, a major contention of stratification theory too often neglected is that the inequalities of gender status continue to operate through the class categories most important in the system of social stratification in the particular society (Ferree and Hall 1996). Put another way, no doubt much of the income inequality between men and women can be explained by historical conditions of sexism and discrimination against women in our society (England et al. 1988; England and Farkas 1986). Like racism, as we will see, once sexism is established, much of this sex discrimination operates through the established class system (Wright 1997: Chapter 9; Ferree and Hall 1996).

Several studies described in previous chapters have shown that in addition to occupational skill level, income inequality in general is related to positions within authority structures, ownership of the means of production, periphery versus core employment, and unionization. Thus, if we find sex differences in relation to these other factors affecting income inequality in general, we have located other sources of sex inequality operating through the class system. Several studies show this is in fact the case.

In Chapter 2 we saw that women and minorities tend to have lower occupational status than white men. Thus, for whatever reason, being kept out of higher-status positions in the occupational structure produces income and other types of inequalities. But we have also seen from Table 2-3 in Chapter 2 that even when women have the same occupational status and education as men, their incomes are lower. To help understand this situation, we must return to Wright's class categories first described in Chapter 5 (Wright 1997; Wright 1978a, 1978b; Wright and Perrone 1977; Wright et al. 1982; Wright and Martin 1987).

Considering racial and sexual distribution of class in terms of authority positions, Table 10-7 shows that black males, white females, and black females are all more likely to be found in Wright's working-class or unskilled category (Wright 1997:68; Wright

## T A B L E   1 0 - 7

### Wright's Class Categories by Race and Sex (Ownership, Authority, and Skill Level)

|  | Whites | | Blacks | |
| --- | --- | --- | --- | --- |
|  | **Males** | **Females** | **Males** | **Females** |
| 1. Capitalists | 3.0% | 0.7% | 0.0% | 0.0% |
| 2. Small employers | 8.2 | 4.9 | 0.0 | 1.3 |
| 3. Petty bourgeoisie | 6.4 | 8.8 | 3.6 | 0.0 |
| Total self-employed | 17.6 | 14.4 | 3.6 | 1.3 |
| 4. Expert managers | 8.5 | 2.8 | 5.1 | 0.0 |
| 5. Skilled managers | 5.7 | 2.4 | 2.0 | 0.0 |
| 6. Nonskilled managers | 2.3 | 3.9 | 1.0 | 6.3 |
| 7. Expert supervisors | 4.2 | 1.7 | 1.3 | 1.7 |
| 8. Skilled supervisors | 7.9 | 4.3 | 7.5 | 2.0 |
| 9. Nonskilled supervisors | 5.0 | 9.3 | 4.6 | 7.7 |
| 10. Experts | 3.2 | 3.5 | 2.9 | 1.8 |
| 11. Skilled workers | 17.4 | 7.7 | 23.3 | 10.9 |
| 12. Nonskilled workers | 28.2 | 50.0 | 47.7 | 68.4 |

SOURCE: Wright (1997:68).

and Perrone 1977; Wright et al. 1982; Robinson and Kelley 1979). This is especially so with both black and white females because this working-class category includes clerical and service workers. Then, at the top we find that white males dominate the categories, but more females and blacks appear as we go lower and lower in these class categories in Table 10-7. Several studies have shown that less authority and ownership explain a significant amount of the lower income for females and minorities (Wright and Perrone 1977; Wright 1997; Kluegel 1978; Wright 1978b, 1979; Wolf and Fligstein 1979; Treiman and Roos 1983). And more recent research comparing the status of women in 22 industrial societies has found this is the case even with government intervention to reduce gender inequality (Mandel and Semyonov 2006). Laws and programs against gender discrimination can increase the occupational status of women but seem to have less impact on getting women into higher occupational authority positions. In Chapter 8 we also found that core or periphery position in the dual economy has an effect on job security, promotion changes, and certainly income inequality. Several studies have shown that females and minorities have less income, in part because they are more often employed in periphery industries (Beck et al. 1978; Tolbert et al. 1980; Kaufman 1983). Finally, the dual-economy research indicates that unionization is a factor in lower female and minority income, with other studies more directly showing that females and minorities are more often employed in industries that are less unionized (Beck et al. 1980).

Other studies, however, indicate that more traditional factors like simple discrimination account for sex inequalities in income. These studies take into consideration all of the factors such as authority position, job tenure, educational level, and so on that can account for sex and race income inequalities. They still find income differences that must be attributed to racism and sexism (England et al. 1988; Parcel and Mueller 1989; Wellington 1994; Waldfogel 1997). One detailed study has shown that jobs labeled "women's work" bring less income despite educational level, occupational skill level, authority, and other factors that are usually associated with income attainment (McLaughlin 1978; Bellas 1994). Other studies have found that even when men and women do the same job, women are often given a different job title with less pay (Bielby and Baron 1986; Peterson and Morgan 1995). In a large-scale study, Marini and Fan (1997) found that individual characteristics of women—or human capital variables such as education level, job skills, and aspirations—account for less than half of the gender gap in wages for people's first job. In contrast, employment networks, in which women are more often left out, and the characteristics and practices of corporations account for about 40 percent of the difference in the income of women.

With respect to sex inequalities, there are some signs that these inequalities will be reduced further in the future. As we have seen, there is, for example, a substantial increase in women holding jobs traditionally seen as men's jobs. Perhaps more significant, we have seen there have been important changes in the fields of study chosen by college women. No longer do we find women studying only for degrees in education, home economics, recreation, or social work. Many women now study law, medicine, engineering, accounting, and other subjects traditionally seen as male-dominated.

Still, there are other signs of less improvement with respect to the authority structure. Limitations of this type for women as well as minorities are described with the concept of a **glass ceiling.** The concept suggests that while women and minorities may be showing some improvements in occupational status and even moving into greater positions of authority in important governmental and corporate bureaucracies, they still are kept out of the very top of these authority structures—thus, a glass ceiling above which they are unable to rise.

We can return to Wright's (1997) massive research on social stratification in major nations around the world for further evidence of this glass ceiling effect. Table 10-8 shows how many men and women are in various levels of authority within large organizations. The highest authority position is top manager, then upper manager, then down to supervisor, and finally nonmanagement. As can be seen in Table 10-8, in the seven industrial nations in the data set, there is consistency; women are much more likely to be in nonmanagement positions, and few are in higher management positions. Compared to women in these other societies, American women are slightly better off with respect to being in higher management, but we must stress only slightly better off.

We have one final topic of importance that pertains to the position of women and other minorities in the class structure of industrial societies such as the United States—chances for and restrictions to upward social mobility. Again, we will find that traditional sources of racism, sexism, and discrimination operate through the established class categories. But before we consider the situation for women and minorities, we must consider the question of social mobility and status attainment more generally in Chapter 12.

**T A B L E  1 0 - 8**

**Comparative Data on Males and Females in Management Positions**

| | Top manager | | Upper manager | | Middle manager | | Lower manager | | Supervisor | | Nonmanagement | |
|---|---|---|---|---|---|---|---|---|---|---|---|---|
| | Men | Women | Men | Women | Men | Women | Men | Women | Men | Women | Men | Women |
| United States | 3.3% | 2.8% | 4.5% | 1.5% | 5.7% | 3.6% | 3.3% | 2.2% | 20.7% | 15.9% | 62.4% | 74.1% |
| Australia | 3.0 | 1.9 | 5.9 | 2.1 | 8.7 | 4.1 | 2.4 | 2.6 | 30.3 | 29.1 | 49.6 | 60.1 |
| United Kingdom | 3.9 | 0.9 | 1.2 | 0.2 | 8.6 | 1.8 | 4.9 | 1.1 | 20.2 | 18.4 | 61.3 | 77.6 |
| Canada | 3.7 | 0.9 | 5.2 | 0.9 | 5.4 | 3.0 | 2.3 | 2.0 | 18.9 | 11.9 | 64.6 | 81.2 |
| Sweden | 1.9 | 1.0 | 2.3 | 0.0 | 6.2 | 1.7 | 4.9 | 2.6 | 18.8 | 11.1 | 65.9 | 83.7 |
| Norway | 5.0 | 0.9 | 5.5 | 0.9 | 5.1 | 0.5 | 0.5 | 0.2 | 23.4 | 8.3 | 60.6 | 89.3 |
| Japan | 1.2 | 0.0 | 4.3 | 0.0 | 2.8 | 0.0 | 1.6 | 0.0 | 37.2 | 3.5 | 53.0 | 96.5 |

*SOURCE:* From data in Wright (1997:337).

# Summary

After supplying basic definitions of gender and sex differences, this chapter began with information on the level of inequalities for women in the United States. While we have found some improvements in the levels of inequality based on gender in the United States, considerable inequality remains. In the case of reduced gender income, we found that reductions in income inequality between men and women have occurred mainly because the income of men has been going down in recent years. With respect to comparative gender inequalities, we have seen that inequality in the United States remains lower than in most other societies today but is still higher than in many industrial societies.

After an extensive historical discussion of gender inequalities in the world and in the United States, the chapter turned to major theories of gender inequalities. Structural functional and conflict theories, including new feminist theories of gender inequality, were summarized followed by a discussion of how much gender inequalities today continue to operate through the primary dimensions of class in advanced industrial societies.

# Inequalities of Race and Ethnicity: The Persistence of Ascription

The top photo is of Smith Plantation slaves in 1862. The second photo needs no explanation. Though these contrasting photos tell a story of substantial change in the United States, many race and ethnic inequalities remain in the United States and around the world.

*SOURCES:* Top: Library of Congress; bottom: courtesy of the White House.

# Chapter Outline

❖ **Race and Ethnicity: Some Definitions**

❖ **The Inequalities of Race and Ethnicity**

❖ **A History of Race and Ethnic Stratification**

❖ **Global Immigration: A Comparative View of the New Dimensions of Global Race and Ethnic Conflicts**

❖ **Theoretical Explanations of Race and Ethnic Inequalities**

❖ **Summary**

Anyone growing up in the United States during the 1950s and 1960s, especially in the southern part of the United States, can tell you that race and ethnic relations have changed dramatically since then. In many ways, the United States at the time had something like an *apartheid* system of race relations resembling that of South Africa. There were signs on drinking fountains, restrooms, and restaurants proclaiming "whites only." I remember signs outside restaurants in Oklahoma saying "no Indians allowed." Until the civil rights legal cases were successful, it was lawful to require black students to attend separate schools. And when the courts finally forced some universities to accept black students, they were sometimes kept in specific sections of the classrooms, in an area roped off to separate them from white students.

As we will see in this chapter and the next on social mobility, there have been significant changes in many aspects of race and ethnic relations since that time. There have been improvements in educational opportunities and income disparities (at least in some cases), and a rather solid black middle class has developed. And, of course, in 2008 the people of the United States elected an African American president. (In reality President Obama is half black and half white, but he is still referred to as an African American by almost everyone in the United States.) But for some groups, things have not improved substantially, or at all. For minorities living below the poverty line, for example, there was no improvement until the very last years of the 20th century.

Three decades ago, William Julius Wilson became noted for one of his books, *The Declining Significance of Race* (1980). In it he argued that today racial inequality in the United States is more a matter of class inequality than of racial discrimination per se. In other words, past racism has left blacks and other minorities disproportionately in lower-class positions, where many remain, just as anyone is likely to remain because of the disadvantages of being poor, whether one is black or white. From the perspective of the 21st century, it may seem that the "declining significance of race" was overestimated. Research still indicates that many factors reducing the quality of life for blacks are not class related (Hughes and Thomas 1998). Still, it is accurate to suggest that many, if not most, of the racial and ethnic inequalities that exist today are rooted in systems of social stratification examined throughout previous chapters. In the case of black–white inequalities, Wilson (1987, 1996) has shown how the structure of inequality within the black community has changed, creating a greater gap between poor and middle-class blacks and making it more difficult for poor blacks to escape poverty today. That is, continuing levels of racism and sexism that produce inequalities do so through the occupational, authority, and property structures we have already examined. Also, conflict theory in a general sense can be employed to help us understand inequalities associated with gender, race, and ethnicity in the United States, or again, to help us explain "who gets what, and why."

This same conflict perspective can help us understand global race relations as well. Americans tend to look inward, often thinking that race and ethnic relations are unique in this country, and that there is nothing to learn from situations in other countries. Nothing could be further from the truth. There is a wide variety of race and ethnic relations around the world and through history. Much can be learned from countries where race and ethnic relations have been worse, producing more inequality and conflict, as well as where race and ethnic relations have been more positive. A couple of examples will be useful.

Equality between racial and ethnic groups remains rare around the world, but there is considerable variation. Among developing countries, Thailand and Malaysia provide interesting contrasts. Thailand is an ethnically diverse country of Mon, Khmer, Malay, Karen, Indians, Chinese, and Lao, to name only a few of the ethnic groups (Keyes 1979, 1989:201). Compared with most other nations, these diverse ethnic groups coexist relatively well, though there are status differences (Pasuk and Baker 1998:13–17). It is the case of ethnic Chinese in both Thailand and Malaysia that provides the most interesting contrast. As is common throughout Southeast Asia, the immigrant Chinese in Thailand and Malaysia are the most wealthy and economically successful people in the country (Hatch and Yamamura 1996:82; Huntington 1996:169). Such a situation can at times produce intense resentment and open conflict among ethnic groups with a longer history in the country. In Malaysia, conflict with and legal discrimination against ethnic Chinese has been extensive. But in Thailand the conflict is much less apparent, and even intermarriage between ethnic Chinese and other Thais is more common than marriage within the ethnic Chinese community (Pasuk and Baker 1998).

Then, of course, there is the contrast between Japan and the United States. The United States has a worldwide reputation for race and ethnic violence and discrimination. Japan, on the other hand, is viewed as a nation of harmony and relative equality. But Japan is also a nation of extensive homogeneity. Standing in front of a Japanese classroom to call the roll is a striking lesson in national contrasts. With roughly 97 percent of the people living in Japan all racially and ethnically Japanese for many generations back, the American-style diversity seems extreme (Kerbo and McKinstry 1998, 2011). One wonders how race and ethnic conflicts in the United States have not been worse. The Japanese situation, however, is misleading in many ways: Ethnic Chinese and Koreans, who make up almost all of the other 3 percent of the population, have experienced extreme discrimination, and the Japanese have continued the most extensive discrimination against a group of about 1 million people with ancient outcaste origins who can be distinguished from other Japanese only through detailed background research. Private detective agencies all over the country specialize in the exhaustive research often needed to identify these people. With respect to our current topic of race and ethnic inequalities, we must admit that humans and human societies can seem rather peculiar.

In addition to the historical and comparative perspective on race and ethnic relations that will be maintained in this chapter, we must also recognize the growing impact of globalization. And we will see that the American legend of "a nation of immigrants" is not such a unique one any longer. There are some major industrial nations that actually have a population that has a higher percentage of foreign born individuals than does the United States, and several other major industrial nations where the percentage of foreign born individuals is quite similar to that of the United States. Much of this change has been rather recent. We will see that as the inequality between the rich and poor has been increasing steadily in recent decades, reaching its highest point in world history at the beginning of the 21st century, a wave of migration (some say 12 million people at any one point in time) has occurred and is occurring from the poorer countries to the richer countries. It is this wave of world migration that has resulted in the United States losing its unique status as a nation of immigrants. How these immigrants have been received and treated in the richer nations around the world provides us with additional material in studying race and ethnic relations.

As in the previous chapter on gender inequalities, our intent here is not to examine everything there is to know about race and ethnic discrimination and inequality. Rather, our purpose is to consider how, and to what extent, discrimination and inequalities are related to systems of social stratification. Some of this task has been started in earlier chapters. Here our goal is to add to this previous material and to focus discussion on the ascriptive aspects of race and ethnic inequalities. We do so, much like the plan of this book in general, by first exploring additional empirical and historical data on these ascriptive inequalities, then considering theoretical explanations of the persistence of race and ethnic discrimination and inequalities in modern industrial societies. But before doing all of this, there is the usual matter of definitions and concepts.

# ⚔ Race and Ethnicity: Some Definitions

Because we find conflicting and even distorted meanings given to the terms *race* and *ethnicity,* it is important for us to define these terms before proceeding. Race in particular might seem a rather simple concept: There are whites, blacks, Asians, and so on. In reality, though, it is impossible to locate any "pure" races of people. For years scientists tried to establish a logical classification of racial types through such characteristics as skin color, head shape, and facial features. There are, of course, tendencies for people with Asian, African, and Western origins to have certain common characteristics like skin color and facial features, but the mixture within each broad racial category defies classification. For example, where would we place East Indians—people with dark skin but Caucasian features? The reality is that race does not exist. Now that biologists have been able to map the complete DNA of humans, comparisons of the complete DNA of thousands of living humans all over the world have shown that dividing humans into racial categories makes no biological sense (Olson 2003; Chanda 2007). The DNA maps taken from humans considered to be white, black, or Asian show individuals across these "racial" categories are more often similar than the DNA within these "racial" categories.

It is now well established through DNA mapping and comparisons of living individuals throughout the world that all humans originated in Africa. Some 50,000 years ago *Homo sapiens* began moving out of Africa, going north and east, with one group arriving in what is now Australia some 46,000 years ago. After several thousand years, there were superficial changes among these humans in things like skin color to adapt to new climates around the world. But as the old saying goes, we now know these differences are in fact only skin deep.

Despite all of this, of course, race is not a meaningless concept. As one of the old American sociological masters, W. I. Thomas, put it, "Situations defined as real are real in their consequences." **Race** is a social category rather than a biological category. "Racial" differences are only important (1) because people have defined them as important and acted upon these socially defined definitions, and (2) because cultural and subcultural differences are often associated with race due to the long-term separation of groups with socially defined racial differences.

An **ethnic group,** in contrast to a racial group, refers to a group that is relatively distinct in cultural background compared with dominant groups in the society. Many separate ethnic groups may be considered racially identical. Europeans are similar in socially defined racial characteristics, yet they represent diverse cultural groups. Among Americans are ethnic groups such as Polish Americans, German Americans, Japanese Americans, Chinese Americans, and so on.

## ❧ The Inequalities of Race and Ethnicity

We have examined basic indicators of race inequalities in earlier chapters, especially in Chapter 2. In this section, however, we must add to this information and explore additional details of such inequalities. We begin with basic inequalities of income and wealth.

Much like the male–female inequalities described in the previous chapter, there is also "good news and bad news" with respect to black–white and Hispanic–white inequalities. In contrast to what most Americans believe, and in contrast to the belief that affirmative action has been very successful and is no longer needed, many types of inequalities remain, and until very recently have been getting worse. As indicated in Table 11-1, from 1972 to 2009 there was very little change in the black–white household income ratio. The median income for blacks stayed between 57 and 60 percent of the white median income through most of these years. The only improvement came between 1995 and 2000 when the income ratio moved up to 66.3 percent of the white income. It took the longest economic boom in America history for the black–white income ratio to finally improve only slightly. As expected, though, when that long economic boom was over, the income gap between blacks and whites eroded rapidly. The drop in income for blacks compared to whites from 2000 to 2009 was almost as large as the gains made between 1995 and 2000.

The Hispanic–white income ratio was better than the black–white income ratio in 1972. However, as shown in Table 11-1, that ratio has eroded since 1972, only to improve again between 1995 and 2000 and then drop back by 2003 and 2009. The ratio is still

## TABLE 11-1

### Black–White and Hispanic–White Household Income Ratios, 1972–2009

| Year | Black–white income ratio | Hispanic–white income ratio |
|------|--------------------------|------------------------------|
| 1972 | 57.5% | 74.4% |
| 1975 | 59.5 | 71.3 |
| 1980 | 56.6 | 71.7 |
| 1985 | 58.1 | 68.6 |
| 1990 | 58.4 | 69.8 |
| 1995 | 60.2 | 61.5 |
| 2000 | 66.3 | 72.8 |
| 2003 | 62.0 | 69.0 |
| 2009 | 61.0 | 68.3 |

*SOURCES*: Calculated from U.S. Bureau of the Census, *Money Income in the United States, 2000* (2001: Table A-1); U.S. Bureau of the Census, *Income, Poverty, and Health Insurance Coverage in the U.S. 2009* (2010a: Figure 1).

lower than it was in 1972. As we will see, the worsening Hispanic–white income ratio is no doubt related to the continuing rate of Hispanic immigration into the United States. Most of the immigration involves lower-income and lower-skilled Hispanics from Latin American countries, which lowers the median Hispanic income (McCall 2001).

We have seen in previous chapters that blacks and other minorities are more concentrated in lower-income jobs and periphery industries rather than core industries in the economy. These are the job sectors where real income lost ground most since the 1980s and early 1990s. With higher numbers of minorities in these jobs, the income ratios would be expected to decline. But we have also seen big job losses in the middle-income core sectors of America's major industries, such as autos and steel. To the extent that some minorities were breaking into the middle-income positions in the United States, the decline of these industries hurt minorities proportionately more than whites. It was only with the long economic boom of the 1990s that unemployment rates significantly improved for blacks and Hispanics, therefore showing improvements in the income figures as well.

Figure 11-1 shows much the same pattern. We find few gains in median income for Hispanics and blacks compared to whites from 1967 until the mid-1990s; here we can plainly see the bigger improvement in black incomes allowing blacks to slightly narrow the gap with whites in the later years of the 1990s. Asian Americans pulled further ahead of whites during this long economic boom of the 1990s. With the boom over, however, all groups lost real median income up to 2008, but the losses were greater for blacks and Hispanics, widening the gap with whites again.

Table 11-2 explains much of the story. Unemployment rates for blacks and Hispanics moved up and down at about the same rate as whites until after 1995. In other words, the *gap* in the unemployment rate between whites and minorities remained about even from year to year. From 1995 we find the black and Hispanic unemployment rates dropping more than the white unemployment rate. Thus, we can see that the longest boom in American history finally led employers to seek out more and more black and

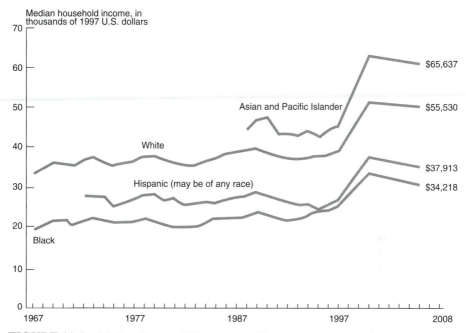

**FIGURE 11-1**    *Median Household Income and Change, by Race and Ethnic Status, 1967–2008*

*SOURCE:* Figure constructed from data presented in U.S. Bureau of the Census, *Measuring 50 Years of Economic Change* (1998:36–37); U.S. Bureau of the Census, *Income, Poverty, and Health Insurance Coverage in the U.S. 2008* (2009a: Figure 1).

## TABLE 11-2

### Unemployment Rates for Blacks, Whites, and Hispanics, 1980–2010

| Year | White unemployment | Black unemployment | Hispanic unemployment |
|---|---|---|---|
| 1980 | 6.3% | 14.3% | 10.1% |
| 1985 | 6.2 | 15.1 | 10.5 |
| 1990 | 4.8 | 11.4 | 8.2 |
| 1995 | 4.9 | 10.4 | 9.3 |
| 1998 | 3.9 | 8.9 | 7.2 |
| 1999 | 3.7 | 8.0 | 6.4 |
| 2000 | 3.5 | 7.6 | 5.7 |
| 2001 | 4.2 | 8.6 | 9.3 |
| 2002 | 5.1 | 10.2 | 7.5 |
| 2004 | 5.0 | 10.1 | 7.0 |
| 2006 | 4.1 | 9.2 | 5.6 |
| 2010 | 8.8 | 16.5 | 12.6 |

*SOURCES:* Table constructed from data in the U.S. Bureau of the Census, *Statistical Abstracts of the United States, 2003* (2004:406); Bureau of Labor Statistics, Monthly Reports (http://www.bls.gov).

Hispanic employees to keep their booming companies running during the second half of the 1990s. After this long economic boom, the black and Hispanic rate jumped back up quickly beginning in 2001. Then with the great recession beginning in 2008, by early 2010 the white unemployment rate had doubled, with almost equal rates increasing for blacks and Hispanics.

But there is more to the story of income changes between whites, blacks, and Hispanic Americans in recent decades: Detailed studies of income distributions and the black–white income ratio in particular have indicated an even larger problem contributing to black–white income inequality. Analysis by the U.S. Census Bureau during the early 1990s pointed to the more rapid breakup of traditional families in the black community as the biggest cause of growing income inequality (U.S. Bureau of the Census, *Studies in the Distribution of Income,* 1992:42.) With respect to all families in the United States, some 30 years ago only about 5 percent of children were living in female-headed households, compared with more than 20 percent by the early 1990s. Among blacks, the figure started at 20 percent of children in female-headed households over 30 years ago; by the early 1990s it was approaching 60 percent. Not only do the children of such female-headed households find it more difficult to achieve higher educational levels and thus more income in the future, but also the present income capabilities of such families are more limited. For example, as we saw earlier, with declining incomes for lower- and working-class Americans in recent decades, more wives were "thrown into the fight" for income in the workplace. Single-parent families have no one else to throw into the battle.

Still another factor in the continuing low black–white and Hispanic–white income ratios is related to government transfer payments in the form of welfare and other non-cash benefits. To some extent this factor of income inequality overlaps with the effects of family breakup described above, but we can focus on the impact of welfare benefits alone. U.S. Census figures during the early 1990s indicated that the black–white median household income gap would be about 5 percent greater if cash benefits from welfare were excluded (U.S. Bureau of the Census, *Income, Poverty, and Wealth in the United States: A Chart Book,* 1992:22). We have already seen in a previous chapter that welfare benefits were reduced about 40 percent in the early 1980s, which accounts for some of the increasing black–white income ratio in these years. Now, with the old welfare system in the United States eliminated and aid recipients restricted to 2 years of benefits at the state government level, as described in Chapter 9, this black–white income gap is likely to increase further, especially since the economic boom of the late 1990s has receded and more of the poor—black, white, and Hispanic—will be without benefits when they become unemployed, especially since 2008. With a higher level of female-headed households and reduced welfare benefits, hunger among blacks, and especially female-headed households, shot up in 2008 more than for any other group (Nord, Andrews, and Carlson, 2009).

## Income Inequalities within Race and Ethnic Communities

What is often missed in any discussion of racial and ethnic inequalities is the level of inequality *within* racial and ethnic communities in the United States. To the degree that the American stratification system has some equality of opportunity built into it, we might expect differing levels of equality of opportunities within racial and ethnic communities, leading some to move up the stratification system and leave others behind. It is of course a positive development if such racial and ethnic mobility occurs, as we will see in more detail in Chapter 12 on social mobility and status attainment in the United States. However, to the degree that only some segments of racial and ethnic communities are able to be upwardly mobile, thus leaving others behind, the position of those left behind will likely worsen and a growing gap within minority communities can lead to conflict and divisions harming the overall interests of race and ethnic minorities.

We should begin our examination in the Asian American community. The basic impression that most Americans have is one of Asians as the "model minority." Indeed, we saw above and in Chapter 2 that the average income of Asian American families is actually now above the average income of white families. But this image is only partially correct because it does not recognize the real diversity among Asian Americans (Okamoto 2003; Zeng and Xie 2004).

Within the black community, there has been considerable concern in recent decades about the rapid increase in income inequality and other conditions of life between a growing black middle class and an urban black poor being left behind. Improving educational levels for a segment of the black community, the continued advantage of two-income, two-parent families among some in the black community, along with the selective effects of government interventions such as affirmative action programs, were among the forces creating more income inequality within the black community since the civil rights movement from the 1960s. There are serious outcomes of this growing black income inequality: One is certainly more conflict within the black community between the "haves" and "have-nots." But an even more serious outcome, as noted in Chapter 9 on poverty, has been the increasing absence of successful black role models for poor young blacks as middle-class blacks leave poor neighborhoods (Wilson 1987, 1996; Harding 2003). Wilson also notes that a deficit of "social capital" has resulted from the growing gap between middle-class and poor blacks. The black middle class has been leaving the mostly all-black areas of central cities, removing social connections with better-off blacks that could be used by poor blacks to find jobs. Also, the exodus of middle-class blacks reduces potential pressure on urban governments for better services, especially education.

Figure 11-2 shows the percentage change in the Gini coefficient of income inequality within the black and Hispanic communities between the early 1970s and 1997, the most recent data from the U.S. Census Bureau. As can be seen in Figure 11-2, there was indeed a growing level of inequality within the black community between the mid-1970s and mid-1990s. Fortunately, however, this trend was altered from the mid-1990s to show a new trend of reduced inequality within the black community. Improvements in educational attainment (discussed below) and a long economic boom in the United States have no doubt been forces reducing black income inequality. As always, there is danger of the new trend reversing itself again to produce more income inequality within the black community as the American economic boom has slowed since 2001 and with income supports from a welfare system severely reduced since the 1996 welfare reform. But the more serious concern lies within the Hispanic community.

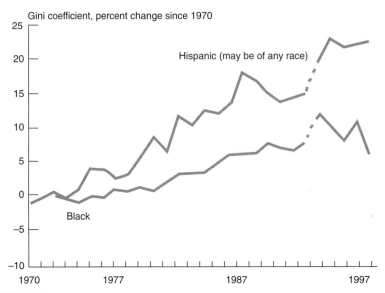

Gini coefficient, percent change since 1970

**FIGURE 11-2**     *Changes in Income Inequality within Race and Ethnic Categories, 1970–1997*

*SOURCE:* Figure constructed from data presented in U.S. Bureau of the Census, *Measuring 50 Years of Economic Change* (1998:40).

Figure 11-2 also shows that in contrast to shrinking inequality among blacks, income inequality among Hispanics has increased more rapidly since the early 1970s, and continues to increase. This is despite the fact that the median income is higher for Hispanic Americans compared to black Americans, and despite the fact that the Hispanic–white income ratio shown in Table 11-1 is better than the black–white income ratio. What Figure 11-2 therefore indicates is that the income figures for Hispanics are misleading in that the general figures mask the wider income disparity within the Hispanic community. The increase in inequality among Hispanic Americans is no doubt related to the continuing, even increasing, immigration of people from Latin America into the United States. Gains have been made among many Hispanic Americans, but the continuing immigration of poorer Hispanics from Latin America has produced dramatic changes in inequality (McCall 2001). The big question is whether or not the new immigrants from Latin America can move up the stratification ladder in future generations as many longer-term Hispanic Americans have done.

## Educational Inequalities

We can begin consideration of educational inequalities with Table 11-3, which indicates the level of education among whites, blacks, Asian Americans, and Hispanics from 1960 to 2008. As can be seen, all three groups have had rather steady educational increases since 1960, though blacks and Hispanics continue to lag behind the

## TABLE 11-3

### Educational Attainment among Whites, Blacks, Hispanics, and Asian Americans, 1960–2008

| Year | Total | White | Black | Asian and Pacific Islander | Hispanic |
|------|-------|-------|-------|------|----------|
| **High School Graduate or More** | | | | | |
| 1960 | 41.1 | 43.2 | 20.1 | (NA) | (NA) |
| 1970 | 52.3 | 54.3 | 31.4 | (NA) | 32.1 |
| 1980 | 66.5 | 68.8 | 51.2 | (NA) | 44.0 |
| 1990 | 77.6 | 79.1 | 66.2 | 80.4 | 50.8 |
| 1995 | 81.7 | 83.0 | 73.8 | (NA) | 53.4 |
| 2000 | 84.1 | 84.9 | 78.5 | 85.7 | 57.0 |
| 2002 | 84.1 | 84.8 | 78.7 | 87.4 | 57.0 |
| 2003 | 84.6 | 85.1 | 80.0 | 87.6 | 57.0 |
| 2004 | 85.2 | 85.8 | 80.6 | 86.8 | 58.4 |
| 2008 | 86.6 | 87.1 | 83.0 | 88.7 | 62.3 |
| **College Graduate or More** | | | | | |
| 1960 | 7.7 | 8.1 | 3.1 | (NA) | (NA) |
| 1970 | 10.7 | 11.3 | 4.4 | (NA) | 4.5 |
| 1980 | 16.2 | 17.1 | 8.4 | (NA) | 7.6 |
| 1990 | 21.3 | 22.0 | 11.3 | 39.9 | 9.2 |
| 1995 | 23.0 | 24.0 | 13.2 | (NA) | 9.3 |
| 2000 | 25.6 | 26.1 | 16.5 | 43.9 | 10.6 |
| 2002 | 26.7 | 27.2 | 17.0 | 47.2 | 11.1 |
| 2003 | 27.2 | 27.6 | 17.3 | 49.8 | 11.4 |
| 2004 | 27.7 | 28.2 | 17.6 | 49.4 | 12.1 |
| 2008 | 29.4 | 29.8 | 19.6 | 52.6 | 13.3 |

*SOURCE:* U.S. Bureau of the Census, *Current Population Survey, www.census.gov.*

white educational attainment. However, for high school graduation blacks have made significant strides in closing the gap. Table 11-3 indicates that in 1960, for example, the rate of high school completion for blacks was only half that for whites. By 2008 the rate for blacks was only about 4 percentage points different from the rate for whites. With respect to attaining a college degree, the gap between blacks and whites has increased slightly in recent years. Blacks gained just over 2 percentage points between 2000 and 2005, whereas whites increased by almost 4 percentage points. Considering the continued improvement in the high school graduation rate for blacks, it is likely that much of the lag in college graduation is related to the elimination of affirmative action programs. Hispanics, though, have continued to lag further behind both blacks and whites in high school and college completion. However, the considerably lower improvement for Hispanics since 1960 is again mostly explained by the high rate of immigration by the lower educated from Latin American countries into the Hispanic community. As shown in Figure 11-3, for U.S.-born Hispanics the rate of high school completion in 2003 was 73.5 percent, while the rate of college completion was 13.5 percent, compared to about 44 percent and 10 percent for foreign-born Hispanics. Figure 11-3 also indicates that the gap between the educational attainment of native versus foreign-born whites and Asian Americans is much less, and the college completion rate for foreign-born Asians is actually higher than native-born Asian Americans.

For the subject of educational attainment it is also important to consider differences within age groups because the figures for all adults in Table 11-3 contain people of the older generations who were much less likely to finish high school or college when they were in their late teens or early 20s. Figure 11-4 lists data from another survey of the 25 and older age group and the 25- to 29-year-olds for whites, blacks, and Hispanics. As can be seen, this estimate indicates that the high school completion rate for whites and blacks at the younger age cohort is continuing to rise, with blacks continuing to gain on whites. Younger Hispanics continue to lag behind whites and blacks in high school completion, but the 25- to 29-year-old Hispanics are starting to narrow the gap in high school completion. The highest high school completion rate, however, is found among young Asian Americans at 93 percent.

The college completion rate, however, is another story. Figure 11-4 indicates that the college completion rate for 25- to 29-year-old blacks and Hispanics has fallen back slightly, while the completion rate for whites has continued to show a rise among the younger age group. The Asian American college completion rate is substantially higher than any other group and is rising even faster among young Asian Americans. There is no clear explanation yet for the drop in college completion among young blacks and Hispanics, but likely explanations are the reductions in grants and scholarships awarded and the elimination of affirmative action programs in some states targeting blacks and Hispanics during the 1990s.

Another set of less optimistic figures is shown in Table 11-4. Despite educational gains for blacks and Hispanics, there is a continuing gap in income at each level of educational attainment compared to whites. For high school dropouts the gap in income is not very significant—it is extremely low for all groups. However, as we move from high school completion through a BA degree and finally advanced college degree, the gap in income compared to whites increases to its highest level with the advanced college degree, except in the case of Hispanic Americans. Among the possible explanations for the increasing gap are the subjects studied in college and type of job obtained—private business sector, private professional, or public sector employment (Grodsky and Pager 2001). But as earlier studies have suggested, it is likely that simple discrimination at all job levels still explains some of the income differences (U.S. Bureau of the Census, *What's It Worth? Educational Background and Economic Status,* 1992).

## Other Inequalities of Race and Ethnicity

As shown in Chapter 2, inequalities of income, wealth, and education are certainly not the only inequalities of importance generated by the stratification system. Virtually all valued goods, services, and conditions of life can be unequally distributed through a stratification system, and the same must be said for inequalities among race and ethnic groups

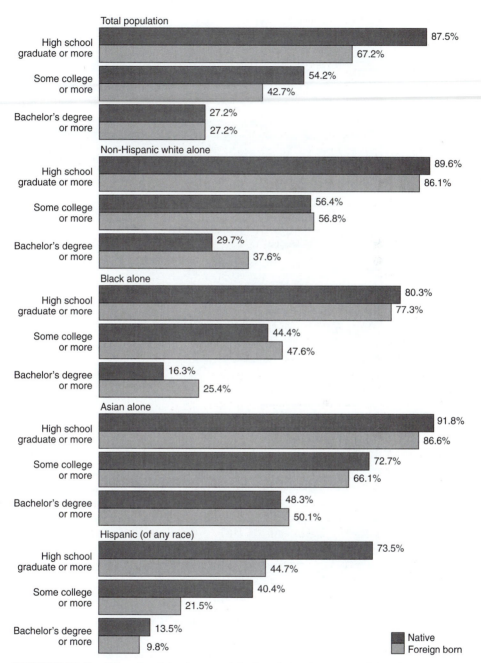

**FIGURE 11-3** *Educational Attainment of the Population 25 Years and Over by Nativity, Race, and Hispanic Origin: 2003*

*SOURCE:* Table constructed from data in U.S. Bureau of the Census, *Educational Attainment in the United States, 2003* (2004:6).

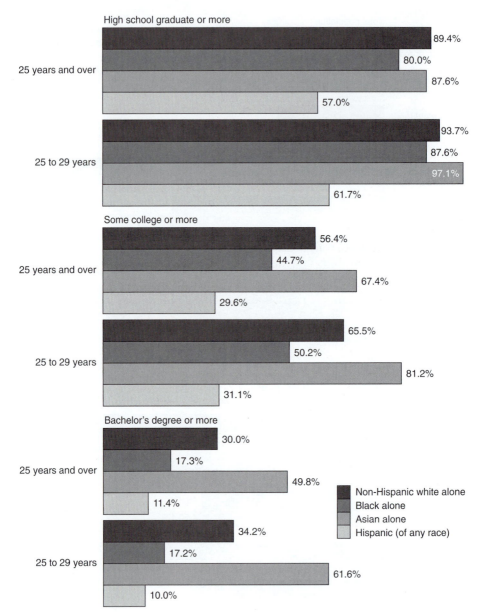

**FIGURE 11-4**    *Educational Attainment of the Population 25 Years and Over by Race, Hispanic Origin, and Age: 2003*

*SOURCE:* Table constructed from data in U.S. Bureau of the Census, *Educational Attainment in the United States, 2003* (2004:5).

# TABLE 11-4

## Blacks, Hispanics, and Whites Income Differentials by Education, 2007

| Characteristic | Total persons | Not a high school graduate | High school graduate only | Some college, no degree | Associate's | Bachelor's | Master's | Professional | Doctorate |
|---|---|---|---|---|---|---|---|---|---|
| | | | | Mean earnings by level of highest degree (dol.) | | | | | |
| All persons[1] | 42,064 | 21,484 | 31,286 | 33,009 | 39,746 | 57,181 | 70,186 | 120,978 | 95,565 |
| White[2] | 43,139 | 22,289 | 32,223 | 33,465 | 40,373 | 58,652 | 71,321 | 122,885 | 97,254 |
| Male | 51,781 | 25,886 | 38,214 | 40,508 | 48,444 | 73,477 | 89,678 | 144,371 | 110,480 |
| Female | 32,899 | 15,278 | 24,276 | 26,007 | 33,223 | 42,846 | 54,532 | 82,758 | 69,778 |
| Black[2] | 33,333 | 17,439 | 27,179 | 31,318 | 36,445 | 46,502 | 56,398 | 96,049 | 96,092 |
| Male | 35,668 | 19,705 | 29,640 | 32,236 | 38,921 | 53,029 | 63,801 | (B) | (B) |
| Female | 31,317 | 14,869 | 24,724 | 30,599 | 34,774 | 41,560 | 51,695 | (B) | (B) |
| Hispanic[3] | 29,910 | 21,303 | 27,604 | 29,384 | 35,348 | 44,696 | 68,040 | 84,512 | (B) |
| Male | 33,040 | 23,923 | 30,932 | 33,643 | 42,140 | 50,805 | 81,069 | 95,907 | (B) |
| Female | 25,262 | 15,574 | 22,283 | 24,884 | 29,279 | 38,584 | 54,263 | (B) | (B) |

B Base figure too small to meet statistical standards for reliability of a derived figure.

[1]Includes other races not shown separately.

[2]For persons who selected this race group only. See footnote 2, Table 224.

[3]Persons of Hispanic origin may be any race.

SOURCE: U.S. Census Bureau, Current Population Survey; http://www.census.gov/population/www/socdemo/educ-attn.html.

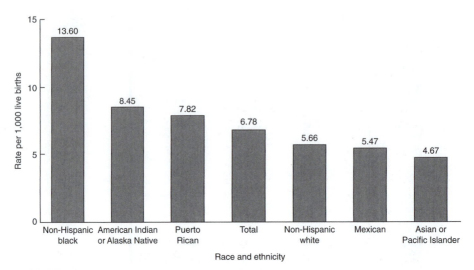

**FIGURE 11-5**   *Infant Mortality Rates by Race and Ethnic Origin, 2004*

*SOURCE:* U.S. Centers for Disease Control, 2007 (www.cdc.gov).

in countries such as the United States. Inequalities in health care are indicated by infant mortality rates, a condition that can be easily reduced with better medical care for the mother and child. As shown in Figure 11-5, there are considerable disparities in the infant mortality rates especially of blacks and whites but also other racial and ethnic groups.

Another kind of disparity involving life and death is indicated in Figure 11-6. The homicide rate for black men is far greater than that for both white and Hispanic men of the same age group.

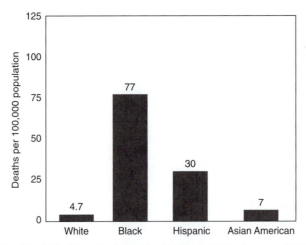

**FIGURE 11-6**   *Homicide Rates for Men 15 to 24 Years Old by Race and Ethnicity, 2004*

*SOURCE:* Figure constructed from data presented in Centers for Disease Control, *Health, United States, 2006* (2007:227).

Before attempting further explanations of the inequalities of race and ethnicity in the United States it is time to turn to another subject, a history of race and ethnic stratification in the world, and the United States more specifically. Then we can consider theories of race and ethnic stratification and discrimination.

# ⚔ A History of Race and Ethnic Stratification

Contrary to common assumptions, the history of racial stratification is comparatively short. Our *Homo sapiens* ancestors began moving around the world only a few thousand years ago. Before that time, the best evidence suggests there was only one "race"—that is, unless you count other species such as Neanderthals, which coexisted for a few thousand years with *Homo sapiens* in Europe. In this case there is even evidence of interspecies conflict, though with small populations such conflict was believed to be rather low (Olson 2003). In fact, one of the most interesting pieces of evidence using mitochondrial DNA analysis is that we all seem to descend from a group of people who lived in western Africa about 100,000 to 200,000 years ago. (The Neanderthal line died out soon after *Homo sapiens* arrived in Europe.) It was only after our ancestors began moving around the world, living in different climates, that the superficial biological changes associated with skin color, hair, and facial shapes occurred. It was even more recently that people of these different "races" had extensive contact with each other.

Before transportation technology allowed extensive mobility around the globe, or even a few miles from home, the homogeneity of community life for most people precluded much racial or ethnic inequality and conflict. There were, of course, the old civilizations in places like the Middle East, where centuries have created separate religious and ethnic communities in conflict, but for most of the world race and racism were still limited until more recently in human history.

We can begin exploration of this history with the history of racism itself—a belief system defining groups of people as either superior or inferior owing to their believed biological characteristics. People, of course, have come into conflict with and developed hatreds toward other people throughout human history. As sociologists made clear long ago, people tend to form a strong sense of in-group and out-group, with beliefs about the superiority of the in-group usually associated with these group divisions. This is especially the case when there is competition over scarce resources. Until recently in human history, though, these beliefs of in-group superiority were not associated with racial differences.

There is some evidence that the ancient Hindu caste system in India was originally associated with racial divisions, but the basis of the caste divisions was established in religious, not racist, beliefs (Dumont 1970; Dube 1998; Sekhon 2000). There is also some weak evidence that racism existed more than 2,000 years ago in the Middle East because of a few passages in the Bible. At one point in the Bible, for example, a person refers to feeling shame because his skin is dark (Solomon 1:5–6). But such minor reference can hardly be convincing when none of the ancient Middle Eastern countries had ever developed a racial caste system or a system of racist beliefs. The most extensive and systematic racist beliefs have developed in countries with European origins and have done so only in the past few hundred years (van den Berghe 1967).

When Europeans first came into more extensive contact with dark-skinned people in the late 15th century, systematic racist beliefs had not yet developed. But racism was soon to develop, especially in England, The Netherlands, and the colonial societies these countries established. The Spanish were somewhat less likely to accept racism, and today less racism is found in Latin American countries compared with countries with British and Dutch roots. Although racism certainly existed in France and its territories as well, even there it was relatively less prevalent. The former British colonies, especially the United States and Australia, and the Dutch and British territory later to become South Africa, along with the later German racism, have led the world in racist ideologies. This link between colonialism and racism needs further examination.

When Europeans began exploring the world during the 15th and 16th centuries, they believed they were "superior" to other peoples in terms of technology and moral values. The Europeans had the new warships and guns, as well as many other material goods and the scientific knowledge made possible by the new enlightenment in Europe. It was easy for some people to make the next assumption that such technological superiority was due to racial differences.

There are, of course, at least two major flaws in this reasoning for white superiority: First, whites have not always been the most advanced in science and technology, and second, the reasons for the technological advance of European nations in recent centuries have nothing to do with race. An elementary understanding of history easily indicates the first point. With the decline of the Roman Empire around a.d. 500, there was more technological advance among darker-skinned people in the Middle East, and there was the rise of the Islamic empire. At about the same time, China was more advanced in science and technology than was Europe, and the Mongol tribes under Attila the Hun and later Genghis Khan conquered most of Asia, the Middle East, and much of what is now Russia and formerly was the Soviet Union. We also know that Asian economies were more dominant in the world until as recently as 1820 when the European economies finally moved ahead (Kerbo 2006; Kristof and WuDunn 2000; World Bank 2000).

As for the second point, we must understand that the rise of the West during the period shortly before industrialization had nothing to do with race. (We consider this process more fully in Chapter 14.) Whites were simply in a position where geography made the process of industrialization most likely at that stage of history. Thus, although the rise of the West and the expansion of the modern world system had nothing to do with race per se, they did create a climate for racism as whites began moving about the world dominating other people. We will return to this theme when introducing conflict theories of racism and racial discrimination.

## A Comparative History of American Diversity

After spending considerable time in other countries, I have never quite gotten used to the images upon returning to the Los Angeles International Airport. After living in Asia for some months, the mixture of European Americans, Latin Americans, and African Americans is always striking. (Even looking into a mirror each morning to see blue eyes after months in Asia is an interesting experience.) The same thing could be said before

1990 after returning from months in Germany: In this case it is the mixture of Asian Americans, Latin Americans, and African Americans that appears striking. Yes, there are other countries with mixtures of racial and ethnic groups, and as we will see, this is especially so since the early 1990s. The European countries that had extensive colonial empires—England, France, and Holland—have their mixtures. An American expatriate walking through parts of Paris or Amsterdam, for example, can almost feel at home. And Germany is rapidly becoming a more diverse country with the influx of immigrants from Turkey, northern Africa, and eastern Europe since the fall of communism. In some places in Asia—in Hong Kong, Malaysia, and Indonesia, for example—there is something of a mixture of peoples in remnants of the colonial empires. The former Soviet empire has made Russia a more diverse country, with migrants from the many ex-Soviet territories. And, of course, though they are rather localized around the huge country, China has the biggest number of ethnic groups of any nation. But until recently, very few countries had a racial and ethnic mix throughout the country, on college campuses, and in major cities as has the United States for many decades. Americans are always told in their history classes that this is a nation of immigrants. Historically this is an accurate statement. (For an excellent collection of books, articles, and many other documents on the history of race and ethnic relations in the United States, see Harvard University's Web site: http://ocp.hul.harvard.edu/immigration/.) But as we will also see, the United States is becoming less unique as a nation of immigrants. For the subject of race and ethnic relations, however, this makes an understanding of the history of race and ethnic relations even more important because many other countries are now looking to the United States for clues of what may be in store for them.

We can begin with Native Americans and by noting that the ethnic diversity, in fact, began long before the European settlers came to North America. The number and variety of native peoples in the Americas are seldom given sufficient recognition. After Asian people crossed over to North America perhaps 13,000 years ago and spread through the Americas, there developed a richness of cultures, including economies, a variety of foods, and political systems, that had an impact on the rest of the world when transcontinental contacts became common (Chanda 2007; Wissler 1966). Many claim, that the federalism in the American political system, with small-town caucuses, was derived from Native Americans (Weatherford 1988).

The first contacts between Europeans and Native Americans were rather positive. Christopher Columbus wrote of Native Americans as "generous" people who "show as much lovingness as though they would give their hearts" (Hraba 1994:214). Of course, all Americans know that Thanksgiving Day is in honor of the first pilgrim settlers of 1620, who were saved from starvation by the Wampanoag Indians. However, Americans are seldom told that less than 100 years after the Wampanoag Indians saved the Europeans, almost all were killed in the first "Indian wars." When the first Europeans arrived in North America, there was little racism directed toward Native Americans, and relations are best described as accommodation. By the 1700s this had all changed—the flood of European immigrants required land. Prior to 1784, white settlers had taken land along the East Coast and down through the Gulf Coast. By 1850, however, almost all territory east of the Mississippi River had been taken, and by 1890 whites had taken most of the remaining lands. It was also during 1890 that the last major battle occurred, which was a massacre of 300 Sioux at Wounded Knee, North Dakota (Brown 1970).

It is also important to recognize how racism toward Native Americans developed through this period, and how this racism allowed for, or helped justify, the massacres. In many cases these attacks can only be called genocide. Though never as systematic as the German attempt to exterminate Jews during World War II, there was an unofficial and sometimes semiofficial policy by the U.S. Army to kill as many Native Americans as possible. Some were killed by methods such as distributing clothing known to be infested with smallpox to reservation Indians (Wax 1971:17–18; Brown 1970). When Europeans first came to North America, there were an estimated 850,000 Native Americans living in what is now the United States. By 1860 the number had been reduced to 250,000 (Hraba 1994:215). Today, while some Native Americans have achieved a middle-class standard of living, many tribes continue to be the poorest of American minorities (U.S. Bureau of the Census, *Characteristics of American Indians by Tribe and Language,* 1993; Sorkin 1978).

The history of African Americans in the United States is perhaps better known than that of any other minority group. There are, however, a few lesser-known points, and there are some basic facts that need restating to put it all in perspective.

While land was being taken from Native Americans, blacks were being transported to America to work on this land for the new white owners. Slave-trading companies sent boats to Africa, where blacks were captured, sometimes with the assistance of rival tribes, then shipped to the new lands in the Americas to be sold beginning in the 1600s. Overall, about 8 million arrived in this fashion, while an estimated 9 million died on ships in passage (Clark 1969:323). Only about 400,000 were sold in the United States, but through reproduction the number of slaves reached about 4 million by 1860 (Genovese 1974:5).

In many respects, black slavery in the Americas was the most brutal in human history. In contrast to slavery elsewhere, these people were torn from their families when captured, then torn from new families again and again as they were resold in the Americas. We have seen that slavery has existed from the beginning of agricultural societies, when it first became profitable to own another human for labor. But in earlier history, slaves were more likely to be respected as humans, with rights and usually the chance of eventual freedom. Soon after slavery became extensive in the United States, a racist belief system developed to justify the holding of slaves by claiming they were subhuman (Turner and Singleton 1978). It has been argued that slaves in the United States were taken care of adequately in a physical sense. Like farm animals that must be kept healthy to serve an economic function, slaves were usually well fed and adequately sheltered (Fogel and Engerman 1974). But though the basic physical needs of slaves might have more often than not been taken care of, psychological and social deprivation was immense. And, it should be noted, farm animals are taken care of only as long as they are productive or do not cost too much to make well if they become ill.

After the Civil War slaves were legally freed, though total freedom was hardly the lot of former slaves. Although slavery had been an issue in the Civil War, it was not necessarily the primary issue. The Civil War was a conflict between elites in the North who were pushing for political policies supporting their industrial economy and elites in the South who were trying to protect their agrarian-based economy. When the Civil War was over, political bargains were struck that allowed southern states to deal with blacks in their own way in exchange for the support of southern politicians on other issues. Thus, in response to black "freedom," southern states rapidly enacted "Jim Crow" legislation, which eliminated the right to vote for most blacks, curtailed their access to courts, and segregated them in schools and other public places.

The National Association for the Advancement of Colored People (NAACP) was founded in 1910. Protest movements in the early 1900s with capable black leaders like W.E.B. Du Bois were in many ways similar to the civil rights movement of the 1950s and 1960s. But African Americans had to wait for other changes in America before these protest movements had a chance of any success. The most important of these changes, internal migration, emerged slowly in the early 1900s, but then came like a flood after World War II. In 1910 almost 90 percent of black Americans lived in the South and in rural areas. By 1940, 77 percent still lived in the South, but by 1970 over half of African Americans lived outside of the South and in major urban areas. This migration was due in part to a "pull" in that jobs were opening up in urban areas, but there was also a big "push" in that farm mechanization eliminated most jobs previously held by blacks. In many ways, blacks today are like the new immigrants who arrived poor and uneducated from Europe in the late 1800s and early 1900s in the United States (Sowell 1981).

It was in this context that the civil rights movement of the 1950s and 1960s began. People generally assume that the black protest movement and riots that followed were born of frustration and desperation. The frustration and desperation were certainly there, but social movements do not come from deprivation alone. It takes new resources in the form of the ability to organize, material support, publicity, along with much more that makes a social movement (McCarthy and Zald 1977). The urban crowding, large black churches, some civil rights protection when away from small towns, and national political elites who needed black votes all combined to make the civil rights movement possible (Jenkins, Jacobs, and Agnone 2003; Morris 1981; Piven and Cloward 1977; McAdam 1982).

Hispanic Americans are the most rapidly growing minority group in the United States. At the current rate of increase, Hispanics can be expected to overtake African Americans as the largest ethnic or racial group in a few decades. In many states, especially California, Hispanics may soon come to outnumber whites. Mexican Americans make up the largest group of Hispanics in the United States, and first became part of the American population through conquest and annexation following war with Mexico in 1848. More recently, immigration from Latin America has increased with the civil wars, revolutions, and previous dictatorships in that region of the Americas. Still, the vast majority of immigrants come from Mexico, with 80 percent living in California and Texas. Because of the importance of agriculture in these states, and because of the political attention directed toward illegal immigrants working in agriculture, it is assumed by many that most Mexican Americans work in agriculture. In reality, however, only about 5 percent are in agricultural occupations.

Though small in numbers compared with European immigrants, Asian Americans made up a significant part of the overall immigration to the United States between 1850 and 1920. They came at first almost exclusively from China, but by the 1890s Japanese immigrants became more numerous. The Japanese immigrants, though originally better off than the Chinese, experienced the same level of discrimination and racism in the American West. From time to time legislation restricted their right to own land and become U.S. citizens. By the 1920s, laws were passed by Congress that all but eliminated Japanese and other Asian immigration until after World War II. The most drastic action against Japanese Americans was their internment during World War II.

The most recent Asian arrivals to the United States have come from Southeast Asia (primarily Vietnam, Cambodia, and Laos), with currently more than one million immigrants from these countries. As noted earlier in this chapter, the first wave came during the middle of the 1970s with the end of the Vietnam War. These immigrants were usually middle class, with educations and occupational skills needed in the United States. The second wave of Southeast Asian immigrants in the late 1970s and early 1980s came under different circumstances. These people were often poor farmers or from fishing villages, and they had no money or education. These were primarily the lower classes who could not leave Southeast Asia at first and had to come as boat people.

In the early history of blacks, Hispanics, and Asians in the United States there were high levels of segregation. When slavery was abolished after the American Civil War, there was little change in the living arrangements of these freed slaves. But as noted above, after World War II there was a massive migration of blacks from rural areas into major cities across the United States, though still mostly to big cities in the southern United States. Hispanics were first concentrated in small cities and rural areas not far from the Mexican border. Asian immigrants, particularly Chinese and then Japanese, were concentrated in the western United States at first. The Chinese immigrants were primarily in "China towns" in large cities, while early Japanese immigrants were more likely to settle in farming areas in the western coastal areas. But in the second half of the 20th century we find shifts in these living arrangements that indicate the levels of class mobility and acceptance by dominant whites.

Despite the civil rights movement and many antidiscrimination laws, African Americans remain highly segregated (Wilson 2007). The post–World War II immigration of blacks to large cities actually resulted in increased segregation up to 1970 (Massey 2001). Since 1970 there has been only a small decrease in segregation. Several studies have used a "segregation index" to measure the degree of segregation, ranging from 0 for full integration to 100 for complete segregation. In 2000, the average black–white segregation index in U.S. metropolitan areas was 65, and 74 in the Northeast and Midwest, with relatively lower scores in southern U.S. cities today (Iceland, Weinberg, and Steinmetz 2002). Hispanic segregation in metropolitan areas remains lower than that of black Americans, but increased somewhat between 1970 and 1990, with average segregation scores ranging from 46 to 55 (Denton and Massey 1989). Asian American segregation, on the other hand, is now lower, as is segregation of Native Americans, except for Native Americans still living in reservation areas in the western United States (Massey 2001; Snipp 1992).

Finally, we must consider the white ethnic groups in the United States. Except for Native Americans, who were not yet really incorporated into the society, and slaves, the United States was a rather homogeneous place until the 1860s. Of the 5 million immigrants who came to the United States between 1820 and 1860, 90 percent were from England, Ireland, and Germany. These immigrants were basically white Anglo-Saxon Protestants (WASPs) and blended easily with the original European settlers. After the Civil War, however, this changed dramatically. There was a flood of over 30 million immigrants from central and eastern Europe between 1860 and 1920. The earlier immigrants discriminated against the new white ethnics, who had to begin at the bottom of the stratification system, with the lowest pay and lowliest jobs, when jobs could be found. But as the American ideology has it, at least to some extent, the second and third generations of white ethnics were able to "move up the ladder of success." Although most of the later generations blended with the overall white population and culture, there are still pockets of white ethnics in the United States, especially in some large cities, where Italian, Polish, German, and other traditions are maintained.

Despite all of this history and other ethnic or racial groups that followed, the descendants of the original settlers and others coming later from the same countries still dominate. It was this "old stock" of Americans, the WASPs, who therefore established the basic political and economic institutions and continue to dominate them. Research on the backgrounds of corporate elites has found large majorities to be WASP, with the same found among the graduates of the elite universities (Alba and Moore 1982). Studies of particular industries have found today's economic elites are likely to have ancestors among the earliest British immigrants (Ingham 1978). And while Congress is not quite so dominated by politicians of WASP background, studies of the president's cabinet from 1897 to 1973 have found almost exclusive WASP dominance (Mintz 1975). In addition to showing the exclusion of all other racial and ethnic groups in general, these studies show the inaccuracy of the widespread belief that Jews hold extensive political and economic power in the United States. In their study of institutional elites in the United States, Alba and Moore (1982) found only media elites to have significant Jewish backgrounds, but even there the figure was a mere 25 percent.

## ✖ Global Immigration: A Comparative View of the New Dimensions of Global Race and Ethnic Conflicts

In contrast to the issue of gender stratification and inequalities, it is much more difficult to obtain comparative figures on race and ethnic stratification and inequalities around the world. In the past the United States had been somewhat unique among industrial nations in its population mix of many race and ethnic groups. Countries such as India and China, of course, have a rich mixture of ethnic groups, and until the breakup of the old Soviet Union, their mix of racial and ethnic groups was greater than that of the United States. But among major industrial nations able and willing to place government resources into examining and perhaps attempting to reduce race and ethnic inequalities, the United States has had a relatively unique history. Furthermore, the racial and ethnic groups that did exist in other industrial nations were unable to effectively pressure national governments as in the United States, especially since the civil rights movement of the 1950s and 1960s. Thus, the governments of other industrial nations had been less likely to track race and ethnic inequalities or focus research attention on the problem.

The issue of race and ethnic inequalities, however, is quickly becoming a hot topic in most rich industrial nations around the world. This lack of information and concern among other rich nations is changing fast because of situations such as the following.

Every evening as the sun is setting, hundreds of people can be seen hiding in bushes along the waterfront preparing to make their trip across the water when darkness helps them elude border police. The dream of these people is to make it safely into the richer country to the north where unskilled laborer jobs can be found for as much as 10 times the wages back home—if, that is, jobs could be found in their home country. Most of these poor people on any given night are not successful: They are caught by the border police and quickly deported. Their dreams, however, are seldom deterred by capture and deportation and soon they will try again. Many die each year in the process, but many more arrive day after day to take their chances of obtaining a better life for themselves and their families in a global economy that divides the rich and poor to a greater extent than at any time in world history.

The body of water these poor people are trying to cross is not the Rio Grande river separating the United States and Mexico but the Sea of Alboran between Spain and Morocco at the western end of the Mediterranean Sea. Thousands attempt the crossing each year because once they make it freely across this sea and into Spain there is the chance of jobs in Spain or other European Union countries they can move to from Spain. The nightly ritual of dashing across the water to a rich country, however, can be found around the globe: Similar scenes could be described for Mexicans and other people from poor Latin American countries dashing across the Rio Grande, which separates much of Mexico from the United States, or the Adriatic Sea, which separates Italy from the new states that were once part of the old Yugoslavia, or even boatloads of people from poorer sections of China trying to make their way into Japan.

In later chapters of this book we will see in more detail that the gap between the rich and poor has increased dramatically in recent decades. Some 200 years ago it is estimated that the majority of people around the globe had a roughly similar standard of living (World Bank, *Global Economic Prospects and the Developing Countries,* 2002:31). By the end of the 20th century, however, the gap between the world's rich and poor was huge. For example, a United Nations–sponsored report for the first time was able to estimate world wealth inequality. The top 2 percent of the world's population own over half of the world's wealth (Davis et al. 2006). The bottom half of the world's population own about 1 percent of the world's wealth. The annual per capita income of people in rich countries like the United States was $30,600 compared to $500 in many poor countries such as Sierra Leone, Tanzania, and Ethiopia. With respect to income, the top 20 percent of the world's population received 150 times the income of the bottom 20 percent: Just 30 years before this income gap had been 60 to 1. Even worse, it is estimated that some *1.3 billion people* in the world today live on less than $1 per day, and *2.8 billion people,* almost half the world's population, live on less than $2 per day (World Bank, *World Development Report, 2000/2001,* 2000; United Nations, *A Better World for All,* 2000; United Nations Development Program, *Overcoming Human Poverty,* 2000).

As this divide between the rich and poor of this world jumped dramatically in the second half of the 20th century, more and more people have been willing to risk their lives to escape poverty, often escaping death from war or starvation, by illegal immigration to richer countries. The migration is primarily from south to north because it is the north–south divide that separates most of the world's rich and poor. The biggest percentage of this south to north migration is found between North and South America and Africa and the countries of Europe. But much of it can also be found from the former communist eastern European nations to western European countries, and even in countries such as those in Southeast Asia where poor Indonesians seek a better life in Malaysia or Burmese, Laotians, and Cambodians seek a better life in Thailand.

What this surge of world migration means is that most rich countries are becoming much more diverse with respect to race and ethnicity. Countries once assuming they had no racism or racial and ethnic conflicts must suddenly confront a kind of diversity and conflict with which countries such as the United States are more familiar. It also means that one of the most important factors of global stratification determining who gets what and why involves citizenship rights. Those people in the bottom half of the world's humanity, the 2.8 billion people living on less than $2 per day, will be increasingly "pounding on the doors" of those in rich countries. A "green card" or any kind of work visa, if they cannot get citizenship, is their dream. As long as this world inequality remains, the world is going to become more racially and ethnically diverse whether people in rich countries like it or not. We must consider the impact of these immigration flows in rich countries in more detail before considering how some of the world's richest countries are handling the problem.

## Journeys for Survival: Migration of the World's Poor

Not surprisingly, when these poor people of the world can do so, they are on the move from areas of hunger and hopelessness to richer countries. The International Organization of Migration estimated that there were 214 million migrants in 2010, mostly people from poorer countries seeking income in richer countries (www.iom.int/). In 2006 the World Bank estimated these international migrants were sending $166 billion back to mostly poorer countries to take care of family members (World Bank 2006b). The estimates of illegal immigrants in the United States range widely, from around 1 or 2 million to perhaps five times as many. The massive border between Mexico and the United States especially makes detection and thus estimations difficult. We do know, however, that the number of illegal immigrants has been high for many decades. Europeans, in contrast, have been shocked with the rate of increase since 1990. As indicated in Figure 11-7, illegal immigration into the European Union countries increased from 30 thousand to half a million people between 1993 and 1999. As shown in Figure 11-8, Germany had the most dramatic rise in residents born outside of Europe between 1981 and 2000.

Throughout its history the United States considered itself alone as a nation of immigrants. While immigration has often produced conflict and hostility, there has also been much pride in this statement that America is a nation of immigrants, with most Americans interested in knowing about and tracing the history of their particular racial or ethnic group in early American history. It would be misleading, though, to assume this American legacy of a nation of immigrants is old history: In recent decades immigration has again picked up. As seen in Figure 11-9, the number of foreign-born Americans

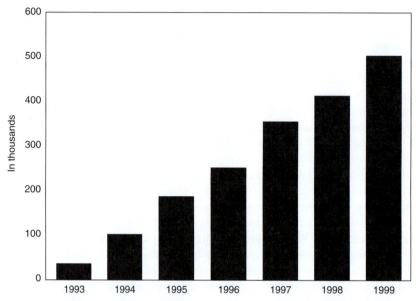

**FIGURE 11-7**    *Illegal Immigration into the European Union Nations, 1993–1999*

*SOURCE:* Constructed from U.S. Bureau of the Census data and OECD data compiled in United States Central Intelligence Agency, *Growing Global Migration and Its Implications for the United States* (2001:12).

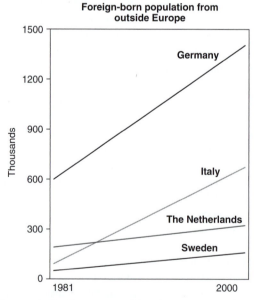

**FIGURE 11-8**    *Changes in the Percentage of Foreign-Born Population from Outside Europe among European Union Countries, 1981–2000*

*SOURCE:* United Nations, *U.N. Human Development Report, 2004* (2005:30).

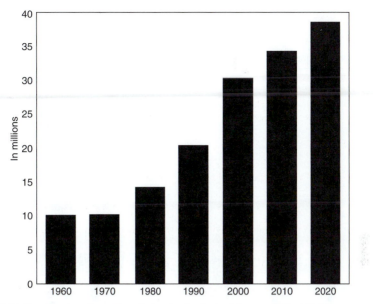

**FIGURE 11-9**    *Foreign-Born Population in the United States, 1960–2020\**

*2010 and 2020 are estimates.

*SOURCE:* Constructed from U.S. Bureau of the Census data and OECD data compiled in United States Central Intelligence Agency, *Growing Global Migration and Its Implications for the United States* (2001:12).

increased from 10 million in 1970 to 30 million by 2000. The number is expected to reach 38 million by 2020. Figure 11-10, however, indicates that the United States is not alone with respect to rapid immigration in recent years. Indeed, Europe as a whole has been far ahead of North America in the number of immigrants for a couple of decades. And as Table 11-5 indicates, while the percentage of foreign workers has increased in the United States, this increase does not represent a large share of the U.S. workforce in recent decades.

Americans, however, can no longer claim such uniqueness as a nation of immigrants: Canada, Australia, and Switzerland have far surpassed the United States in the percentage of foreign-born people in the country (U.S. Central Intelligence Agency 2001:12). The change has been quite dramatic in Australia and Switzerland. Long considered one of the more racist nations with policies excluding virtually all nonwhite immigration, Australia has extensively opened its borders to the skilled labor from its Asian neighbors. A nationalist, anti-immigration political party has gained some strength in Australia in recent years, but never has there been a serious threat of change compared to what shocked the French in April of 2002 when an anti-immigration candidate for president received the second-highest number of votes. Switzerland, long priding itself as a neutral country, has been most affected by the fall of communism and immigration to rich western European nations. Serious debate has been ongoing in Switzerland over how to cope with the large immigration problem, but there has been no credible solution put in place, nor have there been attacks on foreign residents.

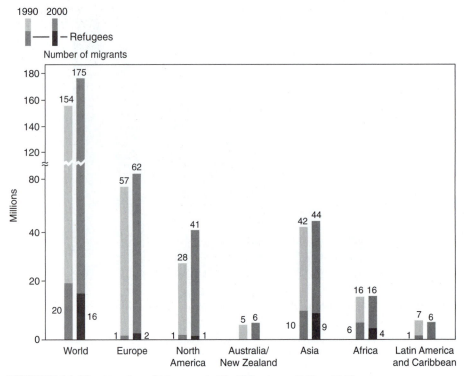

**FIGURE 11-10**    *Number of Migrants in World Regions, 1990 to 2000*

SOURCE: United Nations, *Human Development Report, 2004* (2005:100).

---

## TABLE 11-5

### Share of Mexican and Other Immigrants in U.S. Workforce, 1940–2005

|  | Share of workforce (decennial census) | | | | | | | Share of workforce (CPS) | |
|---|---|---|---|---|---|---|---|---|---|
|  | 1940 | 1950 | 1960 | 1970 | 1980 | 1990 | 2000 | 2000 | 2005 |
| **Total** | | | | | | | | | |
| All immigrants | 9.8% | 7.3% | 6.0% | 5.2% | 6.5% | 8.8% | 13.2% | 13.4% | 14.9% |
| Mexican immigrants | 0.3 | 0.4 | 0.4 | 0.4 | 1.1 | 2.0 | 4.0 | 3.9 | 4.6 |
| Other immigrants | 9.5 | 6.9 | 5.6 | 4.8 | 5.4 | 6.8 | 9.2 | 9.6 | 10.3 |

*Data from 1940 to 2000 are from the U.S. census conducted every 10 years, while the last two columns are from the quarterly Current Population Surveys conducted by the U.S. Census Bureau.

SOURCE: Mishel, Bernstein, and Allegretto (2007: Table 3-31).

## Theoretical Explanations of Race and Ethnic Inequalities

It is time to turn to some theoretical explanations for what they offer in understanding the underlying causes of the inequalities described here. Several points, or rather cautions, are in order before we do so. There is no doubt that racism and the conflicts and inequalities associated with racial and ethnic divisions are many-sided and complex. At this point we cannot try to explain it all. What we can do is remain with the focus of the book: social stratification and the underlying questions of who gets what, and why, with our attempts at explanation. We will also continue the focus on macro-level conflict theory in attempting to explain major issues of social stratification, though as before we must not neglect what other theoretical perspectives have to offer.

Also with respect to the theoretical focus of this chapter, note that I have subtitled this chapter "The Persistence of Ascription." This is not to suggest that Weber's description of a status dimension of social stratification primarily explains race, ethnic, and gender inequalities as was done with the divisions of caste in the Indian caste system. You will remember that in Chapter 3 we noted some important distinctions between the Indian caste system and racial inequalities. Again, what is meant by the persistence of ascription is that the more modern trend toward achievement variables influencing where a person ends up in the stratification system continues to apply less to people of other race and ethnic categories and to women. Thus, it will be argued that the continued stress on ascription for these people is likely to involve economic and power interests of the dominant group, and less of a status dimension per se.

So far in this chapter we have accomplished two major objectives: We have examined some of the most important statistical information pertaining to race and ethnic inequalities, and we have considered these subject matters from a historical and comparative dimension. We have, so to speak, presented the contemporary and historical realities in need of explanation. It is now our task to see what a multidimensional conflict theory of social stratification can do for us.

### Theories of Race and Ethnic Stratification

Given the atrocities of the 19th and 20th centuries involving racial and ethnic strife, the social sciences abound with theories of racism and discrimination. It is worthwhile to briefly note some of the more important theories before we contrast them with the theories of social stratification we have followed throughout this book.

Even a brief discussion with a hard-core racist can clearly indicate there is a psychological dimension to racism and discrimination. Racism, as the concept was defined in the beginning of this chapter, can be a passionately held part of a person's overall worldview. Two *psychological theories* of racism and discrimination have been most respected in the social sciences.

The **frustration-aggression** theory of noted psychologists such as Dollard (Dollard et al. 1939) and Allport (1958) claims that racism and prejudice are the result of frustrations projected upon others who are weak in the society. The true source of frustration experienced by individuals may be unknown, or the individuals may be unable to strike out at the true source of their frustrations. However, frustration is believed to produce a psychological need for aggressive behavior that can reduce the stress of frustration. Thus, if the aggression cannot be directed toward the true source of frustration, frustrated individuals will direct their aggression toward another convenient group in the society: that is, a weaker group considered an out-group with less ability.

There is plenty of evidence supporting the general theory of frustration-aggression. To cite some historical examples, in large part, frustration-aggression was behind the attack on Jews in Germany prior to and during World War II. In the context of economic disaster and defeat after World War I, the old existence of anti-Semitism was picked up and became extreme, with beliefs that Jews were somehow responsible for Germany's problems. Once, when asked what would have happened had Jews not been a convenient target of attack for mobilizing people in Germany, Hitler replied that another group would have been found (Hoffer 1966). This also helps us understand why Jews have so frequently been the targets of discrimination throughout history. Jews have often been in a particular society, but not completely a part of it, at times on the fringes of social networks, remaining focused within their own group. They are thus convenient targets—close by, but not really part of the in-group.

History is filled with scapegoating attacks on other people when the frustration level among the dominant group becomes high. In another striking case, Koreans were attacked in Japan after that country's most severe earthquake in 1923. About 100,000 Japanese were killed by the earthquake and fires that followed, primarily in Tokyo. In the context of fear and frustration, rumors of Koreans taking advantage of Japanese spread, resulting in attacks that by some estimates killed as many as 5,000 Koreans living in Japan (Mitchell 1967).

Another theory of racism describes what is called an **authoritarian personality** as a major cause. Adorno et al. (1950) are most noted for developing this theory soon after World War II in an attempt to explain the existence of anti-Semitism in Germany and the Holocaust, but also racism found all over the world. Some of the thinking behind the theory existed in German critical literature before World War II, with Heinrich Mann's *Man of Straw* one of the best examples before the war and Gunter Grass's *The Tin Drum* a more recent example. The basic characteristics of this personality type include respect for force, submission toward superiors, rigidity of outlook, and intolerance of ambiguity.

In general, social psychological theories of racism and discrimination can help explain why some individuals are more prone to racism. But these theories beg the questions of who or what group is picked as the target of racism and discrimination and why racism and discrimination are much greater in some historical periods and in some countries. Thus, to best explain racism we must consider the nature of these societies and the historical events giving rise to racism.

## Conflict Theory

A simple but important point is that at the heart of major causes of racism and discrimination is conflict between two or more groups. Consider Northern Ireland: Why do Catholics attack Protestants, and vice versa? Is it really because of religion? A better explanation involves the control of resources, exploitation, and inequality. The

Protestant British led by Cromwell in the 1600s invaded Ireland, taking the land and resources of the defeated Irish Catholics; to this day, the Protestants in Northern Ireland still control the best jobs and most of the wealth because of this history. The case of South Africa is even more obvious: White British, and then the white Dutch, took the land and resources during colonialism and made black Africans work for them at extremely low wages. To change the situation means that the standard of living for most white South Africans will eventually go down. The reason most South Africans have finally gone along with change is that it became obvious that by not changing they risked losing everything, including their lives. Finally, among the thousands of other examples, consider white Americans: Black slaves were brought as cheap labor, and to a large extent continue to be a source of cheap labor when dirty work is to be done. In the case of American Indians, it is even more simple: Whites wanted land for expansion. It is in the context of conflict, exploitation, and domination that we must understand racism and discrimination.

One of the best comparative and historical theories on racism is still that by van den Berghe (1967). Through examination of the major cases of racism in modern history, he concludes that economic conflict during the development of colonialism is primarily responsible for much of the widespread racism today. Van den Berghe believes three factors were most important.

First, racism developed with economic exploitation as industrial societies began to emerge and dominate colonies. But economic conflict has existed throughout history, and some colonial nations were more prone to racism; thus, there must be additional factors.

Second, racism in European nations and their colonies emerged in the context of Darwin's theory of evolution. Though scientifically Darwin's theory did not suggest the racial superiority of any one group, which even Darwin himself stressed, it was easy for some people to draw such a conclusion. If humans evolved from other animals, then it might be argued that some humans had evolved further and were thus "superior."

Third, ironically, it was the new liberal and egalitarian value system developing with new industrial democracies that helped racism spread in this context. "Faced with the blatant contradiction between the treatment of slaves and colonial peoples and the official rhetoric of freedom and equality, Europeans and white North Americans began to dichotomize humanity between men and submen" (van den Berghe 1967:17–18). In so doing, their exploitation of people could be justified, and the contradiction with liberal values ignored, if these people were not really human. Once the system of racism becomes tradition in a society, it can be taught and passed on to individuals who have no characteristics of an authoritarian personality and no particular need to exploit the minority group for economic gain.

The focus of van den Berghe's theory is economic exploitation and the development of racism to justify the exploitation in a grand sweep of history; it does not claim to explain every case of racism and exploitation. More recent economic conflict theories, however, address specific cases of race and ethnic exploitation and distinguish between those most exploited and those less so. One of the most useful theoretical concepts is **internal colonialism,** which distinguishes between minorities who are "conquered peoples" and those who have not been conquered. Thus, a distinction is made between **colonized minority** and **immigrant minority** (Blauner 1972). Within the United States, for example, included in the category of colonized minority would, of course, be American Indians, black slaves and their descendants, as well as Mexican Americans. Immigrant minorities would include Asians, Latin Americans, and white immigrants such as Irish, Polish, and East European Jews. There is obviously some overlap and degrees of differences among all of these groups, but the concept of internal colonialism is useful. The groups whose members have experienced the status of a colonized minority have been more harshly treated, and experience more prejudice and discrimination, which tends to lead to more social problems for these people and subsequent generations. This helps us understand why many immigrant groups to countries such as the United States are able to "make it" after a few years (Powers and Seltzer 1998), while colonized minorities remain poor, with less education and more social problems such as family disruption, crime, and substance abuse (Mirande 1987). There remains controversy, however, over the exact psychological forces that may harm colonized minority children (Ainsworth-Darnell and Downey 1998). Also, it is clear that immigrant minorities often bring much with them when they immigrate to a country such as the United States—things such as wealth, social, and human capital (in the form of education, occupational skills, and simply a strong family structure). For example, as Zulfacar (1998) found with Afghan immigrants to Germany and the United States, social capital in the form of a network of family and friendship ties in the new country is critical to achievement in the new country. Research on Asian and Hispanic immigrants to the United States shows the similar effects of family and friendship ties in obtaining help to prosper with self-employment (Sanders and Nee 1996).

Another economic theory of race and ethnic inequality and discrimination focuses on what is called the **split labor market.** Because of successive waves of immigration to this country from different parts of the world, new immigrants often produce new competition for the previous immigrants who are still toward the bottom of the occupational ladder. The competition has often resulted in ethnic hostilities that divide the working class and keep the more recent immigrants poor because the earlier immigrants in better positions work to keep their higher positions (Bonacich 1972, 1975, 1976; Wilson 1978). Even today one of the most important causes of racial income inequality is the concentration of minorities in types of jobs with lower salaries (Huffman and Cohen 2004).

These theories raise the interesting question of who benefits from these forms of prejudice and discrimination. In the case of the split labor market concept, in the short term the advantaged workers, usually working-class whites, are able to maintain higher wages over the lower-status workers who are kept out of the better jobs. However, in the long run there is evidence that it is the more affluent whites, especially capitalists, who win. For example, in research by Szymanski (1976) it was found that states with relatively high racial inequality also had lower average wages for white workers and more income inequality overall. In other words, by keeping the wages of minorities down, in the long run there is downward pressure on all wages. Similar historically oriented research has shown that as income inequality between whites and blacks increased, in the longer run white workers' incomes also decreased, and the profits of business owners increased (Reich 1981). The split labor market concept suggests that part of the problem for workers, therefore, is that they keep themselves divided and weak because of their internal conflicts and prejudices, but the capitalists have played a part in all of this. One reason that labor unions have always been weaker in the United States compared with Europe is that capitalists have used these racial and ethnic differences among workers to keep them divided (Aronowitz 1974). To cite one concrete example, during a strike against United States Steel in 1919, loyal employees were asked "to stir up as much bad feeling as you possibly can between the Serbians and the Italians. . . . Call up every question you can in reference to racial hatred between two nationalities" (Goldman 1953:305).

## *Maintenance of Racial and Ethnic Inequalities*

It is important to recognize that these theories tend to focus on the sources of racial and ethnic discrimination and inequalities. Once the discrimination and inequality start, however, they can take on a life of their own. Thus, questions of whether more people have racist beliefs in a society are not always what is most important. For example, research indicates that since the 1970s fewer whites seem to believe blacks are innately inferior (Kluegel 1990). In contrast to what some people believe, there has not been an increase in racist attitudes among young white Americans in the 1990s (Steeh and Schuman 1992). But this does not mean that racial and ethnic inequalities and forms of discrimination will be reduced. This is how the class system, or whatever general system of social stratification that exists in the society, operates to maintain racial and ethnic inequalities, and creates what can be called "institutional discrimination."

**Institutional discrimination** refers to the way in which primary institutions in the society (e.g., economy, schools, political system) produce discrimination through their normal operations when racial and ethnic inequalities are high because of past discrimination and racism. For example, occupational and income inequality between races may exist because the minority has low educational achievement. In a traditional manner for an industrial society, the best jobs and income go to those who achieve a certain level of education. Higher education may not be as likely among the minority group for several reasons: the need to work before high school is completed; lack of money to attend college; and poor academic achievement in high school because parents are less able to help due to their own low education, job demands, or family disruption. Poor achievement in high school may also be related to factors such as attending lower-quality schools in poor areas of the city where poor minorities must live, classmates with lower aspirations, and various social problems that disrupt the normal school routines. The point should be clear by now: As we have already seen, poverty breeds poverty, and lower-working-class children are likely to end up in the lower working class like their parents. Thus, because of past discrimination (and usually continuing discrimination), minority children are more likely born into lower-class families; because they are born into lower-class families, it is difficult to move out of the lower class simply because of how the stratification system normally operates. We have seen some of how this operates in the previous chapter on poverty; we will see more in the next chapter on social mobility and the status attainment process.

We can conclude this section by returning to the idea of "the declining significance of race" by Wilson (1978). Whether or not racism and racial or ethnic discrimination have declined, his key point is basic and powerful: The past effects of discrimination are compounded and maintained by the stratification system in its normal functions. To this we can add the distinction between colonized and immigrant minorities. It is the colonized minority that has more psychological damage, less hope, and social problems such as family breakup, parents with low education, and the long-term despair of racism and discrimination. It is often easy to forget that just because recent immigrants from places like Southeast Asia may come in poverty it does not follow that they have no "human capital": They often come with hope and determination, but also some education and, perhaps most important, the lasting effects of a strong, supportive family when they were young.

## Class Effects on Race and Ethnic Income Inequality

As we described in the earlier chapter on poverty, despite the specialized theories of the causes of poverty, the fact remains that much of why people are poor can be understood through the standard operation of the class system in the country. Likewise, no matter which theory of race and ethnic discrimination or oppression described earlier is most accurate or useful, a major contention of stratification theory that most people neglect is that the inequalities of race and ethnic status continue to operate through the class categories most important in the system of social stratification in the particular society (Ferree and Hall 1996). Put another way, no doubt much of the income inequality between men and women and whites and minorities can be explained by historical conditions of racism and sexism in our society (England et al. 1988; England and Farkas 1986). Once the racism and sexism is established, however, much of this race and sex discrimination operates through the established class system (Wright 1997: Chapter 9; Ferree and Hall 1996).

Several studies described in previous chapters have shown that in addition to occupational skill level, income inequality in general is related to positions within authority structures, ownership of the means of production, periphery versus core employment, and unionization. Thus, if we find sex and race differences in relation to these other factors affecting income inequality in general, we have located other sources of sex and race inequality operating through the class system. Several studies show this is in fact the case.

As we have seen in Chapter 2, minorities tend to have lower occupational status than white men. Thus, for whatever reason, being kept out of higher-status positions in the occupational structure produces income and other types of inequalities. But we have also seen that even when women and minorities have the same occupational status as white men, their incomes are lower. To help understand this situation we must return to Wright's class categories first described in Chapter 5 (Wright 1997; Wright 1978a, 1978b; Wright and Perrone 1977; Wright et al. 1982; Wright and Martin 1987). Considering the racial and sexual distribution of class in terms of authority positions, in Chapter 10, Table 10-7 shows that black males, white females, and black females are all more likely to be found in Wright's working-class or unskilled category (Wright 1997:68; Wright and Perrone 1977; Wright et al. 1982; Robinson and Kelley 1979). This is especially so with both black and white females because this working-class category includes clerical and service workers. Then, at the top of Table 10-7 we found that white males dominate the categories, but more females and blacks appear as we go lower in the class categories. Like the case of gender inequalities, several studies have shown that less authority and ownership explain a significant amount of the lower income for minorities (Wright and Perrone 1977; Wright 1997; Kluegel 1978; Wright 1978b, 1979; Wolf and Fligstein 1979; Treiman and Roos 1983). In Chapter 8 we also found that core or periphery position in the dual economy has an effect on job security, promotion changes, and certainly income inequality. Several studies have shown that minorities have less income, in part because they are more often employed in periphery industries (Beck et al. 1978; Tolbert et al. 1980; Kaufman 1983). Finally, the dual-economy research indicates that unionization is a factor in lower minority income, with other studies more directly showing that minorities are more often employed in industries that are less unionized (Beck et al. 1980).

It is time to turn to the subject of social mobility and status attainment in the stratification system in our next chapter. The chances people have of moving up the stratification system is one of the most important issues over the generations. Again, we will find that traditional sources of racism, sexism, and discrimination operate through the established class categories, restricting access to the higher position for minorities and women.

## Summary

After supplying basic definitions of race and ethnicity, this chapter began with information on the level of inequalities based on these ascriptive status positions in the United States. While we have found some improvements in the levels of inequality based on race and ethnicity in the United States, considerable inequality remains. After an extensive historical discussion of race and ethnic inequalities in the world and in the United States, the chapter considered the new dimensions of race and ethnic relations in rich nations caused by the new wave of immigration from poor to rich countries since the early 1990s. The chapter then turned to major theories of race and ethnic inequalities. Preceding a discussion of sociopsychological theories of race and ethnic discrimination, we focused on conflict, and especially economic conflict theories of race and ethnic discrimination.

# The Process of Social Stratification

# Social Mobility: Class Ascription and Achievement

During the last 100 years or more in the United States, as the two photos above suggest, it was very common for people born into rural farm and working-class families to move into the middle class or higher. As we will see in this chapter, in more recent years, those born into the working class or middle class are increasingly less likely to experience social mobility relative to their parents' class position. And when there is social mobility today, it is most often downward mobility.

*SOURCES:* Left: Library of Congress, Prints and Photographs Division (LC-USF33-011445-M5); right: Justin Horrocks/ Getty Images.

## Chapter Outline

While certainly mild by the standards of many countries, England has also had periods of political violence and revolution. One high point came in the early 1600s during the English civil war, with King Charles I finally losing his head over the situation in 1649. Recent historical research has supported what had previously been assumed by many social scientists (Bearman and Deane 1992): From 1590 to the outbreak of the English civil war in 1640 there was extensive *downward* social mobility in England, indicating the hardships and lost dreams of the British population. During the preceding period, from 1548 to 1589, there was political stability associated with the extensive upward social mobility in England at the time. As noted several times in previous chapters, and as Charles I discovered most dramatically, social mobility is one of the most important and serious subjects in the study of social stratification. The potential for revolution and turmoil, or the prospects for stability and social order, can be judged by the direction of mobility patterns in a society.

On the individual level, in the everyday lives of people in a highly competitive capitalist society, in a society that stresses universalistic success norms, it is hardly surprising that the question "Who gets ahead?" has received much popular attention as well. Early in this century the attention was expressed through the wide appeal of "the Horatio Alger stories of the news-boy who 'made it' by reason of personal virtues" (Mills 1953:337). More recently this popular attention is expressed through the many best-selling books describing how success can be achieved through intimidating others, dressing right, investing in real estate, getting right with God, or getting right with your psyche.

In the sociological literature, the study of social mobility and status attainment is most related to this popular concern. **Social mobility** research concentrates on the extent and patterns of vertical movement up and down the occupational structure. That is, compared with our parents' position, we want to know how many people moved up or down or were immobile in their adult lives. In a related area of study, **status attainment research** asks why such mobility does or does not take place. What factors account for the patterns of vertical mobility or lack of mobility? In other words, we want to know "Who gets ahead, and why?"

As is common in all industrial societies, social mobility in the United States is based on both ascription and achievement. But given our social value of equality of opportunity, we are concerned with the exact mixture of ascription and achievement (Phelan et al. 1995). We want to know the extent to which success or failure is related to personal qualities such as talent, motivation, and hard work, in contrast to ascriptive qualities such as family background, sex, race, or ethnic status. Equally important, because mythology has it that this is the land of opportunity, we want to know how the present United States compares with its past and with other industrial nations in terms of social mobility.

With reference to our success values, the long standing sociological interest in the study of social mobility can be understood. Earlier in this century, however, this sociological interest brought more theoretical speculation than detailed empirical research. The first real breakthrough in social mobility research came with Rogoff's (1953a) study of movement in the occupational structure using measures of occupational status (see Tyree and Hodge 1978). But Blau and Duncan's (1967) work brought a virtual explosion of research in this area. Blau and Duncan were able to compile a massive set of data on the subject with the help of the U.S. Bureau of the Census, and through new statistical methods of causal analysis produced a work that has become the model for almost all subsequent works on the subject.

It can be said with only some overstatement that since the 1960s the empirical study of social stratification *has been* the study of social mobility and status attainment. As described in the previous chapter, our rediscovery of poverty and inequality in the 1960s, combined with the new empirical methods of social research, brought many attempts to explain the existence of extensive and persistent inequality. The major sociology journals became filled with research on social mobility and status attainment (Pease et al. 1970; Huber and Form 1973).

As research conducted for this book shows, of all articles (2,487) published in five major sociology journals between 1965 and 1975, 453 (18 percent) were primarily concerned with some aspect of social stratification. Then, from 1984 to 1994, of all articles published in three major sociology journals (1,447), 220 (15 percent) were primarily concerned with some aspect of social stratification. In the first period, 143 (or 32 percent) of all social stratification articles were mainly concerned with some aspect of social mobility or status attainment, while the figure for the second period, at 46 percent, was even higher.

Research on the subject of inequality of opportunity, whether the focus was on poverty or class inequality in general, was in demand. This was especially true for research with an individualistic rather than a structural focus (see Kerbo 1981a). The individualistic bias in most status attainment research demands further comment later in this chapter.

The rather recent and rapid development of social mobility and status attainment research is clearly impressive. Much of the detail we have about these subjects has come from research that began only about 30 years ago. But, as will be seen in this chapter, we have much to learn. Much of what explains class attainment remains unspecified. And only recently has the individualistic or sociopsychological bias in status attainment research been widely recognized. The 1990s brought new structurally oriented research that shows great promise in further expanding our knowledge of the subject. However, as we will also see, the massive studies of social mobility that were funded in the 1960s and 1970s in the United States have not been repeated. Smaller studies using the old occupational categories to measure mobility have refined our understanding of the subject, but there has been a new trend; because of studies suggesting the old occupational measures of class are inadequate, more of the research on social mobility has turned to "income mobility" from one generation to the next.

The first task of this chapter is to present a summary of what we have learned about social mobility in the United States. We want to know how much vertical movement there is within the class system, what the nature of this mobility is, and the extent of class inheritance. As much as possible, the present patterns of social mobility in the United States are compared historically and cross nationally. Next we consider the recent status attainment research that is more related to functional theory for what it has to offer in explaining who gets ahead in the United States. Last, current status attainment models are examined critically and more recent theory and research is presented that adds to our knowledge of who gets ahead and why.

# ⚔ Social Mobility

Social mobility can be studied from several different vantage points. A first major distinction is made between horizontal and vertical mobility. **Horizontal social mobility** is movement from one position to another of equal rank in the occupational structure. For example, an electrician employed by General Motors who leaves his or her job for a similar position with Boeing would be considered horizontally mobile in the occupational structure. In another case we may consider a move from electrician to railroad engineer. Because both occupations are ranked equally in prestige, this again would be horizontal mobility (also referred to as a move from one situs to another when different but equally ranked occupations are involved; see Sorokin 1959:7; Hauser and Featherman 1977:217).

Of primary concern in the study of social stratification, however, is vertical mobility. **Vertical social mobility** may be defined as the movement from one occupational position to another of higher or lower rank. An example of upward vertical mobility would be movement from police officer to public school teacher. From studies of occupational prestige (see Nakao and Treas 1994) we find the occupation of police officer given a score of 50, whereas that of a public school teacher is given a score of 64 (see Chapter 5). An example of downward vertical mobility would be movement from the position of police officer (scored 50) to barber (scored 36).

It is easy to understand why vertical mobility is of special concern in the study of social stratification; the overall extent of vertical mobility can tell us something about the openness of the class system. However, a simple analysis of vertical mobility up and down the class system can be misleading. Social scientists also want to distinguish between structural mobility and circulation mobility. **Structural mobility** can be defined as the amount of mobility accounted for by changes in the occupational structure (for example, relatively more jobs created at the top than at the bottom alone would force some social mobility). **Circulation mobility** is the amount of mobility explained by exchange movements up and down the occupational structure, what some also call *fluidity* (Erikson and Goldthorpe 1992). With this measure of social mobility we are able to control for look beyond the effects of changes in the occupational structure so that we can compare societies at different points in history and compare different countries. While both kinds of social mobility are no doubt beneficial to a society, it is circulation mobility that more accurately indicates the level of equality of opportunity in a society.

A final distinction must be made between intergenerational and intragenerational mobility. **Intergenerational mobility** is studied by comparing the occupational position of parents with that of their offspring. For example, we want to know if a son or daughter has achieved a higher, lower, or equal occupational position in comparison with that of his or her parents. **Intragenerational mobility** is studied by comparing the occupational position of a person over an extended period of time. For example, we want to know if the occupational status of a person's first job is higher than, lower than, or equal to that of the person's second, third, or fourth job—or if the occupational status of a person has changed after, say, 10 or 20 years.

Both intergenerational and intragenerational mobility may be able to tell us something about the degree of openness in the stratification system. Most often, however, the focus of research has been on intergenerational mobility because the inheritability of occupational status from parents to offspring is considered a key indicator of ascription versus achievement.

Before we proceed to our main objective, an outline of mobility patterns in the United States, a brief note on how mobility studies are conducted is in order. It is important to recognize first that most mobility and status attainment studies are grounded mainly in measures of *occupational prestige*. Remember from our discussion in Chapter 5 that occupational prestige is based on the assumption (from functional theories of social stratification) that the key dimension of class is occupational *status*. Following the studies of occupational prestige (such as that of Hodge et al. 1966), different occupations have been ranked from high to low with respect to the amount of status associated with a particular occupation. Studies of status attainment (discussed later) use a direct variation of such a status ranking of occupations, whereas mobility studies traditionally employ a cruder ranking such as upper nonmanual, lower nonmanual, upper manual, and so on (or professionals, managers, clerical workers, operatives, and service workers).

But, such a status ranking creates problems for an adequate understanding of social stratification in industrial societies. On one hand, we have argued, the status of an occupation may be less important in determining who gets what in the society than the skill level, complexity, or marketability of the occupational skill. The idea of a status ranking neglects the conflict nature of the occupational structure as well as restrictions on free competition in the occupational structure. On the other hand, in addition to divisions in the occupational structure, we have shown the importance of divisions with respect to authority and property. These divisions are not always measured adequately in current studies of social mobility and status attainment. It is partly because of these problems that we have fewer studies of social mobility in the old style of research. Rather, as we will see, more research has turned simply to income mobility from one generation to the next because of fewer measurement problems and a much greater availability of data. These new studies estimating income mobility confirm the higher levels of intergenerational mobility in the past, as well as confirm the findings of recent smaller studies using occupational categories that social mobility has now slowed considerably in the United States.

The biggest problem, however, is found with studies of status attainment because of their more direct use of occupational prestige measures. The 1990s have brought new studies of social mobility and status attainment that overcome these problems using Wright's (1978a, 1978b, 1979, 1997) class categories discussed in Chapter 5. We will see how this new research has considerably improved our understanding of status attainment and social mobility. Still, focusing on the occupational structure and Wright's class categories as they are measured in mobility studies means that the very top of the stratification system in the United States is inadequately represented. In other words, the mobility that is measured in these studies is *mobility below the very top*.

Another introductory note is important before examination of social mobility patterns in the United States. Until recently most studies of social mobility were based on data from employed males. In the past women were excluded from these studies because it was assumed that (1) the family was the most important unit in social stratification, (2) males determined the status of the family, and (3) the status of women was determined by the status of their husbands. These assumptions have been questioned on several grounds (see Acker 1973; Powers and Seltzer 1998; Powers 1982; Powers and Holmberg 1978; Wright 1997:176), most importantly because there are more women in the occupational structure and more female-headed families. Although most of the research is focused on males, when possible we present the new data on female patterns of social mobility.

## Social Mobility in the United States

The most detailed studies of social mobility in the United States following the old functionalist categories were conducted by Blau and Duncan (1967), and then 11 years later by Featherman and Hauser (1978). Since the 1973 data there has been no research as comprehensive from a functionalist perspective, though we have smaller studies providing updated information. Blau and Duncan's mobility data were collected with the help of the U.S. Bureau of the Census in 1962, with detailed information on the family backgrounds, educational experience, and occupational history of over 20,000 males in the labor force. Without a doubt, Blau and Duncan's study (*The American Occupational Structure,* 1967) must be considered the landmark study of social mobility in the United States. The Featherman and Hauser study (*Opportunity and Change,* 1978) was designed as a replication of this landmark study, with a similar sample of over 30,000 employed males in 1973. Hout (1988) has updated this research with new data from 1972 to 1985.

In summary, these large studies published in 1967 and 1978 showed that (1) occupational inheritance from father to son was highest at the top occupational categories. In both studies almost 60 percent of sons stayed in the high occupational level of their fathers. The next highest level of occupational inheritance was at the bottom. Some 40 percent of the sons of low-skilled laborers stayed low-skilled laborers through their adult lives. But (2) in between the upper-middle class and low-skilled occupations, there was an extensive amount of social mobility. Only about 20 percent of sons from fathers with occupations in the middle stayed at that level. And (3) while some of these sons moved down the occupational scale in their adult lives, more moved up.

There are two main explanations for the higher rate of upward compared to downward intergenerational mobility in both 1962 and 1973 (Featherman and Hauser

1978:217). One factor is the changing occupational structure. In this earlier time period, as our society became more advanced technologically, more jobs were being created toward the top of the occupational structure than toward the bottom. Thus, relatively more people are needed toward the top. Combined with this, because of class fertility differences, we find that families have slightly more children as we move down the occupational structure. Thus, with the lower-occupation families producing more children and with the relative number of lower occupations being reduced, there is less room at the bottom and more room toward the top of the occupational structure.

The two time periods can also be compared in terms of structural and circulation mobility. In 1962 the rate of structural mobility was 22.0 percent compared to 18.8 percent in 1973. Putting these figures together for 1973, of the total sample (100 percent) we find 31.9 percent were nonmobile, 18.8 percent were mobile due to occupational structural changes, and 49.3 percent were mobile due to exchanges or circulation mobility.

We noted in beginning this discussion of social mobility in the United States that the 1972 data have been updated, but we do not have research as comprehensive as that by Featherman and Hauser (1978). In previous chapters we have seen changes in the American occupational structure and level of inequality that have most likely affected the pattern of social mobility since 1972. Specifically, in the 1980s and 1990s we have seen the growth of upper-middle-class jobs, the shrinkage of middle-paying jobs, and big increases in jobs paying poverty wages. These changes in the occupational structure and the related increase in inequality must have some effect on the patterns of social mobility, primarily the rate of structural mobility. In contrast to the time period covered in the Featherman and Hauser (1978) study, when the occupational structure was growing more at the top than at the bottom, the 1980s and 1990s most likely brought structural mobility in a downward direction.

Our speculation as to the trends in occupational social mobility for the 1980s can be partially supported by research reported by Hout (1988). However, the period of time included in this study was 1972 to 1985, thus covering more years in the 1970s than the 1980s, and not showing the full impact of the changes in the 1980s and none for the 1990s. But this research does indicate that the patterns of social mobility are changing in the direction we have suggested. For example, Hout (1988) found that the overall rate of social mobility was slowing for the first time in the years we have data on the subject. He also found that, while there was still more upward than downward social mobility, the upward social mobility had slowed.

## Income Mobility

We have seen earlier that there are many problems with the old occupational status measures of class. While Jonsson et al. (2009) show occupational inheritance is still important, Kingston (2000) and Weeden and Grusky (2005) have shown that the old occupational status categories have limited explanatory power with respect to values, lifestyle, and income differences among Americans today. We have also seen in Chapters 2 and 8 that there is a shrinking middle class in the United States measured both in terms of occupations in the middle and people in the income middle. Also, recent studies have shown there is increasing income inequality within occupational categories (Kim and Sakamoto 2008). For these reasons, more research has turned to intergenerational income mobility to judge whether or not the United States is a more or less open class society.

With a sample of over 6,000 American families, Hertz (2004) found considerable drops in upward social mobility and increases in the inheritance of low income over the generations. Other research has found that the rate of income mobility dropped between 1979 and 1998. In this time period almost 70 percent of sons remained in the same 20 percentile income position as their fathers. At the top 20 percent income group, however, most sons had attained more income than their fathers, indicating only significant upward mobility for those born toward the top (see *The Economist,* January 1, 2005). Other research shows the United States has dropped below Canada and several European countries with respect to income mobility in recent decades (Solon 2002, 1992).

Figure 12-1 shows the pattern of intergenerational income inheritance in the United States from 1950. As we would expect with increasing inequality and a shrinking middle class in the United States in recent years, there has been a significant change in income inheritance since 1980. By 1990 and 2000 we find there is less movement from the income position of one's parents in contrast to earlier years; in other words, less social mobility with respect to income. Figure 12-2 indicates what we would also expect considering the growing inequality and shrinking middle class in the United States. Only Great Britain has more intergenerational income inheritance than the United States. As we have seen in earlier chapters, Great Britain is closest to the United States in income inequality as well as the shrinking middle class.

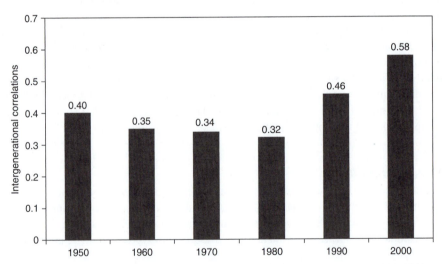

**FIGURE 12-1**    *Intergenerational Income Inheritance in the United States, 1950–2000*

SOURCE: Mishel, Bernstein, and Allegretto (2007: Figure 2c).

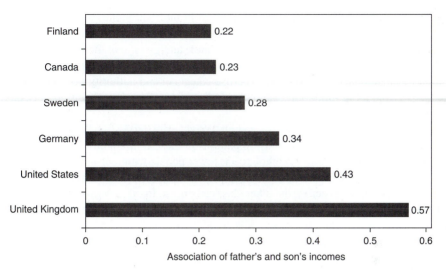

**FIGURE 12-2**    *Comparative Income Inheritance, United States and European Union Countries*

*SOURCES:* Solon (2002); Mishel, Bernstein, and Allegretto (2007: Figure 2G).

## Social Mobility and Wright's Class Categories

As noted before, one of the limitations of previous research on social mobility has been the exclusive focus on occupational status. In earlier chapters we have followed recent theory and research on class categories by Wright (1979, 1985, 1997) in arguing that three primary dimensions of class are important—capitalist property ownership, bureaucratic authority position, and occupational ranking. The capitalist ownership category and the authority category have been completely missed in previous studies of social mobility patterns in the United States and other countries, while the occupational status measures in the previous studies do not capture all important aspects of occupational ranking either.

Recent research has filled in some of the gaps in our knowledge of social mobility by employing some other dimensions of class as outlined by Wright. Using a large data set from the United States, Canada, Norway, and Sweden, Wright (1997:169–201; Western and Wright 1994) found that the capitalist property boundary is the least permeable, while the authority boundary is the most permeable in all four countries. In other words, there is more intergenerational mobility into higher positions of authority than mobility into the category of capitalist property ownership. This is especially so for the United States (and to some extent Canada), which in many ways is the most capitalist of all the industrial societies, has more inequality based on the ownership of property, and has more power in the hands of capitalists and the corporate class than other industrial nations (Wright 1997:186–190).

In this research they also investigated what they call the expertise category, which we can generally call a category of professionals and technical experts. The likelihood of moving into this expertise category was mixed in the four countries, but generally between the capitalist property category and authority category in permeability. Thus, given the importance of wealth in the United States, and given that there are different chances of mobility into the capitalist (or owner) class than into a higher occupational position (occupational skill level and expertise category) and authority positions, it is here that we find a big limitation of the old studies of social mobility focused only on occupational status.

In an interesting addition to this research, Wright (1997:203–222; Wright and Cho 1992) has also examined cross-friendship patterns in these four countries with respect to these class categories. As we might expect, fewer people from outside the capitalist property boundary had friendship ties to people in this capitalist class category compared with friendship ties across the other class categories. In other words, it is not only harder to break into the capitalist class, but it is even more difficult to form friendship ties with people in this class if the person is not already in it.

## Social Mobility at the Top

As already noted, traditional mobility studies have been unable to provide us with an adequate picture of the top of the stratification system. By the top of the stratification system, we are referring to the upper and corporate classes. The upper class is defined primarily by property relations; it consists of the families who own *large amounts* of the major means of production in the society, and thus not even adequately captured in Wright's (1997) research. The corporate class is defined primarily by authority relations; its members are the top corporate officials who control the major means of production. When referring to the corporate class, it will be remembered, we are referring to the top corporate officials in *major* corporations (that is, the 250 to 500 biggest corporations in the United States).

Standard mobility studies (such as those reviewed earlier) include the corporate class in the upper nonmanual or managerial and professional categories. However, such categories are rather broad, including everyone from the chairman of the board at Bank of America to doctors, lawyers (wealthy and poor), and managers of small local factories. The corporate class, though extremely powerful, accounts for only a small proportion of those in upper nonmanual positions. Thus, traditional mobility studies provide no insight into mobility patterns at the very top of the stratification system.

Along with the mobility data already described, what we want to know is (1) the extent of inheritability of upper-class and corporate-class positions, and (2) the extent of recruitment into these positions from positions below the top. It is generally assumed that for both of these top classes (and especially the upper class) inheritability is quite high and recruitment from below is severely restricted. Unfortunately, however, research pertaining to mobility at the very top is limited. But we do have some research that, though by no means conclusive, is suggestive.

We can begin with the upper class. One reason mobility into or out of the upper class is assumed to be very low is that by their very nature, upper-class institutions are designed to prevent such mobility. As described in Chapter 6, upper-class institutions such as the *Social Register,* elite prep schools, and exclusive social clubs function to restrict the membership of upper-class circles (see Baltzell 1958, 1964; Amory 1960; Domhoff 1967, 1970, 1974, 2002). They are designed to keep the new rich, until they "qualify," from penetrating the upper class, and to ensure that upper-class members marry within the upper class. Debutante balls and exclusive upper-class clubs in elite universities also operate to further class intramarriage. Thus, to the extent that upper-class institutions operate as they are designed to operate, mobility into or out of the upper class is severely restricted.

A number of descriptive studies by insiders indicate that these upper-class institutions do operate in such a manner (for example, Baltzell 1958, 1964; Amory 1960). Also, studies suggesting extensive overlap in membership patterns in prep schools, the *Social Register,* and upper-class social clubs provide indirect evidence of continuing restrictive boundaries around the upper class (Domhoff 1998). We do hear of many complaints by upper-class members that upper-class membership is not as restrictive as it should be or once was (Amory 1960)—although this seems to be a constant complaint of upper-class members over the past 100 years or so.

Finally, we do have some old but direct research on upper-class intramarriage. Blumberg and Paul (1975) studied upper-class wedding announcements and found a high degree of upper-class endogamy. Using the Philadelphia *Social Register* as an indicator of upper-class membership, Rosen and Bell (1966) found 31 percent and 21 percent of all upper-class marriages were within the upper class in 1940 and 1961 (that is, both marriage partners were listed in the *Social Register*), respectively. These figures are lower than might be expected, given the description of Baltzell (1958) and others, but it must be recognized that the marriage partners not listed in the Philadelphia *Social Register* could have been from outside the city (and on another *Social Register)* or simply from another upper-class family not listed in a *Social Register.*

That the marriage partner not previously listed in the Philadelphia *Social Register* was usually acceptable to the upper class is indicated by the finding that only 13 percent in 1940 and 11 percent in 1961 were not included in the Philadelphia *Social Register* the following year. This could mean that the previously unlisted marriage partner was already in the upper class (and simply not listed in the *Social Register),* or that marriage is a means of breaking into the upper class. Baltzell's (1958) qualitative research would indicate the former is more typical, although more research is needed.

These studies are concerned with social indicators of upper-class membership. Wealth, especially old wealth, however, is also an important criterion of upper-class membership. More extensive data are needed, but figures on the most wealthy families in the United States show that today most inherit their wealth. For example, of the 66 wealthiest people in 1970, 82 percent were from upper-class origins (Dye 1983). As Dye (1995:53) likes to stress, there has been much movement into the category of "billionaire" during the 1980s, and neither a majority of these people nor their parents were in that category before. Yes, some people get very rich in the United States, more than in other countries, and especially in the 1980s. But this does not indicate movement into the upper class as a class category described in Chapters 6 and 7, nor does it mean that most rich (defined more broadly as millionaires) fail to come from second, third, or more generations.

Estimating inheritance and recruitment into the corporate class presents more complex problems. Most important, problems stem from a lack of clear agreement on what constitutes corporate class boundaries. A summary of relevant studies indicates that when a broad definition of the corporate class is assumed, recruitment into the corporate class from below is higher than if more restrictive boundaries are assumed (Kerbo and Della Fave 1979). That is, if all corporate officers of, say, the biggest 500 corporations are assumed to be members of the corporate class, there is more mobility into the corporate class than if the boundary is only top corporate officers of the biggest 200 corporations. Another problem is that previous research has seldom made a distinction between the upper class and the corporate class (as was made in Chapters 6 and 7). Despite these problems, let us turn to some of the research to see what, if any, conclusions can be made.

Thomas Dye (1995) has collected background information on the presidents and directors of the nation's 201 top corporations (3,572 people). Dye's research indicates that 30 percent of the corporate class had upper-class origins (roughly including the 1 percent of the population in the upper class and corporate class as defined previously) and another 59 percent had upper-middle-class origins (roughly equal to the upper nonmanual occupations in Featherman and Hauser's research). These data are similar to those found in an inflow mobility table (that is, they indicate recruitment into the corporate class).

We can combine these figures to suggest that almost 90 percent of the corporate class had family origins at or close to the top of the stratification system. For a better understanding of corporate-class mobility patterns, we would also like to see data similar to those found in an outflow mobility table (showing the rate of intergenerational corporate-class inheritance), but no such data are presented.

Other studies have suggested that the corporate class has even more restricted class origins. For example, Domhoff (2002) examined the family origins of the directors of the top 20 industrial, top 30 financial, and top 30 transportation and utility corporations. In each case he found that more than 50 percent had upper-class origins. Using Domhoff's indicators of upper-class membership, Mintz (1975) found that 66 percent of all cabinet members between 1897 and 1973 show evidence of upper-class origins. (About 75 percent of these cabinet members were also officials of top corporations at some point; Freitag 1975.) Research by Useem (1978, 1979b, 1984) and Soref (1976) shows a significant relationship between multiple corporate directorships and upper-class origins.

In summary, the available studies leave us with no firm conclusions about intergenerational inheritance or recruitment into the corporate class. A rough estimate that corporate-class inheritance is substantially higher than the 59.4 percent found by Featherman and Hauser (1978) for upper nonmanual occupations in 1973 seems reasonable. A rough estimate that recruitment into the corporate class is more restricted than that of upper nonmanual occupations found by Featherman and Hauser also seems reasonable.

As noted earlier, Dye's (1995) study found that about 90 percent of the corporate elite came from origins at or above the nonmanual level. A rough estimate is usually better than none, but more research is needed for any firm conclusions. Clearly, intergenerational mobility into the corporate class from below does exist, and it is no doubt greater than mobility into the wealthy upper class. But it also seems clear that corporate-class recruitment from below is much more restricted than with upper nonmanual positions in general. It should be remembered also that Featherman and Hauser (1978) found upper nonmanual positions the most closed of those they studied.

## Black Mobility Patterns

To what degree do the mobility patterns of blacks resemble those of the general population? More specifically, what effect have racism and a history of discrimination had on the chances of blacks to be upwardly mobile? Equally important, when blacks have achieved some success in the occupational structure, to what degree have they been able to pass occupational advantages on to their offspring? These questions are of critical importance in understanding racial class inequality in the United States. The studies conducted by Blau and Duncan (1967) and by Featherman and Hauser (1978) contain information relevant to these questions.

Table 12-1 presents standard outflow mobility data for blacks in 1962 and 1973. These data show the class system to be *much more rigid* for blacks (especially in 1962) than for the general population. Beginning with the 1962 data, Table 12-1 shows that

## TABLE 12-1

**Outflow Mobility for Black Men from Father's (or other family head's) Broad Occupation Group to Son's Current Occupation Group, 1962 and 1973**

| Father's occupation | Son's current occupation | | | | | |
| --- | --- | --- | --- | --- | --- | --- |
| | Upper nonmanual | Lower nonmanual | Upper manual | Lower manual | Farm | Total |
| **1962** | | | | | | |
| Upper nonmanual | 13.3% | 10.0% | 13.7% | 63.0% | 0.0% | 100% |
| Lower nonmanual | 8.3 | 14.0 | 14.0 | 63.7 | 0.0 | 100 |
| Upper manual | 8.2 | 10.9 | 10.9 | 67.0 | 3.0 | 100 |
| Lower manual | 6.7 | 9.1 | 11.1 | 71.0 | 2.1 | 100 |
| Farm | 1.2 | 5.4 | 7.1 | 66.3 | 19.9 | 100 |
| Total | 4.5% | 7.7% | 9.4% | 67.9% | 10.5% | 100% |
| **1973** | | | | | | |
| Upper nonmanual | 43.9% | 11.8% | 8.3% | 36.0% | 0.0% | 100% |
| Lower nonmanual | 19.5 | 20.8 | 13.4 | 45.5 | 0.8 | 100 |
| Upper manual | 16.3 | 13.9 | 15.8 | 53.7 | 0.2 | 100 |
| Lower manual | 12.1 | 12.2 | 13.7 | 61.0 | 1.0 | 100 |
| Farm | 5.1 | 6.8 | 16.5 | 63.2 | 8.4 | 100 |
| Total | 11.6% | 10.8% | 14.7% | 59.4% | 3.5% | 100% |

*SOURCE:* Featherman and Hauser (1978:326). The samples include American black men in the experienced civilian labor force aged 21 to 64.

occupational inheritance at the top was severely limited for blacks. For example, black fathers who had attained upper nonmanual positions were seldom able to pass this advantage on to their sons. Among blacks in 1962, only *13.3 percent* of the sons who had fathers with upper nonmanual positions were able to attain such a position. This compares with a 56.8 percent inheritance rate for upper nonmanual positions in the general population.

With lower nonmanual positions, the black inheritance rate was 14.0 percent in 1962, compared with the 23.7 percent rate for the general population. What is more significant, in the general population 43.1 percent of sons with lower nonmanual fathers moved up to upper nonmanual positions. For blacks, this rate of upward movement was only 8.3 percent.

Where, then, did the sons of black upper nonmanual fathers go? For the clear majority, the movement was *down*—way down. In 1962, *63.0 percent* of black sons with upper nonmanual fathers moved all the way down to lower manual positions. The same figure for the general population was 13.8 percent. What this means is that when a black did make it in the occupational structure, say to a position as a doctor or lawyer, this black father, unlike whites, was seldom able to pass his success on to his children. In the white world this would be comparable to 63 percent of the children of doctors ending up on an assembly line doing unskilled blue-collar labor.

These findings describe one of the most tragic conditions for blacks since slavery in the United States, and help us in part to understand why blacks for the most part have remained poor and in the worst jobs, when not in the unemployment lines. Unlike white ethnic groups who often came to this country in poverty, blacks have not had a second and third generation that substantially moved out of poverty. In short, the 1962 figures show almost no accumulated advantages for blacks. A black middle and upper middle class does exist, but these figures demonstrate in part why it has remained very small.

Returning to the 1962 data in Table 12-1 for a moment, we do find greater occupational inheritance for blacks in relation to whites in one part of the occupational structure—at the bottom. For black sons with lower manual fathers, 71.0 percent remained in lower manual occupations. The comparable figure for the general population (primarily white) was 43.4 percent. In fact, what Table 12-1 shows is that *no matter what the father's occupation,* a majority of black sons ended up in lower manual or unskilled blue-collar work.

Moving to the 1973 figures for blacks in Table 12-1, we find at least one significant improvement. At the top of the occupational structure, intergenerational inheritance has increased. For example, in 1973, 43.9 percent of the black sons with upper nonmanual fathers were able to inherit their father's occupational advantage (this compares with 13.3 percent for blacks in 1962). Blacks remain behind the 59.4 percent upper nonmanual inheritance for whites, but a 30 percent improvement is quite significant. Hout (1984) has updated these data to the end of the 1970s, and we continue to find an improved position for stability in this black middle class. Less corresponding improvement for blacks is shown for other occupational positions in 1973, but there has been some improvement.

Comparing 1962 with 1973 in Table 12-1, we find a bit more occupational inheritance for blacks in lower nonmanual and upper manual positions, with somewhat less inheritance in lower manual positions. In essence, the black doctor and black teacher

## TABLE 12-2

### Movement from Bottom to Top 25 Percent Blacks and Whites

|  | Bottom to top quartile | Top to bottom quartile |
|---|---|---|
| All | 7.3% | 9.2% |
| White | 10.2 | 9.0 |
| Black | 4.2 | 18.5 |
| Black–white difference | 26.0% | 9.5% |

*SOURCE:* Mishel, Bernstein, and Allegretto (2007: Table 2.4).

were better able to give their sons an occupational boost in 1973, although they remained less able to do so than whites.

The 1973 figures indicate that barring major setbacks, *at least those blacks able to break into higher occupational positions* will be able to form a more stable black middle class. In contrast to the past, middle- and upper-middle-class status may not be a fading dream for *some* blacks.

The improvements just described for the period before the 1980s may seem to contradict the continuing high rate of black–white income inequality, black unemployment, and the poverty described in the previous chapter, but they do not. Table 12-1 shows only a little of what is happening because for the most part poor and unemployed blacks are not found on this table (Willhelm 1979).

But even in Table 12-1 we continue to find a much higher concentration of blacks in lower manual occupations. Reading down the lower manual column in Table 12-1 for 1973, we find that blacks were still *much* more likely to fall into lower manual occupations no matter what their fathers' occupation. For black sons with higher occupational fathers there was less downward mobility in 1973 but when they were downwardly mobile, they fell much farther than whites. Also, the figure for lower manual inheritance for blacks remained substantially higher than that for whites in 1973 (61.0 percent versus 40.1 percent). As for whites and blacks in 1973, the class structure for blacks is even more rigid at the top and bottom—although for blacks it is still more rigid at the bottom.

Table 12-2 shows a similar pattern with 2000 data. While it is rare for anyone to move from the bottom 25 percent income category where they were born to the top 25 percent income category, 10.2 percent of whites are able to do so compared to 4.2 percent of blacks. Likewise, while it is equally rare for people to fall from the top 25 percent income category to the bottom 25 percent income category, the rate for whites falling is 9 percent compared to 18.5 percent for blacks. This unfortunately fits the earlier occupational mobility research indicating that no matter where blacks are born in the United States, their chances of falling to the bottom are much higher.

### *Mobility Patterns among Women*

As with blacks, our main question at present is whether the mobility patterns observed for women differ from those for white males. Because of the availability of data, our focus must be on white women. In beginning our examination of social mobility, we noted that most studies have been concerned with men (Powers 1982). However, there has been enough research on women to allow for some reasonably firm conclusions with respect to the mobility patterns of white women.

We will begin with a comparison between men and women who are in the labor force. One of the first studies of this type (De Jong, Brawer, and Robin 1971) found the mobility patterns of women to be quite similar to those of men. That is, comparing their occupations with those of their fathers, women had patterns of occupational inheritance and recruitment very close to those of men.

However—perhaps because it was one of the first studies of this type—there is wide agreement that several major problems were contained in the study (see Hauser and Featherman 1977:195). One problem was created because there was no indication of which job (first, second, or third) was being measured for women. Careers do change, and the data must be comparable in this respect. A person's first job is often of lower status than later jobs.

The most important problem, however, involved the broad occupational categories employed in the study. As noted in an earlier chapter, because women tend to be concentrated in particular occupations (such as clerical workers), broad occupational categories (such as lower nonmanual and upper manual) are not able to detect important differences between the mobility patterns of men and women.

When examining mobility patterns using 18 occupational categories, several significant differences between men and women are found. For example, Tyree and Treas (1974) found that daughters of professional fathers were more likely to be in white-collar occupations than were sons of professional fathers. Also, daughters of farmworkers were more likely to be in white-collar occupations and less likely to be in blue-collar occupations than were sons of farmworkers. Further, Hauser and Featherman (1977:204) found that, overall, working women are less likely to be in an occupational status close to their father's when compared with men.

As might be expected when comparing the different occupational distributions of men and women (noted in Chapter 8), most of the difference in mobility patterns between men and women is due to this differing occupational distribution (Hauser and Featherman 1977:203). Following the previous statement that working women are less likely to keep their fathers' occupational status than are men, this occurs because women are both more downwardly and more upwardly mobile (compared with their fathers) than are men.

Women are more concentrated in lower nonmanual or lower white-collar occupations, such as clerical work. Thus, no matter whether their fathers are higher or lower in occupational rank, women are frequently pushed up to, or down to, the lower white-collar positions. There is a sex as well as a race bias in the occupational structure. Black men are often pushed down to lower manual positions no matter what the occupational position of their fathers.

There are, however, two mobility patterns among women, using the occupational status definition. Thus far, we have considered only the intergenerational mobility patterns of women in the labor force. But as noted earlier, the status of women in the stratification system has traditionally been assumed to follow that of their husbands. With more than 50 percent of married women now in the labor force, this assumption must increasingly be questioned.

It also means that slightly less than 50 percent of married women are not in the labor force. To the extent that the occupational structure shapes life chances and the distribution of rewards in the society, the occupational structure more clearly affects this second group of women through the occupational attainment of their husbands. In this case we can consider the intergenerational mobility patterns of women with reference to the occupational position of their fathers vis-à-vis that of their husbands.

Such a mobility analysis of married women not in the labor force has been conducted by Chase (1975), Tyree and Treas (1974), and Glenn et al. (1974). In this respect the intergenerational mobility patterns of women were found to be much closer to those of men. In other words, women tend to marry men who hold occupational positions close to those of their brothers more than they tend to enter occupational positions close to those of their brothers (when women are employed). Put another way, father–son mobility patterns are closer to father–husband mobility patterns than to father–daughter mobility patterns (Hauser and Featherman 1977:197). Thus, for a significant number of women the marriage market more closely reproduces the intergenerational mobility patterns of men. Why this is so is in part suggested by recent research on class intermarriage. Men and women who marry are now even more likely to have similar educational attainments than similar class backgrounds, though this is usually the case as well (Kalmijn 1991). What this means is that if a brother is upwardly mobile through education and occupational status, then the sister is likely to have similar educational attainment and to marry someone with similar educational attainment whether or not the sister joins the labor force herself.

However, these studies have found some differences between the mobility patterns of women (through their husbands) and those of men. One important difference is that mobility for women through marriage remains slightly greater than mobility for men through occupation. It was commonly believed that women had more upward mobility through marriage than did men through occupations (Glenn et al. 1974)—the old story of the poor but attractive girl marrying a rich man. On the contrary, women are as likely to marry down as to marry up. The overall effect is slightly more intergenerational mobility for women through marriage than for men through occupation, but the mobility goes both up and down (Chase 1975).

Finally, we must stress again that the research on the social mobility patterns for women described previously are from the older functionalist perspective using occupational *status* measures. In addition to the limitations of not directly measuring occupational skill level, ownership, and authority positions as the new research has done (Wright 1997), there is research indicating that including women in the studies measuring occupational status actually alters the occupational status scores (Powers and Holmberg 1978). In other words, even the measures used in these studies would slightly change if women had been included in the original estimates of occupational status scores.

In his large study of social mobility in the United States, Canada, Sweden, and Norway using the class categories of property ownership, skill level, and authority, Wright (1997) included women as well as men in the samples, and measured the class positions of women themselves as well as that of the family if they were married. Compared to the overall findings mentioned earlier, there were mostly similarities comparing men and women on patterns of social mobility, though some differences exist. For both men and women, the property class boundary was most impermeable (that is, few could cross it into the capitalist class of owners if not born there). Then occupational skill level was a less restricted barrier, and authority level was the least restricted barrier for women. About the same percentage of women as men move across these class barriers or did not as in most cases. However, an interesting difference is that the property class boundary was somewhat less of a barrier for women (Wright 1997:192). What the research found is that women do on occasion marry into the upper propertied class, more so than men. One additional difference was found, this time when comparing women across the four countries. Women in the United States are more able to move up in occupational skill level than in the other countries (Wright 1997:194). We have earlier seen that women in the United States have lower income compared to men than is the case in other countries. This optimistic finding for American women (at least compared to the other three countries in the data set) indicates a higher occupational position in the future may bring other improvements, such as income. Recent figures on educational attainment for American women also suggest optimism. For example, by 2003, among the 25- to 29-year age group, women had a higher rate of college completion than men (30 percent compared to 26 percent). Further, the percentage of women in college majors normally leading to higher-paying jobs has increased significantly. For example, the percentage of women in business management programs increased from only 9 percent in 1971 to 48 percent by 1996, while the percentage of women majoring in biology (and likely going to medical school) increased from 29 percent to 52 percent, and the percentage of women in majors considered pre-law increased from 5 percent to 73 percent (U.S. Bureau of the Census, *Educational Attainment in the United States, 1999,* 2000:3). Still, of course, there are glass-ceiling effects described in the previous chapter that will limit income coming from the higher authority positions within the occupations of women.

With the new trend of income mobility studies, we have data in Figure 12-3 indicating differences in intergenerational income inheritance for men and women in six industrial nations. Following what we found above, in all countries the chances of women moving out of the bottom 20 percent income group is slightly higher than for men. In the United States, however, men are even more likely to stay in the bottom 20 percent income category than women, mainly because men in the United States are more likely stuck in the bottom compared to men in these other countries.

## Social Mobility: Historical and Comparative

Having examined the more contemporary patterns of social mobility in the United States, we have two remaining questions of considerable importance. First, we want to know how the patterns of social mobility described before compare with those in earlier periods of U.S. history. Our traditional ideology claims that this is a country of opportunity. At least with respect to the occupational structure and positions between the very top and bottom before the 1980s, there has been some support for this ideological claim among white males. Although most mobility is short range (that is, not far from

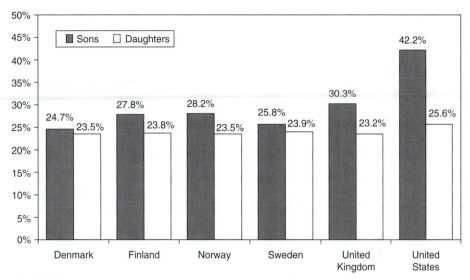

**FIGURE 12-3**    *Comparative Income Inheritance at the Bottom 20 Percent, Sons Compared to Daughters*

*SOURCES:* Jantti et al. (2006); Mishel, Bernstein, and Allegretto (2007: Figure 2H).

occupational origins), the 1962 and 1973 data show that mobility has existed and that there has been more upward than downward mobility. With recent studies on the social mobility patterns described previously, white women generally show similar patterns. What we now want to know is whether it has always been so in the United States. In the past, has the extent of social mobility been less, greater, or the same?

Second, the ideological claims in this country suggest that the United States has more opportunities for people than do other countries. This is one reason so many immigrants came to this country in the past and why so many refugees from countries such as Mexico, Cuba, Vietnam, Cambodia, and Haiti continue to view the United States as the most inviting country among industrialized nations. To what extent are these views correct? Currently, does the United States have more social mobility than other industrialized nations such as England, France, Germany, and Japan?

## Historical Patterns of Mobility in the United States

We do have some evidence of the extent of social mobility in earlier periods of U.S. history, although the evidence is less systematic and extensive than that gained from recent studies. The sociological study of social stratification did not even exist before the late 1800s in the United States; and even before the mid-1900s empirical investigation of mobility patterns was almost totally neglected. Thus, researchers have been forced to design indicators of earlier mobility patterns from various types of historical records. Some of this research is quite ingenious, but it must also be accepted with caution.

In a study concerned with one of the earliest periods of U.S. history, Thernstrom (1970) examined social mobility in Boston during the second half of the 1800s using census records, marriage license applications, and tax records. Thernstrom's data show that of sons born between 1850 and 1879, 36 percent of their fathers were in white-collar occupations, while 56 percent of the sons ended up in white-collar occupations. This may indicate more upward than downward mobility. In terms of occupational inheritance, sons of white-collar fathers were about twice as often found in white-collar occupations as were sons of blue-collar workers. Thus, the sons of white-collar fathers were advantaged, but in the face of extensive European immigration, so were the sons of white Anglo-Saxon Protestants no matter what their fathers' occupations.

The most extensive study of early social mobility in the United States was conducted by Rogoff (1953a, 1953b). In this study Rogoff compared mobility patterns in Indianapolis between 1910 and 1940 using a sample of about 10,000 marriage license applications. At this time the marriage license applications required a listing of the male's occupation and that of his father. Rogoff's findings were that intergenerational mobility was very similar in 1910 and 1940. More specifically, the rate of occupational inheritance was about the same in both years, and when changes in occupational distribution are considered (some jobs were reduced, others increased), upward and downward mobility were about the same in both years.

Rogoff's data have been subjected to extensive reanalysis by Duncan (1966) and Hauser and Featherman (1977) using more sophisticated statistical methods. Both studies have concluded that the mobility patterns between 1910 and 1940 were quite similar, although there were some minor variations not detected in Rogoff's analysis. Furthermore, Tully, Jackson, and Curtis (1970) have provided more recent mobility data for Indianapolis. Comparing the years 1910, 1940, and 1967, these researchers again conclude that the pattern of social mobility in Indianapolis has varied only slightly over these years.

Guest, Landale, and McCann (1989) were able to estimate the patterns of social mobility during the late 1800s in the United States through innovative use of the census data. From the 1880 census and the 1900 census they were able to match information from the fathers' 1880 occupational positions to that of 4,041 of the sons' positions in the 1900 census. Using these matched cases, they found that upward mobility was lower, and occupational inheritance was higher, in the late 1800s when compared with the 1962 and 1973 data studied by Blau and Duncan (1967) and by Featherman and Hauser (1978). However, when restricting the analysis to nonfarm families only, Guest et al. (1989) found only small differences in the amount of upward mobility and occupational inheritance during the late 1800s and 1962 or 1973.

Another method of detecting possible changes in mobility patterns over the years is *cohort analysis*. Using this method we compare workers of different ages to see if their mobility patterns have differed. Duncan (1965) has used such an analysis to compare workers entering the labor force between 1942 and 1952 and between 1952 and 1962. Hauser and Featherman (1977) have extended this analysis to workers entering the labor force between 1962 and 1972. These studies have indicated a slight increase in upward mobility since World War II, primarily due to an increase in higher-level occupations compared with lower-level occupations. This trend in the occupational structure, as we have seen, reversed in the 1980s, leading to the speculation that upward mobility had decreased and downward mobility had increased even further than Hout (1988) had found up to 1985.

Remember that traditional mobility studies do not give us an accurate picture of the top of the stratification system. There have been a few historical studies of the business elite that continue to show that mobility into the very top is quite restricted. For example, Mills (1963) examined the family backgrounds of the 19th-century business elite using biographical sources. He found that only 9.8 percent of the business leaders born before 1907 were from blue-collar origins, while 13.2 percent of the business leaders born between 1820 and 1829 had blue-collar origins.

In her sample, Keller (1953) found that only 3 percent of business leaders born around 1820 had lower white-collar or blue-collar origins. In another study, Bendix and Howton (1959) found that only about 1 to 2 percent of business leaders born between 1801 and 1890 had working-class origins. And in a massive study of the upper class in six steel and iron industry communities (Philadelphia, Bethlehem, Pittsburgh, Wheeling, Youngstown, and Cleveland) at the turn of the century, Ingham (1978) found mobility into the upper class to be almost nonexistent. All these studies were limited to small samples or local areas, but it is reasonable to conclude that mobility into the top of the stratification system has been very restricted over the years, especially for those below the upper nonmanual level.

## Comparative Mobility Studies

The primary task of cross-national studies of social mobility is to compare the differing rates or patterns of social mobility among nations. We want to know, for example, if the United States has more or less social mobility than France, Germany, or any other nation. Such a task would seem quite simple, involving nothing more than measuring the overall amount of social mobility in each country, then ranking the countries in terms of these measures. But the task is not so simple.

To begin with, comparative social mobility can be measured in many ways, with each measure telling us something different about the subject. There is little agreement as to which of the measures are most useful, or even which questions are most important to ask. Furthermore, if we are to compare nations with respect to movement up and down ranks in the occupational structure, the occupational structure of each nation must be somewhat comparable. If one nation has more occupational ranks than another, or if the gaps between ranks in one nation are larger or smaller than in another, a simple indicator comparing movement up and down the occupational ranks in two nations will be misleading (Matras 1980:413).

Finally, traditional mobility studies, and especially comparative studies (Matras 1980:408), are concerned with movement in the occupational structure. The assumption is that the occupational structure of each nation is equally important in the stratification system, that the conflict over valued resources in each society is focused on the occupational structure. Such an assumption, however, is not necessarily valid. Societies may differ with respect to how the distribution of rewards depends on a mixture of political authority, the ownership of property, racial caste, and occupational position. Recent research has indicated this is clearly the case in urban China (Lin and Bian 1991). As for another example, in Japan income is more related to a person's age and the size of the company where employed, and less to education and occupational status, compared with the United States (Ishida 1993).

Comparative studies of social mobility, therefore, must be interpreted with caution. The task is somewhat simplified when restricted to Western industrial nations with roughly the same level of economic development, but even here some tough questions remain. Can we say a physician's occupational position in the United States is comparable to that of a physician in England when their economic rewards differ greatly? Would intergenerational movement from college professor to physician in the United States and Germany be considered upward mobility in both countries? This is an even bigger question when comparing Japan and the United States. Physicians have similar incomes in Japan and the United States, but the income of college professors is much lower in Japan. However, the status of and respect for a college professor in Japan are much higher. Thus, should we consider the son of a physician in Japan who became a college professor to have experienced upward or downward mobility?

Comparative mobility studies are not meaningless. They can tell us something about stratification and social mobility in the United States compared with other industrial nations. For example, they can tell us if there is or is not a common pattern of social mobility shaped by the process of industrialization. They also can tell us if things can or cannot be done to influence the rate and direction of social mobility in the society to create more equality of opportunity. These types of questions can be answered with at least some degree of confidence with new studies of comparative social mobility published in the 1980s.

Some of the earlier, cruder comparative studies simply compared the overall rates of social mobility for countries, or compared rates of movement in and out of certain occupational positions in the society (for example, Miller 1960; Fox and Miller 1965a, 1965b; Lenski 1966). We know now, however, that we must adjust for differences in the level of economic development and differing shapes of the occupational structures. For example, countries in later stages of development tend to have fewer working-class positions and more upper-middle-class positions to move into, thus affecting mobility chances and rates.

Correcting for these differences, however, we can learn some important things about comparative rates of social mobility, as was done by Ishida et al. (1987), and by Ishida (1993) in their studies of the United States, Japan, and western Europe. For example, they found that Japan has a higher rate of upward mobility out of the working class, and less downward mobility into the working class, than the United States or European countries. Most different was the rate of working-class occupational inheritance for Japan (that is, the number of people who must stay in the working class when born there). The figure of working-class inheritance was only 21 percent in Japan, compared with 39 to 78 percent inheritance for the European countries. The overall rate of circulation mobility was not substantially different between Japan and the United States, even though there were differences at specific places in the occupational structure. We need to know why a greater percentage of working-class offspring in Japan move to higher positions, and we will examine the influence of the educational system in Japan (among other things) on opportunities for the working class in Chapter 15.

Much of the comparative mobility research in the 1980s and 1990s was directed toward the "Featherman-Jones-Hauser hypothesis" that nations at roughly similar intervals of economic development also should have similar circulation rates of social mobility once adjustments are made for differences in their occupational distributions (see Featherman, Jones, and Hauser 1975). What this hypothesis claims is that social mobility rates and the chance for people to move up or down are generally the same in all industrial nations, and these chances and rates of circulation mobility are shaped almost exclusively by aspects of industrialization.

Using data from 15 industrial nations, Hazelrigg and Garnier (1976) at first found some weak support for this hypothesis. Another study by Tyree, Semyonov, and Hodge (1979) also found only weak support for the hypothesis that rates of circulation mobility are similar in all advanced industrial nations. Their findings also made them suggest that wealth and power inequalities that differ among industrial nations may affect circulation mobility rates more than the Featherman-Jones-Hauser hypothesis would indicate.

In the most detailed study of comparative social mobility rates, Erikson and Goldthorpe (1992) have rejected some of the main components of the hypotheses (1) that all industrial nations are moving toward a common rate of social mobility, (2) that there is a common trend in all industrial nations of increasing rates of social mobility, and (3) that factors outside of the economy (such as political intervention) do not affect rates of social mobility. In their study of 12 industrial nations, Erikson and Goldthorpe have shown all three hypotheses are generally inaccurate. In their words, "Highly specific, historically formed features of national societies . . . [usually institutional rather than cultural] may create a distinctiveness in their fluidity patterns that cannot be dismissed as merely transient." Also, "Political intervention into social structures and processes is also capable of modifying fluidity patterns, even though the degree of its effectiveness must always be regarded as problematic" (Erikson and Goldthorpe 1992:180–181).

Other less extensive studies in the 1980s suggest similar rejection and modification of the Featherman-Jones-Hauser hypothesis of similar patterns of circulation mobility (Grusky and Hauser 1984; Slomczynski and Krauze 1987; Hauser and Grusky 1988). More specifically, these studies have found that the level of democracy and level of inequality can have more effect on the rates of circulation mobility than most sociologists had believed in the past. The important implication is that political action and government policy can create more equality of opportunity and that higher levels of inequality impede circulation mobility.

Some social scientists still have doubts about the ability of government policy to affect rates of social mobility and argue that the Featherman-Jones-Hauser thesis of no significant differences between industrial nations is correct (for example, Breen 1997). However, this is more the minority view, and most recently Wright's large multination study has given further evidence for the effects of government policies and other social factors on rates of social mobility. As Wright (1997:199) put it, "Our findings are also consistent with the view that social democratic welfare states can influence the operation of capitalist class mechanisms toward greater equality." Wright notes especially that in the United States, the most capitalist of the nations in his study, the wealthy are most able to protect their positions and the boundaries keeping others out are strongest.

A final issue of comparative mobility rates can now be addressed that was impossible to address before the massive Erikson and Goldthorpe (1992) study and Wright's (1997) class categories research—comparative rates of social mobility for women. In five of the European nations in their study—France, Germany, Hungary, Poland, and

Sweden—there were enough data on the social mobility patterns of women to make some reasonable generalizations. While there is variation across the nations in actual rates of mobility (fluidity), as noted earlier for men, they did find two patterns that were very close to what we previously described for women in the United States. If the family unit of women is considered (thus the position of the husband entered into the measure), what is most significant "is the evidence of how *little* women's experience of class mobility differs from that of men" (Erikson and Goldthorpe 1992:275). On the other hand, when we consider the occupations of women themselves in these five European nations, there is more social mobility compared with men, but much of it is downward to the lower white-collar or manual employment. As we saw in the previous chapter on the position of women in the United States, compared with men, these European women tend to experience more limited prospects of moving into top positions in the society, even when born into families at or close to the top of the occupational structure.

As we have already seen in discussing Wright's (1997) extensive research on social mobility, using property, occupational skill, and authority class categories, Wright has found some differences in the social mobility patterns for women across countries. For example, higher authority positions are *slightly* less difficult for women to attain in the United States compared to Europe (Wright 1997:192). Recent research in the United States on women engineers has also suggested that the glass-ceiling effect for American women may be becoming less of a problem for younger women (Morgan 1998). Across all nations studied, it is important to note, many factors such as cultural expectations and what could be called higher or lower levels of sexism affect the mobility chances of women. However, these other factors then interact with the system of social stratification, or class categories outlined here, in making their effects (Wright 1989).

Finally, with the new trend in income mobility studies we have already seen in Figures 12-2 and 12-3 that the overall income mobility for the United States today is lower than in European nations (except for Britain), that income mobility out of the bottom for men is lower in the United States, and that income mobility out of the bottom for women is similar in the United States compared to several other industrial societies.

The United States has the reputation of being the land of opportunity among many people in the world. The preceding studies, however, indicate that the United States is only about average with respect to its rate of circulation mobility, or equality of opportunity in general. In fact, none of the advanced capitalist societies are radically different with respect to their overall rates of circulation mobility. But in some places in the stratification system, especially toward the bottom, the chances of moving up are below average for the United States. In one sense, though, people who view the United States as the land of opportunity are correct: More than in most industrial nations, we can say that outsiders can get into the United States to compete for the chance of upward mobility.

## Social Mobility: A Conclusion

Our concern in the first half of this chapter has been social mobility—the pattern of vertical movement up and down the occupational structure. The importance of the subject cannot be overstressed, for the dynamics of class tell us a good deal about the mixture of ascription and achievement operating in a society. The social values of this country prescribe that achievement is good, and thus extensive mobility (when based on achievement) is good.

An examination of world history can also suggest that a relatively open society is usually good because it helps maintain social stability. Even extreme inequalities and class exploitation may be endured by those at the bottom when there is hope for a better future, if not for oneself, then at least for one's offspring. When inequality is high, the loss of such hope can have violent consequences, as it has throughout history and, as noted in beginning this chapter, Charles I found out in 1649 (Bearman and Deane 1992). With hope, those at the bottom are encouraged to work for individual solutions to their misery.

When hope of individual mobility is reduced, those at the bottom may conclude that the solution to their misery is found in collective challenge to the overall system of stratification, and violent class conflict may be the result. Therefore, social mobility, especially below the elite level, is functional for those at the top. Without it, their positions and rewards may be threatened.

We have noted that social mobility is somewhat extensive—at least in the occupational structure, and at least in the middle of the occupational structure—in virtually all Western industrial societies. A major part of this mobility is upward rather than downward, another condition that is productive of social stability. So far, most industrial societies have continued to expand and advance economically so that changes in the occupational structure (more jobs created at the top) have produced more upward than downward mobility (Matras 1980:412). Marx's prediction of the destruction of capitalism, at least so far, has been most incorrect on this point. But with inequality quite high in these capitalist societies, widespread and long-term economic stagnation leading to a sharp reduction of mobility could be dangerous, and we have noted that the United States may be moving in this direction, though very slowly at present.

A short summary of what we have discovered about social mobility in this country is now in order.

**1.** Occupational inheritance in the United States is fairly high at the top and bottom of the occupational structure. Between these extremes, inheritance is less and intergenerational mobility is relatively greater. But even at the top, movement (or recruitment) into the top occupational positions exists in the face of inheritance. This occurs because the positions toward the top are increasing (though not as much as positions at the bottom in recent years), with fewer offspring at the top helping produce more room for those below. Overall, most social mobility in the United States, both up and down, is short-range mobility. That is, when people are mobile, they usually rise or fall only to positions close to those of their family origins. This helps explain, for example, why those who move into the top positions are more likely to be close to the top in their origins.

**2.** We have very limited and inadequate information on mobility patterns at the very top. This lack of research seems surprising until we recognize that the bias of mobility research has led to a focus on occupational status, neglecting the importance of positions of ownership and/or control of the dominant means of production in the society. The research we do have is sometimes contradictory because of conflicting indicators of elite positions. There is some agreement that inheritance is very high among the upper and corporate classes, but the extent of recruitment into these classes below the elite level is in more dispute.

Whatever the rate of recruitment into the very top, it is no doubt what Domhoff (1998) and others call *sponsored mobility*. That is, recruitment is very selective to ensure that those brought into the very top will be supportive of the class inequalities and privilege attached to top positions. (Put another way, we would expect to find few top officers at General Motors who are in favor of extensive equality and restrictions on corporate-class power.)

**3.** Extensive data from 1962 and 1973 suggest that the mobility patterns for white males were very stable in that time period. Less extensive data also suggest that mobility patterns have been rather stable for at least 50 to perhaps 150 years. The major exception to this stability has been with farm occupations because they have been reduced sharply over the years. A slight exception to this stability was the very slow increase in upward mobility over the years. During the 1980s and 1990s, however, this pattern was changing with the shrinkage of middle-level jobs, and the most growth occurring in lower manual and low-paying jobs. This indicates that social mobility most likely slowed in the 1980s and 1990s, and there actually may have been more downward than upward mobility by the 1990s.The new trend in income mobility studies has confirmed this slowdown in upward mobility. Now, compared to almost all other industrial nations, there is more intergenerational income inheritance in the United States, and it is harder to move out of low-income positions in the United States compared to other countries.

**4.** The patterns of mobility for blacks and women have diverged from those of white males. The occupational structure has been much more rigid at the bottom for blacks. Occupational inheritance at the bottom has been the rule, but with extensive disinheritance at the top for blacks. But the 1973 figures did show some change, so the offspring of blacks at the top have a better chance to stay at the top, although still not as good a chance as whites. Again, however, recent data indicate that black improvements found in the late 1960s and 1970s were slowed or reversed in the 1980s.

**5.** Until recently, women have been neglected in mobility studies. But we now have more research showing that two mobility patterns must be distinguished for women. On one hand, when considering women in the labor force, their mobility diverges from that of white males because women are concentrated in lower nonmanual occupations. No matter where women originate (in terms of their fathers' occupations), they are likely to move up or move down to lower nonmanual positions. On the other hand, when we consider the occupational status of women to follow that of their husbands, the intergenerational mobility pattern is more similar to that of white males. The exception is that there is slightly more upward and downward mobility through marriage for women than through occupation for men.

## ✂ The Attainment Process

The primary focus of mobility research is on the amount and patterns of movement in the occupational structure. The studies, however, raise very important questions that cannot be answered directly through examination of mobility patterns alone. For example, in Blau and Duncan's study, what distinguishes the 56.8 percent who inherited their fathers' upper nonmanual positions from the 43.2 percent who were downwardly mobile? What distinguishes the 43.1 percent of sons with lower nonmanual fathers who moved up to upper nonmanual positions from those not upwardly mobile? In other words, what factors account for the attainment of positions in the occupational structure? We can conclude from many of the data presented in the preceding section that family background contributes a good deal to occupational attainment. But what is it about family background that influences attainment? And because it seems clear that family background factors alone do not determine attainment, what other factors influence attainment?

These questions are the province of what is usually called *status attainment* research. The focus, again, is on the process of attainment in the occupational status structure, although the attainment of income and education is included in much of this research. Despite a serious bias in functional theory, which we will examine at the end of this chapter, this research can help us understand a lot about why some people are favored over others by the stratification system. Common knowledge may tell us that educational attainment, intellectual ability, motivation, and the economic and educational standing of one's parents help influence occupational attainment. But we want to know which of these factors, among others, are more important. The question becomes extremely complex when we find that most of the significant factors—such as family background, education, performance on achievement tests, and aspirations—are interrelated.

## Status Attainment Models

In addition to achieving a breakthrough in mobility research, Blau and Duncan (1967) contributed much to early research on the process of status attainment. They did so primarily by employing a method of data analysis (path analysis) that allows us to disentangle the direct and indirect effects of a number of interrelated independent variables.

In this research Blau and Duncan were most concerned with the effects of father's education, father's occupation, and the son's education and first job on the occupational status of their respondents in the massive data collected in 1962. In summary, Blau and Duncan (1967:170) found that (1) father's education affects son's occupation through the son's educational attainment, (2) father's occupation also affects son's occupation through the son's educational attainment and the son's first job (with father's occupation having a small independent effect on son's 1962 occupation), and (3) of all the variables, the son's educational attainment produced the strongest effect on the son's 1962 occupation (partially through the effect of the son's education on the first job attained). In other words, fathers were able to influence their sons' 1962 occupation primarily by influencing their sons' educational achievement, and the sons' educational achievement also had a strong independent effect (independent of family background) on their 1962 occupational status. Together, the four independent variables explain about 43 percent of the variance in sons' 1962 occupational status. (About 57 percent of the variance, or what causes sons' occupational status, was not explained.)

Although Blau and Duncan's research on the status attainment process represented a significant breakthrough, much was left unexplained. For example, we want to know how the father's education and occupation affect the son's education, and we want to understand the other factors explaining the respondent's occupational status and education that were not included in the model. The Blau and Duncan model was soon expanded into what has come to be known as the *Wisconsin model* of status attainment.

## The Wisconsin Model

The Wisconsin model of status attainment adds several psychological variables to the original Blau and Duncan model. The addition of these sociopsychological variables can be seen as an attempt to specify how family background affects educational and occupational achievement, as well as an attempt to explain the model more fully. More specifically, these sociopsychological variables include the son's educational and occupational aspirations and the influence of significant others on these aspirations. Also included in the Wisconsin model are indicators of mental ability and academic performance.

Figure 12-4 represents the most cited path model of the Wisconsin school (see Sewell and Hauser, 1975, for the complete study). Several important findings are worth noting: First, in this model all the effects of the parents' socioeconomic status (SES), measured as discussed in Chapter 5, on the son's educational and occupational attainment operate through other variables. Most important, the parents' SES affects the son's significant others (for example, peer relations), which in turn strongly affect the son's educational (path = .508) and occupational (path = .441) aspirations.

Occupational aspirations have a weak effect on occupational attainment (path = .152), but educational aspirations have a strong effect on actual educational attainment (path = .457), with educational attainment having a strong direct effect on occupational attainment (path = .522). Also of note is that mental ability has a strong effect on academic performance, with academic performance directly (though more weakly) affecting aspirations and actual educational attainment. Overall, the model explains about 40 percent of the variance in occupational attainment and 57 percent of the variance in educational attainment.

Several studies using differing samples from the United States and other countries have generally confirmed the basic findings described here (see Wilson and Portes 1975; Alexander, Eckland, and Griffin 1975; Ishida 1993). And in a reexamination of the Wisconsin model, Warren and Hauser (1997) have confirmed the original research, but demonstrate that the effects of parents on their children are not extended to grandparents. In other words, high or low levels of income or education attained by grandparents have no effect on their grandchildren when the direct effects of parents' income and education are considered. In summary, what these studies indicate is that there is a mixture of ascriptive and achievement factors that helps explain educational and occupational attainment. The ascriptive effect of family SES works most importantly through significant others on aspirations, while aspirations, in turn, directly affect educational attainment. But educational attainment has the strongest effect on occupational attainment, and educational attainment, it is argued, is in part an achievement variable (not completely determined by family SES).

Studies from the Wisconsin tradition of status attainment research have made important contributions to our understanding of how significant others influence who

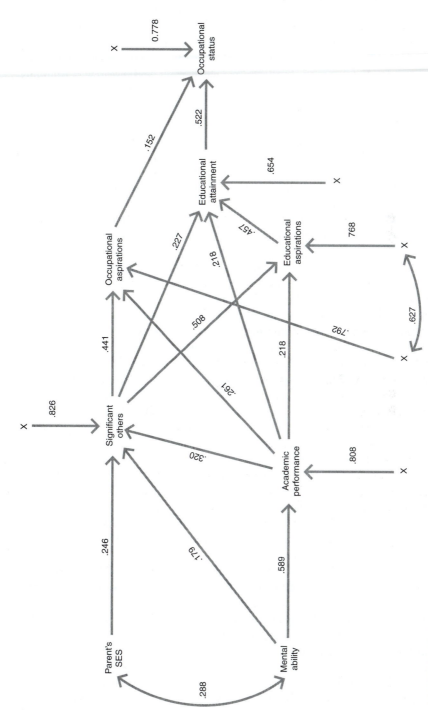

**FIGURE 12-4** *Path Model of Status Attainment Process from the Wisconsin School*

*SOURCE:* Sewell, Haller, and Ohlendorf (1970:1023).

375

gets ahead. Also, the importance of educational and occupational aspirations in the process of status attainment has been demonstrated by this research tradition. However, the status attainment perspective in general contains several shortcomings, many of which are related to the individualistic perspective of the tradition (Horan 1978; Smith 1990; Sorensen 1990). The status attainment perspective has neglected the extent to which the structure of unequal opportunity sets limits on achievement, and researchers from this perspective have often underestimated the full effect of ascriptive factors such as family background. In addition, status attainment models have been very weak in their attempts to explain income attainment (see Sewell and Hauser 1975).

As we have seen, the Wisconsin model of status attainment has primarily added psychological or attitude variables to explain why some people attain more education and occupational status. Recent research, however, is showing that nonpsychological variables are much more important than assumed by the Wisconsin model. For example, research is increasingly showing the importance of what is called *social capital* and *cultural capital*. "Capital" means something a person owns, but not what would first come to mind—property. Social capital refers to interpersonal networks, friendship networks, and such things as networks of family relations. Research shows that the more of these personal ties people have, the more help they are able to get finding jobs, getting references to jobs, and even help learning the job (McDonald and Elder 2006; Granovetter 1995; Portes 1998; Podolny and Baron 1997; Bian 1997; De Graaf, and Flap 1988; Okamoto 2003; Mouw 2003). As Wilson has found, for example, one problem for poor blacks today is that the upwardly mobile black families have left poor neighborhoods, taking away valuable social connections (Wilson 1996). Cultural capital refers not only to what a person knows in the sense of math and science, but also "higher culture" such as knowledge of art, music, classical dance, and so on. In the process of being evaluated by significant others, such as school teachers, the possession of such cultural capital can give a child a more favorable evaluation, which can lead to favorable treatment and a cycle producing more actual educational achievement (Bourdieu 1977; Bourdieu and Passeron 1990; DiMaggio 1982; DiMaggio and Mohr 1985; Aschaffenburg and Mass 1997). Both cultural capital and social capital are strongly related to a person's class background, and thus the class background effects of class and status attainment (or rather class ascription) are greater than the status attainment models have estimated in the past.

As for the underestimation of ascriptive factors in the attainment process, a reanalysis of several studies from the status attainment perspective found that family background, in fact, explains almost *50 percent* of the variance in occupational status attainment (Jencks et al. 1979:214–217). In addition, this reanalysis of the data suggests that education is not the great avenue of achievement in our society the status attainment perspective would have us believe (see Jencks et al. 1972:135; 1979:225). For example, recent studies show that the advantage of being born into a more highly educated family has a greater impact on children's academic achievement than previously known. If the educational attainments of mothers are added to that of fathers (which was not done in earlier studies), the advantage or disadvantage of their offspring is even greater (Beller 2009). In summarizing all their findings from reanalysis of status attainment research, Jencks et al. (1979:82) wrote, "If we define 'equal opportunity' as a situation in which sons born into different families have the same chances of success, our data show that America comes nowhere near achieving it."

Before pursuing a more general critique of status attainment research, we need to give more attention to education as a mediating structure in the attainment process. By doing so, we can see how some of the education-related factors found to be important by the status attainment perspective operate and how educational attainment helps further inequality and class inheritance in our society.

## Education as Mediating Structure

All sides in the debate agree on the importance of education both in promoting achievement and in reproducing class inequalities through inheritance (Aschaffenburg and Mass 1997; Bourdieu and Passeron 1990). They also agree that education is becoming more important for both achievement and ascription as our society becomes more advanced and the education level of the general population increases (Featherman and Hauser 1978:227–233). Recent historical research has suggested that in European countries during the first two-thirds of the 20th century, higher educational attainment for lower-class children was a realistic means for higher occupational attainment compared to their parents (Breen et al. 2009). But to the extent this was also the case in the United States, it has become less so in recent years. In this section we examine briefly some of the factors that influence educational attainment, beginning with the earliest years of schooling and following this process through the college years.

### *The Early Years of Schooling*

The road to higher educational attainment begins very early (Entwisle, Alexander, and Olson 2005). Children from higher-class families are more likely to have a home environment that provides the intellectual skills they need to do well in school (Duncan et al. 1998; Jencks et al. 1972:138; Mercy and Steelman 1982). In a similar fashion, children from two-parent families are advantaged (Biblarz and Raftery 1993; Astone and McLanahan 1991). They have toys and books that give them an early advantage, and they are more likely to see their parents engaged in activities such as reading and writing—thus, the image that these are valued skills. Because of all this, studies indicate that middle-class children are already ahead of lower-class children in intellectual ability before the first year of school (Jencks et al. 1972). Intellectual capacity (as distinguished from educational achievement) is to some degree biologically inherited, but the best estimate is that only about 45 percent of IQ is biologically determined, and IQ is only weakly related to social class (Jencks et al. 1972:65, 81; Martin 1998).

By the time children are in school and even preschool and first grade (Entwisle, Alexander, and Olson 2005), the process of separating the winners from the losers, and what is expected of boys versus girls, becomes even clearer (Jencks et al. 1979). An important factor in this process is teacher expectations; several studies have shown that teachers expect more of children from higher-class backgrounds and that the differential treatment of children in terms of teacher expectations leads to better performance among these children (Rosenthal and Jacobson 1968; Rist 1970; Stein 1971; Good and Brophy 1973). There have been some negative reports on the importance of teacher expectations in children's performance (see Claiborn 1969), but the weight of evidence remains in favor of this argument.

Perhaps more important in separating the winners from the losers in the early years of schooling is the practice of tracking. Even though tracking may be more extensive in European nations with long histories of class restrictions on educational attainment (Rubinson 1986), it has been estimated that about 85 percent of U.S. public schools follow the practice of placing children in different tracks that prepare some students for college and others for vocational skills that do not lead to college (Jencks et al. 1972:33).

There have been numerous studies on both the factors that influence track placement and the outcomes of track placement. Recent research indicates the complexity of tracking by showing how schools are not all alike in what determines track placement of children (Gamoran 1992) and how characteristics of the teachers and school organization themselves affect track placement (Kilgore 1991). As for the factors that help determine track placement, it was commonly believed that track placement is directly influenced by the class background of children. But such a direct influence of class must be rejected as overly simple. Measured intellectual skills have been found to be most responsible for track placement (Jencks et al. 1972:35; Heyns 1974), although class background is also involved (Alexander, Cook, and McDill 1978:65). But the effect of track placement, because cognitive skills and academic performance are influenced by class background, is the same; tracking tends to separate children by class background and race (Lucas 2001; McPortland 1968; Jencks et al. 1972:35).

Many outcomes of track placement have been found. Some studies indicate that children in the college preparatory track, or higher track, improve in academic achievement over the years, while those in the lower track perform at lower levels (Rosenbaum 1975; Persell 1977; Alexander and Cook 1982), although a few studies show that this is not always the case (see Jencks et al. 1972:106–107). But also important, children in the higher track are less likely to drop out of school (Schafer and Olexa 1971; Gamoran and Mare 1989), have higher educational aspirations (Alexander et al. 1978), and are more likely to attend college (Ainsworth and Roscigno 2005; Jencks et al. 1972:34; Alexander et al. 1978). In conclusion, we can say that tracking works to reinforce class differences and has an independent effect of further differentiating children in terms of family background (Alexander et al. 1978:57; Gamoran and Mare 1989).

Finally, much has been written about the importance of school quality on later educational attainment. The assumption has been that lower-class children more often attend schools of poor quality that prepare them less well for higher educational attainment. This assumption, however, was challenged in a famous study by Jencks et al. (1972). More recent research, however, using a long-term panel study following children over the course of their education shows that where one goes to school (inner-city slum, suburbs, or rural areas) does in fact matter extensively (Roscigno, Tomaskovic-Devey, and Crowley 2006). Children in inner cities are more likely to do poorly in the school environment and drop out before finishing high school. Also, recent research has shown that how long a child lives in poverty and an inner city has a big impact on educational attainment (Wagmiller et al. 2006). The longer a child lives in poverty, the lower the educational attainment.

School quality, however, is difficult to measure with much precision. Research has found some differences in occupational and income attainment due to school quality. Griffin and Alexander (1978) conducted a 1970 follow-up study of 947 males originally studied in 1955. They found that school quality accounted for 11 percent of the variance in occupational attainment and 15 percent of the variance in income attainment among the sample. More recently, Mayer (2001) examined the impact of growing income inequality since the 1970s on inequalities of educational attainment. She found that inequality in educational attainment increased by income level, mostly because of differences in school quality where low-income versus higher-income children went to school.

## *Family Background and College Attendance*

With access to higher occupational positions becoming more dependent on educational attainment, college attendance is a key mechanism of class achievement or ascription. Those who finish college have a 49 percent occupational advantage over those who do not, while those who finish high school have only a 15 to 29 percent advantage over those who do not (Jencks et al. 1979). With respect to income, the advantage of college graduates is even greater, and growing. According to Census Bureau figures, for example, in 1979 a male college graduate received 49 percent more in income compared with someone with only a high school education. By 1999 college graduates received almost 100 percent more income than high school graduates (U.S. Bureau of the Census, *Educational Attainment in the United States, Update,* 2000). This income gap between high school graduates and college graduates has continued to expand as of 2009 (U.S. Bureau of the Census 2010a). The most important questions, therefore, become what influences college attendance and college completion.

Several of the class-related factors described previously are important in college attendance. Figure 12-5 shows that family income is certainly a key to attending a top university in the United States. It is not until the upper 25 percent income category that more young people go to a top university compared to a junior college, and at that level, almost 75 percent of offspring do so. But despite the fact that university tuition is generally much more costly in the United States compared to Japan and Europe (where tuition is almost free), it is more than just parents' income. As the Wisconsin model of status attainment indicates, much of the effect of class background on college attendance may be through educational aspirations. Sewell and Hauser (1975:186) found that sociopsychological variables such as aspirations explain about 60 to 80 percent of the relationship between class background and educational attainment.

Educational aspirations, which show an important relationship to college attendance, are influenced by parents and significant others such as the peer group. Higher-class parents are more likely to encourage their children to go to college and provide role models leading to higher educational aspirations (Sewell et al. 1970). But close in importance to parents in influencing educational aspirations are the peer group (Sewell 1971) and class differences in youth subcultures (Hagan 1991). When the peer group is made up of children whose parents are doctors, lawyers, and other higher professionals, the higher aspirations of this peer group will affect others in the group. Thus, access to privileged peers is almost as important as access to privileged parents in educational attainment.

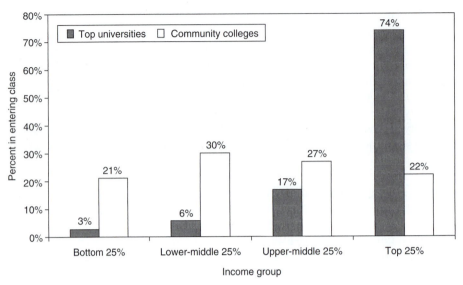

**FIGURE 12-5** *Income Category of Students Entering Top Universities Compared to Community Colleges in the United States*

*SOURCES:* Carnevale and Rose (2004); Mishel, Bernstein, and Allegretto (2007: Figure 2E).

If college attendance were based primarily on intellectual skills, there would be much less class inheritance than exists today. But class inequality operates to retard the relationship between intellectual ability and college attendance. In a study of 9,007 high school students, Sewell and Shah (1968) found that 91.1 percent of the students with high intelligence and high-class backgrounds attended college. However, only 40.1 percent of the students with high intelligence but low-class backgrounds attended college.

Looking at the other end of the intelligence rank, 58 percent of the students with low intelligence and high-class backgrounds attended college, but only 9.3 percent of those with low intelligence and low-class backgrounds attended college. No matter what their intelligence, 84.2 percent of the students from higher-class backgrounds attended college, and only 20.8 percent of those with lower-class backgrounds attended college. In other words, class background is strongly related to college attendance (Featherman and Hauser 1978:309). Part of the reason for class background effects simply involves money: Steelman and Powell (1991) have found parents' income level and how many other children they have are most important in the parents' willingness to pay for their children's college education. The next important factor was whether or not the parents themselves had parents who supported them while in college, thus indicating cross-generational class background effects.

A final question pertains to college completion. A good indicator of completing college is a student's college grade point average (GPA) (Barger and Hall 1965; Stanfiel 1973). Several studies, however, have found class background to be a very weak predictor of college GPA (Barger and Hall 1965; Bayer 1968; Labovitz 1975). Figure 12-6,

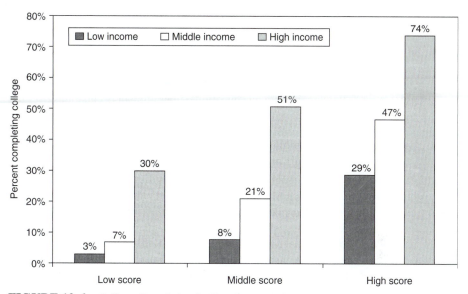

**FIGURE 12-6** *College Completion by Test Scores and Parents' Income*

SOURCES: Fox, Connolly, and Snyder (2005); Mishel, Bernstein, and Allegretto (2007: Figure 2F).

though, suggests there is still something about class, or at least parents' income, that is related to university completion. University entrance exam scores are related to university completion, but at every test score level, parents' income is also important for college completion. Thus, both intelligence (or whatever is measured by college entrance exams) and parents' class background are important in college educational achievement.

## A Conflict Perspective of Education

We have seen that education can promote both ascription and achievement. Functional theory stresses the achievement aspect of education whereby important skills are attained by the most talented, who are then prepared to fill important positions in the society (Davis and Moore 1945). The full validity of this functional view of education must be questioned, however, when we find (as noted earlier) that the offspring of higher-class families are much more likely to go to college no matter what their intellectual ability. Furthermore, the functional view must be questioned when we find that getting a college degree is much more important than just attending college in attaining higher occupational status and income. In other words, it is questionable whether the only function of college is providing skills when we find that the final year of college completed is much more important for occupational attainment than the third or second year of college.

Finally, Collins (1971) has provided evidence showing that the educational upgrading of occupations over the years is not always explained by any increase in the technical requirements of these occupations. Thus, more education is needed to obtain most jobs, but this is not simply explained by the technical requirements of the job. What, then, is most important about college completion?

A conflict view of education is partially supported by the research showing that higher-class offspring are much more likely to go to college. This may indicate that education is a means of class conflict; that is, in the conflict over valued rewards, the higher-class members are better able to ensure that their offspring win through education (Bourdieu and Passeron 1990).

Furthermore, following the data on educational upgrading of occupations over the years, Collins (1971) argues that education is a means of maintaining class boundaries. For example, in the past, when college degrees were much more limited and the middle class typically had only high school degrees, middle-class occupations required a high school degree. But as more of the middle class obtained college degrees and more of the working class obtained high school degrees, middle-class occupations were typically upgraded so that a college degree was required for employment. Thus, the class boundaries of middle-class occupations were maintained through an upgrading of educational requirements.

Collins's data indicate that the same process has occurred with working-class, upper-middle-class, and elite occupations. As might be expected, this process of educational upgrading of occupations has produced a reduction in the occupational and income return for each year of education (Featherman and Hauser 1978:223; Jencks et al. 1979:228). Whereas a college degree once brought an elite occupational position with elite pay, it now brings a middle-class position with middle-class pay. From the conflict perspective, education is a certification of class membership more than of technical skills.

However, even to the extent that some lower-class offspring are upwardly mobile through education, the conflict view of education may be supported when we consider what the educational system does. If the educational system does not function primarily to teach occupationally related skills, as the data indicate (Diamond and Bedrosian 1970; Jencks et al. 1972:187; Rawlins and Ulman 1974), it certifies that people have learned to respect the authority and accept the values, ideals, and system of inequality in the occupational structure (Bowles and Gintis 1976). As Collins (1971:1011) puts it, "Educational requirements for employment can serve both to select new members for elite positions who share the elite culture and, at a lower level of education, to hire lower and middle employees who have acquired a general respect for these elite values and styles."

Education does provide some knowledge and skills, and certainly needs to do more of this in the United States compared with other industrial nations. But because the educational system requires some conformity to authority, those who succeed in the educational system—no matter what their class background—are certified as potential workers who can respect authority divisions in the occupational structure. Thus, education provides two important services for higher-class members: It is a means of class inheritance and a means of selecting responsible new recruits for higher occupational positions.

## The Conflict Perspective: A Critique and Reinterpretation of Status Attainment Research

We began this chapter by noting the relatively short history of status attainment research. Since the early 1960s much progress has been made, but since the mid-1970s critical research also has increased rapidly. The general critiques of status attainment research fall into four main (though overlapping) categories: (1) Status attainment models have limited explanatory power; (2) they attempt to explain the wrong thing (that is, occupational status); (3) they are focused on individual characteristics or human capital variables rather than equally important structural variables; and (4) most of the findings from this research can be better (or at least equally) explained by a conflict (or allocation) perspective rather than a functional theory of social stratification. We will consider each of these general critiques in turn.

## *Limited Explanatory Power*

As noted earlier, in his now famous work Jencks brought together data from several status attainment studies. Jencks's (see primarily Jencks et al. 1972) reanalysis of the combined data stressed how little we really know about the process of getting ahead in the United States. The limited explanatory power of status attainment models was shown in two ways. First, taking the current methodological perspective of these models, combining all the variables explains only about 50 percent of the variance in occupational status and 40 percent of the variance in income attainment. Second, from another methodological perspective, when we compare the variance in intergenerational attainment within occupational and income divisions, the data show almost as much variance within categories as between categories.

The first point is not difficult to understand, but an example of the second point may be helpful. Consider the general occupational categories of upper nonmanual and lower nonmanual. What Jencks's research shows is that the family backgrounds and current income of those *within* upper nonmanual positions differ almost as much as the backgrounds and income *between* upper nonmanual and lower nonmanual position holders.

In another work (Jencks et al. 1979) Jencks reanalyzed additional data to conclude that almost 50 percent of the variance in occupational status is explained by family background alone. Still, much of what we know about who gets ahead is unexplained. In the face of this lack of explanatory power, Jencks first emphasized (Jencks et al. 1972) that luck is very important in attaining occupational status and income. In his second major work on the subject (Jencks et al. 1979:306–311), Jencks has admitted that structural economic forces not measured in his work may help explain much of the inequality in occupation and income, although luck in a limited sense is again given some credit.

The process of attainment is very complex, involving much of what can be called luck on a personal level. We can use the example of two brothers, each with a college degree. One brother finishes college to become a low-level manager in a firm that goes out of business in a couple of years, leaving him unemployed for a time and forced to take a lower-level job. The other brother has difficulty finding a job at first, but happens to hear about a possible job opening as a low-level manager with a rapidly growing firm. In the interview for this job, the second brother finds the boss to be from his old college fraternity. This brother's luck again holds out when he unknowingly says the right things to impress his future boss during the interview. But this brother's luck becomes even greater when events in the modern world system become more favorable to his new company. Specifically, the Asian economic crisis hits in the late 1990s, putting several competing firms in South Korea, Taiwan, and Japan out of business, and Europe stays in economic stagnation, harming other competing firms in that part of the world. This second brother gets the job, and because of the rapid expansion of the firm, is soon promoted to fill a mid-level management position in a new factory opened by the firm. A few years after graduating from college, the first brother has a low-status job making $25,000 a year, while the second brother has a mid-level management position paying $150,000 a year.

In a very general sense we might say that these two brothers are separated by luck—luck in joining the right firm in a new global economy, in saying the right thing during an interview, and in one having a boss who respects the old school ties. Many such factors beyond the control of specific people can influence occupational and income attainment. However, if we move from the individualistic focus of current status attainment models, we find political and economic forces that can be measured and that can help us explain more of the variance in occupational and income attainment.

In other words, luck may lead a person to be in the right place at the right time in order to land a job with the right firm. But when we move from an individual level to a higher level of sociological analysis, various structural and world system variables can help us explain more of the variance in occupational and income attainment. These other structural variables will be considered later. But first there is a problem with the traditional focus on occupational status that leads to limited explanatory power in status attainment research.

## The Limitations of Occupational Status

Earlier chapters have noted the problems associated with the functional theory's concept of occupational status or prestige. These problems have two main roots.

**1.** Within the occupational structure, status ranks do not always correspond to more important ranks based on job complexity or skill and authority (Wilson 1978; Spaeth 1979; Robinson and Kelley 1979; Lord and Falk 1980; Kalleberg and Griffin 1980; Wright 1997). Also, the functional view of stratification based on status ranks assumes a free, open market (see, for example, Davis and Moore 1945). But as Horan's (1978) critique demonstrates, such an assumption must be questioned. For example, two occupations may be ranked equally in terms of status, but competition in one may be restricted, making it more difficult to enter the occupation and making it higher paying.

**2.** Previous chapters have stressed that the stratification system includes inequalities based on authority and property as well as occupation. Thus, even to the extent that status attainment models have furthered our understanding of attainment with respect to the occupational structure, as Wright's (1997) research shows, authority and property divisions have been neglected. The neglect of these other divisions is important because they, too, have an influence on income and occupational attainment.

Considering the first problem, we can begin by noting that in one sense it can be quite misleading to suggest that intergenerational mobility has occurred when a son moves from his father's upper manual or skilled blue-collar position to a lower nonmanual or lower white-collar position (Willhelm 1979). The son's lower nonmanual or white-collar position may very well be lower in job complexity, authority, and pay than the father's upper manual or skilled blue-collar position. True, the lower nonmanual position is most likely ranked higher in prestige; but there is much more to occupational divisions than prestige. Let us look at some research.

Spaeth (1979) measured vertical occupational divisions in three ways—occupational status, job skill level or complexity, and authority. He found that the authority and complexity measures were more strongly correlated to each other than to occupational status. Thus, occupational status cannot be assumed to be an indicator of job authority or skill level. More specific to the process of educational attainment, Spaeth (1976) has also shown that father's job complexity has an important independent effect on the educational attainment of offspring.

Other research has examined how the traditional focus on occupational status has resulted in an inability to explain much of the variance in income attainment. The full Wisconsin status attainment model presented by Sewell and Hauser (1975) could explain only a very small part of the variance in income. If occupational status is important, including occupational status in the model should explain a good deal more than 7 percent of the variance in income. In a more limited study, Wilson (1978) constructed an index of *occupational power* and an index of education based on the curriculum needed to attain positions of occupational power (rather than occupational status). Using these new measures, Wilson was able to explain 46 percent of the variance in income in his sample.

We noted the research by Kalleberg and Griffin (1980), Robinson and Kelley (1979), and Wright (1997; Wright and Perrone 1977) in a previous chapter. These studies examined the relationship between income attainment and stratification divisions based on occupational authority and ownership of the means of production (property relations), as well as occupational status. All these studies showed that we can explain much more of the variance in income attainment by including authority and property divisions, although more than half of the variance in income remains unexplained by all of these factors. Equally important, Robinson and Kelley (1979) found that the variance in occupational authority attainment is explained more by the father's level of occupational authority than by the father's occupational status. In other words, the process of occupational authority attainment and the process of occupational status attainment are not identical. The same conclusion was supported when this study was conducted in France (Robinson and Garnier 1985), and also when Kerckhoff, Campbell, and Trott (1982) examined the multidimensional aspects of status attainment in England. Attainment in occupation, education, authority position, and capitalist property ownership were affected by different combinations of factors, and this was especially so for the attainment of property. Finally, in a five-nation study by Robinson (1984), we find that status attainment differs for each of the class categories described by Wright (1978a, 1978b). For example, education is important in attaining occupational authority, but education is not much help in attaining ownership and control of property or a position in the petite bourgeoisie.

Other research (Wright 1978b; Wolf and Fligstein 1979; Treiman and Roos 1983) has shown that the process of income attainment for women and blacks differs from that of white males in part because of the effects of occupational authority. Even when women and blacks have occupational status equal to that of white males, their income tends to be lower because their occupational authority tends to be lower. With respect to education, equal amounts of education (compared with that of white males) gained less occupational authority for women and blacks.

## Global and Economic Structural Influences on the Attainment Process

It was noted earlier that Jencks (Jencks et al. 1979) to some degree now recognizes the impact of economic structural variables on the attainment process; Hauser (1980) has also admitted as much, at least for income attainment. In our imaginary example of two equally educated brothers, part of the luck that separated these brothers was in being employed by different firms: one firm did well; the other went under. The dual-economy research discussed in previous chapters is directly relevant to income attainment, as is recent research on the differing organizational structures of specific firms.

The problem with standard status attainment models in this respect is that they are focused on personal characteristics. The human capital resources of people—such as job skills, education, experience, intelligence, and perhaps even aspirations—are assumed by these models to be the most important, if not the only, factors relevant to the attainment of occupational status and income (Knottnerus 1987; Smith 1990). But impersonal economic forces beyond the control of most people have a hand in determining the payoff of human capital resources. For example, Grusky (1983) and South and Xu (1990) have shown that regional economic differences can produce differences in the occupational attainment process.

Briefly reviewing the dual-economy research, corporations can be divided roughly between core and periphery organizations. The core firms are bigger, make more profits, have more control over their markets, pay higher wages, and are more likely to be unionized than periphery firms. The dual-economy research has found that workers with the same occupational status may receive differing incomes, depending on core or periphery location, even when other human capital variables such as education and experience are controlled (see Beck et al. 1978; Tolbert et al. 1980; Beck et al. 1980; Weakleim 1990; South and Xu 1990; Sakamoto and Chen 1991). Also, this research has shown that education brings different amounts of income, depending on core or periphery location, and that movement from periphery to core employment is restricted if the family background or a person's first job is located in the periphery sector (Tolbert 1982; Jacobs 1983).

Other research has shown that characteristics of individual firms besides core or periphery location have an impact on the occupational and income attainment process (Stolzenberg 1978; Baron and Bielby 1980, 1984; Kalleberg and Van Buren 1996; DiPrete and McManus 1996). One important difference between firms is the degree of bureaucratization. When firms are more bureaucratized, there are more occupational ranks from top to bottom, thus allowing an employee to move farther in terms of occupational and income attainment (compared with someone in a less bureaucratized firm). Also important is whether or not jobs are in new growth industries or in declining industries (Hachen 1992).

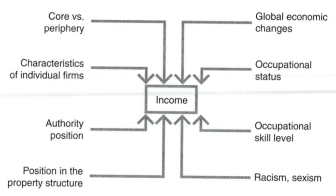

**FIGURE 12-7**    *Structural and Individual Variables Affecting Income Attainment*

With respect to income and occupational attainment, Baron and Bielby (1980) suggest that at least five levels of analysis are important—the general economy, the industry sector (for example, the core-periphery division), individual firms, specific occupations across firms, and individual workers. At each level of analysis above individual workers, there are influences that can affect the occupational income and income attainment of employees independent of their human capital resources. The conclusion is that much of the unexplained variance in occupation and income found by traditional status attainment research is due to these structural-level variables.

Figure 12-7 summarizes what a number of studies have shown to be important in helping explain income attainment. But some variables in Figure 12-7 have been neglected by previous studies of occupational and income attainment. For example, it seems obvious that racism and sexism continue to have their effects in this country and others. We have seen how much of the effects of racism and sexism operate through the stratification system, but still there are independent effects of both that reduce the opportunities of nonwhites and women. As we have seen already, and will see in more detail in Chapter 14, changes in the modern world system certainly affect people's life chances. Much of the growing income inequality in the United States has been caused by changes in the position of the United States in this modern world system. Further research is needed that combines the effects of all these variables on income attainment, but the development of research critical of status attainment models has yet to reach this stage.

## A Conflict Perspective: Allocation versus Attainment

A *final* critique of status attainment research is more general. In this critique the findings and variables included in status attainment research are less the issue than the *interpretation* of the findings. From the perspective of status attainment research, the individual is considered "relatively free to move within the social system, his attainments being determined by what he chooses to do and how well he does it" (Kerckhoff 1976:369; see also Knottnerus 1987; Kerckhoff 1989).

This assumption is directly confronted by a conflict perspective that considers *allocation* rather than attainment to be the most important process: "An allocation model views the individual as relatively constrained by the social structure, his attainments being determined by what he is permitted to do" (Kerckhoff 1976:369). Also, class power inequalities are of central importance (Goldthorpe 1987; Wong 1992). The most important aspect of social structure that constrains the free movement of people is the corporate structure (Collins 1975; Willhelm 1979; Beck et al. 1980). The needs of this corporate structure and capitalism, rather than the desires of individual actors, determine what positions require occupants, and people are selected in terms of what is needed in filling these positions (Goldman and Tickamyer 1984). Put another way, the focus of the allocation perspective is on control by dominant agencies; the selection process is based on their needs.

Another argument usually associated with the allocation perspective pertains to the criteria relevant to the selection process. Status attainment models stress that occupational attainment is based on marketable skills obtained through the educational system (although, of course, occupational status is measured in this research). The allocation perspective, in contrast, stresses that selection is based on class cultural criteria.

As Collins (1975:452) puts it, "The conflict model proposes that careers take place within an ongoing struggle of cultural groups to control positions by imposing their standards upon selection. Success comes to individuals who fit into the culture of those who hold the resources to control old positions or create new ones." Class inheritance in the occupational structure doesn't always prevail. The mobility data would not support such a view. Rather, Collins is saying that when upward intergenerational mobility does occur, it is because the mobile person fits the cultural criteria of the higher-class position.

The most important certifying agent in this process is the educational system. As we saw earlier, the conflict view is that success in the educational system comes not solely with cognitive ability but also with the ability to learn higher-class values and lifestyles. As Collins (1975:454) again states, "The evidence best fits the interpretation that education is important, not for providing technical skill but for membership in a cultural group which controls access to particular jobs" (see also Collins 1971, 1979).

Thus, occupational inheritance is relatively high because the offspring of higher-occupational fathers are better able to succeed in the educational system. But upward mobility does occur because some of the lower-class offspring have been able to acquire higher-class cultural traits through the educational system. Both the status attainment and the allocation perspectives agree that education is the key to occupational inheritance and mobility—but for different reasons.

We can now point up the differing perspectives with an example. Consider the case of a young man whose father is an unskilled factory worker. This young man was able to work his way through college to attain an advanced degree and a job as a chemical engineer. The status attainment perspective would view this case as one in which social mobility occurred because of the aspirations and talent of this young man. In other words, through free competition the motivation and talent of this individual led to his success.

The allocation perspective, in contrast, would argue that the corporate structure at the time had a need for chemical engineers. This young man was selected for the position because he was able to show acceptance and conformity to the dominant class values through success in the educational system. His entry into this particular occupational career was influenced because, while in college, he recognized that he could make a living by pursuing this career rather than one as a social worker. Social workers were not needed at the time because the poor were not rioting and the welfare system was contracting. Thus, the needs of the corporate structure in global competition strongly influenced the occupational career of this young man, and the class system and its criteria influenced the selection of this young man.

In an excellent summary of the status attainment and allocation perspectives, Kerckhoff (1976) has shown that to a large degree both perspectives fit the existing *individual-level* data generated by the status attainment research. As noted in our earlier discussion of social scientific paradigms, social reality is complex, and it is the purpose of theory to explain as much of this reality as possible. We have described the many problems associated with the status attainment perspective. Because of these problems, and because of the additional research reviewed earlier, the allocation perspective contained within a conflict theory of social stratification in an increasingly global economy has been favored.

# The Conflict View of Attainment: A Conclusion

In the second half of this chapter we have reviewed one of the most impressive bodies of empirical research in the study of social stratification. In the past 30 years or so, our knowledge of who gets ahead has grown rapidly. Most of this impressive growth in knowledge began through the use of causal analysis by researchers concerned with building models of the status attainment process. This development was first stimulated by Blau and Duncan (1967), but it was later expanded by the Wisconsin school through the addition of sociopsychological variables that linked family background variables to educational and occupational attainment. The Wisconsin model of status attainment stresses that significant others, ability, and aspirations link family background to educational and occupational attainment.

The Wisconsin model, however, was shown to have limitations. First, its stress on occupational status creates problems in that status is not most important in the occupational structure. Second, the Wisconsin model has limited explanatory power. Much of this problem results from a stress on individual-level human capital resources. The effects of the corporate structure (such as the dual economy and authority relations), as well as the modern world system, are also necessary in understanding occupational and, especially, income attainment.

At present much more research is needed that combines the variables traditionally included in status attainment models with these structural and global effects. When such research is done, we would expect that much more of the variance in occupational and income attainment can be explained. Luck is doubtless a factor in who gets ahead, but a good deal of this luck can be explained by a more careful consideration of structural features in our stratification system.

Finally, we described how an allocation perspective based on a conflict view of social stratification can explain the data generated by status attainment research. Because the status attainment perspective is based on a functional view of social stratification and because a functional view has been shown to be inadequate in several other respects in previous chapters, we have concluded that the allocation perspective should be favored.

People do compete for and achieve some success through their motivation and abilities. But it is competition for success structured by the needs of the overall corporate structure. From a more individualistic level of analysis, both achievement and ascription can be found. In his analysis of attainment research, however, Jencks et al. (1979) concluded that almost 50 percent of the variance in occupational attainment is explained by family background. In the process of getting ahead, those with parents who are already ahead have the edge.

Chapters 6 through 11 examined the characteristics, structural bases, rewards, and power of the major class groupings in the United States. This chapter examined the dynamics of class in this country—the amount and means of class inheritance and mobility. We have a final important point to examine about our class system and social stratification in general. We need to know how class inequalities are maintained. The question becomes important when we find that those on top receive a highly disproportionate share of the rewards and are in a much better position to ensure that their offspring inherit their favored position. What prevents those toward the bottom from resisting such a state of affairs? What prevents them from trying to achieve a basic change in the stratification system? We will turn to these questions with a review of the legitimation process.

## Summary

This chapter has been divided into the interrelated subjects of social mobility and status attainment. The study of social mobility is more directed to analysis of the overall level and types of social mobility in a society. Large studies of social mobility in the United States have shown rather extensive amounts of social mobility, especially when the very top and very bottom of the stratification system are excluded from the analysis. At the top and the bottom, we find there is much more occupational inheritance, meaning that those born at the top and bottom are more likely to stay where they are in later life compared with those born between these extremes. However, more recent but still less complete data indicate that the overall rate of social mobility is slowing down with the relative decline of the United States in the world economy and a reduction of middle-paying jobs since the early 1980s. The patterns of social mobility for blacks and women diverge in different ways from the patterns of white men. For blacks there has been much more occupational inheritance at the bottom and very little occupational inheritance at the top. In other words, blacks have had more difficulty escaping low-skilled employment, but when they have, it has been difficult to pass the advantages on to their children, who tend to fall to the bottom. However, data since the 1960s have shown much improvement in the social mobility chances for blacks in the United States. For women there is more overall social mobility than for white men, though this social mobility is both upward and downward mobility. Women tend to be pushed up to or pulled down to low-skilled white-collar jobs regardless of whether they were born in higher or lower positions in the stratification system. Finally, extensive comparative studies of social mobility indicate that the United States is not the land of opportunity any more than other industrial nations with respect to the social mobility chances for people born in this country.

The focus of status attainment research is on questions such as why some people have moved up or down the stratification system. Such research was pioneered by Blau and Duncan in the 1960s, and progressed with the Wisconsin model, which added psychological and aspirational variables to the model. Status attainment research has indicated that family class background factors (such as parents' occupation, education, and income) are important in the process, though other factors affecting aspirations (such as the peer group) are equally important. However, there are many criticisms of this research. Among the most important objections are that very little of the variance (or why mobility occurs) is actually explained in the status attainment models, that the exclusive focus on occupational rank misses other dimensions of rank in a stratification system, and that these models tend to miss various kinds of institutional or structural restraints on social mobility.

# The Process of Legitimation

Research conducted by such respected polling organizations as Gallup and Pew show that in recent decades U.S. news programs have become highly polarized. The American people now mostly watch TV news with either the left- or right-wing political views they favor and are less accurately informed today about the world and their own country than people in other major postindustrial nations.

*SOURCE:* The McGraw-Hill Companies, Inc./Jill Braaten, Photographer.

# Chapter Outline

❖ **The Microprocess of Legitimation**
❖ **The Macroprocess of Legitimation: Building Support for Specific Forms of Inequality**
❖ **Summary**

Imagine a society with an extremely high degree of inequality—much higher than that in the United States. Imagine further that within this society those at the bottom of the stratification system are extremely deprived both materially and psychologically. This low-status group lives in the worst conditions with respect to basic necessities and is allowed to perform only the dirtiest and most degrading jobs (such as collecting and disposing of human feces in baskets).

In addition to having poor material conditions, this group is held in extreme contempt by the rest of the society. Its status is such that its members are considered socially unclean and are prohibited from almost any contact with respectable members of the society (that is, everyone except members of their own status group). They cannot be under the same roof as respectable members of the society, much less eat or work in their presence. When passing respectable people on the street, they must hide or, if this is not possible, bow with their face in the dirt. Finally, imagine that the members of this unclean lower-status group have almost no hope of ever leaving their low status—at least in their lifetime.

Given Western assumptions of human nature, we might expect this low-status group to reject its status and, when possible, rebel. We might assume that its condition is so unbearable and without hope that its members would be extremely discontent, would reject the system of social stratification that led to their position, and would collectively attempt to change this system.

All these assumptions may be false, however. The conditions just described are comparable to those experienced over the centuries by untouchables in India. While there were some revolts by untouchables in previous centuries (Sekhon 2000; Fuller 1996; Srinivas 1996), for the most part these untouchables accepted their status (Dumont 1970). As noted in an earlier chapter, it was primarily the incredibly strong cultural and religious reinforcement of the Indian caste system that brought about such stability and passive acceptance of extreme inequality.

In modern societies, of course, ideological support for such high levels of all kinds of inequalities is lacking or weak. Indeed, the situation is generally the opposite: Cultural values of democracy and equality of opportunity suggest such high levels of inequality and lack of opportunities are to be condemned. Why, then, do we continue to find societies with high inequality, lack of freedom, or living conditions much worse than they could be if elites got less or were less in control? In the old communist countries, of course, there was extensive information control—what the masses don't know can't hurt the elites. As Orwell put it in *Animal Farm,* "Ignorance is bliss"—or, we might add, bliss at least for the elites.

In the modern information age, it is not so easy to keep the population ignorant, at least if the population does not want to be ignorant. This has been one of the weaknesses hastening the fall of communism. The problem certainly exists in communist China, even with its less developed media infrastructure compared with those in the fully industrialized societies. To their dismay, in 1989 the Chinese dictators found that the educated urban population knew much more about what was happening in the world and in their own country than these old men wanted them to know. Even with control of television and print news media, educated Chinese people were receiving accurate information through such mechanisms as cheap photocopy machines and fax links with their friends in the United States and other places and now the Internet (Salisbury 1989; Liu, Ming, and Gang 1989). After the aging dictators killed a few hundred, if not several hundreds, of their young people in Tiananmen Square, they hunted down those fax machines and put more controls on the copy machines and now the Internet. Currently the Burmese military dictators are taking no chances: Today it is even a crime to own a personal computer, much less log on to the Internet in Burma.

Free access to information about major issues of the day affecting inequality and elite power in modern industrial societies is not always a problem for elites. There continues to be some means of countering or slanting information, causing enough doubt and confusion that people don't know what to do, or whom or what to blame for their troubles. In some countries, we must honestly admit, it is much easier to mislead and confuse major segments of the population when people care little about being accurately informed. Newspaper readership in the United States is about half (and in many cases less than half) what it is in Europe and Japan, and far fewer books are published and read in the United States compared to European countries and Japan (World Bank, 2000:310; Keizai Koho Center 2006:125). Further, studies show that American newspapers and TV news programs have reduced their coverage of serious news in the past decade, and have especially reduced news about the outside world, which was already the lowest for all industrial nations 20 years ago (*International Herald Tribune,* October 23, 2001, March 15, 2002; *Los Angeles Times,* September 27, 2001).

Some outcomes of this are understandable: In a 1994 *Los Angeles Times* survey, a sample of people in eight countries were asked five basic questions about current events of the day (*Los Angeles Times,* March 16, 1994). Of people in these countries— the United States, Canada, Mexico, Britain, France, Spain, Germany, and Italy—the Americans were dead last. For example, while 94 percent of Germans could correctly identify Boris Yeltsin, only 50 percent of Americans could do so. Likewise, 79 percent of Germans knew that the Israelis had recently signed a peace accord with the Palestinians, while only 40 percent of Americans knew. Only 3 percent of Germans got all five questions wrong; 37 percent of the Americans missed them all. With respect to questions of geography, a 1988 Gallup poll found Americans in their late teens and early 20s ranked last compared with young people in other industrial societies. Even when people in all of these countries were asked questions about geography of the United States, Americans were ahead of only two other countries in the percentage of correct answers (Shapiro 1992:69). An international opinion poll conducted during December of 2001 showed that Americans were especially shocked by the September 11, 2001, terrorist attacks because, unlike people in other nations, few Americans realized that a large percentage of the world's population blames the United States for many of the world's problems such as poverty. For example, less than 20 percent of Americans believed that U.S.

policies could motivate foreigners to be angry at the United States, while over half of the people in other world regions believed U.S. policies motivated people to be angry at Americans. Likewise, over half of the American public thought the rest of the world admired the United States because the country does so much good around the world: Only 12 to 23 percent of the people in other countries throughout the world thought the United States is admired because it "does good in the world" (*International Herald Tribune*, December 20, 2001; also see *International Herald Tribune*, December 5, 2002, June 3, 2003). An important implication of all this, of course, is that Americans know comparatively less about the outside world, and even what is happening in their own country, making it relatively easier to mislead a large segment of the American public. Several years of opinion polls by the Pew Research Center indicate that this lack of basic knowledge is increasing among Americans (Pew Research Center 2004). In recent decades there has been increased reliance by Americans on "news" from cable TV programs that explicitly cater to either right-wing conservatives or the left, with fewer people watching more serious, unbiased news programs. The Pew Research Center annually polls Americans on their knowledge of some basic facts, and they find that people who primarily rely on Fox News programs have the least factual knowledge, with people relying mostly on CNN having only slightly more knowledge, and people relying on the PBS News Hour having the most factual knowledge. In a 2004 CNN poll just before the election, a majority of Bush supporters still believed Saddam Hussein had connections with Al Qaeda terrorists and weapons of mass destruction even after the CIA and the Bush administration admitted it was not the case. On the subject of inequality in industrial nations, Osberg and Smeeding (2006) surveyed Americans and people living in several European nations. To their surprise, Osberg and Smeeding found that Americans and Europeans are equally opposed to very high corporate salaries. But the big difference was that in contrast to Europeans, Americans were mostly ignorant of the very high corporate salaries in the United States. Europeans are pressing their politicians to do something about it; Americans are not doing so mostly because of their ignorance in the matter.

All of these factors influence how people will or will not accept high levels of inequality and other conditions of life that are unequally distributed in modern societies. And all of this is related to the important process of **legitimation** of social stratification in human societies—that is, how the system of social stratification, the level of inequality, and the power of elites in the society are made acceptable to the general population.

Of course, high levels of inequality and exploitation may exist for extensive periods of time without the population accepting them as legitimate. Force has more often than not been successful in maintaining inequalities throughout history. But in the long run, force is inefficient and costly, especially in more recent history, as white South Africans finally realized. However, in addition to force there are material incentives for obedience and support of the status quo. This method is most common, although it also has limitations. What prevents nonelites from deciding that their obedience is bought too cheaply? What happens when material incentives become limited for a time? And what prevents nonelites from deciding that other elites with a new status quo can provide more material incentives?

The point is that force and material incentives as methods of promoting obedience and maintaining the status quo have serious limitations. The most efficient means for the job involves somehow convincing nonelites that inequality is morally right, and that those most advantaged are justified in giving orders and receiving a greater proportion of valued goods and services or, if nothing else, creating doubts about the alternatives. This method of maintaining obedience and structured inequality can be referred to as the *process of legitimation.*

The task of legitimation, however, is more complex than simply justifying the rewards and function of a particular set of elites or inducing people to respect authority and submit to their commands. Moving from the more specific to the more general, we can identify legitimation of inequality and authority with respect to (1) individual elites and their status, (2) a particular regime in power and its authority and policies, (3) a particular system of social stratification or political economy, and (4) stratification and inequalities of wealth and authority in principle (see Della Fave 1974c, 1980).

This chapter examines the process of legitimation on two levels. First, we consider the microlevel legitimation process. Our concern will be the sociopsychological processes that produce legitimacy for inequality and authority divisions in a more general sense. Second, we consider the more macrolevel or social-level legitimation process. Our concern at this point will be the process by which particular elites gain legitimacy for their policies and the particular political economy they represent. The first process is more basic, for only if social stratification and inequality in general enjoy support can particular elites and a particular political economy hope to maintain any allegiance.

Before turning to the microlevel process of legitimation, it is worth noting that all theoretical perspectives in the study of social stratification recognize the importance of a legitimation process (Della Fave 1980, 1986). What were described as theories from functional, uncritical-conflict, and critical-conflict paradigms of social stratification agree that some process of legitimation is required for social order. They agree that norms and ideologies must produce allegiance to elites or some form of social organization if society is to be possible.

These theoretical perspectives, however, part ways on the question of the outcome and exact nature of the legitimation process. For functional theory, social stratification and elite legitimacy are considered necessary and beneficial for all in the society. For uncritical-conflict theory, elite legitimation is a means of elite dominance that is not always beneficial for all in the society. And for critical-conflict theory, legitimation is a means of elite dominance that prevents acceptance of a political economy resulting in much less inequality and exploitation.

## The Microprocess of Legitimation

It is seldom easy to totally separate sociopsychological processes from more general or macro sociological processes. Society is a collective of actors who are individually shaped and influenced by group forces, while themselves contributing to these group forces. When the level of analysis (or study) is the individual—his or her behavior, self-concept, belief system—a more general level of analysis is also implied. When the level of analysis is the general society or some structural aspect of the society—of a concentration of power—a microlevel analysis is implicit.

In the first case, because we are social animals, we must recognize that the group or society has a hand in shaping individual behavior. In the second case, because society is a collection of individuals, any collective process must be grounded in individual understandings and motives. But we can choose to focus on one level while holding the other level implicit. When we want to understand a more general-level phenomenon, such as inequality and social stratification, we benefit most from a macrolevel analysis. From time to time, however, we can also benefit from touching base with a more socio-psychological level of analysis. In examining the maintenance of social stratification, such an analysis will be helpful.

Let us begin by restating two basic questions: Why do some people often willingly accept a smaller share of goods and services than others in the society? And why do people often willingly accept the legitimacy of authority figures and follow their orders? We must emphasize *willingly* in these two questions because our concern at present is behavior in the absence of direct coercion.

A conflict relationship may be at the heart of social stratification, but when societies are relatively stable, when overt conflict does not threaten major rebellion and social change, this conflict relationship is pushed into the background. What the preceding questions ask, in short, is how such conflict is pushed into the background. The first half of this chapter examines how basic legitimacy is maintained through **norms of distributive justice,** self-evaluation, and ideology (more specifically, equality of opportunity).

## Norms of Distributive Justice

As we saw in our review of the history of inequality, there is evidence that most people came to accept social and material inequality as small agricultural settlements emerged about 10,000 to 15,000 years ago (Wells 1971:193; Pfeiffer 1977:21). As one theory has it, when food became more difficult to find or produce, a norm of distributive justice emerged along with human societies (Pfeiffer 1977). The idea is that because human beings must somehow cooperate when conditions force them to live in close proximity, a sense of elementary justice or fairness in sharing goods and services will be established to reduce overt conflict. One way of establishing fairness is to sanction greater rewards for those who contribute most to the well-being of the collective. We can imagine that in the earliest societies the best hunter or the person believed able to influence supernatural forces was given greater rewards for his or her greater contribution.

From another perspective, many social scientists have argued that because people strive for cognitive consistency (Festinger 1957) they will develop principles of fairness, such as distributive justice, which maintain that rewards should be proportional to investments and contributions. This psychological need for cognitive consistence present in all human beings accounts for the apparently universal norm of distributive justice (Homans 1961, 1974).

But there appears to be another side to human psychology that has an effect on distribution norms. Because of our ability to understand the feelings of others, to understand their suffering and needs, there is at least some support for distribution based on need. Thus, Moore (1978:37) argues that all societies have distribution norms based on both need and contribution.

There is abundant evidence for the existence of norms of distributive justice (Younts and Mueller 2001). Most evidence has been obtained with research on small groups (see Ofshe and Ofshe 1970; Homans 1974; Leventhal 1975). A typical pattern in this research is to bring several subjects together to do some collective task. The task is structured in such a way as to make it evident that one person contributes most in completing the task, others about equally, and still others contribute least. When subjects are asked how rewards should be distributed among the members of this small group, they consistently opt for rewards distributed in terms of contribution (see Leventhal, Michaels, and Sanford 1972).

In other research, subjects have been asked to judge the fairness of income distributions when given descriptions of various individuals and families (Jasso and Rossi 1977; Alves and Rossi 1978). The findings are that people make judgments in terms of both merit and need, and there is some consistency in the judgments among research subjects.

For example, in terms of merit, those with a higher-level occupation and education are judged to deserve more income. In terms of need, those with a larger family are judged to deserve more income. The research subjects also show some agreement on the fairness of maximum and minimum income levels. Computing the maximum and minimum levels for a husband-and-wife household with lowest need and merit to the highest need and merit, Alves and Rossi (1978:557) established an average fairness judgment that ranged from $7,211 to $44,466 in yearly income—in mid-1970s dollars—and an income distribution, they note, that was much narrower than the actual level of income inequality at the time.

What can be concluded from such evidence? The most obvious conclusion is that norms of distributive justice do exist, and that there is at least some agreement among people with respect to these norms (Younts and Mueller 2001). Evidence from other industrial societies makes such a conclusion even stronger (Grandjean and Bean 1975). In the context of the present discussion, there is support for inequality based on norms of distributive justice. But despite some wide agreement, there are differences among people in applying the justice norms. For example, Alves and Rossi (1978:559) found that those higher in the class system tend to focus more on merit when making fairness judgments, while those lower in the class system tend to focus more on need.

A fundamental problem with the idea of distributive justice, however, is that such norms are rather ambiguous in concrete application. The task of defining which contributions are most important and the *degree* of reward justified for particular contributions remains. Among small groups this problem is minimized. But in large societies, where contribution can seldom be judged with much accuracy, the problem is extensive. There is the potential for elites to manipulate judgments of contribution so that their greater rewards seem justified (Moore 1978:40; Della Fave 1980:960). Thus, while we do find support for "fair" inequality with norms of distributive justice, we must look further to understand how extensive inequality comes to be accepted by many people.

## The Socialization Process and Self-Evaluation

One of the most basic sociopsychological theories (microprocesses) of legitimation has been outlined by L. Richard Della Fave (1980, 1986). Following what we know about socialization and the development of a self-concept, we can understand how a person's *self-evaluation* is constructed so that the person comes to view himself or herself as one who deserves a higher or lower position in the stratification system. Within more specific social contexts (or positions), we examine how a person comes to have a higher or lower view of his or her abilities and is or is not deserving of more rewards (Stolte 1983).

From the work of George Herbert Mead (1935) we recognize that a self-concept is first developed through interaction with significant others, and later through interactions with members of the wider society. In essence, we become aware of what others expect of us by how they react to us. "People, in general, see us as bright or dull, attractive or ugly, strong or weak, capable or incapable. This amalgam of perceived generalized expectations and reactions constitutes the generalized other" (Della Fave 1980:959). Thus, through this generalized other we come to define who we are; this constitutes our self-evaluation. The key is that those toward the bottom of the stratification system usually come to have a lower self-evaluation; they come to view themselves as less deserving. Let us consider how a low self-evaluation is produced.

Beginning with our earliest socialization experiences, we described in Chapter 8 how child-rearing methods differ by class. Working-class children, for example, are more likely to be taught to respect authority per se, without questioning the reason or purpose of commands from authority. Middle- and upper-middle-class children are taught by their parents to be more self-reliant, to have greater confidence in themselves and their abilities.

When children reach school age, their self-concept and self-evaluation are developed further by a wider social circle. We described in Chapter 12 how the educational system tends to treat children differently by class background. How the peer group and teachers react to children, their track placement and other such experiences, all help to foster the self-evaluation process of children. The status attainment research described in the previous chapter shows how class background shapes educational and occupational aspirations through the influences of significant others. But aspirations are only one outcome of this process; self-evaluations are another outcome.

The self-evaluation process does not end when a person completes his or her education; it is an ongoing process that continues throughout life. One of the most important sources of feedback from others in the self-evaluation process during adulthood is the occupational structure. A person's relation to authority, how he or she is treated by the boss and coworkers, contributes to the self-evaluation. Research has shown that class position is more strongly related to self-esteem or self-evaluation in adults than in children (see Rosenberg and Pearlin 1978; Demo and Savin-Williams 1983). This seems a result of adults' contacts with a wider range of other class members, making their own class positions more significant. Children, in contrast, are more likely to interact with children from the same class background because of class-segregated neighborhoods and schools. Thus, an adult's occupation and education come to have an important effect on his or her self-esteem (Jacques and Chason 1977).

More specific to authority relations in the workplace, qualitative studies suggest that when workers are treated in a dependent and degraded manner, when work is organized so that workers cannot come to feel self-reliant, self-esteem among the working class is low (Sennett and Cobb 1973; Pfeffer 1979). Those in higher authority positions, especially in the United States, have seldom assumed that workers can be counted on to perform their work obligation properly and that they have the intelligence or good sense to perform their jobs without consistent supervision (Turner 1992; Lincoln and Kalleberg 1985, 1990). Thus, the lower we move down occupational authority ranks, the lower the self-evaluations.

When we move from the family and work relations to the wider society, we find other sources of feedback that contribute to a lower self-evaluation as we move down the class system. Here the feedback becomes more generalized in depicting images of class members as a group. From the mass media—from movies, news stories, and television—people pick up the general images of class members held by the more general society.

We have already seen how the degrading views of welfare recipients and the poor help contribute to their low self-concept (see Piven and Cloward 1971; Kerbo 1976b). Others have argued that the working class also receives negative images of itself through the representation of working-class characters in films (Miliband 1969; Aronowitz 1974:108; Gitlin 1979). For example, television and movie heroes are seldom from the working class or lower class, and when working-class and lower-class members are presented, they usually conform to dominant stereotypes that lead to low self-evaluation.

Thus far we have focused on the self-evaluation of people in positions toward the bottom of the class system. However, the self-evaluation of those toward the top can be understood as a complement of this process. While those in lower-class positions usually receive more negative feedback, those in higher-class positions usually receive more positive feedback simply because they are in higher positions.

But there is an added ingredient. Those in higher-class positions usually have a wider audience from which to receive feedback contributing to their self-evaluation. They have a wider audience through interacting with more people in their occupation and with more subordinates below them, and they are likely to be more widely known in the community (or even nation). This wider audience may appear to be made up of more objective outside observers than more immediate significant others. In other words, your family, friends, and peers may provide positive feedback, but you can seldom escape the feeling that these significant others have a positive bias. Thus, the more positive feedback obtained from a wider audience can contribute even more to a person's self-evaluation (Della Fave 1980:962).

Higher-status people have another advantage in the self-evaluation process. From the work of symbolic interaction theorists such as Goffman (1959), we can view the interaction process as similar to a stage production. Various stage props and image-creating mechanisms are used by people to form the best possible presentation of the self to others. Interaction rituals can also be viewed as a conflict relation, with each party attempting to present a more favorable view of the self, but with the higher-status person having greater power and resources to do so (Collins 1975:115).

For example, the wealthier can display higher status in personal appearance and in the setting in which encounters take place (such as in the home or office; see Della Fave 1980:963). Higher-status people are better able to give the appearance of being calm and in control (Hall and Hewitt 1970). There is the power to dictate explicitly or implicitly where a meeting will take place. Equally important, the superior often requires the subordinate to wait, signifying that his or her time is more important than that of the lower-status person (Schwartz 1974). All this means that a higher-status person can usually manage a better performance, contributing to a higher self-evaluation (Della Fave 1980:963).

In large societies people are often required to make status judgments of someone else with only a few clues to the status of the other person (Berger et al. 1972; Webster and Driskell 1978). The interaction rituals described earlier, therefore, become even more important in enhancing the status of higher-class members in the eyes of lower-class members. If greater rewards are to be justified, following the norm of distributive justice described earlier, a person must be seen as making a greater contribution to the society. But because higher-status people have more resources to make a favorable impression, *their contribution can appear to be greater.* "What is crucial is that the entire process through which the appropriate level of reward is determined is *circular,* in that the very fact of being wealthy or powerful influences our assessment of 'contribution' and, on the basis of such assessment, we judge that person worthy of such a high reward" (Della Fave 1980:961).

It is time to summarize how the process of self-evaluation and self-efficacy contributes to a legitimation of inequality in a very general sense. It is important to remember that at this point we are not concerned with the legitimation of a particular political economy, specific policies, or specific elites, but simply inequalities of wealth and authority in and of themselves.

Della Fave's (1980:962) primary proposition is as follows: "The level of primary resources that an individual sees as just for him/herself, relative to others, is directly proportional to his/her level of self-evaluation." That is, when a person, for all the reasons noted previously, comes to have a lower self-evaluation, *he or she will come to view his or her own low rewards and the high rewards of others as just.*

In relation to the wider society, "The strength of legitimacy of stratification in any society is directly proportional to the degree of congruence between the distribution of primary resources and the distribution of self-evaluations" (Della Fave 1980:962). In other words, taken as a whole, *when the people with fewer rewards are generally those with lower self-evaluations, social inequality is more likely to be viewed as legitimate.*

## The Effects of Individualism and "Equality of Opportunity"

It is often difficult for people in modern industrial societies to appreciate the powerful influence our belief in equality of opportunity can have in maintaining the class system. Modern people are so accustomed to the ideology that a society without such a belief system is hard to imagine. But such societies have existed, and in fact only a very small proportion of the societies that have ever existed have had a value of equality of opportunity.

In those societies without this revolutionary new ideology, the maintenance of class inequalities fell to other ideologies—religion in the hands of political and economic elites tended to be the most favored. But once these old ideologies were broken in that turbulent period between feudal and industrial societies, the belief in equality of opportunity proved a new and powerful tool for the legitimation of inequality.

This new belief in equality of opportunity, however, provides both a strong support and a danger for higher-class privilege, because the value must have at least some basis in reality if it is to legitimate the class system. With the hope and expectations of a population raised, if reality does not appear to show at least some support for this value, the consequences could be revolutionary.

As we found in Chapter 12, thus far most industrial societies have been expanding at a rate that provides generally more upward than downward social mobility. Where the modern idea of equality of opportunity has been exported to underdeveloped nations with more rigid class boundaries, the consequence has usually been more overt class conflict. And where the value has less basis in reality for minorities in modern industrial societies, like the United States with respect to blacks and Latinos, a consequence has been more overt class conflict along racial lines.

In the case of the United States, we must add the effects of the value of **individualism** to the ideology of equality of opportunity. As is well known, the United States was "founded" by immigrants from Europe beginning in the early 1600s. But people often forget that these people were religious refugees in many respects; they were often members of extreme Protestant religious sects who believed in strict independence and individualism. Later waves of immigrants in the 1800s and early 1900s made this earlier value system imported to the "new land" more complex, but the elements of this radical individualism remained strong.

Contributing to this was the geography of the North American continent. The vast territory, especially to the west, and the gradual settlement of this territory led many social scientists to support Frederick Turner's famous thesis in his work *The Significance of the Frontier in American History.* In no other modern industrial nation could so many people break from their family roots, load the family on a covered wagon, and move west to make a new life, a very independent life, as in the new United States of America. The radical individualism and independence of the European founders were strengthened and also transformed from an ideology to reality as the new country expanded into these vast territories.

A result of this history is a rather unique value system often referred to as *the American Creed* (Lipset 1996:19)—a value system stressing liberty, egalitarianism, individualism, populism, and laissez-faire. The liberty (or freedom) and individualism should be evident from what we have previously said. The Protestant religious sects, which taught that all are equal in the eyes of God, gave these new Americans this ideology of egalitarianism; the frontier made it more of a reality. Breaking from family roots, those who moved to this country and then moved westward lost the old status ranking of family origins, and the frontier made people more equal in the fight to survive. Populism and laissez-faire are the manifestations of these values directed toward the political system; the people, it is believed, should be a populist force controlling the government, and the government should stay out of their lives to the greatest extent possible.

Research on the attitudes and values of people throughout nations today continues to indicate the existence of rather different American values. In his famous study using questionnaires from some 15,000 people in 53 countries around the world, Hofstede (1991) found *Americans scoring the highest in the world on his index of individualism.* Other comparative opinion polls indicate Americans are less likely to support government action to solve social problems of various kinds, or do such simple things as help maintain health care systems for all citizens (Lipset 1996:75–76). Compared to major industrial nations in Europe, people in the United States are much more likely to reject government intervention to help the poor and reduce inequalities, and show by far the highest percentage believing that equality of opportunity in fact exists (Ladd and Bowman 1998:118–123), in contrast to the reality of that fact that there is no more social mobility in the United States than in other industrial nations, which we found in the previous chapter (also see the *New York Times,* January 20, 2003). In 2001 a sample of over 128,000 Americans and Europeans indicated that there is much more "unhappiness" about inequality and poverty in Europe than in the United States (Alesina, Di Tella, and MacCulloch 2001). A key reason for this difference is that Americans (incorrectly) believe there is more "equality of opportunity" in their country and more movement out of poverty and into higher-income positions. Recent research by Osberg and Smeeding (2006) concur. They question the extent of American uniqueness in value orientations, but have found that Americans are much more likely than Europeans to be unconcerned about poverty because of (inaccurate) beliefs about "equality of opportunity" in the United States.

A national poll by the *New York Times* (2005) clearly shows this overwhelming belief in equality of opportunity in the United States. When asked "Is it possible to start out poor, work hard, and get rich?" 80 percent of Americans said yes. When asked the likelihood of moving to a higher social class in America compared to 30 years ago, 40 percent said it is greater today, while 35 percent said it is the same as 30 years ago. When asked about the chances for upward mobility in the United States compared to Europe, 45 percent of Americans said it is easier in the United States. And finally, when those who do not consider themselves financially well off were asked about their chances of becoming financially well off in the United States, 45 percent said it is very likely or somewhat likely. In an age of growing inequality, a shrinking middle class, and less social mobility in the early 21st century in the United States, the myth of America as the land of greatest opportunity remains remarkably strong.

Our discussion of equality of opportunity has yet to consider the sociopsychological effect on class legitimation. This is our present task, which can be accomplished with reference to Lane's (1962) now classic study of working-class men in a northeastern industrial city. In Lane's detailed interviews with 15 white blue-collar workers, he found a strong belief in equality of opportunity that had profound effects on what these men thought about their position in life. Perhaps the most important effect of this belief is that it leads people to *find some defect in themselves* when explaining their relatively low status. Lane (1962:59) found that these men felt they had more opportunities than they were using; in short, they felt they had let opportunities slip away.

The importance of education, of course, is a key ingredient in the belief in equality of opportunity in the United States. As one man stated, "If I had gone to college . . . I would be higher up in this world" (Lane 1962:70). But it was an opportunity he believed was wasted. The low self-evaluation of these men, at least with respect to lost educational opportunities, helps them explain their low status. But it does so with some face-saving as well: "At least it is only the fault of an irresponsible youth, not a grown man" (Lane 1962:71).

Another key in understanding the acceptance of inequality among these men is that they have much invested in the present system. They may be relatively low in the class system, but they feel they have worked hard for what they have achieved. They have had some opportunities for more pay and security they believe their fathers did not have; so although they are not on top, neither are they on the bottom.

In this respect we can understand why these men even fear greater equality (Lane 1962:73). These men may gain with more equality, but they believe all their life's hard work would be of little value if the poor below them, whom they view with contempt, were given equal rewards—which returns us to a point noted in the chapter on poverty in the United States. When the poor are viewed with contempt, this abstract category of the "undeserving poor" serves the function of legitimating inequality by making those just above the poor feel better about their own low rewards (Gans 1972).

A final aspect of the worldview of these men is worth exploring. For the most part these men are distrustful of human nature. If all in the society were assured equal rewards, they have the feeling there would be no incentive; there would be nothing to work for, and the "lazy" side of human nature would prevail (people, they believe, would not "put forth their best efforts," Lane 1962:76). Thus, they see equality of opportunity as a fair and necessary policy in providing incentive, which is to say their worldview is close to the ideal put forth in the Davis and Moore (1945) functional theory of social stratification.

What is interesting, however, is that none of these men ever considered the idea that inequality could be reduced from its present levels (Lane 1962:78) with no adverse effects. The ideological debate has been safely limited to inequality versus equality. A more reasonable controversy over *degrees* of inequality is not on the agenda, in large measure because of the manner in which their worldview has been shaped by wider forces in the society. (We consider such forces in the second half of this chapter.)

It was noted earlier that every society must provide some legitimating ideology for inequality if the stratification system is to remain stable. It seems reasonable to conclude that historical circumstances have led the United States to stress the mythology of equality of opportunity more than other nations. Although more comparative data are needed for any firm conclusions in this respect, we do have data comparing British and American views of inequality.

Robinson and Bell (1978) found acceptance of inequality to be similar in both nations, but they conclude that this acceptance is in part related to differing ideological supports. In England people are "taught at an early age to reconcile themselves to their lot in life" (Robinson and Bell 1978:141); their historical traditions have led them to a greater acceptance of ascription (Turner 1960; Devine 1997:75–103). But in the United States, our historical traditions preclude aristocratic privilege, and ascription must be denied with the belief that anyone can achieve success through hard work (Lipset 1963, 1996). Thus, although in England people more often are taught to accept inequality, in the United States people come to accept inequality because an ideology of equality of opportunity has led those less successful to partially blame themselves for their lower position.

Before concluding this discussion of the micro supports for inequality, we must mention briefly the sociopsychological effects of solidarity rituals. Our concern at this point is the emotional support for society's basic institutions and values gained through collective rituals. For many years social theorists (most notably Durkheim) have recognized that collective emotional rituals can strengthen social bonds and provide an almost godly respect for human institutions. In the face of such strong emotional support, traditions of unequal power and wealth may come to appear almost sacred in nature. It becomes most difficult for someone to question the legitimacy of these conditions while continuing to desire membership in the surrounding community.

Raising the idea of emotional rituals brings religion to mind. Religion has often been used to support inequality, as Marx was one of the first to stress. But, as noted earlier, such a view is overly simple because religion can be used equally to support or challenge inequalities of power and privilege. One of the most interesting examples in this respect is the mixing of fundamentalist Christian ideals and socialism by the rural poor in Oklahoma protesting exploitation by wealthy landlords between 1912 and 1920 (Burbank 1976).

Many comparative opinion polls on religious beliefs, along with statistics on church attendance, indicate that the United States is clearly the most religious of all industrial societies (see Gallup Poll International, 2000; Lipset 1996). Thus, the mixture of religion and Americanism often provides emotional support for the basis of inequality. Religion in the United States has come to be a **civil religion** (Bellah 1970) in praise of country, the flag, anticommunism, and Americanism, as much as any pure religious ideals. Even before the rise of fundamentalist Christian political action during the 1980s and 1990s, this quality of American religious beliefs was widely recognized by sociologists (see Herberg 1960). An outcome of this civil religion or the mixing of religious ideals with Americanism is that national values and institutions are sometimes given emotional support to such a degree that to question such values and social arrangements is kin to immorality. Thus, civil religion in the United States must be recognized as making a significant contribution to the legitimation of inequality and authority.

The source of ritual solidarity must be considered when we recognize its existence in virtually all human societies. Because human beings can think abstractly, they seek meaning in the world; a meaningless world is an insecure world. Thus, there is a social construction of reality that becomes possible and is maintained through collective rituals (Berger and Luckman 1966).

Emotional collective rituals are important because such emotional arousal makes the reality people seek more meaningful or unquestioned (Collins 1975:153); their reality comes to seem more transcendental rather than simply human-made. It is understandable that when collective rituals take place people emphasize their commonality—the social values, institutions, and social relations they have in common. What this means for the legitimation of power and inequality is that the form of social stratification the society has developed, for whatever historical reasons, can be given positive meaning through rituals of solidarity.

Elites often seek control of solidarity rituals for obvious reasons (Collins 1975), but control by elites is not always necessary. If power and privilege by an elite are a firm aspect of the common reality, they will most often be supported as the overall social reality and given legitimacy through rituals of solidarity. But if the power and privilege of elites are threatened or weakening, a call for support through rituals is a useful tool. This call is most often made by finding or manufacturing some threat to the general society, as historical research on the Salem witch hunts of the 1600s indicates (Erikson 1966). At a time when the authority of religious elites was being questioned, the fear of witches was used to create an "outside" threat, which then helped restore support for authority.

One of the most soundly supported sociological ideas is that out-group conflict tends to produce in-group solidarity (Coser 1967). In some capitalist societies, communism was as functional as the devil was for highly religious societies, which is why many scholars predict a search for new devils now that communism no longer provides this function.

## The Basis of Legitimation: A Summary

Thus far we have found that norms of distributive justice, the process of self-evaluation, solidarity rituals, and the ideology of equality of opportunity in this country help provide an underlying base for the support of inequality in industrial societies. The main focus has been on people and the factors leading them to reason that the pattern of inequality in a society is somehow fair and necessary.

Our major concern, of course, has been the micro process of legitimation among nonelites, although we did consider how those high in the class system may come to have a higher self-evaluation (and thus feel justified in receiving greater rewards). The legitimation process among elites needs less explanation—because they are most advantaged in the stratification system, legitimation is less problematic at this level.

One point requires restatement. Up to this point we have considered only micro-processes that lead to *a tendency to accept inequality in a very general or abstract sense*. Many social scientists make the claim that inequality exists in all societies, except perhaps the most elementary, and assume that some startling fact has been revealed. But the issue of real importance is not the simple existence of inequality; it is the extent of differential rewards and the span of inequality that exists within societies. What we have examined here helps us understand a tendency to accept inequality in principle. It does not help us understand the *degree* of inequality that can be maintained, or its exact form. To understand the degree and form of inequality that may be maintained, we must look to how elites build on this sociopsychological base to establish legitimacy for themselves and the particular political economy they represent.

A related point requires emphasis. The processes and factors described here only help produce tendencies to accept inequality. There is no automatic acceptance of inequality by everyone; neither is everyone willing to accept the same level of inequality or accept inequality for the same reasons. There can be and is variation around the world with respect to the level of inequality that is found acceptable (Ladd and Bowman 1998). Comparative research on the United States, Sweden, and Japan has found much less acceptance of high inequality in the latter two countries (Verba et al. 1987). Opinion polls from nine European nations and the United States also show that Americans are far more likely to accept high inequalities of income and wealth than people in these other nations (Alesina et al. 2001; Ladd and Bowman 1998:118–123). It will be remembered that Alves and Rossi (1978) found higher-class people more willing to accept inequality based on merit, while lower-class people are more willing to accept inequality based on need. In another study of the acceptance of inequality, Robinson and Bell (1978) found that in the United States the young, minorities, and those lower in occupational status are more likely to favor greater equality. Research by Kelley and Evans (1993) using data from nine industrial nations shows similar results. For example, older people in higher occupational positions, and people who claim to be more conservative politically prefer much higher pay for higher occupational positions. Both of these sets of research suggest that it is more difficult to convince those toward the bottom of the stratification system that the present level of inequality is just.

The tendency to accept inequality in a particular society may also be related to a person's *perception* of the degree of inequality that exists in that society. In other words, people may believe the level of inequality that exists is legitimate because they underestimate the degree of inequality in the society. Bell and Robinson (1980) have found perceptions of inequality to vary. For example, in both the United States and England, minorities are more likely to perceive greater income inequality, and in the United States there is more overall variance in the perception of income inequality than in England (people more often differ in their estimates of inequality in the United States). As noted earlier, this is exactly what Osberg and Smeeding (2006) found with a survey of several European nations compared to the United States. Americans are less likely to know the level of inequality that actually exists in their country. What this says is that many people in the United States may accept the present level of inequality because they do not recognize, or have been misled about, its extent. The misconception of the extent of inequality is a subject we must examine in our next section.

There are at least four levels on which legitimation may vary (Della Fave 1980, 1986). The acceptance of inequality or social stratification per se is most abstract. We become more specific as we consider the legitimacy of a particular system of political economy (such as capitalism, democratic socialism, or communism), a particular group of elites and their policies, and particular elites themselves (for example, their honesty or competence).

The sociopsychological tendency to accept inequality we have examined pertains primarily to inequality on an abstract level. Inequality per se may be accepted, but this does not mean that more specific kinds of inequality will be accepted. For example, studies have found that the working class may accept inequality in principle, but it often objects to exact levels of income inequality and particular authority relations (Liebow 1967; Sennett and Cobb 1973).

Because inequality and social stratification in principle are usually accepted, elites are able to achieve legitimacy for their particular place in a particular system of social stratification. Without the legitimacy of inequality, if even only in principle, they would have no hope. However, this also means that if elites seek legitimacy for their particular rule within a particular system of social stratification, *they must work for it.* There is no automatic acceptance. How do elites work for legitimacy on a more specific level? What means do elites have for maintaining such legitimacy? It is to these questions that we now turn.

## ✵ The Macroprocess of Legitimation: Building Support for Specific Forms of Inequality

From a sociopsychological base, helping to make the acceptance of inequality among the general population more likely, the job for elites begins. Their task is now to turn the general or abstract acceptance of inequality into the specific acceptance of their high rewards, the policies that favor their interests, and the general political and economic system that provides their base of power and privilege.

In short, an abstract legitimacy for inequality is only a beginning. The next step requires what can be called a *macroprocess* of legitimation—macro in the sense that elites must move beyond a sociopsychological tendency for the acceptance of inequality to legitimation of social arrangements that lead to their power and privilege. For example, if capitalism is the base of elite power and privilege, the population must be convinced that private ownership and private profit are just and in the best interests of all in the society. If communism is the base of elite power and privilege, the population must be convinced that this political economy is just and in the best interests of all in the society, if not at present, then at least when a mature communist state becomes a reality, after present sacrifice.

With respect to more specific policies, a particular foreign policy or economic policy to fight inflation may be in the best interests of economic elites. But because alternative policies (all equally possible within a given political economy) may be employed, and because other policies may favor the interests of nonelites, the task becomes that of creating acceptance for the policy that favors economic elite interests.

To maintain their power and privilege, elites have learned to use the norms of distributive justice by convincing nonelites that (1) elite contributions to the society are in proportion to the rewards they receive and (2) the abilities of elites are superior to those of nonelites (Moore 1978:40). To put it crudely, in the case of clear exploitation by elites, the legitimation process resembles a con game or sting operation. The trick is to exploit nonelites without their realizing they are being exploited. In the terminology of the con artist, this requires "cooling out the mark." More typically, where elites do perform some important function for the general society, the task becomes one of convincing nonelites that this function is even more important than it actually is, thereby justifying a greater "take" of valued goods and services than would otherwise be possible (except, of course, by overt force).

Throughout history, we have noted, some form of ideology has been used to justify elite privilege. Most often, past elites have used some religiously based ideology (Pfeiffer 1977:21, 104). A case in point was the use of religion to justify slavery in the southern United States (Aptheker 1963:57). Ideological legitimation, however, tells us little about the *process* of legitimation. Ideologies are not automatically accepted, and any particular ideology can be used to justify other elites and different policies. Thus, we must look further. In what follows we will consider how legitimacy is maintained through the educational system, the mass media, and opinion-influencing organizations. Our focus will be on the United States in particular, although most of what we consider applies to industrial societies in general.

In beginning this examination, we must acknowledge that by considering each of the means of legitimation separately we are oversimplifying the overall process of legitimation to some extent. The various means must be considered in concert; they tend to overlap and reinforce each other. To use functional terminology, the process of legitimation is an interrelated process or system. If one part of the system is not performing, the whole process may be weakened; it becomes more difficult for each part to serve its overall function. If the parts are all functioning well, the task becomes easier for each part. For example, if the educational system is performing its legitimation function adequately, it becomes much easier for the mass media to serve their legitimation function. If this overall process is kept in mind, however, examination of each part separately presents less of an oversimplification.

Another issue must be clarified before proceeding. When we say that the educational system or the mass media are performing a legitimating function, we are suggesting that they are passing on information that helps support a particular set of elites, their policies, or a particular system of political economy. To put it bluntly, we are saying that these institutions are involved in propaganda and indoctrination.

Americans don't like to do anything that is thought of as "something communists do." But by propaganda, or persuasion if you will, we simply mean the practice of convincing others of your particular point of view. We are not saying that the information offered is inaccurate, although it is often biased or slanted to favor the view and interests of those providing the information. Most simply, it must be recognized that the act of attempted persuasion implies a conflict relationship. As we have suggested throughout previous chapters, human organization is full of conflict relations. For example, there is often an immediate conflict relation between parent and child. The parent wants the child's behavior to conform to his or her expectations, but the child may have other ideas. Parents use propaganda and indoctrination to make the child conform. Propaganda and indoctrination are not unique to any political or economic system.

## The Legitimation Function of Education

Our schools perform much more than a legitimation function (for inequality, capitalism, democratic principles, or particular elites) by passing on important knowledge of all kinds. But schools do provide a legitimation function. Consider a most blatant example. At the beginning of each school day, teachers in virtually every school conduct the flag salute and pledge of allegiance. Five days a week throughout the school year, at about 8:30 or 9:00 in the morning, one can visualize millions of children standing, placing their right hands over their hearts, facing the flag, and reciting, "I pledge allegiance to the flag of the United States of America. . . ." This is a political ritual designed to maintain political legitimacy. Few, if any, people object to this elementary form of indoctrination. The general political economy is considered legitimate by most Americans; the legitimation process has been successful.

Consider, however, a more controversial practice that exists, or existed, in most American schools—the morning prayer. This practice is more controversial because the Christian religion is not accepted, or considered legitimate in a personal sense, by all Americans. Jews, Muslims, atheists, and others may object to Christian religious rituals in public schools. The issue has been oversimplified purposely to make a point; the legitimation of our political economy is accepted by most as an important function of public schools because our political economy itself is accepted by most adults. Most adults, even if only in a vague way, recognize the legitimation function of public schools. This is why there is so much conflict over what is taught in schools and what books are used. Adults want to make certain that their values are taught, or at least not rejected.

In the previous chapter we suggested how the educational system helps support the stratification system by teaching children to respect authority and accept their places in the stratification system—a function that contributes to the self-evaluation process described earlier. Our concern in this section, however, is the content of information obtained in the educational system. Many studies of textbooks have been conducted (for example, Kane 1970; Bowker 1972) that consistently show the views of upper-middle-class whites dominate these works, while those of minorities are almost totally neglected.

But for the present discussion what is most important in terms of content requires no systematic study to detect; the American past and its institutions are idealized. Schoolchildren are seldom told of the almost successful attempt to exterminate Native Americans in early American history (see Brown 1970) or of the total brutalizing effects of slavery. Children may read about early communist influence in labor unions but will learn little of the systematic and violent attempts by the state and corporations to prevent union organizing. If civil disorder is given any attention, children do not learn that most violence has come not from demonstrators or social movement members but from authorities against those who voice dissent (Gamson 1975; Stohl 1976).

Children do read about a few political and corporate scandals, but these scandals are portrayed as isolated products of greedy men rather than as any systemic defects. They are unlikely to read about the support for fascism by some big business leaders (Sampson 1973) before World War II or the congressional evidence suggesting that some business leaders were planning to seize the government illegally during Franklin Roosevelt's early years as president (Archer 1973) because they thought he was turning to communism.

None of this is very surprising, and we do not need more examples. Throughout history children have been socialized to accept the dominant values and institutions of their society. Once a political economy has been established, the socialization process gives it momentum. But the legitimation process is not ignored by those most advantaged in the society. Legitimacy can be eroded over time, and in the event of a major crisis, the extent of political legitimacy can be an insurance policy preventing basic change. Because of this, elites have often taken steps to ensure that the educational system is performing its legitimation function "properly" (Wells 1971:718).

This is especially true since societies have become more secular and the major task of shaping loyalty has been transferred from the churches to the public schools (Collins 1975:378). As we will see later, economic elites in this country have not been willing to assume that the educational system is doing its job in teaching the "proper" views of our economic system. They have spent millions to train teachers and provide books and teaching aids (Domhoff 2006a).

The relationship between education and conservative attitudes, however, is not always consistent. As noted previously, the less educated are more likely to blame the poor for poverty and to hold negative welfare stereotypes (Feagin 1975). This attitude is no doubt related to the need for working-class people to feel better about their own low status. But on more general political views, Huber and Form (1973) have found that those with lower incomes (and presumably less education) are more likely to believe that a power elite is in control of the country and less likely to believe that personal attributes account for wealth. In his analysis of the American class structure with a large data set of respondents, Wright (1997:407–458) has found much the same attitudes differing with class levels—the lower we go in the stratification system, the more people are skeptical of the rich and powerful.

A problem with studies such as those cited here is that we cannot say confidently that more support for elite policy is shaped directly by the educational system. But in a unique study by Cummings and Taebel (1978), we do have a bit more confidence about the direct efforts of education. In this study 370 schoolchildren were questioned to see if their support for dominant capitalist ideology increased as they advanced in grade level.

The findings show that increasing support does occur, sometimes dramatically. For example, on the issue of state intervention in the economy (along the lines of democratic socialism), 66 percent of the 6th-grade students favored such intervention, but by the 12th grade only 31 percent did. With respect to private ownership of major corporations, only 25 percent of the 6th-grade students thought this was right, while 63 percent of the 12th-grade students thought it was proper. Finally, only 29 percent of the 6th graders expressed negative views toward unions, although by the 12th grade 59 percent expressed such views.

Thus far we have considered schools in general. Perhaps special mention is necessary for higher education. The information is quite clear that the corporate class and upper class dominate formal positions of authority in most universities. In addition, the biggest and most respected universities depend on the wealthy and corporations for their funding (Smith 1974).

For example one-third of the trustees in the 30 top universities in the nation, were listed in the *Social Register,* and 45 percent were corporate directors or executives (Domhoff 2006a). About one-half of the largest 200 industrial and financial corporations had a representative among the trustees of these 30 leading universities. Many of these top 30 universities are not state supported. However, trustees of state-supported universities are no less members of the corporate and upper-class. For example, of the 24 trustees of the University of California's multicampus system, 4 are public officials. But the other 20 appointed regents are represented on 60 major corporate boards (Dye 1995).

As suggested in an earlier chapter, major universities serve important functions for the corporate class and upper class by conducting valuable research and formulating ideas for government policy (Domhoff 2006a; Dye 1995). But many theorists also argue that the funding and formal positions of authority in universities held by the wealthy and corporate leaders have a significant, if not always immediate, influence on the ideas that reach students.

Universities, above all, are seen as institutions in which the marketplace of ideas should be open. Limits are enforced from time to time, however. Trustees have the power to call for dismissal of university employees, and funding by the wealthy and corporations can be withheld. There are enough known cases in which members of the faculty have been fired for teaching "radical" ideas, or funding is threatened because "antibusiness speakers" have been brought on campus to make universities cautious (Szymanski 1978:251). The control of "acceptable" materials of instruction is less apparent in universities than in secondary and elementary schools, but there are limits on what can be taught, and these limits are sometimes enforced. The instruction provided in universities is supposed to be balanced and objective. But definitions of what is balanced and objective are certainly in dispute.

## The Legitimation Function of the Mass Media

The role of the mass media in the process of legitimation is difficult to demonstrate directly (Domhoff 2010:139–144), in part because long-run effects on public opinion are most important, and these are difficult to measure in the face of other influences on public opinion. But it is more clear that "newspeople decide what the news will be, how it will be presented, and how it will be interpreted. Newspeople have the power to create some national issues and ignore others, elevate obscure people to national prominence, reward politicians they favor, and punish those they disfavor" (Dye 1995:111–112). The most important role of the mass media in supporting overall legitimacy and elite policy, it is argued, is found with (1) supporting new government policy directly by "getting the word out" (Domhoff 1975, 2006a; Dye 1995); (2) shaping more general worldviews favorable to the dominant political economy; and (3) ridiculing alternatives to the present political economy (Miliband 1969; Domhoff 1970, 1979, 2010). The first function was considered in some detail in Chapter 6. Thus, at this point our focus will be on the latter, more abstract, functions.

In recent years I have been doing field work on poverty and corruption in Thailand, Vietnam, Laos, and Cambodia. In one of the most corrupt and dictatorial countries in Asia (after North Korea and Burma), I have learned that journalists, labor union leaders, and opposition party members have been imprisoned, beaten, and sometimes killed in Cambodia (Kerbo 2011). The mass media in the United States are not censored, nor are they completely controlled by corporations and the wealthy. This somewhat free environment within which the mass media operate, it is argued (Miliband 1969:219), produces more acceptance for what is presented. There is, in other words, a critical line that must be recognized. Media that are totally independent and unbiased may undermine legitimacy for elites and the political economy, but media that are overly controlled by elites may undermine the legitimacy of the media itself.

Much like universities, many of the mass media are under the influence of the wealthy and corporate class. As with universities, the several means of influence are not always noticed in the day-to-day operation of the major mass media. But such influence is in the background, to be used when limits are violated. There are enough instances in which this influence has been used to keep the media aware of the limits. We can begin by considering some of the means of influence over the media held by corporations and the wealthy.

As Dye (1995:125) put it, "A few private corporations (CBS, NBC, ABC, and Turner Broadcasting, Inc.) largely determine what the people will see and hear about their world; they feed 1,099 local TV stations that account for 80 percent of the news and entertainment broadcasts." (Turner stations and CNN are now owned by AOL Time Warner.) More important, we must recognize that the major mass media organizations in the United States today are big corporations owned by other big corporations. For example, Disney Corporation owns ABC, General Electric owns NBC, and Westinghouse owns CBS (Domhoff 2002:114). Table 13-1 shows the top six media

## TABLE 13-1

### Top Six Media Conglomerates in the United States, 2010

| Corporation | 2008 Revenues (in billions $) | Holdings |
|---|---|---|
| General Electric | $183 | Television networks NBC and Telemundo; Universal Pictures; Focus Features; 26 television stations in the United States and cable networks MSNBC, Bravo, and the Sci Fi channel; 80% of NBC Universal |
| Walt Disney | 37.8 | ABC television network; cable networks ESPN, the Disney Channel, SOAPnet, A&E, and Lifetime; 277 radio stations; music and book publishing companies; production companies Touchstone, Miramax, and Walt Disney Pictures; Pixar Animation Studios; the cellular service Disney Mobile; theme parks around the world |
| News Corporation | 33 | Fox Broadcasting Company; television and cable networks Fox, Fox Business Channel, National Geographic, and FX; *Wall Street Journal, New York Post,* and *TVGuide; Barron's, SmartMoney,* and *The Weekly Standard;* HarperCollins; production companies 20th Century Fox; Fox Searchlight Pictures, and Blue Sky Studios; numerous Web sites including MarketWatch.com; the National Rugby League |
| Time Warner | 29.8 | CNN, the CW (a joint venture with CBS), HBO, Cinemax, Cartoon Network, TBS, and TNT; America Online; MapQuest; Moviefone; Warner Bros. Pictures, Castle Rock, and New Line Cinema; more than 150 magazines including *Time, Sports Illustrated, Fortune, Marie Claire,* and *People* |
| Viacom | 14.6 | MTV, Nickelodeon/Nick-at-Nite, VH1, BET, and Comedy Central; Paramount Pictures, Paramount Home Entertainment, Atom Entertainment, and music game developer Harmonix; Viacom 18, a joint venture with Indian media company Global Broadcast news |
| CBS Corporation | 14 | CBS Television Network, CBS Television Distribution Group, the CW (a joint venture with Time Warner), and Showtime; Simon & Schuster; 29 television stations; CBS Radio, Inc., which has 140 stations; leading supplier of video to Google's new Video Marketplace |

*SOURCE*: www.freepress.net.

conglomerates as of 2010 and some of their ownership of media in America. Together these six media conglomerates control about 75 percent of all prime-time viewing in the United States today (Khan 2003).

As noted in the beginning of this chapter, fewer people read newspapers in the United States than in any other industrial nation. And the number has been declining steadily in the last 30 years, from 36 percent of the population to just 25 percent. As the numbers drop, the concentration of newspaper ownership becomes even greater. Currently, "fifteen newspaper empires account for more than one half of the total newspaper circulation in the United States" (Dye 1995:113).

It is widely recognized and admitted that our major mass media make news in the sense that they select what will be presented and *how* it will be presented (Gans 1979; Lester 1980; Dye 1995). Thus we get a view of our nation and the world that is structured by media elites. As noted earlier, the mass media are free in the United States, but there are limits. With the potential corporate influence described previously, and with their operating funds coming primarily from corporate advertising (Marger 1987:220–224), the media cannot afford to alienate major corporations.

The media must report corporate and political scandals, but they must be careful to be "objective" (as this is defined by those in power), or not to present these events "too extensively" or in such a way as to challenge the more general political economy. Put another way, they must report that the airline industry or oil companies have been involved in price fixing but be careful not to say something like "This is another example of what can result from the structure of corporate concentration unrestrained by government regulation."

In an extensive examination of how the media elites are led to censor news and slant what is presented to protect corporate and upper-class interests in the United States, Herman and Chomsky (1988) studied major news stories and other events that were not presented as major news stories by media elites. For example, they wanted to know why it was more "newsworthy" (that is, much more news coverage given) when a religious leader was killed by government officials in Poland during the early 1980s than when many, many more religious leaders were killed during the same time period by government officials in Latin American countries supported by the U.S. government (Herman and Chomsky 1988:40).

In their examination of many cases such as the preceding, Herman and Chomsky developed a model focusing on five factors that create a slant in the news favoring U.S. corporate and government interests. First, they note, as we have earlier, how much of the news media in the United States is owned by the upper class and major corporations and is directed by interests of profits.

Second, because the major mass media primarily depend on advertising to stay in business, this leaves the media open to pressure from corporate elites, who can withdraw this economic means of the media's existence. Herman and Chomsky cite many cases throughout their book of when this has happened. For example, in 1985, when a public television station showed a documentary called "Hunger for Profit" that was critical of specific U.S. multinational corporations' activities in third world countries that helped to produce more hunger in these countries, Gulf & Western complained that the program was "virulently anti-business if not anti-American" and cut all funding previously given to the station (Herman and Chomsky 1988:17).

Third, Herman and Chomsky (1988:2) note that "the reliance of the media on information provided by government, business, and 'experts' funded and approved by these primary sources and agents of power" leads to limits placed on information we receive, and a slant toward supporting the interests of these powerful groups in the news that is presented.

Fourth, there are "flak-generating" organizations that will create so many problems for the media if they present information corporate and top political elites find "objectionable," that mass media organizations learn what must be "self-censored." Again, Herman and Chomsky (1988) describe many actual cases in which this happened in the 1980s and before, and list organizations that have established these "flak-producing" agencies. For example, in the 1970s and 1980s, "the corporate community sponsored the growth of institutions such as the American Legal Foundation, the Capital Legal Foundation, and Accuracy in Media" (Herman and Chomsky 1988:27), among others, to intimidate the mass media through lawsuits and publicity campaigns attacking the media if they disliked their presentation of the news. More recently there are examples of large corporations simply trying to censor the content of movies and TV programs of media companies they own. One famous case was the attempt to prevent release of Michael Moore's *Fahrenheit 9/11;* another was the attempt to stop release of Michael Cain's movie *The Quiet American* because it presented a critical (though accurate) picture of U.S. involvement in terrorist activities during America's entrance into the Vietnam War (*International Herald Tribune,* November 13, 2003; BBC, November 8, 2002, May 5, 2004).

Finally, in many news stories of foreign events and U.S. foreign policy, Herman and Chomsky (1988:2) found that "anticommunism" is like "a national religion and control mechanism" that can be used to mislead the public and justify what is done in U.S. corporate and government interests.

Concerning all five of these "filters" on the news, Herman and Chomsky (1988:2) write that "the elite domination of the media and marginalization of dissidents that results from the operation of these filters occurs so naturally that media news people, frequently operating with complete integrity and goodwill, are able to convince themselves that they choose and interpret the news 'objectively' and on the basis of professional news values." However, the "constraints are so powerful, and are built into the system in such a fundamental way, that alternative bases of news choices are hardly imaginable."

In the context of the preceding, it is interesting to examine the old Soviet news media. It will probably come as a surprise to most Americans, influenced by the U.S. news "filters" described earlier, that Dan Rather, Peter Jennings, and Tom Brokaw's counterpart in the old Soviet Union, Vladimir Dunayev, did not have his news scripts approved by the state before his evening news broadcast (*Time,* June 23, 1980:58). Dunayev, of course, was not free to say anything he liked; neither, for that matter, were Rather, Jennings, and Brokaw. They all knew the limits, and they all wanted to keep their jobs. But it is more complex than this because they had all learned to respect what it means to be "professional" and "responsible." That is one reason they were at the top of their profession. They all work within the norms of their profession that prescribe limits. These limits are developed through a history of events that have brought pressure from the state, courts, and private citizens or corporations when the limits were seen as violated.

We think that the news media in communist and other totalitarian states are not free because of state domination. This is more clearly the case with books and magazines, for which state review before publication is the norm. For the most part this is accepted. (See Solzhenitsyn's very interesting description [1980] of the battles by the magazine *Novy Mir* to get his works published in the Soviet Union.) But professional journalists in the former Soviet Union did not think that the United States news media were free because of the influence of corporate domination. The "real facts," of course, are subject to interpretation. They are interpreted through differing worldviews established through the process of legitimation in each country. The top media professionals in every country, because they are a part of their society and its worldview, practice self-censorship (consciously and unconsciously).

Also, the marketplace of ideas in the United States is free to the extent that one has money—lots of it. Major corporations can buy advertising time to tell us how good their companies are and what they are doing to help the country. We continually hear how oil companies are helping us by finding oil with "inadequate" profits, how chemical companies are giving us better lives and how safe all their products are, how drug companies need their very high profits to discover new drugs, and so on. Corporate advertising is designed to sell large companies' view of economics as well as their products (Miliband 1969:215).

In addition to the ad campaigns by individual corporations, the Advertising Council is an arm of major corporations that attempts to present a favorable image of corporations in general and influence public opinion about economic issues. A good example of this is the Ad Council's radio and television advertising campaign to "upgrade" the public's "economic quotient" by showing how "free enterprise really works in the best interest of the country" (see Domhoff 1979:183–191). Of course, in none of the Ad Council's advertisements do we find out about the extent of market concentration, the concentration of corporate ownership, interlocking directorates, or other such matters.

In considering the ability of television to shape worldviews, we must remember that most of what people see is not news or advertising but entertainment programs. Cerulo (1984) has found that the images and symbols presented in all the major forms of mass media have become more standardized since World War II, primarily because of television's becoming widespread in the 1950s. The exact influence of these programs is most difficult to measure, but many social scientists have argued that what people see works to emphasize class stereotypes, degrade minorities, make "radical" ideas appear ridiculous, and praise dominant American values (Miliband 1969:228; Sallach 1974; Gitlin 1979). The heroes almost never express unaccepted political and economic ideas; in fact, they are usually "antiradical." The working-class characters are usually unintelligent, bigoted, and superpatriotic. The old Archie Bunker character from one of the longest-running shows in American television, of course, was meant to present a satire. But Vidmar and Rokeach (1974) found that people who enjoyed watching the show tended to be more rather than less prejudiced (Dye 1979:109).

The mass media cannot be accused of dominating or constructing worldviews for the public in favor of accepted corporate values. The mass media are only part of the legitimation process, and they are as much a product of the legitimation process as they are a part of it. If the mass media step out of line in presenting views critical of the corporate structure, America in general, or major values held by the population, they must answer to influential corporations as well as to the public. The legitimation process is cyclic, and the public that has come to accept the legitimacy of our political economy expects to see it supported by the mass media.

## Opinion-Influencing Organizations

The educational system and the mass media are the most recognized means of shaping opinions, but many organizations are formed by interest groups to get their point across to the public. The struggle for minds is carried on by many voluntary organizations that use the media, distribute books and pamphlets, and sponsor discussion seminars.

When an interest group has wealthy backers or a very wide following among the population, it can usually get plenty of money for such activities. When an interest group has no wealthy backers and only a relatively small following (or even a large following of relatively poor people), it is at a disadvantage. When the latter is the case, however, there is at least some hope of getting the point across by "using" the media. Demonstrations, sit-ins, marches, and even lawsuits will often bring media attention, although there is a chance of discrediting the aims of the group by using such tactics.

There is also a strong possibility that a group going against the power structure will be discredited through the activities of government agencies. Such activities include planting false information about the group in the press, using blackmail, planting false information within the group to promote infighting, and using agent provocateurs to create violent incidents that are blamed on social movement members. The CIA and the FBI have admitted doing all these things in the United States (see Marx 1974; Mintz and Cohen 1976:367–385; Domhoff 1979:196).

The concern at this point is opinion-influencing organizations supported by corporations or agencies of the federal government that attempt to support the status quo. We begin by examining corporate and upper-class organizations. In Chapter 6 the functions of the Council on Foreign Relations (CFR) and the Committee for Economic Development (CED) were described. It is the job of these organizations to influence government policy. But these groups also have affiliations that attempt to shape public opinion (Domhoff 2010:104–105).

For example, with the CFR there is the Foreign Policy Association (FPA), whose directors are mostly CFR members and corporate officials (Rosenau 1961; Domhoff 1970:151). The FPA sponsors World Affairs Councils, discussion groups, and speakers for local gatherings (like the League of Women Voters) to discuss the views of corporate leaders on matters of world affairs.

The CFR also sponsors Committees on Foreign Relations that meet about once a month to hear speakers provided by the CFR or the government (Shoup and Minter 1977; Domhoff 1979:174). The goal of Committees on Foreign Relations is to inform local community elites on the CFR's view of foreign affairs so these local elites, in turn, can inform citizens in their communities. In addition to these activities, the FPA and CFR are linked with the American Assembly and the United Nations Association, which organize discussion groups around the country and foreign affairs institutes at universities to "spread the word" (Domhoff 2010:104–107).

With respect to domestic economic issues, the CED, like the CFR, has affiliated organizations that attempt to influence opinion on economic questions. Remembering our discussion of the importance of public schools in shaping ideas about economic issues, it is perhaps understandable that the CED formed an organization to make sure students are "properly taught."

The Joint Council on Economic Education was formed in 1949 by the CED with funding by the Ford Foundation (Schriftgiesser 1967). "Its biggest donors in 1975 were the American Bankers Association, AT&T, International Paper Company Foundation, the J. M. Foundation, Northern Natural Gas Company, the Sears Roebuck Foundation, the Sloan Foundation and the Department of Health, Education and Welfare" (Domhoff 1979:180). The Joint Council conducts minicourses and summer workshops to train teachers in economics (with 19,500 participants in 1974), and helps develop textbooks and curricula to be used by teachers (Domhoff 1979:181). Through activities such as these, corporate leaders can influence public school teachers and, through them, their students.

We have no direct research on the outcome of ad campaigns, discussion groups, seminars, teacher training, or books and pamphlets sponsored by these groups. We must assume that corporations and wealthy families believe they have some effect because they continue to spend millions of dollars on such efforts. These organizations are only one part of the legitimation process geared toward specific issues and support for the general political economy. But they are most likely an important part. Corporate elites cannot simply hope that support for their views will be forthcoming. They must work for support and do so through a large network of organizations that lead from corporate boardrooms to the general public.

We do know, however, that the most conservative and corporate-sponsored think tanks are much more likely than liberal or union-sponsored groups to get their views expressed in the mass media (Domhoff 2002:115). Studies show that TV news programs and talk shows, as well as other mass media, are more likely to interview and present experts who are in favor of U.S. government policies.

## The Macro Legitimation Process: A Conclusion

It would be incorrect to view the legitimation process in the United States as a simple conspiracy. There are, of course, behind-the-scenes plans to induce the public to accept what elites are doing or plan to do. But the process usually falls short of what we generally think of as a conspiracy for several reasons. First, in contrast to the situation in totalitarian societies, the *overall* process of legitimation in the United States is unplanned. There is planning on specific issues and policies—to maintain public acceptance of military and economic intervention in other countries, of specific economic policies in this country, of nuclear energy, of pollution policies, and so on—but such planning is usually uncoordinated.

Second, no overall plan is accepted by all elites because there are often divisions among elites (as noted in Chapters 6 and 7). One segment of elites may strongly favor a specific policy (for example, foreign intervention supported by multinationals and defense industries) while other elites have less interest in the policy or even oppose it.

In such a case elites may compete for public favor. There are issues on which all elites agree, such as private profit and support of the overall political economy, but even here they may disagree on how the issues should be defended or even whether a defense is needed.

Third, the process of legitimation for specific issues usually falls short of what would be called a conspiracy because most of the process is not secret. Most people are unaware of the process, but the information on what is being done by elite organizations is obtainable. There are cases of hidden operations, as with the CIA's work to legitimate foreign policy or with undisclosed corporate organizations intended to mislead the public on certain issues. Elites do plan behind the scenes to manipulate public opinion. There are charges that the George W. Bush administration was censuring government reports from agencies like the Department of Education and U.S. Census Bureau to a greater extent than any administration in many decades. In 2004 the Union of Concerned Scientists issued a report signed by 20 Nobel Prize winners charging that the Bush administration was manipulating public opinion and harming the progress of science in the United States (*New York Times,* February 19, 2004). But the process cannot usually be described as a conspiracy, even though it is often quite effective and unrecognized by the public.

It would also be incorrect to assume that elites can make anything they do appear legitimate in the eyes of nonelites. There are limits, although these are seldom clearly defined or unchanging (Moore 1978). Cultural and historical forces operate to establish limits, but these forces are subject to change. During the late 1960s and early 1970s, for example, big tax breaks for corporations and drastic cutbacks in government social spending would have been difficult to defend. But as we now know, the 1980s brought new limits in this respect, which were continued through the 2000s. An enlightened elite learns to work with cultural and historical forces in its favor. When the public, for whatever reason, seems ripe for some kind of change, elites will be ready with the changes they want and will attempt to make the changes appear to be in the national interest.

Finally, we must recognize that everything done by elites need not be accepted as legitimate. On one hand, most of the public is often unaware of what is being done by elites. In this respect, a highly informed public would be threatening to elites—despite elite rhetoric to the contrary. From the perspective of rational self-interest, the game is to keep as much information from the public as possible, especially if the information might be controversial. And when pressed for information by the public, the game is to let out as little information as possible (Schattschneider 1960).

On the other hand, even when a policy that goes against public opinion is known by the public, elites will be able to continue the policy unless there is a strongly organized interest group or social movement to challenge it. The task for elites in this case is to prevent an organized challenge by discrediting their opponents, creating confusion, or discouraging the hope that change is possible.

For the most part, however, the public is apathetic unless it recognizes that an issue affects it strongly. We have seen evidence indicating the general public favors much more income equality than presently exists. But more income equality would most benefit relatively powerless groups and harm the interests of relatively powerful

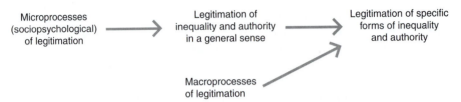

**FIGURE 13-1**     *The Interaction of Micro- and Macroprocesses of Legitimation*

groups, which means most of the population remains apathetic. Besides, efforts to reduce income inequality can be opposed by elites on procedural issues. A bill may be introduced in Congress to reduce income inequality, but before it passes (if ever) it will be so altered as to render it ineffective.

In the second half of this chapter we have examined how legitimacy for specific policies, for specific elites, and for a specific form of political economy can be maintained. Building on a sociopsychological base of acceptance for inequality in general, the educational system, the mass media, and specific opinion-shaping organizations can work to legitimate more specific forms of inequality. The overall process operates in the manner outlined in Figure 13-1. The trick is for elites to use the sociopsychological process of legitimation to their advantage. They learn to play upon the public's acceptance of inequality in an abstract sense to make what they do acceptable. They usually do this by making what elites do appear to be in the interests of nonelites and by making their contributions appear to be greater than those of others.

All of what has been described in this chapter implies that a delegitimation process can occur as well. The legitimation process is an ongoing process that can be weakened or reversed. The legitimation of inequality and stratification in general is simpler to maintain (Mann 1970; Della Fave 1980); but, as described, there are at least four levels of legitimation, and delegitimation at lower levels of abstraction may coexist with legitimation on a higher level.

For example, the failure of elites to maintain social order or economic well-being *may* produce delegitimation at progressively higher levels (Mankoff 1970; Della Fave 1980). Disorder (political and/or economic) may result in a loss of legitimacy for specific elites and their policies if not corrected. And through time, if other elites and new policies cannot restore order, the political economy itself may lose legitimacy, with the population willing to support a new form of political economy (for example, socialism or fascism). We say disorder *may* result in a loss of legitimacy because for at least a period of time elites may be able to successfully blame outside forces for the disorder. Perhaps for this reason there is a natural tendency for all elites to seek scapegoats.

Throughout history inequality has generally been accepted. But it is not always accepted, especially on lower levels of abstraction. As we saw in our review of inequality in the history of human societies, elites are rejected from time to time, as are particular forms of social stratification. As we also saw at many points in earlier chapters, the level of inequality is quite high in the United States. Given this high level of inequality, the biggest question is not why people rebel but why people rebel so seldom. In this chapter we have attempted to provide some answers to the second question.

## Summary

The subject of this chapter has been the legitimation process, or the process by which the nature of social stratification and the level of inequality in a society are made legitimate or at least relatively acceptable to the population. The subject is divided into the microprocess and the macroprocess. In the microprocess, we examined how norms of distributive justice, self-evaluations, and the ideology of equality of opportunity can be manipulated to maintain acceptance for a certain type of social stratification and inequality. In the macroprocess, we focused on how information about what exists in a society that will legitimate inequality can be shaped by the educational system, mass media, and opinion-influencing organizations, all of which can be influenced in many ways by the more wealthy and powerful in the society.

# Social Stratification beyond the United States

# The World Stratification System: Dominance and Competition among Core Nations

The huge temple of Borobudor (left) on the island of Java in Indonesia is from one of the oldest civilizations in Southeast Asia. People from this civilization were the most advanced seafaring people in the world 1,500 years ago. The ruins of an old fort (right) in the city of Malacca on the western coast of Malaysia was occupied 500 years ago. This area was first taken by Portuguese colonials, then about a century later by Dutch colonials, and finally by the British. Malaysia did not gain independence until the mid-20th century. Westerners have little realization that their world dominance has been quite recent and is likely to be relatively short-lived. The ups and downs of world regions over the centuries is one of the subjects of this chapter and the next two chapters as well.

*SOURCES:* © Harold Kerbo.

## Chapter Outline

As I wrote in the introduction to this chapter for the 4th edition, I can again write that in many ways the world is a different place than it was when I completed the previous edition. In the previous edition I was referring to the accumulative changes brought about by the fall of communism around the world. In some ways it is again a different world after the September 11, 2001, terrorist attacks on the United States. But these events in part can also be understood as flowing from changes taking place in the world system from the post–World War II era through the 1980s and 1990s.

As other capitalist industrial nations were in ashes after World War II, by default the United States was left as the only capitalist power that could defend capitalist interests against the emerging communist nations. Then, with the fall of communism beginning late in the 1980s, the United States was left as the world's only superpower. In the world stratification system, this means that it is up to the United States and American political and economic elites to maintain the world stratification system for the interests of themselves and their capitalist allies among the other rich nations. To understand this sufficiently we must recognize that much like the domestic class conflicts within nations we have focused on throughout previous chapters, there is international "class conflict." Within the international stratification system, there are "upper-class" nations trying to maintain their advantages while lower-class nations are often struggling to change the stratification system or their place within it. This situation, of course, gives the United States and American elites an advantage in the world's international class conflicts. The United States and its elites have extensive power to protect their interests and maintain their favored positions. There are, however, negatives, such as the human and financial costs of attempting to be the world's watchdog to protect oil supplies in the Middle East as well as being the target of attacks by groups angry about many conditions in the world today. An international opinion poll some 3 months after the September 11 attacks on the United States, for example, found that a majority of people in less-developed countries blame the United States for many of the world's ills. International opinion polls between 2001 and 2005 showed a growing fear of the United States as one of the biggest threats to world peace (see, for example, various BBC polls [http://www.bbc.co.uk], and The Pew Research Center [pewresearch.org]). An international poll by the Pew Research Center in 2009 and another by Gallup in 2010 found more favorable views of the United States around the world, but also that the United States was not seen as the world leader that it used to be (www. gallup. com).

In this chapter we begin an examination of the world stratification system, or modern world system. This chapter first considers the nature and history of this world stratification system, then competition among the richer nations in the world during the last 500 years, but with a focus on the present. As mentioned in earlier chapters, we will see in more detail why much of the inequality and life chances for differing classes in the United States are affected by this system of global stratification.

Chapter 15 examines the stratification systems of the second and third largest economies in the world today. In important ways, Japan and Germany differ significantly from the world's capitalist leader, the United States. We will see that their political, economic, and stratification systems lead to advantages and disadvantages in global competition for the 21st century. And we will see that their differences have profound consequences for the well-being of people in Japan and Germany when compared to the United States.

Finally, in Chapter 16 we consider the world's poor and the impact of the world stratification system on their prospects of moving out of desperate poverty. Theory and research on the modern world system, along with antiglobalization protesters, suggest that much of the world's poverty is caused by the actions of rich nations and their multinational corporations in search of profits. As we will see, there is much evidence supporting these views, but as always the world is rather more complex. With comparisons of less-developed countries in Latin America, Africa, and Asia, we find that people in these world regions are affected differently by the modern world system, with some key characteristics of many less-developed nations in Asia allowing them to slowly overcome their situations of poverty.

Before we take up these subjects, though, a review of recent world history is useful. We need to put these events into perspective and consider how they are driven by characteristics of the world stratification system before we can examine the modern world system in more detail.

## *The Fall of Communism*

In the last 50 years no other event has changed the world more profoundly than the fall of communism around the world. It happened so rapidly and unexpectedly that few people at the time understood why it happened, or the full consequences of the transformation.

On August 19, 1989, one of Poland's Solidarity leaders (Tadeusz Mazowiecki) became the first noncommunist prime minister of an eastern European country since World War II. This occurred soon after the communist government of Poland allowed the labor union, Solidarity, to legally exist for the first time, and then called for national elections. Solidarity candidates took a majority of seats in Poland's parliament in this national election during June 1989. Many of the Solidarity candidates who won office had recently been in jail.

Then, in November and December 1989, more such events occurred with a rapidity that caused the world to look on in amazement. On November 10 the Berlin Wall fell and the East German communist government resigned; on November 28 the communist government in Czechoslovakia resigned and gave power to opposition leader Vaclav Havel; on December 23 a popular revolution led to the fall of the communist government in Romania; and other communist governments in eastern Europe were promising reforms and scheduling multiparty elections. Then, on October 3, 1990, Germany was reunified and East Germany ceased to exist, potentially producing an even more dominant German economy for some Europeans to worry about.

The biggest in this chain of events, however, came in 1991: The Soviet Union suddenly ceased to exist. The collapse left the central country of Russia with a noncommunist government and many independent states that had broken off from the old Soviet Union. The world was left with China as the last major "communist" country, but a country recording the most rapid economic growth of the last 20 years, and doing so in a most uncommunist fashion.

## The Reemergence of Asia

Even before all of this, of course, there was the new economic threat for Western powers from Japan. Japan was the first, and as yet only, advanced industrial nation in the world from Asian traditions and culture. Until quite recently the world economy had been European-centered. Yes, the 20th century had been dominated by the United States, but this North American economic power was only an extension of the European-centered core that started in the 1500s. Few people realize, though, that Asia accounted for more of the world's economy until as recently as 1820 (Kristof and WuDunn 2000:30).

About 1,000 years ago China and India dominated the economic world (Frank 1998). While Japan has remained in economic stagnation for the past 15 years, according to World Bank estimates the world's third (and soon to be second) largest economy is now China. India is also moving up and is ahead of other European nations in overall size of GDP. Neither China nor India will have an average standard of living for its people comparable to European Union countries or the United States any time soon (Meredith 2007; Luce 2007). But the overall size of their economies, and especially China being the largest exporter of goods in the world, have again made Asian economies (along with Japan, South Korea, and Taiwan) dominate in the world economy. Just 50 years ago China had been mired in civil war, revolution, and Japanese invasion for decades. Many millions of Chinese died in these wars, and millions more starved. Mothers in the United States were telling their children "finish the food on your plate, think of all the starving children in China." We saw in the beginning of Chapter 3 that China closed its borders and dismantled those "treasure ships" that were sailing through much of the world, making Chinese merchants rich. The upper classes in China were afraid the newly wealthy merchant class would come to dominate them (Menzies 2002; Levathes 1994). After 300 to 400 years, European nations surpassed China in trade, science, and technology, leading to China's rapid decline and European colonization of Asia by the 1800s. But as we will see in the final chapter of this book, several countries in today's modern world system, primarily in Asia, have discovered how to reestablish their older civilizations and state authority, developing an Asian form of capitalism poised to overtake many Western economies.

## Capitalist Competition

Now that communist economies are gone, however, we have discovered capitalisms. While we used to be told it was "them" (them being the Soviet Union and their allies), and "us" (us being all of the other industrial nations), we find it is no longer so clear. As we saw in Chapter 7 (Table 7-5), the three largest industrial nations at the end of the 20th century—the United States, Japan, and Germany—had very different forms of what we used to think of as democratic capitalism. Japan, among other things, has elites who are more unified and influential than anywhere else, and in many ways has much less democracy than Western industrial nations. Theirs is a planned economy organized by government bureaucrats still dominating a corporate class united in powerful monopolistic groups without significant private family ownership of the means of production that is supposed to exist with capitalism.

China continues to have an undemocratic communist political system, but with a more free market economy that is rapidly moving up in the world. State ownership of the economy is now less than 50 percent and is being steadily reduced. China is the largest exporter of goods in the world and has loaned the United States trillions of dollars to bail out our government's debt. Vietnam is in many ways a smaller copy of China today, continuing with its communist political system, but moving rapidly to a more free market economic system. Slowly recovering from its wars with the French colonials and then the United States, Vietnam also realized by the late 1980s that a communist economy would not work. As we will see in the last chapter of this book, Vietnam opened its economy to private ownership and to corporations of the world with economic reforms called *Doi Moi*. Vietnam quickly moved away from mass hunger to become one of the world's fastest growing economies by the 1990s and 2000s, and just as quickly the world's second largest exporter of rice and coffee (Kerbo 2006: Chapter 9).

The other major economic power, Germany, is also different when compared with the United States. Since World War II, Germany has had extensive labor laws—such as the Works Constitution Act, co-determination laws, and strong works councils in every company—along with powerful labor unions. All of these things give German workers much influence in how each company is managed and operated, as well as much influence in how the overall economy is run. This situation, most capitalists in America would tell us, cannot create a strong competitive economy. But it is with these labor laws and powerful unions that Germany rebuilt after World War II to become the third largest economic power after Japan and the United States, and the world's biggest exporter of goods and services until China overtook them in 2010.

In many ways, in fact, contrary to what most Americans would think, it is the United States that is the odd capitalist country. Some of this oddity is related to the characteristics needed for economic dominance at the beginning of the 20th century—abundant land, cheap resources, a motivated but not so educated workforce, and a minimum of government involvement in the economy (Thurow 1991). To this day the United States has much less government involvement in the economy than Japan and most of Europe. But the United States is also different in that there is still more private ownership of corporate stock in the United States than in Japan and especially Europe, where large percentages of corporations have much government ownership. There are only limited labor laws in the United States compared with Europe and Japan, and, as we have seen, labor unions are extremely weak in the United States compared with other industrial nations. Not least in importance, the United States has much more income inequality, in fact the highest among industrial nations, while Germany has one of the lowest rates of inequality in the world. The key differences between the different types of capitalism today and implications for competition among rich nations in the 21st century will be considered in more detail after we examine the main characteristics of the modern world system.

## World Poverty

While rich countries were competing with each other the last 200 years, the gap between the rich and poor of this world became immense. A World Bank estimate noted that "As late as 1820, per capita incomes were quite similar around the world—and very low, ranging from around $500 in China and South Asia to $1,000–1,500 in the richest countries of Europe" (World Bank 2000:45). As the 21st century began, the annual per capita income of people in rich countries like the United States was $30,600 compared to $500 in many poor countries such as Sierra Leone, Tanzania, and Ethiopia.* Close to 20 percent of the world's population (over 1 billion people) lived on less than $1 a day at century's end. Almost half of the world's population (2.8 billion people) lived on less than $2 per day. In another report, the United Nations figures that the number of people existing on less than $1 a day has increased directly with globalization during the 1990s (United Nations, *A Better World for All,* 2000); United Nations Development Program, *Overcoming Human Poverty,* 2000). As we have seen, the first ever estimate of global wealth inequality indicates that the top 2 percent of people in the world own over half of all the world's wealth, while the bottom 50 percent of people own less than 1 percent (Davis et al. 2006). As for income, the top 20 percent of people receive 150 times the income of the bottom 20 percent of people. Just 30 years ago this gap was 60 to 1 instead of 150 to 1. The United Nations' Food and Agriculture Organization estimates that there are 800 million chronically undernourished people in the world, with another 2 billion people experiencing crucial deficiencies in nutrients. UNICEF reports that malnutrition is a factor in about 55 percent of the 12 million preventable deaths among children younger than five every year. The rich are getting richer while many of the poor are getting poorer, not just in the United States but even more so worldwide (Korzeniewicz and Moran 1997; Kerbo 2006).

The causes of World Wars I and II, the fall of communism, competition among the world's economic powers, the steady rise of inequality within the United States, increasing world poverty and inequality, and even terrorist attacks against the rich countries—none of these events of recent years can be fully understood without reference to the system of global stratification often referred to as the **modern world system.** It is now time to consider modern world system theory and research in more detail before we return to these subjects.

# ✵ Characteristics of the World Stratification System

Soon after the first industrial societies took root in the declining bed of Western feudalism, there was no doubt an increasing awareness that separate nations were more and more tied through economic exchange. But the extent of these economic

---

*World Bank, *World Development Report, 2000 2001* (2000:274–275). Note that these figures are calculated in the new Purchasing Power Parity Index, which more accurately takes into account lower prices for basic necessities in poor countries compared to rich countries in North America, Europe, and Japan. Using the standard measures of per capita income there are dozens of countries listed as having annual per capita incomes of $200 and $300.

ties grew more rapidly than the full awareness of their importance. In the early works of economists such as Adam Smith, for example, such awareness was not yet sufficient. In the mid-1800s Karl Marx did have something to say about the worldwide growth of capitalism (see Chase-Dunn 1975:721–722; 1989), but he left the task of specifying how advanced capitalist nations would dominate others to Lenin (1965) some 50 years later. Still, Lenin's work on imperialism remained incomplete in many details. It was not until after the middle of the 20th century that an abundance of literature on what we know as the world stratification system emerged. Indeed, it has been only in the last couple of decades that the full extent of what is often commonly called "globalization" has been widely recognized. While the extent and speed of globalization is often exaggerated, there is abundant data showing the spread of economic as well as cultural globalization, a process bringing even the previously most remote people into the world stratification system (Chase-Dunn, Kawano, and Brewer 2000; Held et al. 1999).

To understand the basic nature of the world stratification system, we must begin by recognizing the worldwide division of labor. As differentiated from the traditional view of economic systems corresponding with political or national boundaries, an economic division of labor cuts across these boundaries, bringing national territories within a worldwide economic system (see Wallerstein 1974:348–349).

Snyder and Kick (1979:1099–1100) summarize three main points in the world-system perspective:

> First, the world system is the appropriate point of conceptual orientation. The behavior and experiences of its constituent geopolitical units depend fundamentally on features of the system as a whole (e.g., a capitalist world economy) which reflect transnational linkages. Second, the modern world system is composed of three structural positions: core, semiperiphery, and periphery. Third, these labels are not merely descriptive. They indicate an international division of labor in which the core is linked to the periphery (and semiperiphery) in dynamic and exploitative ways.

We will have much more to say about the structural positions in this modern world system (that is, core, semiperiphery, and periphery). But for now we must stress the important implications of this world system for understanding world stratification. In earlier chapters we showed how a capitalist property structure and occupational division of labor (along with a bureaucratic power structure) can be located behind the system of social stratification in the United States. Among the results of interaction between property and occupational relations are the following:

**1.** Rather distinct classes are found in relation to the objective divisions created by ownership of the means of production and position in the occupational structure.

**2.** There is an upper class that owns and/or controls the means of production, with a working class having no ownership and performing occupational tasks for owners. In between these two classes we find a middle class with little or no ownership of the means of production, but with a higher occupational position.

**3.** The distribution of valued resources is in large measure based on these class positions.

**4.** There are dynamics of class conflict and change based on the differing distribution of rewards in the class system.

**5.** Finally, there are various mechanisms to maintain the favored position of those on top of the stratification system.

The key point is that once we recognize that capitalist property relations and an occupational division of labor *exist beyond national boundaries,* we must also recognize that there is a *world stratification system* with characteristics similar to the five listed here. The primary unit of analysis, however, has shifted from classes within nations to nations that are in many respects like classes (see Wallerstein 1974:351; Rubinson 1976; Chirot 1977:8). We must caution, however, there remain class divisions within each nation with differing interests with respect to these international ties. Let us proceed by examining the three primary class positions in the world stratification system.

What can be considered as similar to the upper class are the **core nations** (for the characteristics of all three, see Wallerstein 1974:349–351; Chirot 1986; Chase-Dunn 1989; Bornschier and Chase-Dunn 1985; Bornschier 1995). Among the core nations we find those that are most economically diversified, wealthy, and powerful (economically and militarily). These core nations are highly industrialized; they specialize in information, finance, and service industries, and they produce manufactured goods rather than raw materials for export. They also have a more complex occupational structure with generally less income inequality compared with the other nations, with the exception of the United States. In addition, these core nations have relatively more complex and stronger state institutions that help manage economic affairs internally and externally. Finally, these core nations have many means of influence over noncore nations but are themselves relatively independent of outside control (see Table 14-1 for examples of these nations).

## TABLE 14-1

### Examples of Core, Semiperiphery, and Periphery Nations in the World System, 2010*

| Core | Semiperiphery | Periphery |
|---|---|---|
| United States | Mexico | Chad |
| Japan | Argentina | Uganda |
| Germany | South Korea | Burma |
| The Netherlands | Ireland | Laos |
| England | Chile | Bolivia |
| France | Thailand | Philippines |
| Italy | Taiwan | El Salvador |
| Canada | India | Haiti |
| Austria | Pakistan | Dominican Republic |

*This table is a representative listing for nations in the structural positions in the world system from older data presented in research by Snyder and Kick (1979) for a more complete list of 118 nations. The partial list of nations in this table is from Snyder and Kick's study using trade relations, military interventions, and diplomatic and treaty ties as indicators of world system positions.

Similar to the lower or working class are the **periphery nations.** Among the periphery nations we find those that are the least economically diversified. They tend to depend on one type of economic activity, such as extracting and exporting raw materials to the core nations. These nations are relatively poor economically, with less division of labor and a high level of income inequality. There is commonly a wide division between wealthy elites and a poor common mass of people in the country. These nations have relatively weak state institutions, and are strongly influenced by outside nations (both economically and militarily).

**Semiperiphery nations** represent those midway between the core and periphery, similar to a middle class. These are primarily nations moving toward industrialization and a diversified economy. They also can be considered as midway between core and periphery nations with respect to state strength, a complex occupational structure, national wealth, and income inequality. In short, "While they are weaker than core societies, they are trying to overcome this weakness and are not as subject to outside manipulation as peripheral societies" (Chirot 1977:13).

It is worth emphasizing that the world stratification system is a type of class system based on the relationship of a nation to world production forces. Class position in the world system is defined with respect to (1) Marx's perspective of class (ownership versus nonownership of the means of production) and (2) Weber's perspective of class, which, in addition to ownership, stressed economic exchange relations and occupational skill level in the production process.

The core nations (through their major corporations) primarily own and control the major means of production in the world and perform the higher-level production tasks (for example, the more complex industrial production of cars, computers, aircraft, and electronic equipment). The periphery nations own very little of the world's means of production (even when these are located in periphery nations) and provide the less-skilled labor of, for example, extracting raw materials (which are usually exported to core nations for processing into a finished product). The semiperiphery nations are in a mixed or middle position in the world's production system.

Like a class system within a nation, class positions in relation to the world economic system result in an unequal distribution of rewards or resources. The upper-class or core nations receive the greatest share of surplus production, while periphery nations receive the least. Furthermore, because of the economic power of core nations, they are usually able to purchase raw materials and other goods from the noncore nations at low prices, while demanding higher prices for their exports to noncore nations. Chirot (1986) lists the five most important benefits coming to core societies from their domination of the periphery: (1) access to a large quantity of raw material, (2) cheap labor, (3) enormous profits from direct capital investments, (4) a market for exports, and (5) skilled professional labor through migration of these people from the noncore to the core.

For noncore nations, and especially the periphery, there is an unequal exchange or exploitative relationship with core domination. It might appear (and the ideology pushed by core nations maintains) that periphery nations benefit from their relation with core nations. For example, the periphery nations get a market for their raw materials, military aid, factories built (and owned) by core multinational corporations providing jobs for their people, and technical equipment and expertise—all of which could help further economic development in the poor nations.

However, although some benefits for periphery nations may be realized, the total impact of core domination often harms the economic and political well-being of people in periphery nations, especially in the long run. There are certainly differences among the noncore nations, especially in the noncore Asian nations compared with those in South America and Africa, as we will see in Chapter 16.

We should conclude this section on basic characteristics of the modern world system by again stressing the importance of economic factors behind the conflicts and changes in this world system. In his influential book, *The Clash of Civilizations and the Remaking of World Order,* Samuel Huntington (1996) has argued that civilizational divisions are again becoming more important after the fall of the old Soviet Union and at the end of the cold war. No doubt these civilization ties are important in shaping national alliances. Most major nations have old cultural ties with either the Western/Christian, Islamic, Orthodox Christian, Asian/Buddhist, or Hindu civilization, to name some of the most important. Russia's continuing support in the late 1990s of Serbs in the old Yugoslavia despite all their atrocities against Muslims, Croatians, Albanians, and others can best be understood because of the old Orthodox Christian civilizational ties between Russia and Serbs. However, while such civilizational ties are important, a major point of the modern world system is that economic forces are still most important and are becoming more important to what happens to nations and people in the world today.

## Development of the Modern World System

It should be noted in beginning this section that Wallerstein (1974, 1980, 1989) argues that there have been only two types of world systems in existence. The first type has existed in several periods of world history, as what he calls a *world empire.* Although never covering such a large area of the world as today's *world economic system* (using Wallerstein's term), these world empires did include major parts of the world—for example, the Roman Empire, the Near Eastern empire of Alexander the Great, and the Egyptian and Babylonian empires much earlier.

The major distinction between a world empire and a world economy is that in the former a main goal is political as well as economic domination (see Wallerstein 1974:60). As Chirot (1977:20) puts it, "In classical empires, a political elite, as opposed to a business elite, dominated policy. This elite was composed of soldiers, glory-seeking emperors, and learned but antibusiness religious officials." Core elites in the modern world system, by contrast, are economic elites concerned with economic *profit.* A subjected country in the modern world system is not usually controlled in every detail by core elites, occupied by a foreign army, or forced to pay taxes to the dominant country. All of this is rather inefficient in terms of the main goal, which is to extract profits for dominant core elites.

The distinction between world empires and the modern world system is also important in understanding the *development* of the world economic system. When conditions became ripe for a world economic system in about 1450, Spain and Portugal took the lead. They were the first to establish extensive overseas colonies and explore the world for new territories. But Spain and Portugal soon lost their early lead, with England, The Netherlands, and France becoming dominant. Primarily this occurred because the latter nations learned a lesson that Spain and Portugal did not: It becomes too expensive to dominate many countries politically and militarily around the world (Wallerstein 1974:157–179; Chirot 1977:18–20). In short, Spain and Portugal became overextended with empire building and lost their earlier positions of power in the modern world system.

This is not to say that some core countries within the modern world system today never attempt to gain extensive control over periphery nations, and to control them as their colonies. It is a matter of degree when comparing the control a dominant country tried to achieve in a world empire (say, the Roman Empire) with the modern world system. Research by Boswell (1989) on historical trends in the world system since the 1600s has shown that there is variance in the amount of control over periphery nations and colonization. Boswell (1989) found that when the world economy is expanding and core nations are experiencing good economic times, there is less colonization, meaning core nations are not trying to achieve as much control over "their periphery nations." But during poor economic times these core nations tend to attempt more extensive colonial control to keep other core nations from having economic relations with their periphery nations.

# ✎ A Brief History of Core Conflict and Hegemony

As described earlier, the modern world system is in many ways similar to an international stratification system, with conflict over competing interests, much like class conflict. This conflict is centered especially around the differing interests of rich and poorer nations, but it is also clearly evident among the core nations themselves. It must be stressed that not all core nations are equal in wealth and power, and the processes of change in this modern world system lead to continual alterations in the fortunes of the core nations. This places these core nations in conflict with each other, especially over their competing claims of hegemony in periphery areas of the world.

We will consider briefly this history of core conflict, some results of this conflict for the rise and fall of core nations, and some of the political and economic principles that Wallerstein and others believe are behind the changes in the modern world system. As a related issue, we will consider the current position of the United States in the modern world system, along with this country's relative economic decline and growing inequality.

Since the beginning of this modern world system, there has always been a collection of core nations in competition with each other for economic dominance, hegemony over periphery nations, and access to the world's resources. At times the conflict is more overt and deadly, with shifting core alliances as nations try to gain better positions in the process of core conflict. At other times, however brief, there has been one core nation with clear economic dominance over other core nations in the world system.

Wallerstein (1980) considers a core nation as dominant over all others when it has a simultaneous lead in three economic rankings over an extended period. First, *productivity dominance* is important. The nation with productivity dominance can produce products of higher quality and at a lower price compared with other nations. Second, productivity dominance can lead to *trade dominance*. In this situation the balance of trade favors the dominant nation because more nations are buying the products of the dominant nation than it is buying from them. Third, trade dominance can lead to *financial dominance*. With a favorable balance of trade, more money is coming into the nation than is going out. The bankers of the dominant nation tend to become the bankers of the world, with greater control of the world's financial resources.

When a nation achieves these three forms of economic dominance, military dominance is also likely. With a stronger economic base, and with interests tied to a world status quo worth protecting, the dominant core nation tends to build a strong military. However, it must be stressed that during this modern world system no country has been able to use military strength as a *means to gain* economic dominance. In fact, each of the previously dominant core nations has achieved economic dominance with relatively small levels of military spending as each rose to the top, and each began to lose economic dominance with later military expansion (Kennedy 1987).

From the time that this modern world system began in the 1400s to 1500s, Wallerstein (1980) argues, there have been only three brief periods in which one core nation has come to dominate, with each period lasting less than 100 years. The first country to have this clear dominance was The Netherlands during the 1600s. As noted earlier, Spain and Portugal tried to achieve this dominant position but failed when they became overextended, with too many military commitments and colonial territories to protect around the world (Kennedy 1987:47–48). By the 1600s, however, the Dutch achieved this dominance after their political revolution led to a modernized state supporting capitalists, a new financial system some historians call "revolutionary" (Kennedy 1987:76), and the development of new technologies, especially with respect to efficient shipbuilding (Chirot 1986:36). The Dutch shipbuilding industry also helped foster an economic lead through more exports to other nations, and the Dutch fleet provided an advantage in the race for colonies (Wallerstein 1974; Kennedy 1987:67–86).

By becoming the dominant core nation, however, The Netherlands set in motion a process that eventually led to its relative economic decline. First, other nations were able to copy the innovative production and banking methods created by the Dutch. With even newer production methods that were developed since the rise of the Dutch, and knowledge of what originally worked and did not work for the Dutch, other industrializing nations began to challenge Dutch economic dominance, particularly England and France. The productivity edge held by the Netherlands also declined with the rise in its standard of living, a result of its dominant core status. This relatively high standard of living pushed up production costs, making Dutch products somewhat less competitive (Wallerstein 1980:268–269). With loss of productivity dominance, the Dutch trade dominance was soon lost, and with trade dominance gone, financial dominance was eroded.

Although The Netherlands continued to hold financial power, its bankers, seeking profitable investments, went outside the country to a greater degree than in the past. With the development of other industrial nations, Dutch bankers saw more profit potential in these other nations, and the flow of investment capital moved, especially to England (Kennedy 1987:81). This outflow of investment capital further harmed the Dutch economic position even though it helped the profits of Dutch bankers.

With the Dutch in relative decline by the end of the 1600s, conflict among the core nations increased. There had always been wars among core nations, but now (1) the power of the Dutch to enforce world order was reduced, and (2) other nations were fighting for advantage to take the lead once held by the Dutch. The two main nations in this conflict at the time of Dutch decline were England and France. The Dutch had often fought the British, but by the early 1700s they were allies. It was Dutch financial investment that helped the English advance in productivity and trade, and it was Dutch military support that helped the English defeat the French.

It should also be noted, however, that it was an outdated political structure and a rigid stratification system still dominated by the old agrarian aristocracy that hurt the French. The Dutch had what has been called the first "bourgeois revolution" in the 1560s, which gave them more independence from the Hapsburgs in Spain, resulting in a new political system that favored the new capitalist class (Wallerstein 1974:181). In England the capitalist class had achieved dominance over the old landed aristocracy by the 1700s, though this had happened more slowly, over an extended period compared with the Netherlands. But in France, the bourgeois revolution of 1789 came too late for French dominance in the new era of the modern world and capitalist competition (Skocpol 1979). Before 1789 the French government was still dominated by the old landed aristocracy, which resisted economic policies and financial reform that could have made its economy more competitive with England.

With British dominance there was again relative stability in the world system during the 1800s. It was especially a time of British expansion all over the world, with many colonies in Asia, Africa, and the New World. But following the earlier pattern of the Dutch, the British also slid into a relative economic decline. The overextended colonial system placed a strain on the British military, the cost of which also contributed to British economic decline. Thus, like the Dutch, the British held clear dominance in the world system for a relatively short time—from about 1815 to the 1870s (Kennedy 1987:226).

As in the 1700s, there was again extensive core conflict after the English lost their clear dominance. This time Britain and France were allies, with Germany, and later Japan and Italy, providing the new threat to their hegemony in the world. Germany, and then Japan and Italy, were late developers among the industrial nations. It was German and Italian unification in the late 1800s that helped the rise of these two nations, and the Meiji Restoration beginning in 1864 that brought industrialization to Japan (as we will see in the next chapter).

By 1900, however, there was a major difference in the modern world system compared with 100 or 200 years before. Most of the periphery areas of the world had already been claimed by one of the older core nations (Chirot 1986). In 1800 the old European core claimed 35 percent of the world's territory, whereas by 1914 this European core claimed an amazing 85 percent of the world's territory (Kennedy 1987:150). This meant that if a new core nation wanted periphery areas to exploit for economic resources as the French, Dutch, and British had done before, the areas would have to be taken from one of the core nations. This the Germans, and then the Italians and Japanese, began to do in the first half of the 20th century, setting the stage for World War I and World War II.

While the Germans, Italians, and Japanese were moving into core status in the world system in the late 1800s, of course, so was the United States. The defeat of the agrarian South in the American Civil War led to more power for northern industrial elites, who could pressure the government for policies favoring industrial expansion. British bankers at this time were also directing more of their financial investment toward the United States, as the British economy was in relative decline (as did the Dutch bankers when their relative decline was in process). And, like the Dutch and British at the time of their rise to core dominance, the United States had a very small military budget compared with those of all other industrial nations (Kennedy 1987:248).

It was the American entry into World Wars I and II that resulted in Allied victory over Germany, and then Italy and Japan. A key factor in the Allied victory during World War II was the early capture of the secret coding machine developed by the Germans, who also gave it to the Japanese. The result of this was that the U.S. and British forces had advance knowledge of most German and some Japanese military moves (with the major exception of the Battle of the Bulge in December of 1944; see Winterbotham 1974). But it was U.S. industrial capacity by the time of World War II that was most important in defeating the Germans, Italians, and Japanese. By 1943 the United States was producing military equipment at a breathtaking pace. For example, a new airplane was produced every 5 minutes and a new ship every day (Kennedy 1987:355).

The United States began taking the place of England as the new dominant core nation after World War I. But with Europe and Japan in ruins after World War II, the United States was able to dominate the world system more than any other nation in the history of this world system. For example, soon after World War II, the United States alone accounted for over half of all the industrial production in the world, supplied one-third of all the world's exports, and owned two-thirds of the world's supply of gold reserves (Kennedy 1987:358). Along with this economic dominance, the United States took over military dominance, becoming watchdog of the world in protecting periphery areas seen as important to U.S. economic elites and their capitalist allies around the world (Kolko 1988).

## Postwar Competition: The Rise and Fall of the Soviet Union

The new situation known as the cold war was what the United States was primarily involved in as watchdog of the world for its capitalist allies. By agreement at the end of World War II, the American and British forces met in Berlin, cutting Germany in half, with the American, British, and French forces occupying western Europe while Soviet forces occupied eastern Europe. At the very end of World War II, the Soviet Union also moved quickly to take parts of northeastern Asia from the defeated Japanese. The Soviets, however, had in mind to create a new alliance against the capitalist bloc of the core after World War II. Core competition in the modern world system had entered a new stage.

While the Russian Revolution of 1917 is a fascinating subject worthy of considerable study, we must give it only brief attention at this point. It was the conscious intent of Lenin, Stalin, Trotsky, and other Bolsheviks to create a communist state without private ownership of the means of production. But history is not made with only the conscious intent of individual leaders. Before the revolution of 1917, Russia was a rather backward country struggling to modernize and industrialize. A push toward industrialization was begun by Alexander II in the 1860s, and although some gains were made, Russia remained behind most of Europe, with much of its industrial capacity foreign-owned (Crankshaw 1976:218; Salisbury 1977:115–119; Skocpol 1979; Kennedy 1987:233–234). It was a weak economic system in the face of foreign competition that, combined with World War I, led the czar's government to fall to angry masses in February 1917 (Skocpol 1979). Lenin and his party had no direct hand in this fall, but they were organized to pick up the pieces in their revolution of October 1917 (Payne 1964; Keep 1976; Solzhenitsyn 1976).

A communist state became possible in part because of the absence of a strong capitalist class (Moore 1966), and forced industrialization became necessary for the state's survival in the face of foreign and internal threats (Skocpol 1976, 1979:215). There has seldom been a revolution resulting in such a thorough break with the past (Skocpol 1979:206), but even in Russia the old traditions had a hand in shaping the future. These old traditions were an authoritarian state, a strong secret police, and forced labor camps (Crankshaw 1976:63–69). There is abundant evidence (see Fischer 1982) that Lenin, before his death soon after the revolution, attempted to stem the power of a centralized bureaucracy (and Stalin in particular). But, of course, he failed (Payne 1964; Ulam 1973:217; Howe 1978:86). One reason for differing outcomes of revolution can be found in historical forces rooted in the old regime (Skocpol 1976:284). These forces, along with military invasion from the West and civil war, resulted in a centralized, authoritarian bureaucracy that controlled the means of production. In our terms, the political authority structure and property structure were merged.

With Stalin's forced industrialization beginning in the late 1920s, the Soviet Union did achieve rapid industrialization to the point where it was second only to the United States in GNP in the early years of the cold war. By the 1990s, however, the Soviet Union had collapsed, in one of the most amazing events, to symbolically bring an end to this cold war just before the new century began. The timing of the collapse was predicted by no one. But with hindsight we can see that the fall of the Soviet Union was not such a strange new event in the modern world system.

Much like France in its wars and economic competition against Britain during the 1700s, the Soviet economy was weakened due to military competition with the United States. The Dutch, British, and Americans, you will remember, all had comparatively small military budgets when they were rising to core dominance: Military power came later. The Soviets, on the other hand, tried to achieve dominance in the modern world system through military might, without first achieving the economic base to do so.

The "house of cards" that once was the Soviet bloc in eastern Europe fell as well. From the study of social movements, revolutions, and political violence, we know that these events do not occur only because people have become angry and fail to continue accepting exploitation. Resource mobilization theory (McCarthy and Zald 1977; Kerbo 1982) tells us, for example, that rebellions and revolutions usually become massive events and are successful due to changes in the balance of power between rebels and political authorities.

During 1953, 1956, and 1968 there were major rebellions in East Germany, Poland, Hungary, and finally Czechoslovakia. During these rebellions against communism and Soviet dominance, the Soviet tanks came in to crush the protest. In 1981, in the face of rebellion and the growing strength of the Solidarity movement in Poland, the Polish army itself stopped the movement and put leaders such as Lech Walesa in jail so that Soviet tanks would not come in again. But much had changed in the Soviet Union before the next round of east European rebellion occurred. By the late 1980s, the Solidarity movement was rising again. As east Europeans waited in fear, and the whole world watched in amazement, the Soviet tanks did not come in. Rather, Mikhail Gorbachev, who had taken over rule of the Soviet Union in 1985, began taking tanks out of Hungary in 1989. Before the end of the decade, the Berlin Wall had fallen, and so had communist governments all over eastern Europe. As in previous centuries of the modern world system, international competition among the core had led to the downfall of a major power.

The other side in the cold war did not come out of it economically stronger, in contrast to the period right after World War II, even though the United States was the only military superpower after the fall of the Soviet Union. The American economy was badly damaged by years of focus on military spending, research and development for military production rather than consumer production, and a foreign policy oriented toward military competition rather than economic interests around the world. In a popular saying of the time, "The cold war is over; Japan won." In many respects, however, we should mention other winners as well, such as Germany. But with the cold war over, as we will see, the U.S. economic dominance returned—at least for a while. Of course the end of the cold war did not end U.S. action as the watchdog of the world for capitalist industrial nations. Again and again, it was the United States that had to take the lead in protecting the capitalist nations' oil supplies in places like the Middle East, reestablishing stability in the former Yugoslavia, and now fighting terrorism directed against rich nations.

## The Relative Decline, Then Reemergence of the United States

The 1970s came as a big shock to the United States. From the heights of world military and economic dominance during the 25 years immediately after World War II, the U.S. economy hit a period of relative decline, while the nation also lost its first war, in Vietnam. This is not the place to go into all the details of this relative economic decline during the 1970s and 1980s (for discussions of this economic decline, see Vogel 1979, 1985; Blumberg 1980; Bluestone and Harrison 1982; Etzioni 1984; Halberstam 1986; Dore 1987; Harrison and Bluestone 1988; Reich 1981; Thurow 1991; Dietrich 1991). We have already seen the relative economic declines of previous core leaders, which were never able to hold core dominance for as long as 100 years (and actually only between 50 and 75 years). This is what Bornschier (1988, 1995; Bornschier and Suter 1992) refers to as *common cycles* and *long waves of development,* followed by the relative economic decline of previously leading nations.

Table 14-2 indicates the relative decline of U.S. productivity by the end of the 1970s. Looking at the base year of 1967 for all these countries in Table 14-2, we can see

## TABLE 14-2

### Comparative Productivity Growth, 1970–1979 (Base Productivity in 1967 = 100)*

|  | 1970 | 1975 | 1979 |
|---|---|---|---|
| United States | 104.5 | 118.2 | 129.2 |
| Canada | 114.7 | 133.3 | 156.3 |
| France | 121.2 | 150.7 | 189.9 |
| West Germany | 116.1 | 151.3 | 183.8 |
| Japan | 146.5 | 174.6 | 230.5 |
| United Kingdom | 108.8 | 124.2 | 133.0 |

*Note that the base year of productivity in 1967 is set at 100 for every nation. Then each following year's productivity is compared with this base year. Thus, for the United States the 104.5 productivity figure in 1970 showed a slight increase over the 100 level for the 1967 base year.

SOURCE: U.S. Bureau of the Census, *Statistical Abstracts of the United States, 1979* (1980: Table 1591, p. 913).

that U.S. productivity was growing, but not nearly at the rate of some of the other industrial nations in the world, especially Japan. U.S. corporate elites lost the competitive edge due to, among other things, a lack of real competition in a highly concentrated domestic economy, examined in Chapters 6 and 7; a lack of reinvestment as well as research and development; and high costs because of the highest standard of living in the world.

After this relative decline in U.S. productivity became evident in the 1970s, the U.S. trade deficit grew to huge proportions in the 1980s. The U.S. trade imbalance was negative every year in the 1980s, and was well over $100 billion in the red for most years of the decade. During the first half of the 1990s there was only slight improvement in this trade imbalance. Added to this was the loss of U.S. financial dominance. At the beginning of the 1980s, the United States had the largest banks in the world, and more banks listed as among the 10 largest in the world than any other nation. By the end of the decade, however, the United States had only 1 bank among the world's top 10, while the top 8 banks in the world were all Japanese.

With the end of the cold war beginning in 1990, however, the U.S. economic decline was quickly reversed. Indeed, the United States began its longest economic boom in history, which did not slow until 2001. As can been seen in Table 14-3, the United States led the seven largest industrial economies with annual growth in the economy (GNP), percent increases in domestic investment rate increases per year, and annual productivity increases, while maintaining the lowest unemployment rate (with the exception of Japan, which keeps unemployment artificially low even in times of economic stagnation). The U.S. stock market increased its value more than 100 percent in just a few years of the 1990s (Mishel et al. 1999:268).

A primary question at this point is, *how did the United States create this turn-around in its economic competitiveness relative to other industrial nations?* It is time to again consider this question because it is directly related to the nature of social stratification in the United States.

**TABLE 14-3**

**Core Nation Economic Indicators, 1990–2000**

| Nation | Annual GNP growth 1990–2000 | % Growth domestic investment 1990–2000 | Average productivity increases 1995–2000 | Unemployment 1995–2000 |
|---|---|---|---|---|
| United States | 3.4% | 7.0% | 2.6% | 4.5% |
| Japan | 1.4 | 1.1 | 1.8 | 4.2 |
| Germany | 1.5 | 0.5 | 1.7 | 8.6 |
| Great Britain | 2.2 | 1.8 | 1.5 | 5.3 |
| France | 1.7 | −1.6 | 1.4 | 11.1 |
| Italy | 1.2 | −1.0 | 0.6 | 11.5 |
| Canada | 2.3 | 2.6 | 1.2 | 7.2 |

*SOURCES:* World Bank, *World Development Report, 2000* (2000); U.S. Bureau of the Census, Statistical Abstracts of the United States, 2001 (2002).

## American Inequality and the Future of Core Conflict

Much of the increasing inequality over the past 30 years within the United States we have discussed throughout previous chapters was related to the relative economic decline of the United States in the 1970s and 1980s. Because many U.S. industries were no longer as competitive compared with some in other countries, millions of well-paying working-class jobs were lost (Harrison and Bluestone 1988; Reich 1991; Thurow 1991). But jobs were also lost due to automation and robots that American companies were introducing into the workplace in an attempt to reduce labor costs, thus increasing global competitiveness. Other American workers had to accept lower pay because of domestic competition among workers for a smaller number of jobs, but also because of competition from low-wage labor in periphery and semiperiphery nations as U.S. multinational corporations began moving to other countries.

By the 1990s, however, there was an important new element. The growing inequality in the United States was not a result of the relative U.S. economic decline but of the new national strategy by American business leaders and conservative politicians to "make America more competitive again." "Lean production," cutting wages, cutting benefits (such as health insurance), making jobs temporary, with longer working hours for less pay to those who had the jobs, became a reality during the 1990s (Mishel et al. 1999, 2001). We saw in Chapter 7 that as a result of the U.S. economic decline the corporate elite became more politically active during the late 1970s and early 1980s (Useem 1984). Corporate elite pressure for more and more support from the government (through lower taxes, fewer labor laws, less government support for unions, etc.) continued throughout the 1980s but became even more focused after 1994, when conservative

Republicans gained control of both the House and the Senate for the first time since the 1950s (Kalleberg 2009; Tope and Jacobs 2009).

Innovations in technology and improved production processes due to new high-tech manufacturing methods certainly helped the U.S. economic resurgence during the 1990s. But one of the most important elements in the U.S. economic resurgence and longest economic boom in American history was simply the ability of U.S. corporations to *get more work from American workers at less cost* compared to earlier periods and compared to other industrial nations. What is called the "total unit labor cost" (the cost of labor including wages, benefits, and taxes) dropped dramatically during the 1990s in the United States, falling below all the other seven largest capitalist countries except France by the end of the 1990s (Keizai Koho Center 2002:103). As we have already seen in previous chapters, by the end of the 1990s the average wages of American workers were substantially below the average of other industrial nations, benefits were lowest among major industrial nations, and the average work week and year for American workers finally became the longest of all industrial nations, and with the least vacation time, by the second half of the 1990s (Mishel et al. 2001:400–401). This trend of lower wages and benefits, with longer working hours, continued into the 21st century. What was new for the first years of the 21st century, though, was an accelerated loss of American jobs overseas. In contrast to European nations, it is much easier for American corporations to close operations in the United States and move these jobs to countries where wages are a fraction of U.S. wages. Unlike figures on unemployment rates, wages, and poverty levels, there is no U.S. government agency that keeps track of job losses overseas—what is called outsourcing. Several studies, however, now show that almost half a million American jobs were outsourced in 2004 alone (*International Herald Tribune,* November 18, 2004). In short, the conditions of work in America underwent a quiet revolution that allowed U.S. corporations to make and sell things around the world and at home for less than could be done in other major industrial nations.

## ⚔ Capitalist Models and Core Competition in the 21st Century

The Japanese, but particularly the Europeans, have certainly taken notice of signs the U.S. economy has become more competitive again in relation to their own, and of how American corporations have been doing it. Great Britain had been following the U.S. lead, with some economic improvement, since the first years of Reaganomics. By the end of the 1990s, Britain, like the United States, had the same trend of increasing income inequality, lower worker pay, and fewer benefits (Mishel et al. 1999, 2001). As indicated in Table 14-3 above, compared to the 1970s and 1980s when Britain was often seen as the economically sick relative of Europe, the 1990s brought better economic figures, though not for the British working class. For Europe in general, however, the focus on economic unification had been their major strategy to improve economic competitiveness (Bornschier 1994, 1995). The idea is that more economic cooperation among European Union nations will make their economies more efficient and competitive with other industrial nations. But with far greater welfare and unemployment benefits than the United States, more generous pay and benefits to workers, and much shorter working hours as we have seen in previous chapters, Europeans are now becoming worried that they will be left behind if the new conservative American strategy continues to succeed in making the U.S. economy much more competitive again.

Whether or not the renewed American stress on cutting wages, benefits, and jobs, while increasing working hours for those with jobs, will in fact help maintain U.S. economic dominance in the long run, however, is far from certain. A growing, though still limited, number of scholars and economists in the United States have been arguing that America can regain economic strength, not to mention a society with fewer social problems, only by moving in the opposite direction (see especially Thurow 1991; Reich 1991). In a similar manner, others have argued that the United States should look closely at how Germany is able to train its workforce and obtain more worker involvement in corporate decision making as a way to improve competitiveness (Thelen 1991; Turner 1991; Wever 1993). The argument, in short, is that America needs a better-educated, better-trained, better-paid, and more motivated and loyal workforce in a world economy that increasingly rewards nations that are able to compete in high-tech industries. As Thurow (1991) puts it, America must compete in a new high-tech world economy by worrying more about the education and motivation of the bottom 50 percent of workers and families, rather than by beating down wages and labor, as has been done in the past. In the view of many, it is the better-educated, more skilled, and more loyal workers (because of more labor participation and union involvement) of Europe and Japan who will give those countries the edge in future economic competition if the United States does not make big changes in these directions.

Whether or not the above is correct about competitive strategies for the future, an important point is that the systems of social stratification in the United States, Continental Europe, and Asian nations are significantly different, allowing differing classes to push through agendas favoring their interests relative to those in other class positions. As we saw at the end of Chapter 7 (see especially Table 7-5), there are what some refer to as competing models of "welfare capitalism," or simply different types of capitalist systems, with different relations between the government, the capitalist class, and the middle and working class (Esping-Andersen 1990; Goodin et al. 1999). The United States, and to a lesser degree Britain, have what some refer to as a neo-liberal system in which the government stays relatively uninvolved in the economy (with little economic planning and almost no government ownership of industry), resulting in more freedom for a corporate class to run the economy as they see fit to do so. I prefer to call the U.S. model corporate-dominated capitalism. Implied in this description of a neo-liberal economy or corporate-dominated capitalism is a relatively weak working class, and especially a working class lacking influence in the government and in obtaining government protection (with labor laws, income protection, social benefits). A significantly different capitalist system found in varying degrees in Continental European countries (especially Germany and France) is called a corporatist system, or what I call cooperative capitalism. In a corporatist system the corporate class and working class, in alliance with government, have arrived at a sort of power-sharing agreement so that the government helps organize the economy and protect the interests of all parties. A central component of the corporatist system in contrast to the neo-liberal U.S. system is strong labor unions and labor laws restricting what corporate elites can do in the economy and political system. Finally, less studied by Western social scientists, the most rapidly growing economies of the world have what can generally be called an *Asian development model* (Kerbo 2006: Chapter 3; Kerbo and McKinstry 1995; Kerbo and Slagter 2000a, 2000b; Dierichs and Kerbo 1999). In this model of capitalism the state has more independent, or autonomous, political power, as well as more control over the economy. As in the case of the second largest economy in the world, Japan, there is little government ownership of industry, but the private sector is rigidly guided and restricted by bureaucratic government elites. Indeed, these bureaucratic government elites are not elected officials and are thus less subject to influence by either the corporate class or working class through the political process. The argument from this perspective has been that a government ministry can have the freedom to plan the economy and look to long-term national interests without having their economic policies disrupted by either corporate-class or working-class short-term and narrow interests.

In the next chapter we examine how the German and Japanese forms of capitalism are different from each other and that of the United States. We also will see how these differences lead to different strategies for competing in today's global economy, with differing positive and negative outcomes for people in each country. Just as Britain, Holland, and France were competing with each other from different political and economic institutions in the 1700s, by the middle of the 21st century we will likely find out which of the three current forms of capitalism will be able to take or continue the lead in today's modern world system.

## Summary

The nature of social stratification in a particular country can no longer be understood without reference to the position of that country in the modern world system, or world stratification system. In this chapter we began with a description of the main characteristics of the world stratification system. Most important in this description, we outlined the ranks of core, semiperiphery, and periphery nations within the modern world system and the basic characteristics of nations in each of these three positions. We then turned to a brief history of the modern world system, which began around the 1500s and included almost all of the world's area by the 20th century. It was this latter situation that helped explain the massive wars of the 20th century, when late-developing core nations—Germany, Japan, and Italy—tried to create their own colonial systems that required taking territory from other core nations. Also in this historical discussion we examined what helped the leading core nations attain dominance and then what led to their relative decline. With this historical perspective we considered the current competition among major core nations as we begin the 21st century and how the United States was able to regain its economic dominance.

# Social Stratification in Japan and Germany: Contrasting Forms of Political Economy

Germany's new parliament building with its glass dome (*top*) symbolically represents the transparency of Germany's political system. The bottom photo shows the Japanese pyramid-shaped Parliament in Tokyo with the emperor's palace grounds behind it, all surrounded by tall buildings. Germany and Japan are advanced industrial democracies like the United States, but these three countries have significant differences with respect to their political, economic, and stratification systems.

*SOURCES:* © Harold Kerbo and Patrick Ziltener.

## Chapter Outline

❖ **Ranking in Japan: Some Preliminary Observations**

❖ **The Structural Bases of Social Stratification in Japan**

❖ **Japan's Power Elite**

❖ **Social Stratification in Germany: Some Similarities—and Key Differences**

❖ **German Workers and Codetermination Laws**

❖ **Variation in Modern Systems of Social Stratification: A Conclusion**

❖ **Summary**

Although there has been much comparative information throughout this book, with the exception of the previous chapter our primary focus has been on the United States. The United States is still the largest capitalist industrial nation, with Japan and Germany the second and third largest, respectively. It seems logical to include a chapter on social stratification in these two countries, one the first fully postindustrial society in Asia, and the other the biggest economic power in Euorpe. There are important reasons to include a chapter on social stratification in Japan and Germany. As noted previously, since the cold war, Americans have tended to assume that all capitalist nations are basically alike with respect to such characteristics as wage inequalities, the wealth and power of capitalists, and the influence of workers. Some exceptions might be understood in the case of Japan, because it is Asian. But, one might think, the main competitor to the United States in Europe, located in the general geographic area where capitalism and industrialization began, should certainly conform to the American model of political economy. Otherwise, how could Germany have such a strong economy? This assumption, however, is wrong on many points; in fact, Japan is in some respects is more similar to the United States than is Germany. In contrast to what I have called a more corporate-dominated political economy in the United States, comparative research has shown that Germany has a more cooperative form of political economy. Japan established a more uniquely Asian model that emerging political economies in Asia (including China) are following in most respects. As we have seen in Chapters 7 and 14 (see especially Table 7-5), these different types of political economies have profound effects on the nature of stratification systems.

## ⚔ Ranking in Japan: Some Preliminary Observations

A Western traveler to Japan encounters a country that at first sight seems like any other modern nation. True, the written language on the signboards and trucks is certainly different than that found in any Western advanced industrial society, and everything seems somehow smaller to Americans—the trucks, the rooms, portions of food in the restaurants, and even the people (at least the older people). Still, the people go about their work much like we would expect in other industrial societies. They talk about marketing, problems with financing, the technical problems associated with designing a new product, conflict between management and labor in wage discussions, and the ever-present advanced society problems such as traffic, pollution, smog, and urban crowding. Upon closer analysis, however, there are what some people might see as puzzling aspects of the society. With respect to our subject of social stratification, for example, it is interesting to note how the Japanese seem obsessed with ranking and hierarchy (Pharr 1990; Eisenstadt 1996; Kerbo and McKinstry 1998; Christopher 1983; Taylor 1983:42). Corporations are ranked; universities are ranked; all educational programs are ranked; in fact, almost anything that can be ranked is ranked, with magazines and newspapers reporting on the ranking. One of the first things a foreigner may learn to say is *Ichi ban,* which means, roughly, "Number one!"

This stress on ranking and hierarchy is not limited to things and institutions—it carries over to people. There is concern with a relative status ordering of people that makes it difficult for Japanese people to interact with each other as equals. Japanese people are unable to sit, talk, eat, or drink with other people until the relative ranking order of those present has been reasonably ascertained. Within this social context the practice of exchanging business cards (or something like them), called *meishi,* has developed (Nakane 1970:30). There is a ritual involved with the exchange of these meishi. The point is to carefully study the business card so that each person can show the proper level of respect to the other. (After *ichi ban,* one of the next things a foreigner is likely to learn to say is *Watashi no meishi des*—"Here is my business card.") Once the status-relevant markers such as age, gender, education, occupation, and place of employment have been established among all present, the business of eating, talking, drinking, or whatever can proceed in an orderly manner that is unlikely to offend someone who expects greater status deference. It is to be expected that in such a society the language will be well developed to express deference, respect, and informality or formality as the situation calls for. There are, in fact, few languages that are as extensive as Japanese in allowing people to express levels of status, respect, and formality (Miller 1967; Goldstein and Tamura 1975). It is not an overstatement to say that almost every word uttered by one Japanese person to another indicates some aspect of their relative status ranking (whether that rank is superior, inferior, or equal to that of the person spoken to).

With this concern for ranking and formality that could easily disorient a laid-back Californian, we might expect Japan to be a society with a high degree of inequality in every aspect of life. But such expectations are far from accurate. There has been some flux in the income inequality of Japan in the last three decades, with inequality in Japan dropping in the 1960s (Mouer and Sugimoto 1986) to one of the lowest levels in the world, then rising slightly with the "bubble economy" of the late 1980s to the present. With economic slowdown and even stagnation since the "bubble burst" in the early 1990s, there was some indication that income inequality was again going down in Japan (Shirahase 2001:2), but as we will see later in this chapter, by 2010 inequality and poverty are up again. While incomes of top corporate executives in the United States continued their rapid rise in the 1990s and 2000s, the incomes of Japanese executives actually dropped by almost 8 percent, and the gap between corporate executives and the average worker in Japan was reduced. By one recent estimate, while the average top executive in Japan has an income 12 times that of the average Japanese worker, the average U.S. executive has an income 300 times or more that of the average American worker (see Table 2-6). Furthermore, much of the recent increase in inequality in Japan is accounted for by the rapid increase in the percent of the population over 65 years of age that does not have the Social Security protection found in the United States (Shirahase 2001). A main point, therefore, is that income inequality in Japan has been consistently lower than in the United States since the 1960s, and generally low among other industrial nations. Although it increased during the bubble economy of the late 1980s and early 1990s, when the economy slowed, the top executives took cuts in pay along with workers rather than lay off workers.

It is tempting to conclude that the primary difference with Japan is simply that the Japanese have a tradition of unequal status ranking, but with relatively more equality in material things. We must not, however, be tempted to draw such a conclusion. Yes, the language showing deference and status ranking has developed over the centuries, but the income inequality figures for Japan were rather different less than 100 years ago. Going back only to the 1920s, we find not a 17-to-1 gap or an 8-to-1 gap within major corporations in Japan but a 100-to-1 gap (Hara and Seiyama 2005:xxi; Abegglen and Stalk 1985:191). During the 1930s in Japan, about 16 percent of the people had over 50 percent of the income, and the top 0.0019 percent of the people had 10 percent of all income (Hane 1982:11).

## Social Stratification in Germany: Some Preliminary Observations

While there is a rich mixture of similarities and differences between Japan, Germany, and the United States with respect to aspects of social stratification, let's begin with a description of one set of key differences in Germany. We can do so by presenting a fictitious example of a German industrial corporation that, like any other in the capitalist world, is making decisions about increasing competitiveness through more efficient production and the introduction of new production technology.

> The company in question will be called IG Hintzmann, a publicly owned corporation with many financial and family stockholders, that produces mostly spark plugs for a wide variety of German automobiles. There are more than 4,000 employees of IG Hintzmann, most of whom are machine workers producing the spark plugs in two large plants located in Duisburg and Essen. In recent years the company has experienced a decline in profits and productivity compared to its competitors, primarily, it seems, because of new production technology that IG Hintzmann is yet to utilize.
>
> The corporate supervisors for IG Hintzmann (similar to the U.S. corporate board of directors) have recently met for many hours analyzing information related to productivity and the effects new production machinery would have on productivity. The impact such machinery would have on IG Hintzmann's workers—for example, whether redundancies (i.e., layoffs) would occur, whether work hours and wages would be affected, as well as whether new training would be required—has been considered in detail because of questions by one-half of IG Hintzmann's board of supervisors who are *by law* workers elected by their fellow workers as representatives.
>
> After these supervisors have been assured that changes are in the best interests of the workers, and that workers' jobs and pay will be protected, the next step is to consult with the powerful labor union, IG Metall, for its support.

Finally, before new machinery is purchased and sent to the shop floor, it is equally important, and the laws require, that the 15 works council representatives on the shop floors of both large plants in Duisburg and Essen be consulted. As stipulated by German labor laws, these works councils, made up of shop floor workers elected by their fellow employees, must be consulted about anything affecting workers on the shop floor, such as the hiring and firing of workers by management, changes in the hours worked, the organization of work, criteria for promotions, and so on. Only with great difficulty, time, and resources can management of a corporation such as IG Hintzmann go against a decision of the works council. Thus, management must keep the works council fully advised and assured that the interests of shop floor workers will be protected by any management decision.

As in most other German corporations of this size, average pay is much higher than it is in other countries, especially the United States, and IG Hintzmann's employees work an average of just over 35 hours a week. Most IG Hintzmann employees have been with the company for more than 20 years and realistically expect to be employed by the company until they retire with a comfortable pension.

IG Hintzmann, though imaginary, is typical of the thousands of large to medium-sized corporations all over Germany, and about as untypical of American corporations as one could find in the world. Moving away from the imaginary, we have already seen some of the figures indicating that German workers have obtained benefits and conditions of employment far better than those of workers in the United States. Table 15-1

## TABLE 15-1

### Hourly Labor Costs for Industrial Workers Compared to the United States, 2007*

| | |
|---|---|
| Norway | 180 |
| Germany | 166 |
| Denmark | 156 |
| Austria | 141 |
| Finland | 130 |
| The Netherlands | 129 |
| Belgium | 127 |
| Sweden | 127 |
| Switzerland | 125 |
| France | 123 |
| United Kingdom | 120 |
| Ireland | 117 |
| Italy | 105 |
| United States | 100 |
| Spain | 80 |
| All European Union | 129 |

*Base income is set at 100 percent of U.S. industrial worker hourly wages.

SOURCE: U.S. Bureau of the Census, *Statistical Abstracts of the United States, 2010* (Table 1318).

shows that working-class hourly wages in Germany are among the highest in the world. In addition, while the average hours worked per year in the United States was almost 1,804 in 2006, and 1,784 for Japanese, the average for Germans was just over 1,400 (Mishel, Bernstein, and Shierholz 2009: Table 8.4).

By the late 1990s and early 2000s, however, corporate leaders and conservative politicians in Germany were painting a different picture of what is happening in the typical German corporation such as our imaginary IG Hintzmann. Faced with increasing competition from the U.S. corporate resurgence, these German corporate elites were charging that the high German wages and benefits are making their products too expensive compared to those of other countries. Also, corporate and individual income taxes (at about 50 percent for most), which are needed to pay for the high level of welfare, medical, and other benefits to the German people, are said to hinder German corporate performance. Further, the power of German labor unions, plus work laws giving workers extensive influence within each company, are making it almost impossible to lay off workers in order to cut costs and keep corporate profits up, again in contrast to what American companies are able to do. In addition, these corporate leaders in Germany claim that the continuing high unemployment in Germany, even in the face of strong improvements in the German economy in the early 21st century, is caused by these German work laws preventing easy layoff of workers. They claim this keeps German companies from hiring new employees they would not be able to get rid of later, again as U.S. companies can do easily. Finally, these corporate leaders are threatening (with some threats already carried out) to move factories out of Germany to low-cost countries, such as the United States.

By 2010, however, union and worker influence in Germany was not diminished significantly. The German people elected a liberal Social Democratic and Green Party coalition government in 1998 and again in 2003. (I should probably clarify that in 1998 Germans voted in a new government specifically *to keep* welfare programs, government spending, and taxes at their previously high levels.) The more conservative party, Christian Democrats, were able to win back a conservative coalition in the parliament (*Bundestag*) with national elections in 2005 and again in 2009, but there have been only small reductions in the wages and benefits of German workers, and their average working hours remain among the lowest in the world. Neither have they seen a massive loss of jobs like the outsourcing experienced by American workers in recent years. They still have the power to make it much too costly for German companies to close plants and move them to countries such as China.

# ✖ The Structural Bases of Social Stratification in Japan

We have seen that the most important bases of social stratification in the United States are the occupational structure, authority structure (economic and political), and property structure. We found that most kinds of rewards (such as income) are distributed through these structures, and that the intersections of these three structures form the bases for the class positions in our industrial society.

What about Japan? If the theories are correct that advanced industrial societies, especially capitalist industrial societies, have these similar bases in their stratification systems, then Japan should also fit. Japan is clearly an advanced industrial society, as figures on Japan's GDP (gross domestic product) and competitive position in the world economy indicate today. And it should be noted that Japan was closest to the United States with respect to the percentage of private (in contrast to state) ownership of basic industries.

In summary, Japan does generally fit the pattern, but with some important differences. As pointed out in previous chapters, all advanced industrial societies are expected to have relatively minor differences in their systems of social stratification. Japan has more of these differences than most, but the differences, as we will see, are as much related to the timing of Japan's economic development as to its differing cultural values. It is time to examine Japan's occupational structure, authority structure, and property structure, in turn.

# Occupational Structure

Like all industrial societies, Japan has doctors, lawyers, corporate managers, scientists, medical technicians, computer programmers, truck drivers, and so on. This much is rather obvious when we consider how well the Japanese make cars, stereos, DVD players, and just about any other product sold in the United States. But we need to consider other aspects of the occupational structure in Japan that are not so apparent. For example, we need to know the distribution of these different kinds of occupations, how people are placed in them, and the relationship between important rewards in the society (such as income) and these occupational positions.

## *Occupational Distribution*

The occupational distributions of Japan and the United States are roughly similar. There are some differences, and these differences do matter; but again, they are relatively minor. For example, we find that more people are in farming occupations in Japan (Hara and Seiyama 2005: Chapter 3; Ishida 1993; Ishida et al. 1987). Another significant difference in the Japanese occupational distribution is the larger number of retail workers and small shop owners (or petite bourgeoisie). As any visitor to Japan can easily see, Japan is still a country of small shop owners. This image is confirmed by Wright's comparative study of class (Wright 1997:45). Following Wright's class categories we find a much larger petty bourgeoisie in Japan compared to the United States (23.2 percent of Japan's working population compared to 6.8 percent in the United States). But also there is a smaller working class in Japan compared to the United States (47.9 percent versus 56.7 percent) as measured by Wright's class categories, in part because Japan is a late-developing economy that skipped over a stage with a greater number of working-class jobs.

Another way to compare the occupational structures of the United States and Japan is to compare the occupational status scales of the two countries. You will remember from Chapter 5 that occupational status studies of the United States and other industrial nations indicate a remarkable consistency through time and across cultures. The meaning of occupational status and what these studies measure can be questioned, but it must be stressed that whatever they measure, they do so consistently. In comparing the occupational status ranking in the United States and Japan, Treiman (1977:87) has found a 0.90 correlation (1.00 is a perfect correlation) between the occupational status rankings carried out in Japan and the United States. Also significant is the strong 0.85 correlation between the educational level of occupants of similar jobs in Japan and the United States (Treiman 1977:110). Again, when we find that all advanced capitalist industrial societies have these high correlations, it is clear that Japan's occupational structure fits.

## Dual Economy

Japan's dual economy presents another similarity in United States–Japanese occupational structures. To an even greater extent than in the United States, in fact, Japan's economy is divided between large firms with higher profits, more market control, higher wages, and more unionization, and smaller firms having all of these characteristics in much lesser degrees (Hara and Seiyama 2005: 67–69; Ishida 1993:224; Lincoln and Kalleberg 1985, 1990; Kalleberg and Lincoln 1988). This aspect of Japan's dual economy must be kept in mind when we hear stories of lifetime employment and extensive worker benefits, such as company housing, in Japanese corporations. These things do exist in Japan (though we must qualify the "lifetime employment" in discussing age in the following section), but primarily for the 30 percent of Japanese workers in the core sector of the dual economy.

The negative impact of this dual economy for workers in the small firms is actually getting worse. In order to cope with an economy stagnate for over 15 years, smaller firms, and even some larger companies, have reverted to hiring more part-time workers instead of regular employees who are less likely to be laid off. In the past decade the percentage of the labor force in part-time or temporary employment more than doubled to almost 35 percent (*International Herald Tribune* February 8, 2009). This is more than double the rate for the United States, but like the United States, these temporary jobs often pay below Japan's poverty line, which is set at about $25,000 per year for a family of 4 (close to the U.S. poverty line).

## Age Ranking

We now come to an interesting difference in the Japanese occupational structure. As with all advanced industrial societies, there is a positive correlation between education and occupational level in Japan; that is, a higher-level job (doctor, lawyer, accountant, etc.) usually requires a higher level of education. However, at the younger age level (25 years old), workers with less education actually make *more* money than the college-educated (Lincoln 2001:38–41). As we move up the age levels we find that higher education pays off. But this payoff operates primarily by the relationship between higher education and attaining a job in the core sector of the dual economy. Japan is a highly age-ranked society. Thus, there is a stronger correlation between age and income than between education and income (Woronoff 1980:164; Kalleberg and Lincoln 1988).

In what is called the *nenko* system in Japan, once a person lands a good job in a major corporation (because of educational attainment), that person will probably be promoted along with the same age group every year. In other words, merit counts in getting that job, but merit is less important for further promotions in that job (though this is changing in some Japanese corporations but not in public-sector bureaucracies; Clark 1979:45; Abegglen and Stalk 1985; MacMillan 1985).

There is an element of merit always at work in the background, however, that we need to consider. When employees in the core sector reach about age 55 to 60, the jobs toward the top suddenly become fewer. Everyone cannot be promoted together after this. Thus, those employees most highly evaluated by the company are promoted and the others are forced to retire. This is the major amendment to the concept of lifetime employment noted earlier.

## *Income Inequality*

One last aspect of the occupational structure in Japan must be explored. It is in contrast to that of the United States, though not necessarily in equal contrast to other industrial nations (which suggests that the United States is as much or more the deviant case compared with other nations as is Japan). While inequality increased in the late 1980s and early 1990s, during the early 1980s Japan had the lowest level of income inequality of any industrial nation. As can be seen from Table 15-2, the Gini index of income inequality in Japan stayed in the low 0.30 range from 1961 to the late 1980s, moved to the 0.36 range through most of the 1990s, then moved up to the 0.38 range after that. (Remember that 0.0 means complete equality, while 1.0 means one person or family has all the income.) It is difficult to get more recent data on the Gini index in Japan, but the figure for Japan is likely much closer to that high figure for the United States today. During this time the Gini index moved from 0.38 to 0.46 by 2009 in the United States.

## TABLE 15-2

### Gini Index of Income Inequality in Japan, 1961–2002*

| | |
|---|---|
| 1961 | 0.344 |
| 1967 | 0.328 |
| 1972 | 0.314 |
| 1975 | 0.346 |
| 1978 | 0.338 |
| 1981 | 0.314 |
| 1984 | 0.343 |
| 1987 | 0.338 |
| 1990 | 0.364 |
| 1993 | 0.365 |
| 1996 | 0.361 |
| 1999 | 0.381 |
| 2002 | 0.381 |

*Income distribution after taxes and transfers.

*SOURCE:* Tachibanaki (2006).

Unlike what we saw in Chapter 2, this is in contrast to European nations, which keep income inequality lower through government policies. In Japan, most of this changing income inequality is produced within the economy rather than through government action, such as tax and welfare policies (Verba et al. 1987:274). For example, the minimum wage in Japan is now lower than the U.S. rate of just over $7 per hour. Also, as noted above, there has been a big increase in temporary workers in Japan with very low wages (about 35 percent of the labor force today). As a result of all this, Japanese were shocked to learn that the relative poverty rate (below half of median income) in Japan has risen to 15 percent of the population, which compares to about 19 percent for the United States (*International Herald Tribune* April 21, 2010). It turns out that the Japanese government ministry bureaucrats had been withholding this poverty data for years. However, it is important to note that the rising income inequality in Japan since the late 1980s has not been exclusively due to the occupational structure but is also an aspect of age stratification in Japan. While age brings status and respect in Japan, it does not bring as much political power as in the United States, which is to say Japan lacks the kind of Social Security system that, as we saw in Chapter 9, has been successful in reducing poverty among older Americans.

Currently Japan has over 22 percent of its population over 65 of age compared to 13 percent in the United States, with 32 percent of the population in Japan projected to be over 65 by 2050 (U.S. Bureau of the Census 2010b: Tables 8 and 1298; Keizai Koho Center 2002:13). Thus, because the Japanese population is aging rapidly, there are more elderly people as a percentage of the population, resulting in more income inequality (Hara 2007; Shirahase 2001).

Finally, we have seen figures showing that the gap between top executives' salaries and the new employees' salaries in Japan is much smaller than in the United States, which has the largest gap. Figures like these suggest that income inequality in Japan is rising because the bottom (temporary workers and the aged) is getting less, and not because the top is getting more. One recent estimate is that the average Japanese top executive makes from $300,000 to a high of $500,000, compared to more than $10 million for the average U.S. executive in the top 300 corporations. The figures cannot be dismissed by saying that the many fringe benefits Japanese executives receive are ignored. While U.S. executives receive many extras, such as stock options, which increase their total income, stock options for Japanese executives are prohibited by Japanese law (Hara and Seiyama 2005; Abegglen and Stalk 1985:187; Kerbo and McKinstry 1995: Chapters 1 and 4). Thus, when we consider these extras, the income gap between U.S. and Japanese executives becomes much larger.

## Bureaucratic Authority Structures

When most people think of bureaucracy, they think of countless rules and legions of bureaucrats enforcing these rules, so that it takes a longer time to get anything done, at much greater effort. We think of the rules at the U.S. Post Office, where packages must be the correct size and weight, and we must fill out many forms if anything out of the ordinary is requested. Any U.S. citizen who has lived for a time in Japan will tell you that you haven't experienced anything like bureaucracy in a post office until you come to Japan. The postal service in Japan, however, should not be singled out, as such bureaucracy is a characteristic of all government and corporate agencies in Japan. We will look at bureaucratic authority structures first in the economy and then in the Japanese government agencies.

## Corporate Bureaucracies

Like any other industrial capitalist nation, Japan has large corporate bureaucracies. There are top managers, mid-managers, supervisors, and so on. However, compared to the United States, Japan has relatively fewer managers (Wright 1997:45). In other words, in the United States there are more people watching over other people doing the work. In this case, though, it is the United States that is untypical when compared to Canada, Norway, Sweden, and England in Wright's study (1997). But compared to the United States, corporate bureaucracies in Japan are noted for having more ranks and levels than in most other nations (Lincoln and Kalleberg 1990; Gerlach 1992). In other words, while the United States has more people managing others, Japan creates more rank divisions among the people doing the managing.

This would follow observations made earlier that the Japanese seem particularly concerned with ranking, and that extensive age ranking exists in core corporations in Japan (that is, there must be many ranks to keep promoting people into). But it is also interesting that there tend to be fewer observable rank distinctions in Japanese corporations (Clark 1979:215), even in overseas operations of Japanese corporations with foreign employees (Kerbo et al. 1994a, 1994b; Lincoln et al. 1995). In many ways, higher management is not treated so differently; managers eat in the same places as workers, they do not have large and separate offices, or executive washrooms. However, as we will discuss later, the status difference given to top executives by lower-ranking employees in Japan is more extensive than in the United States.

## Political Authority Structures

Like the United States, Japan today has a political authority structure in which questions of who gets what, and why, are influenced by a process of conflict. And, as in the United States, some groups have more resources with which to try to influence the state to protect their interests. But the Japanese political system is by no means a carbon copy of the U.S. system. All political systems have their unique aspects, with Japan having probably more than its share. As the Liberal Democratic Party and the *Diet* (parliament) in general were in disarray because of scandal in the early 1990s, a 1994 political cartoon in Japan described the situation quite well: Under a picture showing emergency workers and medical personnel running around outside the office building for Diet members, one emergency worker says to another, "It is too bad about that gas leak killing all Diet members at their desks." The other emergency worker responds, "Yes, but it is lucky no important functions of government were harmed."

As we will see later when considering the nature of Japan's power elite, in a major contrast to the United States, the most powerful agents of government in Japan are unelected ministry bureaucrats. In each government agency in Japan, such as the Ministry of Finance, Ministry of International Trade and Industry (MITI), Ministry of

Justice, and so on, the vice ministers and their employees are far more powerful than elected politicians in the Diet (Colignon and Usui 2003; Koh 1989; Johnson 1982; Kerbo and McKinstry 1995: Chapters 5 and 6; Hartcher 1998; Gibney 1998). The minister of each government bureaucracy is a temporary political appointee and therefore is no match to the power of the vice minister of each agency. These vice ministers are the people who write most of the laws and then decide how to administer the laws. These ministry officials are career bureaucrats with much more experience than politicians and many more staff to carry out government functions. Another way to understand this difference between Japan and the United States is to consider how many people a new American president appoints after being elected to office compared to a new Japanese prime minister coming into office. A new American president appoints as many as 4,000 people (often from corporate positions) to help run the government. A new Japanese prime minister appoints about 20, all elected officials from the parliament. As one after another prime minister in Japan comes and goes, the government ministry civil servants remain, running the most important functions of government.

In Japan today, therefore, the competition to obtain favorable government action or protection is carried on by corporate elites and Diet members elected by citizens who must go to powerful government ministers for favors and protection. In this sense, while Japanese people vote in far greater numbers than Americans (over 70 percent compared with 50 percent or less), there is less democracy in Japan. A new political party took control of the Japanese parliament (Diet) in 2009 and has taken a few successful steps to reduce some of the power of these unelected government bureaucrats. But it will take many years, if not decades, before the power of ministry bureaucrats is effectively reduced in the Japanese political system.

## Property Structure

In the United States one of the major sources of inequality is the ownership of the major means of production by a few versus the lack of such ownership by most people. There are certainly degrees of ownership (in terms of overall amounts), but because most privately held corporate stock is concentrated in the hands of less than 1 percent of the U.S. population, it can realistically be divided into those who own major amounts of corporate stock (which gives them much wealth, income, and power) and those who have very little or none.

Japan, like the United States, is a capitalist industrial society. This means that there is little government ownership and/or control of the major means of production. But it becomes a bit more complex in the case of Japan. Families who could be said to make up an upper class in Japan (either old upper class or new upper class) today own much less stock than in the United States. Whereas half of all corporate stock is still controlled by families and individuals in the United States, this number is estimated to be 25 to 30 percent in Japan, and much less than this when we look only at the largest 1,000 or so Japanese corporations (Kerbo and McKinstry 1995:63–68). As we saw in Chapter 2, while the most wealthy 10 percent of Americans owned 70 percent of the wealth in the United States, the richest 10 percent of Japanese owned only 39 percent of the wealth in their country, the lowest wealth inequality of all industrial nations (Davis et al. 2006). There are some Marxian analyses of Japan that continue to use the old term *upper class* in the original Marxian sense of capitalist ruling families (Halliday 1975; Steven 1983), but this terminology has much less application to postwar Japan. Let's consider some of the data.

As early as 1966, data on the stock ownership patterns of the largest 466 companies (all with assets of more than 5 billion yen) show that only 8.8 percent (or 41) of these companies have enough family-held stock to be considered family or individually controlled. Dore (1987:112) presents data on stock ownership by various categories of owners for all the corporations listed on the stock exchanges in Japan for 1983. We find that of all this corporate stock, only 27 percent of shares are held by families or individuals. The next biggest share is the 26 percent held by industrial and other commercial corporations, then 18 percent held by banks, and 17 percent held by insurance companies. Counting the amounts owned by stockbroking companies and investment and other financial companies, we find that 66 percent of all corporate stock is owned by corporations in Japan.

Research by Kerbo and Nakao (1991) considered ownership patterns in the largest 100 industrial corporations and 25 largest banks in Japan. Focusing on the number one stockholder in each of the 100 largest industrial corporations, we found only 10 of these companies had a family or individual as the number one stockholder: 47 companies had an insurance company or other financial firm as the number one stockholder, while in 16 it was a bank, and in 19 it was another industrial corporation. As for the top 25 banks, 84 percent had an insurance company or other financial institution as the number one stockholder, while in 12 percent of the cases it was another bank, in 4 percent an industrial corporation, and in no case was the number one stockholder an individual or family. Further, we found only 8 families or individuals had much corporate stock in these 100 top industrial corporations and none among the top 25 banks who had 10 percent or more of the stock in a company.

Finally, in comparison to the United States we must stress a key point: This stock is *owned* by these other corporations, in contrast to the huge amounts of stock *controlled* by U.S. financial firms that are in reality owned by worker pension funds. Before World War II most major corporations in Japan were owned or controlled by a few wealthy family firms combined into groups called **zaibatsu**. Wealthy families were forced to sell off their holdings and reduce their control of the economy by the U.S. Occupation reforms. These firms that were once controlled by families are still in operation and have partially reformed their groups of powerful corporations now called *keiretsu,* but family ownership is no longer significant (Clark 1979:75; Abegglen and Stalk 1985:189). As an example, Table 15-3 lists the main corporations in the Mitsubishi group and the stock they control in each other. The primary reasons for the lack of ownership by families and individuals today must begin with the forced breakup of the old zaibatsu after World War II. When this stock was forced to be sold to break up these family groups, other corporations were among the only ones in a position to buy. Second, unlike in the United States, top corporate managers are prevented by law from being paid with stock options in their companies (Abegglen and Stalk 1985:187). Thus, while this practice accounts for some of the individually owned stock in the United States, there is almost none of this manager-owned stock in Japan. Finally, in Japan, when a corporation has important business deals with another corporation (as a supplier, retailing the product, holding or

**TABLE 15-3**

## The Mitsubishi Group of Interlocked Corporations

| Company of stock issue | Percentage of stock owned by other top 20 firms in the Mitsubishi group |
| --- | --- |
| Mitsubishi Bank | 26.9% |
| Mitsubishi Trust Bank | 32.3 |
| Tokyo Marine | 21.7 |
| Mitsubishi Heavy Industries | 23.2 |
| Mitsubishi Corporation | 42.2 |
| Mitsubishi Electric | 16.3 |
| Asahi Glass | 29.3 |
| Kirin Beer | 12.7 |
| Mitsubishi Chemical | 24.5 |
| N.Y.K. Shipping | 27.5 |

SOURCES: Table constructed from data presented in Lincoln (2001:193); Clark (1979:75).

giving financial loans, etc.), the practice is to buy significant amounts of stock in the corporate business partner (and vice versa) as a show of support and to maintain good relations. A result has been the keiretsu groups of corporations so famous in Japan today, which we discuss in some detail in the next section on power elites in Japan.

During the late 1990s and the first years of the 21st century, however, we must recognize that this Japanese corporate structure is changing. How much it is changing is not yet clear, but there has been a new trend of corporate mergers in Japan that have gone across the old keiretsu circles. Although nothing like the merger wave in the United States in the last two decades, the mergers of large banks from separate keiretsu groups in Japan have made this corporate structure more fuzzy, with less distinct circles by 2010.

In Chapters 6 and 7, we found that institutional investors control most stock in major U.S. corporations. This development has cut into the ownership and power of an old upper class of families and created the basis for what is called the *corporate class* of top executives, who not only control their own corporations but also have extensive influence across major corporations, as well as much influence in the government. To what extent do we find this corporate class in Japan? This is our next subject—Japan's power elite.

# ⚔ Japan's Power Elite

In many ways the configuration of elites in Japan fits the view of a "power elite" described by C. Wright Mills better than the elites in any other country. There is a "triumvirate of elites," what the Japanese often refer to as the "iron triangle," which is more powerful, more united, and more in control of the country than anywhere else among modern industrial societies. Likewise, among nonelites in Japan, there is something closer to a "mass society" of powerless and politically inactive people described by Mills than can be found among any other of the leading modern nations today. The primary qualification in Mills's power elite thesis when applied to Japan is that the triumvirate of elites does not include the military. Rather, the iron triangle is made up of the corporate elite, the bureaucratic elite in the government ministry, with the political elite of leading politicians coming in as a distant third with respect to power in today's Japan. In what follows we present a small part of the evidence indicating the power and unity of Japan's power elite.

## The Corporate Class

The corporate class of this triumvirate of elites is based in Japan's postwar keiretsu corporate structure described earlier. With the fall of the powerful zaibatsu corporate groups soon after World War II, there was a slow emergence of what are today called keiretsu corporate groups. The fundamental difference is that the keiretsu groups of corporations are seldom owned and controlled by wealthy families, but in fact own each other. Sitting on top of the keiretsu groups are corporate executives who collectively run the economy with more authority and independence than can be found in other capitalist nations (Kerbo and McKinstry 1995: Chapter 4).

Before we consider the positions of these corporate executives, the importance of the keiretsu corporate groups themselves must be considered. While the number of keiretsu corporate groups seen as most important may be in dispute, and there are a few mergers going across keiretsu lines in recent years, there is clear agreement over the six most powerful keiretsu. These "big six" contain approximately 193 main corporations, accounting for about 15 percent of all corporate assets in Japan, including 40 percent of all banking assets, 53 percent of all insurance assets, and 53 percent of the real estate business (Ōsono 1991; Gerlach 1992:87; Morioka 1989:49). On average, each of the 193 corporations within one of the big six groups is linked through stock ownership with 54 percent of the other corporations within the group, with an average of 21.6 percent of the stock of each of these corporations held collectively by other corporations within the specific keiretsu. With economic crises and pending bank failures during the late 1990s, the keiretsu system is in something of a flux. Some of the big banks have had to merge, in essence merging some other corporations into the keiretsu as well. But as of 2000, the cross stock holdings among the big six keiretsu had gone down only slightly (Lincoln 2001:192–193).

In addition to the big keiretsu, or what can be called horizontal keiretsu, are many more *vertical keiretsu*. Each of the big corporations within a horizontal keiretsu dominates many smaller corporations, sometimes numbering in the hundreds, who supply the dominant corporations with parts or services vital to operations. Thus, through the interlocking big six keiretsu, there is a web of thousands of corporations tied together when we count the smaller corporations in the vertical keiretsu of the giants. By way of example, Table 15-4 contains the list of the main and affiliate corporations in the powerful Mitsui keiretsu, one of the big six. Selecting Toshiba within this keiretsu for further example, there are more than 200 additional companies in the web that are lower members of the Toshiba vertical keiretsu (Kerbo and McKinstry 1995: Chapter 4; Ōsono 1991; Gerlach 1992:88).

## TABLE 15-4

## Example of Companies in the Mitsui Keiretsu

### Main companies

| | |
|---|---|
| Mitsui Manufacturing | Toshiba |
| Mitsui Real Estate | Toyota |
| Taiyo-Kobe/Mitsui Bank | Mitsukoshi Stores |
| Mitsui Toatsu Chemicals | Mitsui Maritime Casualty |
| Mitsui Storage | Tore Industries |
| Mitsui Trust Bank | Oji Paper Products |
| Mitsui Shipbuilding | Sanki Heavy Industries |
| Osaka Shipping/Mitsui Shipping | Japan Steel Co. |
| Mitsui Metals and Ore | Japan Flour Products |
| Mitsui Construction | Onoma Cement |
| Mitsui Mines | |
| Mitsui Life Insurance | |
| Mitsui Petrochemical Industries | |

### Associate companies

| | |
|---|---|
| Mitsui Leasing Enterprises | Electrochemical Industries |
| Mitsui Information Development | Ishikawajima/Hamima Heavy Industries |
| Mitsui Liquid Gas | Toyo Engineering |
| Mitsui Homes | Tomen Corporation |
| Mitsui Aluminum | General Petroleum |
| Mitsui Agricultural Products | |

| Group | Main companies | Affiliate companies | Presidents' club |
|---|---|---|---|
| Mitsubishi | 28 | 93 | Kinyo kai (Friday Club) |
| Mitsui | 24 | 92 | Nikikai (Two Pillars Club) |
| Sumitomo | 21 | 95 | Hakusuikai (White Water Club) |
| Fuji | 29 | 74 | Fuyo kai (Lotus Club) |
| Daiichi Kangyo | 47 | 45 | Sankinkai (Three Gold Club) |
| Sanwa | 44 | 27 | Sansuikai (Three Waters Club) |

Heading these big keiretsu corporations are executives who run their own companies but also belong to cross-keiretsu organizations that help manage and protect the interests of the keiretsu corporations collectively. Among the most important of the cross-corporate organizations are *shacho-kai,* or "presidents' clubs," found in each keiretsu. The members of the presidents' clubs normally meet once a month to consider common problems, plan business ties, consider the problems of any company having trouble within the keiretsu, and organize joint political action to influence government policy. Table 15-4 lists the big six keiretsu, the number of main corporations and lesser affiliated corporations in each group, and the name of the presidents' club (Kerbo and McKinstry 1995:71–72).

There are a few organizations in the corporate class in Japan, however, that cut across all of the big keiretsu to help deal with common problems and especially direct the political action for them all. *Keidanren* (or Japan Federation of Economic Organizations) is by far the most important, a kind of super business establishment, or, as some say, the "parliament of big business" with the Keidanren chair as the "prime minister" of the business world—and likely the single most powerful person in Japan (Kakuma 1981a; Atsuta 1992; Okumura 1978, 1983; Woronoff 1986:152; Kerbo and McKinstry 1995:Chapter 7). There are approximately 900 members of Keidanren who come from less than 1 percent of the corporations in Japan. However, this inner group of the corporate class who are Keidanren members come from corporations accounting for 40 percent of all sales and 50 percent of all corporate assets in Japan. Until 1997, the chair of Keidanren was Eiji Toyoda, also director and former CEO of Toyota Motor Company. It is especially in Keidanren that the inner group of the corporate class, called the *zaikai* in Japan, coordinates the economy and applies political pressure on the government in ways that often would be illegal in the United States.

## The Bureaucratic Elite

As noted earlier with respect to power in Japanese government, it is the top personnel in the main ministries who are most important and have the most influence. The key government ministries include the Ministry of Finance and the Ministry of International Trade and Industry, with the most powerful person in all of these ministries being the vice ministers, not the ministers. The vice minister and all of the ministry personnel below this person in each ministry are career bureaucrats who started in the ministry right out of college and worked their way to the top. The minister in each government ministry, on the other hand, is a political appointee, knows little about the agency compared with the other personnel, and is in office for only 3 or 4 years at most, and most often in recent years for less than 1 year (Colignon and Usui 2003; Kerbo and McKinstry 1995:Chapter 5; Koh 1989).

Neither can the politicians be considered all that influential over the bureaucratic ministry elite in Japan. Japanese ministers of parliament have few staff, and over 80 percent of the legislation passed in parliament was written and pushed by the ministry elite. The laws that are passed give the ministry elite broad interpretation when acting on their authority, as well as what is called "administrative guidance" to pressure people in all sectors of the society to follow their dictates. But beyond this, the ministry officials issue their own ordinances to direct all sectors of the society, which outnumber the laws from the Diet by nine to one (Koh 1989:206–207).

## The Political Elite

The political elites in Japan today are in retreat, and will be for many years to come. Before 1993, and going back to 1955, the political elites from one political party—the Liberal Democratic Party (LDP)—dominated Japanese politics. But these people finally became so corrupt and such an embarrassment to their corporate elite supporters that the party lost control of the Diet in 1993. It wasn't just the $50 million in gold bars found hidden in leader Kanemaru's home safe from the latest bribery scandal in the late 1980s that did the LDP in—that was only one of the final embarrassments. The corporate elite, often through the big business organization Keidanren, before 1993 had given the LDP over 90 percent of its campaign funds; after 1993 these funds were cut off but only briefly. By 1994 the LDP was back in control of the lower house of the Diet, although its control is less complete compared to the pre-1993 years (Kerbo and McKinstry 1995: Chapter 6). Campaign reform laws, which were finally passed in 1993 and 1994, and the new single-seat districts, which came into effect in 1994, have also left Japanese politics in turmoil. Finally, in 2009 the Democratic Party in Japan won a majority of seats in the lower house of the Diet to stop rule by the LDP. The new prime minister, Yukio Hatoyama, began attempts,—with some limited success as of 2010—to reduce the power of the government ministry. But there is unlikely to be much success for many years, if decades.

The Diet and those politicians in top positions in the Diet are not now, nor were they ever, powerless. Among other things, laws must be passed—even if they are mostly written by ministry officials—and tax revenues must be allocated. But the postwar Japanese political elite can be best described as playing a supportive role for the corporate and ministry elite.

# ❧ Social Stratification in Germany: Some Similarities—and Key Differences

We should begin this section by noting that our reference points are Germany and the United States, with some comparison to material from Japan in the first half of this chapter. This is important to note because many people, including many sociologists in the United States and Europe, have assumed that European class structures are more or less the same, with the United States and England placed in contrast to the continental European countries (Haller 1990:xi). Renewed attention to this question in recent years has brought research indicating the contrary (see especially Teckenberg 1990). There are many significant differences among the nations of continental Europe, though it is generally true that there are more similarities when contrasted to England and the United States.

Throughout the previous chapters of this book we have addressed the many issues of social stratification with comparative data—often with European data. In the first half of this chapter on Japan, we again covered the many issues of social stratification with Japan, the United States, and other Western nations as points of comparison. Thus, in this section we proceed rapidly through a series of major issues in social stratification so as not to belabor points made elsewhere.

## Structures of Social Stratification: Occupation, Authority, and Property

We have noted that all societies have some differences in the distribution of occupational categories that must be taken into consideration when comparing mobility rates.

Compared with the United States, there are some differences in Germany: For example, Germany has more industrial workers compared with a larger service sector in the United States. There is a large difference in the number of managerial workers, with under 5 percent of workers for Germany compared with over 13 percent in the United States (Kappelhoff and Teckenberg 1987:5–8). (This difference is no doubt related to the work laws, which are examined later in this chapter.) However, despite some differences, a main point of recent research on the class structure of Germany is that the class categories made up of occupational position, authority position, and property holdings are equally useful for understanding social stratification in Germany.

Several studies using recent German data have employed the Wright (1985, 1997) class categories we have used in previous chapters (for example, Holtmann and Strasser 1990; Terwey 1987; Haller 1990). As in the United States and other major industrial nations, such issues as the distribution of income by class categories and gender in Germany, as well as class consciousness, can be understood with reference to the class categories outlined by Wright (1985, 1997).

## Corporate and Bureaucratic Elites

As late-developing capitalist powers, defeated and largely destroyed after World War II, Japan and Germany invite all manner of comparisons. With respect to corporate elites, there have been, in fact, a number of similarities—both before and after World War II—but there also have been many differences. Among the similarities are some very wealthy families emerging at about the time of rapid industrialization in the second half of the 1800s, though Germany never had as much concentration of wealth in the prewar period as represented in the largest six Japanese zaibatsu.

Also among the similarities, most of the German upper class lost much of its wealth after World War II. Here, however, the comparison to Japan must certainly be seen as a matter of degree: There was much more continuity of wealth in pre– and post–World War II Germany than in Japan, and very few of the big German corporations were broken up as were the largest zaibatsu in Japan (Broom and Shay 1992; Spohn and Bodemann 1989:85–87). There was the 1952 "equalization of burdens law" (*Lastenausgleichgesetz*), which took some of the wealth from Germans, but only a small percent. Thus, upper-class and corporate-class power remains in Germany, somewhat more like in the present-day United States. But again there are some differences that must be outlined if we are to understand the position and power of current corporate elites in Germany.

While the United States has come to dominate the list of the richest people in the world, there are still wealthy families in Germany. In fact, before the American upsurge because of the booming U.S. stock market and longest economic boom in American history during the 1990s, in 1991 Germany ranked third in the list of world billionaires. In overall numbers the United States has more than twice as many billionaires compared with Japan and Germany, but despite war devastation, Japan and Germany have their share. Also interesting is that Germany actually has a slightly higher concentration of billionaires per population than the United States or Japan, though even with this statistic Germany is still third in billionaires behind Hong Kong and Switzerland.

Equally important to note is that unlike in Japan, where most billionaires today are post-war in origin and generally not the most powerful people in the economy (Kerbo and McKinstry 1995: Chapter 4), German billionaires show much more continuity and have more corporate power. Of the 43 billionaires in Broom and Shay's (1992) data set from Germany (and 1 from Switzerland affected by the Nazis), well over half of the family fortunes date back before World War II, and sometimes much further back. Six of the billionaire families originated before the 19th century. For example, "the youngest billionaire on the *Forbes* and *Fortune* rosters, 8-year-old Prince Albert von Thurn und Taxis, is 12th in a family line that founded the Holy Roman Empire's postal service" (Broom and Shay 1992:4). Another of the richest families in Germany today, the Haniels of the Ruhr industrial area of Germany, "date back 235 years to an ancestor to whom Frederick the Great granted the right to build a Duisburg warehouse" (Broom and Shay 1992:5). Today, Haniel family members hold about $5.3 billion in assets. We should not forget the Krupp family wealth, so important to Germany in arms production during many wars. The last Krupp family member died in 1986, though he had dropped the Krupp family name by 1966 and had renounced his inheritance because of Krupp corporate support of Hitler and building of concentration camps during World War II (though he did agree to keep an annual allowance of $900,000). The Krupp wealth dates back to the Thirty Years' War (1618–1648), when they made gun barrels for the German government. As for a more recent billionaire family, the Bosch family fortune was established by Robert Bosch, who began making such items as spark plugs and other electrical devices in 1886.

The real takeoff for these pre–World War II family fortunes goes back primarily to the second half of the 1800s with Germany's industrial expansion, even for most of the families who had wealth before this time. Three of the most wealthy families after World War II (Krupp, Thyssen, and Haniel), for example, made much of their wealth during the second half of the 1800s in the Ruhr industrial area around Duisburg, Essen, and Düsseldorf. But there was also great wealth emerging from the growth of big German banks at this time. The biggest of them all today, Deutsche Bank, was established by famous upper-class families of today such as Siemens (Broom and Shay 1992:5–6).

We have learned in previous chapters, however, that great wealth does not always equal great economic power. While there is much continuity of wealth in Germany through the past two centuries, there also has been great change in the German corporate structure since World War II. The rise of institutional investor stock control (to an even greater extent than in the United States), interlocked corporations with banks in central positions, and government ownership of much stock in big corporations are among the most important of these changes.

## German Corporate Structure

When we examine large corporations in Germany, family stock control has become less extensive in the post–World War II period. However, a rough examination of the data indicates that there is still more family control of large corporations in Germany than in the United States, and certainly much more than in Japan (Liedtke 1994). As we have already seen in the United States, there has been a rise of institutional investor stock control in the hands of investment banks, trusts, and other institutional investors in Germany. However, we will see later in this chapter that because of German laws, especially labor laws, stock control in a German corporation does not confer quite as much power in many cases as it does in the United States.

There is one more important difference between the German and American corporate structures that must be noted in the beginning: Unlike in the United States, and even Japan, big banks in Germany can also directly own large percentages of stock in big corporations. With the combination of institutional investor stock control and stock directly owned by banks, the big German banks—such as Deutsche Bank, Commerzbank, and Dresdner Bank—are the real powerhouses in today's German economy (Liedtke 1994). It is now not uncommon to hear of Germany's *bank keiretsus* (in reference to the Japanese keiretsu) to describe the groups of German corporations linked by powerful bank stock control, loan dependency from these big banks, and interlocking directorates coming from these big German banks (Thurow 1991:34; Craig 1991:115; Glouchevitch 1992:73–75). One important reason for this is that in contrast to Japan and the United States, German banks are not so restricted in how much stock they can hold in other corporations, plus they also can act directly as stockbrokers to control more stock (Glouchevitch 1992:75).

We can focus on the biggest bank today, Deutsche Bank. To list some examples of powerful corporations, Deutsche Bank holds 25 percent of the stock in Daimler-Benz, 10 percent of the leading insurance company (Allianz), 10 percent of another leading insurance company (Munich Re), 10 percent of Germany's leading department store (Karstadt), about 26 percent of Germany's leading construction company (Philipp Holzmann), among many others, just a few of which are also shown in Table 15-5 (Liedtke 1994). Executives from Deutsche Bank can also be found on the corporate boards (supervisory boards) in over 150 large corporations in Germany (Glouchevitch 1992:73). There is another big difference in Germany's corporate structure compared with those of Japan and the United States: The German government also

---

### TABLE 15-5

### Examples of German Bank *Keiretsu* (% of Stock Owned by Bank)

| Deutsche Bank | Dresdner Bank |
|---|---|
| Allianz (10%) | Allianz (10%) |
| Munich Re (25%) | Bilfinger & Berger (25%) |
| Daimler-Benz (25%) | Hapag-Lloyd (10%) |
| Karstadt (10%) | Verba (5%) |
| Philipp Holzmann (26%) | BMW (5%) |
| Klockner, Humboldt, Deutz (41%) | Munchener Ruck (10%) |
| Linde (10%) | |
| Munchener Ruck (10%) | |
| Sudzucker (17%) | |
| Hapag-Lloyd (10%) | |

*SOURCE:* Data from Liedtke (1994).

owns significant percentages of stock in major corporations. This government owner-ship of stock in Germany is on both the federal and state (Lander) government levels. Overall, the German government owns about 7 percent of all corporate stock in the country (Garten 1992:113), though in many cases the amount held in particular corpora-tions is much higher. For example, the central government owns 52 percent of the big airline, Lufthansa, and large portions of the Bundesbahn (railroad), and Telekom (the national phone system, though much of this government-held stock will be sold soon). For another example, one of the states, Lower Saxony, owns 20 percent of Volkswagen. Overall, the German government directly owns more corporate stock than the govern-ment of any other industrial nation today (Thurow 1991:36).

## The Bureaucratic and Political Elite

At the upper levels of power and social stratification, it is among the bureaucratic elite where we find most similarities between Japan and Germany. While there are some important differences today that must be considered, it is useful to note that Japan spe-cifically used the German state and bureaucratic elite structure as a model for its own development from the early Meiji period when Japan started its industrialization in the second half of the 1800s (Dietrich 1991:273).

In Germany, by the early 1800s it was already assumed that the state needed to direct the economy, and even in some cases to own and control corporations for eco-nomic development (Bendix 1978:413). Also like the Meiji Restoration of the late 1800s in Japan, from the middle 1800s Germany experienced something like a revolution from above, with sections of the elites pushing for basic change so that Germany could catch up to the other dominant powers of Europe at the time (Spohn and Bodemann 1989:76). While it is Bismarck who is often described as the founder of the German bureaucracy, it developed much earlier: Frederick William I, who ruled from 1713 to 1740, in many ways can be better described as the founder (Dietrich 1991:274–278). At that time, of course, most bureaucratic elites came from the *Junker* aristocratic upper class, but even then these people had to be rather well educated and talented to obtain such positions. Probably nowhere else in Europe does the bureaucratic elite continue to have as much respect and status as in Germany (Smith 1984; Dahrendorf 1979). Also like Japan, the German bureaucratic elite survived World War II intact more than did the corporate and certainly the political elite of Germany.

Where German and Japanese bureaucratic elite differ most is in the federal and state government division of responsibility already noted earlier in this chapter. While there are important bureaucratic elite positions on both federal and state (Lander) government levels, more central policy is developed on the federal level, and most of the actual work of guiding the economy and society falls to the state (Lander) levels (Mayntz 1984).

At the federal level, in each of the main government ministries there is only one main political appointee (as in Japan); the remainder are career civil servants. There are 20 main federal ministries with about 20,000 civil servants. Some 5,000 at the top are considered to be the "higher bureaucrats," with only 134 positions considered the very top (Dietrich 1991:278–282). These bureaucratic elites have gone to the best universities in Germany, and while only about 15 percent of Germans graduate from a university, in a figure unbelievable to most Americans, about *50 percent of all university graduates* in Germany start and end their careers with government positions—after they pass another difficult examination to enter the civil service, that is (Conradt 1978:167).

Unlike the preceding, significant differences exist between Japan and Germany with respect to their political elites. As noted earlier, although (and to some degree because) political parties were outlawed by Hitler, they made a big comeback after World War II (Dietrich 1991:282). German politicians actually do much governing and establishing policy, in contrast to their Japanese counterparts. They therefore provide a counterforce to the bureaucratic elite, and cooperation and compromises must be made in running the German state to a much greater extent than in Japan.

# ✎ German Workers and Codetermination Laws

With the preceding description of German corporate elites and the keiretsu-type corporate structure centered around large banks, one might assume that German workers have little influence in such a system. In contrast to the United States, however, such an assumption could not be further from the truth. How else are we to explain the high unemployment benefits cited earlier, or the low inequality figures already cited? At this point it is important to remember that Germany has some of the lowest levels of income inequality among industrial nations. As we saw in Chapter 2, the gap between the typical manufacturing worker's pay and the typical chief executive officer is 11 to 1 in Japan and 10 to 1 in Germany, while it is highest for the United States at 200 to 300 to 1 by various estimates. In other research comparing Germany, Japan, Canada, Italy, France, England, and the United States, the average manufacturing employee's income was highest in Germany, third highest in Japan, and lowest in the United States and England. As for the income of chief executive officers, however, it is highest in the United States, while executives in Germany receive one-half the income of U.S. executives and Japanese executives receive about one-fourth the income (not counting bonuses and stock options which put American corporate executives much further ahead in overall compensation).

While Germany and Japan are rather similar with respect to comparatively low pay for CEOs and high pay for average workers, the two countries line up very differently on some other figures: We have already seen that, except for American workers, Japanese employees work the longest hours per year among advanced industrial nations, while German employees are toward the bottom of average hours worked per year. The point is that German workers have few equals when it comes to wages and other benefits, short working hours, government protection, among many other conditions workers around the world can only look upon with envy. To put it crudely, the wealthy and corporate elites in Germany did not suddenly decide to give workers a better deal because they are "nice guys." It is our task at present to provide some explanation for why German workers are the envy of most workers in the world, and we must begin with a brief history of the "works constitution act," "codetermination laws," and other means of labor influence in Germany.

# A History of German Labor Laws

While conducting research on relations between Japanese managers and German employees in Japanese transplant corporations located in Germany during 1992 and 1993, we asked German personnel managers to explain some of the problems associated with their job in a Japanese corporation. In a common response, one of our informants stated, "Japanese corporate executives here do not think the position of personnel manager is such a complex job." He went on to describe how the job of personnel manager in Germany involves much more than hiring and firing of employees, especially because there must be continuous and complex negotiations with employees on almost every issue (Kerbo et al. 1994a, 1994b; Lincoln et al. 1995). Workers in Germany are not simply told what policies they must follow. Indeed, because of labor laws, it can be said that German workers have more rights and influence in what happens in the workplace, and often in the company generally, than any other workers in the world (see Thelen 1991; Turner 1991). These labor laws apply to any corporation setting up operations in Germany, whether the company is German, American, Russian, or Japanese.

The term **dual system** is used to describe the form of labor representation in Germany that has evolved since World War II. This dual system involves (1) legally mandated equal employee representation on the company board of directors, along with representation on the shop floor level by "works councils," and (2) the continued presence of powerful labor unions representing labor in wider issues above the individual plant level. Soon after World War II, labor unions were able to gain strength after having been destroyed by Hitler. By 1952, however, labor laws first pushed as early as 1848 were finally enacted by the German government, giving workers extensive rights and specific representation in each company, above the very smallest, through worker corporate board representatives and works councils elected by employees of the company (Hoffmeister and Tubach 1992:180). Fearing the consequences of greater labor union influence after World War II, the conservative German government at the time tried to weaken labor unions through laws it believed would isolate worker representatives in each corporation, creating something like "company unions." The idea backfired, however, when labor unions in fact did not decline in influence and worker support but learned to cooperate with works councils and worker board members in each corporation for influence on two fronts, from within each company and from without (Thelen 1991). With a more liberal government in the 1970s, these labor laws, or **codetermination laws,** were expanded in 1972, giving workers even more rights of "codetermination" about what happens in the workplace.

It is important to note that labor influence is said to be more legalistic, or formalized into law, in Germany compared with other industrial nations, even other countries in Europe such as Sweden and Austria that are known for strong labor unions. Compared with several other European nations, Germany, in fact, has a lower rate of unionization; but this is misleading. Despite the lower rate of unionization in Germany, workers have more influence because (1) the ties between works councils and unions are more important than the number of workers who actually join a union in the company, and (2) workers' rights' are more fixed in law and not as dependent on what kind of government happens to be in office at the time. With this situation, a division of labor has developed, especially between union leaders and works councils: The unions work for wage and other agreements affecting German workers generally—often through political action and threats of strike—while the works councils see that these wider agreements and already existing labor rights are upheld on each individual shop floor.

A few examples of the rights afforded workers under the codetermination laws will be useful for American readers, who will find the situation surprising compared with that in their own country. For example, under the expanded 1972 laws, workers must be given extensive information about all matters affecting them and the whole company; works councils must be consulted on any changes in policies affecting work time arrangements, overtime, work breaks, vacation times, plant wage systems, the introduction of new technologies and any other alterations in the work environment, as well as the hiring, transfer, reclassification, or firing of workers. Thus, corporate managers "must secure (in advance) the consent of the works council on a range of personnel decisions affecting individual workers, including job assignments, classifications and reclassification, and transfers [paragraph 99 of the Works Constitutions Act]" (Thelen 1991:101). After consulting with the works council on these issues, it is sometimes possible for managers to go against a vote of the works council; but to do so is very time consuming because of extensive rights for challenge given workers in a labor court system in Germany.

To make the point more clearly, we can provide a few details pertaining to the influence of works councils from the 239-page 1991 English version of the official *Codetermination Laws* (German Federal Ministry of Labour and Social Affairs 1991:18–19):

> [Works councils have] a genuine right of co-determination in a series of matters such as: working hours, e.g. the introduction of short-time work, the introduction and use of technical devices designed to monitor the behaviour or performance of the employees, the assignment of and notice to vacate company-owned accommodation, the fixing of job and bonus rates and comparable performance-related remuneration.
>
> Works councils have a far-reaching right of participation and co-determination in matters concerning the structuring, organization and design of jobs, operation and the working environment, manpower planning and personnel management as well as in-plant training.
>
> In the case of recruitments, gradings, re-gradings and transfers the employer must obtain the consent of the works council. If the works council refuses its consent it can be substituted only by a decision in lieu of consent by a labour court.
>
> Dismissals are effective only if the works council was consulted in advance. The works council may oppose a routine dismissal with the effect that the employer must keep the employee in his employment until a final court decision is given on the case at issue.
>
> The works council has the right to be informed on a large number of matters. Moreover, the finance committee, which is to be established in companies with more than 100 employees, and whose members are all appointed by the works council, has a substantial right to be informed and to be heard in financial matters.
>
> In the case of alterations, such as the reduction of operations, the closure or transfer of an establishment, the works council may require the preparation of a social compensation plan in order to compensate for any financial prejudices sustained by the employees.

Finally, we must also stress that according to the Codetermination Act of 1976, large German corporations must have equal representation of workers on the "supervisory board." The supervisory board in a German company is similar to the board of directors that represents stockholders of the company in an American corporation in that these people have legal authority over corporate managers, and can set their salaries as well as fire managers for poor performance (though we have seen it is more complex than this in the American corporation in Chapter 7). But in striking contrast to the United States, under German law the workers of a corporation are considered to have equal rights, legal protection, and therefore equal authority with the stockholders. As noted earlier, this is where stock control in a German corporation may not bring as much power as it does in the United States or Japan. By German law, in large German corporations the supervisory board must be made up of 10 employee representatives and 10 stockholders' representatives (see Markovits 1986:56). Further, the 10 employee representatives on the supervisory board must include at least 7 staff members, from which at least 1 is a wage earner, 1 a salaried employee, and 1 a management employee, along with 3 union representatives from the shop floor.

With the long hours and low pay of American and other workers, it might seem that German workers would be unable to compete. With low-wage competition from the United States becoming more intense from the 1990s, more German corporate executives are claiming this to be a problem. But the situation is more complex than just comparative wages and benefits. Otherwise the German economy would not be the strongest in Europe, the third largest in the world, and still a strong competitor of the United States and Japan. Because of its importance to the question of world economic competition and the position and standard of living of workers, as well as because little of this is known in the United States, we must now turn briefly to the issue of benefits to German corporations and the German economy from the dual system.

## Labor Power and the Benefits of the Codetermination Laws

When first confronted with the array of German labor laws, legal rights, and labor costs, American, British, and Japanese corporate executives are likely to assume these are harmful to business, and wonder how German corporations are able to survive. But German corporations certainly do survive, and there is evidence that German labor laws, unions, and works councils actually help the competitiveness of German companies. Also, interviews with executives from major German corporations have recently indicated these executives now agree that codetermination laws have helped their business (Wever 1993; Thelen 1991; Kerbo and Strasser 2000:Chapter 4).

To understand one of the major benefits of works councils and strong German unions, the individualistic orientation of workers in Western industrial nations has to be acknowledged. Western child-rearing methods and Western culture will likely never allow the tendency toward identification with the company and the extent of cooperation with the work group found in Asian countries such as Japan (Pye 1985). But neither can all workers seek only their own individual interests without due regard for group needs if a civilization or a particular company is to survive. However flawed some of his ideas, Sigmund Freud outlined this dilemma of human societies in one of his greatest books, *Civilization and Its Discontents,* in 1930. Some means of organization and compromise of conflicting interests must be attained. Early German sociologists such as Georg

Simmel (1905/1955) and later sociologists such as Coser (1956, 1967) outlined similar principles of human societies in dealing with conflicting interests. These sociologists have shown how group conflicts, when properly managed and organized, can in fact have positive benefits for both parties in a conflict.

For example, it has long been pointed out that an organized opponent is much preferable to an unorganized one. With an unorganized opponent, solutions to a conflict or compromise are close to impossible. But with an organized opponent, negotiations and compromises can be made. *And,* most important, the compromise agreement can be carried out with an organized opponent whose leaders are able to keep their members in line. Recent studies of German corporate executives and their attitudes toward strong unions and works councils suggest many have read their Simmel, or more likely simply have discovered a universal principle first outlined by Simmel. As one representative of the Association of German Employers stated (Thelen 1991:34–35):

> As soon as you get splinter groups in the plant, you get unrest in the plant as well. We would rather deal with one union, with a unified works council. A single, unified opponent is more reliable and trustworthy [*verlasslich*]; more than one faction fosters competition among them as each tries to outdo the other. We would rather have a single strong and self-confident union to work with.

A logical calculation of winners and losers in the conflict or cooperation between management and labor supports the attitudes of German managers described above (Wright 2002b). With workers kept weak and uninfluential in the company as in the United States, corporate profits in the short run are higher. Wright (2002b) showed that as working-class power increases to challenge the capitalist-class power, in the short term, productivity and profits decline. But after a period of time there is a positive effect on both higher corporate profits and worker wages and benefits as workers' power helps capitalists solve the various kinds of collective action problems to increase production quality and productivity.

Despite the extensive individualism of Western workers, it is still beneficial *and* possible to obtain worker identification with the company, as well as the long-term needs and survival of the company. But such worker identification and cooperation in Western nations is more likely achieved by giving recognition to individualism rather than trying to suppress it.

This is in contrast to the lingering effects of philosophies such as Confucianism in many Asian nations, including Japan. In these countries subordinates are more likely to submit to authority figures in return for protection and rewards, which they expect will be given because of their submission (Pye 1985). In the more individualistic West, however, subordinates are more likely to demand rights and influence in what authority figures decide in order to assure themselves of benefits and protection. This is not to say Asian subordinates will remain passive when their expectations are violated; they certainly have rebelled throughout history, especially in Japan. But the point is that there are different approaches to authority figures by subordinates, and different ways of ensuring expected benefits.

German codetermination laws could not be further from Confucianism: German employees certainly do not wish to depend on the paternalism of corporate managers. But in providing worker rights and influence in matters affecting their jobs, labor–management cooperation can be achieved. When employees are brought into some of the decision-making process, they feel more confident their interests are being protected, and they are made to feel more loyalty toward the company, tied to the long-term profitability and survival of the company, much like Japanese workers in the most successful Japanese corporations. Because of the past treatment of workers and mutual mistrust between labor and managers in the United States, there is often the attitude of a "zero-sum game"; that is, if one side wins something, it means the other side necessarily loses, rather than both possibly ending up as winners. In our visits to union offices in Germany, on the other hand, we saw and heard many things suggesting a rejection of such a zero-sum game.

# ❧ Variation in Modern Systems of Social Stratification: A Conclusion

As we have seen in several places throughout this book, especially at the end of Chapter 7 (see Table 7-5) and Chapter 14, there are different variations of modern stratification systems today, related to what we can call differing political economies or different capitalisms. In this chapter we have seen more detail about how and why the German system of social stratification is related to what I have called "cooperative capitalism," and the Japanese system fits the "Asian model," both in contrast to the "corporate-dominated" form of social stratification in the United States. All systems of social stratification in modern industrial and postindustrial societies have some fundamental similarities: the occupational, authority, and property structures shape the ranks of modern stratification systems, there is social mobility (though with more variation today), and there is certainly income and wealth inequality in all of them. Still, there are important variations.

Of the three primary actors in modern capitalist systems, in Germany there is more of a balance of power between the corporate elite, the state, and employees. This greater balance of power is what gives German employees a much greater share of the valued resources compared to the United States. In Japan (as well as most other Asian nations), the state has always been more authoritarian, even when some democracy has been achieved. The state is much more involved in regulating aspects of the society, and especially economic activity. And it is primarily unelected bureaucratic officials who direct the state when it comes to economic planning (Kerbo and McKinstry 1995). Other East and Southeast Asian nations that have been experiencing rapid economic development in recent decades have been more or less following this Japanese model (Kerbo 2006, 2005, forthcoming).

With a much weaker state under the neo-liberal philosophy of the United States, a philosophy arguing that the state should be less involved in human affairs (especially economic activity), a corporate elite has come to be much more influential, especially since the Reagan era beginning in 1980 (Kalleberg 2009; Tope and Jacobs 2009; Birchfield 2008). Of course, the differences between the German system, following a more "cooperative capitalist" form, and the more corporate-dominated form found in the United States are aligned more like a continuum, with other Western industrial nations falling somewhere in between. And there has been movement among specific nations through history. Before the 1930s the United States had more of a neo-liberal (smaller state) form, then turned a bit toward the "cooperative capitalism" form during the Great Depression under Roosevelt's "New Deal" programs. Serious political and economic problems for the United States from the 1970s led to more corporate elite political activism in a time of economic insecurities for the general population as well (Useem 1984, 1978, 1979b). With growing inequality, job insecurity, not to mention two wars going badly, the 2008 economic crisis in the United States set the stage for movement back to greater government involvement in the economy (Domhoff 2010). The U.S. form of capitalism and political economy is very unlikely to move very far toward the cooperative capitalism represented in Germany. But it will be interesting to see how far the Obama administration will move away from the Reagan era during this second decade of the 21st century.

## Summary

This chapter has compared the stratification systems of both Japan and Germany to that of the United States today. As the world's second largest economy and the first fully modern postindustrial society in Asia, Japan provides one of the biggest contrasts to the United States. As the third largest economy in the world, and an advanced industrial society outside of both North America and Asia, Germany provides us with a further test of the similarities and differences of systems of social stratification in modern capitalist industrial societies. Among the biggest contrasts to the United States, Japan has less inequality and much greater involvement of the state in the economy. Most of the emerging economies in East and Southeast Asia are more or less following the Japanese form of capitalism. Among the most important differences in Germany are the low levels of inequality and the power of labor unions and the working class. After World War II, labor unions, once outlawed by Hitler, became powerful, and many new labor laws came into effect. These labor laws have given employees what is called codetermination in German corporations through extensive representation of workers on the corporate board and works councils elected by employees in the company or government agencies. Along with these work laws and the power of labor unions in Germany, we must add the expanded welfare state as creating a relatively low level of inequality and poverty in Germany today.

# World Stratification and Globalization: The Poor of This Earth

Squatter slums like these in Bangkok, Thailand (*top*), and near Phnom Penh, Cambodia (*bottom*) are found throughout the developing world. They are much more numerous and harsh in some developing countries than in others. Most of the people living in these scrap wood and metal shacks in Bangkok have village homes to return to and live in Bangkok only temporarily to make extra money. In Cambodia, though, rates of poverty are much higher, and poor people are increasingly losing their land because of corrupt deals between government officials and foreign companies, mainly from South Korea and China. I first interviewed some of these Cambodian poor in a slum in the middle of the capital, Phnom Penh. Their land was later stolen, and these people were dumped in a field about 30 miles away with only these straw huts they made themselves. Some 3,000 people live in this one-square-mile area today. Amnesty International estimates 150,000 additional poor people in Cambodia will have their land stolen in coming years.
*SOURCES:* © Harold Kerbo.

## Chapter Outline

The largest and most dire of Bangkok's slums, Klong Toey, which I described in the beginning of Chapter 9, a slum with some 100,000 poor people crammed into one neighborhood, pales in comparison to "world class" slums in several other countries around the world. In India, for example, the Bombay-Dharavi slum is claimed to be the biggest in the world, with people far more desperate than most people in slums like Klong Toey. It is estimated that 58 percent of the 6.7 million residents of Bombay, India, live in slums such as Dharavi, which itself has perhaps as many as one million people. Then there is the slum located in the Philippines, contained within Manila's huge garbage dump. Thousands of people live there and try to make a living by searching through garbage for anything they can sell. From time to time, as happened in the summer of 2000, parts of the garbage dump explode into flames, killing hundreds of people and injuring many more. There is also, for example, the famous Kibera slum in Nairobi, where all world leaders seem to be taken to show them how bad things can really become. Although it is hard to imagine while walking through the Klong Toey slum in Thailand, those like Kibera are far worse, with people who have much less hope, far fewer options in life, and almost no aid from the national government where they live.

To a far greater extent than Klong Toey, these slums like Dharavi are crime ridden and dangerous, not only for the crime but also because of the extremely unsanitary conditions: There is, for instance, one toilet for every 800 people in the Dharavi slum. In Cambodia conditions for the urban poor are even more desperate, and getting worse. While doing fieldwork on poverty conditions in Southeast Asia between 2006 and 2009, I watched the slums of Phnom Penh (Cambodia's capital city) become fewer and fewer. But the reduction is not because thousands of people have gotten better jobs and homes. The extremely corrupt government in Cambodia is allowing foreign corporations, mainly from China and South Korea, to take over the slum land in the capital to build tourist hotels, condos, and casinos (Kerbo 2011). I located four sites where many of these displaced people now live in "relocation camps." They are miles from the city, and there is no work nor farmland to grow food. They were simply arrested, taken from their slum homes in the city, and dumped in a field. Amnesty International estimates there will be 150,000 people like this in Cambodia (www.amnestyusa.org; also see, http://www.licadho-cambodia.org/, and CHRAC 2009) by 2012. In one of these forced relocation camps, some 3,000 people were living in straw huts all crammed together in a square mile area. I did find one exception, however. A few hundred of these former urban slum people were given small houses about 25 miles from Phnom Penh, right next to a garment sweatshop owned by the South Korean company that had taken their land in the city. But several girls and their parents in this relocation camp told me the sweatshop would only hire teenagers, mostly young girls.

Another way to consider the desperate condition of almost half of the world's population is to contemplate the existence of the now notorious sweatshops around the world (Rosen 2002). But it is not simply that these sweatshops exist with wages sometimes below $1 per day, requiring 10- to 12-hour working days in extremely unhealthy environments. What is even more troubling to consider is that with almost half of the world's population living on less than what $2 per day will buy in the United States, *landing such sweatshop jobs is a big step up for hundreds of millions of people in this world!* American middle-class and working-class parents hope their children will get into a good university and eventually land a good professional position. As many as one or two billion people in the world dream of their children being able to improve their lives through landing a sweatshop job (Kristof and WuDunn 2000). As *New York Times* journalist Nicholas Kristof tried to explain in a purposely shocking opinion article titled "Let's Hear It for Third World Sweatshops," a sad commentary on world inequality is that when international agencies are successful in shutting some of these sweatshops, people end up in greater hunger because sweatshops are their only options (*International Herald Tribune,* June 26, 2002). This is a reality far removed from anything comfortable people in rich countries can imagine.

# ⚔ The Extent of World Poverty

We have already seen some of the figures on poverty in beginning this final Part Five of our look at social stratification worldwide. But a bit more detail is important. Using the Purchasing Power Parity (PPP) measure to make comparisons of world currencies more accurate, agencies such as the World Bank and United Nations estimate that approximately 1.1 to 1.3 billion people in the world today are living on what less than $1 would buy them each day in the United States.* This is about 20 percent of the

---

*It is perhaps useful to make clear what the World Bank and other agencies imply with this new $1 per person per day measure. This $1 per day is estimated using Purchasing Power Parity (PPP), meaning the estimate begins with what goods $1 per day would buy in the United States, then approximates the cost of the same goods in the actual currency of each country. It might be useful to use what a friend of mine came up with—the "sandwich index." Given that $1 in the United States could buy a sandwich (well, a cheap one anyway), we can say that the World Bank estimates that 1.3 billion people in the world do not have enough money to buy one sandwich per day. There are, of course, many factors making this $1 per day only a rough estimate, as the World Bank admits. For example, while in one country the one sandwich per day means the person must go without a place to sleep because all of the daily wage has gone for the sandwich, another country has a tradition of families taking other family members under their roof. Thus, in this other country the person has a sandwich *and* a place to sleep. It seems, nonetheless, that this $1 per day rough indicator of economic means for people in the world gives us a reasonable idea of comparative levels of poverty. For more details see the World Bank, *Technical Notes,* 2000:320.

world's population. Almost 30 percent more of the world's population live on less than $2 per day (United Nations, *A Better World for All,* 2000); United Nations Development Program, *Overcoming Human Poverty,* 2000; World Bank, *Progress in the Fight Against Poverty,* 2004). The PPP measure of the value of different currencies around the world (which the $1 per day estimate is based on) was first done in the early 1990s. The World Bank published its updated report in 2008. Worldwide the World Bank found the percentage and number of people living on less than $1 per day had not changed much, though the percentage was pushed higher in a few countries such as China and Cambodia (also see Haughton and Khandker 2009).

The income and wealth inequalities we have seen are not the only inequalities of importance; we also see extreme inequalities in how the world's food supply is distributed. In 2008 the United Nations World Food Programme estimated almost 1 billion of the world's population were undernourished, an increase of over 100 million people compared to the previous year (United Nations World Food Programme 2009). Part of this increase was due to a jump in world food prices in 2008. No doubt when new reports are published, we will find a big jump in world hunger again because of the global economic crisis during 2009 and 2010.

For the millions of poor living in urban areas in the least-developed countries, this poverty also means only about half of these people have "access to sanitary living conditions" such as clean water and toilets. It means that an average of 107 out of 1,000 babies die by the time they are 5 years old compared to only 6 in richer nations. It means very little education, if any, and almost half the population is illiterate. It means that an average of about 20 percent of the children 10 to 14 years old in low-income nations must be employed for long hours a day, and a much higher percentage in many of these countries (World Bank 2000:276–285; 2004). Poverty also means dying at an earlier age than people in richer countries simply because there is no money for medical treatment. One of the worst examples of this is the spread of AIDS in developing countries. While the disease is still not curable, people infected with HIV that leads to AIDS can expect to live to a normal age with drug treatment. But in poor countries there is no money; in African countries alone some 5,000 people die each day of AIDS, there are 13.2 million children orphaned by AIDS, and in 10 years the deaths from AIDS in Africa alone will exceed all of those killed in World War I and World War II combined. There are African countries that will experience population declines of 30 to 40 percent in coming years because of deaths from AIDS. And in countries such as Namibia, Zimbabwe, Swaziland, and Botswana, one estimate is that in 10 years the life expectancy will be reduced to around 30 years of age instead of 70 (World Bank, *Aid and Reform in* Africa, 2002; United Nations 2004).

It is also important to recognize that in many countries these poverty and inequality figures have been getting worse as globalization proceeds (United Nations, *A Better World for All,* 2000; United Nations Development Program, *Overcoming Human Poverty,* 2000). But many people in low-income countries are experiencing improved conditions compared to people in other countries where conditions are getting worse. These less-well-known statistics are among the most important to consider because, as we will do later in this chapter, understanding why people in some poor countries are experiencing improved conditions can be a key to understanding, and hopefully helping, the people in countries where conditions are worsening.

Table 16-1 shows that the percentage of people living on less than $1 per day varies dramatically in less-developed nations, and the variation in prospects for improvement are even more dramatic. For people living in East Asia and the Pacific (in countries such as China, Thailand, Vietnam, Malaysia, Indonesia, and South Korea), the percentage of people living in extreme poverty (less than $1 per day) has dropped extensively since 1990, and is estimated to drop to 0.9 percent in 2015. (However, many of the countries in the region, such as Laos, Burma, and Cambodia, continue with high levels of extreme poverty.) In other regions, such as south Asia (primarily India), there has been little improvement in rates of extreme poverty in recent years, but conditions are expected to improve. In Latin America there was much less of a drop in extreme poverty up to 2002, though the World Bank expects the drop to increase by 2015 (World Bank 2006b, 2008; also see Firebaugh and Goesling 2004). In sub-Saharan Africa the rate of extreme poverty has been increasing rather than decreasing, with almost half the population living on less than $1 per day in 2002. In a new optimistic forecast, however, the World Bank now thinks there is a chance for enough poverty reduction in a few African nations such as South Africa to bring down the overall rate of extreme poverty in sub-Saharan African slightly by 2015.

Another way in which to consider the extent of world poverty is to compare rates of gross national product (GNP) or income on a per capita basis. Especially now that we have the new Purchasing Power Parity measure of currencies and incomes, comparing rates of GNP per capita gives us a rough idea of the level of poverty, or the general standard of living in countries around the world. Table 16-2 presents such data for a selection of countries around the world for 2008. The differences, of course, are huge. As

## TABLE 16-1

### Percentage of the Population Living on Less Than $1 and $2 a Day by World Region, 1990 to 2015

| Region | Percent of population living on | | | | | |
| | less than $1 per day | | | less than $2 per day | | |
| | 1990 | 2002 | 2015 | 1990 | 2002 | 2015 |
|---|---|---|---|---|---|---|
| East Asia and the Pacific | 29.6 | 14.9 | 0.9 | 69.9 | 40.7 | 12.7 |
| China | 33.0 | 16.6 | 1.2 | 72.6 | 41.6 | 13.1 |
| Rest of East Asia and the Pacific | 21.1 | 10.8 | 0.4 | 63.2 | 38.6 | 11.9 |
| Europe and Central Asia | 0.5 | 3.6 | 0.4 | 4.9 | 16.1 | 8.2 |
| Latin America and the Caribbean | 11.3 | 9.5 | 6.9 | 28.4 | 22.6 | 17.2 |
| Middle East and North Africa | 2.3 | 2.4 | 0.9 | 21.4 | 19.8 | 10.4 |
| South Asia | 41.3 | 31.3 | 12.8 | 85.5 | 77.8 | 56.7 |
| Sub-Saharan Africa | 44.6 | 46.4 | 38.4 | 75.0 | 74.9 | 67.1 |
| Total | 27.9 | 21.1 | 10.2 | 60.8 | 49.9 | 32.8 |
| Excluding China | 26.1 | 22.5 | 12.9 | 56.6 | 52.6 | 38.6 |

*SOURCE:* World Bank, *Global Prospects, Remittances, 2006* (2006b:10).

# TABLE 16-2

## Gross National Income per Capita, Select Countries, PPP Measures, 2008

| Country | Gross national income per capita, PPP |
|---|---|
| Norway | 58,500 |
| United States | 46,970 |
| Switzerland | 46,460 |
| Canada | 36,220 |
| Britain | 36,130 |
| Germany | 35,940 |
| Japan | 35,220 |
| France | 34,410 |
| South Korea | 28,120 |
| Mexico | 14,270 |
| Malaysia | 13,740 |
| South Africa | 9,780 |
| Ecuador | 7,760 |
| China | 6,020 |
| Thailand | 5,990 |
| Angola | 5,020 |
| Philippines | 3,900 |
| Indonesia | 3,830 |
| India | 2,960 |
| Vietnam | 2,700 |
| Laos | 2,060 |
| Cambodia | 1,820 |
| Tanzania | 1,230 |
| Haiti | 1,180 |
| Uganda | 1,140 |
| Rwanda | 1,010 |
| Ethiopia | 870 |
| Malawi | 830 |
| Mozambique | 770 |
| Sierra Leone | 750 |
| Niger | 680 |
| Burundi | 380 |
| Congo, of Democratic Republic | 290 |

*SOURCE:* World Bank (2010:Table 1).

we move down Table 16-2 we move from Norway with an annual gross national income per capita of almost $60,000 per year to the sub-Saharan African countries of Malawi, Burundi, and the Democratic Republic of Congo, with per capita incomes of only $830, $380, and $290 per year, respectively. Remembering the above description of how the $1 per day figure using Purchasing Power Parity is estimated one is reminded that this $290 is the equivalent of what $290 would buy a person in the United States, *not* what $290 U.S. dollars would buy in the Democratic Republic of Congo. In other words, the average person in the Democratic Republic of Congo is trying to live on what one could buy with $290 to last for the whole year. Simply considering the average per capita GNP of a nation, however, can be misleading in one important respect: It assumes the total GNP of a country is divided equally among all of its people.

This $1 a day per person figure is a rough estimate of living conditions. Without any "income-in-kind" such as being able to grow some of your own food (which is not included in these estimates), people would starve to death. Millions of people, of course, do not. In other words, 1.3 billion people living on less than $1 per day does not mean 1.3 billion people are starving to death each year. But as we saw above, almost 1 billion people a day were malnourished in 2008. As I traveled the countryside conducting interviews with village farmers in Cambodia between 2006 and 2008, where 66 percent of the people live on less than $1 per day, I saw little starvation, though plenty of indicators of malnutrition. The difference for Cambodia, and almost all of Southeast Asia, is that most poor peasants have at least a little land to grow their own food. I was told by families in village after village, "we grow *almost* enough food to feed our families." Land inequality in Asia is generally lower than in Africa and especially Latin America, and this is a big advantage for Asia. However, in some countries this advantage is shrinking. Fifteen years ago only 3 percent of farm families were landless in Cambodia, but because of corrupt government officials and the need to sell land for hospital care for sick children, by 2006 this figure was already at 23 percent landless in Cambodia (Kerbo 2011).

It is also clear that differences in rates of extreme poverty are not simply related to rates of economic growth. Some Latin American countries in recent years have had rates of economic growth similar to rates of growth in GNP in East and Southeast Asian countries. What divides most East and Southeast Asian countries from Latin American countries is *even* versus *uneven* economic development. (For most of sub-Saharan Africa, however, it is simply no economic development.) As can be seen in Table 16-3, Gini scores from the mid-2000s show East and Southeast Asian nations generally have much lower income inequality than countries in Latin America or Africa. Brazil, for example, has one of the highest rates of income inequality in the world (at 0.59), while the other Latin American countries where we have data are not far behind Brazil. In Brazil the poorest 20 percent of the population receives only 2.5 percent of the annual income while the richest 20 percent receives 63.8 percent. The situation is even worse for the poor in sub-Saharan African countries because of the low gross national income to begin with, then a highly unequal distribution in most cases. For example, Mozambique had a per capita income of only $1,270 in 2005, but the bottom 20 percent of people got only 6.5 percent of the income pie.

Because the vast majority of people in less-developed countries around the world live in rural areas and depend on some kind of agricultural work for their survival, the

## TABLE 16-3

### Cross-National Comparison of Income Inequality within Nations and Gini Index, mid-2000s

| | Percentage of total household income | | |
|---|---|---|---|
| Country | Poorest 20% | Top 20% | Gini Index |
| Bangladesh | 8.7% | 42.8% | 0.31% |
| India | 8.1 | 46.1 | 0.33 |
| Indonesia | 6.0 | 44.9 | 0.34 |
| Philippines | 5.4 | 52.3 | 0.46 |
| Thailand | 6.4 | 48.4 | 0.40 |
| China | 5.9 | 46.6 | 0.45 |
| Malaysia | 4.5 | 53.8 | 0.49 |
| Vietnam | 8.0 | 44.5 | 0.35 |
| South Korea | 7.5 | 39.3 | 0.32 |
| Ethiopia | 7.1 | 47.7 | 0.30 |
| Egypt | 9.8 | 39.0 | 0.34 |
| Kenya | 5.0 | 50.2 | 0.44 |
| Zambia | 4.2 | 54.8 | 0.53 |
| Mozambique | 6.5 | 46.5 | 0.40 |
| Guatemala | 2.1 | 63.0 | 0.58 |
| El Salvador | 3.4 | 56.5 | 0.50 |
| Peru | 4.4 | 51.2 | 0.50 |
| Costa Rica | 4.0 | 51.8 | 0.48 |
| Brazil | 2.5 | 63.8 | 0.59 |
| Panama | 3.6 | 52.8 | 0.55 |
| Mexico | 3.6 | 58.2 | 0.49 |
| Chile | 3.5 | 60.1 | 0.51 |
| Venezuela | 3.7 | 53.1 | 0.42 |
| Spain | 7.5 | 40.3 | 0.35 |
| Sweden | 9.6 | 34.5 | 0.25 |
| Italy | 8.7 | 36.3 | 0.31 |
| United Kingdom | 6.6 | 43.0 | 0.34 |
| The Netherlands | 7.3 | 40.1 | 0.29 |
| France | 7.2 | 40.2 | 0.31 |
| Germany | 8.2 | 38.5 | 0.28 |
| United States | 5.2 | 46.4 | 0.38 |

*SOURCE:* World Bank (2006a:280–282).

distribution of land is a very important condition. Using a recently developed Gini index of land inequality, Table 16-4 shows even bigger differences between Asia and especially Latin America. Most countries in Latin America have Gini index figures in the 0.80 range, and some even in the 0.90 range. (Remember that 1.00 would mean one person owns all the land.) Asian nations, on the other hand, have Gini index numbers ranging from the 0.30 to 0.50. Typical of less-developed countries with uneven rates of economic development within the country are major differences between rural and urban people. For example, the World Bank lists the urban poverty rate for Brazil as 13 percent compared to 32 percent in rural areas. In Bangladesh it was 14 percent in urban areas versus 40 percent in rural areas, while it was 40 percent versus 65 percent in Peru, 15 percent versus 65 percent in Panama, and 34 percent versus 72 percent in Guatemala. In most East

## TABLE 16-4

### Land Inequality in the Developing World, Gini Index of Land Inequality*

| Country | Gini land concentration index** |
|---|---|
| Southeast Asia | |
| Thailand | 0.47 |
| Burma | 0.44 |
| Indonesia | 0.46 |
| Laos | 0.39 |
| Philippines | 0.55 |
| Africa | |
| Ethiopia | 0.47 |
| Malawi | 0.52 |
| Morocco | 0.62 |
| Uganda | 0.59 |
| Latin America | |
| Argentina | 0.83 |
| Brazil | 0.85 |
| Columbia | 0.80 |
| Honduras | 0.66 |
| Panama | 0.60 |
| Uruguay | 0.79 |
| Nicaragua | 0.93 |
| Paraguay | 0.78 |
| Peru | 0.91 |

*The U.N. Gini land concentration index is based on the same principle as the Gini income inequality index. The higher the number, the higher the concentration of land ownership in the hands of a few people in the country.

**Data were not available for every country, and most recent data available are presented here.

*SOURCE:* World Bank (2006a:280–282).

and Southeast Asian countries these rural versus urban poverty differences are much less. Thailand, for example, has one of the least differences, with the poverty rate at 15 percent in the rural areas compared to 10 percent in urban areas (World Bank 2000:280–281). What this means, of course, is that Latin America and Africa have a higher percentage of landless peasants who must depend on the rich landowners for their means of existence. We also will see that these rich landowners in Latin America especially are tied to the world agriculture markets and big agribusiness firms in the rich countries, often keeping both landowners and agribusiness firms rich at the expense of landless peasants.

There is another important new estimate that helps us understand the problem of world poverty. The World Bank's *World Development Report 2000/2001* includes calculations on how much poverty reduction countries obtain for each percentage of new economic growth each year. This, of course, is a key to *even* compared to *uneven* economic development. If, for example, economic growth does not lead to poverty reduction, this means that some of the population has an improved standard of living because of the economic growth while others in the country have no improvement or even possibly worse living conditions. Figure 16-1 shows the country's rate of GDP growth across the bottom and the rate of poverty reduction along the left side of the figure. Putting the two together we find Asian nations fall along a line going down as we move to the right (toward higher levels of economic growth), thus showing poverty reduction and economic growth are strongly related for most Asian nations (and especially so in Thailand). The World Bank, International Monetary Fund, and other such international capitalist agencies like to claim that economic growth always results in poverty reduction. Their

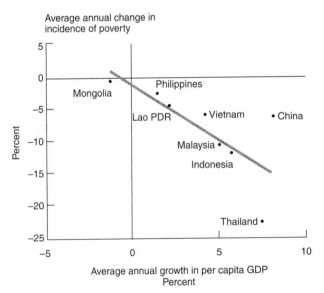

**FIGURE 16-1**    *Poverty Reduction with Economic Growth Since 1980, Asia*

*SOURCE:* World Bank, *World Development Report 2000/2001* (2000: Chapter 3, p. 48).

figures, such as those in the same publication where Figure 16-1 is located, do not make the case. Latin American nations have averaged less economic growth since the early 1980s, but more importantly it has not reduced poverty. South Asia has tended to have a bit more economic growth, but still it did not result in reduced poverty. Africa, on the other hand, has had little economic growth or even negative figures for the economic change and no improvements in poverty rates. When we look to the future, however, Table 16-1 indicates poverty has been getting much worse in Africa in recent years.

# Poverty in World Regions

Before attempting to answer questions of why some countries are so poor while others are improving, it is necessary to understand the commonalities as well as differences of nations in each world region (see Figure 16-2). We can start with the cradle of humanity and the region now deep in crisis—Africa.

## *Sub-Saharan Africa*

Most sub-Saharan countries are among the world's poorest. In fact, of the world's poorest countries in terms of per capita GNP, all but eight are in sub-Saharan Africa. However, not all sub-Saharan countries are in economic stagnation with increasing poverty. Botswana's economy has experienced healthy growth for some years, as has Mozambique after independence from Portugal and the end of civil war. South Africa is the richest nation in sub-Saharan Africa with a per capita GNP (PPP) of over $12,000 (Kerbo 2006:Chapter 7). But almost all of the other countries in the region rank the lowest in the world, from percent of the country's people living on less than $1 per day, to high infant mortality rates and low life expectancy, to levels of political violence and political instability. In Zambia and Nigeria, for example, about 70 percent of the people live on less than $1 per day. Of the 25 countries with the highest infection rates of HIV and AIDS, only one, Haiti at 24th, is not in sub-Saharan Africa (U.S. Central Intelligence Agency, *World Fact Book, 2003,* 2003). In contrast to all of these terrible rankings for sub-Saharan Africa is the continent's wealth of natural resources. As asked by the African author Ali Mazrui (1986), "if Africa is so rich, why are its people so poor?"

## *East and Southeast Asia*

The mostly vibrant countries of East and Southeast Asia present one of the most striking contrasts to African countries. With the major exception of North Korea (one of the world's poorest and most backward countries), as we move from China, South Korea, and Japan down to Taiwan, Thailand, Vietnam, Malaysia, and Indonesia, we encounter countries where economic development is proceeding at high to moderate levels. The striking exceptions, however, are Cambodia, Laos, and Burma (Myanmar). While traveling through the countryside and the largest cities of Cambodia between 2006 and 2008, it was clear that the World Bank reports of 7 to 8 percent or more growth in Cambodia's GNP were accurate (World Bank 2010). But it was also clear that this growth in GNP is very uneven in Cambodia, making just a few rich and making most other Cambodians either no better off or poorer (Kerbo 2011). As we will see below, this will not produce

**FIGURE 16-2** *Poverty Estimates in Countries around the World*

Note: Figures represent country estimates with differing definitions of poverty. These estimates, while not exactly comparable, do give us a rough idea of different levels of poverty around the globe.

*SOURCE:* World Bank, *World Development Report 2000/2001* (2000).

sustainable economic development. Traveling along the flatland areas in Laos up and down the Mekong River during this same time period, I saw less economic development, but more economic development spread more evenly among the population. Laos is just now starting to go more the way of their communist neighbor, Vietnam, and will likely surpass Cambodia with more steady economic development and more poverty reduction in coming years.

Many of the countries of East and Southeast Asia have ancient civilizations going back for thousands of years. Few Westerners realize that east, southeast, and south Asia (primarily India) had the most economically dominant countries in the world a few centuries ago (Levathes 1994; Menzies 2002; Kristof and WuDunn 2000). We will consider the characteristics of Southeast Asian nations in more detail later for clues to what countries can do to rapidly reduce poverty as they attempt economic development.

## *South Asia*

The region called south Asia includes India, Pakistan to the northwest of India, Nepal and Bangladesh to the northeast, and the island country of Sri Lanka to the south of India. India is often called the world's largest democracy because of its parliamentary system inherited from the British colonial period. But India also inherited a colonial administration that turned into one of the most obstructive government bureaucracies in the world (Chibber 2002 Luce 2007; Meredith 2007; Kohli 2004; Prestowitz 2005). India is the second most populous nation with just over 1 billion people, and still one of the world's poorest, with some 44 percent of its population living in what the World Bank defines as extreme poverty, living on less than $1 per day. There is finally hope for economic development and poverty reduction in the future, however, with the number of people living on less than $1 per day expected to shrink by about 50 percent in the next 10 years. Still, India will remain one of the world's poorest countries, with other social problems like AIDS also advancing rapidly—all of this in a country that 300 years ago formed an economic block with China that was at the time the world's most powerful.

It is interesting to note that Pakistan has actually shown more economic growth and poverty reduction than India in recent years, with just over 30 percent of Pakistanis now living on less than $1 per day. Pakistan is certainly not a democracy, but it has a government efficiency rating that is quite high (Evans and Rauch 1999). The future of Pakistan is in doubt, however, because of organized terrorist groups on its borders and many supporters of Osama bin Laden in the country.

Sri Lanka, on the other hand, has the lowest poverty rate of south Asia, with only 6 percent of its people living on less than $1 per day. Sri Lanka is a Buddhist country and the country that helped spread Theravada Buddhism throughout Southeast Asia during the 7th century. Political and religious conflict has raged for the last several decades, with one faction allied with India. Only now has this civil war some hope of cooling, and with it, much better hope for further economic development and poverty reduction.

Finally, Bangladesh and Nepal remain among the world's poorest countries, both having about 30 percent of their people living on less than $1 per day. Although India has a higher rate of extreme poverty, at least prospects for poverty reduction appear greater for the country. In Bangladesh and Nepal per capita GNP increased by only $600 between 1990 and 2001. Bangladesh has at least achieved some political stability and prospects for improvement, whereas Nepal is in the midst of a revolution involving communist rebels.

## Latin America

Colonization ended much earlier in Central and South America than in Africa or Asia. When the European powers began taking territory in Asia and Africa in the early 1800s, most of Latin America was already independent from colonial rule. Countries such as Chile, Argentina, and Brazil were already achieving some economic development in the late 1800s and early 20th century, although economic development was highly dependent on U.S. corporate dominance. For our focus on world poverty, however, it is the nature of these more-developed economies that is most important. Latin American countries have become very unequal societies with extremes of poverty and wealth existing side by side (Kerbo 2006: Chapter 8). Brazil is the world's second most unequal society. It has a modern economy making all kinds of industrial goods, but with 17 percent of its people living on less than $2 per day. The poorest 20 percent of Brazilians receive only 2.5 percent of national income while the richest 20 percent of Brazilians receive about 64 percent of all income. Chile as well has a rather modern industrial society but over 20 percent of its population live on less than $2 per day. Chile is only slightly less unequal, with the bottom 20 percent of people getting about 3.4 percent of income while the top 20 percent get 61 percent of all income. Its most northern Latin American neighbor, Mexico, has about 40 percent of its people living on less than $2 per day, and 17 percent living on less than $1 per day. Like Chile, Mexico is only slightly less unequal than Brazil. Other Latin American countries have even higher levels of extreme poverty: Ecuador has over 50 percent of its population living on less than $2 per day. One of the most important things we need to explore later in this chapter is how more than a century of economic dominance from the United States has affected Latin American economies.

## Eastern Europe and Central Asia

The countries of eastern Europe used to be among the most advanced in Europe. One of the first European empires, the Hapsburg Empire, held much of eastern Europe by A.D. 1200. By the 1500s it contained what is now Austria, Hungary, Slovakia, the Czech Republic, Poland, and much of the old Yugoslavia. Traveling through this part of the world today one sees the old grandeur of the cathedrals and castles of this earlier age. Eastern Europe's problems of the 20th century were related to superpower politics. First they were in the middle of World Wars I and II, and then dominated by the Soviet Union until the beginning of the 1990s. The communist governments put in place by the Soviets crushed economic progress as well as human rights. Still, soon after the end of communism in this part of the world the level of poverty in these countries was very low by African and even Latin American standards. Most of these countries have less than 1 or 2 percent of their people living on less than $1 per day. With the fall of communism, this part of the world has some of the best prospects for renewed economic development.

In 2004, several of these east European countries formally joined the European Union. They are almost certain to get a strong economic boost with open markets throughout all of the European Union countries.

The prospects for Central Asia are more varied and less certain. Central Asia was once the middle of one of the biggest empires in history. Nomadic Asian tribes led by Attila the Hun and his descendants held territory from China and into much of what is Europe today some 1,500 years ago. But this empire was not to last long, and it was dominance by Russia and then the Soviet Union that shaped prospects for people of this region in the 19th and 20th centuries. At the beginning of the 21st century, countries such as Tajikistan, Kyrgyzstan, and Azerbaijan are among the poorest in the region, with well over half their population living in poverty. Tajikistan's 2005 per capita GNP was only $1,500, though per capita GNP was more than $2,000 for other countries in the region, including some with a per capita GNP of over $4,000. Many of these central Asian countries have oil resources, but most also have unstable and very corrupt governments. The mix of Asian and Islamic civilizations has also led to conflict and opposition movements that are likely to keep these countries from achieving much economic development and poverty reduction in the near future.

## The Middle East

We can conclude with a region of the world Western countries hear, but know so little, about. The Middle East, as we know, is a region of ancient civilizations and the birthplace of the most populous monotheistic religions—Christianity, Judaism, and Islam. These religions began some 1,500 to more than 2,000 years ago, and all are interrelated, sharing some of the prophets and religions' leaders in their own religious history. Christianity and Islam have repeatedly clashed as one group spread its following only to decline and have the other reclaim the region. It was the Roman Empire that spread Christianity through much of what is Europe, central Europe, and parts of the Middle East until the Roman Empire collapsed some 1,500 years ago. Mongol invaders from central Asia stepped in to take up some of the power vacuum from the fall of the Roman Empire, about the time Islam was born. An Islamic empire quickly began its spread throughout the Middle East, North Africa, and into much of Europe. But as the Renaissance pulled Christian Europe out of its Dark Ages, the centuries-long clash between Christian Europe and Islam in the Middle East began. One of world history's lowest points began just before A.D. 1100 as the Crusades began with European Christians marching to battle against Islam. There were a total of eight Crusades between A.D. 1097 and A.D. 1212, with many thousands of Muslims killed. One eyewitness account described the religious frenzy: "The slaughter was terrible; the blood of the conquered ran down the streets, until men splashed in blood as they rode" (Wells 1971:564). There was certainly the religious frenzy of European Christians urged on by the pope to massacre Muslims, but it was also a time of expansion of European dominance to arrest its decline, which is no doubt why new banks in Europe financed the Crusades (Thomas 1979:186).

After the Crusades, Islam began losing control in the western realms of its empire, but spread even more to its east, through central Asia, south Asia, and Southeast Asia by the 1400s. The end of World War I in 1918, however, brought down the last of the Islamic empire, the Ottoman Empire based in Turkey, which was allied with Germany. Before and after World War I, the nations and people of the Middle East were almost completely taken over by European colonial regimes. The new oil riches were exploited, and countries in the region had new boundaries drawn to suit the needs of European powers without much regard to natural and historic boundaries. Middle Eastern leaders trying to throw off European dominance were deposed by European, and later American, military or covert actions to keep the low-cost oil flowing (Roosevelt 1979; Mosley 1978). Although the nations of the Middle East are now free of any formal colonial control from Western nations, Islamic countries in the Middle East continue to have little trust of Western nations, but they are also without a central unifying nation able to focus this opposition to the West (Huntington 1996). The region is at conflict within itself as much as with Western nations and Israel. This is especially so after the Israeli revolution in 1948 took control of what was before that time the country of Palestine, sending hundreds of thousands of Palestinians from their homes and into refugee camps around the Middle East.

It is this state of conflict and disarray that has left much poverty in the Middle East, though not nearly as much poverty as many other places in the world (Kerbo 2006: Chapter 7). Not including the very small oil-rich countries such as Kuwait and Qatar, and also not including Israel, Turkey and Iran have the highest per capita GNPs using the PPP estimate for 2005, both around $8,000. Lebanon and Jordan are next at over $5,000 per capita. Syria comes in at almost $4,000. Yemen and Gaza Strip territory (full of Palestinians displaced by Israel) are by far the poorest with per capita GNP at only $700. But while we have less complete data compared to other world regions, even the countries with higher GNPs per capita have high poverty rates by the old World Bank measure. (We do not have $1 per day figures for these countries.) Iran, for example, is listed as having more than 50 percent of its population living in poverty; in Jordan and Lebanon about 30 percent of the people live in poverty.

It is time to return to the review of modern world system theory we began in Chapter 14. This time, however, we focus on how this modern world system or world stratification system affects noncore countries in this world. We will see that there is a logic to *why some countries and most of their people get richer as other people get poorer.* But we will also see that there is a dynamic of power relations and resources in the global stratification system so that countries do not always have to remain poor. Understanding why some countries can reduce their rates of poverty while others have not, of course, is central to understanding how we might reduce world poverty and the many negative outcomes of the current rapid increase in poverty for the world.

---

# ✵ The World System and Economic Development in Periphery Nations: Why Some of the World's Poor Remain Poor

For many years economists had assumed that nations throughout the world would follow a similar pattern of economic development. With some initial capital investment, it was believed, nations would proceed on a path from preindustrial agrarian societies, like the very early history of today's industrial societies, to industrialization (for example, see Rostow 1960). But we now know that these theories of economic development are highly misleading when applied to less-developed nations today (see Frank 1998; Vogel 1991; Johnson 1982; Chase-Dunn 1975; Portes 1976). The realities faced by today's undeveloped and developing societies in the periphery and semiperiphery are far different from those faced by the already developed (or core) nations when they were in the process of economic development. Among these new realities are fewer natural resources, a much larger population, and a poorer climate (see Myrdal 1968:32–37). Perhaps most important, the nations that are now developed economically *did not have other developed nations to contend with in their early process of development.* The result is that the noncore nations today find it much more difficult to achieve economic development (Stiglitz 2002, 2007; Stiglitz and Charlton 2002).

## Barriers to Economic Development and Poverty Reduction

While there is certainly variance among periphery nations, especially in Asia, as we will see in more detail below, several studies have shown that many periphery nations that have extensive aid and investment from the core have *less long-term economic growth* (Chase-Dunn 1975, 1989; Bornschier and Chase-Dunn 1985; Bornschier, Chase-Dunn, and Rubinson 1978; Snyder and Kick 1979; Stokes and Jaffee 1982; Nolan 1983a, 1983b; Rudra 2008). These nations, of course, tend to have some economic growth in the short term (fewer than 5 years) because of the aid and investment coming from the core. But the longer-term prospects for growth may actually be harmed by the kinds of outside aid and investment these nations have received.

Although there are many reasons for these harmful economic effects of outside dominance by core nations, four seem most important (Kerbo 2006, forthcoming). The first involves a problem of *structural distortion in the economy.* In an "undistorted" economic process some natural resource, human or nonhuman, leads to a chain of economic activity creating jobs, profits, and economic growth. We can use the case of a core nation with extensive copper deposits. Mining the copper provides jobs and profits. The copper is refined into metal, again providing some people with jobs and profits. The metal is then used by other firms to make consumer products, providing jobs and profits. Finally, the products are sold by retail firms, again providing jobs and profits. From the mining process to the retail sales of the products there is a chain of jobs and profits providing economic growth and revenues that can be used for infrastructure development (roads, electric power, educational institutions).

Now consider what usually happens when the copper is mined in a periphery nation with extensive ties to the core. The copper may be mined by native workers, but the ore or metal is shipped to core nations where the remainder of the economic chain is completed. The additional jobs and profits from the chain of economic activities are lost to the periphery nation—they go to the core (Chase-Dunn 1975). The periphery nation, in other words, loses the chain of economic activity that comes from its natural resources, which means no economic development because of structural distortion in the economy.

A second negative effect on the economy of periphery nations is related to *agricultural disruption.* Export agriculture often becomes an important economic activity of a periphery nation brought into the modern world system. Before this time, traditional

agriculture was directed toward local consumption, and there was no incentive to introduce capital-intensive (labor-saving) methods of farming. As a result of traditional agricultural methods and lack of an extensive market for agricultural products, some land
was left for poor peasants, food was cheaper, and jobs were more plentiful. But with
export agriculture and capital-intensive farming methods, food is now more expensive,
poor peasants are being pushed off the land so more land can be used to grow crops for
the world market, and more machines are doing the work, resulting in fewer jobs for
poor peasants. This also means exaggerated urbanization as peasants lose jobs and land,
since they move to the cities in hopes of finding work there (Kentor 1981). Again, profits
go to a small group of wealthy landowners and large multinational agribusinesses, with
peasants (a majority of people in the country) losing jobs, income, and land, preventing
them from being active consumers needed if an economy is to naturally develop.

In addition to these problems, which can be called technical economic problems,
there is a third, more serious difficulty involving internal class conflicts within poor
nations, what we might call *the class struggle within.* Quite often political and economic
elites in poor nations become more tied to, and accommodating to, corporate elites from
rich nations who have investments in their country. When we think about it, this situation is not surprising. The local political and economic elites receive handsome profits
because multinational corporations have investments in the country. These elites in poor
countries are certainly smart enough to know that multinational corporations are making investments in the poor nation because labor costs are low, unions are nonexistent,
taxes are low, and other things such as lax environmental controls are favorable to multinational corporate interests. Thus, to keep their material rewards coming in, the local
elites must keep the multinationals in the country. For self-serving elites this creates
a *direct conflict of interest* between them and the masses of people in the poor nation.
The people of least-developed nations want less poverty, better wages, more humane
working conditions, and so on. But if these things are realized, it can mean multinational
corporations will leave. Considered another way, the problems of structural distortion in
the economy and agricultural disruption noted above could, with difficulty, be reduced.
It is often the "will" to overcome these problems that is lacking, at least lacking on the
part of local elites.

A recent example from Mexico is instructive. After the North American Free
Trade Agreement (NAFTA) went into effect in 1994, thousands of export factories from
the United States, Europe, and Japan moved into Mexico to take advantage of the low
wages and free access to the North American market. By 2000 there were almost 4,000
of these new factories. By 2002, however, the foreign factories began moving out, with
500 closed and 250,000 jobs lost in 1 year as the foreign factories began moving to
countries such as China where beginning wages for low-skill factory jobs are as low
as $0.25 an hour compared to $1.50 in Mexico (*International Herald Tribune,* June 21,
2002; Rosen 2002). Another example comes from El Salvador. After years of working
in sweatshop conditions, often working 18 hour days for $0.50 an hour, several workers
employed by a small company making clothing for The Gap and other Western retailers
finally began a strike. Normally the strike would have been put down with little significant effort or media attention. The timing of the strike was fortunate for the workers,
however, because Western clothing firms such as The Gap were under heavy criticism

from North American protestors and labor groups. Under this outside pressure The Gap gave in, and demanded some improvements in working conditions and increased wages $0.05 an hour. However, as representatives of The Gap reported, the small sweatshop, which was actually owned by Taiwanese investors, made few of the changes The Gap demanded, and local government officials made sure such strike activity did not happen again. Because of the negative publicity and potential for increased labor costs, several companies making clothing for retailers such as JC Penney, Eddie Bauer, and Target canceled contracts and moved to other locations with more controlled laborers.

A fourth basic problem from most periphery nations is more directly linked to power imbalances in the global stratification system, and the dominant ideology of "free markets" pushed most strongly by the United States and the agency influenced heavily by the United States, the International Monetary Fund, or IMF (Rudra 2008). One of the most difficult things for rich nations and agencies like the IMF to understand is that in critical ways the world economy is very different than it was 100, 200, or 300 years ago. Free markets back then were extremely rare. Free and open markets can contribute to competitiveness and economic efficiency in the already rich countries today. For poor countries struggling to develop, however, the world economy today does not provide them with the same open market as the rich nations. In essence, open markets do not always help poor countries when there are now already rich countries over them, rich countries able to distort open markets with billions of dollars in subsidies to their own large corporations, preventing infant industries in poorer countries from having an even chance of survival (Stiglitz and Charlton 2005). These harmful forces were not around when most of the already rich countries were becoming rich because they were the first to become rich. Most of those countries that became rich in the second wave of develop- ment more than 100 years ago (such as Germany and Japan) did so with decidedly unfree domestic markets protecting their infant industries. But now the worldwide stratifica- tion system gives core nations the power to enforce rules of the global economy (and avoid some for themselves) that help them while harming periphery nations. A bit more explanation will be useful.

Despite all the rhetoric, rich nations want open markets in other countries, but not in their own country. Then, the rich nations can buy cheap resources and sell their manu- factured goods especially in poor countries. Global trade has increased some 60 percent in the past 10 years, but it has declined for the least-developed nations because of trade barriers placed on their goods by the rich nations. The United States has one of the highest tariffs on imported agricultural products to protect American farmers, though the European Union has its share. For some examples, duties on imported textiles into the United States are relatively high, that is, unless the clothing is made abroad using American-made textiles by companies such as The Gap, JC Penney, Eddie Bauer, and Target. In the European Union the duties on agricultural products are usually less than in the United States, but there are restrictions to protect European producers. African countries, for instance, can export coco beans to European manufacturers such as Nestlé, but if the African countries process the beans themselves and attempt to sell chocolate to Europe (a more profitable venture) the tariffs are high. Companies like Nestlé want the profits from processing the coco beans and selling the finished products; but of course they need the coco beans coming from countries in Africa.

Figure 16-3 presents the average tariff rates for rich and middle-income versus poor nations in the world today. Despite their free-market ideology, the rich countries, led by the United States, in reality seem to think that open markets are best in poor countries rather than their own. Core nations and their global corporate class (discussed in Chapter 14) have the power through agencies such as the IMF, World Bank, and to a lesser degree the World Trade Organization to protect their domestic industries, but then use their global power to make sure poor countries open their borders to products produced and processed in the rich countries. One estimate is that the 49 least-developed nations in the world lose about $2.5 billion a year due to tariffs and quotas placed on their products by rich nations. To cite just one of more than a hundred examples, the aid agency Oxfam estimates the United States gets back $7 for every $1 given in aid to Bangladesh because of import barriers. Oxfam also estimates that rich countries subsidize their own agribusinesses at a level of about $1 billion per day, which floods the world market with cheap food, while the IMF pushes these least-developed countries to keep their markets open to these agricultural products (Watkins 2001). In other words, rich nations give subsidies to their farmers so they can produce farm products more cheaply and with more profits, but disallow poor countries to do so, even when the government of the poor country could afford to provide subsidies. Another estimate by the United Nations suggests that rich nations subsidize their industries (of all kinds) to the tune of $100 billion each year to make them more competitive (Stiglitz and Charlton 2005). The least-developed nations have no means of doing this. When forced to open their markets to products from rich nations backed by government subsidies, they cannot compete. In actuality, as we will see in more detail, when left to themselves, *world*

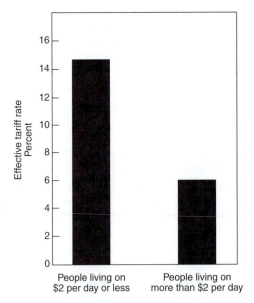

**FIGURE 16-3**  *Comparative Tariff Barriers Faced by Rich versus Poor Nations*

*SOURCE:* World Bank, *Global Prospects for Development* (2002:57).

*"market forces" can make people in some countries poorer than they otherwise would be.* A free world market where multinational corporations can come and go at will, and without controls on their behavior in poor nations, can increase poverty and inequality in many if not most nations.

The above provides only a sampling of important factors leading to less economic development, and is by no means a complete description. Neither is it meant to suggest that all periphery nations are equally hurt by investments from the core, or are hurt in the same way. Likewise, it is not being suggested that multinational corporate investments in poor nations cause all of their problems. But, as we will see, research over the last 30 years has suggested that many, and in some world regions most, periphery nations are significantly harmed over the long run by outside multinational corporate investments.

# ✬ Global Corporations Can Do Harm: Some Evidence

Soon after the utility of modern world system theory became recognized in the 1970s it generated an impressive amount of quite sophisticated empirical research, most showing consistent results. One of the most important research questions, of course, is whether or not poorer countries have less long-term economic growth when they become extensively tied to multinationals from rich nations as predicted by the theory. While there is certainly variability among periphery nations, especially in Asia, as we will see, several studies have shown that many periphery nations that have extensive aid and investment from the core do in fact have less long-term economic growth (Chase-Dunn 1975, 1989; Bornschier and Chase-Dunn 1985; Bornschier et al. 1978; Snyder and Kick 1979; Stokes and Jaffee 1982; Nolan 1983a, 1983b). These poor nations receiving extensive multinational corporate investments of course tend to have some economic growth in the short term. But the longer-term prospects for growth (over 5 years or more) are in many cases actually harmed by the kinds of outside aid and investment these nations have received.

After the first wave of empirical research on the effects of multinational corporate investments in poor countries, however, more recent research has shown less consistent and even some contradictory results. One new piece of research using a larger and more recent data set of poor nations has found extensive multinational corporate investment tends to produce some positive economic growth in the long term, while another using recalculations of older data also finds outside investment results in more long-term economic growth (de Soysa and Oneal 1999; Firebaugh 1992, 1996). Other research has shown that outside corporate investment in poor countries per se does not lead to less economic development when consideration is taken for the types of goods imported from or exported to the poor nations (Bollen and Appold 1993). Still other studies have questioned the negative effects of multinational investments in poor nations, such as increases in income inequality and a lower standard of living among the poor masses of people in many of these countries. They suggest there is a more complex relationship between multinational corporate investment and income inequality, and there is evidence that the poor in many of these periphery nations do have improved lives because of multinational investment (Kentor and Boswell 2003; Alderson and Nielsen 1999; Firebaugh and Beck 1994).

## Methodological Considerations

To help explain some of the new research findings that seem to contradict the original research we must consider several factors (Kerbo 2006). First, most of this new research uses more recent data on poor nations, mostly from the 1980s to 1990s, compared to the original data sets using 1960s and 1970s data. So far the explanations of new research findings have been surprisingly ahistorical given that the social scientists are examining a historically grounded theory. It is quite possible, even likely, that new forces in the world have produced some change in the relationship or balance of power between rich core nations and some developing nations. For example, we know that more direct foreign investments going to developing nations today involve high-tech industries. There is evidence these high-tech investments lead to more sustainable economic growth for these nations than previous low-tech investments. Further, with the cold war over and rich nations focused more on profits and less on fighting communism, some poorer nations are courted by rich nations, giving the poorer countries more leverage when playing one rich nation off against another. However, we must make clear the type of research that has been conducted on the subject of the modern world system and economic development and its limitations as well as its strengths. Some of the more recent research suggesting there are no *statistical* relations between multinational corporate investment and less economic growth does *not* mean that now *all* poor nations are equally helped by outside multinational corporate investment.

The typical methodology of world system research today involves a sample of 50 to 100 less-developed nations. Data on a number of independent variables are collected, such as the extent of outside multinational corporate investment in each country, the amount of foreign aid flowing into each country, outstanding debt to richer nations and international agencies, trade flows, and so on. Then data on dependent variables are collected, measuring such things as growth in GNP, income inequality, and various indicators of standards of living such as poverty levels, life expectancy, and infant mortality. Using lagged time intervals of 5 or 10 years to give the dependent variables (such as multinational corporate investment) time to have their theorized effects, statistical correlations are made to see if relationships can be found between these variables (such as multinational corporate investments related to less economic development and higher levels of income inequality after 10 years).

This type of research has always been complex because there can be disputes over the correct measures of variables and even the correct indicators of important factors from world system theory such as what constitutes direct outside investments. Despite these problems, and despite all of the disputes and controversy, 30 years of research on the modern world system has shown impressive results. Many of the details of the theory have been supported and other parts revised in response to this research. But we must be clear on what this research has shown and has not shown, and we must be clear on the inherent limitations of the comparative time-series methodology generally used in the past 30 years.

The first point we must be clear about is that a statistically significant relationship between, say, multinational investment at one point of time and slower economic growth at a later time (10 years later), means quite simply that *most* nations with heavy amounts of multinational corporate investments have reduced economic growth rates later. It does not mean this happens in all nations, only that there is this tendency for it to occur when looking across the sample of 50, 75, or 100 nations. This means, of course, that some nations within the sample have high levels of outside multinational corporate investments *and* strong economic growth in later years. Quite often in this research the authors will note that some countries (at times not even identified) are "outliers," meaning they are located out on the margins of where the other countries line up on the variables. But then the subject is dropped. Why are they outliers? What is different about these countries that do not conform to the statistically significant relationship between the important variables studied? We will see that quite often in this world system research the outliers are Asian nations.

Second, we must recognize that the methodologies used by most world system research follow a Durkheimian tradition (Ragin and Zaret 1983; Smelser 1976). It was Durkheim who first assumed there are "natural laws" of human behavior and social organization that span across all societies and then showed how these laws might be discovered in his masterful work *Suicide* in 1897 (Durkheim 1951). Following this Durkheimian methodology the research can uncover important tendencies across nations, for example, but at the same time much of the detail about what is happening within each nation is ignored. This methodology has brought recent charges that world system research is missing "internal processes" within nations that help produce differing outcomes among these nations with the same level of outside multinational investments (Alderson and Nielsen 1999). The comparative-historical research of Max Weber, in contrast, rejected such single-dimensional laws of the Durkheimian perspective and called instead for the recognition of complex and somewhat unique combinations of historical forces interacting to produce important outcomes for each nation. Even further, Weber recognized that a certain outcome could have varied causes in differing nations (Smelser 1976:142). To the extent this is true, it is obvious that a qualitative historical and comparative analysis of specific nations or groups of relatively similar nations is best suited to detect important differences within nations or groups of nations that affect their chances for economic development (Ragin 2000). "Qualitative" research means research that does not rely primarily on numbers or things that can be easily measured and compared across many nations. Qualitative research means the researcher must seek to uncover more specific details about each particular case (such as how a nation's political system operates, or past effects of colonialism) that are studied before attempting comparisons to other nations which have also been studied with qualitative research methods. It is this type of analysis that will be considered below to identify important characteristics and historical influences on some East and Southeast Asian nations that result in economic development or stagnation.

Finally, a major theme of the latter pages of this chapter is that none of these studies has so far considered that *multinational corporate investments can have different effects in different parts of the world.* For example, are there generally different outcomes when considering multinational corporate investments going to Asian nations in contrast to Latin American or African nations? As most people are fully aware, during the 1980s and 1990s most East and Southeast Asian countries experienced rapid economic growth while growth in Latin America has been much slower, and even slower yet in most African nations (Haggard and Kaufman 2008; Jomo 2001; Jalilian and Weiss 2003). More multinational corporate investment has gone to Asian countries than all other poor nations since the 1980s. Further, we know that nations with more human capital (i.e., a more educated population) are better able to use multinational corporate investment for positive long-term economic growth (Kentor and Boswell 2003; de Soysa and Oneal 1999). The logical next question, therefore, seems to be: Is there something different about East and Southeast Asian nations trying to maintain economic development compared to poorer nations in Latin America or Africa? Before we consider this question, though, we need to examine other aspects of the impact of the world system on less-developed countries in the world.

# ⚔ World System Effects on Noncore Stratification Systems

In addition to research described above on the effects of core influence on economic development in noncore nations, we know the position of noncore societies in the world system has a very important impact on (1) the existence and power of a small group of elites, (2) the degree of working-class powerlessness, (3) the type of political system maintained, and (4) the level of income inequality within noncore nations. These four factors are important aspects of the overall stratification system within a nation. They all tend to be interrelated and influence many other conditions, such as a lack of *evenly distributed economic development,* but also inequalities of ownership or wealth, health and health care, social services for those in need, opportunities for social mobility, and so on through a long list of conditions often related to the nature of stratification within a society. In this section we focus on the four interrelated aspects of social stratification that have received most research attention.

We may begin with a basic condition of income inequality. In our review of history (Chapter 3), we followed Lenski's (1966, 1984) description of the significant change in the degree of material inequality as societies move from agrarian, or less economically developed, societies to industrial societies. It will be helpful at this point to review more recent empirical studies of this relationship between economic development (that is, level of technology or industrialization) and level of inequality, then add the new reality for many noncore nations today.

Using various measures of economic development and inequality within nations, a number of comparative studies have reached similar results; there is a strong tendency for inequality to be reduced once nations become fully industrialized (Jackman 1975; Hewitt 1977; Stack 1978a; Weede 1980). These findings help explain some of the variance in income inequality we found in Table 16-3, though as also noted, the Asian difference (generally less income inequality at even lower levels of economic development) has not been recognized in this research. Equally important, this relation between economic development and less inequality remains strong even when the possible effects on inequality from other variables (such as type of political system) are eliminated statistically (although a nation's place in the world stratification system does have an effect on inequality independent of economic development; see Breedlove and Nolan 1988).

In Chapter 3 we also reviewed Lenski's (1966, 1984) description of a number of factors helping to produce less material inequality in industrial societies. One of the most important factors is the changing nature of the occupational structure. With industrialization the occupational structure is expanded, creating more occupations in the middle (that is, between the rich and the poor) that require more skills, thus producing a greater range of economic rewards.

For many periphery nations today, however, the factors described earlier as new to nations dominated by core nations of the modern world system slow or block long-term economic development, thus prolonging or making permanent the high levels of inequality that are more characteristic of preindustrial nations.

The *internal class relations* shaped by the world system must also be recognized as influencing income inequality and other aspects of domestic stratification (Breedlove and Nolan 1988). Of critical importance is the *power of elites* in noncore societies. These elites have a strong interest in keeping multinational corporations in the nation, primarily because their favored economic position is dependent on multinational investment and trade. One outcome of domestic elite ties to multinationals is that wages are kept low to attract multinational investment and trade. Furthermore, these domestic elites work to keep corporate taxes and other duties low. This helps attract multinationals but also keeps government redistribution to the poor very low.

On the other hand, *the power of the working and lower classes is very low.* This occurs because industrial workers are a smaller proportion of the labor force and are kept unorganized (unions are usually lacking or very weak due to repression), while agricultural workers are often isolated, unorganized, and powerless (see Paige 1975). This produces a lower class with little political and economic influence. The state bureaucratic structures, which could help produce less income inequality, are usually dominated by wealthy elites (domestic or core elites). A typical result is a very low level of democracy, with the state working to serve the interests of elites rather than other classes in noncore societies (Huber et al. 2006; Lee 2007; Martin and Brady 2007). We must now examine what research indicates with respect to these internal class dynamics.

Chase-Dunn's (1975) study of economic stagnation in heavily dependent periphery nations was discussed earlier. In this study Chase-Dunn also examined the relation between core influence in the economy and income inequality. His most important finding is that both heavy foreign investment and foreign debt dependency are related to greater income inequality.

Also of major interest is that in periphery nations with more foreign investment in the economy and greater debt dependence on the core, the top 5 percent of the population had a much higher income. This latter finding conforms to the argument that a small elite is formed in periphery nations that depends on core multinationals and that has strong interests in continued core domination.

In a similar but somewhat more detailed study, Rubinson's (1976) findings support those of Chase-Dunn's reported earlier. With a sample of 47 nations, Rubinson measured core influence on other nations by (1) the degree of foreign control over internal economic production, (2) dependence on external markets, and (3) the magnitude of foreign debt dependence in the economy. All three conditions were significantly related to greater income inequality in periphery nations.

In addition, Rubinson (1976) was able to specify further the relation between economic development and income inequality. A large study by Jackman (1975) has shown that greater economic development is related to less income inequality over time. The effect of economic development on reduced income inequality has been an important historical factor shaping the nature of social stratification in today's industrial societies. However, as we have already discussed, the poorer and less-developed nations have a reality not faced by today's developed nations when they were in the process of development many years ago. This new reality for less-developed nations is the influence of core or already developed nations.

Rubinson's (1976) data from 47 nations did find that greater economic development is related to less income inequality (as did Jackman 1975). But—and this is the key point—when we divide nations into core and noncore standing in the world system, the effect of economic development on less income inequality is greatly reduced. Even when noncore nations are able to achieve some economic growth, the effect of the world system (and core interests) on their economy in large measure prevents more economic development from resulting in less income inequality (see also Fiala 1983; Nolan 1983a, 1983b).

Bornschier et al. (1978) have examined several studies similar to the preceding two. All these studies are consistent in showing that greater foreign investment and greater aid or debt dependency in a noncore nation produce more income inequality. These studies have been criticized in part because they tend to ignore the internal class processes (in large part also related to world system influences) that affect income inequality. For example, Nielsen (1994) has shown that we must also consider the effects of educational systems, population growth, and the occupational structure within each society, though these factors are also affected by position in the world system. Thus, we find more information on how world system position affects inequality.

Another suggested area of neglect in these studies is class influences on the political system. As noted earlier, when a small but wealthy and powerful elite is able to dominate the state (no doubt because of its role in core dominance), we may expect less democracy and less state aid (or at least no reform measures) to reduce income inequality. With this in mind, Stack (1978b) reanalyzed Rubinson's (1976) data from a smaller sample of 36 nations. This reanalysis continued to support Rubinson's findings that core influence in the economy (investment and debt dependency) produces greater income inequality. But Stack found that the democratic performance of the state in these nations also was related independently to the degree of income inequality; that is, less democracy was significantly related to greater income inequality. More recent research has given even more support to the relations between income inequality and the level of democracy and unionization in less developed countries (Lee 2007; Martin and Brady 2007; Huber et al. 2006; Simpson 1990).

One study is especially useful in specifying the internal class process that produces greater income inequality in noncore nations. In our examination of the U.S. stratification system, we pointed out that (1) the property structure (ownership or nonownership of the means of production), (2) bureaucratic authority structures, and

(3) the occupational structure are all important in producing class divisions and shaping the nature of social stratification. Most of these world system studies discussed above focus on the first—significant ownership of the means of production by core multinationals—as related to income inequality.

With data from 50 nations, Bornschier and Ballmer-Cao (1979) conducted a more complete examination of factors producing noncore income inequality:

**1.** In line with previous studies, they found that greater multinational investment in the noncore economy was related to more income inequality.

**2.** They found that less bureaucratic development in the noncore nations was related to greater income inequality. In other words, with fewer ranks within bureaucratic power structures or a greater separation between bureaucratic elites and the masses, there is greater income inequality. And in relation to the bureaucratic power of the state, when there was more multinational influence in the nation, Bornschier and Ballmer-Cao found that state resources are used to help industry more than to meet the needs of the poor. This strongly suggests the influence of class interests on state behavior.

**3.** The less-developed occupational structure in noncore societies was found to be related to greater income inequality. In this study, the less-developed occupational structure was indicated by fewer technical experts and a smaller, powerless, and controlled industrial labor force. Thus, Bornschier and Ballmer-Cao's study specified in more detail the internal class process that helps produce more income inequality in noncore societies. This study conforms in large degree to our earlier review of the important processes (the three structures) producing class inequality in the United States. But all the structures producing income inequality in noncore nations are influenced to a large degree by each nation's position in the world stratification system (as indicated in Figure 16-4).

We may conclude this section by noting briefly some negative and positive effects of core dominance of the world system for core nations themselves. As suggested by the

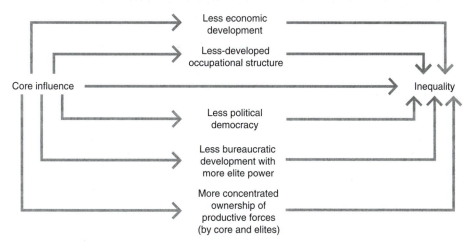

**FIGURE 16-4**    *World System Influences on Internal Stratification in Noncore Societies*

unequal exchange and power relation between core and periphery nations, core nations are favored. However, the benefits flowing to core nations are not equally distributed within core nations, and in many respects the working class in core nations is harmed by core dominance.

For corporate elites in core nations, there are greater profits, cheap raw materials, and a market for export, all of which strengthen core economic performance. Some of these benefits work their way down to nonelites in core nations in the form of a higher standard of living and some cheaper consumer goods. But as we have seen in earlier chapters, there are important negative effects for core nonelites in the form of over a million jobs lost because of multinational moves to periphery nations with cheap labor costs (for earlier studies of this, see Barnet and Müller 1974:303–304; Stillman 1980:76; Blumberg 1980:128–129). We also have data showing that corporate investment in poor countries has reduced the wages of workers in core countries because they are more in competition with low-wage workers in these poor countries to keep their jobs (Mahler 2001). And of course, as we saw in Chapter 14, there are military costs (in tax dollars and lives lost) of maintaining core dominance in the world system.

Figure 16-5 presents a summary of some of the means of core dominance over periphery nations and some of the consequences of this dominance for both core and periphery nations. Given the unequal exchange between core and periphery nations, we might

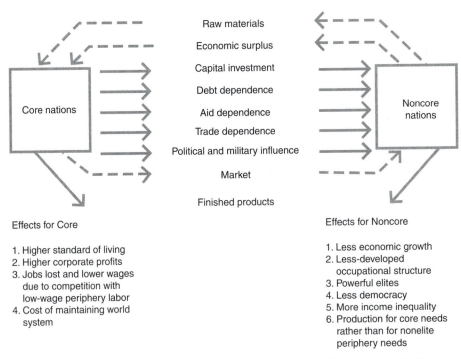

| Effects for Core | Effects for Noncore |
|---|---|
| 1. Higher standard of living<br>2. Higher corporate profits<br>3. Jobs lost and lower wages due to competition with low-wage periphery labor<br>4. Cost of maintaining world system | 1. Less economic growth<br>2. Less-developed occupational structure<br>3. Powerful elites<br>4. Less democracy<br>5. More income inequality<br>6. Production for core needs rather than for nonelite periphery needs |

**FIGURE 16-5**    *Summary of the Means of Core Dominance and Its Outcomes for Core and Periphery Nations*

expect that nonelites (as opposed to the elites in periphery nations who usually profit from this dominance) in periphery nations would attempt to resist core dominance. Before we consider the prospects of change for periphery nations, we must consider some major exceptions to much of the preceding in Asia. But as we will find, they are exceptions that fit the rule. Many Asian nations have been able to avoid having the characteristics described above that harm the chances of long-term economic development in noncore nations.

## The Rise of East and Southeast Asia: Exceptions That Fit the Rule

Traveling through East and Southeast Asia, it is difficult to miss the huge presence of multinational corporations from the major core nations. Walking through the streets of Seoul, Taipei, Bangkok, and the special economic zones of China (Kerbo 2006; Vogel 1989), for example, one is impressed by the number of buildings displaying the logo of corporations from the United States, Japan, Germany, France, and a few others of the Western industrial powers. But walking through these cities, one is also impressed by the massive economic development in progress. The Seoul I visited in 2001 looked more like the Tokyo I visited first in 1984 than the Seoul I also saw in 1984. Bangkok, for another example, looked much more developed and was growing even more rapidly in 1997 than just 10 years earlier, and by 1999 had resumed its growth after the "Asian economic crisis." By 2002 Thailand was back to 4 percent growth in GNP and comparatively *evenly distributed* economic development reducing poverty in the country.

The economic statistics strongly concur with these personal observations: With some exceptions, these nations of East and Southeast Asia through most of the 1990s and 2000s had the highest rates of economic growth in the world (World Bank 2010; Kerbo 2006). With core nations in North America and Europe experiencing annual rates of 2 to 3 percent in good years, many of these nations of East and Southeast Asia were often growing at 10 percent or more annually.

But unlike other periphery nations trying to develop economically, the nations of East and Southeast Asia, such as Korea, Taiwan, China, Thailand, and Malaysia, have had much less of the *uneven development* found in Latin America. Yes, inequality increased in China as the economic boom raced along in the 1900s and 2000s. But this inequality is not because the rich are getting rich and the poor are getting poorer. Inequality is increasing because the rich are getting richer faster than the poor are becoming less poor. Infrastructure investment and open markets are making the rural people less poor, and account for most of the poverty reduction in China (Prestowitz 2005). Much the same can be said for Southeast Asian nations that are reducing poverty. Even though inequality is rising (though not to U.S. levels of inequality), lower-income people are seeing many benefits (Doner 2009). Uneven development, which causes more inequality and poverty, is the big problem of most countries in Latin America and Africa. (A look at the figures for Brazil in Table 16-3 will show one of the worst cases.) There are certainly sections of homeless people from places such as rural northeastern Thailand around Bangkok, but there is much less of this than in Latin America, Africa, or India. The economic growth among these "Asian tigers" has been producing jobs, and the labor shortages in many of these countries has been bringing up average wages. In

Latin America, by contrast, even though there was some significant economic growth for some of these countries in the 1990s and 2000s unemployment and poverty continued to rise, as does inequality (World Bank 2010).

The figures in Table 16-3, for example, generally show less income inequality in this part of the world compared with Latin America and Africa. Most important, we have seen in Table 16-1 that only East and Southeast Asia have a strong record of reducing extreme poverty and will continue this trend in coming years. In Latin America there has been almost no poverty reduction in the last 20 years, and in Africa poverty is expected to increase dramatically in coming years.

Beginning in July of 1997, as noted earlier, many of these Asian nations were hit by what has been called the Asian economic crisis. Economic growth slowed dramatically in South Korea, Taiwan, Thailand, Indonesia, and Malaysia. In some of these countries such as Thailand, the 1990s had earlier brought some increasing inequality with the very rapid economic development (Doner 2009; Kerbo 2006; Pasuk and Baker 1998; Slagter and Kerbo 2000), though the level of poverty kept falling. But by the end of 1999, however, their economies were mostly moving upward again. What the Asian economic crisis beginning in 1997 brought can best be described as an economic correction to what has been called the "golf course capitalism boom" fueled by too much money in the hands of corrupt financial elites in these countries (Slagter and Kerbo 2000). By 1999 the governments of Thailand, South Korea, and Malaysia had taken greater control of the failed financial institutions and made economic adjustments that have restarted the Asian economies toward the 21st century predicted to be dominated by Asia (Frank 1998).

The point is that according to research described in the previous sections of this chapter, extensive investment and economic ties from core nations are supposed to harm the economies of periphery nations and create more inequality and poverty. The discrepancy revealed by statistics as those presented earlier was first considered in an article titled "Dependency Theory and Taiwan: Analysis of a Deviant Case" (Barrett and Whyte 1982). Since this article appeared, it has become evident that there are other deviant cases, primarily in East and Southeast Asia (Kerbo 2006; Kristof and WuDunn 2000; Jomo 2001; Jalilian and Weiss 2003). We will consider Taiwan first.

Among other reasons, Taiwan is considered a deviant case because the Taiwanese state is stronger, more involved with economic planning, and more concerned with domestic economic development for the country as a whole, not just for a group of elites and the small middle class, as is more typical of many periphery nations. For several decades the Taiwanese state has had the influence and motivation, and has been working to make sure that multinationals do not harm the domestic economy when economic ties are allowed (Gold 1986). These characteristics and policies of the Taiwanese state developed after the Nationalist Party of China, fleeing Mao's revolution on mainland China in 1949, took control of the island. Learning from past mistakes on the mainland, the leaders of the new government on Taiwan were motivated to help ensure long-term economic development as a means of regaining popular support, which they had lost before the communist takeover of the mainland. But it was also a strong state supported by the United States as a showcase against communism, which brought many special benefits to the country (Barrett and Whyte 1982, 1984; Hammer 1984). Also cited as important for Taiwan's economic development, however, is land redistribution, which made consumers of the farmers making up the vast majority of the population in earlier years, and the agricultural infrastructure created by the Japanese when they held the island as a colony from 1895 until 1945.

Taiwan, however, now seems to have much company as a deviant case in Asia. South Korea, for example, also has a strong state active in economic planning, relatively low inequality helped by land redistribution, and an economic infrastructure started by Japanese occupation in the first half of the 20th century (Kohli 2004; Kim 1997; Vogel 1991; McNamara 1989; Nahm 1988; Pye 1985:218). Others in East and Southeast Asia—such as Malaysia, Thailand, Vietnam, and now China—are exceptions to the rule for different reasons (Kerbo 2006, 2011). It is important to consider some of these reasons because they can help us understand the continued high levels of world poverty in other regions, and how, in fact, modern world system theory and dependence theory have been rather accurate in other world regions about the reasons for economic stagnation or unevenly distributed economic development responsible for increasing world inequality. Following this we will focus on the example of Thailand in recent decades because Thailand has been cited by the United Nations and World Bank as the international leader in reducing poverty among developing nations.

# ✖ The Characteristics of East and Southeast Asian Nations: The Exceptions behind the Asian Economic Miracles

Before considering what characteristics of developing nations (particularly those in East and Southeast Asia) seem most responsible for promoting economic development and poverty reduction, it is important to consider one aspect often given as the main reason, but a characteristic that is considerably overestimated. When contemplating the condition of poverty around the world, there seems a natural tendency for many people in rich countries to wonder "What is wrong with those people?" "They seem so slow, no one appears to work very hard, nor could they with all of those 'siestas.'" Comfortable people in rich nations know they themselves have worked hard for what they have achieved; "Why can't these other people do the same?" Put another way, the more affluent tend to judge others from realities of their own lives, from the logic of how human behavior brings rewards and punishment in their own day-to-day interactions. As we have already seen in Chapter 9, again and again it has been shown that most people in the United States tend to blame the poor for their poverty. A "culture of poverty" theory is most popular in the United States because it complies with these assumptions of blaming the poor for their poverty because of "irresponsible and lazy" behavior. When looking beyond rich nations, it is even more difficult for the affluent of this world to understand the everyday realities and options of the world's poor.

## A Resurgence of Cultural Explanations

It is in this context that cultural explanations for world poverty have reemerged in recent years, especially since the World Trade Organization protests in Seattle during the fall of 1999 placed more blame directly on rich countries and corporations themselves. To name just a few of the indicators of the resurgence of cultural explanations, a book first published in 1985, *Underdevelopment Is a State of Mind,* by Lawrence Harrison—a book highly critical of dependency theory and Spanish Catholic values inherited by Latin American countries—was updated and reissued in 2000 (Harrison 2000). Samuel Huntington then collaborated with Harrison on an edited volume titled *Culture Matters: How Values Shape Human Progress,* also published in 2000 (Harrison and Huntington 2000). At the same time, the World Bank suddenly started picking up the theme of cultural barriers to economic development, pouring millions of dollars into new books on the subject, international conferences on the subject, and aid projects in developing countries designed to change cultural values believed to be detrimental to economic development.*

Traditional values in many developing countries certainly can have negative effects on economic development. There can be impediments to economic development from present-time orientations and an inability to save and plan for the future, just as we saw in Chapter 9 with the very similar culture-of-poverty explanation for domestic poverty. But just as the culture-of-poverty theory in the United States has neglected structural barriers to getting out of poverty, and how the present situation of people has only a short-term effect on their attitudes (as research from the "situational view" of poverty has shown), other factors related to economic opportunities in poor countries are more important. Much of the same criticism we have seen against the culture-of-poverty theory in the United States has been leveled at this resurgence of cultural explanations for world poverty (see Pye 2000:254).

In this international context there is also a serious problem with the Asian values many claim are responsible for the Asian economic miracles in recent decades. Not all East and Southeast Asian nations that have been successful with economic development and poverty reduction have these Asian values claimed most important, and some nations with the Asian values have not achieved significant economic development or much poverty reduction. Within Southeast Asia, for example, Malaysia (the most economically advanced country in the region) is majority Islamic, as is Indonesia, which has achieved considerable economic growth in recent decades. In the northern half of Southeast Asia, Burma, Laos, Cambodia, and Thailand have almost identical Theravada Buddhist cultural heritages (Kerbo 2006: Chapter 6, forthcoming; De Casparis and Mabbett 1999:294; Osborne 1995). Thailand has one of the best records of poverty reduction and economic development in the world; Burma, Laos, and Cambodia are among the poorest countries in the world with still no prospects of moving out of that status. Vietnam is the only country in Southeast Asia with the type of Asian values (a mix of Confucianism and Buddhism imported from China centuries ago) most often cited as encouraging economic development. But Vietnam is only now starting on the road to economic development after being among the poorest countries in the world like its neighbors Laos and Cambodia. There are obviously other factors, mostly related to the

---

*All of these projects, as well as dozens of conference papers, can be found on the World Bank Web site, http://www.worldbank.org.

world stratification through history, that strongly affect why some countries are able to develop and others are not, even with the same cultural traditions shaping their current value orientations. It is time to examine some of the most important of these factors and then consider how Thailand has been able to achieve strong economic development and poverty reduction in recent decades.

# ✴ Asian Traditions and Forms of Social Organization: Some Commonalities

In contrast to the image held by most Westerners, Asian nations are not "all alike." In fact, while moving from, say, Japan to Korea, from Korea to China, and then from China into Southeast Asian nations, one encounters more variety and contrast of cultures than if one were to travel through modern Europe. Having said this, among the variety of Asian cultural values, forms of social organization, and other historical traditions, we can identify some characteristics of Asian societies that in combination help us understand why some have had significant economic development even with the outside intervention from the modern world system found harmful to other nations (for more detail see Kerbo 2006, 2005). Three characteristics are interrelated and most important.

## Ancient Civilizations

People who live in countries with ancient civilizations (both the elites and common people) tend to have a much stronger identity with and pride in their nation and recognize their common national interests. This general characteristic of Asian nations can be suggested by Hanoi's Temple of Literature, which is in fact one of the first "universities" in Vietnam. In the large courtyards of what remains of the original structures there are still today what look like many tombstones, but are in fact engraved records of graduates who obtained their degrees in the first centuries of this university. What is most remarkable to contemplate are the dates; it turns out this university is some 1,000 years old, a fact that should humble Oxford graduates, or graduates of the University of Salamanca in Spain who think of themselves as graduating from the oldest universities in Europe.

Thinking in a broader context we can begin to imagine some of the underlying differences between developing nations in Asia and those in Latin America and Africa. Of course, Latin America and Africa are continents that contained ancient civilizations; the key word is "contained." About all that exists of the ancient civilizations in South and Central America are the stone pyramids. Just a few hundred years ago Europeans began carving out new national boundaries with colonialism so that the nations of South and Central America today are nominally only 300 years or so old, at the oldest. Of course, most of the people in Central and South America today are descendants of people from ancient civilizations such as the Maya and Incas. But it is the ancestors of recent immigrants from Europe during the Spanish and Portugese colonial period who are mostly in control. There are fractured nations where these people of European ancestry feel less identity with the original people of the continent and are less likely to promote development and poverty reduction for all people in the country (Kohli 2004).

In Africa, of course, we also find ancient civilizations and the cradle of human evolution. But again, except for a few cases in northern Africa and the horn of Africa, these old civilizations were mostly destroyed, and finally erased in one sense by the European colonialists. With the Berlin Conference of 1884–1885 the European nations partitioned Africa into what would become nations that make no sense socially, culturally, or ethnically. These are the roots of African political instability today with tribal conflicts helping to spark one civil war after another (Mazrui 1978, 1986).

In contrast to Latin America and Africa, we find countries throughout most of Asia that come from or were once central parts of ancient civilizations. None of these was as dominant as the Chinese civilization or Indian civilization, of course, but most Asian nations today have strong roots in ancient civilizations of which they were members hundreds if not thousands of years ago. In a similar vein, in contrast to Latin America and Africa, colonialism in Asia was less likely to result in new countries with boundaries cutting across old civilizations or ethnic groups. Most Asian nations today are therefore more likely to make "sociological sense" with respect to rather natural societal boundaries (Myrdal 1968:64).

There are nations in Asia today that do not fit this general rule, but these are in most cases precisely the Asian nations with most instability and least economic development. Indonesia, for example, has had the highest levels of political violence since the end of the 1990s, and a once healthy economy has been harmed. Indonesia today is in reality a collection of many old civilizations put together by the Dutch during their colonial dominance of the region. Laos, one of the poorest countries of Southeast Asia today, was a product of the end of French colonialism in Indochina. It was created by the French out of smaller kingdoms existing before colonialism. The national boundaries of Burma, or Myanmar as the military dictators now demand it be called, were largely a construct of British colonialism, and during most of that time attached to Britain's greater Indian colonial territory. Before giving up Burma after World War II, the British fashioned national boundaries, which included many tribal people from differing old civilizations. Burma, since independence, has been contested territory with these various groups all seeking independence. Cambodia was once the center of an ancient empire, but is just now regaining some stability after the Indochina wars involving the French, then the Japanese, then again the French, and finally Americans. The Philippines is the nation in the region with least claim to an ancient civilization and most dominated and changed by Western colonialists, the Spanish and then Americans, losing comparatively more of its indigenous culture. Like Indonesia, the national boundaries of the Philippines today, which were created by the colonial powers, include extensive Muslim areas among the dominant northern Christian areas, creating the roots of the Islamic separatist rebellion that continues to break into open warfare from time to time. Finally, British treatment of Malaysia at the end of colonialism was in stark contrast to Burma. The British worked hard to form a nation out of many Islamic sultanates for years after World War II, not thrusting the nation into independence to fend for itself until 1957 (Taylor 1999; Turnbull 1999; Stockwell 1999; Cheong 1999; Keay 1997; Osborne 1995; Hall 1999).

Finally, there is new empirical evidence of the impact of ancient civilizations on successful economic development and poverty reduction today. It is clear that what the World Bank calls "good governance" is important today. Many studies have shown that good governance and government efficiency are strongly correlated with poverty reduction and economic development for less-developed countries in recent decades (Kerbo 2006: Chapter 5). But no one has effectively figured out how to produce good governance if a country doesn't already have it. Countries with ancient civilizations were more likely to have at least some functioning government institutions before European colonials took them over 200 or 300 years ago. These countries are concentrated in Asia. The data show that these ancient civilizations were usually able to reestablish better government in recent years after the colonials were forced to give the country independence (Kerbo and Ziltener forthcoming; Chanda and Putterman 2005).

## Traditions of Authority and Elite Responsibility

In addition to a greater sense of national identity among the population, the older civilizations of Asia are more likely to have retained ancient traditions of authority, national identity, and elite responsibility. In Myrdal's description, in Asia, European colonialism was less likely to harm "the indigenous system of rights and obligations among the population" (Myrdal 1968:212). As noted, outside intervention by rich multinational corporations often presents a situation today in which wealthy or powerful elites can enrich themselves, often at the expense of long-term economic development, and the continued poverty of the people in their country. In contrast to this, *with these traditions of rights and obligations in place, when faced with the dilemma of pleasing outside multinationals or pushing for some protection and benefits for their nation and the common people, elites in countries with these ancient traditions of obligations will more likely temper their narrower self-interests to protect the nation and people.*

Even in the ancient Asian civilizations, of course, throughout history and today, elites sometimes ignore these traditions of elite responsibility, but they do so at their own peril. As Barrington Moore (1978) demonstrated in his famous book, *Injustice: The Social Bases of Obedience and Revolt,* throughout history, when these elite obligations are violated various types of protest or even revolution were likely forthcoming. The three obligations most important for elites to uphold, Moore's historical works suggest, are (1) protection from outside forces, (2) internal peace and order, and (3) material security. Much the same is described in the historical analysis of political violence and rebellion in European feudal societies by Charles Tilly (see Tilly 1978, 1981; Tilly et al. 1975).

The same can be found in the ancient civilizations in Asia. In his comparative history of "the mandate to rule" and modernization in Europe and Asia, Reinhard Bendix noted that from at least 2000 B.C. there was the idea of a "heavenly mandate" for emperors in China. But emperors were obligated to take care of the nation and "perform," in a sense, or the mandate would be lost. The earlier emperors were believed to deserve their rule because they alone had the power to control ancestor spirits for the good of the nation (Bendix 1978:49–56). Later, around 500 B.C., Confucius worked out his philosophy of rights and obligations between rulers and subjects in response to a preceding period of almost 200 years of social disorder. These old traditions of rights and obligations in China held the nation more or less together and maintained emperor rule for centuries until the emperors began to have greater difficulty meeting their obligations with social change and European colonialism beginning around 1800. These were the changes that led eventually to massive revolution in China during the 20th century (Fairbank 1986).

Most kingdoms in Southeast Asia are relatively more recent when compared to those of India and China, but still centuries old. Some of the first were found in Cambodia (Angkor), Sumatra (Srivijaya), and Burma (Pagan) around A.D. 800. But like other Asian empires, these "Buddhist kingdoms," along with Vietnam's Confucian model inherited from China, had strong traditions of obligations and rights developed and amended over the centuries. Most of these traditions of elite obligations survived European colonialism, though there are some exceptions, such as in the Philippines, which was more dominated and changed by Spanish rule (Osborne 1995:17–27, 45–50).

## A Hard State

In Volume II of his famous work, *Asian Drama: An Inquiry into the Poverty of Nations,* the Nobel Prize–winning economist Gunnar Myrdal (1968:896) wrote in reference to south Asia, "[T]hroughout the region, national governments require extraordinarily little of their citizens. There are few obligations either to do things in the interest of the community or to avoid actions opposed to that interest." Myrdal, of course, was referring to the problem of "soft states" primarily in India, Pakistan, and Sri Lanka (Ceylon) soon after independence from British colonialism. He was not yet aware of how multinational corporations spreading more widely in poor countries in the early 1960s could be harmful to the long-term development interests of these poor nations. But his idea of the need for "hard states" has become one of the most important aspects of his massive work on the problems of poor nations.

What is also given more recognition since Myrdal's time is that *late-developing nations,* or nations that have achieved economic development since the nations in Europe and North America, have often required extensive state intervention, planning, and even state ownership of many industries (Thurow 1991; Fallows 1994). One of the best examples of this late development is found with Germany. The many German territories were not even united into a single nation until the late 1800s under the leadership of Bismarck. Already behind most of Europe by this time, the German state used extensive intervention in the economy in the form of planning, state-directed loans, economic incentives to businesses, and extensive government ownership of corporations, to push Germany rapidly ahead to finally achieve the position of the largest economy in Europe (Craig 1991; Kennedy 1987; Chirot 1986; Dietrich 1991; Raff 1988).

Nations trying to develop in the second half of the 20th century Vogel calls "late, late developers" and are even more in need of state assistance in overcoming obstacles created for them by the new global economy. The "four Asian tigers" (Taiwan, South Korea, Hong Kong, and Singapore) achieved rapid economic growth in the 1980s, Vogel (1991) shows, with extensive state intervention. As many scholars have shown, it was Japan that led the way as an Asian late-developing nation with extensive state intervention from the late 1800s to become the second largest economic power in the world after the United States. It was Japan that more or less perfected what is now known as the

"Asian development model" copied in one form or another by Asian nations that have recently achieved at least some success with economic development (Johnson 1982).

Specifically, what is meant by a *hard state* is a government with sufficient rational organization and power to achieve its development goals. There must be a state with the ability to provide consistent economic guidance, rational organization to efficiently achieve its goals, and the power to back up its long-range economic policies. All of this is needed because the state must be able to *resist external demands from outside corporations to do things for its short-term gain, overcome internal resistance from strong groups trying to protect short-term narrow interests, reduce corruption, and control infighting within the nation over who will most benefit from development projects.* What this hard state comes down to primarily is leadership and bureaucracy—bureaucracy that is comparatively honest, efficient, and has the power to back up policy decisions.

The characteristics of Asian nations described already should be recognized as the stuff making a hard state more likely in East and Southeast Asia. Because of ancient traditions and a sense of identification with their nation and its government, people recognize their common interests as a nation and are more willing to make some sacrifices for these common interests. Very importantly, with restraint from ancient traditions of obligations to the nation and people, elites in these countries are also more likely to restrain their selfish interests and use their power to protect the long-term interests of their nation and people.

Evans and Rauch (1999) created what they called a Weberianness Scale, referring to the most important characteristics of rational and efficient bureaucratic organizations defined in the famous works of Max Weber some 100 years ago. Of the 37 nations in the sample, seven were Asian, and they all ranked above average on their Weberianness Scale (with the exception of the Philippines), while the four tigers clustered at the top four positions (Taiwan, South Korea, Hong Kong, Singapore). Also of importance, they found this Weberianness Scale positively related to economic development. Unfortunately, as is typical in Western sociological research, the interesting fact that the four Asian tigers are at the top was mentioned, but no consideration was given as to why the Asian nations tend to rank so well on this scale.

Before leaving this topic of a hard state, it is important to underscore what is not a key or required component of a hard state. A hard state is not to be equated with a military dictatorship, and in fact it is generally the opposite. Military dictatorships in third world countries often develop because the state is unable to provide basic support for the health, welfare, and infrastructure needed by the nation. It is in response to the resulting political instability that an oppressive military dictatorship may come into existence, such as in Burma (Myanmar) today. A hard state can be right wing, left wing, repressive, or relatively democratic. Most important, a hard state is *a state able to implement and carry out policies protecting national interests, thus giving more assurance of long-term economic development.*

Despite all the evidence of the importance of a hard state first described by Myrdal almost 40 years ago, some international aid agencies are just now publicly recognizing the fact. The United Nations Development Project, for example, published a report in April of 2000, *Overcoming Human Poverty: UNDP Poverty Report, 2000,* which focuses on "good governance" in poor countries as a key to economic development and overcoming the selfish interests of wealthy elites often behind state actions in developing nations. The report concludes that "Without good governance, reliance on trickle-down economic development and a host of other strategies will not work." It seems it has taken quite some time for the Western-dominated international development agencies to acknowledge that bad governing and the collusion between Western multinationals and third world governments have been part of the problem. Thailand provides us with just one classic case of how even and sustainable development has been achieved because through history the nation and its state have been able to protect the country from the negative impact of outside corporate penetration of the economy.

# ⚔ The Case of Thailand

With the exception of a 2-year setback and slowdown from the 1997 Asian economic crisis, Thailand has had a steady record of not only economic development but also poverty reduction in recent decades. In contrast to earlier world system theory predictions, this growth and poverty reduction coincided with huge amounts of foreign direct investment (FDI) from the world's rich multinational corporations. Thailand, in fact, has the best record in Asia of poverty reduction for each increase in gross domestic product (World Bank, 2000: Chapter 3, p. 48). Today the percentage of the population living on less than $1 a day in Thailand (0.1 percent) is far below almost all other developing countries. Thailand has reduced its national poverty rate from around 50 percent of the population in the 1960s to about 13 percent today. In simple terms, Thailand has brought up the overall standard of living for its citizens, but the bottom economic group in Thailand has been reduced even more compared to other countries.

As with all other developing countries in the world, though, we must look outside the central cities of Thailand, primarily Bangkok. The vast majority of the world's people continue to be rural, agricultural workers (International Fund for Agricultural Development 2001). At the beginning of the 21st century, 79 percent of the Thai population was still listed as rural people and more than half of the labor force still works in agriculture. The contrast between Thailand and other developing countries is again striking. As we saw in the beginning of this chapter, the typical developing country pattern shows major disparities in the standards of living between rural and urban people. In Thailand, however, the poverty rate is listed at 10 percent in the urban areas compared to 15 percent in rural areas (World Bank 2000:280–281).

To understand how all this has been possible it is important to begin with a short examination of Thai political and economic history, a history that parallels the outline of Asian nations described in the previous section.

## A Brief History of Thailand

*Tai* ethnic people from southern China began populating what is now Thailand over 2000 years ago (Wyatt 1984; Osborne 1995). Some 1000 years ago Burma (Myanmar) and Cambodia were dominant countries in Southeast Asia. During the 1800s both Thailand and Vietnam had become dominant regional powers as Burma and Cambodia were in decline. But then came the threat of colonialism. It was King Monkut and his son

King Chulalongkorn (Rama V) who astutely led the nation during the most crucial period of confrontation with the West from the 1850s until the turn of the century—a period in which the kingdom began its transformation into a modern nation-state. The Western powers, and Britain in particular, forced the integration of Thailand into the economic system dominated by the West (Chaiyan 1994). The French stripped away some Thai territory in the east for colonies in Laos and Cambodia. But unlike all other countries in Southeast Asia, Thailand kept its independence and strengthened and modernized its institutions in the process. Under the leadership of King Chulalongkorn the government administration was transformed from the old household system to a modern bureaucratic form in which the civil servants worked for the king.

In June of 1932, 49 military officers and 65 civilians, most educated in the West, staged a coup, deposing King Rama VII as the last absolute monarch of Thailand. The "promoters" were motivated by their conviction that the absolute monarchy was an obstacle to further modernization and development of Thailand. Rather than attempting to run the country themselves, however, the military quickly turned executive functions over to the increasingly competent government ministry bureaucrats. Since 1932 various factions of the military and royal circles have been maneuvering for power, with brief periods of more or less civilian government since the 1970s (Handley 2006). But through it all the unelected well-educated bureaucratic government ministry has been running most functions of government. After the longest period of civilian government rule that began in 1992, in 2006, with the backing of this bureaucratic elite and supporters of the old royalty, another military coup deposed the popular government of Prime Minister Thaksin. Thaksin was an American-educated sociologist who later became a billionaire with an electronics and cell phone business, selling mainly to the government and military at first. There were several issues behind the military coup (such as the usual corruption), but it seems clear that the biggest issue was that the bureaucratic ministry and royal elites were losing control (Pasuk and Baker 2004; McCargo and Pathmanand 2005). During the 1997 Asian economic crisis, these governmental elites had agreed to a new constitution that increased democracy in Thailand by such means as a strong electoral commission to reduce voter fraud and making the upper house of parliament fully elected, as is the more powerful lower house. As we will see below, the Thai government, especially with pressure from the popular king who had no formal power, had been reducing poverty and promoting economic development for more than three decades. But as prime minister, Thaksin began even more programs for the rural and working-class poor to gain their support in elections. The problem for the nonelected elite was that Thaksin became increasingly powerful and began helping himself and his inner circle as to become more wealthy. He was also reducing restrictions on multinational corporations, restrictions the elite believed were needed to help long-term economic development in Thailand. Thus after the military coup of 2006, the ruling elites again rewrote the Thai constitution, taking out some of the measures promoting more democracy, such as full popular election of the upper house of parliament, which again allowed the unelected elites to appoint half of the seats after 2007.

The low-income rural and urban working-class Thais who had benefited from Thaksin's poverty reduction programs (such as free medical care, economic development loans to villages, and micro loans to the poor) were angered by the 2006 military coup and their loss of influence in government. Thus began the "red shirt" movement, which has created violence and political instability in Thailand since 2007. After the military restored elections in 2008, supporters of Thaksin again won national elections but were deposed through legal maneuvers by the unelected government elite and protests by "yellow shirts," made up of the educated urban elite opposed to so much political influence by the rural poor and working class, all of which produced a big increase in political violence in Thailand in 2010.

Western style democracy is not necessarily related to economic development and poverty reduction for less-developed countries today (Kerbo 2006:37; United Nations, *Human Development Report, 2002*: 57–60). There is a correlation between economic development and democracy, but the causal direction is from a longer history of high levels of economic development to democracy. When people become more affluent and better educated in a society, they begin to demand more democracy (Jackman 1974, 1975). It is likely that Thailand is starting to go through this process. The key point is that Thailand achieved its economic development and relatively low poverty under what can be called a "hard state" beginning a few decades ago (Muscat 1994; Kulick and Wilson 1996; Doner 2009).

## Thai Development Policies

It was not long after the military took power during the 1932 coup that the alliance was formed between the Thai military and ministry bureaucrats, and policies for economic development were started. However, because of the worldwide depression and then World War II, during the late 1950s serious efforts were given to economic development policies. When these policies were finally started, one of the most important things to emphasize for our subject of economic development and poverty reduction in Thailand is that relative to other countries, these policies did not mean economic development would proceed on the backs of Thai peasants (Muscat 1994:245). For most countries trying to catch up to the industrialized West in the last 150 years or more, rapid economic development meant a focus on urban industry with surpluses extracted from peasants to fuel the industrial expansion. This is how Stalin achieved economic development for the Soviet Union in the 1930s, and how Japanese governments did it in the early 20th century. In these two countries, as well as the others, peasants rebelled, but mostly just got poorer and often died.

Not so in Thailand. As one of the leading economic teams of researchers in Thailand put it, in contrast to countries like South Korea and Taiwan, "Thailand had lots of unused land and lots of people to work it. . . . The government saw it had the opportunity—and the duty to the large peasant population—to grow by pumping up agriculture" (Pasuk and Baker 1996:58). In later years there was also the Rural Employment Generation Program, which gave each *tambon,* or group of villages, in the country a substantial annual grant that could be spent on agricultural development projects of their choosing, a policy that provided a "'bottom-up' approach to rural development" (Muscat 1994:138–139). In addition to this focus on agriculture, the first 5-year plan called for "raising the standard of living" as the main objective, along with care that "increased output should be equitably distributed so that, to the extent possible, all citizens, and not merely a privileged few, derive benefit from it" (Muscat 1994:95). All lofty ideas, of course, but given the track record of poverty reduction and economic development with a relatively smaller gap between rural and urban standards of living, we can say that at the time Thai government and ministry officials did a fairly good job of pulling it off.

Aside from agriculture, from the beginning of these Thai development policies the focus was also on *import substitution*. In this critical strategy, a hard state (or at least semihard state) must be able to tell multinational corporations from rich countries that goods will be imported, if at all, with tariffs as high as 80 to even 150 percent to prevent these goods from competing with goods made in (at least at first) less efficient infant factories in the poorer country. It is a hard state that must do this because only a hard state can have the influence to enforce such a policy on rich multinational corporations (and their governments who will almost certainly try to resist), and only a hard state can have the influence to enforce such a policy against the demands of its own rich citizens who want the imported goods, "and want them now," at a cheaper price, not waiting for infant domestic industries to produce suitable products. Thailand was especially successful with this strategy in the auto industry. From the 1970s Thailand began placing tariffs of 150 percent on imported autos, but at the same time telling the foreign auto industries that if they came to Thailand to create joint ventures with a Thai company to build cars—and thus hire Thai employees, pay Thai taxes, and keep some profits within Thailand—the auto company would get many forms of government assistance (Muscat 1994:148; Doner 2009). With the major exception of American auto companies, they came in big numbers. With more than 20,000 additional autos on the streets of Bangkok every month during many years, the foreign auto makers and Thais did quite well.

By the early 1970s economic growth based on agricultural export growth and the expansion of the domestic market had reached its limits. From the 1980s, the most successful development policies began to stress *exports*. It became evident that South Korea and Taiwan were becoming the most successful countries in expanding their economies, and were doing so through attracting foreign investment that was focused on manufacturing goods for export. It was then that Thai bureaucrats shifted policy toward attracting foreign investment in all kinds of manufacturing and to exporting cheap manufactured goods and textiles. By the 1990s, however, the export focus shifted to high-tech electronic goods. During the mid-1990s, the largest employer in Thailand, for example, was Seagate, the American firm manufacturing computer components.

It is important to stress that during the 1980s and 1990s, Thailand continued to protect its economy despite the flood of foreign investment the country had attracted. This is especially important because, as we have seen from the modern world system research, without protections that a hard state can enforce, long-term economic growth can actually be reduced by extensive foreign investment in the country. Thus, Thai bureaucrats initiated rules such as those demanding a sufficient percentage of domestic content in goods manufactured by foreign companies in Thailand and the famous *51 percent rule* (Muscat 1994:80). While I learned firsthand in interviews with Thai bureaucrats in the Bureau of Investment, as well as Japanese and American executives operating in Thailand, that the 51 percent rule is not always evenly applied and that with certain exceptions, it has worked. Under this 51 percent rule, a foreign company setting up production operations in Thailand must form a joint venture with a Thai company.

The result is that a Thai company with 51 percent control is better able to keep jobs and profits in the country. Among other things, it was the relaxation of rules on foreign investment under Thaksin that angered the bureaucratic elite and brought about the military coup deposing him in 2006 (Pasuk and Baker 2004). One might assume that faced with such rules the multinational corporations would simply leave the country or never invest there to begin with. Countries such as Thailand, however, have been able to keep foreign investors because the government has maintained more infrastructure investment to provide good transportation and a rather educated labor force, enhancing productivity. In large part because of all this, Thailand has kept its domestic economy growing at such a rate that foreign investors want to keep their presence in the country to make and sell things in a booming market. These specific development policies, however, were not what ensured the rural people were pulled out of poverty.

## Thai Peasants and Political Action

One afternoon during the spring of 1998 I sat with a group of students along Ratchadamnoen Road in Bangkok, just past Democracy Monument, watching thousands upon thousands of Thai peasant farmers marching by on their way to Government House (the Thai Parliament building). Most were walking, though many were piled into village pickup trucks. The mood was quite Thai, which is to say there was a lot of *sanuk* (joking and having fun). These people from the countryside seemed as interested in watching us *farangs* (Western foreigners) as we were them; many waved and said *"hullo,"* and some even shook our hands as they marched by. A few were singing protest songs, and we had to smile when some of the people marching by wore T-shirts with pictures of the former Cuban revolutionary, Che Guevara, on the front. (We later asked some farmers who had Che's picture on their pickup truck if they knew who he was; the answer was "no.")

What we had stumbled on that day was a massive protest organized by the Forum for the Poor to make sure farmers were protected as the Asian economic crisis raged around them. Even before the "red shirts" in 2006 there have been many such protests by rural Thais, in recent years mostly lead by the Forum for the Poor, a broad-based social movement organization involved in all kinds of rural and environmental issues (Missingham 2003). The most active of these protests by Thai villagers began in the 1970s when the economic development policies such as those we saw above were being implemented. By the mid-1990s it is estimated that there were at least two rural protest movements going on each day in Thailand (Pasuk and Baker 1996:206, 162). As in most countries, especially developing countries, there is often a rural–urban split in political and economic interests. The urban population of Bangkok has become an increasing political force in recent decades. But with peasants living in villages making up most of the Thai population, and a large percentage of these people relatively well organized politically, rural issues have been kept before Thai politicians.

To understand the somewhat unique position of Thai peasants when compared to developing countries in other regions of the world (especially Latin America and Africa) requires a little diversion into the history of rural Thailand. First, we must remember that the concept of national boundaries was foreign to mainland Southeast Asia. The kingdoms of Pagan, Angkor (Cambodia), and Siam (Thailand), for example, extended only as far as their power to enforce rules over villages. As one got farther away from the capital cities, the question of which kingdom holds the area often became less clear. This also meant that *peasants in the areas were relatively independent,* at least until one kingdom or another came in to more strongly press its claims of sovereignty over the people.

Second, when territories were not in dispute, in most Southeast Asian countries the king "theoretically" owned the land (Keyes 1989:31). We must specify theoretically because in reality the kings seldom occupied this land or sent their agents to run plantations for them. Rather, the land was given over to peasants and village people through a sort of lifetime lease that could be passed on to offspring but not sold to others (Pasuk and Baker 1996:7–8). In other words, in a major contrast to the position of peasants in the preindustrial feudal countries of Europe, Latin America, and elsewhere in Asia (especially Japan), mainland Southeast Asian peasants had their own land, *had no feudal lord dominating them,* and were relatively independent of outsiders from urban areas. Even if they did not have an official lease on land from one of the kingdoms, land was plentiful in uncontested areas of Southeast Asia, so the peasant family or even village could move to such land.

Because of these traditions of independence and organizing for themselves, Thai peasants have been able to bring pressure upon the central government to have some protection of their interests in the process of economic development. But also, the traditions of land distribution in Thailand even more directly help us explain the relatively low level of inequality and more evenly spread economic development in Thailand during the second half of the 20th century. As Table 16-4 earlier indicated, Thailand continues to have a relatively low level of land inequality, and the contrast between Southeast Asia in general, Africa, and Latin America is striking. Following old traditions, this land is still leased to individual peasants and small villages at very low cost, which is the reason we today find about 90 percent of rural people with their own land in Thailand (Kulick and Wilson 1996:132). This is why I discovered in interviews with slum dwellers in Bangkok that their lives were for the most part much better than people living in massive slum areas in other parts of the world, such as India, Africa, and Latin America. Many, if not most, of the people living in massive slums in Bangkok like Klong Toey described earlier actually have rural homes to return to. They are living temporarily in Bangkok slum areas to sell produce in the city or work at low-skill jobs to add to their farm income. After the Asian economic crisis hit Thailand, I was at first surprised to learn from Thai aid workers that the number of the 100,000 "homeless" people living in Klong Toey had not expanded. I was told when jobs were harder to find in Bangkok, Klong Toey "residents" simply started going back to their farms.

As many studies have shown, land reform policies that get more land to the cultivators themselves are one of the best ways to reduce poverty in the world (International Fund for Agricultural Development 2001: Chapter 3). When peasants and farmers own their own land, farming is often more productive, agriculture is more labor intensive (which creates more farm jobs), and small farmers and peasants are able to keep more of the profits themselves (obviously helping to reduce poverty rates). Historical traditions have thus given Thailand an advantage in the countryside. Other countries that do not have this historical legacy of low land inequality can achieve it as Japan did after

World War II, but as the International Fund for Agricultural Development *Rural Poverty Report, 2001* indicates, it is seldom an easy task.

## Thailand in World System Perspective

Research and theory from the world system perspective have shown why it is often difficult to have economic development, and especially more evenly distributed economic development benefiting all people in the country. Without traditions of national identity and elite responsibility, elites are often tempted into siding with core multinational investors to keep these investors happy and themselves rich. This also makes it difficult for a hard state to develop with the ability to follow consistent development policies for long-term and even economic development. In most parts of the world, the history of colonialism has helped contribute to all of these negatives for poor countries. There are now more promising techniques to help stimulate sustainable and more even economic development in poor countries, but the most difficult problem is *creating the motivation* to use these techniques of development when domestic elites tied to multinational corporations find the status quo more conducive to their personal short-term interests.

We have seen how Thailand has had a more favorable history that has given the country a greater chance for even economic development. When colonial powers arrived in Asia, Thailand was in a position of strength. The country's leaders skillfully played the European powers against each other to keep their independence—the only country in Southeast Asia able to do so (Slagter and Kerbo 2000; Kerbo 2006). With its independence and nationalistic elites, Thailand was able to maintain at least a semihard state able to carry out development policies and prevent multinational corporate investment from draining their financial and natural resources (with policies like the 51 percent investment rule). Thailand was also fortunate to have quite equitable land distribution so that major land reform was not needed to build a base of citizens with material resources to help drive a domestic economy.

Finally, the case of Thailand shows us that cultural explanations have been overused. Thailand's neighbors (Burma, Laos, and Cambodia) have identical cultural traditions but remain among the poorest countries in the world with little prospects for development. Burma was colonized by the British, who left their colony in disruption from which it has never recovered, in radical contrast to how the British helped their former colony of Malaysia plan for independence and economic development. Since 1946 Burma has been plagued by political violence by many tribal people from old civilizations that were brought into Burmese borders by the British before they left to let the Burmese fall into chaos (see especially Smith 1999; Stockwell 1999; Keay 1997). On the other side of Thailand, Laos and Cambodia were dragged into the first Indochinese War (against the French colonial powers) and then the second Indochinese War (against the United States). Both communist and noncommunist forces devastated these little countries. In Cambodia, after 1975 the Khmer Rouge government ended up killing 1.7 million of its people, targeting the educated population and leaving the whole country with only some 300 college graduates by the 1980s (Kamm 1998; Chandler 1998, 1999). Laos ended up with a more benign, though incompetent, government, but has suffered from French colonialism that has only sapped resources. Between the early 1960s and 1975, Laos then suffered from a huge "secret war" led and organized by the United States, which dropped more tons of bombs on Laos per capita than any country in world history (over two-thirds of a ton for every living person in Laos; see Warner 1995, 1996:352; Evans 1995, 1998). The World Bank and United Nations agencies now stress that "good governance" is a key to economic development. With traditional national borders disrupted by colonial powers and war devastation, any kind of governance is difficult to achieve.

# ✄ The World Stratification System: A Conclusion and Perspective on the Future

We conclude by first emphasizing what has not been suggested by world system theorists. Most important, the world system and multinational corporations cannot be held accountable for all of the world's inequality. Culture, climate, and lack of resources, among many other factors not directly related to world stratification, can help produce and maintain poverty.

However, to a very large degree, all regions of the world are increasingly interrelated in a worldwide economic system. Because of differing economic interests in this system, and differing amounts of power to ensure that these interests are met, there is a world stratification system that produces inequality among nations and inequality among classes within the nations. The data are clear that since globalization has speeded up in the last century, income and wealth inequalities have drastically increased (World Bank 2000:31).

It must also be recognized that no easy solutions to underdevelopment can be identified. Many problems are faced by poor nations that will not be solved by simply removing core dominance (as Myrdal 1968, among others, has shown). The rapid development in *some* Asian countries at least shows that late development for the periphery is not impossible at this stage of the modern world system. The problem for most periphery nations outside East and Southeast Asia, however, is that they often lack key factors that have been crucial to development from the new Asian economic development model, specifically as we showed with the contrasting case of Thailand.

## Social Structure and Technical Tools for Development

In recent years many new techniques for promoting more sustainable and even economic development in poor countries have been perfected, techniques we may call "technical tools" for development. We have long recognized that *land reform* is a key to sustainable and more even economic development. Farmers with their own land produce more, create more jobs and income, all helping to sustain a cycle of economic development. Among the most recent of the new technical tools for development are *micro loans*. Agencies such as the World Bank are taking a closer look at the famous Grameen Bank's "microcredit" program in Bangladesh that gives loans for as low as $100 to poor farmers. A small pump costing only $50, for example, can make a big difference in a village without the means of irrigation. Thousands of farmers can increase their incomes and lead to more even and sustained economic development in a country. Dividing the loan money into thousands of these micro loans has promoted more evenly distributed development in poor nations in contrast to older programs putting millions of dollars into big projects like dams, which tend to provide more economic benefits for multinational corporations and those already rich in developing countries.

Other specific policies include *debt relief,* reducing trade barriers in rich nations, and empowering women. Numerous studies and reports by the International Fund for Agricultural Development, World Bank, and United Nations are now showing clear evidence that *improvements in women's rights* help reduce poverty and speed economic development (World Bank, *Engendering Development,* 2001; World Bank 2000; International Fund for Agricultural Development 2001). There seem to be several reasons for this. Better-educated women contribute more to the economy; when given the chance, rural women seem to manage family budgets and economic resources better than men and are more likely to repay micro loans; and women who have more rights and education are more aware of the importance of population control for the family, with the influence to demand the use of birth control.

However successful these new technical means of sustainable economic development may be, there remain two serious problems. First, there is often not the "will" or motivation among the poor country's elite to employ these technical means for more even development. They are getting rich from the status quo and prefer to keep multinational corporations and actors in the "world markets" happy rather than help their own people. Second, without a change in social structure (e.g., the domestic stratification system, political system, and highly unequal economic system), many of the techniques to provide sustainable development will not work.

During the 1960s the quick-fix scheme was the "green revolution." The basic idea sounded great: Rich nations, especially the United States, would send their agricultural experts to poor countries to teach farmers how to grow crops more efficiently and help supply new strains of crops, new farm equipment, and chemicals to dramatically increase crop yield. One goal was achieved: Food production increased dramatically. But the basic goal (or at least the overtly stated goal) failed badly. Rich landowners became wealthier, but poor peasants typically became poorer. The problem was that landowners began growing different crops to sell on the world market, exporting everything they could to increase their profits, while they stopped growing many other crops used as cheap food for local people. Likewise, the green revolution created an incentive for big landowners to acquire more and more land, thus taking land from small farmers and peasants. Finally, the new capital-intensive agriculture promoted in the green revolution forced peasants out of agricultural jobs. A few years after the green revolution began, many poor countries often exported food while their own poor went hungry.

The obvious need for land reform in most countries, especially in Africa and Latin America, provides another example of the necessity for changes in social structure first. As logical as this sounds, land reform has seldom been followed. The payoff for the more affluent is greater in promoting urban industrialization, and if agricultural development is given much attention it is usually agricultural development for export, which enriches wealthy landowners while impoverishing peasants. Studies of this problem in Africa note that while three-fourths of Africans are farmers, there are almost no policies in Africa attempting to boost agricultural production. Kenya is an example: With the vast majority of its people living off the land, only 4 percent of the Kenyan government budget goes to agricultural programs, and 75 percent of this 4 percent goes to support wasteful state farms. Then there is the case of President Mugabe of Zimbabwe. With falling political support in the late 1990s and early 2000s, Mugabe jumped on the bandwagon of land redistribution for Zimbabwe. The problem was that it was land reform only for his political supporters and was carried out in such an irrational manner that agricultural output dropped. Not exactly the good governance the World Bank has talked about recently.

Finally, as rich nations of the world have taken up the campaign against terrorism since September 11, 2001, many have reminded us that eliminating terrorism cannot be effective without due consideration to the dramatic rise in world inequality and poverty we have seen in this chapter. One cannot make the claim that increases in world poverty alone create political violence, but it is a prime breeding ground. Figures compiled by the World Bank show that between 1990 and 1995 about 90 percent of all cases of "civil war and strife" occurred in poor nations (World Bank 2000:50). But this civil war and strife is not concentrated in any particular region of the world such as the Middle East. It is spread evenly among all world regions with poor nations. A study by the National Defense Council found 59 cases of "serious conflict" in 193 countries around the world in 2001, compared to 35 just over 10 years ago. "Major conflicts" involving 1,000 or more deaths in 1 year were found in 38 of these 193 countries, again a big increase compared to the decade earlier. Research by sociologists has also shown the importance of world inequality for sparking political violence. Measuring the gap between the rich and poor in countries and cities all over the world, several studies have shown a significant correlation between inequality and levels of political violence (Messner 1982; Muller 1985; Blau and Blau 1982; Williams 1984). It seems obvious that any war against terrorism by rich countries cannot stop with arresting or killing famous leaders supporting terrorism. Other bin Ladens will emerge. The United States will increasingly be a target: An international opinion poll conducted at the end of 2001 indicates that most people in the world think that the United States and its policies are the prime reasons for the increase in world poverty today.

## Summary

We have examined data showing a large and increasing gap between the rich and poor of this world. And we have examined how the world stratification system, or modern world system, creates extreme power imbalances among the world's nations. The old theories of economic development, such as the stages of economic growth theory, do not fit the current reality for poor countries trying to achieve economic development in today's global economy. For many poor countries today, investments from rich multinational corporations often make their inequality and poverty greater and their prospects for long-term economic development more difficult. We have seen that there are exceptions to these rules, particularly in several East and Southeast Asian nations. Some of these countries have been able to protect themselves from harmful effects of core domination because ancient traditions have made domestic elites more nationalistic and responsible to the needs of their people. Hard states have been established, which are able to guide successful development policies. With the case of Thailand we outlined how this has been possible and how Thailand has been one of the most successful nations in the world to reduce poverty with economic development in recent decades.

# Glossary

## A

**achievement**   Class or stratum placement based primarily on qualities that can be controlled by individuals, involving merit through living up to certain socially defined ideals or certain achievement rules.

**ascription**   When class or stratum placement is primarily hereditary; in other words, people are placed in positions in a stratification system because of qualities beyond their control (for example, because of race, sex, or class at birth).

**authoritarian personality**   A personality type with basic characteristics including respect for force, submission toward superiors, rigidity of outlook, and intolerance of ambiguity. It is this personality type, shaped in the socialization process in certain cultures, that is believed to be the cause of much racism and discrimination.

**authority structure**   Another of the primary dimensions of class in modern industrial societies, which refers to one's authority position in private or political bureaucratic organizations.

## B

**bourgeoisie**   A Marxian term indicating the owners of the means of production or capital in a capitalist society.

**bureaucracy**   A form of rational social organization, according to Max Weber, based on fixed, written rules and a hierarchy of positions, which has come to dominate in industrial societies.

## C

**caste system**   A system of social stratification based on status rankings and strict ascription.

**charismatic authority**   Authority, according to Weber, that rests on devotion to the specific and exceptional sanctity, heroism, or exemplary character of an individual person.

**circulation mobility**   The amount of social mobility explained by exchange movement up and down the occupational structure.

**civil religion**   A mix of religion and nationalism wherein religion has come to reinforce the dominant political ideologies of the country.

**class**   In one of the most general definitions, a grouping of individuals with similar positions and similar political and economic interests within the stratification system. According to Max Weber, it is a dimension of social stratification based on property ownership or lack of ownership (as in Marxian theory) but also upon occupational skill level.

**class subcultures**   Beliefs, worldviews, values, and behavior associated with these attitudes that may differ with class position and result in somewhat different cultural groupings.

**class system**   A system of social stratification, primarily found in industrial societies, that is based mainly on economic position (though to some extent also on authority position) and involves a mix of ascription and achievement.

**codetermination laws**   The post–World War II German labor laws that provide employees with influence in the decision-making process within corporations through representation on the corporate board and elected works councils on the shop floor.

**colonized minority**    A minority group that has acquired minority status through involuntary means, such as being captured and brought to another country or having their home territory annexed by the dominant group.

**comparable worth**    Laws placing the same value to work requiring similar skill and complexity level for men and women in the labor force.

**conflict theory**    Theory that views conflicting interests and interest groups as the most important dimensions of the society, with social order maintained by an unequal distribution of power.

**continuous class rankings**    Considers class or stratum as ranks on a scale; there are positions from high to low, with numerous grades in between.

**core industries**    Industries within the dual economy that tend to have (1) a high concentration of corporate assets within the industry (a few large corporations do most of the business), (2) higher productivity, (3) higher profits, (4) more capital-intensive production, and (5) less economic competition.

**core nations**    The most economically diversified, wealthy, and powerful nations in the modern world system.

**corporate class**    A group of people with high authority and power in major corporations (through positions in top management or board positions), usually without extensive ownership in these corporations.

**culture-of-poverty theory**    The main points of the theory are that there is a subculture of poverty that has developed to allow the poor to cope with their position, which is in many ways counterproductive to getting out of poverty.

# D

**discontinuous class rankings**    Considers class divisions to have distinct boundaries and sees the divisions between classes as more important than differences within class divisions.

**dual economy**    An economy extensively divided between large, near-monopoly industries (core industries) and industries (periphery industries) with more competing firms, lower profits, less unionization, and lower wages.

**dual system**    The combination of labor representation by unions and legally mandated works councils in post–World War II Germany.

# E

**estate system/feudalism**    An agrarian system of social stratification based on land ownership with a high level of ascription.

**ethnic group**    A group of people relatively distinct in cultural background compared with the dominant group in the society.

# F

**frustration-aggression theory**    A theory that claims that racism and prejudice are the result of frustrations projected upon others who are weak in the society.

**functional theory**    A theory that views societies as holistic systems, with subsystems serving important tasks for the good of the whole, and held together primarily by a general consensus over the major values and norms in the society.

# G

**gender**    Socially acquired and socially defined sex-linked behavior expectations in a particular society.

**Gini index**    An index used to measure the level of inequality in a society by indicating how far the distribution deviates from a completely equal distribution of things such as income or wealth.

**glass ceiling**    The invisible barrier making it difficult for women to be promoted into higher positions of authority in corporate and government bureaucracies.

# H

**historical materialism**    The view that a society must be understood with a focus on the underlying material conditions (level and type of technology, geography, etc.) and how these material conditions have shaped the society.

**horizontal social mobility**   Intergenerational or intragenerational moves to occupations in the occupational structure considered to be of equal rank or status.

# I

**immigrant minority**   A minority group that has acquired minority status through voluntary immigration.

**indirect interlocks**   When two corporations are tied by their board members through a third corporation.

**individualism**   A value system stressing the greater importance of the individual and individual freedoms over groups' needs and restraints.

**industrial reserve army**   Workers who are poor and available to capitalists as cheap labor for maintaining profits in times of boom or periods of economic expansion.

**inner group of the corporate class**   The most powerful members of the corporate class, who have multiple corporate positions and often represent the corporate class in government and civic organizations as well.

**institutional discrimination**   Discrimination operating through primary institutions in the society (e.g., economy, schools, political system) in their normal operations when race and ethnic inequalities are high due to past discrimination and racism.

**intergenerational mobility**   Social mobility by adults from the occupational position of their parents.

**interlocking directorates**   The linking of two or more corporations through at least one of their board members.

**internal colonialism**   A theory of racism and discrimination that distinguishes between minorities who are "conquered peoples" and those who have not been. It is the conquered people within a country or brought to a country by the dominant group that experiences more racism and discrimination.

**intragenerational mobility**   Social mobility experienced by a person during his or her occupational career.

# K

**keiretsu**   Groups of corporations in modern Japan interlocked through mutual ownership, business ties, and corporate directors.

# L

**labor theory of value**   The theory that the value of any article is equal to the amount of labor socially necessary or the labor-time socially necessary for its production.

**legitimation**   A method or belief system for justifying the existence of inequality in a society.

**Lorenz curve**   A graphic measure indicating how much wealth or income is held by various percentages of the total population as opposed to an equal distribution.

**lower class**   Individuals and families with no property, who are often unemployed and have no authority, and are consequently poor.

# M

**means of production**   The type of technology used to produce basic necessities and other valued goods (such as hunting and gathering, agrarian methods of varying sophistication, machine technology).

**mechanical solidarity**   Durkheim's view of a rural or preindustrial society where social organization rests on close contact and common views of moral order.

**middle class**   Individuals and families with relatively little property but high to middle positions in occupation (nonmanual labor) and authority. Further distinction is made with respect to the upper middle class (lesser corporate managers, doctors, lawyers, and so forth) and lower middle class (office workers, clerks, salespeople).

**mode of production**   The overall set of economic factors within the Marxian concept of substructure.

**modern world system**   The system of unequal power and economic roles among nations similar to an international stratification system, which has developed since the 1500s.

**monopoly capitalism**   The later stages of capitalism, according to Marxian theory, where fewer and fewer capitalists own the means of production.

**multidimensional view of social stratification**   The perspective originated by Max Weber which argues that Marx's view of ownership versus nonownership of the means of production as the most important dimension of social stratification is too simple. Rather, Weber stresses that class, status, and power (or party) can be important dimensions behind stratification systems.

# N

**Neolithic revolution**   The emergence of simple horticulture about 10,000 years ago, which led to vast changes in most aspects of societies.

**nominalist definition of *class***   Places emphasis on the common characteristics groups of people may have that influence their life chances and share of valued rewards in the society, such as educational level, occupational position, or bureaucratic power position.

**norms of distributive justice**   Norms found in all societies that define what distribution of valued goods to whom is considered fair.

# O

**objective definition of *class***   A definition of *class* that stresses particular life chances or economic characteristics people may have in common as the most important, whether or not people are aware of these common characteristics.

**occupational structure**   One of the primary dimensions of class position in modern industrial societies, which pertains to a person's occupation and skill level, or what Weber referred to as one's relation to the marketplace.

**organic analogy**   The functionalist perspective of society resembling a living organism.

**organic solidarity**   Durkheim's view of industrial societies, where social order is possible through occupational organizations or guilds.

# P

**paradigms**   General images of reality that shape more specific theories and are based on untested and often unacknowledged assumptions (paradigm assumptions) about the nature of reality.

**pay equity**   Laws making it illegal to pay different wages to women and men doing similar tasks.

**periphery industries**   Industries within the dual economy that tend to have (1) less concentration of corporate assets within the industry (a few large corporations do not do most of the business), (2) lower productivity, (3) lower profits, (4) more labor-intensive production, and (5) more economic competition.

**periphery nations**   The least economically developed and diversified nations within the modern world system.

**postindustrial societies**   The most advanced societies, with economies based less in industrial production than in knowledge-based industries and services.

**poverty line**   An economic definition of poverty established by the Bureau of the Census through a determination of what it costs a family (of a certain size and place of residence) to buy food, housing, and other necessities.

**power/party**   The dimension of stratification, according to Max Weber, that is based on organization and authority as a means to influence others in the society.

**primitive communal societies**   The earliest forms of social organization based on simple hunting and gathering, normally with little inequality and no formal system of social stratification.

**progressive taxes**   Taxes that require the more affluent to pay at a higher percentage of their income or wealth.

**proletariat**   Urban industrial workers in a capitalist system who do not own the means of production.

**property structure**   Another of the primary dimensions of class in modern industrial societies, which refers to ownership or nonownership of the major means of production.

**Purchasing Power Parity (PPP)**   A means of comparing different currencies around the world based on what each currency can buy rather than the old method that used official exchange rates. This makes for a more realistic and stable method of comparing standards of living.

# R

**race**   Socially defined groupings of people assumed to have common biological characteristics that separate them from other people.

**rational-legal authority**   Authority, according to Weber, that rests on a belief in the "legality" of patterns of normative rules and the right of those elevated to authority under such rules to issue commands.

**realist definition of *class***   Places emphasis on clear class boundaries—people identifying themselves as members of a particular class and interacting most with others in the same class.

**regressive taxes**   Taxes that require the less affluent to pay more as a percentage of their income or wealth than do the more affluent.

**relations of production**   The human relationships within a given mode of production, such as the relationships between workers as dictated by the type of production (whether they work together and can interact in a mass-production setting or work in smaller settings or in isolation from other workers), the dominance–submission relationships among workers and authorities, and the ownership and distribution of valued goods in the society.

# S

**semiperiphery nations**   Nations in the modern world system midway between core and periphery with respect to economic development and diversification.

**shogun**   The leader of a military clan that had achieved dominance over most of Japan, backed by the landed aristocracy, with the emperor serving only as a figurehead.

**situational view of poverty**   Main points of the theory are that the poor may sometimes behave differently or have different lifestyles

and preferences *because* they are poor, but these differences are only temporary adjustments to a situation that does not prevent the poor from becoming nonpoor if opportunities to move out of poverty develop.

**slavery**   A system of social stratification in which there is extensive formal ownership of other human beings as a primary dimension of the economy.

**social Darwinism**   Based on the Darwinist idea of "survival of the fittest," the main point of the theory is that people are poor and on the bottom of society because they are unfit to survive the competition, and conversely, the rich and powerful are on top because they are the fittest.

**social differentiation**   The natural distinction among individuals with respect to their characteristics and social roles without the necessity of inequality or ranking.

**social inequality**   The condition whereby people have unequal access to valued resources, services, and positions in the society.

**social mobility**   Individual or group movement within the class system. We can speak of both vertical and horizontal mobility, or the movement of individuals up and down the class system compared with their movement across positions of roughly equal rank.

**social stratification**   The condition in which layered hierarchy and inequality has been hardened or *institutionalized,* and there is a *system of social relationships* that determines who gets what, and why.

**socioeconomic status scales**   Empirical measures of class position usually based primarily on occupational status position.

**split labor market**   A labor market that tends to separate people with certain characteristics and limits their movement into other labor markets.

**status**   Ranking based on honor or prestige within the society. According to Max Weber, the dimension of social stratification based on respect and following a specific honored lifestyle in the society.

**status attainment research**   Studies attempting to measure the exact mixture of achievement versus ascriptive factors that determines where people end up in the class system.

**status inconsistency** The condition in which individuals in the society have contradictory high and low positions on separate dimensions of social stratification.

**structural mobility** The amount of mobility in the stratification system accounted for by changes in the occupational structure.

**structural view of poverty** A perspective that argues that poverty can be understood and explained only with reference to political and economic characteristics of the society rather than any characteristics of the poor.

**subjective definition of** *class* A definition of *class* that argues that classes are real only when they have meaning to the people said to be in a particular class.

**substructure** The Marxian concept of the underlying economic base of the society, which shapes other aspects of a society.

**superstructure** The Marxian concept referring to aspects of societies (such as political systems, family system, religion) that are shaped by the economic substructure of the society.

## T

**traditional authority** Authority, according to Weber, that rests on an established belief in the sanctity of immemorial traditions and the legitimacy of the status of those exercising authority under them.

## U

**upper class** Old established families with significant ownership of major corporations and therefore extensive authority and economic power flowing from such ownership.

## V

**vertical social mobility** Movement from one occupational position to another of higher or lower rank.

## W

**wealthfare** Government services and resources provided for the affluent in the society.

**welfare state** A society in which the state has taken rather broad responsibility for social problems and the general social welfare of the population through direct provision of goods and services.

**working class** Individuals and families with little or no property, middle to low positions in occupation (manual labor), and little or no authority. A further distinction is made with respect to skilled and unskilled working class.

## Z

*zaibatsu* The pre–World War II interlocked groups of major family-owned corporations in Japan.

# References

Abegglen, James C., and George Stalk Jr. 1985. *Kaisha: The Japanese Corporation.* New York: Basic Books.

Abrahamson, Mark. 1973. "Functionalism and the Functional Theory of Stratification: An Empirical Assessment." *American Journal of Sociology,* 78:1236–1246.

Abrahamson, Mark. 1979. "A Functional Theory of Organizational Stratification." *Social Forces,* 58:128–145.

Acker, Joan. 1973. "Women and Social Stratification: A Case of Intellectual Sexism." *American Journal of Sociology,* 78:936–945.

Adorno, T. W., E. Frenkel-Brunswik, D. J. Levinson, and R. N. Sanford. 1950. *The Authoritarian Personality.* New York: Harper & Row.

Ainsworth, James W., and Vincent J. Roscigno. 2005. "Stratification, School-Work Linkages and Vocational Education." *Social Forces,* 84:257–284.

Ainsworth-Darnell, James W., and Douglas B. Downey. 1998. "Assessing the Oppositional Culture Explanation for Racial/Ethnic Differences in School Performance." *American Sociological Review,* 63:536–553.

Alba, Richard, and Gwen Moore. 1982. "Ethnicity in the American Elite." *American Sociological Review,* 47:373–383.

Alderson, Arthur S., and Jason Beckfield. 2004. "Power and Position in the World City System." *American Journal of Sociology,* 109:811–851.

Alderson, Arthur S., and Francois Nielsen. 1999. "Income Inequality, Development, and Dependence: A Reconsideration." *American Sociological Review,* 64:606–631.

Alderson, Arthur S., and Francois Nielsen. 2002. "Globalization and the Great U-Turn: Income Inequality Trends in 16 OECD Countries." *American Journal of Sociology,* 107:1244–1299.

Aldrich, Howard, and Jane Weiss. 1981. "Differentiation within the U.S. Capitalist Class: Workforce Size and Income Differences." *American Sociological Review,* 46:279–289.

Alesina, Alberto, Rafael Di Tella, and Robert MacCulloch. 2001. "Inequality and Happiness: Are Europeans and Americans Different?" National Bureau of Economic Research, Working Paper No. w8198, April, http://www.nber.org/papers/w8198.

Alexander, Karl, and Martha Cook. 1982. "Curricula and Coursework: A Surprise Ending to a Familiar Story." *American Sociological Review,* 47:626–640.

Alexander, Karl, Martha Cook, and Edward McDill. 1978. "Curriculum Tracking and Educational Stratification: Some Further Evidence." *American Sociological Review,* 43:47–66.

Alexander, Karl, Bruce Eckland, and Larry Griffin. 1975. "The Wisconsin Model of Socioeconomic Achievement." *American Journal of Sociology,* 81:324–342.

Allen, Michael. 1974. "The Structure of Interorganizational Elite Cooptation: Interlocking Corporate Directorates." *American Sociological Review,* 39:393–406.

Allen, Michael. 1977. "Economic Interest Groups and the Corporate Elite Structure." *Social Science Quarterly,* 58:597–615.

Allen, Michael. 1978. "Continuity and Change within the Core Corporate Elite." *Sociological Quarterly,* 19:510–521.

Allport, Gordon W. 1958. *The Nature of Prejudice.* New York: Doubleday.

Althusser, Louis. 1969. *For Marx.* Harmondsworth, England: Penguin Books.

Althusser, Louis. 1977. *Politics and History.* London: NLB.

Alves, Wayne, and Peter Rossi. 1978. "Who Should Get What? Fairness Judgments of Distribution of Earnings." *American Journal of Sociology,* 84:541–564.

Ammott, Teresa, and Julie Matthaei. 1996. *Race, Gender, and Work: A Multicultural Economic History of Women in the United States.* Boston: South End Press.

Amory, Cleveland. 1960. *Who Killed Society?* New York: Harper & Row.

Andersen, Margaret L. 1997. *Thinking about Women: Sociological Perspectives on Sex and Gender.* Boston: Allyn & Bacon.

Anderson, Charles. 1974. *The Political Economy of Social Class.* Upper Saddle River, N.J.: Prentice Hall.

Andrews, Frank, and Stephen Withey. 1976. *Social Indicators of Well-Being.* New York: Plenum.

Antonio, Robert. 1979. "The Contradiction of Domination and Production in Bureaucracy: The Contribution of Organizational Efficiency to the Decline of the Roman Empire." *American Sociological Review,* 44:895–912.

Appelbaum, Richard. 1978a. "Marxist Method: Structural Constraints and Social Praxis." *The American Sociologist,* 13:73–81.

Appelbaum, Richard. 1978b. "Marx's Theory of the Falling Rate of Profit: Towards a Dialectical Analysis of Structural Social Change." *American Sociological Review,* 43:67–80.

Aptheker, Herbert. 1963. *American Negro Slave Revolts.* New York: International Publishers.

Archer, Jules. 1973. *The Plot to Seize the White House.* New York: Hawthorn Books.

Aronowitz, Stanley. 1974. *False Promises: The Shaping of American Working Class Consciousness.* New York: McGraw-Hill.

Arrow, Kenneth, Samuel Bowles, and Steven Durlauf (eds.). 2000. *Meritocracy and Economic Inequality.* Princeton: Princeton University Press.

Aschaffenburg, Karen, and Ineke Mass. 1997. "Cultural and Educational Careers: The Dynamics of Social Reproduction." *American Sociological Review,* 62:573–587.

Astone, Nan Marie, and Sara S. McLanahan. 1991. "Family Structure, Parental Practices, and High School Completion." *American Sociological Review,* 56:309–320.

Atkinson, Dick. 1972. *Orthodox Consensus and Radical Alternative.* New York: Basic Books.

Atsuta Masanori. 1992. *Shinzaikai Jinretsuden* (Biography of the New Financial World Lineup). Tokyo: Yomiuri Shimbunsha.

Auletta, Ken. 1983. *The Under Class.* New York: Vintage Books.

Baker, P. M. 1977. "On the Use of Psychophysical Methods in the Study of Social Status: A Replication, and Some Theoretical Problems." *Social Forces,* 55:898–920.

Balkwell, James, Frederick Bates, and Albeno Garbin. 1980. "On the Intersubjectivity of Occupational Status Evaluations: A Test of a Key Assumption Underlying the 'Wisconsin Model' of Status Attainment." *Social Forces,* 58:865–881.

Baltzell, E. Digby. 1958. *Philadelphia Gentlemen: The Making of a National Upper Class.* New York: Free Press.

Baltzell, E. Digby. 1964. *The Protestant Establishment: Aristocracy and Caste in America.* New York: Random House.

Barash, David. 1977. "Reflections on a Premature Burial." *The American Sociologist,* 12:62–68.

Barger, Ben, and Everett Hall. 1965. "The Interaction of Ability Levels and Socioeconomic Variables in Prediction of College Dropouts and Grade Achievement." *Educational and Psychological Measurement,* 25:501–508.

Barnet, Richard, and Ronald Müller. 1974. *Global Reach.* New York: Simon & Schuster.

Baron, James, and William Bielby. 1980. "Bringing the Firms Back In: Stratification, Segmentation, and the Organization of Work." *American Sociological Review,* 45:737–766.

Baron, James, and William Bielby. 1984. "The Organization of Work in a Segmented Economy." *American Sociological Review,* 49:454–473.

Barrett, Richard, and Martin King Whyte. 1982. "Dependency Theory and Taiwan: Analysis of a Deviant Case." *American Journal of Sociology,* 87:1064–1089.

Barrett, Richard, and Martin King Whyte. 1984. "What Is Dependency? Reply to Hammer." *American Journal of Sociology,* 89:937–940.

Bayer, Alan. 1968. "The College Dropout: Factors Affecting Senior College Completion." *Sociology of Education,* 41:305–316.

Bearman, Peter S., and Glenn Deane. 1992. "The Structure of Opportunity: Middle-Class Mobility in England, 1548–1689." *American Journal of Sociology,* 98:30–66.

Beck, E. M., Patrick Horan, and Charles Tolbert. 1978. "Stratification in a Dual Economy: A Structural Model of Earnings Determination." *American Sociological Review,* 43:704–720.

Beck, E. M., Patrick Horan, and Charles Tolbert. 1980. "Social Stratification in Industrial Society: Further Evidence for a Structural Alternative." *American Sociological Review,* 45:712–719.

Beckfield, Jason. 2006. "European Integration and Income Inequality." *American Sociological Review,* 71:964–985

Behrendt, Christina. 2000. "Holes in the Safety Net? Social Security and the Alleviation of Poverty in Comparative Perspective." Luxembourg Income Study Working Paper No. 259.

Bell, Daniel. 1976. *The Coming of Post-Industrial Society.* New York: Basic Books.

Bell, Wendell, and Robert Robinson. 1980. "Cognitive Maps of Class and Racial Inequalities in England and the United States." *American Journal of Sociology,* 86:320–349.

Bellah, Robert. 1970. *Beyond Belief.* New York: Harper & Row.

Bellah, Robert N., Richard Madsen, William M. Sullivan, Ann Swidler, and Steven M. Tipton. 1985. *Habits of the Heart: Individualism and Commitment in American Life.* New York: Harper & Row.

Bellas, Marcia L. 1994. "Comparable Worth in Academia: The Effects on Faculty Salaries of the Sex Composition and Labor-Market Conditions of Academic Disciplines." *American Sociological Review,* 59:807–821.

Beller, Emily. 2009. "Bringing Intergenerational Social Mobility Research into the Twenty-First Century: Why Mothers Matter." *American Sociological Review,* 74:507–528.

Bendix, Reinhard. 1960. *Max Weber: An Intellectual Portrait.* New York: Doubleday.

Bendix, Reinhard. 1978. *Kings or People: Power and the Mandate to Rule.* Berkeley: University of California Press.

Bendix, Reinhard, and Frank Howton. 1959. "Social Mobility and the American Business Elite." Pp. 114–143 in Reinhard Bendix and Seymour Lipset (eds.), *Social Mobility in Industrial Society.* Berkeley: University of California Press.

Benini, Aldo. 2000. *Modern Switzerland.* New York: McGraw-Hill.

Berger, J., M. Zelditch, B. Anderson, and B. P. Cohen. 1972. "Structural Aspects of Distributive Justice: A Status Value Formulation." Pp. 111–129 in J. Berger, M. Zelditch, and B. Anderson (eds.), *Sociological Theories in Progress,* vol. 2. Boston: Houghton Mifflin.

Berger, Peter, and Thomas Luckman. 1966. *The Social Construction of Reality.* Garden City, N.Y.: Doubleday.

Berle, Adolf. 1959. *Power without Property.* New York: Harcourt Brace Jovanovich.

Berle, Adolf, and Gardiner Means. 1932. *The Modern Corporation and Private Property.* New York: Macmillan.

Berlin, Isaiah. 1963. *Karl Marx: His Life and Environment.* New York: Oxford University Press.

Beteille, Andre. 1996. *Caste, Class and Power: Changing Patterns of Stratification in a Tanjore Village.* 2nd ed. New Delhi: Oxford University Press.

Betz, Michael. 1974. "Riots and Welfare: Are They Related?" *Social Problems,* 21:345–355.

Bian, Yanjie. 1997. "Bringing Strong Ties Back In: Indirect Ties, Network Bridges, and Job Searches in China." *American Sociological Review,* 62:366–385.

Biblarz, Timothy J., and Adrian E. Raftery. 1993. "The Effects of Family Disruption on Social Mobility." *American Sociological Review,* 58:97–109.

Bielby, William T., and James N. Baron. 1986. "Men and Women at Work: Sex Segregation and Statistical Discrimination." *American Journal of Sociology,* 91:759–799.

Birchfield, Vicki. 2008. *Income Inequality in Capitalist Democracies: The Interplay of Values and Institutions.* University Park, PA: Pennsylvania State University Press.

Blair, Margaret M. 1995. Ownership and Control: Rethinking Corporate Governance for the Twenty-First Century. Washington, D.C.: Brookings Institution Press.

Blank, Rebecca. 1997. *It Takes a Nation.* Princeton, N.J.: Princeton University Press.

Blau, Judith, and Peter Blau. 1982. "The Cost of Inequality: Metropolitan Structure and Violent Crime." *American Sociological Review,* 47:114–129.

Blau, Peter, and Otis Dudley Duncan. 1967. *The American Occupational Structure.* New York: John Wiley & Sons.

Blauner, Robert. 1972. *Racial Progression in America.* New York: Harper & Row.

Bloch, Marc. 1961. *Feudal Society.* London: Routledge & Kegan Paul.

Block, Fred, Richard A. Cloward, Barbara Ehrenreich, and Frances Fox Piven. 1987. *The Mean Season: The Attack on the Welfare State.* New York: Pantheon.

Bloomquist, Leonard, and Gene Summer. 1982. "Organization of Production and Community Income Distributions." *American Sociological Review,* 47:325–338.

Bluestone, Barry. 1988. "The Great U-Turn: An Inquiry into Recent U.S. Economic Trends in Employment, Earnings and Family Income." Paper presented to the Sapporo Seminar in American Studies, Sapporo, Japan. Hokkaido University, August 1988.

Bluestone, Barry, and Bennett Harrison. 1982. *The Deindustrialization of America.* New York: Basic Books.

Blumberg, Paul. 1980. *Inequality in an Age of Decline.* New York: Oxford University Press.

Blumberg, Paul, and P. W. Paul. 1975. "Continuities and Discontinuities in Upper-Class Marriages." *Journal of Marriage and Family,* 37:63–77.

Blyth, Mark. 2002. *Great Transformations: Economic Ideas and Institutional Change in the Twentieth Century.* New York: Cambridge University Press.

Bolin, Robert, and Susan Bolton Bolin. 1980. "Sociobiology and Paradigms in Evolutionary Theory." *American Sociological Review,* 45:154–159.

Bollen, Kenneth A., and Stephen J. Appold. 1993. "National Industrial Structure and the Global System." *American Sociological Review,* 58:283–301.

Bonacich, Edna. 1972. "A Theory of Ethnic Antagonism: The Split Labor Market." *American Sociological Review,* 37:547–559.

Bonacich, Edna. 1975. "Abolition, the Extension of Slavery, and the Position of Free Blacks: A Study of Split Labor Markets in the United States, 1830–1863." *American Journal of Sociology,* 81:601–628.

Bonacich, Edna. 1976. "Advanced Capitalism and Black/White Relations in the United States: A Split Labor Market Interpretation." *American Sociological Review,* 41:34–51.

Bornschier, Volker. 1988. *Westliche Gesellschaft im Wandel* (Western Society in Transition). Frankfurt: Campus.

Bornschier, Volker. 1994. "The Rise of the European Community: Grasping toward Hegemony? or Therapy against National Decline?" *International Journal of Sociology,* 24:62–96.

Bornschier, Volker. 1995. *Western Society in Transition.* New Brunswick, N.J.: Transaction Press.

Bornschier, Volker, and Christopher Chase-Dunn. 1985. *Transnational Corporations and Underdevelopment.* New York: Praeger.

Bornschier, Volker, Christopher Chase-Dunn, and Richard Rubinson. 1978. "Cross-National Evidence of the Effects of Foreign Investment and Aid on Economic Growth and Inequality: A Survey of Findings and a Reanalysis." *American Journal of Sociology,* 84:651–683.

Bornschier, Volker, and Christian Suter. 1992. "Long Waves in the World System." Pp. 15–50 in Volker Bornschier and Peter Lengyel (eds.), *Waves, Formations and Values in the World System: World Society Studies,* vol. 2. New Brunswick, N.J.: Transaction Press.

Bornschier, Volker, and Thank-Huyen Ballmer-Cao. 1979. "Income Inequality: A Cross-National Study of the Relationships between MNC-Penetration, Dimensions of the Power Structure and Income Distribution." *American Sociological Review,* 44:487–506.

Boswell, Terry. 1989. "Colonial Empires and the Capitalist World Economy: A Time Series Analysis of Colonization, 1640–1960." *American Sociological Review,* 54:169–180.

Bottomore, Thomas B (ed.). 1973. *Karl Marx.* Upper Saddle River, N.J.: Prentice Hall.

Bougle, C. 1958. "The Essence and Reality of the Caste System." Pp. 64–73 in Dipankar Gupta (ed.), *Social Stratification.* Delhi: Oxford University Press, 1991.

Bourdieu, Pierre. 1977. "Cultural Reproduction and Social Reproductions." Pp. 487–511 in J. Karabel and A. H. Halsey (eds.), *Power and Ideology in Education.* New York: Oxford University Press.

Bourdieu, Pierre. 1984. *Distinction: A Social Critique of the Judgement of Taste.* Cambridge, Mass.: Harvard University Press.

Bourdieu, Pierre. 1993. *The Field of Cultural Production: Essays on Art and Leisure.* New York: Columbia University Press.

Bourdieu, Pierre. 1996. *The State Nobility.* Palo Alto, Calif.: Stanford University Press.

Bourdieu, Pierre, and Jean-Claude Passeron. 1990. *Reproduction in Education, Society, and Culture.* 2nd ed. London: Sage.

Bowker, Lee. 1972. "Red and Black in Contemporary American History Texts: A Content Analysis." Pp. 101–109 in Howard Bahr, Bruce Chadwick, and Robert Day (eds.), *Native Americans Today: Sociological Perspectives.* New York: Harper & Row.

Bowles, S., and H. Gintis. 1976. *Schooling in Capitalist America: Educational Reform and the Contradictions of Economic Life.* New York: Basic Books.

Bradburn, N. M., and David Caplovitz. 1965. *Reports on Happiness.* Chicago: Aldine.

Brady, David. 2003a. "The Politics of Poverty: Left Political Institutions, the Welfare State, and Poverty." *Social Forces,* 82:557–588.

Brady, David. 2003b. "Rethinking the Sociological Measurement of Poverty." *Social Forces,* 81:715–751.

Brady, David. 2005. "The Welfare State and Relative Poverty in Rich Western Democracies, 1967–1997." *Social Forces,* 83:1329–1364.

Brady, David. 2006. "Economic Globalization, Industrialization and Deindustrialization in Affluent Democracies." *Social Forces,* 85:297–329.

Brady, David, Jason Beckfield, and Martin Seeleib-Kaiser. 2005. "Economic Globalization and the Welfare State in Affluent Democracies, 1975–2001." *American Sociological Review,* 70:921–948.

Brady, David, and Ryan Denniston. 2006. "Economic Globalization, Industrialization and Deindustrialization in Affluent Democracies." *Social Forces,* 85:297–329.

Breedlove, William L., and Patrick D. Nolan. 1988. "International Stratification and Inequality 1960–1980." *International Journal of Contemporary Sociology,* 25:105–123.

Breen, Richard. 1997. "Inequality, Economic Growth, and Social Mobility." *British Journal of Sociology,* 48:429–449.

Breen, Richard, Ruud Luijkx, Walter Müller, and Reinhard Pollak. 2009. "Nonpersistent Inequality in Educational Attainment: Evidence from Eight European Countries." *American Journal of Sociology,* ll4:1475–1521.

Briar, Scott. 1966. "Welfare from Below: Recipients' Views of the Public Welfare System." Pp. 73–95 in Jacobus Ten Broek (ed.), *The Law of the Poor.* San Francisco: Chandler.

Brinton, Mary C., Yean-Ju Lee, and William Parish. 1995. "Married Women's Employment in Rapidly Industrializing Societies: Examples from East Asia." *American Journal of Sociology,* 100:1099–1131.

Brooks, Clem, and Jeff Manza. 1997a. "The Social and Ideological Bases of Middle-Class Political Realignment in the United States, 1972–1992." *American Sociological Review,* 62:191–208.

Brooks, Clem, and Jeff Manza. 1997b. "Social Cleavages and Political Alignments: U.S. Presidential Elections, 1960–1992." *American Sociological Review,* 62:937–946.

Brooks, Clem, and Jeff Manza. 2006. "Social Policy Responsiveness in Developed Democracies." *American Sociological Review,* 71:474–494.

Broom, Leonard, and Robert Cushing. 1977. "A Modest Test of an Immodest Theory: The Functional Theory of Stratification." *American Sociological Review,* 42:157–169.

Broom, Leonard, and William L. Shay Jr. 1992. "German Billionaires and the Fortunes of War." Unpublished working paper.

Brown, Dee. 1970. *Bury My Heart at Wounded Knee: An Indian History of the American West.* New York: Holt, Rinehart and Winston.

Brownstein, Ronald, and Nina Easton. 1983. *Reagan's Ruling Class: Portraits of the President's Top One Hundred Officials.* New York: Pantheon.

Brunt, P. A. 1971. *Social Conflicts in the Roman Republic.* London: Chatto & Windus.

Budig, Michelle J., and Paula England. 2001. "The Wage Penalty for Motherhood." *American Sociological Review,* 66:204–225.

Burbank, Garin. 1976. *When Farmers Voted Red: The Gospel of Socialism in the Oklahoma Countryside, 1910–1924.* Westport, Conn.: Greenwood Press.

Burch, Philip H. 1981. *Elites in American History,* vols. 1–3. New York: Holmes and Meier.

Burger, Thomas. 1977. "Talcott Parsons, the Problem of Order in Society, and the Program of an Analytical Sociology." *American Journal of Sociology,* 83:320–334.

Burris, Val. 2005. "Interlocking Directorates and Political Cohesion among Corporate Elites." *American Journal of Sociology,* 111:249–283.

Burris, Val. 2008. "Interlocking Directorates and Political Cohesion among Corporate Elites." *Research in Political Sociology,* 17:3–42.

Burt, Ronald S., Kenneth P. Christman, and Harold C. Kilburn Jr. 1980. "Testing a Structural Theory of Corporate Cooptation: Inter-Organizational Directorate Ties as a Strategy for Avoiding Market Constraints on Profits." *American Sociological Review,* 45:821–841.

Calhoun, Craig, Edward Lipuma, and Moishe Postone (eds.). 1993. *Bourdieu: Critical Perspectives.* Chicago: University of Chicago Press.

Carnevale, Anthony P., and Stephen J. Rose. 2004. *Socioeconomic Status, Race/Ethnicity, and Selective College Admissions.* New York: A Century Foundation Paper.

Casper, L., and L. E. Bass. 1998. *Voting and Registration in the Election of November 1996.* Washington D.C.: Current Population Reports, pp. 20–504.

Casper, Lynne M., Sara S. McLanahan, and Irwin Garfinkel. 1994. "The Gender-Poverty Gap: What We Can Learn from Other Countries." *American Sociological Review,* 1994:594–605.

Cerulo, Karen. 1984. "Television, Magazine Covers, and the Shared Symbolic Environment: 1948–1970." *American Sociological Review,* 49:566–570.

Chafetz, Janet Saltzman. 1984. *Sex and Advantage: A Comparative, Macro-Structural Theory of Sex Stratification.* Totowa, N.J.: Rowman & Allanheld.

Chafetz, Janet Saltzman. 1988. *Feminist Sociology: An Overview of Contemporary Theories.* Itasca, Ill.: Peacock Publishers.

Chafetz, Janet Saltzman. 1990. *Gender Equity: An Integrated Theory of Stability and Change.* Newbury Park, Calif.: Sage.

Chaiyan, Rajchagool. 1994. *The Rise and Fall of the Thai Absolute Monarchy.* Bangkok: White Lotus Press.

Chan, Tak Wing, and John Goldthorpe. 2007a."Class and Status: The Conceptual Distinction and Its Empirical Relevance." *American Sociological Review,* 72:512–532.

Chan, Tak Wing, and John Goldthorpe. 2007b. "Social Status and Newspaper Readership." *American Journal of Sociology,* 122:1095–1134.

Chanda, Areendam, and Louis Putterman. 2005. "State Effectiveness, Economic Growth, and the Age of States." Pp. 69–91 in Matthew Lange and Dietrich Rueschemeyer (eds.), *States and Development: Historical Antecedents of Stagnation and Advance.* New York: Palgrave MacMillian.

Chanda, Nayan. 2007. *Bound Together: How Traders, Preachers, Adventurers, and Warriors Shaped Globalization.* New Haven: Yale University Press.

Chandler, David P. 1998. *A History of Cambodia.* Chiang Mai, Thailand: Silkworm Books.

Chandler, David P. 1999. *The Tragedy of Cambodian History: Politics, War, and Revolution Since 1945.* Chiang Mai, Thailand: Silkworm Books.

Charles, Maria, and Karen Bradley. 2002. "Equal but Separate? A Cross-National Study of Sex Segregation in Higher Education." *American Sociological Review,* 67:573–599.

Chase, Ivan. 1975. "A Comparison of Men's and Women's Intergenerational Mobility in the United States." *American Sociological Review,* 40:483–505.

Chase-Dunn, Christopher. 1975. "The Effects of International Economic Dependence on Development and Inequality: A Cross-National Study." *American Sociological Review,* 40:720–738.

Chase-Dunn, Christopher. 1989. *Global Formation: Structures of the World-Economy.* Oxford: Basil Blackwell.

Chase-Dunn, Christopher, Yukio Kawano, and Benjamin D. Brewer. 2000. "Trade Globalization Since 1795: Waves of Integration in the World System." *American Sociological Review,* 65:77–95.

Cheffins, Brian R. 2003. "Will Executive Pay Globalise Along American Lines?" *Corporate Governance,* 11:1.

Cheong, Yong Mun. 1999. "The Political Structures of the Independent States." Pp. 59–138 in Nicholas Tarling (ed.), *The Cambridge History of Southeast Asia: From World War II to the Present,* vol. 4. Cambridge, England: Cambridge University Press.

Chibber, Vivek. 2002. "Bureaucratic Rationality and the Development State." *American Journal of Sociology,* 107:951–989.

Childe, V. Gordon. 1952. *New Light on the Most Ancient East.* London: Routledge & Kegan Paul.

Chirot, Daniel. 1977. *Social Change in the Twentieth Century.* New York: Harcourt Brace Jovanovich.

Chirot, Daniel. 1984. "The Rise of the West." *American Sociological Review,* 50:181–195.

Chirot, Daniel. 1986. *Social Change in the Modern Era*. New York: Harcourt Brace College Publishers.

Chodorow, Nancy. 1978. *The Reproduction of Mothering: Psychoanalysis and the Sociology of Gender*. Berkeley: University of California Press.

CHRAC (Cambodian Human Rights Action Committee). 2009. *Losing Ground: Forced Evictions and Intimidation in Cambodia*. http://www.chrac.org/eng/.

Christopher, Robert. 1983. *The Japanese Mind: The Goliath Explained*. New York: Simon & Schuster.

Claiborn, W. L. 1969. "Expectancy Effects in the Classroom: A Failure to Replicate." *Journal of Educational Psychology,* 60:377–383.

Clark, Kenneth. 1969. *Civilization*. New York: Harper & Row.

Clark, Rodney. 1979. *The Japanese Company*. Tokyo: Tuttle.

Clark, Ronald. 1971. *Einstein: The Life and Times*. New York: Times Mirror World Publishing.

Clark, Terry Nichols, and Seymour Martin Lipset (eds.). 2001. *The Breakdown of Class Politics: A Debate on Post-Industrial Stratification*. Washington, D.C.: Woodrow Wilson Center Press.

Clark, Terry Nichols, Seymour Martin Lipset, and Michael Rempel. 2001. "The Declining Political Significance of Social Class." Pp. 77–104 in Terry Nichols Clark and Seymour Martin Lipset (eds.), *The Breakdown of Class Politics: A Debate on Post-Industrial Stratification*. Washington, D.C.: Woodrow Wilson Center Press.

Coe, Richard. 1978. "Dependency and Poverty in the Short and Long Run." In G. J. Duncan and J. N. Morgan (eds.), *Five Thousand American Families—Patterns of Economic Progress,* vol. 6. Ann Arbor: Institute for Social Research, University of Michigan Press.

Cohen, Albert K., and Harold Hodges. 1963. "Characteristics of the Lower-Blue-Collar Classes." *Social Problems,* 10:303–334.

Cohen, Jere, Lawrence Hazelrigg, and Whitney Pope. 1975. "De-Parsonizing Weber." *American Sociological Review,* 40:229–241.

Cohen, Mark. 1977. *The Food Crisis in Prehistory: Overpopulation and the Origins of Agriculture*. New Haven: Yale University Press.

Cohen, Percy. 1968. *Modern Sociological Theory*. New York: Basic Books.

Cohen, Philip N., and Matt L. Huffman. 2003. "Occupational Segregation and the Devaluation of Women's Work Across U.S. Labor Markets." *Social Forces,* 81:881–908.

Cole, Stephen, and Robert Lejeune. 1972. "Illness and the Legitimation of Failure." *American Sociological Review,* 37:347–356.

Colignon, Richard A., and Chikako Usui. 2003. *Amakudari: The Hidden Fabric of Japan's Economy*. Ithaca, N.Y.: Cornell University Press.

Collier, Peter, and David Horowitz. 1976. *The Rockefellers: An American Dynasty*. New York: Holt, Rinehart and Winston.

Collins, Randall. 1971. "Functional and Conflict Theories of Educational Stratification." *American Sociological Review,* 36:1002–1019.

Collins, Randall. 1975. *Conflict Sociology*. New York: Academic Press.

Collins, Randall. 1979. *The Credential Society: A Historical Sociology of Education and Stratification*. New York: Academic Press.

Collins, Randall. 1997. "Religious Economy and the Emergence of Capitalism in Japan." *American Sociological Review,* 62:843–865.

Collins, Robert. 1977. "Positive Business Responses to the New Deal: The Roots of the Committee for Economic Development, 1933–1942." *Business History Review,* 22:103–119.

Coltrane, Scott. 1989. "Household Labor and the Routine Production of Gender." *Social Problems,* 36, No. 5:473–490.

Connell, B. W. 1987. *Gender and Power*. Palo Alto, Calif.: Stanford University Press.

Conradt, David P. 1978. *The German Polity.* New York: Longman.

Cookson, Peter W., Jr., and Caroline Hodges Persell. 1985. *Preparing for Power: America's Elite Boarding Schools.* New York: Basic Books.

Corcoran, Mary. 2001. "Mobility, Persistence, and the Consequences of Poverty for Children: Child and Adult Outcomes." Pp. 127–161 in Sheldon H. Danziger and Robert H. Haveman (eds.), *Understanding Poverty.* Cambridge, Mass.: Harvard University Press.

Cornfield, Daniel B. 1991. "The U.S. Labor Movement: Its Development and Impact on Social Inequality and Politics." *Annual Review of Sociology,* 17:27–49.

Correll, Shelley. 2001. "Gender and the Career Choice Process: The Role of Biased Self-Assessments." *American Journal of Sociology,* 106:1691–1730.

Correll, Shelley. 2004. "Constraints into Preferences: Gender, Status, and Emerging Career Aspirations." *American Sociological Review,* 69:93–113.

Coser, Lewis. 1956. *The Functions of Social Conflict.* New York: Free Press.

Coser, Lewis. 1967. *Continuities in the Study of Social Conflict.* New York: Free Press.

Cox, Oliver. 1948. *Caste, Class and Race.* Garden City, N.Y.: Doubleday.

Coxon, A.P.M., P. M. Davies, and C. L. Jones. 1986. *Images of Social Stratification: Occupational Structures and Class.* London: Sage.

Craig, Gordon A. 1991. *The Germans.* New York: Meridian.

Crankshaw, Edward. 1976. *The Shadow of the Winter Palace: Russia's Drift to Revolution, 1825–1917.* New York: Viking Press.

Crippen, Timothy. 1994. "Toward a Neo-Darwin Sociology: Its Nomological Principles and Some Illustrative Applications." *Sociological Perspectives,* 37:309–335.

Cuber, John, and William Kenkel. 1954. *Social Stratification in the United States.* New York: Appleton-Century-Crofts.

Cummings, Scott, and Del Taebel. 1978. "The Economic Socialization of Children: A Neo-Marxist Analysis." *Social Problems,* 26:198–210.

Dahrendorf, Ralf. 1959. *Class and Class Conflict in Industrial Society.* Stanford, Calif.: Stanford University Press.

Dahrendorf, Ralf. 1968. *Essays in the Theory of Society.* Stanford, Calif.: Stanford University Press.

Dahrendorf, Ralf. 1979. *Society and Democracy in Germany.* New York: W.W. Norton.

Daloz, Jean-Pascal.2010. *The Sociology of Elite Distinction: From Theoretical to Comparative Perspectives.* London: Palgrave.

Danziger, Sheldon H., and Peter Gottschalk. 1995. *America Unequal.* New York and Cambridge, Mass.: Russell Sage and Harvard University Press.

Danziger, Sheldon H., and Robert H. Haveman (eds.). 2001. *Understanding Poverty.* Cambridge, Mass.: Harvard University Press.

Danziger, Sheldon, Robert H. Haveman, and Robert D. Plotnick. 1986. "Antipoverty Policy: Effects on the Poor and the Nonpoor." Pp. 50–77 in Sheldon H. Danziger and Daniel H. Weinberg (eds.), *Fighting Poverty: What Works and What Doesn't.* Cambridge, Mass.: Harvard University Press.

Davies, Norman. 1996. *Europe: A History.* New York: Oxford University Press.

Davis, Gerald F., Kristina A. Diekmann, and Catherine H. Tinsley. 1994. "The Decline and Fall of the Conglomerate Firm in the 1980s: The Deinstitutionalization of an Organizational Form." *American Sociological Review,* 59:547–570.

Davis, James, Susanna Sandstrom, Anthony Shorrocks, and Edward Wolff. 2006. "World Distribution of Household Wealth." United Nations, www.un.org.

Davis, Kingsley. 1948. *Human Societies.* New York: Macmillan.

Davis, Kingsley, and Wilbert Moore. 1945. "Some Principles of Stratification." *American Sociological Review,* 10:242–249.

de Beer, Paul, Cok Vrooman, and Jean Marie Wildeboer Schut. 2001. "Measuring Welfare State Performance: Three or Two Worlds of Welfare Capitalism?" Luxembourg Income Study Working Paper No. 276.

De Casparis, J. G., and I. W. Mabbett. 1999. "Religion and Popular Beliefs of Southeast Asia before c. 1500." Pp. 276–339 in Nicholas Tarling (ed.), *The Cambridge History of Southeast Asia, From Early Times to c. 1500, Volume One, Part One.* Cambridge, England: Cambridge University Press.

De Graaf, Nan Dirk, and Hendrik Derk Flap. 1988. " 'With a Little Help from My Friends': Social Resources as an Explanation of Occupational Status and Income in West Germany, the Netherlands, and the United States." *Social Forces,* 67:452–472.

De Jong, Peter, Milton Brawer, and Stanley Robin. 1971. "Patterns of Female Intergenerational Occupational Mobility: A Comparison with Male Patterns of Intergenerational Occupational Mobility." *American Sociological Review,* 36:1035–1042.

Della Fave, L. Richard. 1974a. "Success Values: Are They Universal or Class-Differentiated?" *American Journal of Sociology,* 80:153–169.

Della Fave, L. Richard. 1974b. "The Culture of Poverty Revisited: A Strategy for Research." *Social Problems,* 21:609–621.

Della Fave, L. Richard. 1974c. "On the Structure of Egalitarianism." *Social Problems,* 22:199–213.

Della Fave, L. Richard. 1980. "The Meek Shall Not Inherit the Earth: Self-Evaluation and the Legitimacy of Stratification." *American Sociological Review,* 45:955–971.

Della Fave, L. Richard. 1986. "Toward an Explication of the Legitimation Process." *Social Forces,* 65:476–500.

Demo, David, and Ritch Savin-Williams. 1983. "Early Adolescent Self-Esteem as a Function of Social Class: Rosenberg and Pearlin Revisited." *American Journal of Sociology,* 88:763–774.

Demos. 2002. *New Opportunities?: Public Opinion on Poverty, Income Inequality, and Public Policy, 1996–2001.* New York: Demos: A Network for Ideas and Action, http://www.demos-usa.org.

Denton, Nancy, and Douglas Massey. 1989. "Residential Segregation of Blacks, Hispanics, and Asians by Socioeconomic Status and Gender." *Social Science Quarterly,* 69:797–818.

de Soysa, Indra, and John R. Oneal. 1999. "Boon or Bane?: Reassessing the Productivity of Foreign Direct Investment." *American Sociological Review,* 64:766–782.

de Tocqueville, Alexis. 1969. *Democracy in America.* New York: Doubleday.

Devine, Fiona. 1997. *Social Class in America and Britain.* Edinburgh, Scotland: Edinburgh University Press.

Devine, Fiona. 2004. *Class Practices: How Parents Help Their Children Get Good Jobs.* Cambridge: Cambridge University Press.

Devine, Joel A. 1983. "Fiscal Policy and Class Income Inequality: The Distributional Consequences of Governmental Revenues and Expenditures in the United States, 1949–1976." *American Sociological Review,* 48:606–622.

Diamond, D. E., and H. Bedrosian. 1970. *Hiring Standards and Job Performance.* Washington, D.C.: U.S. Government Printing Office.

Dierichs, Claudia, and Harold Kerbo. 1999. "Japan's Political Class." In Jens Borchert (ed.), *Politics as a Vocation: The Political Class in Western Democracies.* Oxford, England: Oxford University Press.

Dietrich, William S. 1991. *In the Shadow of the Rising Sun: The Political Roots of American Economic Decline.* University Park: Pennsylvania State University Press.

DiMaggio, Paul. 1982. "Cultural Capital and School Success: The Impact of Status Culture Participation on Grades of U.S. High School Students." *American Sociological Review,* 47:189–201.

DiMaggio, Paul, and John Mohr. 1985. "Cultural Capital, Educational Attainment, and Marital Selection." *American Journal of Sociology,* 90:1231–1261.

DiMaggio, Paul J., and Walter W. Powell. 1983. "The Iron Cage Revisited: Institutional Isomorphism and Collective Rationality in Organizational Fields." *American Sociological Review,* 48:147–160.

DiPrete, Thomas A., and Patricia A. McManus. 1996. "Institutions, Technical Change, and Diverging Life Chances: Earnings Mobility in the United States and Germany." *American Journal of Sociology,* 102:34–79.

Di Tella, Rafael, and Robert MacCulloch. 2001. "Inequality and Happiness: Are Europeans and Americans Different?" National Bureau of Economic Research, http://www.nber.org/papers/w8198.

Dollard, John, et al. 1939. *Frustration and Aggression.* New Haven: Yale University Press.

Domhoff, G. William. 1967. *Who Rules America?* Upper Saddle River, N.J.: Prentice Hall.

Domhoff, G. William. 1970. *The Higher Circles.* New York: Random House.

Domhoff, G. William. 1974. *The Bohemian Grove and Other Retreats.* New York: Harper & Row.

Domhoff, G. William. 1975. "Social Clubs, Policy-Planning Groups, and Corporations: A Network Study of Ruling-Class Cohesiveness." *The Insurgent Sociologist,* 5:173–184.

Domhoff, G. William. 1979. *The Powers That Be.* New York: Vintage Press.

Domhoff, G. William. 1983. *Who Rules America Now?: A View for the '80s.* Upper Saddle River, N.J.: Prentice Hall.

Domhoff, G. William. 1990. *The Power Elite and the State.* New York: Aldine.

Domhoff, G. William. 1998. *Who Rules America?: Power and Politics in the Year 2000.* Mountain View, Calif.: Mayfield.

Domhoff, G. William. 2002. *Who Rules America?: Power and Politics.* 4th ed. New York: McGraw-Hill.

Domhoff, G. William. 2006a. *Who Rules America.* 5th ed. New York: McGraw-Hill.

Domhoff, G. William. 2006b. "Mills's *The Power Elite* 50 Years Later." *Contemporary Sociology,* 35:547–550.

Domhoff, G. William. 2010. *Who Rules America?: Challenges to Corporate and Class Dominance.* 6th ed. New York: McGraw-Hill.

Domhoff, G. William, and Hoyt Ballard (eds.). 1968. *C. Wright Mills and "The Power Elite."* Boston: Beacon Press.

Doner, Richard. 2009. *The Politics of Uneven Development: Thailand's Economic Growth in Comparative Perspective.* Cambridge: Cambridge University Press.

Dore, Ronald. 1987. *Taking Japan Seriously.* Stanford, Calif.: Stanford University Press.

Downes, Bryan T. 1970. "A Critical Reexamination of the Social and Political Characteristics of Riot Cities." *Social Science Quarterly,* 51:349–360.

Dube, Saurabh. 1998. *Untouchable Pasts: Religion, Identity, and Power among a Central India Community, 1780–1950.* Albany N.Y.: SUNY Press.

Dukas, Helen, and Banesh Hoffman. 1979. *Albert Einstein: The Human Side, New Glimpses from His Archives.* Princeton, N.J.: Princeton University Press.

Dumont, Louis. 1970. *Homo Hierarchius: The Caste System and Its Implications.* Chicago: University of Chicago Press.

Duncan, Greg, and Jeanne Brooks-Gunn (eds.). 1997. *Consequences of Growing Up Poor.* New York: Russell Sage Foundation.

Duncan, Greg J., and Saul D. Hoffman. 1991. "Teenage Underclass Behavior and Subsequent Poverty: Have the Rules Changed?" Pp. 155–174 in Christopher Jencks and Paul E. Peterson (eds.), *The Urban Underclass.* Washington, D.C.: Brookings Institution Press.

Duncan, Greg J., and Willard Rodgers. 1991. "Has Children's Poverty Become More Persistent?" *American Sociological Review,* 56:538–550.

Duncan, Greg J., W. Jean Yeung, Jeanne Brooks-Gunn, and Judith R. Smith. 1998. "How Much Does Childhood Poverty Affect the Life Chances of Children?" *American Sociological Review,* 63:406–423.

Duncan, Otis Dudley. 1965. "The Trend of Occupational Mobility in the United States." *American Sociological Review,* 30:491–498.

Duncan, Otis Dudley. 1966. "Methodological Issues in the Analysis of Social Mobility." Pp. 51–97 in Niel Smelser and Seymour Lipset (eds.), *Social Structure and Mobility in Economic Development.* Chicago: Aldine.

Durkheim, Émile. 1951. *Suicide.* New York: Free Press.

Durkheim, Émile. 1962. *Socialism.* Edited with an Introduction by Alvin Gouldner. New York: Collier Books.

Durkheim, Émile. 1964. *The Division of Labor in Society.* New York: Free Press.

Dutton, Diana. 1978. "Explaining the Low Use of Health Services by the Poor: Costs, Attitudes, or Delivery Systems?" *American Sociological Review,* 43:348–367.

Dye, Thomas R. 1979. *Who's Running America?* Upper Saddle River, N.J.: Prentice Hall.

Dye, Thomas R. 1983. *Who's Running America?: The Reagan Years.* Upper Saddle River, N.J.: Prentice Hall.

Dye, Thomas R. 1990. *Who's Running America?: The Bush Era.* 5th ed. Upper Saddle River, N.J.: Prentice Hall.

Dye, Thomas R. 1995. *Who's Running America?: The Clinton Years.* 6th ed. Upper Saddle River, N.J.: Prentice Hall.

Eckstein, Susan. 2001. "Community as Gift-Giving: Collectivistic Roots of Volunteerism." *American Sociological Review,* 66:829–851.

Effrat, Andrew. 1972. "Power to the Paradigms." Pp. 3–34 in Andrew Effrat (ed.), *Perspectives in Political Sociology.* New York: Bobbs-Merrill.

Ehrenreich, Barbara. 2001. *Nickel and Dimed: On (Not) Getting By in America.* New York: Metropolitan Books.

Eisenstadt, S. N. 1996. *Japanese Civilization: A Comparative View.* Chicago: University of Chicago Press.

Ellis, Dean. 1967. "Speech and Social Status in America." *Social Forces,* 45:431–437.

Ellis, Godfrey, Gary Lee, and Larry Peterson. 1978. "Supervision and Conformity: A Cross-Cultural Analysis of Parental Socialization Values." *American Journal of Sociology,* 84:386–403.

Ellis, Lee. 1977. "The Decline and Fall of Sociology, 1975–2000." *The American Sociologist,* 12:56–66.

England, Paula, and George Farkas. 1986. *Households, Employment, and Gender: A Social, Economic and Demographic View.* New York: Aldine.

England, Paula, George Farkas, Barbara Stanek Kilbourne, and Thomas Dou. 1988. "Explaining Occupational Sex Segregation and Wages: Findings from a Model with Fixed Effects." *American Sociological Review,* 53:544–558.

Entwisle, Doris, Karl L. Alexander, and Linda Steffel Olson. 2005. "First Grade and Educational Attainment by Age 22: A New Story." *American Journal of Sociology,* 110:1458–1502.

Erikson, Kai T. 1966. *The Wayward Puritans: A Study in the Sociology of Deviance.* New York: John Wiley & Sons.

Erikson, Robert, and John H. Goldthorpe. 1992. *The Constant Flux: A Study of Class Mobility in Industrial Societies.* Oxford, England: Clarendon.

Erlanger, Howard. 1974. "Social Class and Corporal Punishment in Childrearing: A Reassessment." *American Sociological Review,* 39:68–85.

Esping-Anderson, Gosta. 1990. *The Three Worlds of Welfare Capitalism.* Princeton, N.J.: Princeton University Press.

Estioko-Griffin, Agnes, and P. Bion Griffin. 1981. "Woman the Hunter: The Agta." Pp. 121–140 in Frances Dahlberg (ed.), *Woman the Gatherer.* New Haven: Yale University Press.

Etzioni, Amitai. 1984. *An Immodest Agenda: Rebuilding America before the 21st Century.* New York: McGraw-Hill.

Evans, G (ed.). 1999. *The End of Class Politics?: Class Voting in Comparative Context.* Oxford, England: Oxford University Press.

Evans, Grant. 1995. *Lao Peasants Under Socialism and Post-Socialism,* New Haven, Conn.: Yale University Press.

Evans, Grant. 1998. *The Politics of Ritual and Remembrance: Laos Since 1975.* Chiang Mai, Thailand: Silkworm Press.

Evans, Peter, and James E. Rauch. 1999. "Bureaucracy and Growth: A Cross-National Analysis of the Effects of 'Weberian' State Structures on Economic Growth." *American Sociological Review,* 64:748–765.

Evanson, Elizabeth. 1981. "The Dynamics of Poverty." *Focus,* 5:9–11, 19–20.

Fairbank, John King. 1986. *The Great Chinese Revolution: 1800–1985.* New York: Harper & Row.

Fallows, James. 1994. *Looking at the Sun: The Rise of the New East Asian Economic and Political System.* New York: Pantheon.

Feagin, Joe R. 1972. "When It Comes to Poverty, It's Still 'God Helps Those Who Help Themselves.'" *Psychology Today* 6 (November):101–129.

Feagin, Joe R. 1975. *Subordinating the Poor.* Upper Saddle River, N.J.: Prentice Hall.

Featherman, David, and Robert Hauser. 1978. *Opportunity and Change.* New York: Academic Press.

Featherman, David L., F. Lancaster Jones, and Robert M. Hauser. 1975. "Assumptions of Social Mobility Research in the U.S.: A Case of Occupational Status." *Social Science Research,* 4:329–360.

Feldman, Marcus W., Sarah P. Otto, and Freddy B. Christiansen. 2000. "Genes, Culture, and Inequality." Pp. 61–86 in Kenneth Arrow, Samuel Bowles, and Steven Durlauf (eds.), *Meritocracy and Economic Inequality.* Princeton, N.J.: Princeton University Press.

Ferree, Myra Marx, and Elaine J. Hall. 1996. "Rethinking Stratification from a Feminist Perspective: Gender, Race, and Class in Mainstream Textbooks." *American Sociological Review,* 61:929–950.

Festinger, Leon. 1957. *A Theory of Cognitive Dissonance.* Stanford, Calif.: Stanford University Press.

Fiala, Robert. 1983. "Inequality and the Service Sector in Less Developed Countries: A Reanalysis and Respecification." *American Sociological Review,* 48:421–428.

Firebaugh, Glenn. 1992. "Growth Effects of Foreign and Domestic Investment." *American Journal of Sociology,* 98:105–130.

Firebaugh, Glenn. 1996. "Does Foreign Capital Harm Poor Nations? New Estimates Based on Dixon and Boswell's Measures of Capital Penetration." *American Journal of Sociology,* 102:563–578.

Firebaugh, Glenn. 2003. *The New Geography of Global Income Inequality.* Cambridge, Mass.: Harvard University Press.

Firebaugh, Glenn, and Frank D. Beck. 1994. "Does Economic Growth Benefit the Masses? Growth, Dependence, and Welfare in the Third World." *American Sociological Review,* 59:631–653.

Firebaugh, Glenn, and Brian Goesling. 2004. "Accounting for the Recent Decline in Global Income Inequality." *American Journal of Sociology,* 110:283–312.

Fiscella, Kevin, Peter Franks, Marthe R. Gold, and Carolyn M. Clancy. 2000. "Inequality in Quality: Addressing Socioeconomic, Racial, and Ethnic Disparities in Health Care." *Journal of the American Medical Association,* 283:2579–2584.

Fischer, Ruth. 1982. *Stalin and German Communism.* New Brunswick, N.J.: Transaction Press.

Flannery, Kent. 1972. "The Origins of the Village as a Settlement Type in Mesoamerica and the Near East: A Comparative Study." Pp. 117–132 in Peter Ucko, Ruth Tringham, and G. W. Dimbleday (eds.), *Man, Settlement, and Urbanism.* London: Duckworth.

Flynn, James R. 2000. "IQ Trends over Time: Intelligence, Race, and Meritocracy." Pp. 35–60 in Kenneth Arrow, Samuel Bowles, and Steven Durlauf (eds.), *Meritocracy and Economic Inequality.* Princeton, N.J.: Princeton University Press.

*Focus.* 1982. "Valuing In-Kind Transfers," vol. 6, pp. 13–14. Madison: University of Wisconsin, Institute for Research on Poverty.

*Focus.* 1984. "Poverty in the United States: Where Do We Stand Now?" vol. 7, pp. 1–13. Madison: University of Wisconsin, Institute for Research on Poverty.

Fogel, Robert William, and Stanley L. Engerman. 1974. *Time on the Cross: The Economics of American Negro Slavery.* Boston: Little, Brown.

Form, William. 1985. *Divided We Stand: Working-Class Stratification in America.* Urbana: University of Illinois Press.

Fox, M. A., B. A. Connolly, and T. D. Synder. 2005. *Youth Indicators 2005: Trends in the Well-Being of American Youth.* Washington, D.C.: U.S. Department of Education, National Center for Education Statistics.

Fox, Thomas, and S. M. Miller. 1965a. "Intra-Country Variations: Occupational Stratification and Mobility." *Society Transactions,* 1:23–38.

Fox, Thomas, and S. M. Miller. 1965b. "Economic, Political, and Social Determinants of Mobility: An International Cross-Sectional Analysis." *Acta Sociologica,* 9:73–91.

Frank, Andre Gunder. 1969. *Capitalism and Underdevelopment in Latin America.* New York: Monthly Review Press.

Frank, Andre Gunder. 1975. *On Capitalist Underdevelopment.* Bombay: Oxford University Press.

Frank, Andre Gunder. 1978. *Dependent Accumulation and Underdevelopment.* New York: Monthly Review Press.

Frank, Andre Gunder. 1998. *ReOrient: Global Economy in the Asian Age.* Los Angeles: University of California Press.

Franklin, M. N. 1996. "Electoral Participation." Pp. 216–235 in L. LeDuc, R. G. Niemi, and P. Norris (eds.), *Comparing Democracies: Elections and Voting in Global Perspective.* Thousand Oaks, Calif.: Sage.

Frazier, E. Franklin. 1932. *The Negro Family in Chicago.* Chicago: University of Chicago Press.

Freeman, Richard B. 2001. "The Rising Tide Lifts . . . ?" Pp. 97–126 in Sheldon H. Danziger and Robert H. Haveman (eds.), *Understanding Poverty.* Cambridge, Mass.: Harvard University Press.

Freitag, Peter. 1975. "The Cabinet and Big Business: A Study of Interlocks." *Social Problems,* 23:137–152.

Fried, Morton. 1973. "On the Evolution of Social Stratification and the State." Pp. 15–25 in John C. Leggett (ed.), *Taking State Power: The Sources and Consequences of Political Challenge.* New York: Harper & Row.

Friedlander, Walter. 1968. *Introduction to Social Welfare.* Upper Saddle River, N.J.: Prentice Hall.

Friedrichs, Robert. 1970. *A Sociology of Sociology.* New York: Free Press.

Fuller, C. J. (ed.). 1996. *Caste Today.* New Delhi: Oxford University Press.

Galaskiewicz, Joseph, and Stanley Wasserman. 1981. "A Dynamic Study of Change in a Regional Corporate Network." *American Sociological Review,* 46:475–484.

Galaskiewicz, Joseph, Stanley Wasserman, Barbara Rauschenbach, Wolfgang Bielefeld, and Patti Mullaney. 1985. "The Influence of Corporate Power, Social Status, and Market Position on Corporate Interlocks in a Regional Network." *Social Forces,* 64:403–432.

Galbraith, John Kenneth. 1971. *The New Industrial State.* Boston: Houghton Mifflin.

Gallman, R. E. 1969. "Trends in the Size Distribution of Wealth in the Nineteenth Century." Pp. 1–31 in L. Soltow (ed.), *Six Papers on the Distribution of Wealth.* New York: National Bureau of Economic Research.

Gallup Poll International. 2000. *Gallup International Millennium Survey, 2000.* http://www.gallup-international.com.

Gamoran, Adam. 1992. "The Variable Effects of High School Tracking." *American Sociological Review,* 57:812–828.

Gamoran, Adam, and Robert D. Mare. 1989. "Secondary School Tracking and Educational Inequality: Compensation, Reinforcement, or Neutrality?" *American Journal of Sociology,* 94:1146–1183.

Gamson, William. 1975. *The Strategy of Social Protest.* Homewood, Ill.: Dorsey Press.

Gangl, Markus. 2004. "Welfare States and the Scar Effects of Unemployment: A Comparative Analysis of the United States and West Germany." *American Journal of Sociology,* 109:1319–1364.

Gans, Herbert. 1969. "Culture and Class in the Study of Poverty: An Approach to Anti-Poverty Research." Pp. 201–228 in Daniel P. Moynihan (ed.), *On Understanding Poverty.* New York: Basic Books.

Gans, Herbert. 1972. "Positive Functions of Poverty." *American Journal of Sociology,* 78:275–289.

Gans, Herbert. 1979. *Deciding What's News.* New York: Pantheon.

Garfinkel, Harold. 1967. *Studies in Ethnomethodology.* Upper Saddle River, N.J.: Prentice Hall.

Garner, Roberta Ash. 1977. *Social Movements in America.* Chicago: Rand McNally.

Garten, Jeffrey E. 1992. *A Cold Peace: America, Japan, Germany, and the Struggle for Supremacy.* New York: Times Books.

Genovese, Eugene D. 1974. *Roll, Jordan, Roll: The World the Slaves Made.* New York: Pantheon Books.

Gerlach, Michael L. 1992. *Alliance Capitalism: The Social Organization of Japanese Business.* Berkeley: University of California Press.

German Federal Ministry of Labour and Social Affairs (Germany). 1991. *Co-determination in the Federal Republic of Germany (Legal Texts).* Bonn: Der Bundesminister für Arbeit und Sozialordnung Referat Presse.

Gershoy, Leo. 1964. *The French Revolution and Napoleon.* New York: Appleton, Century, Crofts.

Gerth, Hans, and C. Wright Mills. 1946. *From Max Weber: Essays in Sociology.* New York: Oxford University Press.

Ghurye, G. S. 1969. "Features of the Caste System." Pp. 35–48 in Dipankar Gupta (ed.), *Social Stratification.* Delhi: Oxford University Press.

Gibney, Frank (ed.). 1998. *Unlocking the Bureaucrat's Kingdom: Deregulation and the Japanese Economy.* Washington, D.C.: Brookings Institution Press.

Giddens, Anthony. 1973. *The Class Structure of the Advanced Societies.* New York: Harper & Row.

Giddens, Anthony. 1978. *Émile Durkheim.* New York: Penguin Books.

Gilder, George. 1981. *Wealth and Poverty.* New York: Basic Books.

Gitlin, Todd. 1979. "Prime Time Ideology: The Hegemonic Process in Television Entertainment." *Social Problems,* 26:251–268.

Glenn, Norval, Andreain Ross, and Judy Corder Tully. 1974. "Patterns of Intergenerational Mobility of Females through Marriage." *American Sociological Review,* 39:683–699.

Glouchevitch, Philip. 1992. *Juggernaut: The German Way of Business.* New York: Simon & Schuster.

Goesling, Brian. 2001. "Changing Income Inequalities Within and Between Nations: New Evidence." *American Sociological Review,* 66:745–761.

Goffman, Erving. 1959. *The Presentation of Self in Everyday Life.* Garden City, N.Y.: Doubleday.

Gold, Thomas B. 1986. *State and Society in the Taiwan Miracle.* Armonk, N.Y.: M. E. Sharpe.

Goldman, Eric F. 1953. *Rendezvous with Destiny.* New York: Knopf.

Goldman, Robert, and Ann Tickamyer. 1984. "Status Attainment and the Commodity Form: Stratification in Historical Perspective." *American Sociological Review,* 49:196–209.

Goldstein, Bernice, and Kyoka Tamura. 1975. *Japan and America: A Comparative Study in Language and Culture.* Tokyo: Tuttle.

Goldthorpe, John H. 1987. *Social Mobility and Class Structure in Modern Britain.* Oxford, England: Clarendon Press.

Goldthorpe, John H. 2001. "Class and Politics in Advanced Industrial Societies." Pp. 105–120 in Terry Nichols Clark and Seymour Martin Lipset (eds.), *The Breakdown of Class Politics: A Debate on Post-Industrial Stratification.* Washington, D.C.: Woodrow Wilson Center Press.

Good, T., and J. Brophy. 1973. *Looking in Class-Rooms.* New York: Harper & Row.

Goodin, Robert E., Bruce Headey, Ruud Muffels, and Henk-Jan Dirven. 1999. *The Real Worlds of Welfare Capitalism.* Cambridge, England: Cambridge University Press.

Goodwin, Leonard. 1972. *Do the Poor Want to Work? A Social-Psychological Study of Work Orientations.* Washington, D.C.: Brookings Institution Press.

Gordon, Milton. 1963. *Social Class in American Sociology.* New York: McGraw-Hill.

Gortmaker, Steven. 1979. "Poverty and Infant Mortality in the United States." *American Sociological Review,* 44:280–297.

Gouldner, Alvin. 1970. *The Coming Crisis in Western Sociology.* New York: Basic Books.

Gouldner, Alvin. 1973. *For Sociology: Renewal and Critique in Sociology Today.* New York: Basic Books.

Grandjean, Burke, and Frank Bean. 1975. "The Davis-Moore Theory and Perceptions of Stratification." *Social Forces,* 54:166–180.

Granovetter, Mark. 1995. *Getting a Job: A Study of Contacts and Careers.* 2nd ed. Chicago: University of Chicago Press.

Griffin, Larry, and Karl Alexander. 1978. "Schooling and Socioeconomic Attainments: High School and College Influences." *American Journal of Sociology,* 84:319–347.

Griffin, Larry, Michael Wallace, and Beth Rubin. 1986. "Capitalist Resistance to the Organization of Labor before the New Deal: Why? How? Success?" *American Sociological Review,* 51:147–167.

Grodsky, Eric, and Devah Pager. 2001. "The Structure of Disadvantage: Individual and Occupational Determinants of the Black–White Wage Gap." *American Sociological Review,* 66:542–567.

Grusky, David. 1983. "Industrialization and the Status Attainment Process: The Thesis of Industrialism Reconsidered." *American Sociological Review,* 48:494–506.

Grusky, David, and Robert Hauser. 1984. "Comparative Social Mobility Revisited: Models of Convergence and Divergence in 16 Countries." *American Sociological Review,* 49:19–38.

Guest, Avery M., Nancy S. Landale, and James C. McCann. 1989. "Intergenerational Occupational Mobility in the Late 19th Century United States." *Social Forces,* 68:351–378.

Guppy, L. Neil. 1982. "On Intersubjectivity and Collective Conscience in Occupational Prestige Research: A Comment on Balkwell-Bates-Garbin and Kraus-Schild-Hodge." *Social Forces,* 60:1178–1182.

Guppy, L. Neil, and John C. Goyder. 1984. "Consensus on Occupational Prestige: A Reassessment of the Evidence." *Social Forces,* 62:709–726.

Gupta, Dipankar (ed.). 1991. *Social Stratification.* New Delhi: Oxford University Press.

Gusfield, J. R., and M. Schwartz. 1963. "The Meanings of Occupational Prestige: Reconsideration of the NORC Scale." *American Sociological Review,* 28:265–271.

Habermas, Jurgen. 1975. *Legitimation Crisis.* Boston: Beacon Press.

Habermas, Jurgen. 1984. *Reason and the Rationalization of Society.* Boston: Beacon Press.

Hachen, David S., Jr. 1992. "Industrial Characteristics and Job Mobility Rates." *American Sociological Review,* 57:39–55.

Hacker, Andrew. 1975. "What Rules America?" *New York Review of Books,* 22 (May 1): 9–13. Reprinted on pp. 363–371 in Maurice Zeitlin (ed.), *American Society, Inc.,* 2nd ed. Chicago: Rand McNally, 1977.

Hacker, Andrew. 1997. *Money: Who Has How Much and Why.* New York: Scribner.

Hagan, John. 1991. "Destiny and Drift: Subcultural Preferences, Status Attainments, and the Risks and Rewards of Youth." *American Sociological Review,* 56:567–582.

Haggard, Stephan, and Robert Kaufman. 2008. *Development, Democracy, and Welfare States: Latin America, East Asia, and Eastern Europe.* Princeton: Princeton University Press.

Halberstam, David. 1986. *The Reckoning.* New York: Morrow.

Hall, Kenneth R. 1999. "Economic History of Early Southeast Asia." Pp. 183–275 in Nicholas Tarling (ed.), *The Cambridge History of Southeast Asia, From Early Times to c. 1500, Volume One, Part One.* Cambridge, England: Cambridge University Press.

Hall, P. M., and J. P. Hewitt. 1970. "The Quasi Theory of Communication and Management of Dissent." *Social Problems,* 18:17–26.

Haller, Max (ed.). 1990. *Class Structure in Europe: New Findings from East-West Comparisons of Social Structure and Mobility.* Armonk, N.Y.: M. E. Sharpe.

Halliday, Jon. 1975. *A Political History of Japanese Capitalism.* New York: Monthly Review Press.

Hamilton, Richard. 1972. *Class and Politics in the United States.* New York: John Wiley & Sons.

Hammer, Heather-Jo. 1984. "Comment of 'Dependency Theory and Taiwan: Analysis of a Deviant Case.'" *American Journal of Sociology,* 89:932–936.

Handler, Joel, and Ellen Jane Hollingsworth. 1971. *The "Deserving Poor": A Study of Welfare Administration.* Chicago: Markham.

Handley, Paul. 2006. *The King Never Smiles: A Biography of Thailand's Bhumibol Adulyadej.* New Haven: Yale University Press.

Hane, Mikiso. 1982. *Peasants, Rebels, and Outcastes: The Underside of Modern Japan.* New York: Pantheon.

Hara, Junsuke. 2007. "Contemporary Japanese Society and the New Inequalities: A Frontier of Social Stratification and Inequality Research." Pp. 3–17 in Yoshimich Sato (ed.), *Deciphering Stratification and Inequality: Japan and Beyond.* Sendai, Japan: Center for the Study of Social Stratification and Inequality, and Melbourne: Trans Pacific Press.

Hara, Junsuke, and Kazuo Seiyama. 2005. *Inequality amid Affluence: Social Stratification in Japan.* Sendai, Japan: Center for the Study of Social Stratification and Inequality, and Melbourne: Trans Pacific Press.

Harding, David J. 2003. "Counterfactual Models of Neighborhood Effects: The Effect of Neighborhood Poverty on Dropping Out and Teenage Pregnancy." *American Journal of Sociology,* 109:676–719.

Harms, L. S. 1961. "Listener Judgments of Status Cues in Speech." *Quarterly Journal of Speech,* 47:164–168.

Harrington, Michael. 1976. *The Twilight of Capitalism.* New York: Simon & Schuster.

Harrington, Michael. 1984. *The New American Poverty.* New York: Holt, Rinehart and Winston.

Harris, David. 1977. "Alternative Pathways toward Agriculture." Pp. 231–248 in Charles Reed (ed.), *Origins of Agriculture.* The Hague, Netherlands: Mouton.

Harrison, Bennett, and Barry Bluestone. 1988. *The Great U-Turn: Corporate Restructuring and the Polarizing of America.* New York: Basic Books.

Harrison, Lawrence E. 2000 (updated edition). *Underdevelopment Is a State of Mind: The Latin American Case.* Lanham, Md.: Madison Books.

Harrison, Lawrence E., and Samuel P. Huntington (eds.). 2000. *Culture Matters: How Values Shape Human Progress.* New York: Basic Books.

Hartcher, Peter. 1998. *The Ministry: How Japan's Most Powerful Institution Endangers World Markets.* Boston, Mass.: Harvard Business School Press.

Hatch, W., and K. Yamamura. 1996. *Asia in Japan's Embrace: Building a Regional Production Alliance.* Cambridge, England: Cambridge University Press.

Haughton, Jonathon, and Shahidur Khandker. 2009. *Handbook on Poverty and Inequality.* World Bank, www.worldbank.org.

Hauser, Robert. 1980. "On Stratification in a Dual Economy." *American Sociological Review,* 45:702–711.

Hauser, Robert, and David Featherman. 1977. *The Process of Stratification.* New York: Academic Press.

Hauser, Robert, and David Grusky. 1988. "Cross-National Variation in Occupational Distributions, Relative Mobility Chances, and Intergenerational Shifts in Occupational Distributions." *American Sociological Review,* 53:723–741.

Hazelrigg, Lawrence, and Maurice Garnier. 1976. "Occupational Mobility in Industrial Societies: A Comparative Analysis of Different Access to Occupational Ranks in Seventeen Countries." *American Sociological Review,* 41:498–510.

Hechter, Michael, and William Brustein. 1980. "Regional Modes of Production and Patterns of State Formation in Western Europe." *American Journal of Sociology,* 85:1061–1094.

Heise, David, Gerhard Lenski, and John Wardwell. 1976. "Further Notes on Technology and the Moral Order." *Social Forces,* 55:316–337.

Held, David, Anthony McGrew, David Goldblatt, and Jonathan Perraton. 1999. *Global Transformations: Politics, Economics, and Culture.* Palo Alto, Calif.: Stanford University Press.

Heller, Celia (ed.). 1969. *Structured Social Inequality.* New York: Macmillan.

Heller, Celia S (ed.). 1987. *Structured Social Inequality: A Reader in Comparative Social Stratification.* 2nd ed. New York: Macmillan.

Herberg, Will. 1960. *Protestant, Catholic, Jew.* New York: Doubleday.

Herman, Edward. 1975. *Conflicts of Interest: Commercial Bank Trust Departments.* New York: Twentieth Century Fund.

Herman, Edward S., and Noam Chomsky. 1988. *Manufacturing Consent: The Political Economy of the Mass Media.* New York: Pantheon.

Herrnstein, Richard, and Charles Murray. 1994. *The Bell Curve: Intelligence and Class Structure in American Life.* New York: Free Press.

Hertz, Thomas, 2004. "Rags, Riches and Race: The Intergenerational Economic Mobility of Black and White Families in the United States." In Samuel Bowles, Herbert Gintis, and Melissa Osborne (eds.), *Unequal Chances: Family Background and Economic Success.* New York: Russell Sage and Princeton University Press.

Hewitt, Christopher. 1977. "The Effect of Political Democracy and Social Democracy on Equality in Industrial Societies: A Cross-National Comparison." *American Sociological Review,* 42:450–463.

Hewlett, Barry S. 1991. *Intimate Fathers: The Nature and Context of Aka Pygmy Paternal-Infant Care.* Ann Arbor: University of Michigan Press.

Heyns, B. 1974. "Social Selection and Stratification within Schools." *American Journal of Sociology,* 79:1434–1451.

Hicks, Alexander, Roger Friedland, and Edwin Johnson. 1978. "Class Power and State Policy: The Case of Large Business Corporations, Labor Unions and Governmental Redistribution in the American States." *American Sociological Review,* 43:302–315.

Higham, Charles. 2001. *The Civilization of Angkor.* London: Weidenfeld and Nicolson.

Higham, Charles. 2002. *Early Cultures of Mainland Southeast Asia.* Bangkok: River Books.

Hill, Martha. 1981. "Some Dynamic Aspects of Poverty." In M. Hill, D. Hill, and J. N. Morgan (eds.), *Five Thousand American Families—Patterns of Economic Progress,* vol. 9. Ann Arbor: Institute for Social Research, University of Michigan Press.

Hirsch, Glenn. 1975. "Only You Can Prevent Ideological Hegemony: The Advertising Council and Its Place in the American Power Structure." *Insurgent Sociologist,* 5:64–82.

Hodge, Robert, Paul Siegel, and Peter Rossi. 1964. "Occupational Prestige in the United

States." *American Journal of Sociology,* 70:286–302.

Hodge, Robert, Paul Siegel, and Peter Rossi. 1966. "Occupational Prestige in the United States, 1925–1963." Pp. 322–334 in R. Bendix and S. M. Lipset (eds.), *Class, Status, and Power.* New York: Free Press.

Hodge, Robert, and Donald Treiman. 1968a. "Social Participation and Social Status." *American Journal of Sociology,* 33:578–593.

Hoffer, Eric. 1966. *The True Believer.* New York: Harper & Row.

Hoffmeister, Gerhart, and Frederic C. Tubach. 1992. *Germany: 2000 Years: From the Nazi Era to German Unification,* vol. 3. New York: Continuum.

Hofstede, Geert. 1991. *Cultures and Organizations: Software of the Mind.* New York: McGraw-Hill.

Hollingshead, August. 1949. *Elmtown's Youth.* New York: John Wiley & Sons.

Hollingshead, August, and Frederick Redlich. 1958. *Social Class and Mental Illness.* New York: John Wiley & Sons.

Hollister, Matissa N. 2004. "Does Firm Size Matter Anymore? The New Economy and Firm Size Wage Effects." *American Sociological Review,* 69:659–676.

Holmes, Henry, and Suchada Tangtongtavy. 1995. *Working with the Thais: A Guide to Managing in Thailand.* Bangkok: White Lotus.

Holtmann, Dieter, and Hermann Strasser. 1990. "Comparing Class Structures and Class Consciousness in Western Societies." Pp. 3–23 in Max Haller (ed.), *Class Structure in Europe: New Findings from East-West Comparisons of Social Structure and Mobility.* Armonk, N.Y.: M. E. Sharpe.

Homans, George. 1961. *Social Behavior: Its Elementary Forms.* New York: Harcourt, Brace & World.

Homans, George. 1974. *Social Behavior: Its Elementary Forms.* Rev. ed. New York: Harcourt Brace & World.

Hope, Keith. 1982. "A Liberal Theory of Prestige." *American Journal of Sociology,* 87:1011–1031.

Horan, Patrick. 1978. "Is Status Attainment Research Atheoretical?" *American Sociological Review,* 43:534–541.

Horton, John. 1966. "Order and Conflict Theories of Social Problems as Competing Ideologies." *American Journal of Sociology,* 71:701–713.

Hout, Michael. 1984. "Occupational Mobility of Black Men: 1962 to 1973." *American Sociological Review,* 49:308–322.

Hout, Michael. 1988. "More Universalism, Less Structural Mobility: The American Occupational Structure in the 1980s." *American Journal of Sociology,* 93:1358–1400.

Hout, Michael, Clem Brooks, and Jeff Manza. 1995. "The Democratic Class Struggle in the United States, 1948–1992." *American Sociological Review,* 60:805–828.

Hout, Michael, Clem Brooks, and Jeff Manza. 2001. "The Persistence of Classes in Post-Industrial Societies." Pp. 55–76 in Terry Nichols Clark and Seymour Martin Lipset (eds.), *The Breakdown of Class Politics: A Debate on Post-Industrial Stratification.* Washington, D.C.: Woodrow Wilson Center Press.

Houtman, D. 2001. "Class, Culture, and Conservatism: Reassessing Education as a Variable in Political Sociology." Pp. 161–196 in T. N. Clark and S. M. Lipset (eds.), *The Breakdown of Class Politics: A Debate on Post-Industrial Stratification.* Washington D.C.: Woodrow Wilson Center Press.

Howe, Irving. 1976. *World of Our Fathers: The Journey of the East European Jews to America and the Life They Found and Made.* New York: Harcourt Brace Jovanovich.

Howe, Irving. 1978. *Leon Trotsky.* New York: Viking Press.

Hraba, Joseph. 1994. *American Ethnicity.* Itasca, Ill.: Peacock.

Huber, Evelyne, Francois Nielsen, Jenny Pribble, and John Stephens. 2006. "Politics of Inequality in Latin America and the Caribbean." *American Sociological Review,* 71:943–963.

Huber, Joan, and William H. Form. 1973. *Income and Ideology: An Analysis of the American Political Formula.* New York: Free Press.

Huffman, Matt L., and Philip N. Cohen. 2004. "Racial Wage Inequality: Job Segregation and Devaluation across U.S. Labor Markets." *American Journal of Sociology,* 109:902–936.

Hughes, Michael, and Melvin E. Thomas. 1998. "The Continuing Significance of Race Revisited: A Study of Race, Class, and Quality of Life in America, 1972–1996." *American Sociological Review,* 63:785–795.

Hunter, Floyd. 1953. *Community Power Structure: A Study of Decision Makers.* Chapel Hill: University of North Carolina Press.

Huntington, Samuel P. 1996. *The Clash of Civilizations and the Remaking of World Order.* New York: Simon & Schuster.

Hyman, Herbert, and Charles R. Wright. 1971. "Trends in Voluntary Association Memberships of American Adults: Replication Based on Secondary Analysis of National Sample Surveys." *American Sociological Review,* 36:191–206.

Iceland, John. 2003. *Poverty in America.* Berkeley: University of California Press.

Iceland, John, Daniel Weinberg, and Erika Steinmetz. 2002. "Racial and Ethnic Segregation in the United States, 1980–2000." U.S. Census Bureau. Special Report Series, CENSR #3. Washington D.C.: U.S. Government Printing Office.

Ingham, John. 1978. *The Iron Barons.* Chicago: University of Chicago Press.

Inglehart, R. 1990. *Culture Shift in Advanced Industrial Society.* Princeton, N.J.: Princeton University Press.

International Fund for Agricultural Development. 2001. *Rural Poverty Report, 2001: The Challenge of Ending Rural Poverty.* New York: Oxford University Press.

Isaac, Larry, and William Kelly. 1981. "Racial Insurgency, the State, and Welfare Expansion: Local and National Level Evidence from the Postwar United States." *American Journal of Sociology,* 86:1348–1386.

Ishida, Hiroshi. 1993. *Social Mobility in Contemporary Japan.* Palo Alto, Calif.: Stanford University Press.

Ishida, Hiroshi, John H. Goldthorpe, and Robert Erikson. 1987. "Intergenerational Class Mobility in Post War Japan: Conformity or Peculiarity in Cross-National Perspective." Paper presented to the Research Committee on Social Stratification of the International Sociological Association, Berkeley, August.

Jackman, Robert. 1974. "Political Democracy and Social Equality: A Comparative Analysis." *American Sociological Review,* 39:29–45.

Jackman, Robert. 1975. *Politics and Social Equality: A Comparative Analysis.* New York: John Wiley & Sons.

Jackman, R. W., and R. A. Miller. 1995. "Voter Turnout in the Industrial Democracies During the 1980s." *Comparative Political Studies,* 27:467–492.

Jacobs, David. 1979. "Inequality and Police Strength: Conflict Theory and Coercive Control in Metropolitan Areas." *American Sociological Review,* 44:913–924.

Jacobs, David. 1982. "Competition, Scale, and Political Explanations for Inequality: An Integrated Study of Sectoral Explanations at the Aggregate Level." *American Sociological Review,* 47:600–614.

Jacobs, David. 1985. "Unequal Organizations or Unequal Attainment? An Empirical Comparison of Sectoral and Individualistic Explanations for Aggregate Inequality." *American Sociological Review,* 50:166–180.

Jacobs, David. 1988. "Corporate Economic Power and the State: A Longitudinal Assessment of Two Explanations." *American Journal of Sociology,* 93:852–881.

Jacobs, Jerry. 1983. "Industrial Sector and Career Mobility Reconsidered." *American Sociological Review,* 48:415–421.

Jacques, Jeffrey, and Karen Chason. 1977. "Self-Esteem and Low Status Groups: A Changing Scene?" *Sociological Quarterly,* 18:399–412.

Jain, Shail. 1975. *Size Distribution of Income: A Compilation of Data.* Washington, D.C.: World Bank.

Jalilian, Hossein, and John Weiss. 2003. "Foreign Direct Investment and Poverty in the ASEAN Region." *ASEAN Economic Bulletin,* 19:231–253.

Jantti, Markus, et al. 2006. "American Exceptionalism in a New Light: A Comparison of Intergenerational Earning Mobility in the Nordic Countries, the United Kingdom, and the United States." Discussion Paper No. 2006:1938. Institute for the Study of Labor.

Jargowsky, Paul A., and Mary Jo Bane. 1991. "Ghetto Poverty in the United States, 1970–1980." Pp. 235–273 in Christopher Jencks and Paul E. Peterson (eds.), *The Urban Underclass.* Washington, D.C.: Brookings Institution Press.

Jasso, Guillermina, and Peter Rossi. 1977. "Distributive Justice and Earned Income." *American Sociological Review,* 42:639–651.

Jencks, Christopher. 1991. "Is the American Underclass Growing?" Pp. 28–102 in Christopher Jencks and Paul E. Peterson (eds.), *The Urban Underclass.* Washington, D.C.: Brookings Institution Press.

Jencks, Christopher, et al. 1972. *Inequality: Reassessment of the Effect of Family and Schooling in America.* New York: Harper & Row.

Jencks, Christopher, et al. 1979. *Who Gets Ahead? The Determinants of Economic Success in America.* New York: Basic Books.

Jenkins, J. Craig, and Barbara G. Brents. 1989. "Social Protest, Hegemonic Competition, and Social Reform: A Political Struggle Interpretation of the Origins of the American Welfare State." *American Sociological Review,* 54:891–909.

Jenkins, J. Craig, David Jacobs, and Jon Agnone. 2003. "Political Opportunities and African-American Protest, 1948–1997." *American Journal of Sociology,* 109:277–303.

Jenkins, J. Craig, and Charles Perrow. 1977. "Insurgency of the Powerless: Farm Worker Movements." *American Sociological Review,* 42:249–268.

Jenkins, Richard. 1992. *Pierre Bourdieu: Key Sociologists.* New York: Routledge.

Jennings, Edward T. 1983. "Racial Insurgency, the State, and Welfare Expansion: A Critical Comment and Reanalysis." *American Journal of Sociology,* 88:1220–1236.

Johnson, Chalmers. 1982. *MITI and the Japanese Miracle.* Stanford, Calif.: Stanford University Press.

Jomo, K. S. 2001. "Globalisation, Liberalisation, Poverty and Income Inequality in Southeast Asia." Technical Paper No. 185, OECD.

Jonsson, Jan O., David B. Grusky, Matthew Di Carlo, Reinhard Pollak, and Mary C. Brinton. 2009. "Microclass Mobility: Social Reproduction in Four Countries." *American Journal of Sociology,* 114:977–1036.

Kahn, Alfred, and Sheila Kamerman. 1977. *Not for the Poor Alone: European Social Services.* New York: Harper Colophon Books.

Kakuma Takashi. 1981a. *Nihon no Shihai Kaikyū, Jokan* (Japan's Ruling Class, Part One). Tokyo: PHP Kenkyūjo.

Kalleberg, Arne. 2009. "Precarious Work, Insecure Workers: Employment Relations in Transition." *American Sociological Review,* 74:1–22.

Kalleberg, Arne, and Larry Griffin. 1980. "Class, Occupation, and Inequality in Job Rewards." *American Journal of Sociology,* 85:731–768.

Kalleberg, Arne L., and James R. Lincoln. 1988. "The Structure of Earnings Inequality in the United States and Japan." *American Journal of Sociology,* 94:5121–5153.

Kalleberg, Arne L., and Mark E. Van Buren. 1996. "Is Bigger Better? Explaining the Relationship between Organization Size and Job Rewards." *American Sociological Review,* 61:47–66.

Kalmijn, Matthijs. 1991. "Status Homogamy in the United States." *American Journal of Sociology,* 97:496–523.

Kamata, Satoshi. 1982. *Japan in the Passing Lane: An Insider's Account of Life in a Japanese Auto Factory.* New York: Pantheon Books.

Kamm, Henry. 1998. *Cambodia: Report from a Stricken Land.* New York: Arcade.

Kane, Michael. 1970. *Minorities in Textbooks.* Chicago: Quadrangle.

Kaplan, H. Roy, and Curt Travsky. 1972. "Work and the Welfare Cadillac: The Function and Commitment to Work among the Hard-Core Unemployed." *Social Problems,* 19:469–483.

Kappelhoff, Peter, and Wolfgang Teckenberg. 1987. "Intergenerational and Career Mobility in the Federal Republic and the United States." Pp. 3–52 in Wolfgang Teckenberg (ed.), *Comparative Studies of Social Structure: Recent Research on France, the United States, and the Federal Republic of Germany.* Armonk, N. Y.: M. E. Sharpe.

Kaufman, Robert L. 1983."A Structural Decomposition of Black–White Earnings Differentials." *American Journal of Sociology,* 89:585–611.

Kaufman, Robert L. 2002. "Assessing Alternative Perspectives on Race and Sex Employment Segregation." *American Sociological Review,* 67:547–572.

Keay, John. 1997. *Last Post: The End of Empire in the Far East.* London: John Murray.

Keep, John. 1976. *The Russian Revolution: A Study in Mass Mobilization.* New York: Norton.

Keister, Lisa A. 2000. *Wealth in America: Trends in Wealth Inequality.* Cambridge, England: Cambridge University Press.

Keizai Koho Center. 2002. *Japan 2001: An International Comparison.* Tokyo: Keizai Koho Center (Japan Institute for Social and Economic Affairs).

Keizai Koho Center. 2007. *Japan 2006: An International Comparison.* Tokyo: Keizai Koho Center. http://www.kkc.or.jp/english/.

Keller, Suzanne. 1953. "The Social Origins and Career Lines of Three Generations of American Business Leaders." Unpublished PhD dissertation, Columbia University.

Keller, Suzanne, and M. Zavalloni. 1964. "Ambition and Social Class: A Respecification." *Social Forces,* 43:58–70.

Kelley, Jonathan, and M.D.R. Evans. 1993. "The Legitimation of Inequality: Occupational Earnings in Nine Nations." *American Journal of Sociology,* 99:75–125.

Kellner, Douglas. 1990. *Television and the Crisis of Democracy.* Boulder, Colo.: Westview Press.

Kelly, William, and David Snyder. 1980. "Racial Violence and Socioeconomic Changes among Blacks in the United States." *Social Forces,* 58:739–760.

Kennedy, Paul. 1987. *The Rise and Fall of the Great Powers: Economic Change and Military Conflict from 1500 to 2000.* New York: Random House.

Kentor, Jeffrey. 1981. "Structural Determinants of Peripheral Urbanization: The Effects of International Dependence." *American Sociological Review,* 46:201–211.

Kentor, Jeffrey, and Terry Boswell. 2003. "Foreign Capital Dependence and Development: A New Direction." *American Sociological Review,* 68:301–313.

Kerbo, Harold. 1976a. "Marxist and Functionalist Theories in the Study of Social Stratification: A Comment." *Social Forces,* 55:191–192.

Kerbo, Harold. 1976b. "The Stigma of Welfare and a Passive Poor." *Sociology and Social Research,* 60:173–187.

Kerbo, Harold. 1981a. "Characteristics of the Poor: A Continuing Focus in Social Research." *Sociology and Social Research,* 65:323–331.

Kerbo, Harold. 1982. "Movements of Crisis' and Movements of Affluence': A Critique of Deprivation and Resource Mobilization Theories." *Journal of Conflict Resolution,* 26:645–663.

Kerbo, Harold. 2002. "Review of 'Classless Society,' by Paul Kingston," *Contemporary Sociology,* 31:267–268.

Kerbo, Harold. 2005. "Foreign Investment and Disparities in Economic Development and Poverty Reduction: A Comparative-Historical Analysis of the Buddhist Countries of Southeast Asia." *International Journal of Comparative Sociology,* 46:425–459.

Kerbo, Harold. 2006. *World Poverty in the 21st Century: The Modern World System and the Roots of Global Inequality.* New York: McGraw-Hill.

Kerbo, Harold. 2011. *The Tragedy of Cambodian Poverty: From the Killing Fields to Deprivation in the 21st Century.* London: McFarland Press.

Kerbo, Harold, and L. Richard Della Fave. 1979. "The Empirical Side of the Power Elite Debate: An Assessment and Critique of Recent Research." *Sociological Quarterly,* 20:5–22.

Kerbo, Harold, and L. Richard Della Fave. 1983. "Corporate Linkage and Control of the Corporate Economy: New Evidence and a Reinterpretation." *Sociological Quarterly,* 24:201–218.

Kerbo, Harold, and L. Richard Della Fave. 1984. "Further Notes on the Evolution of Corporate Control and Institutional Investors: A Response to Niemonen." *Sociological Quarterly,* 25:279–283.

Kerbo, Harold, and Juan J. Gonzalez. 2003. "Class and Non-Voting in Comparative Perspective: Possible Causes and Consequences in the United States." Pp 175–196 in Betty Dobratz, Lisa Waldner, and Timothy Buzzell (eds.), *Political Sociology for the 21st Century, Research in Political Sociology, Volume 12.* Boston: JAI.

Kerbo, Harold, and John McKinstry. 1995. *Who Rules Japan?: The Inner-Circles of Economic and Political Power.* Westport, Conn.: Praeger.

Kerbo, Harold, and John McKinstry. 1998. *Modern Japan: A Volume in the Comparative Societies Series.* New York: McGraw-Hill.

Kerbo, Harold, and Keiko Nakao. 1991. "Corporate Structure and Modernization: A Comparative Analysis of Japan and the United States." *International Review of Sociology,* 3:149–174.

Kerbo, Harold, and Richard A. Shaffer. 1986a. "Unemployment and Protest in the United States: 1890–1940: A Methodological Critique and Research Note." *Social Forces,* 64:1046–1056.

Kerbo, Harold, and Richard A. Shaffer. 1986b. "Elite Recognition of Unemployment as a Working Class Issue in the United States, 1890–1940." *Sociology and Social Research,* 70:294–298.

Kerbo, Harold, and Robert Slagter. 2000a. "Thailand, Japan, and the 'East Asian Development Model': The Asian Economic Crisis in World System Perspective." Pp. 119–140 in Frank-Jürgen Richter (ed.), *The East Asian Development Model: Economic Growth, Institutional Failure and the Aftermath of the Crisis.* London: Macmillan.

Kerbo, Harold, and Robert Slagter. 2000b. "The Asian Economic Crisis and the Decline of Japanese Leadership in Asia." In Frank-Jürgen Richter (ed.), *The Asian Economic Crisis.* New York: Quorum Press.

Kerbo, Harold, and Hermann Strasser. 2000. *Modern Germany—A Society in Transition: A Volume in the Comparative Societies Series.* New York: McGraw-Hill.

Kerbo, Harold, Elke Wittenhagen, and Keiko Nakao. 1994a. *Japanische Unternehmen in Deutsch: Unternehmenstruktur und Arbeitsverhältnis.* Gelsenkirchen, Germany: Veroffentlichungsliste des Instituts Arbeit und Technik.

Kerbo, Harold, Elke Wittenhagen, and Keiko Nakao. 1994b. "Japanese Transplant Corporations, Foreign Employees, and the German Economy: A Comparative Analysis of Germany and the United States." Duisburger Bettrage zur Soziologischen Forschung. Duisburg, Germany.

Kerbo, Harold, and Patrick Ziltener. Forthcoming. *Sustainable Development and Poverty Reduction in the Modern World System: Southeast Asia and the Negative Case of Cambodia.*

Kerckhoff, Alan. 1976. "The Status Attainment Process: Socialization or Allocation?" *Social Forces,* 55:368–381.

Kerckhoff, Alan C. 1989. "On the Social Psychology of Social Mobility Processes." *Social Forces,* 68:17–25.

Kerckhoff, Alan, Richard Campbell, and Jerry Trott. 1982. "Dimensions of Educational and Occupational Attainment in Great Britain." *American Sociological Review,* 47:347–364.

Keyes, Charles F. 1989. *Thailand: Buddhist Kingdom as Modern Nation-State.* Boulder, Colo.: Westview Press.

Keyes, Charles R. (ed.). 1979. *Ethnic Adaptation and Identity: The Karen on the Thai Frontier with Burma.* Philadelphia: Institute for the Study of Human Issues.

Khan, Mafruza. 2003. "Media Diversity at Risk." Corporate Research Project, May 29, http://www.corpwatch.org.

Kilgore, Sally. 1991. "The Organizational Context of Tracking in Schools." *American Sociological Review,* 56:189–203.

Kim, ChangHwan, and Arthur Sakamoto. 2008. "The Rise of Intra-Occupational Wage Inequality in the United States." *American Sociological Review,* 73:129–157.

Kim, Eun Nee. 1997. *Big Business, Strong State: Collusion and Conflict in South Korean Development, 1960–1990.* Albany: State University of New York Press.

Kim, Hwanjoon. 2000. "Anti-Poverty Effectiveness of Taxes and Income Transfers in Welfare States." Luxembourg Income Study Working Paper No. 228.

Kimmel, Michael S. 2000. *The Gender Society.* New York: Oxford University Press.

Kingston, Paul W. 2000. *The Classless Society.* Palo Alto, Calif.: Stanford University Press.

Kluegel, James. 1978. "The Causes and Cost of Racial Exclusion from Job Authority." *American Sociological Review,* 43:285–301.

Kluegel, James R. 1990. "Trends in White's Explanations of the Black-White Gap in Socioeconomic Status, 1977–1989." *American Sociological Review,* 55:512–525.

Knoke, David, and Michael Hout. 1974. "Social and Demographic Factors in American Political Party Affiliations." *American Sociological Review,* 39:700–713.

Knottnerus, J. David. 1987. "Status Attainment Research and Its Image of Society." *American Sociological Review,* 52:113–121.

Koh, B. C. 1989. *Japan's Administrative Elite.* Berkeley: University of California Press.

Kohli, Atul. 2004. *State-Directed Development: Political Power and Industrialization in the Global Periphery.* New York: Cambridge University Press.

Kohn, Melvin. 1969. *Class and Conformity.* Homewood, Ill.: Dorsey Press.

Kohn, Melvin. 1976. "Occupational Structure and Alientation." *American Journal of Sociology,* 82:111–130.

Kohn, Melvin, and Carmi Schooler. 1982. "Job Conditions and Personality: A Longitudinal Assessment of Their Reciprocal Effects." *American Journal of Sociology,* 87:1257–1286.

Kolko, Gabriel. 1988. *Confronting the Third World: United States Foreign Policy, 1945–1980.* New York: Pantheon.

Komarovsky, Mirra. 1962. *Blue-Collar Marriage.* New York: Random House.

Korenman, Sanders, and Jane E. Miller. 1997. "Effects of Long-Term Poverty on Physical Health of Children in the National Longitudinal Survey of Youth." Pp. 70–99 in Greg J. Duncan and Jeanne Brooks-Gunn (eds.), *Consequences of Growing Up Poor.* New York: Russell Sage.

Korzeniewicz, Reberto Patricio, and Timothy Patrick Moran. 1997. "World-Economic Trends in the Distribution of Income, 1965–1992." *American Journal of Sociology,* 102:1000–1039.

Krader, Lawrence. 1975. *The Asiatic Mode of Production: Sources, Development and Critique in the Writings of Karl Marx.* Assen, The Netherlands: Van Gorcum.

Kristof, Nicholas D., and Sheryl WuDunn. 2000. *Thunder from the East: Portrait of a Rising Asia.* New York: Knopf.

Kropi, Walter. 1989. "Power, Politics, and State Autonomy in the Development of Social Citizenship: Social Rights during Sickness in Eighteen OECD Countries Since 1953." *American Sociological Review,* 54:309–328.

Kuczynski, Jürgen. 1967. *The Rise of the Working Class.* New York: McGraw-Hill.

Kuhn, Thomas. 1962. *The Structure of Scientific Revolutions.* Chicago: University of Chicago Press.

Kuhn, Thomas. 1970. *The Structure of Scientific Revolutions.* 2nd ed. Chicago: University of Chicago Press.

Kulick, Elliot, and Dick Wilson. 1996. *Time for Thailand: Profile of a New Success.* Bangkok: White Lotus.

Kutz, Myer. 1974. *Rockefeller Power: America's Chosen Family.* New York: Simon & Schuster.

Labovitz, Eugene. 1975. "Race, SES Contexts and Fulfillment of College Aspirations." *Sociological Quarterly,* 16:241–249.

Ladd, Everett Carll, and Karlyn H. Bowman. 1998. *Attitudes toward Economic Inequality.* Washington, D.C.: AEI Press.

Lane, Robert. 1962. *Political Ideology.* New York: Free Press.

Lasson, Kenneth. 1971. *The Workers: Portraits of Nine American Job Holders.* New York: Grossman.

Laumann, Edward, David Knoke, and Yon-Hak Kim. 1985. "An Organizational Approach to State Policy Formation: A Comparative Study of Energy and Health Domains." *American Sociological Review,* 50:1–19.

Leakey, Richard, and Roger Lewin. 1977. *Origins.* New York: Dutton.

Leakey, Richard, and Roger Lewin. 1978. *The People of the Lake.* New York: Doubleday.

Leavy, Marvin. 1974. "Commentary." *American Journal of Sociology,* 80:723–727.

LeDuc, L., R. G. Niemi, and P. Norris (eds.). 1996. *Comparing Democracies: Elections and Voting in Global Perspective.* Thousand Oaks, Calif.: Sage.

Lee, Changsoo, and George De Vos. 1981. *Koreans in Japan: Ethnic Conflict and Accommodation.* Berkeley: University of California Press.

Lee, Cheol-Sung. 2005. "Income Inequality, Democracy, and Public Sector Size." *American Sociological Review,* 70:158–181.

Lee, Cheol-Sung. 2007. "Labor Unions and Good Governance: A Cross-National, Comparative Analysis." *American Sociological Review,* 72:585–609.

Lee, George. 1985. *The Dobe !Kung.* New York: Harcourt Brace Jovanovich.

Lengermann, Patricia Madoo, and Jill Niebrugge-Brantley. 1992. "Contemporary Feminist Theory." Pp. 447–496 in George Ritzer (ed.), *Sociological Theory.* New York: McGraw-Hill.

Lenin, V. I. 1965. *Imperialism: The Highest Stage of Capitalism.* New York: International Publishers.

Lenski, Gerhard. 1966. *Power and Privilege.* New York: McGraw-Hill.

Lenski, Gerhard. 1977. "Sociology and Sociobiology: An Alternative View." *The American Sociologist,* 12:72–75.

Lenski, Gerhard. 1984. *Power and Privilege: A Theory of Social Stratification.* Chapel Hill: University of North Carolina Press.

Lenski, Gerhard. 2005. *Ecological-Evolutionary Theory: Principles and Applications.* Boulder, Colo.: Paradigm.

Lenski, Gerhard, Jean Lenski, and Patrick D. Nolan. 1991 *Human Societies: An Introduction to Macrosociology.* 6th ed. New York: McGraw-Hill.

Lepowsky, Maria. 1993. *Fruit of the Motherland: Gender in an Egalitarian Society.* New York: Columbia University Press.

Le Roy Ladurie, Emmanuel. 1979. *Carnival in Romans.* New York: George Braziller.

Lester, Marilyn. 1980. "Generating Newsworthiness: The Interpretive Construction of Public Events." *American Sociological Review,* 45:984–994.

Levathes, Louise. 1994. *When China Ruled the Seas.* New York: Oxford University Press.

Leventhal, G. 1975. "The Distribution of Rewards and Resources in Groups and Organizations." Pp. 132–143 in L. Berkowitz and E. Walster (eds.), *Advances in Experimental Social Psychology.* New York: Academic Press.

Leventhal, G., J. W. Michaels, and C. Sanford. 1972. "Inequality and Interpersonal Conflict: Reward Allocation and Secrecy about Rewards as Methods of Preventing Conflict." *Journal of Personality and Social Psychology,* 23:88–102.

Levinson, Andrew. 1975. *The Working-Class Majority.* New York: Penguin Books.

Levy, Fred. 1977. "How Big Is the American Underclass?" Working Paper 0090-1, Urban Institute, Washington, D.C.

Lewis, Oscar. 1959. *Five Families: Mexican Case Studies in the Culture of Poverty.* New York: Basic Books.

Lewis, Oscar. 1961. *The Children of Sanchez.* New York: Random House.

Lewis, Oscar. 1966. *La Vida: A Puerto Rican Family in the Culture of Poverty.* New York: Random House.

Lewontin, R. C., Steven Rose, and Leon J. Kamin. 1984. *Not in Our Genes.* New York: Pantheon.

Lichter, Daniel T., Felicia B. LeClere, and Diane K. McLaughlin. 1991. "Local Marriage Markets and the Marital Behavior of Black and White Women." *American Journal of Sociology,* 96:843–867.

Liebow, Elliot. 1967. *Tally's Corner.* Boston: Little, Brown.

Liedtke, Rudiger. 1994. *Wem Gehort die Republik?* (Who Owns the Republic?). Frankfurt: Eichborn.

Lin, Nan, and Wen Xie. 1988. "Occupational Prestige in Urban China." *American Journal of Sociology,* 93:793–833.

Lin, Nan, and Yanjie Bian. 1991. "Getting Ahead in Urban China." *American Journal of Sociology,* 97:657–688.

Lincoln, Edward J. 2001. *Arthritic Japan: The Slow Pace of Economic Reform.* Washington, D.C.: Brookings Institution Press.

Lincoln, James R. 1978. "Community Structure and Industrial Conflict: An Analysis of Strike Activity in SMSAs." *American Sociological Review,* 43:199–220.

Lincoln, James R., and Arne L. Kalleberg. 1985. "Work Organization and Work Force Commitment: A Study of Plants and Employees in the U.S. and Japan." *American Sociological Review,* 50:738–760.

Lincoln, James R., and Arne L. Kalleberg. 1990. *Culture, Control, and Commitment: A Study of Work Organization and Work Attitudes in the United States and Japan.* New York: Cambridge University Press.

Lincoln, James R., Harold R. Kerbo, and Elke Wittenhagen. 1995. "Japanese Companies in Germany: A Case Study in Cross-Cultural Management." *Journal of Industrial Relations,* 25:123–139.

Lipset, Seymour. 1963. "The Value Patterns of Democracy: A Case Study in Comparative Analysis." *American Sociological Review,* 28:515–531.

Lipset, Seymour Martin. 1981. *Political Man: The Social Bases of Politics.* Baltimore: Johns Hopkins University Press.

Lipset, Seymour Martin. 1996. *American Exceptionalism: A Double-Edged Sword.* New York: W. W. Norton.

Liu Binyan, Ruan Ming, and Xu Gang. 1989. *"Tell the World": What Happened in China and Why.* New York: Pantheon Books.

Lobao, Linda, and Gregory Hooks. 2003. "Public Employment, Welfare Transfers, and Economic Well-Being across Local Populations: Does a Lean and Mean Government Benefit the Masses?" *Social Forces,* 82:519–556.

Lorber, Judith. 1994. "Guarding the Gates: The Micropolitics of Gender."

Pp. 270–294 in Michael S. Kimmel (ed.), *The Gendered Society Reader.* New York: Oxford University Press, 2000.

Lord, George, and William Falk. 1980. "An Exploratory Analysis of Individualist versus Structuralist Explanations of Income." *Social Forces,* 59:376–391.

Loscocco, Karyn, and Arne L. Kalleberg. 1988. "Age and the Meaning of Work in the United States and Japan." *Social Forces,* 67:337–356.

Lucas, Samuel R. 2001. "Effectively Maintained Inequality: Educational Transitions, Track Mobility, and Social Background Effects." *American Journal of Sociology,* 106:1642–1690.

Luce, Edward. 2007. *In Spite of the Gods: The Strange Rise of Modern India.* New York: Doubleday.

Lukes, Steven. 1973a. *Émile Durkheim: His Life and Work: A Historical and Critical Study.* New York: Penguin Books.

Lukes, Steven. 1973b. *Individualism.* New York: Harper & Row.

Lundberg, Ferdinand. 1968. *The Rich and the Super-Rich.* New York: Bantam Books.

Lynd, Robert, and Helen Lynd. 1929. *Middletown.* New York: Harcourt Brace Jovanovich.

Lynd, Robert, and Helen Lynd. 1937. *Middletown in Transition.* New York: Harcourt Brace Jovanovich.

MacMillan, Charles J. 1985. *The Japanese Industrial System.* New York: Walter de Gruyter.

MacMullen, Ramsay. 1974. *Roman Social Relations.* New Haven, Conn.: Yale University Press.

McAdam, Doug. 1982. *Political Process and the Development of Black Insurgency, 1930–1970.* Chicago: University of Chicago Press.

McCall, Leslie. 2001. "Sources of Racial Wage Inequality in Metropolitan Labor Markets: Racial, Ethnic, and Gender Differences." *American Sociological Review,* 66:520–541.

McCargo, Duncan, and Ukrist Pathmanand. 2005. *The Thaksinization of Thailand.*

Denmark: Nordic Institute of Asian Studies.

McCarthy, John D., and Mayer N. Zald. 1977. "Resource Mobilization and Social Movements: A Partial Theory." *American Journal of Sociology,* 82:1212–1241.

McClain, James L. 2002. *Japan: A Modern History.* N.Y.: W. W. Norton.

McDonald, Steve, and Glen H. Elder Jr. 2006. "When Does Social Capital Matter? Non-Searching for Jobs across the Life Course." *Social Forces,* 85:521–549.

McLaughlin, Steven. 1978. "Occupational Sex Identification and the Assessment of Male and Female Earnings Inequality." *American Sociological Review,* 43:909–921.

McLellan, David. 1973. *Karl Marx: His Life and Thought.* New York: Harper & Row.

McLeod, Jane D., and Michael J. Shanahan. 1993. "Poverty, Parenting, and Children's Mental Health." *American Sociological Review,* 58:351–366.

McNall, Scott. 1977. "Does Anybody Rule America?: A Critique of Elite Theory and Method." Paper presented at the annual meeting of the America Sociological Association, Chicago.

McNamara, Dennis. 1989. "The Keish and the Korean Business Elite." *Journal of Asian Studies,* 48:310–323.

McPortland, J. 1968. *The Segregated Students in Desegregated Schools: Sources of Influence on Negro Secondary Students.* Baltimore, Md.: Johns Hopkins University Press.

Mahler, Vincent A. 2001. "Economic Globalization, Domestic Politics, and Income Inequality in the Developed Countries." Luxembourg Income Study Working Paper No. 273.

Mahler, V. A. 2002. "Exploring the Subnational Dimension of Income Inequality: An Analysis of the Relationship between Inequality and Electoral Turnout in Developed Countries." *Luxembourg Income Study* Working Paper No. 292.

Mandel, Ernest. 1971. *The Formation of the Economic Thought of Karl Marx: 1843 to "Capital."* New York: Monthly Review Press.

Mandel, Hadas, and Moshe Semyonov. 2006. "A Welfare State Paradox: State Interventions and Women's Employment Opportunities in 22 Countries." *American Journal of Sociology,* 111:1910–1949.

Mankoff, Milton. 1970. "Power in Advanced Capitalist Society: A Review Essay on Recent Elitist and Marxist Criticism of Pluralist Society." *Social Problems,* 17:418–429.

Mann, Michael. 1970. "The Social Cohesion of Liberal Democracy." *American Sociological Review,* 35:423–439.

Marcuse, Herbert. 1964. *One-Dimensional Man.* Boston: Beacon Press.

Marcuse, Herbert. 1971. "Industrialization and Capitalism." Pp. 133–150 in Otto Stammer (ed.), *Max Weber and Sociology Today.* New York: Free Press.

Mare, Robert D., and Christopher Winship. 1991. "Socioeconomic Change and the Decline of Marriage for Blacks and Whites." Pp. 175–202 in Christopher Jencks and Paul E. Peterson (eds.), *The Urban Underclass.* Washington, D.C.: Brookings Institution Press.

Marger, Martin. 1987. *Elites and Masses: An Introduction to Political Sociology.* 2nd ed. Belmont, Calif.: Wadsworth.

Marini, Margaret Mooney, and Pi-Ling Fan. 1997. "The Gender Gap in Earnings at Career Entry." *American Sociological Review,* 62:588–604.

Mariolis, Peter. 1975. "Interlocking Directorates and the Control of Corporations: The Theory of Bank Control." *Social Science Quarterly,* 56:425–439.

Markovits, Andrei S. 1986. *The Politics of the West German Trade Unions: Strategies of Class and Interest Representation in Growth and Crisis.* Cambridge, England: Cambridge University Press.

Marmot, Michael. 2004. *The Status Syndrome: How Social Standing Affects Our Health and Longevity.* New York: Henry Holt.

Martin, Karin A. 1998. "Becoming a Gendered Body: Practices of Preschools." *American Sociological Review,* 63:494–511.

Martin, Nathan, and David Brady. 2007. "Workers of the Less Developed World Unite? A Multilevel Analysis of Unionization in Less Developed Countries." *American Sociological Review,* 72:562–584.

Marx, Gary T. 1974. "Thoughts on a Neglected Category of Social Movement Participant: The Agent Provocateur and the Informant." *American Journal of Sociology,* 80:402–442.

Marx, Karl. 1906. *Capital: A Critique of Political Economy.* New York: Random House.

Marx, Karl. 1964. *Karl Marx: Early Writings.* Edited by T. B. Bottomore. New York: McGraw-Hill.

Marx, Karl. 1971. *The Grundrisse.* Edited by David McLellan. New York: Harper Torchbooks.

Marx, Karl, and Friedrich Engels. 1965. *The German Ideology.* New York: International Publishers.

Maryanski, Alexandra. 1994. "The Pursuit of Human Nature in Sociobiology and Evolutionary Sociology." *Sociological Perspectives,* 37:375–389.

Maryanski, Alexandra, and Jonathan Turner. 1992. *The Social Cage: Human Nature and the Evolution of Society.* Stanford, Calif.: Stanford University Press.

Massey, Douglas. 2001. "Residential Segregation and Neighborhood Conditions in U.S. Metropolitan Areas." Pp. 391–434 in Neil Smelser, William Julius Wilson, and Faith Mitchell (eds.), *America Becoming: Racial Trends and Their Consequences,* vol. I. Washington, D.C.: National Academy Press.

Matras, Judah. 1980. "Comparative Social Mobility." *Annual Review of Sociology,* 6:401–431.

Mayer, A. J., and T. F. Hoult. 1955. "Social Stratification and Combat Survival." *Social Forces,* 34:155–159.

Mayer, Susan E. 2001. "How Did the Increase in Economic Inequality between 1970 and 1990 Affect Children's Educational Attainment?" *American Journal of Sociology,* 107:1–32.

Mayntz, Renate. 1984. "The Higher Civil Service of the Federal Republic of Germany." Pp. 46–101 in Bruce Smith (ed.), *The Higher Civil Service in Europe and Canada.* Washington, D.C.: Brookings Institution Press.

Mazrui, Ali A. 1978. *Africa's International Relations: The Diplomacy of Dependency and Change.* Boulder, Colo.: Westview Press.

Mazrui, Ali A. 1986. *The Africans: A Triple Heritage.* New York: Little, Brown.

Mead, George Herbert. 1935. *Mind, Self, and Society.* Chicago: University of Chicago Press.

Mead, Margaret. 1935, 1950, 1963. "Sex and Temperament in Three Primitive Societies." Pp. 38–43 in Michael S. Kimmel (ed.), *The Gendered Society Reader.* New York: Oxford University Press, 2000.

Menzies, Gavin. 2002. *1421: The Year China Discovered the World.* New York: Bantam Books.

Mercy, James, and Lala Carr Steelman. 1982. "Familial Influence on the Intellectual Attainment of Children." *American Sociological Review,* 47:532–542.

Meredith, Robyn. 2007. *The Elephant and the Dragon: The Rise of India and China and What It Means for All of Us.* New York: Norton.

Messner, Steven F. 1982. "Societal Development, Social Equality, and Homicide: A Cross-National Test of a Durkheimian Model." *Social Forces,* 61:225–240.

Micklethwait, John, and Adrian Wooldridge. 2004. *The Right Nation: Conservative Power in America.* New York: Penguin.

Miliband, Ralph. 1969. *The State in Capitalist Society.* New York: Basic Books.

Miliband, Ralph. 1977. *Marxism and Politics.* New York: Oxford University Press.

Miller, Delbert. 1977. *Handbook of Research Design and Social Measurement.* New York: David McKay.

Miller, Roy Andrew. 1967. *The Japanese Language.* Chicago: University of Chicago Press.

Miller, S. M. 1960. "Comparative Social Mobility." *Current Sociology,* 9:81–89.

Miller, S. M. 1975. "Notes on Neo-Capitalism." *Theory and Society,* 2:1–36.

Miller, S. M. 1976. "The Political Economy of Social Problems: From the Sixties to the Seventies." *Social Problems,* 24:131–141.

Miller, S. M., David Riessman, and A. Seagull. 1971. "Poverty and Self-Indulgence: A Critique of the Non-Deferred Gratification Pattern." Pp. 285–302 in Louis Ferman, Joyce Kornbluh, and Alan Harber (eds.), *Poverty in America.* Ann Arbor: University of Michigan Press.

Miller, Walter. 1971. "Is the Income Gap Closed—No!" Pp. 61–66 in Louis Ferman, Joyce Kornbluh, and Alan Harber (eds.), *Poverty in America.* Ann Arbor: University of Michigan Press.

Mills, C. Wright. 1953. *White Collar.* New York: Oxford University Press.

Mills, C. Wright. 1956. *The Power Elite.* New York: Oxford University Press.

Mills, C. Wright. 1962. *The Marxists.* New York: Dell.

Mills, C. Wright. 1963. *Power, Politics, and People.* Edited by I. L. Horowitz. New York: Oxford University Press.

Mintz, Beth. 1975. "The President's Cabinet, 1897–1972: A Contribution to the Power Structure Debate." *Insurgent Sociologist,* 5:131–148.

Mintz, Beth. 1989. "United States." Pp. 207–226 in Tom Bottomore and Robert J. Brym (eds.), *The Capitalist Class: An International Study.* New York: New York University Press.

Mintz, Beth, Peter Freitag, Carol Hendricks, and Michael Schwartz. 1976. "Problems of Proof in Elite Research." *Social Problems,* 23:314–324.

Mintz, Beth, and Michael Schwartz. 1985. *The Power Structure of American Business.* Chicago: University of Chicago Press.

Mintz, Morton, and Jerry Cohen. 1976. *Power, Inc.: Public and Private Rulers and How to Make Them Accountable.* New York: Viking Press.

Mirande, Alfredo. 1987. *Gringo Justice.* Notre Dame, Ind.: University of Notre Dame Press.

Mishel, Lawrence, and Jared Bernstein. 1993. *The State of Working America, 1992–1993.* Armonk, N.Y.: M. E. Sharpe/Economic Policy Institute.

Mishel, Lawrence, Jared Bernstein, and Sylvia Allegretto. 2007. *The State of Working America, 2006/2007.* Ithaca, N.Y.: Cornell University Press.

Mishel, Lawrence, Jared Bernstein, and Heather Boushey. 2003. *The State of Working America: 2002/2003.* Ithaca, N.Y.: Cornell University Press.

Mishel, Lawrence, Jared Bernstein, and John Schmitt. 1999. *The State of Working America, 1998–99.* Ithaca, N.Y.: Cornell University Press.

Mishel, Lawrence, Jared Bernstein, and John Schmitt. 2001. *The State of Working America, 2000/2001.* Ithaca, N.Y.: Cornell University Press.

Mishel, Lawrence, Jared Bernstein, and Heidi Shierholz. 2009. *The State of Working America: 2008/2009.* Ithaca, N. Y.: Economic Policy Institute, Cornell University Press.

Missingham, Bruce D. 2003. *The Assembly of the Poor in Thailand: From Local Struggles to National Protest Movement.* Chiang Mai, Thailand: Silkworm Books.

Mitchell, Richard. 1967. *The Korean Minority in Japan.* Berkeley: University of California Press.

Mitzman, Arthur. 1969. *The Iron Cage.* New York: Grosset and Dunlap.

Mizruchi, Mark S. 1992. *The Structure of Corporate Political Action: Interfirm Relations and Their Consequences.* Cambridge, Mass.: Harvard University Press.

Moller, Stephanie, David Bradley, Evelyne Huber, Francois Nielsen, and John Stephens. 2003. "Determinants of Relative Poverty in Advanced Capitalist Democracies." *American Sociological Review,* 68:22–51.

Moore, Barrington. 1966. *Social Origins of Dictatorship and Democracy: Lord and Peasant in the Making of the Modern World.* Boston: Beacon Press.

Moore, Barrington. 1978. *Injustice: The Social Bases of Obedience and Revolt.* White Plains, N.Y.: M. E. Sharpe.

Moran, Timothy Patrick. 2006. "Statistical Inference and Patterns of Inequality in the Global North." *Social Forces,* 84:1799–1818.

Morgan, Edmund. 1956. *The Birth of the Republic, 1763–89.* Chicago: University of Chicago Press.

Morgan, Laurie A. 1998. "Glass-Ceiling Effect or Cohort Effect?: A Longitudinal Study of the Gender Earnings Gap for Engineers, 1982–1989." *American Sociological Review,* 63:479–483.

Morioka, Koji. 1989. "Japan." Pp. 140–176 in Tom Bottomore and Robert J. Brym (eds.), *The Capitalist Class: An International Study.* New York: New York University Press.

Morris, Aldon. 1981. "Black Southern Student Sit-In Movement: An Analysis of Internal Structure." *American Sociological Review,* 46:744–767.

Morris, Robert. 1979. *Social Policy of the American Welfare State.* New York: Harper & Row.

Mosley, Leonard. 1978. *Dulles.* New York: Dial Press.

Mouer, Ross, and Yoshio Sugimoto. 1986. *Images of Japanese Society.* London: Kegan Paul International.

Mouw, Ted. 2003. "Social Capital and Finding a Job: Do Contacts Matter?" *American Sociological Review,* 88:868–898.

Muennig, Peter, Kevin Fiscella, Daniel Tancredi, and Peter Franks. 2010. "The Relative Health Burden of Selected Social and Behavioral Risk Factors in the United States: Implications for Policy." *American Journal of Public Health,* January, www.ajph.aphapublications.org/.

Muller, Edward. 1985. "Income Inequality, Regime Repressiveness, and Political Violence." *American Sociological Review,* 50:47–61.

Mullins, Nicholas. 1973. *Theories and Theory Groups in Contemporary American Sociology.* New York: Harper & Row.

Murdock, George. 1949. *Social Structure.* New York: Macmillan.

Murdock, George. 1957. "World Ethnographic Sample." *American Anthropologist,* 59:664–687.

Murray, Charles. 1984. *Losing Ground: American Social Policy, 1950–1980.* New York: Basic Books.

Muscat, Robert J. 1994. *The Fifth Tiger: A Study of Thai Development.* Armonk, N.Y.: M. E. Sharpe.

Myrdal, Gunnar. 1968. *The Challenge of World Poverty.* New York: Pantheon.

Nahm, Andrew C. 1988. *Korea: Tradition and Transformation.* Elizabeth, N.J., and Seoul, Korea: Hollym International.

Nakane, Chie. 1970. *Japanese Society.* Berkeley: University of California Press.

Nakao, Keiko, and Judith Treas. 1990. "Occupational Prestige in the United States Revisited: Twenty-Five Years of Stability and Change." Paper presented at the annual meetings of the American Sociological Association. Washington, D.C., August.

Nakao, Keiko, and Judith Treas. 1994. "Updating Occupational Prestige and Socioeconomic Scales: How the New Measures Measure Up." *Sociological Methodology,* 24:1–72.

Naoi, Atsushi, and Carmi Schooler. 1985. "Occupational Conditions and Psychological Functions in Japan." *American Journal of Sociology,* 90:729–752.

Neary, Ian. 1997. "Burakumin in Contemporary Japan." Pp. 50–78 in Michael Weiner (ed.), *Japan's Minorities: The Illusion of Homogeneity.* London: Routledge.

Needham, Joseph. 1983. *Science and Civilization in China.* Cambridge, England: Cambridge University Press.

Nielsen, Francois. 1994. "Income Inequality and Industrial Development: Dualism Revisited." *American Sociological Review,* 59:654–677.

Nielsen, Joyce McCarl. 1990. *Sex and Gender in Society: Perspectives on Stratification.* Prospect Heights, Ill.: Waveland Press.

Nieuwbeerta, Paul. 2001. "The Democratic Class Struggle in Postwar Societies: Traditional Class Voting in Twenty Countries, 1945–1990." Pp. 121–136 in Terry Nichols Clark and Seymour Martin Lipset (eds.), *The Breakdown of Class Politics: A Debate on Post-Industrial Stratification.* Washington, D.C.: Woodrow Wilson Center Press.

Nisbet, Robert. 1959. "The Decline and Fall of Social Class." *Pacific Sociological Review,* 2:11–17.

Nolan, Patrick, and Gerhard Lenski. 1998. *Human Societies: An Introduction to Macrosociology.* New York: McGraw-Hill.

Nolan, Patrick D. 1983a. "Status in the World Economy and National Structure and Development." *International Journal of Contemporary Sociology,* 24:109–120.

Nolan, Patrick D. 1983b. "Status in the World System, Income Inequality, and Economic Growth." *American Journal of Sociology,* 89:410–419.

Nord, Mark, Margaret Andrews, and Steven Carlson. 2009. "Household Food Security in the United States, 2009," U.S. Department of Agriculture, www.usda.gov.

North, C. C., and P. K. Hatt. 1947. "Jobs and Occupations: A Popular Evaluation." *Opinion News,* 9:3–13.

Ofshe, L., and R. Ofshe. 1970. *Utility and Choice in Social Interaction.* Upper Saddle River, N.J.: Prentice Hall.

Okamoto, Dina G. 2003. "Toward a Theory of Panethnicity: Explaining Asian American Collective Action." *American Sociological Review,* 68:811–842.

Okumura Hiroshi. 1978. *Kigyō Shūdan no Keieisha* (Leaders in an Era of Industrial Groups). Tokyo: Nikei Shinsha.

Okumura Hiroshi. 1983. *Shin-Nihon no Roku Dai Kigyō Shūdan* (Six Great Industrial Groups of Laterday Japan). Tokyo: Daiyamondosha.

Olsen, Nancy. 1973. "Family Structure and Independence Training in a Taiwanese Village." *Journal of Marriage and Family,* 35:512–519.

Olson, Steve. 2003. *Mapping Human History: Genes, Race, and Our Common Human Origins.* New York: Houghton Mifflin.

Oppenheimer, Martin. 1969. *The Urban Guerrilla.* Chicago: Quadrangle Books.

Orloff, Ann Shola, and Theda Skocpol. 1984. "Why Not Equal Protection? Explaining the Politics of Public Social Spending in Britain, 1900–1911, and the United States, 1800s–1920." *American Sociological Review,* 49:726–750.

Osberg, Lars, and Timothy Smeeding. 2006. "'Fair' Inequality? Attitudes toward Pay Differentials: The United States in Comparative Perspective." *American Sociological Review,* 71:450–473.

Osborne, Milton. 1995. *Southeast Asia: An Introductory History.* Brisbane: Allen and Unwin.

Ōsono Tomokazu. 1991. *Kigyō Keiretsu to Gyōkai Chizu* (Map of Industrial *Keiretsu* and Other Big Business Circles). Tokyo: Nihon Jitsugyo Shuppansha.

Ostrander, Susan A. 1984. *Women of the Upper Class.* Philadelphia: Temple University Press.

O'Sullivan, Mary A. 2000. *Contests for Corporate Control: Corporate Governance and Economic Performance in the United States and Germany.* New York: Oxford University Press.

Page, Charles H. 1969. *Class and American Sociology.* New York: Schocken Books.

Paige, Jeffrey. 1975. *Agrarian Revolution.* New York: Free Press.

Pampel, Fred, and John Williamson. 1985. "Age Structure, Politics and Cross-National Patterns of Public Pension Expenditures." *American Sociological Review,* 50:782–799.

Pampel, Fred C., and John B. Williamson. 1988. "Welfare Spending in Advanced Industrial Democracies, 1950–1980." *American Journal of Sociology,* 93:1424–1456.

Parcel, Toby. 1979. "Race, Regional Labor Markets and Earnings." *American Sociological Review,* 44:262–279.

Parcel, Toby L., and Charles W. Mueller. 1989. "Temporal Change in Occupational Earnings Attainment, 1970–1980." *American Sociological Review,* 54:622–634.

Parkin, Frank. 1971. *Class Inequality and Political Order: Social Stratification in Capitalist and Communist Societies.* New York: Praeger.

Parsons, Talcott. 1937. *The Structure of Social Action.* New York: Free Press.

Parsons, Talcott. 1951. *The Social System.* New York: Free Press.

Parsons, Talcott. 1960. "Authority, Legitimization, and Political Action." Pp. 170–198 in *Structure and Process in Modern Societies.* New York: Free Press.

Parsons, Talcott. 1964. *Essays in Sociological Theory.* New York: Free Press.

Parsons, Talcott. 1968. "The Distribution of Power in American Society." Pp. 60–87 in G. William Domhoff and Hoyt B. Ballard (eds.), *C. Wright Mills and the Power Elite.* Boston: Beacon Press.

Parsons, Talcott. 1970. "Equality and Inequality in Modern Society, or Social Stratification Revisited." Pp. 13–72 in Edward O. Laumann (ed.), *Social Stratification.* New York: Bobbs-Merrill.

Parsons, Talcott. 1977. "Comment on Burger's Critique." *American Journal of Sociology,* 83:335–339.

Pasuk, Phongpaichit, and Chris Baker. 1996. *Thailand: Economy and Politics.* Kuala Lumpur: Oxford University Press.

Pasuk, Phongpaichit, and Chris Baker. 1998. *Thailand's Boom and Bust.* Chiang Mai, Thailand: Silkworm Books.

Pasuk, Phongpaichit, and Chris Baker, 2004. *Thaksin: The Business of Politics in Thailand.* Chaing Mai, Thailand: Silkworm Books.

Pasuk, Phongpaichit, Piriyarangsan Sungsidh, and Treerat Nualnoi. 1998. *Guns, Girls, Gambling, Ganja: Thailand's Illegal Economy and Public Policy.* Chiang Mai, Thailand: Silkwood Books.

Patterson, James T. 1986. *America's Struggle against Poverty, 1900–1985.* Cambridge, Mass.: Harvard University Press.

Pavetti, Ladonna A. 2001. "Welfare Policy in Transition: Redefining the Social Contract for Poor Families with Children and for Immigrants." Pp. 278–313 in Sheldon H. Danziger and Robert H. Haveman (eds.), *Understanding Poverty.* Cambridge, Mass.: Harvard University Press.

Paxton, Pamela, Melanie M. Hughes, and Jennifer L. Green. 2006. "The International Women's Movement and Women's Political Representation, 1893–2003." *American Sociological Review,* 71:898–920.

Payne, Robert. 1964. *The Life and Death of Lenin.* New York: Simon & Schuster.

Pearl, Meyer, and Partners. 2006. "2006 CEO Compensation Report." www.pearlmeyer.com.

Pearlin, Leonard. 1971. *Class Context and Family Relations: A Cross-National Study.* Boston: Little, Brown.

Pease, John, William Form, and Joan Huber. 1970. "Ideological Currents in American Stratification Literature." *American Sociologist,* 5:127–137.

Persell, C. H. 1977. *Education and Inequality: A Theoretical and Empirical Synthesis.* New York: Free Press.

Peterson, Trond, and Laurie A. Morgan. 1995. "Separate and Unequal: Occupation-Establishment Sex Segregation and the Gender Wage Gap." *American Journal of Sociology,* 101:329–365.

Pew Research Center. 2004. *News Audiences Increasingly Polarized.* http://pewresearch.org/.

Pfautz, Harold. 1953. "The Current Literature on Social Stratification: Critique and Bibliography." *American Journal of Sociology,* 58:391–418.

Pfeffer, Richard. 1979. *Working for Capitalism.* New York: Columbia University Press.

Pfeiffer, John. 1977. *The Emergence of Society: A Prehistory of the Establishment.* New York: McGraw-Hill.

Pharr, Susan J. 1990. *Losing Face: Status Politics in Japan.* Berkeley: University of California Press.

Phelan, J., Bruce G. Link, Ann Stueve, and Robert E. Moore. 1995. "Education, Social Liberalism, and Economic Conservatism: Attitudes toward Homeless People." *American Sociological Review,* 60:126–140.

Phillips, Peter. 1994. *A Relative Advantage: Sociology of the San Francisco Bohemian Club.* PhD dissertation, University of California, Davis.

Piven, Frances Fox, and Richard Cloward. 1971. *Regulating the Poor: The Functions of Public Welfare.* New York: Pantheon Books.

Piven, Frances Fox, and Richard Cloward. 1977. *Poor People's Movements: Why They Succeed, Why They Fail.* New York: Pantheon Books.

Piven, Frances Fox, and Richard Cloward. 1982. *The New Class War: Reagan's Attack on the Welfare State and Its Consequences.* New York: Pantheon Books.

Piven, Frances Fox, and Richard Cloward. 1988. *Why Americans Don't Vote.* New York: Pantheon Books.

Piven, Frances Fox, and Richard Cloward. 2000. *Why Americans Still Don't Vote: And Why Politicians Want It That Way.* Boston: Beacon Press.

Podolny, Joel M., and James N. Baron. 1997. "Resources and Relationships: Social Networks and Mobility in the Workplace." *American Sociological Review,* 62:673–693.

Pornchokchai, Sopon. 1992. *Bangkok Slums: Review and Recommendations.* Bangkok: Agency for Real Estate Affairs.

Portes, Alejandro. 1976. "On the Sociology of National Development: Theories and Issues." *American Journal of Sociology,* 85:55–85.

Portes, Alejandro. 1998. "Social Capital: Its Origins and Applications in Modern Sociology." *Annual Review of Sociology,* 24:1–24.

Poulantzas, Nicos. 1973. *Political Power and Social Classes.* London: Verso.

Poulantzas, Nicos. 1975. *Classes and Contemporary Capitalism.* London: NLB.

Powers, Mary G. 1982. *Measures of Socioeconomic Status: Current Issues.* Boulder, Colo.: Westview Press.

Powers, Mary G., and Joan J. Holmberg. 1978. "Occupational Status Scores: Changes Introduced by the Inclusion of Women." *Demography,* 15:183–204.

Powers, Mary G., and William Seltzer. 1998. "Occupational Status and Mobility among Undocumented Immigrants by Gender." *International Migration Review,* 32:21–55.

Pressman, Steven. 2001. "The Decline of the Middle Class: An International Perspective." Luxembourg Income Study Working Paper No. 280.

Preston, Samuel H., and Cameron Campbell. 1993. "Differential Fertility and the Distribution of Traits: The Case of IQ." *American Journal of Sociology,* 98:997–1019.

Prestowitz, Clyde. 2005. *Three Billion New Capitalists: The Great Shift of Wealth and Power to the East.* New York: Basic Books.

Putnam, Robert. 1976. *The Comparative Study of Elites.* Upper Saddle River, N.J.: Prentice Hall.

Pye, Lucian W. 1985. *Asian Power and Politics: The Cultural Dimensions of Authority.* Cambridge, Mass.: Belknap Press/Harvard University Press.

Pye, Lucian W. 2000. "'Asian Values': From Dynamos to Dominoes?" Pp. 244–254 in Lawrence E. Harrison and Samuel P. Huntington (eds.), *Culture Matters: How Values Shape Human Progress.* New York: Basic Books.

Quadagno, Jill. 1979. "Paradigms in Evolutionary Theory: The Sociobiological Model of Natural Selection." *American Sociological Review,* 44:100–109.

Quadagno, Jill S. 1984. "Welfare Capitalism and the Social Security Act of 1935." *American Sociological Review,* 49:632–647.

Raabe, Phyllis Hutton. 1973. *Status and Its Impact: New Orleans' Carnival. The Social Upper Class and Upper-Class Power.* PhD dissertation, Department of Sociology, Pennsylvania State University.

Radcliffe-Brown, A. R. 1948. *The Andaman Islanders.* New York: Free Press.

Raff, Diether. 1988. *A History of Germany: From the Medieval Empire to the Present.* Hamburg, Germany: Berg.

Ragin, Charles C. 2000. *Fuzzy-Set Social Science.* Chicago: University of Chicago Press.

Ragin, Charles C., and David Zaret. 1983. "Theory and Method in Comparative Research: Two Strategies." *Social Forces,* 61:731–754.

Rainwater, Lee. 1969. "The Problem of Lower-Class Culture and Poverty-War Strategy." Pp. 229–259 in Daniel P. Moynihan (ed.), *On Understanding Poverty.* New York: Basic Books.

Rasmussen, Susan. 2001. "Pastoral Nomadism and Gender: Status and Prestige, Economic Contribution, and Division of Labor among the Tuareg of Niger." Pp. 280–293 in Caroline B. Brettell and Carolyn F. Sargent (eds.), *Gender in Cross-Cultural Perspective.* Upper Saddle River, N.J.: Prentice Hall.

Rawlins, V. L., and L. Ulman. 1974. "The Utilization of College Trained Manpower in the United States." In M. S. Gordon (ed.), *Higher Education and the Labor Market.* New York: McGraw-Hill.

Redman, Charles. 1978. *The Rise of Civilization: From Early Farmers to Urban Society in the Ancient Near East.* San Francisco: Freeman.

Reich, Michael. 1991. *Racial Inequality: A Political-Economic Analysis.* Princeton, N.J.: Princeton University Press.

Reich, Robert. 1981. *The Work of Nations: Preparing Ourselves for 21st Century Capitalism.* New York: Vintage Books.

Rein, Martin. 1971. "Problems in the Definition and Measurement of Poverty." Pp. 116–131 in Louis Ferman, Joyce Kornbluh, and Alan Harber (eds.), *Poverty in America.* Ann Arbor: University of Michigan Press.

Reischauer, Edwin O., and Albert M. Craig. 1978. *Japan: Tradition and Transformation.* New York: Houghton Mifflin.

Reiss, Albert, O. D. Duncan, Paul Hatt, and C. C. North. 1961. *Occupations and Social Status.* New York: Free Press.

Reskin, Barbara F. 1988. "Bringing the Men Back In: Sex Differentiation and the Devaluation of Women's Work." *Gender and Society,* 2, No. 1:58–81.

Rist, R. C. 1970. "Student Social Class and Teacher Expectations: The Self-fulfilling Prophecy in Ghetto Education." *Harvard Educational Review,* 40:411–450.

Ritzer, George. 1975. *Sociology: A Multiple Paradigm Science.* Boston: Allyn & Bacon.

Ritzer, George. 1980. *Sociology: A Multiple Paradigm Science.* Rev. ed. Boston: Allyn & Bacon.

Ritzer, George. 2004. *Sociological Theory.* 8th ed. New York: McGraw-Hill.

Robinson, Robert, and Wendell Bell. 1978. "Equality, Success, and Social Injustice in England and the United States." *American Sociological Review,* 43:125–143.

Robinson, Robert, and Jonathan Kelley. 1979. "Class as Conceived by Marx and Dahrendorf: Effects on Income Inequality, Class Consciousness, and Class Conflict in the United States and Great Britain." *American Sociological Review,* 44:38–58.

Robinson, Robert V. 1984. "Reproducing Class Relations in Industrial Capitalism." *American Sociological Review,* 49:182–196.

Robinson, Robert V., and Maurice A. Garnier. 1985. "Class Reproduction among Men and Women in France: Reproduction Theory on Its Home Ground." *American Journal of Sociology,* 91:250–281.

Rodman, Hyman. 1963. "The Lower Class Value Stretch." *Social Forces,* 42:205–215.

Rogoff, Natalie. 1953a. "Recent Trends in Occupational Mobility." Pp. 442–454 in Reinhard Bendix and Seymour Lipset (eds.), *Class, Status, and Power.* New York: Free Press.

Rogoff, Natalie. 1953b. *Recent Trends in Occupational Mobility.* New York: Free Press.

Roosevelt, Kermit. 1979. *Counter Coup: The Struggle for the Control of Iran.* New York: McGraw-Hill.

Roscigno, Vincent J., Donald Tomaskovic-Devey, and Martha Crowley. 2006. "Education and Inequalities of Place." *Social Forces,* 84:2121–2145.

Rose, R., and I. McAllister. 1986. *Voters Begin to Choose: From Closed-Class to Open Elections in Britain.* London: Sage.

Rosen, Ellen Israel. 2002. *Making Sweatshops: The Globalization of the U.S. Apparel Industry.* Berkeley: University of California Press.

Rosen, Lawrence, and Robert Bell. 1966. "Mate Selection in the Upper Class." *Sociological Quarterly,* 7:157–166.

Rosenau, James. 1961. *Public Opinion and Foreign Policy.* New York: Random House.

Rosenbaum, J. E. 1975. "The Stratification of the Socialization Processes." *American Sociological Review,* 40:48–54.

Rosenberg, Morris, and Leonard I. Pearlin. 1978. "Social Class and Self-Esteem among Children and Adults." *American Journal of Sociology,* 84:53–77.

Rosenstone, Steven J., and John Mark Hansen. 1993. *Mobilization, Participation, and Democracy in America.* New York: Macmillan.

Rosenthal, R., and L. Jacobson. 1968. *Pygmalion in the Classroom.* New York: Holt, Rinehart and Winston.

Rossi, Peter, and Katharine Lyall. 1976. *Reforming Public Welfare.* New York: Russell Sage.

Rostow, Walter. 1960. *The Stages of Economic Growth.* New York: Cambridge University Press.

Roy, William G. 1981. "The Vesting of Interests and the Determinants of Political Power: Size, Network Structure, and Mobilization of American Industries, 1886–1905." *American Journal of Sociology,* 86:1287–1310.

Rubin, Beth. 1986. "Class Struggle American Style: Unions, Strikes, and Wages." *American Sociological Review,* 51:618–631.

Rubinson, Richard. 1976. "The World Economy and the Distribution of Income within States: A Cross-National Study." *American Sociological Review,* 41:638–659.

Rubinson, Richard. 1986. "Class Formation, Politics, and Institutions: Schooling in the United States." *American Journal of Sociology,* 92:519–538.

Rubinson, Richard, and Dan Quinlan. 1977. "Democracy and Social Inequality: A Reanalysis." *American Sociological Review,* 42:611–623.

Rudra, Nita. 2008. *Globalization and the Race to the Bottom in Developing Countries: Who Really Gets Hurt?* New York: Cambridge University Press.

Ryan, William. 1971. *Blaming the Victim.* New York: Vintage Books.

Sadker, Myra, and David Sadker. 1994. *Failing at Fairness; How America's Schools Cheat Girls.* New York: Scribner's.

Sahlins, Marshall, and Elman Service. 1960. *Evolution and Culture.* Ann Arbor: University of Michigan Press.

Sakamoto, Arthur, and Meichu D. Chen. 1991. "Inequality and Attainment in a Dual Labor Market." *American Sociological Review,* 56:295–308.

Salamon, Lester, and John Siegfried. 1977. "Economic Power and Political Influence: The Impact of Industry Structure on Public Policy." *American Political Science Review,* 71:1026–1043.

Salert, Barbara, and John Sprague. 1980. *The Dynamics of Riots.* Ann Arbor, Mich.: Inter-University Consortium for Political and Social Research.

Salisbury, Harrison. 1977. *Black Night, White Snow: Russia's Revolutions, 1905–1917.* New York: Doubleday.

Salisbury, Harrison E. 1989. *Tiananmen Diary: Thirteen Days in June.* New York: Little, Brown.

Sallach, David. 1974. "Class Domination and Ideological Hegemony." *Sociological Quarterly,* 15:38–50.

Sampson, Anthony. 1973. *The Sovereign State of I.T.&T.* New York: Stein and Day.

Sanday, Peggy. 1981. *Female Power and Male Dominance: On the Origins of Sexual Inequality.* New York: Cambridge University Press.

Sanders, Jimy M., and Victor Nee. 1996. "Immigrant Self-Employment: The Family as Social Capital and the Value of Human Capital." *American Sociological Review,* 61:231–249.

Sanderson, Stephen, D. Alex Heckert, and Joshua K. Dubrow. 2005. "Militarist, Marxian, and Non-Marxian Materialist Theories of Gender Inequality: A Cross-Cultural Test." *Social Forces,* 83:1425–1441.

Schafer, W. E., and C. Olexa. 1971. *Tracking and Opportunity: The Locking-Out Process and Beyond.* Scranton, Pa.: Chandler.

Schama, Simon. 1989. *Citizens: A Chronicle of the French Revolution.* New York: Knopf.

Schattschneider, E. E. 1960. *The Semi-Sovereign People: A Realist's View of Democracy in America.* New York: Holt, Rinehart and Winston.

Schneider, Eric C., Alan M. Zaslavasky, and Arnold M. Epstein. 2002. "Racial Disparities in the Quality of Care for Enrollees in Medicare Managed Care." *Journal of the American Medical Association,* 287:1288–1294.

Schooler, Carmi, and Atsushi Naoi. 1988. "The Psychological Effects of Traditional and of Economically Peripheral Job Settings in Japan." *American Journal of Sociology,* 94:335–355.

Schram, Sanford F., and J. Patrick Turbett. 1983. "Civil Disorder and the Welfare Explosion: A Two Step Process." *American Sociological Review,* 48:408–414.

Schriftgiesser, Karl. 1967. *Business and Public Policy.* Upper Saddle River, N.J.: Prentice Hall.

Schwartz, B. 1974. "Waiting, Exchange, and Power: The Distribution of Time in Social Systems." *American Journal of Sociology,* 79:841–870.

Scott, John. 1991a. "Networks of Corporate Power: A Comparative Assessment." *Annual Review of Sociology,* 17:181–203.

Scott, John. 1991b. *Who Rules Britain?* Cambridge, England: Polity.

Sekhon, Joti. 2000. *Modern India: A Volume in the Comparative Societies Series.* New York: McGraw-Hill.

Sennett, Richard, and Jonathan Cobb. 1973. *The Hidden Injuries of Class.* New York: Vintage Books.

Sewell, William. 1971. "Inequality of Opportunity for Higher Education." *American Sociological Review,* 36:793–809.

Sewell, William, and Robert Hauser. 1975. *Education, Occupation, and Earnings: Achievement in the Early Career.* New York: Academic Press.

Sewell, William, and Vimal Shah. 1968. "Parents' Education and Children's Education Aspirations and Achievements." *American Sociological Review,* 33:191–209.

Sewell, William, A. O. Haller, and G. W. Ohlendorf. 1970. "The Educational and Early Occupational Status Attainment Process: A Replication and Revision." *American Sociological Review,* 35:1014–1027.

Shaffer, Richard A., and Harold R. Kerbo. 1987. "Welfare Development in the United States, 1890–1940: An Empirical Test of Competing Theories." Paper presented at the meetings of the Research Committee on Social Stratification of the International Sociological Association. Berkeley, August.

Shapiro, Andrew L. 1992. *We're Number One: Where America Stands—and Falls—in the New World Order.* New York: Vintage Books.

Shipler, David K. 2004. *The Working Poor: Invisible in America.* New York: Knopf.

Shirahase, Sawako. 2001. "Japanese Income Inequality by Household Types in Comparative Perspective." Luxembourg Income Study Working Paper No. 268.

Shoup, Laurence. 1975. "Shaping the Postwar World: The Council of Foreign Relations and U.S. War Aims during WW II." *Insurgent Sociologist,* 5:9–52.

Shoup, Laurence, and William Minter. 1977. *Imperial Brain Trust.* New York: Monthly Review Press.

Shulman, Beth. 2003. *The Betrayal of Work: How Low-Wage Jobs Fail 30 Million Americans.* New York: New Press.

Siegel, Paul. 1971. "Prestige in the American Occupational Structure." PhD dissertation, the University of Chicago.

Simkus, Albert, and Peter Robert. 1989. "Attitudes toward Inequality under a Kind of Socialism: Hungary, 1987." Paper presented at the meeting of the Research Committee on Social Stratification of the International Sociological Association. Stanford University, August.

Simmel, Georg. 1905/1955. *Conflict and the Web of Group Affiliations.* Edited by Kurt H. Wolff and Reinhard Bendix. New York: Free Press.

Simmel, Georg. 1908/1971. "The Poor." In D. Levine (ed.), *Georg Simmel.* Chicago: University of Chicago Press.

Simpson, Miles. 1990. "Political Rights and Income Inequality: A Cross National Test." *American Sociological Review,* 55:682–693.

Sio, Arnold. 1969. "Interpretations of Slavery: The Slave Status in the Americas." Pp. 63–73 in Celia Heller (ed.), *Structured Social Inequality.* New York: Macmillan.

Skinner, Elliot. (Ed.). 1973. *Peoples and Cultures of Africa.* New York: Doubleday.

Skocpol, Theda. 1976. "Old Regime Legacies and Communist Revolutions in Russia and China." *Social Forces,* 55:284–315.

Skocpol, Theda. 1979. *States and Social Revolutions: A Comparative Analysis of France, Russia, and China.* New York: Cambridge University Press.

Skocpol, Theda. 1992. *Protecting Soldiers and Mothers: The Political Origins of Social Policy in the United States*. Cambridge, Mass.: Harvard University Press.

Skocpol, Theda, and Edwin Amenta. 1985. "Did Capitalists Shape Social Security?" *American Sociological Review*, 50:572–575.

Slagter, Robert, and Harold Kerbo. 2000. *Modern Thailand: A Volume in the Comparative Societies Series*. New York: McGraw-Hill.

Slomczynski, Kazimierz, and Tadeusz K. Krauze. 1987. "Cross-National Similarity in Social Mobility Patterns: A Direct Test of the Fatherman–Jones–Hauser Hypothesis." *American Sociological Review*, 52:598–611.

Slomczynski, Kazimierz, Joanne Miller, and Melvin Kohn. 1981. "Stratification, Work, and Values: A Polish–United States Comparison." *American Sociological Review*, 46:720–744.

Smeeding, Timothy M. 1997. "Financial Poverty in Developed Countries: The Evidence from LIS." Luxembourg Income Study, Working Paper No. 155.

Smeeding, Timothy M., Lee Rainwater, and Gary Burtless. 2001. "United States Poverty in a Cross-National Context." In Sheldon H. Danziger and Robert H. Haveman (eds.), *Understanding Poverty*. New York and Cambridge, Mass.: Russell Sage and Harvard University Press.

Smelser, Neil J. 1976. *Comparative Methods in the Social Sciences*. Upper Saddle River, N.J.: Prentice Hall.

Smith, Adam. 1950/1776. *The Wealth of Nations*. London: Dent.

Smith, Bruce. 1984. "The Higher Civil Service in Comparative Perspective." Pp. 203–257 in Bruce Smith (ed.), *The Higher Civil Service in Europe and Canada*. Washington, D.C.: Brookings Institution Press.

Smith, David. 1974. *Who Rules the Universities?* New York: Monthly Review Press.

Smith, Martin. 1999. *Burma: Insurgency and the Politics of Ethnicity*. Bangkok: White Lotus Press.

Smith, Michael R. 1990. "What Is New in 'New Structuralist' Analyses of Earnings?" *American Sociological Review*, 55:827–841.

Snipp, C. Mathew. 1992. "Sociological Perspectives on American Indians." *Annual Review of Sociology*, 18:351–371.

Snyder, David. 1975. "Institutional Setting and Industrial Conflict: Comparative Analysis of France, Italy, and the United States." *American Sociological Review*, 40:259–278.

Snyder, David, and Edward Kick. 1979. "Structural Position in the World System and Economic Growth, 1955–1970: A Multiple Analysis of Transnational Interactions." *American Journal of Sociology*, 84:1096–1128.

Soboul, Albert. 1974. *The French Revolution, 1787–1799: From the Storming of the Bastille to Napoleon*. New York: Random House.

Solon, Gary. 1992. "International Income Mobility in the United States." *American Economic Review*, 82:393–408.

Solon, Gary. 2002. "Cross-Country Differences in Intergenerational Earning Mobility." *Journal of Economic Perspectives*, 16:59–66.

Solzhenitsyn, Aleksandr. 1976. *Lenin in Zurich*. New York: Farrar, Straus, and Giroux.

Solzhenitsyn, Aleksandr. 1980. *The Oak and the Calf*. New York: Harper & Row.

Somers, Margaret R., and Fred Block. 2006. "From Poverty to Perversity: Ideas, Markets, and Institutions over 200 Years of Welfare Debate." *American Sociological Review*, 70:260–287.

Soref, Michael. 1976. "Social Class and a Division of Labor within the Corporate Elite: A Note on Class, Interlocking, and Executive Committee Membership of Directors of U.S. Firms." *Sociological Quarterly*, 17:360–368.

Sorensen, Aage B. 1990. "Throwing the Sociologists Out? A Reply to Smith." *American Sociological Review*, 55:842–845.

Sorenson, Jesper, and Olav Sorenson. 2007. "Corporate Demography and Income

Inequality." *American Sociological Review,* 72: 766–783.

Sorkin, Alan. 1978. "The Economic Base of Indian Life." *The Annals,* 436:1–12.

Sorokin, Pitirim. 1959. *Social and Cultural Mobility.* New York: Free Press.

South, Scott J., and Weiman Xu. 1990. "Local Industrial Dominance and Earnings Attainment." *American Sociological Review,* 55:591–599.

Sowell, Thomas. 1978. *Essays and Data on American Ethnic Groups.* Washington, D.C.: Urban Institute.

Sowell, Thomas. 1981. *Ethnic America: A History.* New York: Basic Books.

Sowell, Thomas. 1994. *Race and Culture: A World View.* New York: Basic Books.

Spaeth, Joe. 1976. "Cognitive Complexity: A Dimension Underlying the Socioeconomic Achievement Process." Pp. 153–189 in William Sewell, Robert Hauser, and David Featherman (eds.), *Schooling and Achievement in American Society.* New York: Academic Press.

Spaeth, Joe. 1979. "Vertical Differentiation among Occupations." *American Sociological Review,* 44:746–762.

Spohn, Willfried, and Y. Michel Bodemann. 1989. "Federal Republic of Germany." Pp. 73–108 in Tom Bottomore and Robert J. Brym (eds.), *The Capitalist Class: An International Study.* New York: New York University Press.

Srinivas, M. N. (ed.) 1996. *Caste: Its Twentieth Century Avatar.* New Delhi: Viking Press.

Stack, Steven. 1978a. "The Effect of Direct Government Involvement in the Economy on the Degree of Income Inequality: A Cross-National Study." *American Sociological Review,* 43:880–888.

Stack, Steven. 1978b. "Internal Political Organization and the World Economy of Income Inequality." *American Sociological Review,* 42:271–272.

Stanfiel, James. 1973. "Socioeconomic Status as Related to Aptitude, Attrition, and Achievement of College Students." *American Sociological Review,* 46:480–488.

State Attorney General of New York. 2009. *No Rhyme or Reason.* www.oag.state.ny.us/ media_center/2009/july/pdfs/Bonus%20 Report%20Final%207.30.09.pdf.

Steeh, Charlotte, and Howard Schuman. 1992. "Young White Adults: Did Racial Attitudes Change in the 1980s?" *American Journal of Sociology,* 98:340–367.

Steelman, Lala Carr, and Brian Powell. 1991. "Sponsoring the Next Generation: Parental Willingness to Pay for Higher Education." *American Journal of Sociology,* 96:1505–1529.

Stein, A. 1971. "Strategies for Failure." *Harvard Educational Review,* 41:158–204.

Steiner, Gilbert. 1971. *The State of Welfare.* Washington, D.C.: Brookings Institution Press.

Steven, Rob. 1983. *Classes in Contemporary Japan.* Cambridge, England: Cambridge University Press.

Stiglitz, Joseph. 2007. *Making Globalization Work.* New York: W. W. Norton.

Stiglitz, Joseph. 2002. *Globalization and Its Discontents.* New York: W. W. Norton.

Stiglitz, Joseph, and Andrew Charlton. 2005. *Fair Trade for All: How Trade Can Promote Development.* New York: Oxford University Press.

Stillman, Don. 1980. "The Devastating Impact of Plant Relocations." Pp. 72–88 in Mark Green and Robert Massie (eds.), *The Big Business Reader: Essays on Corporate America.* New York: Pilgrim Press.

Stockwell, A. J. 1999. "Southeast Asia in War and Peace: The End of European Colonial Empires." Pp. 1–58 in Nicholas Tarling (ed.), *The Cambridge History of Southeast Asia: From World War II to the Present, Volume 4.* Cambridge, England: Cambridge University Press.

Stohl, Michael. 1976. *War and Domestic Political Violence.* Beverly Hills, Calif.: Sage.

Stokes, Randall, and David Jaffee. 1982. "Another Look at the Export of Raw Materials and Economic Growth." *American Sociological Review,* 47:402–407.

Stolte, John F. 1983. "The Legitimation of Structural Inequality: Reformulation and Test of the Self-Evaluation Argument." *American Sociological Review,* 48:331–342.

Stolzenberg, Ross. 1978. "Bringing the Boss Back In: Employer Size, Employee Schooling, and Socioeconomic Achievement." *American Sociological Review,* 43:813–828.

Strasser, Hermann. 1976. *The Normative Structure of Sociology: Conservative and Emancipatory Themes in Social Thought.* London: Routledge & Kegan Paul.

Szymanski, Albert. 1976. "Racial Discrimination and White Gain." *American Sociological Review,* 41:403–414.

Szymanski, Albert. 1978. *The Capitalist State and the Politics of Class.* Cambridge, Mass.: Winthrop Publishers.

Tachibanaki, Toshiaki. 2006. "Inequality and Poverty in Japan." *The Japanese Economic Review,* 57:1–27.

Tax, Sol. 1978. "The Impact of Urbanization on American Indians." *The Annals,* 436:121–136.

Taylor, Jared. 1983. *Shadows of the Rising Sun: A Critical View of the "Japanese Miracle."* Tokyo: Tuttle.

Taylor, Keith W. 1999. "The Early Kingdoms." Pp. 137–182 in Nicholas Tarling (ed.), *The Cambridge History of Southeast Asia, From Early Times to c. 1500, Volume One, Part One.* Cambridge, England: Cambridge University Press.

Teckenberg, Wolfgang. 1990. "The Stability of Occupational Structures, Social Mobility, and Interest Formation." Pp. 24–60 in Max Haller (ed.), *Class Structure in Europe: New Findings from East-West Comparisons of Social Structure and Mobility.* Armonk, N.Y.: M. E. Sharpe.

Teixeira, R. A. 1987. *Why Americans Don't Vote: Turnout Decline in the United States, 1960–1984.* New York: Greenwood Press.

Terkel, Studs. 1972. *Working.* New York: Pantheon Books.

Terwey, Michael. 1987. "Class Position and Income Inequality: Comparing Results for the Federal Republic with Current U.S. Research." Pp. 119–171 in Wolfgang Teckenberg (ed.), *Comparative Studies of Social Structure: Recent Research on France, the United States, and the Federal Republic of Germany.* Armonk, N.Y.: M. E. Sharpe.

Thelen, Kathleen A. 1991. *Union of Parts: Labor Politics in Postwar Germany.* Ithaca, N.Y.: Cornell University Press.

Therborn, Göran. 1978. *What Does the Ruling Class Do When It Rules?* London: NLB.

Thernstrom, Stephen. 1964. *Poverty and Progress: Social Mobility in a Nineteenth Century City.* Cambridge, Mass.: Harvard University Press.

Thernstrom, Stephen. 1970. "Immigrants and Wasps: Ethnic Differences in Occupational Mobility in Boston, 1890–1940." Pp. 125–164 in Stephen Thernstrom and Richard Sennett (eds.), *Nineteenth Century Cities.* New Haven, Conn.: Yale University Press.

Thomas, Hugh. 1979. *A History of the World.* New York: Harper & Row.

Thurow, Lester. 1987. "A Surge in Inequality." *Scientific American,* 256:31–37.

Thurow, Lester. 1991. *Head to Head: The Coming Economic Battle between the United States, Japan, and Europe.* New York: Morrow.

Tigges, Leann M. 1988. "Age, Earnings, and Change within the Dual Economy." *Social Forces,* 66:676–698.

Tilly, Charles. 1978. *From Mobilization to Revolution.* Reading, Mass.: Addison-Wesley.

Tilly, Charles. 1981. *As Sociology Meets History.* New York: Academic Press.

Tilly, Charles, Louise Tilly, and Richard Tilly. 1975. *The Rebellious Century, 1830–1930.* Cambridge, Mass.: Harvard University Press.

Tilly, Chris, and Charles Tilly. 1998. *Work under Capitalism.* Boulder, Colo.: Westview Press.

Tiryakian, Edward. 1975. "Neither Marx Nor Durkheim . . . Perhaps Weber." *American Journal of Sociology,* 81:1–33.

Tolbert, Charles. 1982. "Industrial Segmentation and Men's Career Mobility." *American Sociological Review,* 47:457–477.

Tolbert, Charles, Patrick Horan, and E. M. Beck. 1980. "The Structure of Economic Segmentation: A Dual Economy Approach." *American Journal of Sociology,* 85:1095–1116.

Tompkins, Gary. 1975. "A Causal Model of State Welfare Expenditures." *Journal of Politics,* 37:392–416.

Tope, Daniel, and David Jacobs. 2009. "The Politics of Union Decline: The Contingent Determinants of Union Recognition Elections and Victories." *American Sociological Review,* 74:842–864.

Toyo Keizai Shinposha. 1989. *Japan Company Handbook* (2 volumes). Tokyo: Toyo Keizai Shinposha.

Trattner, Walter I. (ed.). 1983. *Social Welfare or Social Control? Some Historical Reflections on "Regulating the Poor."* Knoxville: University of Tennessee Press.

Treas, Judith. 1983. "Trickle Down or Transfers?: Post War Determinants of Family Income Inequality." *American Sociological Review,* 48:546–559.

Treiman, Donald J. 1977. *Occupational Prestige in Comparative Perspective.* New York: Academic Press.

Treiman, Donald J., and Patricia Roos. 1983. "Sex and Earnings in Industrial Society: A Nine-Nation Comparison." *American Journal of Sociology,* 89:612–650.

Tufte, Edward. 1978. *Political Control of the Economy.* Princeton, N.J.: Princeton University Press.

Tully, J. C., E. F. Jackson, and R. F. Curtis. 1970. "Trends in Occupational Mobility in Indianapolis." *Social Forces,* 49:186–200.

Tumin, Melvin M. 1953. "Some Principles of Stratification: A Critical Analysis." *American Sociological Review,* 18:387–394.

Tumin, Melvin M. 1963. "On Inequality." *American Sociological Review,* 28:19–26.

Turnbull, C. M. 1999. "Regionalism and Nationalism." Pp. 257–318 in Nicholas Tarling (ed.), *The Cambridge History of Southeast Asia: From World War II to the Present, Volume 4.* Cambridge, England Cambridge University Press.

Turnbull, Colin. 1961. *The Forest People.* New York: Simon & Schuster.

Turner, Jonathan. 1970. "Entrepreneurial Environments and the Emergence of Achievement Motivation in Adolescent Males." *Sociometry,* 33:147–166.

Turner, Jonathan, and Royce Singleton Jr. 1978. "A Theory of Ethnic Oppression: Toward a Reintegration of Cultural and Structural Concepts in Ethnic Relations Theory." *Social Forces,* 56:1001–1018.

Turner, Jonathan, and Charles Starnes. 1976. *Inequality: Privilege and Poverty in America.* Santa Monica, Calif.: Goodyear.

Turner, Lowell. 1991. *Democracy at Work: Changing World Markets and the Future of Labor Unions.* Ithaca, N.Y.: Cornell University Press.

Turner, Lowell. 1992. *Democracy at Work: Changing World Markets and the Future of Labor Unions.* Ithaca, N.Y.: Cornell University Press.

Turner, Ralph. 1960. "Sponsored and Contest Mobility and the School System." *American Sociological Review,* 25:855–867.

Tyree, Andrea, and Robert Hodge. 1978. "Editorial Foreword: Five Empirical Landmarks." *Social Forces,* 56:761–769.

Tyree, Andrea, Moshe Semyonov, and Robert Hodge. 1979. "Gaps and Glissandes: Inequality, Economic Development, and Social Mobility in 24 Countries." *American Sociological Review,* 44:410–424.

Tyree, Andrea, and Judith Treas. 1974. "The Occupational and Marital Mobility of Women." *American Sociological Review,* 39:293–302.

Ulam, Adam. 1973. *Stalin: The Man and His Era.* New York: Viking Press.

United Nations. 2000. *A Better World for All.* New York: Oxford University Press.

United Nations. 2005. *Human Development Report, 2004.* New York: United Nations Development Programme.

United Nations. 2006. *Human Development Report, 2006.* http://hdr.undp.org/.

United Nations. 2009. *Human Development Report, 2009.* http://hdr.undp.org/.

United Nations Development Programme. 2000. *Overcoming Human Poverty.* New York: United Nations.

United Nations World Food Programme.2009. *Annual Report, 2009.* http://documents.wfp.org.

U.S. Bureau of Labor Statistics. 2010. *Current Employment Statistics.* www.bls.gov/ces/home.htm.

U.S. Bureau of the Census. 1960. *Historical Statistics of the United States.* Washington, D.C.: U.S. Government Printing Office.

U.S. Bureau of the Census. 1980. *Statistical Abstract of the United States, 1979.* Washington, D.C.: U.S. Government Printing Office.

U.S. Bureau of the Census. 1992. *Studies in the Distribution of Income. Current Population Reports, Consumer Income,* series P–60, no. 183. Washington, D.C.: U.S. Government Printing Office.

U.S. Bureau of the Census. 1992. *What's It Worth? Educational Background and Economic Status, Spring 1990. Current Population Reports,* series P–70, no. 32. Washington, D.C.: U.S. Government Printing Office.

U.S. Bureau of the Census. 1993. *Asians and Pacific Islanders in the United States. 1990 Census of the Population,* CP–3–5. Washington, D.C.: U.S. Government Printing Office.

U.S. Bureau of the Census. 1993. *Characteristics of American Indians by Tribe and Language. 1990 Census of the Population,* CP–3–7. Washington, D.C.: U.S. Government Printing Office.

U.S. Bureau of the Census. 1998. *Measuring 50 Years of Economic Change.* Washington, D.C.: U.S. Government Printing Office.

U.S. Bureau of the Census. 2000. *Educational Attainment in the United States (Update).* Washington, D.C.: U.S. Government Printing Office.

U.S. Bureau of the Census. 2000. *Statistical Abstract of the United States, 1999.* Washington, D.C.: U.S. Government Printing Office.

U.S. Bureau of the Census. 2001. *Money Income in the United States, 2000.* Washington, D.C.: U.S. Government Printing Office.

U.S. Bureau of the Census. 2001. *Poverty in the United States, 2000.* Washington, D.C.: U.S. Government Printing Office.

U.S. Bureau of the Census. 2002c. *Statistical Abstract of the United States, 2001.* Washington, D.C.: U.S. Government Printing Office.

U.S. Bureau of the Census. 2004. *Educational Attainment in the United States.* Washington D.C.: U.S. Government Printing Office.

U.S. Bureau of the Census. 2004. *Statistical Abstract of the United States, 2003.* Washington, D.C.: U.S. Government Printing Office.

U.S. Bureau of the Census. 2006b. *Income, Earnings, and Poverty Data from the 2005 American Community Survey.* Washington, D.C.: U.S. Government Printing Office. www.census.gov.

U.S. Bureau of the Census. 2007b. *Statistical Abstract of the United States, 2007.* Washington, D.C.: U.S. Government Printing Office. www.census.gov.

U.S. Bureau of the Census. 2009a. *2008 Community Survey Data.* www.census.gov.

U.S. Bureau of the Census. 2009b. *Reported Voting and Registration of Family Members, by Age and Family Income: November 2008.* www.census.gov.

U.S. Bureau of the Census. 2010a. *Income, Poverty, and Health Insurance Coverage Report, 2009.* www.census.gov.

U.S. Bureau of the Census. 2010b. *Statistical Abstracts of the United States, 2010.* www.census.gov.

U.S. Central Intelligence Agency. 2001. *Growing Global Migration and Its Implications for the United States.* Washington, D.C.: U.S. Government Printing Office.

U.S. Central Intelligence Agency. 2003. *World Fact Book, 2003.* http://www.cia.gov/cia/download.html.

U.S. Department of Agriculture. 2000. *Household Food Security Survey, 1999.* Washington, D.C.: U.S. Government Printing Office.

U.S. Department of Commerce. 2004. *Statistical Abstract of the United States, 2003.* Washington, D.C.: U.S. Government Printing Office.

U.S. Department of Health and Human Services, Center for Disease Control. 2008. *Health, the United States, 2008.* http://www.cdc.gov/nchs/data/hus/hus08.pdf.

U.S. Federal Government. 2001. *Budget of the Federal Government, 2001.* Washington, D.C.: U.S. Government Printing Office.

U.S. Senate Committee on Governmental Affairs. 1978a. *Voting Rights in Major Corporations.* Washington, D.C.: U.S. Government Printing Office.

U.S. Senate Committee on Governmental Affairs. 1978b. *Interlocking Directorates among the Major U.S. Corporations.* Washington, D.C.: U.S. Government Printing Office.

U.S. Senate Committee on Governmental Affairs. 1980. *Structure of Corporate Concentration.* 2 vols. Washington, D.C.: U.S. Government Printing Office.

Useem, Michael. 1976a. "State Production of Social Knowledge: Patterns in Government Financing of Academic Social Research." *American Sociological Review,* 41:613–629.

Useem, Michael. 1976b. "Government Influence on the Social Science Paradigm." *Sociological Quarterly,* 17:146–161.

Useem, Michael. 1978. "The Inner Group of the American Capitalist Class." *Social Problems,* 25:225–240.

Useem, Michael. 1979b. "The Social Organization of the American Business Elite." *American Sociological Review,* 44:553–571.

Useem, Michael. 1984. *The Inner Circle: Large Corporations and the Rise of Business Political Activity in the U.S. and U.K.* New York: Oxford University Press.

Useem, Michael, John Hoops, and Thomas Moore. 1976. "Class and Corporate Relations with the Private College System." *Insurgent Sociologist,* 5:27–35.

Valentine, Charles. 1968. *Culture and Poverty.* Chicago: University of Chicago Press.

Valentine, Charles. 1971. "The 'Culture of Poverty': Its Scientific Significance and Its Implications for Action." Pp. 193–225 in E. B. Leacock (ed.), *The Culture of Poverty: A Critique.* New York: Simon & Schuster.

van den Berghe, Pierre. 1963. "Dialectic and Functionalism: Toward a Theoretical Synthesis." *American Sociological Review,* 28:695–705.

van den Berghe, Pierre. 1967. *Race and Racism: A Comparative Perspective.* New York: John Wiley & Sons.

van den Berghe, Pierre. 1974. "Bringing Beasts Back In: Toward a Biosocial Theory of Aggression." *American Sociological Review,* 39:777–788.

van den Berghe, Pierre. 1977. "Response to Ellis' 'The Decline and Fall of Sociology.'" *American Sociologist,* 12:76–79.

van den Berghe, Pierre. 1978. *Man in Society: A Biosocial View.* New York: Elsevier.

Vanneman, Reeve, and Lynn Weber Cannon. 1987. *The American Perception of Class.* Philadelphia: Temple University Press.

Veblen, Thorstein. 1899. *The Theory of the Leisure Class.* New York: Macmillan.

Verba, S., N. H. Nie, and J. Kim. 1978. *Participation and Political Equality: A Seven-Nation Comparison.* Cambridge, England: Cambridge University Press.

Verba, Sidney, and Gary R. Orren. 1985. *Equality in America: The View from the Top.* Cambridge, Mass.: Harvard University Press.

Verba, Sidney, et al. 1987. *Elites and the Idea of Equality.* Cambridge, Mass.: Harvard University Press.

Vidmar, Neil, and Milton Rokeach. 1974. "Archie Bunker's Bigotry: A Study in Selective Perception and Exposure." *Journal of Communication,* 38:36–47.

Vogel, Ezra. 1979. *Japan as Number One: Lessons for America.* Cambridge, Mass.: Harvard University Press.

Vogel, Ezra. 1985. *Come Back: Building the Resurgence of American Business.* New York: Simon & Schuster.

Vogel, Ezra F. 1989. *One Step Ahead in China: Guangdong under Reform.* Cambridge, Mass.: Harvard University Press.

Vogel, Ezra F. 1991. *The Four Little Dragons: The Spread of Industrialization in East* Asia. Cambridge, Mass.: Harvard University Press.

Wacquant, Loic J. D. 1993 . "Bourdieu in America: Notes on the Transatlantic Importation of Social Theory." Pp. 235–262, in Craig, Calhoun, Edward Lipuma, and Moishe Postone (eds.), *Bourdieu: Critical Perspectives.* Chicago: University of Chicago Press.

Wagmiller, Robert L., Jr., Mary Clare Lennon, Li Juang, Philip Alberti, and J. Lawrence Aber. 2006. "The Dynamics of Economic Disadvantage and Children's Life Chances." *American Sociological Review*, 71:847–866.

Waldfogel, Jane. 1997. "The Effect of Children on Women's Wages." *American Sociological Review,* 62:209–217.

Wallace, Ruth A., and Alison Wolf. 1999. *Contemporary Sociological Theory.* Upper Saddle River, N.J.: Prentice Hall.

Wallerstein, Immanual. 1974. *The Modern World-System.* New York: Academic Press.

Wallerstein, Immanual. 1977. "How Do We Know Class Struggle When We See It?" *Insurgent Sociologist,* 7:104–106.

Wallerstein, Immanual. 1980. *The Modern World-System II: Mercantilism and the Consolidation of the European World Economy, 1600–1750.* New York: Academic Press.

Wallerstein, Immanual. 1989. *The Modern World-System III: The Second Era of Great Expansion of the Capitalist World-Economy, 1730–1840s.* New York: Academic Press.

Wallerstein, Immanual. 1999. *The End of the World as We Know It: Social Science for the Twenty-First Century.* Minneapolis: University of Minnesota Press.

Ward, Martha C. 1999. *A World Full of Women.* Boston: Allyn & Bacon.

Warner, Rodger. 1995. *Back Fire: The CIA's Secret War in Laos and Its Link to the War in Vietnam.* New York: Simon & Schuster.

Warner, Rodger. 1996. *Shooting at the Moon: The Story of America's Clandestine War in Laos.* South Royalton, Vermont: Steerforth Press.

Warner, W. Lloyd. 1953. *American Life.* Chicago: University of Chicago Press.

Warner, W. Lloyd, and Paul S. Lunt. 1941. *The Social Life of a Modern Community.* Yankee City Series, vol. I. New Haven, Conn.: Yale University Press.

Warren, John Robert, and Robert M. Hauser. 1997. "Social Stratification across Three Generations: New Evidence from the Wisconsin Longitudinal Study." *American Sociological Review,* 62:561–572.

Watkins, Kevin. 2001. "More Hot Air Won't Bring the World's Poor in from the Cold." *International Herald Tribune,* May 16.

Wax, Murray. 1971. *Indian Americans.* Upper Saddle River, N.J.: Prentice Hall.

Weakleim, David L. 1990. "Relative Wages and the Radical Theory of Economic Segmentation." *American Sociological Review,* 55:574–590.

Weakliem, David L. 2001. "Special Class and Voting: The Case against Decline." Pp. 197–224 in Terry Nichols Clark and Seymour Martin Lipset (eds.), *The Breakdown of Class Politics: A Debate on Post-Industrial Stratification.* Washington, D.C.: Woodrow Wilson Center Press.

Weatherford, Jack. 1988. *Indian Givers: How the Indians of the Americas Transformed the World.* New York: Crown Books.

Weber, Marianne. 1975. *Max Weber: A Biography.* Translated by Harry Zohn. New York: John Wiley & Sons.

Weber, Max. 1947. *The Theory of Social and Economic Organization.* Edited by Talcott Parsons. New York: Free Press.

Weber, Max. 1958. *The Protestant Ethic and the Spirit of Capitalism.* Translated by Talcott Parsons. New York: Scribner's.

Webster, M. J., and J. E. Driskell. 1978. "Status Generalization: A Review of Some New Data." *American Sociological Review,* 43:220–236.

Weede, Erich. 1980. "Beyond Misspecification in Sociological Analysis of Income Inequality." *American Sociological Review,* 45:497–501.

Weeden, Kim A. 2002. "Why Do Some Occupations Pay More than Others?: Social Closure and Earnings Inequality in the United States." *American Journal of Sociology,* 108:55–101.

Weeden, Kim A., and David B. Grusky. 2005. "The Case for a New Class Map." *American Journal of Sociology,* 111:141–212.

Weeden, Kim A., Young-Mi Kim, Matthew Di Carlo, and David Grusky. 2007. "Social Class and Earnings Inequality." *American Behavioral Scientist,* 50:702–736.

Weinberg, Martin, and Colin Williams. 1980. "Sexual Embourgeoisement? Social Class and Sexual Activity: 1938–1970." *American Sociological Review,* 45:33–48.

Wellington, Alison J. 1994. "Accounting for the Male/Female Wage Gap among Whites: 1976 and 1985." *American Sociological Review,* 59:839–848.

Wellington, Sheila, and Katherine Giscombe. 2001. "Women and Leadership in Corporate America." Pp. 87–106 in Cynthia B. Costello and Anne J. Stone (eds.), *The American Woman 2001–2002.* New York: W. W. Norton.

Wells, H. G. 1971. *The Outline of History.* New York: Doubleday.

Wenke, Robert. 1980. *Patterns in Prehistory: Mankind's First Three Million Years.* New York: Oxford University Press.

West, J. C. 1945. *Plainville, USA.* New York: Columbia University Press.

Wessel, David. 2009. *In Fed We Trust: Ben Bernanke's War on the Great Panic.* New York: Crown Books/Random House.

Western, Bruce, Meredith Kleykamp, and Jake Rosenfeld. 2006. "Did Falling Wages and Employment Increase U.S. Imprisonment?" *Social Forces,* 84:2291–2311.

Western, Mark, and Erik Olin Wright. 1994. "The Permeability of Class Boundaries to Intergenerational Mobility among Men in the United States, Canada, Norway, and Sweden." *American Sociological Review,* 59:606–629.

Wever, Kirsten. 1993. "Codetermination and Competitiveness: What German Employers Think." Paper presented at the Industrial Relations Research Association, Anaheim, Calif.

Whitt, J. Allen. 1979. "Toward a Class-Dialectical Model of Power: An Empirical Assessment of Three Competing Models of Political Power." *American Sociological Review,* 44:81–99.

Wilderdink, Nico, and Rob Potharst. 2001. "Socioeconomic Inequalities in the World Society: Trends and Regional Variations, 1950–1998." Paper presented at the meeting of International Sociological Association, Research Committee on Social Stratification. Berkeley, Calif., August.

Wilensky, Harold. 1975. *The Welfare State and Equality.* Berkeley: University of California Press.

Willhelm, Sidney. 1979. "Opportunities Are Diminishing." *Society (Trans-action),* 16:5, 12–17.

Williams, Christine L. 1992. "The Hidden Escalator: Hidden Advantages for Men in the 'Female' Professions." *Social Problems,* 39, No. 3:253–267.

Williams, Kirk. 1984. "Economic Sources of Homicide: Reestimating the Effects of Poverty and Inequality." *American Sociological Review,* 49:283–289.

Wilson, Edmond O. 1975. *Sociobiology: The New Synthesis.* Cambridge, Mass.: Harvard University Press.

Wilson, Frank Harold. 2007. "The Sociology of Racial and Ethnic Relations." In Clifton Bryant and Dennis L. Peck (eds.), *The Handbook of 21st Century Sociology.* Thousand Oaks, CA: Sage.

Wilson, Kenneth. 1978. "Toward an Improved Explanation of Income Attainment: Recalibrating Education and Occupation." *American Journal of Sociology,* 84:684–697.

Wilson, Kenneth, and Alejandro Portes. 1975. "The Educational Attainment Process: Results from a National Sample." *American Journal of Sociology,* 81:343–363.

Wilson, William Julius. 1980. *The Declining Significance of Race: Blacks and Changing American Institutions.* 2nd ed. Chicago: University of Chicago Press.

Wilson, William Julius. 1987. *The Truly Disadvantaged: The Inner City, the Underclass, and Public Policy.* Chicago: University of Chicago Press.

Wilson, William Julius. 1991. "Public Policy Research and *The Truly Disadvantaged.*" Pp. 460–482 in Christopher Jencks and Paul E. Peterson (eds.), *The Urban Underclass.* Washington, D.C.: Brookings Institution Press.

Wilson, William Julius. 1996. *When Work Disappears: The World of the New Urban Poor.* New York: Knopf.

Winders, B. 1999. "The Roller Coaster of Class Conflict: Class Segments, Mass Mobilization, and Voter Turnout in the U.S., 1840–1996." *Social Forces,* 77:833–860.

Winterbotham, F. W. 1974. *The Ultra Secret.* New York: Harper & Row.

Wissler, Clark. 1966. *Indians of the United States.* New York: Doubleday.

Wolf, Wendy, and Neil Fligstein. 1979. "Sex and Authority in the Work Place: The Causes of Sexual Inequality." *American Sociological Review,* 44:235–252.

Wolff, Kurt (ed.). 1971. *From Karl Mannheim.* New York: Oxford University Press.

Wong, Raymond Sin-Kwok. 1992. "Vertical and Nonvertical Effects in Class Mobility: Cross-National Variations." *American Sociological Review,* 57:396–410.

World Bank. 2000. *World Development Report, 2000/2001.* New York: Oxford University Press.

World Bank. 2001. *Engendering Development.* New York: Oxford University Press.

World Bank. 2002. *Aid and Reform in Africa: Lessons from Ten Case Studies.* New York: Oxford University Press.

World Bank. 2002. *Global Economic Prospects and the Developing Countries.* New York: Oxford University Press.

World Bank. 2002. *Global Prospects for Development.* New York: Oxford University Press.

World Bank. 2004. *Progress in the Fight Against Poverty.* New York: Oxford University Press. http://www.worldbank.org.

World Bank. 2006a. *World Development Report, 2006.* New York: Oxford University Press. www.worldbank.org.

World Bank. 2006b. *Global Economic Prospects: Economic Implications of Remittances and Migration, 2006.* New York: Oxford University Press. www.worldbank.org.

World Bank. 2007. *World Development Report, 2007.* New York: Oxford University Press. www.worldbank.org.

World Bank. 2008. *Poverty Data: A Supplement to World Development Indicators, 2008.* www.worldbank.org.

World Health Organization. 2000. "World Health Report, 2000: Health Systems and Improving Performance." Geneva, Switzerland: Author.

Woronoff, Jon. 1980. *Japan: The Coming Social Crisis.* Tokyo: Yohan Lotus Press.

Woronoff, Jon. 1986. *Politics the Japanese Way.* Tokyo: Lotus Press.

Wright, Erik Olin. 1978a. *Class, Crisis and the State.* New York: Schocken Books.

Wright, Erik Olin. 1978b. "Race, Class, and Income Inequality." *American Journal of Sociology,* 83:1368–1388.

Wright, Erik Olin. 1979. *Class Structure and Income Determination.* New York: Academic Press.

Wright, Erik Olin. 1985. *Classes.* London: Verso.

Wright, Erik Olin. 1989. "Women in the Class System." *Politics and Society,* 17:35–66.

Wright, Erik Olin. 1997. *Class Counts: Comparative Studies in Class Analysis.* Cambridge, England: Cambridge University Press.

Wright, Erik Olin. 2002a. "The Shadow of Exploitation in Weber's Class Analysis." *American Sociological Review,* 67:832–853.

Wright, Erik Olin. 2002b. "Working-Class Power, Capitalist-Class Interests, and Class Compromise." *American Journal of Sociology,* 105:957–1002.

Wright, Erik Olin, and Donmoon Cho. 1992. "The Relative Permeability of Class Boundaries to Cross-Class Friendships: A Comparative Study of the United States, Canada, Sweden, and Norway." *American Sociological Review,* 57:85–102.

Wright, Erik Olin, Cynthia Costello, David Hachen, and Joey Sprague. 1982. "The American Class Structure." *American Sociological Review,* 47:709–726.

Wright, Erik Olin, and Rachel E. Dwyer. 2003. "The Patterns of Job Expansions in the USA: A Comparison of the 1960s and 1990s." *Socio-Economic Review*, 1:289–325.

Wright, Erik Olin, and Bill Martin. 1987. "The Transformation of the American Class Structure, 1960–1980." *American Sociological Review,* 93:1–29.

Wright, Erik Olin, and Luca Perrone. 1977. "Marxist Class Categories and Income Inequality." *American Sociological Review,* 42:32–55.

Wright, James D., and Sonia Wright. 1976. "Social Class and Parental Values for Children: A Partial Replication and Extension of the Kohn Thesis." *American Sociological Review,* 41:527–537.

Wright, Sonia. 1975. "Work Response to Income Maintenance." *Social Forces,* 53:553–562.

Wrong, Dennis. 1959. "The Functional Theory of Stratification: Some Neglected Considerations." *American Sociological Review,* 24:772–782.

Wrong, Dennis. 1964. "Social Inequality without Social Stratification." *Canadian Review of Sociology and Anthropology,* 1:5–16.

Wyatt, David K. 1984. *Thailand: A Short History.* New Haven, Conn.: Yale University Press.

Yanowitch, Murray. 1977. *Social and Economic Inequality in the Soviet Union.* White Plains, N.Y.: M. E. Sharpe.

You, Jong-Sung, and Sanjeev Khagram. 2005. "A Comparative Study of Inequality and Corruption." *American Sociological Review*, 70:136–157.

Younts, C. Wesley, and Charles W. Mueller. 2001. "Justice Processes: Specifying the Mediating Role of Perceptions of Distributive Justice." *American Sociological Review,* 66:125–145.

Zeitlin, Irving M. 1968. *Ideology and the Development of Sociological Theory.* Upper Saddle River, N.J.: Prentice Hall.

Zeitlin, Maurice. 1974. "Corporate Ownership and Control: The Large Corporation and the Capitalist Class." *American Journal of Sociology,* 79:1073–1119.

Zeitlin, Maurice, Kenneth Lutterman, and James Russel. 1973. "Death in Vietnam: Class, Poverty, and the Risks of War." *Politics and Society,* 3:313–328.

Zeng, Zhen, and Yu Xie. 2004. "Asian-Americans' Earnings Disadvantage Reexamined: The Role of Place of Education." *American Journal of Sociology,* 109:1075–1108.

Ziltener, Patrick, and Hans-Peter Mueller. 2007. "The Weight of the Past—Traditional Technology and Socio-Political Differentiation in African and Asian Societies: A Quantitative Assessment of Their Impact on Socio-Economic Development." *International Journal of Comparative Sociology,* 48:371–415.

Zinn, Howard. 1995. *A People's History of the United States.* New York: HarperCollins.

Zipp, John, Richard Landerman, and Paul Luebke. 1982. "Political Parties and Political Participation: A Reexamination of the Standard Socioeconomic Model." *Social Forces,* 60:1140–1153.

Zorbaugh, H. W. 1929. *The Gold Coast and the Slum.* Chicago: University of Chicago Press.

Zulfacar, Maliha. 1998. *Afghan Immigrants in the USA and Germany: A Comparative Analysis of the Use of Ethnic Social Capital.* Munster, Germany: LIT Verlag.

Zweigenhaft, Richard L., and G. William Domhoff. 2006. *Blacks in the White Elite: Will the Progress Continue?* New York: Rowman and Littlefield.

Zweigenhaft, Richard, and G. William Domhoff. 2008. *Diversity in the Power Elite: How It Happened, Why It Matters.* Lanham, Md: Rowman and Littlefield.

# Name Index

## C

## X

## Y

## Z

# Subject Index

## A

ABD. *See* Aid to the Blind and Disabled
Absolute poverty, 246–248
Accidental death, work conditions and, 220–221
Achievement
    ascription v., 55
    contribution v. actual, 398, 401
    defined, 10, 55
    inequality fairness judged on, 398
    social mobility research on, 10, 12, 348
    status attainment by factors of, 374, 376
    wealth as symbol of, 124
    *See also* Educational attainment; Occupational
        attainment
ADC. *See* Aid to Dependent Children
Adopted children, 3–4, 7
Advertising, mass media corporate control by, 414,
    416
Advertising Council, 416
AFDC. *See* Aid to Families with Dependent
    Children
Africa
    comparative income inequality in, 32, 53
    HIV/AIDS in, 476
    human origin and ancient civilizations in, 315,
        327, 504
    land reform for, 518–519
    poverty in sub-Saharan, 477, 479, 481, 483, 502
    Tuareg tribe in, 299
African Americans
    apartheid and, 312
    civil rights movement and World War II, 331, 332
    class conflict within community of, 319
    educational attainment and ethnicity, 320–322,
        323
    gender inequality and occupational attainment,
        307
    homicide rate of, 326
    income inequality of, 22, 315–318, 319–320, 325

    infant mortality rate for, 326
    Obama as, 312
    in poverty, 260, 278
    slave history of, 330–331
    social mobility of, 359–361
Age
    elderly population comparison, 453
    ranking by, in Japan, 451–452
    *See also* Social Security program
Age of Enlightenment, 84
Aggression
    racism theory based on, 339–340
    scarcity and, 145–146
Agrarian societies
    decline of, 74–76
    early empires of, 70–71
    gender inequality history of, 299–300
    land inequality in, 71, 72–73, 75
    late empires of, 60–61, 71–74
    Neolithic revolution, 54, 67–70
    sociobiology of, 146
Agriculture industry
    government spending on, 48
    green revolution in, 518
    Mexican Americans in, 331
    periphery development barriers in, 489–490
    periphery land reform for, 518–519
    poverty and occupational structure of, 266–267
    Thailand's economic development and, 512–513
    trade tariffs and, 492
    *See also* Hunger and malnutrition
Agta tribes, 299
AIDS, 476
Aid to Dependent Children (ADC), 268
Aid to Families with Dependent Children (AFDC),
    263, 268–269
Aid to the Blind and Disabled (ABD), 268
Alexander II (czar of Russia), 437
Alger, Horatio, 348
Alienation from work phenomenon, 218–220
Allocation, status attainment v., 387–389
Altruism, 145–146, 273–274
AMA. *See* American Medical Association
American Civil War, 330–331, 332, 436